[**TO 1877**]

Experience
HISTORY
INTERPRETING AMERICA'S PAST

Experience History
Guarantees Better Course Performance

Better-prepared students

Imagine the dynamic class discussions you could have or lively lectures you could give if your students came to class prepared.

Enter **McGraw-Hill's LearnSmart™**, the online adaptive learning system that guarantees students come to class prepared. As part of **McGraw-Hill's *Connect*® History** program, LearnSmart assesses students' knowledge of the chapter content and identifies gaps in understanding. Students come to class with a better grasp of the course material, resulting in livelier discussions and the freedom to lecture on what you think is important.

STUDENTS TELL US:

- *"I just wanted to let you know that **I love this Connect thing**. The LearnSmart modules are great and really help me to learn the material. I even downloaded their app for my phone."*
—Colorado State University

AND THE INSTRUCTORS SAY:

- *"Five weeks into the semester, students in my three [course] sections have averages of 99.93, 99.97, and 100% respectively on the LearnSmart modules. **I would NEVER get that kind of learning and accuracy if I just assigned them to 'read the chapter and take notes' or 'read the chapter and reflect'***

or some other reading-based assignment." —Florida State College at Jacksonville

- ***"LearnSmart has won my heart."*** —McLennan Community College

---

Which of the following are true about the Freedmen's Bureau?

The bureau was in charge of settling freedpeople on abandoned lands.

The bureau established schools for black southerners.

The bureau provided emergency food, clothing, and medical care to war refugees.

The bureau was in charge of registering freepeople to vote.

Click one of the buttons below.

Do you know the answer? (Be honest.)

| Yes | Probably | Maybe | No—Just guessing |

Better critical thinking skills

Experience History moves students beyond memorization of names and dates and promotes critical thinking:

- Now, map captions and "Daily Lives" feature more critical thinking prompts.

- Icons in the margins point to *Experience History*'s global, continental, and environmental coverage.

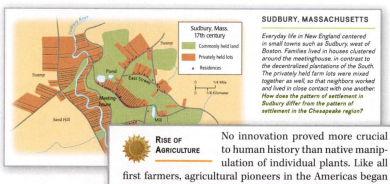

Sudbury, Mass. 17th century
- Commonly held land
- Privately held lots
- Residences

Sudbury River, Swamp, Pond, East Street, Swamp, Meeting-house, Sand Hill, Mill

0   1/4 Mile
0   1/4 Kilometer

SUDBURY, MASSACHUSETTS

Everyday life in New England centered in small towns such as Sudbury, west of Boston. Families lived in houses clustered around the meetinghouse, in contrast to the decentralized plantations of the South. The privately held farm lots were mixed together as well, so that neighbors worked and lived in close contact with one another. **How does the pattern of settlement in Sudbury differ from the pattern of settlement in the Chesapeake region?**

RISE OF AGRICULTURE No innovation proved more crucial to human history than native manipulation of individual plants. Like all first farmers, agricultural pioneers in the Americas began experimenting accidentally. Modern-day species of corn, for example, probably derive from a Mesoamerican grass known as teosinte. It seems that ancient peoples gathered teosinte to collect its small grains. By selecting the grains

WORLDWIDE SPREAD OF AMERICAN CROPS Indeed, ev... the grea... American... ples around the world. In addition to corn, the first Americans gave humanity scores of varieties of squash, potatoes, beans, and other basic foods. Today, plants domesticated by indigenous Americans account for three-fifths of the world's crops, including many that have revolutionized the global

Online activities in *Connect History* place students in an active environment where they develop analytical skills.

- *Connect History* builds advanced thinking and writing skills through "Critical Missions" projects that place students in a pivotal moment in time and ask them to develop a historical argument.

- Expanded and refined *Connect* resources, including new "Dueling Documents" and "Historian's Toolbox" activities, are now easier to assign and heighten the impact of text features.

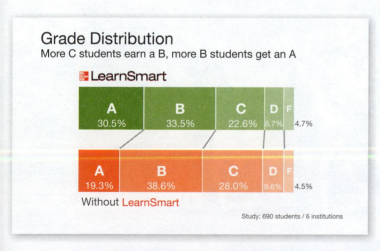

Grade Distribution
More C students earn a B, more B students get an A

LearnSmart

A	B	C	D	F
30.5%	33.5%	22.6%	8.7%	4.7%

A	B	C	D	F
19.3%	38.6%	28.0%	9.6%	4.5%

Without LearnSmart

Study: 690 students / 6 institutions

Better grades

Research shows that students' grades improve using *Connect History* and LearnSmart. Imagine being able to document this type of grade improvement through easily-run reports.

Listen to instructors:

- *"My class that is using Connect scored higher than any other class in my 25 years of teaching."* —University of Colorado Denver

- *"The students really love Connect. They also got the best test scores on their first exam that I have ever seen in my teaching career."* —Georgia Southern University

For a complete list of changes in the 8th edition of *Experience History,* go to **www.mhhe.com/eh8.**

Experience
HISTORY
INTERPRETING AMERICA'S PAST
EIGHTH EDITION

James West Davidson

Brian DeLay
UNIVERSITY OF CALIFORNIA, BERKELEY

Christine Leigh Heyrman
UNIVERSITY OF DELAWARE

Mark H. Lytle
BARD COLLEGE

Michael B. Stoff
UNIVERSITY OF TEXAS, AUSTIN

McGraw Hill Education

EXPERIENCE HISTORY: INTERPRETING AMERICA'S PAST, EIGHTH EDITION

Published by McGraw-Hill Education, 2 Penn Plaza, New York, NY 10121. Copyright © 2014 by McGraw-Hill Education. All rights reserved. Printed in the United States of America. Previous editions © 2011, 2008, and 2005. No part of this publication may be reproduced or distributed in any form or by any means, or stored in a database or retrieval system, without the prior written consent of McGraw-Hill Education, including, but not limited to, in any network or other electronic storage or transmission, or broadcast for distance learning.

Some ancillaries, including electronic and print components, may not be available to customers outside the United States.

This book is printed on acid-free paper.

1 2 3 4 5 6 7 8 9 0 DOW/DOW 1 0 9 8 7 6 5 4 3

ISBN   978-0-07-340701-2 (complete)
MHID   0-07-340701-1 (complete)
ISBN   978-0-07-750472-4 (volume I)
MHID   0-07-750472-0 (volume I)
ISBN   978-0-07-750473-1 (volume II)
MHID   0-07-750473-9 (volume II)

Senior Vice President, Products & Markets: *Kurt L. Strand*
Vice President, General Manager, Products & Markets: *Michael J. Ryan*
Vice President, Content Production & Technology Services: *Kimberly Meriwether David*
Managing Director: *Gina Boedeker*
Director: *Matt Busbridge*
Director of Development: *Rhona Robbin*
Managing Development Editor: *Nancy Crochiere*
Development Editor: *Sarah Remington*
Digital Development Editor: *Meghan Campbell*
Digital Product Analyst: *John Brady*

Brand Coordinator: *Kaelyn Schulz*
Executive Marketing Manager: *Stacy Best Ruel*
Director, Content Production: *Terri Schiesl*
Content Project Manager: *Angela Norris*
Senior Buyer: *Laura M. Fuller*
Design: *Trevor Goodman*
Senior Content Licensing Specialist: *Lori Hancock*
Media Project Manager: *Jennifer Barrick*
Typeface: *9/11 Kepler Std Regular*
Compositor: *Aptara®, Inc.*
Printer: *R. R. Donnelley*

Cover Credits: (buffalo chase by George Catlin): Courtesy National Gallery of Art, Washington; (Heart of the Klondike by Scott Marble): Library of Congress (LC-USZC4-8279); (Pocahontas): Library of Congress Prints and Photographs Division (LC-USZC4-3368); (French map): Library of Congress (ct000656 g3300); (Mrs. Samuel Chandler): Mrs. Samuel Chandler, by Winthrop Chandler, c. 1780. Oil on canvas. Gift of Edgar William and Bernice Chrysler Garbisch, Image, © Gift of Edgar William and Bernice Chrysler Garbisch; (Walt Whitman): Library of Congress (LC-DIG-ppmsca-07143); (Sunday at San Miguel, Santa Fe, New Mexico 1882 by Rudolf Cronau): Courtesy of the Museum of the American West, Autry National Center, 93.99.2; (Tragic Prelude by John Steuart Curry): © Kansas State Historical Society (FK2.1 C.1999*6); (Kansas soldiers with canon): © Kansas State Historical Society (FK2.83*15); (exodusers): Library of Congress; (mural Baptism by Clementine Hunter): Library of Congress (361582c); (protective tariff cartoon): © Fotosearch/Getty Images, Inc.; (Riot at Union Square): © Museum of the City of New York/The Art Archive at Art Resource, NY; (migrant mother): Library of Congress (LC-DIG-fsa-8b29516); (Cesar Chavez): © Arthur Schatz/Time Life Pictures/Getty Images; (Hmong story cloth by Dia, Chue, and Nhia Cha): (Detail) Hmong Story Cloth by Dia Cha and Chue & Nhia Cha. All rights reserved, Image Archives, Denver Museum of Nature & Science; (Sir Francis Drake's West Indian voyage): Library of Congress Geography and Map Division (3291.S12s000B6).

All credits appearing on page or at the end of the book are considered to be an extension of the copyright page.

The Library of Congress has cataloged the single-volume edition of this work as follows

Davidson, James West.
Experience history : interpreting America's past / James West Davidson, Brian DeLay, UNIVERSITY OF CALIFORNIA, BERKELEY, Christine Leigh Heyrman, UNIVERSITY OF DELAWARE, Mark H. Lytle, BARD COLLEGE, Michael B. Stoff, UNIVERSITY OF TEXAS, AUSTIN.—Eighth edition.
       pages cm
   Includes bibliographical references and index.
   ISBN-13: 978-0-07-340701-2 (complete text : acid-free paper)
   ISBN-10: 0-07-340701-1 (complete text : acid-free paper)
   1. United States—History.   2. United States—History—Study and teaching.   I. Title.
E178.1.E94 2014
973—dc23   2013010668

The Internet addresses listed in the text were accurate at the time of publication. The inclusion of a website does not indicate an endorsement by the authors or McGraw-Hill Education, and McGraw-Hill Education does not guarantee the accuracy of the information presented at these sites.

www.mhhe.com

Brief Contents

Contents

Chapter 1

THE FIRST CIVILIZATIONS OF NORTH AMERICA 2

∞∞∞∞ AN AMERICAN STORY ∞∞∞∞

The Power of a Hidden Past 3

After the Fact
Tracking the First Americans   22

Chapter 2

OLD WORLDS, NEW WORLDS 1400–1600 26

∞∞∞∞ AN AMERICAN STORY ∞∞∞∞

Fishing Nets and Far Horizons 27

Chapter 6

IMPERIAL TRIUMPH, IMPERIAL CRISIS 1754–1776   130

∞∞∞ AN AMERICAN STORY ∞∞∞

George Washington and the Half King   131

Chapter 7

THE AMERICAN PEOPLE AND THE AMERICAN REVOLUTION 1775–1783   156

∞∞∞ AN AMERICAN STORY ∞∞∞

"Will He Fight?"   157

Chapter 8
CRISIS AND CONSTITUTION
1776–1789   180

∞∞∞ AN AMERICAN STORY ∞∞∞
"These United States"   181

After the Fact
White and Black Southerners Worshiping Together   204

Chapter 9
THE EARLY REPUBLIC
1789–1824   208

∞∞∞ AN AMERICAN STORY ∞∞∞
"I Felt My Blood Boil"   209

After the Fact
Sally Hemings and Thomas Jefferson   240

Chapter 10
THE OPENING OF AMERICA 1815–1850   244

∞∞∞ AN AMERICAN STORY ∞∞∞

From Boom to Bust with One-Day Clocks   245

Chapter 11
THE RISE OF DEMOCRACY 1824–1840   270

∞∞∞ AN AMERICAN STORY ∞∞∞

*"Wanted: Curling Tongs, Cologne, and
Silk-Stockings . . ."*   271

Chapter 12

Afire with Faith 1820–1850 296

∞∞∞ AN AMERICAN STORY ∞∞∞

The Beechers and the Kingdom of God 297

Chapter 13

The Old South 1820–1860 322

∞∞∞ AN AMERICAN STORY ∞∞∞

Where Is the Real South? 323

Chapter 14

WESTERN EXPANSION AND THE RISE OF THE SLAVERY ISSUE 1820–1850 346

∞∞∞ AN AMERICAN STORY ∞∞∞

Strangers on the Great Plains 347

Chapter 15

THE UNION BROKEN 1850–1861 376

∞∞∞ AN AMERICAN STORY ∞∞∞

The Sacking of a Town in Kansas 377

Chapter 16

TOTAL WAR AND THE REPUBLIC 1861–1865 402

∞∞∞ AN AMERICAN STORY ∞∞∞

Rout at Bull Run 403

After the Fact
What Caused the New York City Draft Riots? 434

Chapter 17

RECONSTRUCTING THE UNION 1865–1877 438

∞∞∞ AN AMERICAN STORY ∞∞∞

The Secret Sale at Davis Bend 439

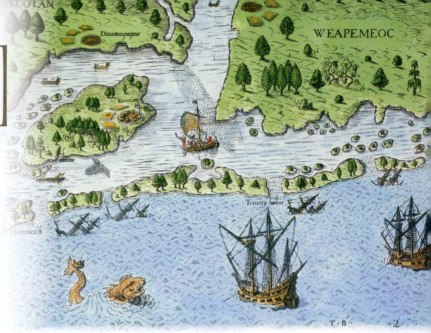

LIST OF
Maps and Charts

From the Authors

How do you make history?

There are two very different answers to the question, depending on whether you're living it or writing it. Yet both actions are more closely connected than appears at first glance. The American past is filled with people who have made history in ways they could not have anticipated when they were younger.

- Jean L'Archevêque, a 12-year-old French servant setting sail across the Atlantic in 1684 (see Chapter 5), could not have predicted that centuries later he would be remembered for his role as a decoy in an assassination plot, for the striking tattoos that were engraved on his face, and for his violent death along the Platte River, half a world away from his place of birth.

- Biology student Rachel Carson (Chapter 30) would have been astonished in 1928 to hear that 30 years later she would challenge the largest chemical companies in the United States, whose pesticides were damaging the environment.

- When a young Filipino soldier named Valentine Untalan (Chapter 26) was captured by the Japanese during World War II, the last thing on his mind, as he was herded into what was later called the Bataan death march, was whether one day his story might be told. He simply wanted to stay alive.

All these people made history—became a part of history—in large ways and small—as you yourself may someday, in a manner that is yet unknowable. However, there is another way to "make" history, and that is by thinking and writing about the past, as historians do.

THE EXPERIENCE OF "MAKING HISTORY"

The operative word is *make*. History is not the past; it is a reconstruction assembled from the past's raw materials. It is not a set of agreed-upon facts. Events happened and are relayed to us through a wide variety of surviving records, but—because we were not there—it is always through the gauze of someone's interpretation.

By nature textbook programs strive to be comprehensive, smooth, and seamless. They project an aura of omniscience; the narrative speaks with a single authoritative voice. But history does

not consist of one voice; it has multiple voices, like our diverse nation. It must take into account the dialogues, disagreements, and diverse actors that all have been a part of American history.

Of course, it is impossible to convey even a fraction of the debates that go into the "making" of history. However, in *Experience History,* we suggest a bit of the substance and flavor of the process by examining some of the debates and disagreements around a particular historical question. We place the reader in the role of historical detective. You are asked to examine historical evidence—whether a cartoon, an artifact, or two conflicting documents—and see what can be made of it. In short, you will learn what it means to make—to construct—history.

EXPERIENCING THE STORIES OF HISTORY

As historians, we use narrative as a way to give life to the past. The choice of narrative puts a great deal of emphasis on the individual and acknowledges that individuals can affect history in surprising ways. Personal decisions, sudden deaths, natural catastrophes, and chance all combine to make history unpredictable. And by telling these unpredictable stories we illustrate what historians refer to as "contingency"—the idea that history is not an inevitable series of events, but is changed and shaped by often-unanticipated events and actions of individuals.

Then, too, these stories fascinate us for the sheer wonder of watching individuals of all kinds grappling with how to shape the worlds around them.

- Take Wingina, chief of the Roanoke Indians, who in 1584 had to decide what to do about the savage, strangely behaved white men who had just landed on his shores;

- Or gaze in wonder at the quirky Henry Ford, who turned out identical Model T automobiles—because, as he put it, "Everybody wants to be somewhere he ain't"—and who also insisted that his factory workers wear identical expressions, which he referred to as "Fordization of the Face."

- Consider young Thurgood Marshall, crisscrossing the South in his own "little old beat-up '29 Ford," typing legal briefs in the backseat, trying to get black teachers to sue for equal pay, hoping to change African American lives for the better. Because (to quote Henry Ford) everybody wants to be somewhere he ain't.

Of course, narrative also allows us to comprehend broad trends—like the transportation revolution that proceeded from canals and steamboats to railroads and automobiles—but it does so without depriving us of history's irreducible details, like Wingina's dilemma or Marshall's dreams.

In *Experience History,* we hope we have combined a narrative whose stories engage you with a set of features that explore what historians do and how history is created. How you reflect upon the past, engage with it, and reconstruct it, will in no small measure determine your understanding and enjoyment of history, as well as your success in it.

Improve
Your
Course

Connect® History is a highly interactive learning environment designed to help students connect to the resources they will need to achieve success. Map activities, primary source exercises, image analysis, key term quizzes, and review questions provide a wealth of assignments to ensure that students are comprehending the reading and will succeed in the course. *ConnectPlus® History* offers all of the above with the addition of an integrated, interactive e-book. Optimized for the web, the e-book immerses students in a flexible, interactive environment.

ConnectPlus® History offers all of the above with the addition of an integrated, interactive e-book. Optimized for the web, the e-book immerses students in a flexible, interactive environment.

LearnSmart, McGraw-Hill's adaptive learning system, helps assess student knowledge of course content and maps out a personalized study plan for success. Accessible within *Connect History*, LearnSmart uses a series of adaptive questions to pinpoint the concepts students understand—and those they don't. The result is an online tool that helps students learn faster and study more efficiently and enables instructors to customize classroom lectures and activities to meet their students' needs.

 **SMARTBOOK™**

Fueled by LearnSmart—the most widely used and intelligent adaptive learning resource—SmartBook is the first and only adaptive reading experience available today.

Distinguishing what a student knows from what they don't, and honing in on concepts they are most likely to forget, SmartBook personalizes content for each student in a continuously adapting reading experience. Reading is no longer a passive and linear experience, but an engaging and dynamic one where students are more likely to master and retain important concepts, coming to class better prepared. Valuable reports provide instructors insight as to how students are progressing through textbook content, and are useful for shaping in-class time or assessment. As a result of the adaptive reading experience found in SmartBook, students are more likely to retain knowledge, stay in class and get better grades. This revolutionary technology is available only from McGraw-Hill Education and for hundreds of course areas as part of the LearnSmart Advantage series.

 **create™**

Design your ideal course materials with McGraw-Hill's **Create—www.mcgrawhillcreate.com!** Rearrange or omit chapters, combine material from other sources, and/or upload your syllabus or any other content you have written to make the perfect resources for your students. Search thousands of leading McGraw-Hill textbooks to find the best content for your students, then arrange it to fit your teaching style. You can even personalize your book's appearance by selecting the cover and adding your name, school, and course information. When you order a Create book, you receive a complimentary review copy. Get a printed copy in three to five business days or an electronic copy (eComp) via e-mail in about an hour. Register today at **www.mcgrawhillcreate.com** and craft your course resources to match the way you teach.

 **CourseSmart** Learn Smart. Choose Smart.

CourseSmart offers thousands of the most commonly adopted textbooks across hundreds of courses from a wide variety of higher education publishers. It is the only place for faculty to review and compare the full text of a textbook online, providing immediate access without the environmental impact of requesting a printed exam copy. At CourseSmart, students can save up to 50 percent off the cost of a printed book, reduce their impact on the environment, and gain access to powerful web tools for learning, including full text search, notes and highlighting, and e-mail tools for sharing notes among classmates. Learn more at **www.coursesmart.com**.

 **Campus**

McGraw-Hill Campus is the first-of-its-kind institutional service providing faculty with true single sign-on access to all of McGraw-Hill's course content, digital tools, and other high-quality learning resources from any learning management system (LMS). This innovative offering allows for secure and deep integration and seamless access to any of our course solutions such as McGraw-Hill *Connect*, McGraw-Hill Create, McGraw-Hill LearnSmart, or Tegrity. McGraw-Hill Campus includes access to our entire content library, including e-books, assessment tools, presentation slides, and multimedia content, among other resources, providing faculty open and unlimited access to prepare for class, create tests/quizzes, develop lecture material, integrate interactive content, and much more.

Online Learning Center for *Experience History*

The **Online Learning Center (OLC)** at **www.mhhe.com/eh8** contains a wealth of instructor resources, including an Instructor's Manual, Test Bank, and PowerPoint presentations for each chapter. All maps and most images from the print text are included.

A **Computerized Test Bank**, McGraw-Hill's EZ Test, allows you to quickly create a customized test using the publisher's supplied test banks or your own questions. You decide the number, type, and order of test questions with a few simple clicks. EZ Test runs on your computer without a connection to the Internet.

Primary Source Documents

The following primary source documents, carefully selected by the authors to coordinate with this program, are available on the Online Learning Center for *Experience History* at www.mhhe.com/eh8 and as assignable assessments on *Connect* at http://connect.mcgraw-hill.com. Documents include an explanatory headnote and are followed by discussion questions.

Choose from many of these documents—or hundreds of others—to customize your print text by visiting McGraw-Hill's Create at www.mcgrawhillcreate.com.

Acknowledgments

We are grateful to the many advisors and reviewers who generously offered comments and suggestions at various stages in our development of this manuscript. Our thanks go to:

Thomas Altherr,
Metropolitan State College of Denver

Melissa Anyiwo,
Curry College

Darren Bardell,
Ohlone College

Daniel Barr,
Robert Morris University

Melissa Biegert,
Temple College

Lisa Blank,
Tarrant County Community College

Margaret Brown,
Brevard College

Owen Chariton,
Metropolitan State College of Denver

Ann Short Chirhart,
Indiana State University

George Fain,
University South Carolina - Upstate

Jessica Feveryear,
Salt Lake Community College

Melody Flowers,
McLennan Community College

Amy Forss,
Metropolitan Community College

Rick Gianni,
Indiana University Northwest

Shawn Gladden,
Community College of Baltimore County

Mark Goldman,
Tallahassee Community College

Wendy Gunderson,
Collin College

David Haney,
Austin Community College

Ken Hansen,
Salt Lake Community College

Carmen Harris,
University of South Carolina - Upstate

Ely Janis,
Massachusetts College of Liberal Arts

Russell Jones,
Eastern Michigan University

Richard Kitchen,
New Mexico Military Institute

John Leland,
Salem International University

Charles Levine,
Mesa Community College

Manuel Medrano,
University of Texas, Brownsville

Mark Mengerink,
Lamar University

Don Mohr,
University of Alaska Anchorage

Kimberly Nichols,
Northeast Texas Community College

Michelle Anne Novak,
Houston Community College - Southeast

Shannon O'Bryan,
Greenville Technical College

Richard Owens,
West Liberty University

David Porter,
Northern Virginia Community College

Gretchen Reilly,
Temple College

John Selby,
Roanoke College

Richard Straw,
Radford University

Michael Thetford,
Lone Star College, Montgomery

Mark Van Ells,
Queensborough Community College

Melissa Weinbrenner,
Northeast Texas Community College

Scott Williams,
Weatherford College

Chad Wooley,
Tarrant County Community College

Digi-posium Attendees

Wayne Ackerson,
Technical College of Low Country

Ceci Barba,
El Paso Community College

Gene Barnett,
Calhoun Community College

Eric Duchess,
High Point University

Caroline Emmons,
Hampden-Sydney College

John Frongillo,
Florida Tech University

Mindy Green Reynolds,
Southern Union State Community College

Phyllis Jestice,
University of Southern Mississippi

Lloyd Johnson,
Campbell University

Haile Larebo,
Morehouse College

Jason Ramshur,
Pearl River Community College

Mark Roehrs,
Lincoln Land Community College

Robert A. Saunders,
Farmingdale State College

Keith Sisson,
University of Memphis

Matt Zembo,
Hudson Valley Community College

One acknowledgment we can never make too often is to the work of our co-author, colleague, and friend, William E. Gienapp. Bill traveled with us on this journey from the book's earliest conception up until his untimely passing in 2003. His insight, erudition, and good humor made him a pleasure to work with, and his contribution to the book will endure no matter how many new revisions appear.

JAMES WEST DAVIDSON, BRIAN DELAY,
CHRISTINE LEIGH HEYRMAN,
MARK H. LYTLE, MICHAEL B. STOFF

About the Authors

James West Davidson

RECEIVED HIS PhD FROM YALE UNIVERSITY. A historian who has pursued a full-time writing career, he is the author of numerous books, among them *After the Fact: The Art of Historical Detection* (with Mark H. Lytle), *The Logic of Millennial Thought: Eighteenth-Century New England*, and *Great Heart: The History of a Labrador Adventure* (with John Rugge). He is co-editor with Michael Stoff of the *Oxford New Narratives in American History*, in which his own most recent book appears: *'They Say': Ida B. Wells and the Reconstruction of Race*.

Brian Delay

RECEIVED HIS PhD FROM HARVARD University and is Associate Professor of History at the University of California, Berkeley. He is a frequent guest speaker at teacher workshops across the country and has won several prizes for his book *War of a Thousand Deserts: Indian Raids and the U.S.-Mexican War*. He is currently at work on the history of guns, business, and freedom in the Americas.

Christine Leigh Heyrman

IS THE ROBERT W. AND SHIRLEY P. Grimble Professor of American History at the University of Delaware. She received a PhD in American Studies from Yale University and is the author of *Commerce and Culture: The Maritime Communities of Colonial Massachusetts, 1690–1750*. Her book *Southern Cross: The Beginnings of the Bible Belt* was awarded the Bancroft Prize in 1998.

Mark H. Lytle

RECEIVED HIS PhD FROM YALE University and is Professor of History and Environmental Studies at Bard College. He served two years as Mary Ball Washington Professor of American History at University College, Dublin, in Ireland. His publications include *The Origins of the Iranian-American Alliance, 1941–1953*, *After the Fact: The Art of Historical Detection* (with James West Davidson), *America's Uncivil Wars: The Sixties Era from Elvis to the Fall of Richard Nixon*, and most recently, *The Gentle Subversive: Rachel Carson, Silent Spring, and the Rise of the Environmental Movement*. He is currently working on a book on the environmental impacts of consumerism in the post–World War II era.

Michael B. Stoff

IS ASSOCIATE PROFESSOR OF HISTORY and Director of the Plan II Honors Program at the University of Texas at Austin. The recipient of a PhD from Yale University, he has been honored many times for his teaching, most recently with the University of Texas System Regents' Outstanding Teaching Award. He is the author of *Oil, War, and American Security: The Search for a National Policy on Foreign Oil, 1941–1947*, co-editor (with Jonathan Fanton and R. Hall Williams) of *The Manhattan Project: A Documentary Introduction to the Atomic Age*, and series co-editor (with James West Davidson) of the *Oxford New Narratives in American History*. He is currently working on a narrative of the bombing of Nagasaki.

Experience
HISTORY
INTERPRETING AMERICA'S PAST

From the air, this serpentine mound fashioned thousands of years ago still stands out in bold relief. Located in southern Ohio, it extends from the snake's coiled tail at the left of the photo to the open mouth at the top right, which is pointed in the direction of the summer solstice sunset. The snake's tail points toward the winter solstice sunrise.

The First Civilizations of North America

⬡⬡⬡⬡⬡ **AN AMERICAN STORY** ⬡⬡⬡⬡⬡

THE POWER OF A HIDDEN PAST

Stories told about the past have power over both the present and the future. Until recently, most students were taught that American history began several centuries ago—with the "discovery" of America by Columbus, or with the English colonization of Jamestown and Plymouth. History books ignored or trivialized the continent's precontact history. But the reminders of that hidden past are everywhere. Scattered across the United States are thousands of ancient archaeological sites and hundreds of examples of monumental architecture, still imposing even after centuries of erosion, looting, and destruction.

Man-made earthen mounds, some nearly 5,000 years old, exist throughout eastern North America in a bewildering variety of shapes and sizes. Many are easily mistaken for modest hills, but others evoke wonder. In present-day Louisiana an ancient town with earthworks took laborers an estimated 5 million work hours to construct. In Ohio a massive serpent effigy snakes for a quarter-mile across the countryside, its head aligned to the summer solstice. In Illinois a vast, earthen structure covers 16 acres at its base and once reached as high as a 10-story building.

Observers in the colonial and revolutionary eras looked on such sites as curiosities and marvels. George Washington, Thomas Jefferson, and other prominent Americans collected ancient artifacts, took a keen interest in the excavation of mounds, and speculated about the Indian civilizations that created them. Travelers explored these strange mounds, trying to imagine in their mind's eye the peoples who had built them. In 1795 the Reverend James Smith traced the boundaries of a mound wall that was strategically placed to protect a neck of land along a looping river bend in the Ohio valley. "The wall at present is so mouldered down that a man could easily ride over it. It is however about 10 feet, as near as I can judge, in perpendicular height. . . . In one place I observe a breach in the wall about 60 feet wide, where I suppose the gate formerly stood through which the people passed in and out of this stronghold." Smith was astonished by the size of the project. "Compared with this," he exclaimed, "what feeble and insignificant works are those of Fort Hamilton or Fort Washington! They are no more in comparison to it than a rail fence is to a brick wall."

But in the 1830s and 1840s, as Americans sought to drive Indians west of the Mississippi and then confine them on smaller and smaller reservations, many observers began thinking differently about the continent's ancient sites. Surely the simple and "savage" people just then being expelled from American life could not have constructed such inspiring monuments. Politicians, writers, and even some influential scientists instead attributed the mounds to peoples of Europe, Africa, or Asia—Hindus, perhaps, or Israelites, Egyptians, or Japanese. Many nineteenth-century Americans found special comfort in a tale about King Madoc from Wales who, supposedly shipwrecked in the Americas in the twelfth century, had left behind a small but ingenious population of Welsh pioneers who built the mysterious mounds before being overrun by Indians. Some observers even thought Indian skin boats resembled Welsh coracles, designs brought over by King Madoc. The Welsh hypothesis seemed to offer poetic justice, because it implied that nineteenth-century Indians were only receiving a fitting punishment for what their ancestors had done to the remarkable mound builders from Wales.

These fanciful tales were discredited in the late nineteenth and twentieth centuries. In recent decades archaeologists working across the Americas have discovered in more detail how native peoples built the hemisphere's ancient architecture. They have also helped to make clear the degree to which prejudice and politics have blinded European Americans to the complexity, wonder, and significance of America's history before 1492. Fifteen thousand years of human habitation in North America allowed a broad range of cultures to develop, based on agriculture as well as hunting and gathering. In North America a population in the millions spoke hundreds of languages. Cities evolved as well as towns and farms, exhibiting great diversity in their cultural, political, economic, and religious organization. ∞∞∞∞

The skilled craftspeople of the Hopewell tradition worked most often with copper but made exquisite objects from a variety of materials. This image of a human hand, discovered in a Hopewell mound, was cut from a single sheet of mica.

A CONTINENT OF CULTURES

IMMIGRANTS FROM ASIA

RECENT BREAKTHROUGHS IN ARCHAEOLOGY AND genetics have demonstrated that the first inhabitants of the Americas arrived from Siberia at least 15,500 years ago BP.* (For more details, see the After the Fact essay "Tracking the First Americans," beginning on page 22). Gradually these **nomads** filtered southward, some likely following

---

*Before the Present, used most commonly by archaeologists when the time spans are in multiple thousands of years. This text will also use CE for Common Era, equivalent to the Christian Era or AD; BCE is Before the Common Era, equivalent to BC.

the Pacific coastline in small boats, others making their way down a narrow, glacier-free corridor along the eastern base of the Rocky Mountains and onto the northern Great Plains. There they found and hunted a stunning array of huge mammals, so-called megafauna. These animals included mammoths that were twice as heavy as elephants, giant bison, sloths that were taller than giraffes, several kinds of camels, and terrifying, 8-foot-long lions. Within a few thousand years the descendants of these Siberians, people whom Columbus would wishfully dub "Indians," had spread throughout the length and breadth of the Americas.

This first colonization of the Americas coincided with, and perhaps accelerated, profound changes in the natural world. The last Ice Age literally melted away as warmer global temperatures freed the great reservoirs of water once locked in glaciers. A rise in sea levels inundated the Bering Strait, submerging the land bridge, and creating new lakes and river systems. The emergence of new **ecosystems**—climates, waterways, and land environments in which humans interacted with other animals and plants—made for ever greater diversity. The first human inhabitants of the Americas had fed, clothed, warmed, and armed themselves in part by hunting megafauna, and some combination of overhunting and climate change resulted in the extinction of most of these giants by the end of the Ice Age. As glaciers receded and human populations increased, the first Americans had to adapt to changing conditions. They adjusted by hunting smaller animals with new, more specialized kinds of stone tools and by learning to exploit particular places more efficiently.

DIVERSIFIED SOCIETIES So it was that between 10,000 and 2,500 years ago distinctive regional cultures developed among the peoples of the Americas. Those who remained in the Great Plains turned to hunting the much smaller descendants of the now-extinct giant bison; those in the deserts of the Great Basin survived on small game, seeds, and edible plants; those in the Pacific Northwest relied mainly on fishing; and those east of the Mississippi, besides fishing and gathering, tracked deer and bear and trapped smaller game animals and birds. Over these same centuries, what seems to have been one original, common language evolved into regional dialects and eventually into a multitude of distinct languages. Linguistic diversity paralleled other sorts of divergences, in social organizations, kinship practices, politics, and religion. Technological and cultural unity gave way to striking regional diversity as the first Americans learned how to best exploit their particular environments. Glimpses of these profound changes may be found today in burials, stone tools, and some precious sites of long-term or repeated occupation.

Civilizations of Ancient Mexico

AGRICULTURAL REVOLUTION To the south, pioneers in **Mesoamerica** began domesticating squash 10,000 years ago. Over the next several thousand years farmers added other crops including beans, tomatoes, and especially corn to an agricultural revolution that would transform life through much of the Americas. Because many crops could be dried and stored, agriculture allowed these first farmers to settle in one place.

By about 1500 BCE, farming villages began giving way to larger societies, to richer and more complex cultures. As the abundant food supply steadily expanded their populations, people began specializing in certain kinds of work. While most continued to labor on the land, others became craftworkers and merchants, architects and artists, warriors and priests. Their built environment reflected this social change as humble villages expanded into skillfully planned urban sites that were centers of trade, government, artistic display, and religious ceremony.

OLMEC CITY-BUILDERS The Olmecs, the first city-builders in the Americas, constructed large plazas and pyramidal buildings, and sculpted enormous heads chiseled from basalt. The Olmec cultural influence gradually spread throughout Mesoamerica, perhaps as a result of their trade with neighboring peoples. By about 100 BCE, the Olmecs' example had inspired the flowering of Teotihuacán from a small town in central Mexico into a metropolis of towering pyramids. The city had bustling marketplaces, palaces decorated with mural paintings that housed an elite of warriors and priests, schools for their children, and sprawling suburbs for commoners. At its height, around 650 CE, Teotihuacán spanned 15 square miles and had a population of nearly 200,000—making it the sixth largest city in the world.

MAYAN CIVILIZATION More impressive still were the achievements of the Mayas, who benefited from their contacts with both the Olmecs and Teotihuacán. In the lowland jungles of Mesoamerica they built cities filled with palaces, bridges, aqueducts, baths, astronomical observatories, and pyramids topped with temples. Their priests developed a written language, their mathematicians discovered the zero, and their astronomers devised a calendar more accurate than any then existing. In its glory, between the third and ninth century CE, the Mayan civilization boasted some 50 urban centers scattered throughout the Yucatán Peninsula, Belize, Guatemala, and Honduras.

DAILY LIVES

PLAY BALL

The band strikes up—trumpets blaring, drums pounding, flutes trilling. Dancers whirl and gymnasts cavort. Then the players parade into the stadium, and the crowd goes wild, cheering their favorites. So many magnificent athletes trained to win, looking all the more formidable in their heavily padded gear. Which team will carry the day? A great deal is at stake for both players and spectators—honor, wealth, perhaps even life itself. The outcome hangs on the arc of a ball.

The Super Bowl? The World Series? Good guesses, because those present-day athletic spectacles bear striking resemblances to the scene described above: the beginning of a ball game in pre-Columbian Mesoamerica. Those contests, with all their accompanying fanfare, consumed the attention of both elites and commoners for many centuries.

It was the Olmecs who got the ball rolling (and flying), around 1500 BCE. In the main plazas of their cities, they built ornate stone ball courts for teams to compete and celebrated star athletes with towering stone sculptures. Even as civilizations rose and fell in Mesoamerica, the passion for playing ball, following the games, and gambling on their outcome not only endured but even spread to the Hohokam in the American Southwest. Archaeological digs have revealed that nearly every city built by the Mayas, Toltecs, and Aztecs boasted its own ball court: the most impressive were larger than present-day football fields, painted in vivid colors, and decorated with intricately carved birds, jaguars, and skeletal heads. Renowned players inspired artists to paint murals or to fashion clay figurines depicting ballplayers in full athletic regalia—kneepads, gloves, and belts festooned with images of their gods or skeletal heads.

In most cultures the rules of the game dictated that players could use only their hips, buttocks, or knees to bounce the ball against the parallel walls of the court and the alley lying between. And after about 800 CE the game became even more challenging: teams earned the most points by shooting hoops—that is, by sending the ball through a stone ring set in the center of the side walls. No mean feat, since players could not use their hands or feet, and the impact of a flying ball—about six pounds of solid rubber—could inflict serious and even fatal injuries.

But it was the ritual significance of these competitions that made for greater danger. In the Southwest, ball games often figured as friendly rivalries, festive occasions intended to strengthen military or trading alliances among neighboring peoples. In Mesoamerica, however, the games typically celebrated military conquests: during postgame rituals, the captain of the losing team—a captive taken in war—was beheaded with an obsidian knife by the winning captain. That practice seems to have stemmed from the religious significance invested in the ball games, which both the winning players and spectators understood as a religious ceremony celebrating their main deity, the Sun, an orb greater than any other celestial body, and encouraging the soil's fertility with a sacrifice of human blood.

Heavy padding protects the internal organs of this Aztec ballplayer from being injured by the heavy, dangerous rubber ball; the player's headdress is a vulture painted brilliant Mayan blue.

Thinking Critically

What similarities and dissimilarities do modern athletic festivals share with ancient ballplaying festivals in the following areas: equipment, social violence, aesthetic appearance, and religious significance?

But neither the earliest urban centers of the Olmecs nor the glittering city-state of Teotihuacán survived. Even the enduring kingdom of the Mayas had collapsed by 900 CE. Like the ancient civilizations of Greece and Rome, they thrived for centuries and then declined. Scholars still debate the reasons for their collapse. Military attack may have brought about their ruin, or perhaps their large populations exhausted local resources.

AZTEC EMPIRE Mayan grandeur was eventually rivaled in the Valley of Mexico. In the middle of the thirteenth century the Aztecs, a people who had originally lived on Mesoamerica's northern frontiers, swept south and settled in central Mexico. By the end of the fifteenth century they ruled over a vast empire from their capital at Tenochtitlán, an island metropolis of perhaps a quarter of a million people. At its center lay a large plaza bordered by sumptuous palaces and the Great Temple of the Sun. Beyond stood three broad causeways connecting the island to the mainland; many other tall temples were adorned with brightly painted carved images of the gods, zoological and botanical gardens, and well-stocked marketplaces. Through Tenochtitlán's canals flowed gold, silver, exotic feathers and

Aztec merchants, or pochtecas, spoke many languages and traveled on foot great distances throughout Mesoamerica and parts of North America. Pictured at left is Yacatecuhtli, Lord Nose, the patron god of merchants. He carries a symbol of the crossroads, with bare footprints. The merchant on the right carries a cargo of quetzal birds.

jewels, cocoa, and millions of pounds of maize—all trade goods and tribute from the several million other peoples in the region subjugated by the Aztecs.

Unsurpassed in power and wealth, in technological and artistic attainments, theirs was also a highly stratified society. The Aztec ruler, or Chief Speaker, shared governing power with the aristocrats who monopolized all positions of religious, military, and political leadership, while the commoners—merchants, farmers, and craftworkers—performed all manual labor. There were slaves as well, some captives taken in war, others from the ranks of commoners forced by poverty to sell themselves or their children.

Farmers, Potters, and Builders of the Southwest

MOGOLLON AND HOHOKAM PEOPLES

Mesoamerican crops and farming techniques began making their way north to the American Southwest by 1000 BCE. At first the most successful farmers in the region were the Mogollon and the Hohokam peoples, two cultures that flourished in New Mexico and southern Arizona during the first millennium CE. Both tended to cluster their dwellings near streams, relying on either floodplain irrigation or a system of floodgates and canals to sustain their crops. The Mogollon came to be the master potters of the Southwest. The Hohokam pioneered vast and complex irrigation systems in arid southern Arizona that allowed them to support one of the largest populations in precontact North America.

THE ANCESTRAL PUEBLO

Their neighbors to the north in what is now known as the Four Corners Region of Arizona, Colorado, New Mexico, and Utah, commonly referred to by the term Anasazi, are today more properly known as the Ancestral Pueblo peoples. The Ancestral

Pueblo peoples adapted corn, beans, and squash to the relatively high altitude of the Colorado Plateau and soon parlayed their growing surplus and prosperity into societies of considerable complexity. Their most stunning achievements were villages of exquisitely executed masonry buildings—apartment-like structures up to four stories high and containing hundreds of rooms at such places as Mesa Verde (Colorado) and Canyon de Chelly (Arizona). Villages in Chaco Canyon (New Mexico), the largest center of Ancestral Puebloan settlement, were linked to the wider region by hundreds of miles of wide, straight roads.

Besides their impressive dwellings, the Ancestral Pueblo people filled their towns with religious shrines, astronomical observatories, and stations for sending signals to other villages. Their craftworkers fashioned delicate woven baskets, beautiful feather and hide sashes, decorated pottery, and turquoise jewelry that they traded throughout the region and beyond. For more than a thousand years, this civilization prospered, reaching a zenith between about 900 and 1100 CE. During those three centuries, the population grew to approximately 30,000 spread over 50,000 square miles, a total area larger than present-day California.

The remains of Pueblo Bonito, one of the nine Great Houses built by Ancestral Puebloans in Chaco Canyon. By the end of the eleventh century, Pueblo Bonito stood four stories high at the rear and contained 800 rooms as well as many towers, terraces, a large central plaza, and several round "kivas" for religious and ceremonial purposes.

Chiefdoms of the Eastern Woodlands

East of the Mississippi, Indian societies prospered in valleys near great rivers (Mississippi, Ohio, Tennessee, and Cumberland), the shores of the Great Lakes, and the coast of the Atlantic. Everywhere the earliest inhabitants depended on a combination of fishing, gathering, and hunting—mainly deer but also bear, raccoon, and a variety of birds. Around 2000 BCE some groups in the temperate, fertile Southeast began growing the gourds and pumpkins first cultivated by Mesoamerican farmers, and later they also adopted the cultivation of maize. But unlike the ancient peoples of the Southwest, most Eastern Woodland peoples continued to subsist largely on animals, fish, and nuts, all of which were abundant enough to meet their needs and even to expand their numbers.

ADENA AND HOPEWELL Indeed, many of the mysterious earthen mounds that would so fascinate Europeans were built by peoples who did not farm. About 1000 BCE, residents of a place now known as Poverty Point in northeastern Louisiana fashioned spectacular earthworks—six semicircular rings that rose 9 feet in height and covered more than half a mile in diameter. Although these structures might have been sites for studying the planets and stars, hundreds of other mounds—built about 2,000 years ago by the Adena and the Hopewell cultures of the Ohio and Mississippi valleys—served as the burial places of their leading men and women. Alongside the corpses mourners heaped their richest goods—headdresses of antlers, necklaces of copper, troves of shells and pearls—rare and precious items imported from as far north as Canada, as far west as Wyoming, and as far east as Florida. All these mounds attest powerfully not only to the skill and sheer numbers of their builders but also to the complexity of these ancient societies, their elaborate religious practices, and the wide scope of their trading networks.

MISSISSIPPIAN CULTURE Even so, the most magnificent culture of the ancient Eastern Woodlands, the Mississippian, owed much of its prominence to farming. By the twelfth century CE these peoples had emerged as the premier city-builders of North America, and their towns radiated for hundreds of miles in every direction from the hub of their trading network at Cahokia, a port city of perhaps 30,000 located directly across from present-day St. Louis at the confluence of the Missouri and Mississippi Rivers. Cahokia's many broad plazas teemed with farmers hawking their corn, squash, and beans and with craftworkers and merchants displaying their wares. But what commanded every eye were the structures surrounding the plazas—more than 100 flat-topped pyramidal mounds crowned by religious temples and the palaces of rulers.

| An artist's reconstruction of the city of Cahokia, ca. 1100 CE, the hearth of Mississippian culture. Note how tiny the human figures are in comparison to the temples.

Life on the Great Plains

MIGRATORY PEOPLES Cahokia's size and power depended on consistent agricultural surpluses. Outside the Southwest and the river valleys of the East, agriculture played a smaller role in shaping North American societies. On the Great Plains, for example, some people did cultivate corn, beans, squash, and sunflowers, near reliable rivers and streams. But more typically plains communities relied on hunting and foraging, migrating to exploit seasonally variable resources. Plains hunters pursued game on foot; the horses that had once roamed the Americas became extinct after the last Ice Age. Sometimes large groups of people worked together to drive the buffaloes over cliffs or to trap them in corrals. The aridity of the plains made it a dynamic and unpredictable place to live. During times of reliable rainfall, bison populations boomed, hunters flocked to the region, and agricultural communities blossomed along major rivers. But sometimes centuries passed with lower-than-average precipitation, and families abandoned the plains for eastern valleys or the foothills of the Rocky Mountains.

Survival in the Great Basin

Some peoples west of the Great Plains also kept to older ways of subsistence. Among them were the Numic-speaking peoples of the Great Basin, which includes present-day Nevada and Utah, eastern California, and western Wyoming and Colorado. Small family groups scoured their stark, arid landscape for the limited supplies of food it yielded, moving with each passing season to make the most of their environment. Men tracked elk and antelope and trapped smaller animals, birds, even toads, rattlesnakes, and insects. But the staples of their diet were edible seeds, nuts, and plants, which women gathered and stored in woven baskets to consume in times of scarcity. Several families occasionally hunted together or wintered in common quarters, but because the desert heat and soil defied farming, these bands usually numbered no more than about 50 people.

The Plenty of the Pacific Northwest

The rugged stretch of coast from the southern banks of present-day British Columbia to northern California has always been an extraordinarily rich natural environment. Its mild climate and abundant rainfall yield forests lush with plants and game; its bays and rivers teem with salmon and halibut, its oceans with whales and porpoises, and its rocky beaches with seals, otters, abalone, mussels, and clams. Agriculture was unnecessary in such a bountiful place. From their villages on the banks of rivers, the shores of bays, and the beaches of low-lying offshore islands, the ancestors of the Nootkans, Makahs, Tlingits, Tshimshians, and Kwakiutls speared or netted salmon, trapped sea mammals, gathered shellfish, and launched canoes. The largest of these craft, from which they harpooned whales, measured 45 feet bow to stern and nearly 6 feet wide.

SOCIAL AND CEREMONIAL DISTINCTIONS By the fifteenth century these fecund lands supported a population of perhaps 130,000. They also permitted a culture with the leisure time needed to create works of art as well as an elaborate social and ceremonial life. The peoples of the Northwest built houses and canoes from red cedar; carved bowls and dishes from red alder; crafted paddles and harpoon shafts, bows, and clubs from Pacific yew; and wove baskets from bark and blankets from mountain goat wool. They evolved a society with sharp distinctions among nobles, commoners, and slaves, the latter being mainly women and children captured in raids on other villages. Those who were free devoted their lives to accumulating and then redistributing their wealth among other villagers in elaborate potlatch ceremonies in order to confirm or enhance their social prestige.

The Frozen North

Most of present-day Canada and Alaska were equally inhospitable to agriculture. In the farthest northern reaches—a treeless belt of Arctic tundra—temperatures fell below

This ornately carved and painted house post once supported the main beams of a dwelling belonging to a Kwakiutl whaler in the Pacific Northwest. Depicting a man of wealth and high rank, the figure has a whale painted on his chest and copper ornaments on his arms. Two smaller figures, in shadow by the whaler's knees, each support one end of a plank seat. These were his household slaves, most likely children captured in an attack on rival tribes.

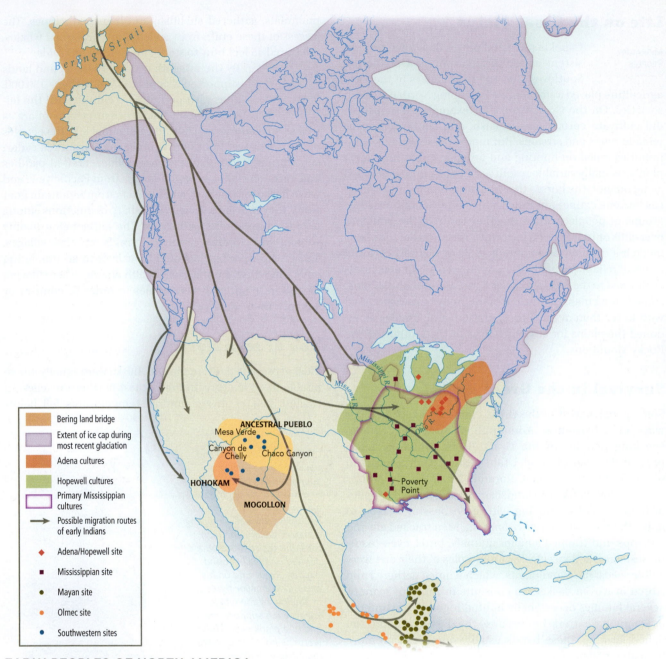

Legend:

- Bering land bridge
- Extent of ice cap during most recent glaciation
- Adena cultures
- Hopewell cultures
- Primary Mississippian cultures
- → Possible migration routes of early Indians
- ◆ Adena/Hopewell site
- ■ Mississippian site
- ● Mayan site
- ● Olmec site
- ● Southwestern sites

Map labels: Bering Strait, ANCESTRAL PUEBLO, Mesa Verde, Canyon de Chelly, Chaco Canyon, HOHOKAM, MOGOLLON, Mississippi R., Missouri R., Ohio R., Poverty Point

EARLY PEOPLES OF NORTH AMERICA

Migration routes across the Bering Strait from Asia were taken by peoples whose descendants created the major civilizations of ancient America. The influence of Mesoamerica is most striking among the cultures of the Southwest and the Mississippians. **Based on the information in After the Fact, "Tracking the First Americans" (pages 22–25), which migration route on this map is being more closely considered due to recent archaeological discoveries?**

freezing for most of the year. The Subarctic, although densely forested, had only about 100 frost-free days each year. As a result, the peoples of both regions survived by fishing and hunting. The Inuit, or Eskimos, of northern Alaska harvested whales from their umiaks, boats made by stretching walrus skin over a driftwood frame and that could bear more than a ton of weight. In the central Arctic, they tracked seals. The inhabitants of the Subarctic, both Algonquian-speaking peoples in the East and Athapaskan

speakers of the West, moved from their summer fishing camps to berry patches in the fall to moose and caribou hunting grounds in the winter.

 REVIEW

How did native cultures differ from region to region, and what accounts for these differences?

INNOVATIONS AND LIMITATIONS

THE FIRST AMERICANS THEREFORE EXPRESSED, governed, and supported themselves in a broad variety of ways. And yet they shared certain core characteristics, including the desire and ability to reshape their world. Whether they lived in forests, coastal regions, jungles, or prairies, whether they inhabited high mountains or low deserts, native communities experimented constantly with the resources around them. Over the course of millennia, nearly all the hemisphere's peoples found ways to change the natural world in order to improve and enrich their lives.

America's Agricultural Gifts

 RISE OF AGRICULTURE   No innovation proved more crucial to human history than native manipulation of individual plants. Like all first farmers, agricultural pioneers in the Americas began experimenting accidentally. Modern-day species of corn, for example, probably derive from a Mesoamerican grass known as teosinte. It seems that ancient peoples gathered teosinte to collect its small grains. By selecting the grains

Teosinte, a Mesoamerican grass. Selective harvesting by native peoples helped transform teosinte into maize (corn).

that best suited them and bringing them back to their settlements, and by returning the grains to the soil through spillage or waste disposal, they unintentionally began the process of domestic cultivation. Soon these first farmers began deliberately saving seeds from the best plants and sowing them in gardens. In this way, over hundreds of generations, American farmers transformed the modest teosinte grass into a staple crop that would give rise to the hemisphere's mightiest civilizations.

 WORLDWIDE SPREAD OF AMERICAN CROPS   Indeed, ever since contact with Europe, the great breakthroughs in Native American farming have sustained peoples around the world. In addition to corn, the first Americans gave humanity scores of varieties of squash, potatoes, beans, and other basic foods. Today, plants domesticated by indigenous Americans account for three-fifths of the world's crops, including many that have revolutionized the global diet. For good or ill, a handful of corn species occupies the center of the contemporary American diet. In addition to its traditional forms, corn is consumed in chips, breads, and breakfast cereals; corn syrup sweeteners are added to many of our processed foods and nearly all soft drinks; and corn is fed to almost all animals grown to be consumed, even farmed fish.

Other Native American crops have become integral to diets all over the world. Potatoes revolutionized northern European life in the centuries after contact, helping to avert famine and boost populations in several countries. Ireland's population tripled in the century after the introduction of potatoes. Beans and peanuts became prized for their protein content in Asia. And in Africa, corn, manioc, and other New World crops so improved diets and overall health that the resulting rise in population may have offset the population lost to the Atlantic slave trade.

Landscapers

Plant domestication requires the smallest of changes, changes farmers slowly encourage at the genetic level. But native peoples in the precontact Americas transformed their world on grand scales as well. In the Andes, Peruvian engineers put people to work by the tens of thousands creating an astonishing patchwork of terraces, dikes, and canals designed to maximize agricultural productivity. Similar public-works projects transformed large parts of central Mexico and the Yucatán. Even today, after several centuries of disuse, overgrowth, and even deliberate destruction, human-shaped landscapes dating from the precontact period still cover thousands of square miles of the Americas.

 CULTIVATED TREES OF THE AMAZON   Recently, scholars have begun to find evidence of incredible manipulation of landscapes and environments in the least likely of places. The vast Amazon rain forest has long been seen by Westerners as an imposing symbol of untouched nature. But it now seems

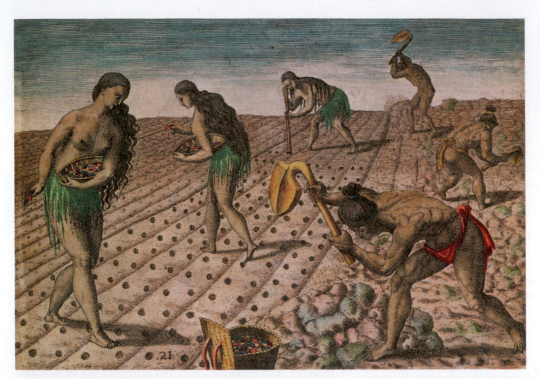

Theodore de Bry, Florida Indians Planting Maize. Both men and women were portrayed as involved in agriculture. Except for the digging stick at the center rear, however, the farming implements drawn by the artist are European in origin.

In both North and South America native peoples used techniques to shape their physical environment, from burning prairies and forests (to harvest/hunt animals) to creating irrigation systems (to control floodwaters for agriculture). This photograph from present-day Peru shows the exquisite terracing Incas employed to maximize agricultural yields amid hills, valleys, and mountains. Some researchers think these circular terraces were used for agronomic experiments.

that much of the Amazon was in fact made by people. Whereas farmers elsewhere in the world domesticated plants for their gardens and fields, farmers in the Amazon cultivated food-bearing trees for thousands of years, cutting down less useful species and replacing them with ones that better suited human needs. All told there are more than 70 different species of domesticated trees throughout the Amazon. At least one-eighth of the nonflooded rain forest was directly or indirectly created by humans. Likewise, native peoples laboriously improved the soil across as much

as a tenth of the Amazon, mixing it with charcoal and a variety of organic materials. These managed soils are more than 10 times as productive as untreated soils in the Amazon. Today, farmers in the region still eagerly search for the places where precontact peoples enriched the earth.

Native North Americans likewise transformed their local environments. Sometimes they moved forests. Ancestral Puebloans cut down and transported more than 200,000 trees to construct the floors and roofs of the monumental buildings in Chaco Canyon. Sometimes they moved rivers. By taming the waters of the Salt and Gila Rivers in present-day Arizona with the most extensive system of irrigation canals anywhere in precontact North America, the Hohokam were able to support large populations in a desert environment. And sometimes they moved the land itself. Twenty-two million cubic feet of earth were moved to construct just one building in the Mississippian city of Cahokia.

FIRE AS A TOOL   Indians also employed fire to systematically reshape landscapes across the continent. Throughout North America's great eastern and western forests, native peoples periodically set low fires to consume undergrowth and fallen trees. In this way the continent's first inhabitants managed forests and also animals. Burning enriched the soil and encouraged the growth of grasses and bushes prized by game animals such as deer, elk, beaver, rabbit, grouse, and turkey. The systematic use of fire to reshape forests helped hunters in multiple ways: it increased the overall food supply for grazing animals, it attracted those animal species hunters valued most, and, by clearing forests of ground debris, fire made it easier to track, kill, and transport game. Deliberate burns transformed forests in eastern North America to such an extent that bison migrated from their original ranges on the plains and thrived far to the east. Thus, when native hunters from New York to Georgia brought down a buffalo, they were harvesting a resource that they themselves had helped to cultivate.

The Shape of a Problem

No matter how great their ingenuity, the first Americans were constrained by certain natural realities. One of the most important is so basic that it is easy to overlook. Unlike Eurasia, which stretches across the Northern Hemisphere along an east-west axis, the Americas fall along a north-south axis, stretching nearly pole to pole. Consequently, the Americas are broken up by tremendous geographic and climactic diversity, making communication and technology transfer far more difficult than it was in the Old World.

Consider the agricultural revolution in Eurasia. Once plants and animals were first domesticated in the Fertile Crescent around 10,000 years ago, they quickly began spreading east and west. Within 1,500 years these innovations had been adopted in Greece and India. A thousand years later the domesticated plants and animals of the Fertile Crescent had reached central Europe, and, from there, it took perhaps 200 years for them to be embraced in present-day Spain. Eurasia's east-west axis facilitated these transfers. Locations at roughly the same latitude share the same seasonal variation, have days of the same length, and often have similar habitats and rates of precipitation, making it relatively easy for plants and animals to move from one place to the next.

In contrast, the north-south orientation of the Americas erected natural barriers to plant and animal transfer. Mesoamerica and South America, for example, are about as far apart as the Balkans and Mesopotamia. It took roughly 2,000 years for plants and animals domesticated in Mesopotamia to reach the Balkans. But because Mesoamerica and South America are separated by tropical, equatorial lowlands, it took domesticated plants such as corn several thousand years to jump between the two regions. Sometimes the transfer never happened at all before European contact. South American potatoes would have thrived in central Mexico, but the tropics stopped their northward migration. Equatorial jungles also denied Mesoamerican societies the llama and the alpaca, domesticated more than 5,000 years ago in the Andes. One wonders what even greater heights the Olmec, Toltec, Mayan, and Aztec civilizations would have achieved if they had had access to these large creatures as draft animals and reliable sources of protein.

TRANSFER OF TECHNOLOGY, AGRICULTURE, AND ANIMALS Dramatic variations in climate likewise delayed the transfer of agriculture from Mexico to regions north of the Rio Grande. Archaeologists have discovered evidence of 10,000-year-old domesticated squash in a cave in southern Mexico, an indication that agriculture began in the Americas nearly as early as anywhere else in the world. Yet squash and corn were not cultivated in the present-day American Southwest for another 7,000 years, and the region's peoples did not embrace a fully sedentary, agricultural lifestyle until the start of the Common Era. Major differences in the length of days, the growing season, average temperatures, and rainfall between the Southwest and central Mexico meant that farmers north of the Rio Grande had to experiment for scores of generations before they perfected crops suited to their particular environments. Corn took even longer to become a staple crop in eastern North America, which is why major urban centers did not arise there until approximately 1000 CE.

By erecting barriers to communication and the spread of technology, then, the predominantly north-south orientation of the Americas made it more difficult for the hemisphere's inhabitants to build on one another's successes. Had American innovations spread as quickly as innovations in Eurasia, the peoples of the Western Hemisphere would likely have been healthier, more numerous, and more powerful than they were when Europeans first encountered them in 1492.

Animals and Illness

One other profound difference between the Eurasian world and the Americas concerned animals and disease. Most diseases affecting humans originated from domesticated animals, which came naturally into frequent and close contact with the humans who raised them. As people across Eurasia embraced agriculture and started living with one another and with domesticated animals in crowded villages, towns, and cities, they created ideal environments for the evolution and transmission of infectious disease. For example, measles, tuberculosis, and smallpox all seem to have derived from diseases afflicting cattle.

 EURASIA'S DEADLY ADVANTAGE Eurasians therefore paid a heavy price for living closely with animals. Yet in the long run, the continent's terrible illnesses hardened its population. Victims who survived into adulthood enjoyed acquired immunity to the most common diseases: that is, if they had already encountered a particular illness as children, their immune systems would recognize and combat the disease more effectively in the event of reinfection. By the fifteenth century, then, Eurasian bodies had learned to live with a host of deadly communicable diseases.

But Native American bodies had not. With a few important exceptions, including tuberculosis, pneumonia, and possibly herpes and syphilis, human populations in the Western Hemisphere seem to have been relatively free from major communicable pathogens. Insofar as most major diseases emerge from domesticated animals, it is easy enough to see why. Indigenous Americans domesticated turkeys, dogs, Muscovy ducks, and guinea pigs but raised only one large mammal—the llama or alpaca (breeds of the same species).

HISTORIAN'S TOOLBOX

An Ancient Calendar

During summer solstice, the spiral is bisected by a single shaft of light.

Why might the Chacoans have used a spiral rather than another image to make this calendar?

On a blazing hot summer day in 1977, Anna Sofaer climbed up to the top of Fajada Butte in Chaco Canyon, New Mexico, spotted three sandstone slabs resting carefully against a wall, and walked over to investigate. What she saw against the wall astounded her: a spiral glyph, bisected by a pure shaft of light. An artist and amateur archaeologist, Sofaer had keen interest in how indigenous American cultures harnessed light and shadow in their architecture. Knowing that it was nearly the summer solstice, she recognized instantly that she'd discovered an ancient Ancestral Puebloan calendar. Later research revealed that the device also marked the winter solstice, the summer and winter equinoxes, and the extremes of the moon's 18–19- year cycle (the major and minor standstills). These discoveries prompted still more research, and scholars now believe that there are structures throughout Chaco Canyon aligned to solar and lunar events.

Thinking Critically

What practical reasons might there have been to build these sorts of sun and moon calendars? Might there have been cultural, religious, or social purposes to track accurately the movements of the sun and moon?

This scarcity of domestic animals had more to do with available supply than with the interest or ability of their would-be breeders. The extinction of most species of megafauna soon after humans arrived in the Americas deprived the hemisphere of 80 percent of its large mammals. Those that remained, including modern-day bison, elk, deer, and moose, were more or less immune to domestication because of peculiarities in their dispositions, diets, rates of growth, mating habits, and social characteristics. In fact, of the world's 148 species of large mammals, only 14 were successfully domesticated before the twentieth century. Of those 14, only one—the ancestor to the llama/alpaca—remained in the Americas following the mass extinctions. Eurasia, in contrast, was home to 13—including the five most common and adaptable domestic mammals: sheep, goats, horses, cows, and pigs.

With virtually no large mammals to domesticate, Native Americans were spared the nightmarish effects of most of the world's major communicable diseases—until 1492. After that date, European colonizers discovered the grim advantage of their millennia-long dance with disease. Old World infections that most colonizers had experienced as children raged through indigenous communities, usually doing the greatest damage to adults

Place and Timing of Pioneering Plant and Animal Domestications

PLACE	PLANT	ANIMAL	APPROX. DATE
Southwest Asia	Wheat, pea, olive	Sheep, goat	8500 BCE
China	Rice, millet	Pig, silkworm	By 7500 BCE
New Guinea	Sugarcane, banana	None	ca. 7000 BCE?
Sahel	Sorghum, African rice	Guinea fowl	By 5000 BCE
Mesoamerica	Corn, beans, squash	Turkey	By 3500 BCE
Andes & Amazonia	Potato, manioc	Llama, guinea pig	By 3500 BCE
Tropical West Africa	African yams, oil palm	None	By 3000 BCE
Eastern North America	Sunflower, goosefoot	None	2500 BCE
Ethiopia	Coffee, teff	None	?

Source: Jared M. Diamond, *Guns, Germs, and Steel: The Fates of Human Societies,* 1st ed. (New York: W.W. Norton, 1997).

whose robust immune systems reacted violently to the novel pathogens. Often native communities came under attack from multiple diseases at the same time. Combined with the wars that attended colonization and the malnutrition, dislocation, and despair that attend wars, disease would kill native peoples by the millions while European colonizers increased and spread over the land. Despite their ingenuity and genius at reshaping plants and environments to their advantage, native peoples in the Americas labored under crucial disadvantages compared to Europe—disadvantages that would contribute to disaster after contact.

✓ **REVIEW**

How did the native inhabitants of the Americas transform their environments, and what natural constraints put them at a disadvantage relative to Europeans?

CRISIS AND TRANSFORMATION

SUDDEN DECLINES

WITH ITS COASTAL PLAINS, ARID deserts, broad forests, and vast grasslands, North America has always been a place of tremendous diversity and constant change. Indeed, many of the continent's most dramatic changes took place in the few centuries before European contact. Because of a complex and still poorly understood combination of ecological and social factors, the continent's most impressive civilizations collapsed as suddenly and mysteriously as had those of the Olmecs and the Mayas of Mesoamerica. In the Southwest, the Mogollon culture went into eclipse around the twelfth century, the Hohokam and the Ancestral Puebloans by about the fourteenth. In the Eastern Woodlands, the story

was strikingly similar. Most of the great Mississippian population centers, including the magnificent city of Cahokia, had faded by the fourteenth century.

Enduring Peoples

TRADING CITY OF PAQUIME

The survivors of these crises struggled to construct new communities, societies, and political systems. In the Southwest, descendants of the Hohokam withdrew to small farming villages that relied on simpler modes of irrigation. Refugees embarked on a massive, coordinated exodus from the Four Corners region and established new, permanent villages in Arizona and New Mexico that the Spaniards would collectively call the Pueblos. The Mogollon have a more mysterious legacy, but some of their number may have helped establish the remarkable trading city of Paquime in present-day Chihuahua. Built around 1300, Paquime contained more than 2,000 rooms and had a sophisticated water and sewage system unlike any other in the Americas. The city included 18 large mounds, all shaped differently from one another, and three ball courts reminiscent of those found elsewhere in Mexico. Until its demise sometime in the fifteenth century Paquime was the center of a massive trading network, breeding macaws and turkeys for export and channeling prized feathers, turquoise, seashells, and worked copper throughout a huge region.

The dramatic transformations remaking the Southwest involved tremendous suffering. Southwesterners had to rebuild in unfamiliar and oftentimes less productive places. Although some of their new settlements endure even to this day, many failed. Skeletal analysis from an abandoned pueblo on the Rio Grande, for example, indicates that the average life expectancy was only 16.5 years. Moreover, drought and migrations increased conflict

The rooms of Paquime, divided by adobe mud walls, help archaeologists estimate population.

over scarce resources. The most successful new settlements were large, containing several hundred people, and constructed in doorless, defensible blocks, or else set on high mesas to ward off enemy attacks. These changes were only compounded by the arrival of Athapaskan-speaking peoples (known to the Spanish as Apaches and Navajos) in the century or two before contact with Europeans. These hunters and foragers from western Canada and Alaska moved in small bands, were sometimes friendly, sometimes hostile toward different Pueblos, and eventually became key figures in the postcontact Southwest.

MUSKOGEAN PEOPLES In the Eastern Woodlands, the great Mississippian chieftainships never again attained the glory of Cahokia, but key traditions endured in the Southeast. In the lower Mississippi valley, the Natchez maintained both the temple mound–building tradition and the rigid social distinctions of Mississippian civilization. Below the chief, or "Great Sun," of the Natchez stood a hereditary nobility of lesser "Suns," who demanded respect from the lowly "Stinkards," the common people. Other Muskogean-speakers rejected this rigid and hierarchical social model and gradually embraced a new, more flexible system of independent and relatively **egalitarian** villages that forged confederacies to better cope with outsiders. These groupings would eventually mature into three of the great southeastern Indian confederacies: Creek, Choctaw, and Chickasaw.

IROQUOIANS To the North lived speakers of Iroquoian languages, roughly divided into a southern faction including Cherokees and Tuscaroras, and a northern faction including the powerful Iroquois and Hurons. Like Muskogeans to the South, these Iroquoian communities mixed farming with a hunting/gathering economy and lived in semipermanent towns. The distinctive feature of Iroquois and Huron architecture was not the temple mound but rather the longhouse (some stretching up to 100 feet in length). Each sheltered as many as 10 families.

ALGONQUINS The Algonquins were the third major group of Eastern Woodlands people. They lived along the Atlantic seaboard and the Great Lakes in communities smaller than those of either the Muskogeans or the Iroquois. By the fifteenth century, the coastal communities from southern New England to Virginia had adopted agriculture to supplement their diets, but those in the colder northern climates with shorter growing seasons depended entirely on hunting, fishing, and gathering plants such as wild rice.

CARIBBEAN CULTURES Cultures of equal and even greater resources persisted and flourished during the fifteenth century in the Caribbean, particularly on the Greater Antilles—the islands of present-day Cuba, Haiti and the Dominican Republic, Jamaica, and Puerto Rico. Although the earliest inhabitants of the ancient Caribbean, the Ciboneys, may have come from the Florida peninsula, it was the Tainos, later emigrants from northern South America, who expanded throughout the Greater Antilles and the Bahamas. Taino chiefs, known as caciques, along with a small number of noble families, ruled island tribes, controlling the production and distribution of food and tools and exacting tribute from the great mass of commoners, farmers, and fisherfolk. Attending to these elites were the poorest Taino peoples—servants who bedecked their masters and mistresses in brilliant diadems of feathers, fine woven textiles, and gold nose and ear pieces and then shouldered the litters on which the rulers sat and paraded their finery.

North America on the Eve of Contact

By the end of the fifteenth century, North America's peoples numbered between 5 and 10 million—with perhaps another million living on the islands of the Caribbean—and they were spread among more than 350 societies speaking nearly as many distinct languages. (The total precontact population for all of the Americas is estimated at between 57 and 112 million.)

DIVERSE LIFEWAYS These millions lived in remarkably diverse ways. Some peoples relied entirely on farming; others on hunting, fishing, and gathering; still others on a combination of the two. Some, like the Natchez and the Iroquois, practiced matrilineal forms of kinship, in which women owned land, tools, and even children. Among others, such as the Algonquins, patrilineal kinship prevailed, and all property and prestige descended in the male line. Some societies, such as those of the Great Plains and the Great Basin in the West, the Inuit in the Arctic, and the Iroquois and Algonquins in the East, were roughly egalitarian, whereas others, like

How Many People Lived on Hispaniola in 1492?

Estimates of the precontact population of the Americas are necessarily speculative. Historians disagree sharply over these estimates, partly because they have used different data and methods and partly because of the moral or political implications that many people associate with high or low figures. The greater the initial population, so the argument goes, the greater the crime of its destruction. The range of estimates is particularly striking for the island of Hispaniola (present-day Haiti and the Dominican Republic), site of Europe's first American colony and of the hemisphere's first demographic catastrophe. Historians Sherburne Cook and Woodrow Borah, relying especially on population estimates in the primary sources, have argued that several million people lived on the island in 1492. The historical demographer Massimo Livi-Bacci, using other methods to estimate the island's precontact population, doubts that it could have exceeded 400,000. These short excerpts cannot capture the complexity of the arguments, but they illustrate some of the differences.

DOCUMENT 1 Sherburne Cook and Woodrow Borah

It is now more than four centuries since [Bartolomé de] las Casas insisted that when Columbus first sighted Hispaniola, the island had 3 to 4 million native inhabitants and perhaps more. This estimate has been denied vigorously. Yet if we accept as substantially correct the count for tribute carried out by Bartolomé Columbus in 1496, and we have seen that there is good evidence for it, we have to concede the reliability of Las Casas. We have set forth previously the reasons for estimating that in 1496 the entire island was inhabited by 3,770,000 souls. There must have been more than this number in 1492, particularly if in 1496 somewhere near 40 percent of the natives were dying annually. Hence we cannot consider a number below 4 million. . . . The most probable number may be put at 7 to 8 million. This is the order of magnitude obtained if we assume that the Columbus' count was relatively accurate, and after we have made all reasonable adjustments for area coverage and the omission of certain population categories. . . . [This figure] would give an average population density for Hispaniola of approximately double the density we found for central Mexico just before the coming of the Europeans. . . . The American Indians in general had available to them food plants of far greater yield per hectare than any cultivated at that time in the Old World except the yams of sub-Saharan Africa and the rice of southeast Asia. The Indians of Hispaniola, relative to the Indians of central Mexico, had cassava, which yields more per hectare than maize and has remarkable storage qualities; they had also the more favorable agricultural conditions of Hispaniola.

Source: Sherburne F. Cook and Woodrow Borah, *Essays in Population History,* 3 vols. (Berkeley and Los Angeles: University of California Press, 1971–1979), 1:405–408.

DOCUMENT 2 Massimo Livi-Bacci

There are many reasons to believe that the contact population could not have exceeded a few hundred thousand people, and to reject recent higher estimates. . . . The crown and the colonists were eager for gold. The Columbuses' failed tribute levy was probably based on rough calculation of the households of the Vega Real and Cibao. On this basis, [historian Luis] Arranz has estimated a total population of 90,000 for 1494 and 60,000 for 1496 in that area, and three times as much (180,000 and 270,000) for the whole of the island. Forcing the indios to work in the mines was a far more efficient way to obtain gold, and gold production reached a peak of 1,000 kg per year in the first years of Ovando's rule. Under the conservative hypothesis that annual individual productivity was 100 g, and that one third of adult males worked in the mines (about 8 percent of the total population), 10,000 laborers would have been needed to produce 1,000 kg, drawn from a total population of 120,000. This figure during Ovando's rule would be consistent with a population twice as large, or more, at the time of contact ten years before, as stipulated by Arranz.

[Another] approach is demographic in nature. It is during [Governor Nicolás de] Ovando's times (1502–1508) that the decline of the native population must have accelerated its pace—the logical consequence of the wars of "pacification," the Spanish occupation of the whole island, the growing number of colonists, and the increased demand for construction, agriculture, and mining labor. At the end of Ovando's rule in 1508, the native population was said to be 60,000: how many could they have been 14 years earlier? A contact population of 400,000—reduced to 200,000 after the high mortality of 1494–1496 and suffering three other major epidemic outbreaks, each one wiping out one third of the total population—would have been reduced to the estimated 60,000 of 1508. Although this is not impossible, epidemics are not mentioned in the abundant available literature prior to the smallpox epidemic of 1518–1519. The repartimiento of 1514 shows an age structure and a children-to-women ratio consistent with rates of decline approaching 5 percent a year. This rate, if carried backward to 1492, would yield a population of about 80,000. More elaborate models would tell an only slightly different story.

These independent methods restrict the plausible range into which the initial contact population could fall. A probability distribution of this elusive number places the most likely figure between 200,000 and 300,000, with levels below 100,000 and above 400,000 both unlikely.

Source: Massimo Livi-Bacci, "Return to Hispaniola: Reassessing a Demographic Catastrophe," *Hispanic American Historical Review* 83, no. 1 (February 2003), pp. 3–51; pp. 48–49.

Thinking Critically

What evidence do Cook and Borah use to produce their population estimate? What evidence does Livi-Bacci employ? Why do you think their approaches produced such dramatically different figures? Do you think that the moral implications of Hispaniola's demographic collapse are different if the original population was 400,000, as opposed to 8 million? Why or why not?

INDIANS OF NORTH AMERICA, CA. 1500

The map shows approximate locations of some Native groups.

many in the Caribbean and the Pacific Northwest, were rigidly divided into nobles and commoners and servants or slaves. Some, such as the Natchez and the Tainos, were ruled by powerful chiefs; others, such as the Algonquins and the Pueblo peoples by councils of village elders or heads of family clans; still others in the Great Basin, the Great Plains, and the far North by the most skillful hunter or the most powerful shaman in their band. Those people who relied on hunting practiced religions that celebrated their kinship with animals and solicited their aid as guardian spirits, whereas predominantly agricultural peoples sought the assistance of their gods to make the rain fall and the crops ripen.

When Europeans first arrived in North America, the continent north of present-day Mexico boasted an ancient, rich, and dynamic history marked by cities, towns, and prosperous farms. At contact it was a land occupied by several million men, women, and children speaking hundreds of languages and characterized by tremendous political, cultural, economic, and religious diversity.

✓ **REVIEW**

What was life like in the Americas on the eve of European contact?

CONCLUSION

THE WORLD AT LARGE

Medieval Scandinavians sailed as far west as Greenland. Then in 1001 a party of men and women under Leif Ericsson established an encampment known as Vinland on the northern tip of Newfoundland. That European outpost in North America may have endured several seasons or even decades, but eventually it was extinguished or abandoned. In contrast, the contact between Eastern and Western Hemispheres that began in 1492 was permanent, and the effects rising out of it were far-reaching. Epidemic diseases and the traumas of colonization would kill millions of Native Americans; animals and vegetables from both hemispheres would transform lives across the globe. And the newcomers from Europe, Africa, and Asia embarked on a series of encounters that reshaped North and South America.

So it is important to grasp the extent of American cultures before 1492, because for most of our nation's short history we have not wanted to remember the Americas as a populous, diverse, and civilized hemisphere when Christopher Columbus first dropped anchor in the Bahamas. In 1830, for example, President Andrew Jackson tried to answer the many critics of his Indian- removal policies. Although "humanity has often wept over the fate of the aborigines of this country," Jackson said, the Indians' fate was as natural and inevitable "as the extinction of one generation to make room for another." Pointing to the mysterious mounds that had so captivated the founding fathers, he proclaimed, "we behold the memorials of a once powerful race, which was exterminated, or has disappeared, to make room for the existing savage tribes." Just as the architects of the mounds supposedly met their end at the hands of these "savage tribes," the president concluded, so, too, must Indians pass away before the descendants of Europe. "What good man would prefer a country covered with forests and ranged by a few thousand savages, to our extensive republic, studded with cities, towns, and prosperous farms . . . and filled with all the blessings of liberty, civilization, and religion!"

Jackson and many others of his era preferred a national history that contained only a few thousand ranging "savages" to one shaped by millions of indigenous hunters, farmers, builders, and inventors. Yet what seems clear from modern research is the rich diversity of American cultures on the eve of contact between the peoples of Eurasia, Africa, and the Americas. We are still struggling to find stories big enough to encompass not only Indians but all those who have forged this complex, tragic, and marvelous nation of nations. ∞∞∞

Chapter Summary

THOUSANDS OF YEARS AFTER SIBERIAN hunters migrated across the Bering Strait to Alaska, their descendants created civilizations that rivaled those of ancient Europe, Asia, and Africa.

- Around 1500 BCE Mesoamerica emerged as the hearth of civilization in the Western Hemisphere, a process started by the Olmecs and brought to its height by the Mayans. Their built cities are remarkable for their art, architecture, and trade.

- The adoption of agriculture gave peoples in the Southwest and the Eastern Woodlands the resource security necessary to develop sedentary cultures of increasing complexity.

- Inhabitants of the Great Plains, the Great Basin, the Arctic, and the Subarctic relied on fishing, hunting, and gathering.

- Peoples of the Pacific Northwest boasted large populations and prosperous economies as well as an elaborate social, ceremonial, and artistic life.

- The first Americans transformed their environments, pioneering crops and terraforming mountains and jungles.

- Nonetheless, the continent's north-south orientation inhibited the spread of agriculture and technology, and a lack of domesticatable animals compared to Europe would leave Native Americans with little protection against Old World diseases.

- North America's most impressive early civilizations had collapsed by the end of the fifteenth century. In their wake a diverse array of cultures evolved.
  - In the Southwest, Pueblo Indians were joined by Athapaskan-speakers eventually known as Apaches and Navajos.
  - In much of eastern North America, stratified chiefdoms of the Mississippian era gave way to more egalitarian confederacies of independent villages.

ADDITIONAL READING

THE MAGAZINE *ARCHAEOLOGY* OFFERS CLEAR explanations of the latest discoveries for nonscientific audiences. The best descriptions of ancient American civilizations are offered by Brian M. Fagan, *Kingdoms of Gold, Kingdoms of Jade: The Americas before Columbus* (1991); and, especially, Charles C. Mann, *1491: New Revelations of the Americas before Columbus* (2005). For North America specifically, see Alice Beck Kehoe, *America before the European Invasions* (2002). For the Southwest, see Stephen Plog, *Ancient Peoples of the Southwest* (2008, 2nd ed.). For the Eastern Woodlands, see George R. Milner, *The Moundbuilders: Ancient Peoples of Eastern North America* (2005). Roger G. Kennedy, *Hidden Cities: The Discovery and Loss of Ancient North American Civilization* (1994), gives a fascinating account of how white Americans responded to the ruins of ancient American cultures. For the consequences of axis alignment and of domesticated animals, see the captivating work by Jared Diamond, *Guns, Germs, and Steel: The Fates of Human Societies* (1998).

For the cultures of precontact Mexico, see Michael D. Coe and Rex Koontz, *Mexico: From the Olmecs to the Aztecs* (5th ed., 2002). For exhaustive surveys of all regional cultures in North America, see William C. Sturtevant, general editor, *Handbook of North American Indians*, 20 volumes projected (1978–).

For a fuller list of readings, see the Bibliography at www.mhhe.com/eh8e.

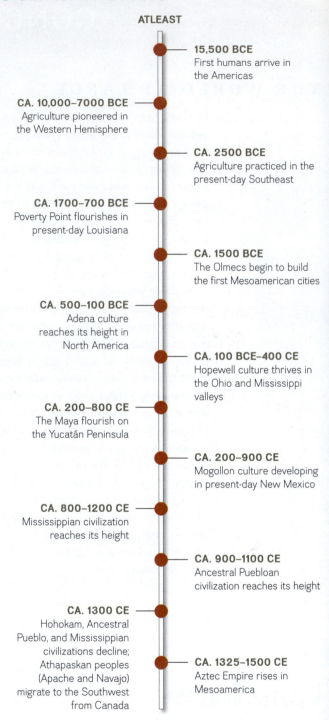

SIGNIFICANT EVENTS

ATLEAST

15,500 BCE
First humans arrive in the Americas

CA. 10,000–7000 BCE
Agriculture pioneered in the Western Hemisphere

CA. 2500 BCE
Agriculture practiced in the present-day Southeast

CA. 1700–700 BCE
Poverty Point flourishes in present-day Louisiana

CA. 1500 BCE
The Olmecs begin to build the first Mesoamerican cities

CA. 500–100 BCE
Adena culture reaches its height in North America

CA. 100 BCE–400 CE
Hopewell culture thrives in the Ohio and Mississippi valleys

CA. 200–800 CE
The Maya flourish on the Yucatán Peninsula

CA. 200–900 CE
Mogollon culture developing in present-day New Mexico

CA. 800–1200 CE
Mississippian civilization reaches its height

CA. 900–1100 CE
Ancestral Puebloan civilization reaches its height

CA. 1300 CE
Hohokam, Ancestral Pueblo, and Mississippian civilizations decline; Athapaskan peoples (Apache and Navajo) migrate to the Southwest from Canada

CA. 1325–1500 CE
Aztec Empire rises in Mesoamerica

	NATURAL ENVIRONMENT	BUILT ENVIRONMENT	PRIMARY SUSTENANCE
Olmecs	Tropical lowlands of south central Mexico	First city-builders: large plazas, pyramidal structures, sculptured heads	Beans, squash, maize (corn)
Mayas	Lowland jungles of the Yucatán Peninsula	Cities contain palaces, bridges, aqueducts, baths, pyramids topped with temples	Beans, squash, maize
Aztecs	Valley of Mexico	Tenochtitlán—an island metropolis with canals, marketplaces, palaces, temples	Beans, squash, maize
Mogollon	Southern New Mexico	Exquisite pottery	
Hohokam	Southern Arizona	Canals, ball courts	Beans, squash, maize
Ancestral Pueblo	Colorado plateau	Masonry buildings	
Eastern Woodlands	Centered in valleys of great rivers, Great Lakes, and Atlantic coast	Mound building, sometimes figurative and monumental	Primarily animals, fish, and nuts; gourds and pumpkins in the southeast; and later maize
Great Plains	Semiarid long- and short-grass plains; rainfall varied and unpredictable	Hide shelters on poles	Primarily hunting and foraging, buffalo stampedes, but some maize, squash, beans, and sunflowers
Great Basin	Plateau between Rocky Mountains and the Sierras	Bands usually numbered less than 50; simple shelters	Elk, antelope trapped; also a wide variety of small game as available; seeds, nuts, and plants
Pacific Northwest	Coastal areas from British Columbia to northern California; abundant rainfall, mild climate	Large and long houses of cedar beams and hand-split boards; complex works of art	Lush forests provide plants and game; rivers and ocean, abundant fish and shellfish
Subarctic and Arctic Peoples	Open boreal forest and tundra stretch across Canada; usually fewer than 100 frost-free days a year	Skin tents and igloos in the arctic winters	Hunting and fishing (including whales, seals, muskrats); moose and caribou

Tracking the First Americans

What methods do historians use to discover the history of a past thousands of years before any humans knew how to write? Archaeological research is key; and by carefully unearthing layer after layer of soil, analyzing artifacts and their relation to these layers, scientists and historians have been able to discover a remarkable amount of information about the first immigrants to the Americas over 15,000 years ago.

But the deductions and inferences made about a past lacking historical documents are often contested. Like millions of other Americans who look to religious texts more than to evolutionary biology or archaeology for their deep history, many Indian people today reject what Western science has to say about their origins. Rather, they insist that their people are truly indigenous to America—that they didn't migrate here but *emerged* here from other planes of existence. A Navajo origin story, for example, explains how their ancestors came into this world, "the changeable world," after a harrowing journey through the Four Dark Worlds. For some these stories are profound metaphors; for others they describe actual events in ancient times. But adherents of either perspective often share an understandable skepticism about scientific "truth" that over the past two centuries has taken so little interest in their oral traditions, has gone through so many massive revisions, and has so often been used to justify native dispossession. After all, Andrew Jackson and other supporters of Indian removal insisted they had "science" on their side.

Archaeologists rarely question the basis of scientific knowledge, but they have continually argued with one another over the scant evidence discovered about early migrations. And progress often depends on accidental finds, such as the one made by an African American cowboy, George McJunkin. McJunkin, a former slave, was a talented rancher, not to mention a capable fiddler, amateur astronomer, and surveyor. Old fossils also fascinated him, and he happened upon one of the most important of the twentieth century.

THE CLOVIS DISCOVERIES

ON HORSEBACK ONE DAY IN 1908 near Folsom, New Mexico, McJunkin spotted some very old bison bones eroding from a slope. Bringing some home, he soon realized that they were far too large—that they must have belonged to an extinct bison species. Professional archaeologists ignored McJunkin's discovery, and only in 1926 after his death did New Mexican locals manage to convince scholars from the University of Colorado to investigate the original site. In doing so, they uncovered an exquisitely crafted stone spear-point embedded in the bison's ribs.

Stone artifacts known as Clovis points have been found with skeletons of mammoths, mastodon, and bison.

The discovery rocked the scientific community, which had long declared confidently that Indians had first arrived in the Americas only about 4,000 BP. Eleven years later another shock followed when archaeologists digging near Clovis, New Mexico, found a different sort of projectile point near butchered mammoth bones. Finally, in 1949, scientists confirmed the great antiquity of both finds by using radiocarbon dating, a method for measuring decay rates of the radioactive isotope of carbon, which exists in organic matter such as bone and starts to break down immediately after an organism dies. Tests revealed that the Folsom site dated to 10,800 BP and that Clovis was nearly a thousand years older still. Soon archaeologists around the continent discovered other sites of comparable antiquity containing stone tools with the same Clovis characteristics. A new consensus emerged: Asian migrants first came to North America around 13,000 BP. These migrants brought with them a common stone-working technology, of the sort found at Clovis. The Clovis people fanned out across the Western Hemisphere and, within one or two millennia, their culture gave way to regionally specific cultural and stone-working traditions, like Folsom.

EVIDENCE OF MIGRATION FROM SIBERIA TO NORTH AMERICA

BUT HOW DID ASIANS GET to North America? According to the long-standing consensus, they walked to Alaska—a region now separated from Siberia by 50 miles of ocean known as the Bering Strait. During the last Ice Age, with much of the world's water locked up in continent-straddling glaciers, ocean levels were far lower. Consequently, between around 25,000 BP and 15,000 BP, a now-submerged landmass called "Beringia" linked Alaska and Siberia. Following game onto and across Beringia, the first Americans gradually occupied this land and, over the course of many generations, some eventually moved east into what is now Alaska. For centuries massive glaciers blocked the way farther south. But geologists have argued that around 15,000 BP an ice-free corridor opened up along what is now the McKenzie River, east of the Canadian Rockies. Game animals and the people hunting them (with Clovis-point tools) eventually began to filter south, gradually emerging into the warmer and totally uninhabited lands of the present-day United States. This scenario enjoyed support for several decades, not only from geologists but also from some geneticists, who found that modern-day Native Americans diverged from Siberians perhaps 15,000 years ago.

Still, several provocative archaeological finds in Tennessee, Pennsylvania, Florida, and elsewhere suggested that humans had been living in the Americas longer—perhaps far longer. For example, a mastodon bone discovered in Washington State, some 800 years older than any Clovis site, had what seemed to be another bone embedded in it—perhaps from a projectile thrown by a human hunter. In the late 1970s researchers from Vanderbilt University discovered an ancient campsite dating to 14,600 BP at Monte Verde, Chile—a full millennium earlier than the oldest known Clovis tools. But the Monte Verde site was thousands of miles to the south and difficult to visit, dating techniques were open to multiple interpretations, and most archaeologists rejected these pre-Clovis claims. The standard story had endured

for decades, and it would take incontrovertible evidence of earlier occupation to overthrow it.

THE NEW CONSENSUS

For most archaeologists, that incontrovertible evidence has finally arrived. A 2008 study demonstrated that fossilized human feces excavated from a cave in Oregon were more than 14,000 years old. In 2011, archaeologist Michael R. Waters (himself once a staunch "Clovis-firster") led a team that confirmed the antiquity of the mastodon bone from Washington State. They found that the invasive bone chip was indeed from another animal and had almost certainly been fashioned into a weapon by an ancient hunter. Most significantly, in 2011 Waters published yet another analysis of a site he excavated on Buttermilk Creek, outside of Austin, Texas. It revealed a typical collection of Clovis tools. But digging deeper into a layer of clay sediments, Waters and his colleagues found dozens of stone tools made with a strikingly different technique. Lacking the organic material necessary for radiocarbon dating, the team instead employed a newer dating technology called optically-stimulated luminescence that can determine when stone was last exposed to the sun by measuring light energy trapped in minerals. The results were remarkable: the oldest tools at the site dated to 15,500 BP.

Most specialists now acknowledge that humans arrived in the present-day United States at least 15,000–16,000 years ago, and that the Clovis stone-working tradition emerged here, long after they arrived. The "shattering" of the Clovis barrier has reinvigorated the study of ancient America, but there now seem to be more questions than ever. Previously excavated sites are being reopened and tested anew in light of the revised theories. Some archaeologists insist that the earliest migrations took place as many as 20,000 or even 40,000 years ago. Though most scholars reject these very early dates, they now do so more tentatively, mindful of the way in which dogmatic loyalty to Clovis-first blinded the field to compelling evidence. And the controversy over dates has reopened the question of the routes Siberians first took into North America. Depending on the date of the first migration, immense glaciers may have made an overland route virtually impossible. For this reason archaeologists have become more interested in the possibility that the first arrivals came in small boats, gradually working their way down the Pacific coast.

Some of the most exciting developments in the study of ancient America are emerging from linguistics and genetics. Previous genetic research on the peopling of the Americas had compared present-day Native Americans and present-day Siberians by examining small regions of their respective genomes, usually Y chromosomes or mitochondrial DNA. These studies confirmed Siberia as the origin of the first migrants and suggested that all native peoples in the Americas descend from a single, ancestral migration. But today new technologies enable the sequencing of entire genomes, making research of this kind far more revealing and complete. In the summer of 2012, researchers unveiled a major new study demonstrating that there were in fact three totally separate migrations from Siberia to the Americas, an idea put forward long ago by linguist Stephen Greenberg but widely dismissed at the time. The first migration, at least 15,000 years ago, populated the entire hemisphere. The vast majority of today's Native Americans are descendants of this first founding group. Millennia later another migration brought the ancestors of the Eskimos and Aleutians who colonized the Arctic, and still another brought the Athapaskans of western Canada and the American Southwest (today's Apaches and Navajos).

It was the most ambitious study of Native American genetics ever undertaken, but the origins debate is hardly settled. Skeptics of the study note that a large majority of the hemisphere's native peoples perished in epidemics and wars in the centuries after contact, making any present-day genetic sample unrepresentative in critical respects. And many indigenous peoples remain deeply distrustful of the motivations behind such studies. They know all too well that stories told about the past have power over both the present and the future. The Genographic Project of the National Geographic Society recently asked all federally recognized tribes in the United States for genetic samples, in order to run an ambitious study on native origins. Out of 565 tribes, only 2 agreed.

Archaeologist Michael R. Waters excavated a site at Buttermilk Creek, near Austin, Texas, which revealed artifacts that are older and of a distinctly different style than the Clovis points found deposited above them, in a more recent layer. Such evidence suggests that migrants into North America arrived much earlier than most archaeologists believed.

With sails bellying in a gale, the Dutch ship in this painting has furled the rest of its canvas. Sailors from western Europe risked much as they crossed the Atlantic in search of fish, silver, gold, and other commodities of trade.

Old Worlds, New Worlds

1400–1600

What's to Come

∞∞∞ **AN AMERICAN STORY** ∞∞∞

FISHING NETS AND FAR HORIZONS

All the world lay before them. Or so it seemed to mariners from England's seafaring coasts, pushing westward toward unknown lands in the far Atlantic.

The scent of the new land came first—not the sight of it, but the smells: the scent of fir trees wafted from beyond the horizon; or the sight of shorebirds wheeling about the masts. Straightaway the captain would call for a lead to be thrown overboard to sound the depths. At its end was a hollowed-out socket with a bit of tallow in it, so that some of the sea bottom would stick when the lead was hauled up. Even out of sight of land, a good sailing master could tell where he was by what came up—"oosy sand" or perhaps "soft worms" or "popplestones as big as beans."

Through much of the fifteenth century the search for cod had drawn West Country sailors north and west, toward Iceland. In the 1480s and 1490s a few English tried their luck farther west, looking for the mythical *Hy-Brasil*—Gaelic for "Isle of the Blessed"—somewhere west of Ireland. These western ventures returned with little to show for their daring until an Italian named Giovanni Caboto, called John Cabot by the English, obtained the blessing of King Henry VII to hunt for unknown lands. From the port of Bristol his lone ship sailed west in the spring of 1497. This time the return voyage brought news of a "new-found" island where the trees were tall enough to make fine masts and the codfish were plentiful. Cabot returned to England to inform His Majesty of his success, received 10 pounds as his reward, and with the proceeds dressed himself in dashing silks. Then he returned to Bristol to undertake a more ambitious search for a northwest passage to Asia. In 1498 his five ships disappeared over the horizon and were never heard from again.

By the 1550s Cabot's island, now known as Newfoundland, attracted 400 vessels annually, fishermen not only from England but also from France, Portugal, and Spain. The harbor of present-day St. John's, Newfoundland, served as the informal hub of the North Atlantic fishery. Sailors dropped anchor to take on supplies in the spring, trade with native peoples, or to prepare for the homeward voyage in autumn. There was a good deal of swapping tales, for these seafarers knew as much as anyone else—if not more—about the new world of wonders that was opening to Europeans. They were acquainted with names like Cristoforo Colombo, the Italian from Genoa whom Cabot might have known as a boy. They listened to Portuguese tales of sailing around the Horn of Africa in pursuit of spices and to stories of Indian empires to the south, rich in gold and silver that Spanish treasure ships were bringing home.

During the sixteenth century, West Country fisherfolk from England sailed from harbors such as Plymouth, shown here in a painting from the 1480s. Can you spot the primitive lighthouse?

Indeed, Newfoundland was one of the few places in the world where so many ordinary folk of different nations could gather and talk, crammed aboard dank ships moored in St. John's harbor, huddled before blazing fires on its beaches, or crowded into smoky makeshift taverns. When the ships sailed home in autumn, the tales went with them, repeated in the tiniest coastal villages by those pleased to have cheated the sea and death one more time. Eager to fish, talk, trade, and take profits, West Country mariners were almost giddy at the prospect of Europe's expanding horizons.

Though most seafarers who fished the waters of Newfoundland remain unknown today, it is well to begin with these ordinary folk, for the European discovery of the Americas cannot be looked on simply as the voyages of a few bold explorers. Adventurers such as Columbus and Cabot were only the tip of a much larger expansion of European peoples and culture that began in the 1450s. That expansion arose out of a series of gradual but telling changes in the fabric of European society. Some of these changes were technological, arising out of advances in the arts of navigating and shipbuilding and the use of gunpowder. Some were economic, involving the development of trade networks like those linking Bristol with ports in Iceland and Spain. Some were **demographic,** bringing about a rise in Europe's population after a devastating century of plague. Other changes were religious, adding a dimension of belief to the political rivalries that fueled discoveries in the Americas. Yet others were political, making it possible for kingdoms to centralize and extend their influence across the ocean. Portugal, Spain, France, and England—all possessing coasts along the Atlantic—led the way in exploration, spurred on by Italian "admirals" such as Caboto and Colombo, Spanish *conquistadores*—"conquerors"—such as Hernán Cortés and Francisco Pizarro, and English sea dogs such as Humphrey Gilbert and Walter Raleigh. Ordinary folk rode these currents, too. The great and the small alike were propelled by forces that were remolding the face of Europe—and were beginning to remold the face of the world. ∞∞∞

EURASIA AND AFRICA IN THE FIFTEENTH CENTURY

 CHINA'S GLORY IN 1450, HOWEVER, THE WESTERN European kingdoms that would one day dominate much of the world still sat at the fringe of an international economy that revolved around China. By a variety of measures Ming China was the richest, most powerful, and most advanced society in the world. All Eurasia sought Chinese goods, especially spices, ceramics, and silks, and Chinese ships sped these goods to faraway ports. Seven times between 1405 and 1433, China's "treasure fleet"—300 ships manned by 28,000 sailors and commanded by Zheng He (pronounced "Jung Huh")—unfurled its red silk sails off the south China coast and traveled as far as the kingdoms of eastern Africa. The treasure fleet's largest craft were nine-masted junks measuring 400 feet long. They boasted multiple decks and luxury cabins with balconies. (By comparison, Columbus's largest ship in 1492 was a mere 85 feet long, and the crew aboard all three of his ships totaled just 90 men.) Chinese leaders soon grounded their trading fleet and put a stop to the long-distance voyages that might eventually have made Zheng He a forerunner to Columbus. But Chinese luxuries, most transported overland, continued to be Eurasia's most sought-after commodities.

ISLAMIC KINGDOMS The next mightiest powers in the Old World were not European kingdoms but rather huge Islamic empires, especially the Ottomans in the eastern Mediterranean. The Ottomans rose to prominence during the fourteenth and fifteenth centuries and expanded aggressively in every direction. Muslim rulers gained control of critical trade routes and centers of commerce between Asia and Europe. The Ottomans' greatest triumph came in 1453, when the sultan Mehmet II conquered Constantinople (now Istanbul), the ancient and supposedly impregnable Christian city that straddled Europe and Asia and was one of the world's premier trading hubs. Mehmet's stunning victory sounded alarms throughout Europe.

Europe's Place in the World

Europe's rulers had good reason for alarm. Distant from Asia's profitable trade and threatened both economically and militarily by the Ottomans, most of the continent remained fractious and vulnerable. During the fourteenth and fifteenth centuries, 90 percent of Europe's people, widely dispersed in small villages, made their living from the land. But warfare, poor transportation, and low grain yields all created food shortages, and undernourishment produced a population prone to disease. Under these circumstances life was nasty, brutish, and usually short. One-quarter of all children died in the first year of life. People who reached the age of 40 counted themselves fortunate.

It was also a world of sharp inequalities, where nobles and aristocrats enjoyed several hundred times the income of peasants or craftworkers. It was a world with no strong, centralized political authority, where kings were weak and warrior lords held sway over small towns and tiny fiefdoms. It was a world of violence and sudden death, where homicide, robbery, and rape occurred with brutal frequency. It was a world where security and order of any kind seemed so fragile that many people clung to tradition, and more than a few used witchcraft in an attempt to master the chaotic and unpredictable world around them.

THE BLACK DEATH But Europe was changing, in part because of a great calamity. Between the late 1340s and the early 1350s, bubonic plague—known as the Black Death—swept away one-quarter of Europe's population. Some urban areas lost 70 percent of their people to the disease. The Black Death disrupted both agriculture and commerce, and provoked a spiritual crisis that resulted in violent, unsanctioned religious movements, scapegoating of marginal groups, even massacres of Jews. Although Europeans seem to have met recurrent outbreaks of the disease with less panic, the sickness continued to disrupt social and economic life nonetheless.

Yet the sudden drop in population relieved pressure on scarce resources. Survivors of the Black Death found that the relative scarcity of workers and consumers made for better wages, lower prices, and more land. These changes intersected in an overall expansion of trade. In earlier centuries Italian merchants had begun building wealth by encouraging commerce across Europe and by tapping into

| *As bubonic plague and other epidemic diseases wracked Europe, it brought the possibility of sudden death closer than ever. This skull pendant dating from the 1600s was designed as jewelry to hang from the wearer's breast. When opened, it revealed a skeleton in a coffin. In England, before the coming of the Black Death, funeral monuments usually portrayed deceased lords and ladies in their finest clothing. Afterward, the monuments increasingly featured death masks, contorted corpses, or skeletons with serpents slinking among their bones.*

A WITCH BOTTLE

Known as a "Bellarmine jar." Why? (Do a little web research!)

Pins and needles. Why might these have been deliberately bent?

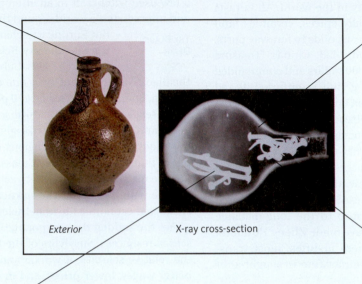

Exterior

X-ray cross-section

Fingernail clippings: well manicured, suggesting someone of higher social standing.

Liquid: analysis shows it to be urine.

Historians often find clues about a culture from material artifacts discarded long ago. A Bellarmine jar was dug up in a cellar in England in 2004. Archaeologists recognized it as a "witch bottle," so called because some English folk used such items to defend against the perceived ill will of witches. "The whole rationale for these bottles was sympathetic magic—so you put something intimate to the bewitched person in the bottle and then you put in bent pins and other unpleasant objects which are going to poison and cause great pain to the witch," explained historian Owen Davies.

When shaken, this bottle splashed and rattled. An X ray showed the objects inside, whose contents were examined in a laboratory. Among other items, the bottle included hair, navel fluff, and a heart-shaped piece of leather with a nail through it. The liquid also contained traces of sulphur (popularly called brimstone in the seventeenth century). An estimated 40,000–60,000 witches were hanged and burned in early modern Europe, demonstrating that despite the Reformation's disdain for "Popish superstitions," supernaturalism and magic remained potent religious strains.

Thinking Critically

Why might brimstone have been added to the witch bottle? What social factors help explain why fifteenth-century Europeans saw witchcraft as a significant part of the way the world worked? Would illnesses such as the plague contribute to attitudes about witchcraft?

---

trade from Africa, the Middle East, and, when able, from Asia. By the late fifteenth century, Europe's merchants and bankers had devised more efficient ways of transferring the money generated from manufacturing and trade and had established credit in order to support commerce across longer distances. Wealth flowed into the coffers of fifteenth-century traders, financiers, and landlords, creating a pool of capital that those investors could plow into new technologies, trading ventures, and, eventually, colonial enterprises.

MONARCHS FORGE NATION-STATES

The direction of Europe's political development also laid the groundwork for overseas colonization. After 1450 strong monarchs in Europe steadily enlarged the sphere of royal power at the expense of warrior lords. Henry VII, the founder of England's Tudor dynasty, Francis I of France, and Ferdinand and Isabella of Spain began the trend, forging modern nation-states by extending their political control over more territory, people, and resources. Such larger, more centrally organized states were able to marshal the resources necessary to support colonial outposts and to sustain the professional armies and navies capable of creating and protecting overseas empires. By the mid-fourteenth century western Europe had commercial networks, private fortunes, strong kingdoms, and ambitions that would lead to a transformative period of expansion.

Africa and the Portuguese Wave

IMPROVED NAVIGATION AND SAILING TECHNIQUES

European expansion began with Africa. For centuries, African spices, ivory, and gold had entered the Eurasian market either westward, through ports on the Indian Ocean, or northward, through the Sahara Desert and into the Mediterranean Sea. Powerful African kingdoms controlled the routes through which these prized commodities moved, and prices ballooned by the time the goods reached cities in Europe. Islamic expansion in the fifteenth century made competition all the more intense. Merchants throughout the continent yearned to access West African markets directly, by ship. But navigational and shipbuilding technology was not yet up to the challenge of the Atlantic's prevailing currents, which sped ships south along Africa's coast but made the return voyage virtually impossible.

Portugal was the first to solve this problem and tap directly into West African markets, thanks in large part to the vision and tenacity of one man. Prince Henry "the Navigator," as he became known, was a passionate advocate for Portugal's maritime interests, an ardent Catholic, and a man who dreamed of turning back Islam's rising tide. He understood that direct commerce with West Africa would allow his kingdom to circumvent the costly trans-Sahara trade. To forward his vision, Henry funded exploratory voyages, established a maritime school, and challenged sailors and engineers to conquer the problem of the current. His advocacy helped the Portuguese develop the caravel, a lighter, more maneuverable ship that could sail better against contrary winds and in rough seas. More seaworthy than the lumbering galleys of the Middle Ages, caravels combined longer, narrower hulls—a shape built for speed—with triangular lateen sails, which allowed for more flexible steering. The caravel allowed the Portuguese to regularly do what few Europeans had ever done: sail down Africa's west coast and return home. Other advances, including a sturdier version of the Islamic world's astrolabe, enabled Portugal's vessels to calculate their position at sea with unprecedented accuracy.

The farther south the Portuguese extended their influence along the Atlantic rim of sub-Saharan Africa, the more likely they were to meet with peoples who had had no earlier encounters with Europeans and, indeed, had no knowledge of the existence of other continents. On catching their first sight of a Portuguese expedition in 1455, the inhabitants of one village on the Senegal River marveled at the strangers' clothing and their white skin. As an Italian member of that expedition recounted, some Africans "rubbed me with their spittle to discover whether my whiteness was dye or flesh."

WEST AFRICAN STATES

But the Portuguese were wrong to mistake such acts of innocence for economic or political naïveté. As they made their way south in stages, the newcomers found mature commercial networks and formidable African states, states eager to trade but intent on protecting their interests. Portugal could not simply take what it wanted from West Africa. With few exceptions, it proved impossible for European powers to colonize territory in West Africa before the nineteenth century because the region's people were too many and too organized. Furthermore, its disease environment was too dangerous. Malaria would kill between one-fourth and one-half of all Portuguese unwise and unlucky enough to try to stay. Hence the newcomers had to seek partners, to forge trading relationships with coastal elites. The Portuguese established forts and trading houses on the coast. They gave tribute or taxes to local powers in return for trading privileges and exchanged textiles, especially, but also raw and worked metal goods, currency (in the form of cowry shells), and beads for prized commodities such as gold, ivory, and malaguetta pepper. Portuguese traders also expressed interest in another commodity, one that would reshape the wider Atlantic world: slaves.

Sugar and the Origins of the Atlantic Slave Trade

Unfree labor has existed in nearly all human societies. Although the norms, characteristics, and economic importance of slavery have varied widely over time and place, men, women, and children have been held as slaves from before recorded history to the present. (U.S. and international organizations estimate that today there are as many as 27 million people held in some form of labor bondage and that nearly 1 million unfree people are sold across international borders every year.)

By the Middle Ages, elites in Europe had largely abandoned the slave culture of the Roman Empire and relied instead on serfs or peasants for labor. Slaves became more important as status symbols than as workers, and most were young white women. Indeed, the word "slave" comes originally from "Slav"; Slavic girls and women from the Balkans and the coasts of the Black Sea were frequent targets of slave raids.

| *Astrolabe*

This African fortune-teller reads the palm of her white client in this seventeenth-century painting by a Franco-Flemish artist, Nicolas Regnier. In early modern Europe, class and religion were more important than color and ethnicity in defining social divisions. Slaves, servants, and free workers of all races often worked and socialized together.

CHANGES IN EUROPEAN SLAVERY

But European slavery began to change again following the Crusades. In 1099 Christian forces captured Jerusalem from the Seljuk Turks (forerunners to the Ottomans). In the Holy Land the crusaders discovered sugar plantations that the Turks had cultivated. At that time some sugar was being produced by Moors in North Africa and Iberia, yet it remained an expensive luxury item coveted by merchants and elites as a medicine and preservative. Crusaders recognized sugar's economic potential, but because it was so labor-intensive they found it a difficult commodity to produce. It required intense work during planting and close tending during the growing season. On maturity the crop had to be harvested and processed 24 hours a day to avoid being spoiled. In short, sugar demanded cheap, pliable labor. The newly arrived crusaders relied in part on slave labor to make their plantations turn a profit.

SPREAD OF SUGAR

Once Islamic forces under the famed leader Saladin reconquered Jerusalem in the twelfth century, European investors established new plantations on eastern Mediterranean islands. In addition to being labor intensive, though, sugar was a crop that quickly exhausted soils and forced planters to move operations regularly. Plantations spread to new islands, and by the early 1400s sugar was even being grown in Portugal. As production expanded, planters had to work harder than ever to obtain the necessary labor because of the Black Death and because Ottoman conquests restricted European access to the traditional slaving grounds of the eastern Mediterranean and the Balkans.

Thus by the fifteenth century the Portuguese were already producing sugar on slave-run plantations, but they were seeking new cropland and new sources of slaves. Once

again Prince Henry's vision enhanced his kingdom's economic interests. While Portugal's merchants were establishing trading posts along the west coast of Africa, Iberian mariners were discovering or rediscovering islands in the eastern Atlantic: the Canaries, Madeira, and the Azores, islands with rich, volcanic soils ideally suited to sugarcane. By the late fifteenth century sugar plantations were booming on the Atlantic islands, staffed by West African slaves. By the middle of the sixteenth century people of African descent accounted for 10 percent of the population of Lisbon, Portugal's capital city.

DIAS AND DA GAMA

Portugal was growing great in wealth and in ambition. Convinced that they could reach coveted Asian markets by sea, bold mariners sailed their caravels farther and farther south. In 1488 Bartolomeu Dias rounded the Cape of Good Hope on the southern tip of Africa, sailing far enough up that continent's eastern coast to claim discovery of a sea route to India. Ten years later Vasco da Gama reached India itself, and Portugal's interests ultimately extended to Indochina and China.

Portuguese geographers had long felt certain that travel around Africa was the shortest route to the Orient, but an Italian sailor disagreed. Cristoforo Colombo was 25 years old when he shipwrecked on the Portuguese coast in 1476. The ambitious young man spent the next 10 years learning from the world's master mariners. He also threw himself into research, devouring Lisbon's books on geography and cartography. Columbus (the Latinized version of his name) became convinced that the fastest route from Portugal to China lay west, across the uncharted Atlantic Ocean. He appealed to Portugal's king to support an exploratory voyage, but royal geographers scoffed at the idea. They agreed that the world was round but insisted (correctly, as it turns out) that the globe was far larger than Columbus had calculated; hence the proposed westward route was too distant to be practical. Almost a decade of rejection had grayed Columbus's red hair, but—undaunted—he packed up in 1485 and took his audacious idea to Spain.

✓ **REVIEW**

Why did Europeans begin to develop commercial networks in the Atlantic, and how did the Portuguese operate in Africa?

SPAIN IN THE AMERICAS

BUT COLUMBUS ARRIVED A FEW years too early. Spain's monarchs, Ferdinand and Isabella, were then engaged in a campaign to drive the Muslims out of their last stronghold on the Iberian Peninsula, the Moorish kingdom of Granada. At first the monarchs rejected Columbus's offer, leading him to make other (failed) overtures to the kings of England, France, and even Portugal again. Then in 1492 Ferdinand and Isabella took Granada and completed their reconquest of Spain, or *reconquista.* Flush with victory and ready to expand their horizons, the pair granted Columbus another audience. The mariner insisted that a westward route to Asia would allow Spain to compete with Portugal and generate sufficient revenue to continue the reconquest, even into the Holy Land itself. Ignoring the advice of their geographers, the monarchs agreed to his proposal.

COLUMBUS REACHES AMERICA

Columbus's first voyage across the Atlantic could only have confirmed his conviction that he was destiny's darling. His three ships, no bigger than fishing vessels that sailed to Newfoundland, plied their course over placid seas, south from Seville to the Canary Islands and then due west. On October 11, a little more than two months after leaving Spain, branches, leaves, and flowers floated by their hulls, signals that land lay near. Just after midnight, a sailor spied cliffs shining white in the moonlight. On the morning of October 12, the *Niña,* the *Pinta,* and the *Santa Maria* set anchor in a shallow sapphire bay, and their crews knelt on the white coral beach. Columbus christened the place San Salvador (Holy Savior).

The Spanish Beachhead in the Caribbean

Like many men of destiny, Columbus mistook his true destination. At first he confused his actual location, the Bahamas, with an island off the coast of Japan. He coasted along Cuba and Hispaniola (today's Haiti and Dominican Republic), expecting at any moment to catch sight of gold-roofed Japanese temples or fleets of Chinese junks. He encountered instead a gentle, generous people who knew nothing of the Great Khan but who welcomed the newcomers profusely. Columbus's journals note that these people wore little clothing (see Daily Lives, "'Barbaric' Dress—Indian and European," page 36), but they did wear jewelry—tiny pendants of gold suspended from the nose. He dubbed the Taino people "Indians"—inhabitants of the Indies.

Columbus would long insist that he had indeed reached the Indies, and it would take some years before other mariners and geographers understood clearly that these newfound islands and the landmasses beyond them lay between Europe and Asia. One of the earliest geographers to do so was the Florentine Amerigo Vespucci, who first described Columbus's Indies as *Mundus Novus,* a "New World." Rather than dub the new lands "Columbia," a German mapmaker called them "America" in Vespucci's honor. The German's maps proved wildly successful, and the name stuck.

WEST AFRICA AND THE CARIBBEAN COMPARED

Whether Columbus had found Asian isles or a new world, Europeans seemed to agree that the simple societies he encountered were better suited to be ruled than partnered with. Unlike the kingdoms of West Africa, the Taino chiefdoms lacked the military power to resist European aggression. Moreover, although the newfound islands would eventually present their own threats to European health, they seemed a good deal more inviting than the deadly coast of West Africa. Hints of gold, a seemingly weak and docile population, and a relatively healthy climate all ensured that Columbus's second voyage would be one of colonization rather than commerce. During the 1490s and early 1500s Spanish colonizers imposed a terrifically brutal regime on

the Tainos, slaughtering native leaders and forcing survivors to toil in mines and fields.

Only a few Spaniards spoke out against the exploitation. Among them was Bartolomé de Las Casas, a man who spent several years in the Caribbean, participating in conquests and profiting from native labor. Eventually, Las Casas had an epiphany, renounced his role in the conquest, and, as a Dominican friar, became a tireless foe of Spanish cruelties toward Indians. He railed against the "unjust, cruel, and tyrannical warfare" waged on Indians, war waged in order to disrupt native societies and force their people into "the hardest, harshest, and most heinous bondage to which men or beasts might ever be bound into." Las Casas's writings, translated throughout Europe and illustrated with gruesome drawings, helped give rise to the "Black Legend" of Spanish oppression in the Americas.

PRINCIPAL ROUTES OF EUROPEAN EXPLORATION

The warnings had some effect, but not for decades. Within a generation of Columbus's landfall, the Taino population had nearly collapsed from war, overwork, malnutrition, despair, and strange new Eurasian diseases. Ambitious Spaniards began scouring the Caribbean basin, discovering new lands and searching for new populations of Indians to subjugate or enslave in place of the vanishing Tainos. Soon the Bahamas were depopulated by Spanish slavers, and conquests had done to present-day Cuba, Jamaica, and Puerto Rico what they had done to Hispaniola.

Conquest of the Aztecs

Would-be conquistadors turned their eyes to the mainland. Spanish sailors surveyed the Yucatán Peninsula and clashed with the formidable Maya. In 1519 an expedition led by the impetuous Hernán Cortés made contact with native peoples on Mexico's gulf coast. They spoke of an oppressive imperial people who occupied a fantastic city to the west. These were the Aztecs.

Aztecs had much in common with Spaniards. Both societies were predominantly rural, with most inhabitants living in small villages and engaging in agriculture. In both places, merchants and specialized craftworkers clustered in cities, organized themselves into guilds, and clamored for protection from the government. Aztec noble and priestly classes, like those in Europe, took the lead in politics and religion, demanding tribute from the common people. Finally, both societies were robustly expansionist, bent on bringing new lands and peoples under their control.

Yet critical differences between these two peoples shaped the outcome of their meeting. The Aztecs lacked the knowledge of ocean navigation, metal tools and weaponry, and firearms. Equally important, the relatively young Aztec empire had not yet established total control over central Mexico. Formidable peoples remained outside Aztec domination, and conquered city-states within the empire bitterly resented Aztec rule. It was a weakness that Cortés exploited ably. Massing an army of disgruntled native warriors, Cortés and his men marched inland to the mighty Aztec capital Tenochtitlán, home to more people (roughly a quarter million) than any city then existing in Europe. When the emperor Moctezuma's ambassadors met Cortés on the road and attempted to appease him with gold ornaments and other gifts, an Indian witness noted that "the Spaniards . . . picked up the gold and fingered it like monkeys. . . . Their bodies swelled with greed." The newcomers were welcomed into the city as honored guests but soon siezed Moctezuma and took him captive. For months Cortés ruled the empire indirectly, but the Aztecs drove the Spanish out after Moctezuma's death.

Both the Aztecs and the Spanish tried to understand the new in terms of the familiar. Hence an Aztec artist portrayed Cortés as an Indian with strange clothes and stranger beard (left), whereas a European artist depicted Moctezuma in the style of a Greco-Roman warrior (right).

"Barbaric" Dress—Indian and European

It was remarkable to sixteenth-century Europeans how many things seemed to be missing from Indian culture. Even more remarkable, the Indians themselves did not seem to notice. Michel de Montaigne, a French philosopher who had never been to America but liked to talk with explorers and read their accounts, managed to compile quite a list. According to Montaigne, Indians had "no kind of traffic [trade], no knowledge of letters, no intelligence of numbers, no name of magistrate, nor of politics, no use of service [servants], of riches, or of poverty, no contracts, no successions, no partitions, no occupation but idle, no apparel but natural. . . ." That last item—clothing—was crucial. European woodcuts, engravings, and paintings regularly showed native peoples either entirely nude or clad in skimpy loincloths or grass skirts.

Some Europeans interpreted the lack of clothing as evidence of "barbarism." André Thevet, a shocked French visitor to Brazil in 1557, voiced this point of view when he attributed nakedness to simple lust. If the Indians could weave hammocks, he sniffed, why not shirts? But other Europeans viewed unashamed nakedness as a badge of innocence. As remnants of a bygone "golden age," they believed, Indians needed clothing no more than government, laws, regular employment, or other corruptions of civilization.

In fact, Indians were no more "naked" than they were without trade, politics, employment, or religion. Although the simplest peoples of the Caribbean and Brazil wore little, the members of more advanced Indian cultures in South, Central, and North America clothed themselves with animal pelts sewn into mantles and robes, breechclouts, leggings, and moccasins. They wrought bird feathers into headdresses and ear decorations and fashioned reptile skins into belts and pouches. Even more formidably clad were the Inuits of the Far North, who dressed head to foot in sealskin suits with waterproofed seams.

If natives struck whites as underdressed, Europeans seemed, by the Indians' standards, grotesquely overdressed. Indeed, European fashion was ill suited to the environment between the Chesapeake and the Caribbean. Elizabethan gentlemen strutted in silk stockings attached with garters to padded, puffed knee breeches, topped by long-sleeved shirts and tight quilted jackets called "doublets." Men of lesser status wore coarse woolen hose, canvas breeches, shirts, and fitted vests known as "jerkins." Women wore gowns with long, full skirts, low-cut bodices, aprons, and hosiery held up by garters. Ladies went about in silk and wore hoods and mantles to ward off the sun, while women from humbler backgrounds dressed in flannels or canvas and covered their heads with linen caps or coifs.

Such fashions complicated life in the American environment, since heavy clothing and even shoes rotted rapidly from sweat and humidity. The pungent aroma of Europeans also compounded the discomfort of natives who came in contact with them—for the whites who swaddled themselves in woolens also disdained regular bathing. To them, Indian devotion to daily washing seemed just another uncivilized oddity.

It would have been natural for Indians to wonder why the barbaric newcomers did not adapt their dress to a new setting. The answer may be that for Europeans the psychological risk of shedding familiar apparel was simply too great. However inappropriate or even unhealthy, heavy, elaborate dress afforded the comfort of familiarity and distinguished "civilized" newcomer from "savage" native in America.

Thinking Critically

From the perspective of Europeans, how did Native American dress seem barbaric? From the point of view of Indian peoples, how did European dress seem barbaric?

Columbus meeting the Tainos on Hispaniola.

DISEASE AND DEFEAT

In the midst of this victory the city encountered another foe—smallpox. Geographically isolated from Eurasia and its complex disease environment, the Aztecs and all other native peoples in the Americas lacked the acquired immunity that gave Europeans a degree of protection against Old World pathogens. The resulting **virgin soil epidemics**—so called because the victims had no prior exposure—took a nightmarish toll. Smallpox claimed millions in central Mexico between 1520 and 1521. This too presented Cortés with opportunities. Supported by a massive Indian force, he put Tenochtitlán to siege, killing tens of thousands before the ragged, starving survivors surrendered in August of 1521. The feared Aztec Empire lay in ruins. Conquistadors fanned out from central Mexico, overwhelming new populations and eventually learning of another mighty kingdom to the south. Again relying on political faction, disease, technological advantages, and luck, by 1532 Spaniards under Francisco Pizarro and his brothers had conquered the Inca Empire in South America, which in certain regards rivaled even the Aztecs.

The Columbian Exchange

Virgin soil epidemics, which contributed to the devastation of the Indian populations, were only one aspect of a complex web of interactions between the flora and fauna of the Americas on the one hand and that of Eurasia and Africa on the other. Just as germs migrated along with humans, so did plants and animals. These transfers, begun in the decades after Columbus first landed in the Caribbean, are known by historians as the **Columbian exchange,** and they had far-reaching effects on either side of the Atlantic. Europeans brought a host of American crops home with them, as seen in Chapter 1 (page 11). They also most likely brought syphilis, an American disease that broke out across Europe in more virulent form than ever before. Europeans brought to the Americas the horses and large dogs that intimidated the Aztecs; they brought oranges, lemons, figs, and bananas from Africa and the Canary Islands. Escaped hogs multiplied so rapidly that they overran some Caribbean islands, as did European rats.

ONGOING EXCHANGES

The Columbian exchange was not a short-lived event. In a host of different ways it continued to reshape the globe over the next half millennium as travel, exploration, and colonization brought cultures ever closer. Instead of smallpox, today H1N1 influenza or the West Nile virus threatens populations worldwide. But the exchanges of the sixteenth century were often more extreme, unpredictable, and far-reaching because of the previous isolation of the two hemispheres.

The Crown Steps In

The proud conquistadors did not long enjoy their mastery in the Americas. Spain's monarchs, who had just tamed an aristocracy at home, were not about to allow a colonial nobility to arise across the Atlantic. The Crown bribed the conquistadors into retirement—or was saved the expense when men such as Francisco Pizarro were assassinated by their own followers. The task of governing Spain's new colonies passed from the conquerors to a small army of officials, soldiers, lawyers, and Catholic bishops, all appointed by the Crown, reporting to the Crown, and loyal to the Crown. Headquartered in urban centers such as Mexico City (formerly Tenochtitlán), an elaborate, centralized bureaucracy administered the Spanish Empire, regulating nearly every aspect of economic and social life.

SPANISH AND INDIAN POPULATIONS

Few Spaniards besides imperial officials settled in the Americas. By 1600 only about 5 percent of the colonial population was of Spanish descent, the other 95 percent being either Indian or African. Even by 1800 only 300,000 Spanish immigrants had come to Central and South America. Indians often remained on the lands that they had farmed under the Aztecs and the Incas, now paying Spanish overlords their taxes and producing livestock for export. More importantly, Indians paid for the new order through their labor, sometimes as slaves but more often through an evolving administrative system channeling native workers to public and private enterprises throughout New Spain. The Spanish also established sugar plantations in the West Indies; these were worked by black slaves who by 1520 were being imported from Africa in large numbers.

SILVER BONANZA

Spain's colonies returned even more spectacular profits to the mother country by the 1540s—the result of silver discoveries of epic proportions in both Mexico and Peru. Silver mining developed into a large-scale capitalist enterprise requiring substantial investment. European investors and Spanish immigrants who had profited from cattle raising and sugar planting poured their capital into equipment and supplies that would mine the silver deposits more efficiently: stamp mills, water-powered crushing equipment, pumps, and mercury. Whole villages of Indians were pressed into service in the mines, joining black slaves and free white workers employed there.

In the last decades of the sixteenth century the economies of Mexico and Peru revolved around the mines. By 1570 the town of Potosí, the site of a veritable mountain of silver, had become larger than any city in either Spain or its American empire, with a population of 120,000. Local farmers who supplied mining centers with food and Spanish merchants in Seville who exported European goods to Potosí profited handsomely. So, too, did the Spanish Crown, which claimed one-fifth of all extracted silver. During the sixteenth century some 16,000 tons of the precious metal were exported from Spanish America to Europe.

The Search for North America's Indian Empires

Riches and glory radicalized Spanish expectations. Would-be conquistadors embarked on an urgent race to discover and topple the next Aztec or Inca Empire, a race to

DUELING DOCUMENTS

HOW DID SPANIARDS AND AZTECS REMEMBER FIRST CONTACT?

The first encounter between the Spaniards under Hernán Cortés and ambassadors of the emperor Moctezuma in 1519 represents a fateful turning point in history. While we have no full contemporary account of that meeting, two remarkable sources present Spanish and Mexican memories of the event written years later. The first selection below was written in the 1560s by one of Cortés's lieutenants, the conquistador Bernal Díaz. The second section comes from a work compiled in the 1540s by the missionary Bernardino de Sahagún, in which indigenous informants recalled Aztec culture, religion, society, and history up to and through the conquest.

DOCUMENT 1   Bernal Díaz

Seeing the big ship with the standards flying they knew that it was there that they must go to speak with the captain; so they went direct to the flagship and going on board asked who was the Tatuan [Tlatoan] which in their language means the chief. Doña Marina who understood the language well, pointed him out. Then the Indians paid many marks of respect to Cortés, according to their usage, and bade him welcome, and said that their lord, a servant of the great Montezuma, had sent them to ask what kind of men we were and of what we were in search. . . . [Cortés] told them that we came to see them and to trade with them and that our arrival in their country should cause them no uneasiness but be looked on by them as fortunate. . . .

[Several days later, one of Montezuma's emissaries] brought with him some clever painters such as they had in Mexico and ordered them to make pictures true to nature of the face and body of Cortés and all his captains, and of the soldiers, ships, sails, and horses, and of Doña Marina and Aguilar, even of the two greyhounds, and the cannon and cannon balls, and all of the army we had brought with us, and he carried the pictures to his master. Cortés ordered our gunners to load the lombards with a great charge of powder so that they should make a great noise when they were fired off. . . . [The emissary] went with all haste and narrated everything to his prince, and showed him the pictures which had been painted. . . .

Source: Bernal Díaz, *The True History of the Conquest of New Spain,* excerpted in Stuart B. Schwartz, ed., *Victors and Vanquished: Spanish and Nahua Views of the Conquest of Mexico* (2000), pp. 85–91.

DOCUMENT 2   Fray Bernardino de Sahagún

When they had gotten up into [Cortes's] boat, each of them made the earth-eating gesture before the Captain. Then they addressed him, saying, "May the god attend: his agent Moteucçoma who is in charge in Mexico for him addresses him and says, 'The god is doubly welcome.'"

Then they dressed up the Captain. They put on him the turquoise serpent mask attached to the quetzal-feather head fan, to which were fixed, from which hung the green-stone serpent earplugs. And they put the sleeveless jacket on him, and around his neck they put the plaited green-stone neckband with the golden disk in the middle. On his lower back they tied the back mirror, and also they tied behind him the cloak called a *tzitzilli.* And on his legs they placed the green-stone bands with the golden bells. And they gave him, placing it on his arm, the shield with gold and shells crossing on whose edge were spread quetzal feathers, with a quetzal banner. And they laid the obsidian sandals before him. . . .

Then the Captain ordered that they be tied up: they put irons on their feet and necks. When this had been done they shot off the cannon. And at this point the messengers truly fainted and swooned; one after another they swayed and fell, losing consciousness. . . . Then [Cortés] let them go.

[Upon returning to Tenochtitlán and reporting to Moteucçoma, he replied] "I will not hear it here. I will hear it at the Coacalco; let them go there." And he gave orders, saying, "Let some captives be covered in chalk [for sacrifice]."

Then the messengers went to the Coacalco, and so did Moteucçoma. There upon the captives died in their presence; they cut open their chests and sprinkled their blood on the messengers. (The reason they did it was that they had gone to very dangerous places and had seen, gazed on the countenances of, and spoken to the gods.) . . .

When this was done, they talked to Moteucçoma, telling him what they had beheld, and they showed him what [the Spaniards'] food was like.

And when he heard what the messengers reported, he was greatly afraid and taken aback, and he was amazed at their food. It especially made him faint when he heard how the guns went off at [the Spaniards'] command, sounding like thunder, causing people to actually swoon, blocking the ears. And when it went off, something like a ball came out from inside, and fire went showering and spitting out. And the smoke that came out had a very foul stench, striking one in the face. And if they shot at a hill, it seemed to crumble and come apart. . . . Their war gear was all iron. They clothed their bodies in iron, they put iron on their heads, their swords were iron, their bows were iron, and their shields were iron.

And the deer that carried them were as tall as the roof. And they wrapped their bodies all over; only their faces could be seen, very white. . . .

And their dogs were huge creatures, with their ears folded over and their jowls dragging. They had burning eyes, eyes like coals, yellow and fiery. . . .

When Moteucçoma heard it, he was greatly afraid; he seemed to faint away, he grew concerned and disturbed.

Source: Fray Bernardino de Sahagún, *The Florentine Codex,* excerpted in Schwartz, ed., *Victors and Vanquished,* pp. 91–99.

Thinking Critically

How did the Aztecs and the Spaniards communicate? Why does Díaz pay so little attention to the gifts the emissaries brought Cortés? Why might the painters be absent from the Nahua account? What principles of critical thinking should be kept in mind when reading such documents?

Fabulous gold and silver discoveries in their New World empire led Spaniards to force Indians and Africans to labor in the mines under dangerous and brutal conditions. This late-sixteenth-century illustration portrays Africans mining for a Spaniard in Panama, but it seems almost pastoral, compared to the dangers of earthen collapses in the mining pits and tunnels or the risks of suffocation or black lung disease from the dust underground.

become the next Cortés or Pizarro. The prevailing mood was captured by the portrait of a Spanish soldier that adorns the frontispiece of his book about the West Indies. He stands with one hand on his sword and the other holding a pair of compasses on top of a globe. Beneath is inscribed the motto "By compasses and the sword / More and more and more and more."

PONCE DE LEÓN Some of the most ambitious adventurers felt certain that more lands and riches would be found in the North. Spanish slavers had been the first to skirt the North American mainland, going as far north as present-day South Carolina. These voyages likely inspired Juan Ponce de León, conquerer of Puerto Rico, to make the first official expedition to the mainland, which he named Florida to mark the day of his landfall, *Pascua Florida* (Easter). Everywhere he went he met armed resistance from Florida's native inhabitants, people who had come to know and despise Spaniards as slave raiders. Ponce de León

sailed back to Puerto Rico and then returned for some years to Spain, until Cortés's early exploits in Mexico rekindled his ambitions. Filled with visions of glory, he returned to Florida in 1521 only to be mortally wounded in a battle with Calusa Indians.

PÁNFILO DE NARVÁEZ AND CABEZA DE VACA Ponce de León died miserably, yet his countrymen still believed that wealthy Indian empires remained undiscovered in the North. In 1526 Spain established a settlement in present-day Georgia, but the endeavor soon collapsed. Two years later Pánfilo de Narváez, a redbearded veteran from the conquest of Cuba, led a major expedition back to Florida. Ignoring advice from his second-in-command, Alvar Núñez Cabeza de Vaca, Narváez separated from his main force near Tampa Bay and led 300 men on a harrowing march in search of riches. For months the force plundered its way through Florida, while the men fell ill or fell victim to Indian archers, whose longbows could bury an arrow six inches into a tree. Disillusioned and desperate, 242 survivors lashed together makeshift rafts and tried to sail along the Gulf Coast to Mexico. Weeks later proud Narváez and most of his men had disappeared at sea, whereas Cabeza de Vaca and a handful of survivors washed up on islands off the Texas coast.

Local Indian groups then turned the tables and made slaves of the Spaniards. Cabeza de Vaca later recalled that his captors were appalled to learn that the starving castaways had eaten their dead. After years as prisoners, Cabeza de Vaca and three others, including a black slave named Esteban, escaped to make an extraordinary trek across Texas and northern Mexico. Somewhere in present-day Chihuahua they passed through what had been the trading hinterland of Paquime, and Cabeza de Vaca noted an enduring regional commerce in feathers and "green stones"—turquoise. Finally, in July 1536 a shocked party of Spanish slavers stumbled across the four rag-tag castaways and brought them to Mexico City.

HERNÁN DE SOTO The stories the four men told of their trek inspired two more massive expeditions to discover and conquer North America's elusive Indian empires. The first was led by Hernán de Soto, who had grown wealthy helping to conquer Peru. Confident that Florida held similar riches, de Soto scoured the Southeast's agricultural villages searching for gold and taking whatever he wanted: food, clothing, luxury goods, even young women whom he and his men "desired both as servants and for their foul uses. . . ." As they raped, stole, and killed their way through the Southeast, de Soto and his men unwittingly had the honor of being the first and last Europeans to glimpse several declining Mississippian chiefdoms, echoes of Cahokia's ancient majesty. Some native communities resisted, inflicting huge losses on de Soto's men. Others shrewdly feigned friendship and insisted that gold and glory could be found in this or that nearby village, thus ridding themselves of a great danger and directing it at enemies instead. De Soto's men ravaged Indian societies through parts of present-day Florida, Georgia, North and

South Carolina, Tennessee, Alabama, Mississippi, Arkansas, Louisiana, and Texas. The expedition never found the treasures it sought, but it did hasten the transformation of the southeastern chiefdoms into decentralized confederacies.

VÁZQUEZ DE CORONADO

Spanish ambition met a similar fate in the West. In 1539, 29-year-old Francisco Vázquez de Coronado led 300 Spaniards and 1,000 Mexican Indian warriors north into the present-day American Southwest. Emboldened by tales of cities more wondrous even than Tenochtitlán, Coronado's brash confidence began to fail him when instead he found only mud and straw pueblos inhabited by modest farmers. Determined to turn his hugely expensive expedition to advantage, Coronado sent men in all directions. Some went west, until they ran into the vastness of the Grand Canyon and had to turn back. Others traveled east, taking up temporary residence among the Pueblo peoples of the upper Rio Grande. The increasingly abusive visitors soon provoked battles with their hosts, forcing them to abandon 13 villages, which the Spaniards then destroyed. Desperate to redeem his reputation and investment, Coronado followed an Indian he dubbed the Turk out onto the Great Plains in search of a rumored kingdom called Quivira. Perhaps the Turk had in mind one of the easternmost Mississippian chiefdoms, but

As Hernán de Soto traveled through North America, he brought a herd of pigs much like this razorback hog. At times the herd numbered more than 700. The animals were an efficient way of providing protein to the expedition. More than 80 percent of a carcass could be consumed, compared with only 50 percent of a cow or sheep. Hogs could be herded on the march as well, foraging for food as they went. But some anthropologists and historians believe that the hogs were also carriers of disease that migrated to humans. The diseases may have sparked the deaths of thousands of Indians, who lacked the immunity built up by Europeans over centuries of exposure to Eurasian illnesses.

Spanish America, ca. 1600

By 1600 Spain was extracting large amounts of gold and silver from Mexico and South America, as well as profits from sugar plantations in the Caribbean. Each year Spanish treasure ships ferried bullion from mines such as the one at Potosí to the Isthmus of Panama, where it was transported by land to the Caribbean coast, and from there to Spain. An expedition from Acapulco sailed annually to the Philippines as well, returning with Asian spices and other trade goods. *For an English "sea dog" (read: pirate) looking to capture Spanish treasure, which geographic location would be the best place to pick off Spanish treasure ships?*

Map legend:
- Extent of Spanish penetration, 1625
- Aztec Empire
- Maya
- Inca Empire
- ○ Sugar plantations
- Silver mining
- Gold mining
- → Spanish treasure fleets

0   250   500 mi
0   500   1000 km

the frustrated conquistador became convinced he had been deceived. He had the Turk strangled somewhere in present-day Kansas and in 1542 returned to Mexico, where Crown authorities brought him to trial for inflicting "great cruelties" on Indians.

SPAIN'S DOMINANCE IN THE AMERICAS — Conquistadors such as Coronado might be ruined by their unfulfilled ambitions, but Spain could afford its failed North American excursions. It had taken vast wealth from the Americas, conquered the hemisphere's mightiest peoples, and laid claim to most of the New World. Spaniards warily expected competition, and yet for most of the sixteenth century rival European powers took little interest in the Americas. England's fishermen continued to explore the North Sea, Labrador, and Newfoundland. Portugal discovered and laid claim to Brazil. France sent expeditions to explore North America's eastern shoreline (Giovanni da Verrazano, 1524) and the St. Lawrence River valley (Jacques Cartier, 1534, 1535, and 1541). These efforts proved important in the long run, but for most of the century Spain could treat the Americas as their own. They owed that luxury, in part, to religious upheaval in Europe. During the second decade of the sixteenth century—the same decade in which Cortés laid siege to Tenochtitlán—religious changes of enormous significance began spreading through Europe. That revolution in Christianity, known as the Protestant Reformation, occupied European attentions and eventually figured as a crucial force in shaping the history of the Americas.

 REVIEW

How did the Spanish respond to the discovery of a "new world"?

RELIGIOUS REFORM DIVIDES EUROPE

DURING THE MIDDLE AGES, THE Roman Catholic church defined what it meant to be a Christian in western Europe. Like other institutions of medieval society, the Catholic church was a hierarchy. At the top was the pope in Rome, and under him were the descending ranks of other church officials—cardinals, archbishops, bishops. At the bottom of the Catholic hierarchy were parish priests, each serving his own village, as well as monks and nuns living in monasteries and convents. But medieval popes were weak, and their power was felt little in the lives of most Europeans. Like political units of the era, religious institutions of the Middle Ages were local and decentralized.

RISE OF THE PAPACY — Between about 1100 and 1500, however, as the monarchs of Europe grew more powerful so, too, did the popes. The Catholic church acquired land throughout Europe, and its swelling bureaucracy added to church income from tithing (taxes

contributed by church members) and from fees paid by those appointed to church offices. In the thirteenth century church officials also began to sell "indulgences." For ordinary believers who expected to spend time after death purging their sins in purgatory, the purchase of an indulgence promised to shorten that punishment by drawing on a "treasury of merit" amassed by the good works of Christ and the saints.

By the fifteenth century the Catholic church and the papacy had become enormously powerful but increasingly indifferent to popular religious concerns. Church officials meddled in secular politics. Popes and bishops flaunted their wealth, while poorly educated parish priests neglected their pastoral duties. At the same time, popular demands for religious assurance grew increasingly intense.

The Teachings of Martin Luther

Into this climate of heightened spirituality stepped Martin Luther, who abandoned studying the law to enter a monastery. Like many of his contemporaries, Luther was consumed by fears over his eternal fate. He was convinced that he was damned, and he could not find any consolation in the Catholic church. Catholic doctrine taught that a person could be saved by faith in God and by his or her own good works—by leading a virtuous life, observing the sacraments (such as baptism, the Mass, and penance), making pilgrimages to holy places, and praying to Christ and the saints. Because Luther believed that human nature was innately evil, he despaired of being able to lead a life that "merited" salvation. If men and women are so bad, he reasoned, how could they ever win their way to heaven with good works?

JUSTIFICATION BY FAITH ALONE — Luther finally broke through his despair with the Bible. It convinced him that God did not require fallen humankind to earn salvation. Salvation, he concluded, came by faith alone, the "free gift" of God to undeserving sinners. The ability to live a good life could not be the *cause* of salvation but its *consequence:* once men and women believed that they had saving faith, moral behavior was possible. Luther elaborated that idea, known as "justification by faith alone," between 1513 and 1517.

Luther was ordained a priest and then assigned to teach at a university in Wittenberg, Germany. He became increasingly critical, however, of the Catholic church as an institution. In 1517 he posted on the door of a local church 95 theses attacking the Catholic hierarchy for selling salvation in the form of indulgences.

The novelty of this attack was not Luther's open break with Catholic teaching. Challenges to the church had cropped up throughout the Middle Ages. What was new were the passion and force behind Luther's protest. Using the blunt, earthy Germanic tongue, he expressed the anxieties of many devout laypeople and their outrage at the church hierarchy's neglect. The "gross, ignorant asses and knaves at Rome," he warned, should keep their distance from Germany, or else "jump into the Rhine or the nearest river, and take . . . a cold bath."

The pope and his representatives in Germany at first tried to silence Martin Luther, then excommunicated him. But opposition only pushed Luther toward more radical positions. He asserted that the church and its officials were not infallible; only the Scriptures were without error. Every person, he said, should read and interpret the Bible for himself or herself. In an even more direct assault on church authority, he advanced an idea known as "the priesthood of all believers." Catholic doctrine held that salvation came only through the church and its clergy, a privileged group that possessed special access to God. Luther asserted that every person had the power claimed by priests.

Although Luther had not intended to start a schism within Catholicism, independent Lutheran churches were forming in Germany by the 1520s. And, during the 1530s, Luther's ideas spread throughout Europe, where they were eagerly taken up by other reformers.

Martin Luther argued that salvation came by faith alone, a free gift of God to undeserving sinners.

The Contribution of John Calvin

The most influential of Luther's successors was John Calvin, a French lawyer turned theologian. Calvin agreed with Luther that men and women could not merit their salvation. But, whereas Luther's God was a loving deity who extended his mercy to sinful humankind, Calvin conceived of God as awesome, all-knowing and all-powerful—the controlling force in human history that would ultimately triumph over Satan. To bring about that final victory, to usher in his heavenly kingdom, God had selected certain people as his agents, Calvin believed. These people—"the saints," or "the **elect**"—had been "predestined" by God for eternal salvation in heaven.

THE "ELECT" Calvin's emphasis on predestination led him to another distinctively Protestant notion—the doctrine of calling. How could a person learn whether he or she belonged to the elect who were saved? Calvin answered: strive to behave like a saint. God expected his elect to serve the good of society by unrelenting work in a "calling," or occupation, in the world. In place of the Catholic belief in the importance of good works, Calvin emphasized the goodness of work itself. Success in attaining discipline and self-control, in bringing order into one's own life and the entire society, revealed that a person might be among the elect.

Calvin fashioned a religion to change the world. Whereas Luther believed that Christians should accept the existing social order, Calvin called on Christians to become activists, reshaping society and government to conform with God's laws laid down in the Bible. He wanted all Europe to become like Geneva, the Swiss city that he had converted into a holy commonwealth in which the elect regulated the behavior and morals of everyone else. And unlike Luther, who wrote primarily for a German audience, Calvin addressed his most important book, *The Institutes of the Christian Religion* (1536), to Christians throughout Europe. Reformers from every country flocked to Geneva to learn more about Calvin's ideas.

The Birth of Spanish Florida and French Huguenots

The Protestant Reformation shattered the unity of Christendom in western Europe. Spain, Portugal, Ireland, and Italy remained firmly Catholic. England, Scotland, the Netherlands, Switzerland, and France developed either dominant or substantial Calvinist constituencies. Much of Germany and Scandinavia opted for Lutheranism. As religious groups competed for political power and the loyalties of believers, brutal wars swept sixteenth-century Europe, and France experienced some of the worst violence. An influential group of Huguenots (Calvin's French followers) saw in North America a potential refuge from religious persecution. Under the leadership of Jean Ribault, 150 Huguenots from Normandy in 1562 established a simple village on Parris Island off present-day South Carolina. That experiment ended in desperation and cannibalism, but two years later Ribault led another, larger group to a site south of present-day Jacksonville, Florida. Here the Huguenots constructed a settlement they named Fort Caroline and nurtured a cordial relationship with the local Timucua Indians. It seemed a promising start.

HUGUENOTS AS A THREAT TO SPAIN But Spanish authorities in the Caribbean took the Huguenots for a triple threat. First, French pirates had long sought to siphon silver from the Americas by waylaying Spanish galleons. Silver shipments rode the Gulf Stream past the Bahamas and up the southeastern coast of North America before turning east toward Spain. In only four years, from 1556 to 1560, French ships preying on this vulnerable route had helped cut Spain's colonial revenues in half. With good reason, Spanish administrators feared that Fort Caroline would entrench the threat of piracy. Second, Spain had to worry that France would plant successful colonies and take a broader interest in the Americas, perhaps eventually making claims on all of North America. Finally, many Spanish Catholics saw Protestantism as a loathsome contagion, to be expunged from Europe and barred from the Americas.

These interlocking concerns prompted Spain to found a permanent colony in Florida. To do so the Crown turned to a focused and unforgiving man named Pedro Menéndez de Avilés. In 1565 Menéndez established a settlement on the coast called St. Augustine (still the United States' oldest continuously occupied, non-Indian settlement) and immediately marched north to destroy Fort Caroline. He and 500 soldiers slogged through the rain and marsh until they found the simple fort. In battle and through later executions, the attackers killed Ribault and about 500 of his Huguenots. Flush with victory, Menéndez established several more outposts on Florida's Atlantic and Gulf coasts, and in 1570 even encouraged a short-lived Jesuit mission just miles from where English colonists would establish Jamestown a generation later. As for the Huguenots, the calamity at Fort Caroline dashed hope that the New World would be their haven. Most had to resign themselves to intensifying persecution in France.

Protestants such as Luther and Calvin placed greater emphasis on the Word of Scripture than on church rituals controlled by priests and bishops. In this seventeenth-century portrait of John Calvin, sacred words from scripture literally help define him.

herself the defender of Protestantism. Elizabeth was no radical Calvinist, however. A vocal minority of her subjects were reformers of that stripe, calling for the English church to purge itself of bishops, elaborate ceremonies, and other Catholic "impurities." Because of the austerity and zeal of such Calvinist radicals, their opponents proclaimed them "**Puritans**."

ELIZABETH'S FEARS

Radical Protestants might annoy Elizabeth as she pursued her careful, moderate policies, but radical Catholics frightened her. She had reason to worry that Spain might try to employ English Catholics to undermine her rule. More ominously, Elizabeth's advisors cautioned that Catholic Ireland to the west would be an ideal base from which Spain or France could launch an invasion of England. Beginning in 1565 the queen encouraged a number of her elite subjects to sponsor private ventures for subduing the native Irish and settling loyal English Protestants on their land. As events fell out, this Irish venture proved to be a prelude to England's bolder attempt to found colonies across the Atlantic.

The English Reformation

While the Reformation wracked northern Europe, King Henry VIII of England labored at a goal more worldly than those of Luther and Calvin. He wanted a son, a male heir to continue the Tudor dynasty. When his wife, Catherine of Aragon, gave birth to a daughter, Mary, Henry petitioned the pope to have his marriage annulled in the hope that a new wife would give him a son. This move enraged the king of Spain, who also happened to be Catherine's nephew. He persuaded the pope to refuse Henry's request. Defiantly, England's king proceeded with the divorce nonetheless and quickly married Anne Boleyn. He then went further, making himself, not the pope, the head of the Church of England. Henry was an audacious but practical man, and he had little interest in promoting reformist doctrine. Apart from discarding the pope, the Church of England remained essentially Catholic in its teachings and rituals.

ENGLISH PURITANS

England's Protestants gained ground during the six-year reign of Henry's son Edward VI but then found themselves persecuted when Edward's Catholic half-sister Mary became queen in 1553. Five years later the situation turned again, when Elizabeth I (Anne Boleyn's daughter) took the throne, proclaiming

REVIEW
How did religious reform divide Europe in the sixteenth century?

ENGLAND'S ENTRY INTO AMERICA

AMONG THE GENTLEMEN EAGER TO win fame and fortune were Humphrey Gilbert and Walter Raleigh, two adventurers with conquistador appetites for more and more. The pair were like most of the English who went to Ireland, ardent Protestants who viewed the native Catholic inhabitants as superstitious, pagan savages: "They blaspheme, they murder, commit whoredome," complained one Englishman, "hold no wedlocke, ravish, steal and commit all abomination without scruple." Thus the English found it easy enough to justify their conquest. They proclaimed it their duty to teach the Irish the discipline of hard work, the rule of law, and the truth of Protestant Christianity. And, while the Irish were learning these civilized, English ways, they would not be allowed to buy land or hold office or serve on juries or give testimony in courts or learn a trade or bear arms.

When the Irish rebelled at that program of "liberation," the English ruthlessly repressed them, slaughtering not only combatants but civilians as well. Most English in Ireland, like most Spaniards in America, believed that native peoples who resisted civilization and proper Christianity should be subdued at any cost. No scruples stopped Gilbert, in an insurgent country, from planting the path to his camp with the severed heads of Irish rebels.

 THE IRISH EXPERIENCE AS A MODEL The struggle to colonize and subdue Ireland would serve as a rough model for later English efforts at expansion. The approach was essentially military, like that of the conquistadors. It also set the ominous precedent that Englishmen could treat "savage" peoples with a level of brutal cruelty that would have been inappropriate in wars between "civilized" Europeans. But the campaigns in Ireland seemed to leave the queen's men with little more than lessons. "Neither reputation, or profytt is to be wonne" in Ireland, concluded Gilbert. He, Raleigh, and many other West Country gentry wanted to take their ambition and their Irish education to North America.

The Ambitions of Gilbert, Raleigh, and Wingina

GILBERT'S UTOPIAN DREAMS In 1578 Gilbert was the first to get his chance for glory when Elizabeth granted him a royal patent—the first English colonial **charter**—to explore, occupy, and govern any territory in America "not actually possessed of any Christian prince or people." The vague, wildly unrealistic charter matched Gilbert's vast ego. It ignored the Indian possession of North America and made him lord and proprietor of all the land lying between Florida and Labrador. In many ways his dreams looked backward. Gilbert hoped to set up a kind of medieval kingdom of his own, where loyal tenant farmers would work the lands of manors, paying rent to feudal lords. Yet his vision also looked forward to a utopian society.

Though Sir Walter Raleigh was a favorite of Queen Elizabeth, her successor, King James I, thought the West Country adventurer lively and dangerous enough to clap him in the Tower of London for fifteen years. When Raleigh defied James a second time, he lost his head.

He planned to encourage England's poor to emigrate by providing them free land and a government "to be chosen by consent of the people." Elizabeth had high hopes for her haughty champion, but a fierce storm got the better of his ship, and the Atlantic swallowed him before he could ever plant a settlement.

WALTER RALEIGH Meanwhile, Gilbert's stepbrother Raleigh had been working more industriously to lay the groundwork for a British American empire. Raleigh enlisted the talents of Richard Hakluyt, a clergyman with a passion for spreading knowledge of overseas discoveries. At Raleigh's bidding, Hakluyt wrote an eloquent plea to Elizabeth for the English settlement of America, titled *A Discourse Concerning Westerne Planting*. The temperate and fertile lands of North America, Hakluyt argued, would prove ideal for growing tropical commodities and would be an excellent base from which to harry the Spanish, search for a northwest passage to the Orient, and extend the influence of Protestantism. He also stressed the advantages of colonies as potential markets for English goods and as havens for the poor and unemployed. Finally, Hakluyt predicted that because the "Spaniardes have executed most outragious and more then Turkishe crueltes in all the west Indies," Indians would greet Englishmen as liberators.

FIRST ROANOKE SETTLEMENT Raleigh's chance to test the prediction finally came in 1584, when Elizabeth granted him a patent nearly identical to Gilbert's. By the summer Raleigh had dispatched an exploratory voyage to the Outer Banks of present-day North Carolina. Expedition leaders reported making friendly contact with a people known as the Roanoke and ruled by a "weroance," or chief, named Wingina. The enthusiastic Hakluyt envisioned a colony that would become the Mexico of England, full of plantations producing sugar and silk and mountains yielding gold. Elizabeth knighted Raleigh and allowed him to name the new land "Virginia," after his virgin queen.

WINGINA'S PLANS But Raleigh was not the only one with grand plans. Almost certainly Wingina had encountered or at least heard of Europeans before 1584. Like most coastal groups in the region, his people would have obtained prized European tools and commodities through indirect trade or by scouring wrecked ships. Preoccupied with the political geography of his own region and eager to fortify his own and his people's power, Wingina recognized that friendly relations with the English would give him privileged access to their trade and influence. Perhaps he believed he would act as patron to the newcomers. After all, they knew little of the region, spoke no Indian languages, and even lacked the basic skills necessary to survive in the area without native assistance. In short, Wingina seems to have welcomed the English and encouraged their return because he believed that they could be useful and that they could be controlled. It was a tragic if understandable miscalculation—one that Indian leaders would make again and again in colonial America.

Raleigh apparently aimed to establish on Roanoke a mining camp and a military garrison. In a stroke of genius, he included in the company of 108 men a scientist, Thomas Hariot, to study the country's natural resources and an artist, John White, to make drawings of the Virginia Indians. *A Briefe and True Reporte of the New Found Land of Virginia* (1588), written by Hariot and illustrated by White, served as one of the principal sources about North America and its Indian inhabitants for more than a century. Far less inspired was Raleigh's choice to lead the expedition—two veterans of the Irish campaigns, Sir Richard Grenville and Ralph Lane. Even his fellow conquistadors in Ireland considered Lane proud and greedy. As for Grenville, he was given to breaking wineglasses between his teeth and then swallowing the shards to show that he could stand the sight of blood, even his own.

The bullying ways of both men quickly alienated the natives of Roanoke. Wingina found the newcomers disrespectful, haughty, and cruel: when a local stole a cup, the English tried to teach everyone a lesson by torching his village and destroying its corn stores. As winter arrived and supplies ran low, the hungry colonists made greater and greater demands. The Roanokes' resentment fueled English anxiety that a revolt was brewing, and these anxieties led only to more brutality and more resentment. The following summer Wingina made a final attempt to regain control of the situation. He had agreed to parlay with Lane about improving relations. But the meeting was a ruse. Lane's men opened fire at the Indian envoys, killed Wingina, and hacked the head from his body. All that averted a massive counterattack was the arrival of England's preeminent privateer, Sir Francis Drake, fresh from freebooting up and down the Caribbean. The settlement's 102 survivors piled onto Drake's ships and put an ocean between themselves and the avenging Roanokes.

A Second Roanoke—and Croatoan

Undaunted, Raleigh organized a second expedition to plant a colony farther north, in Chesapeake Bay. He now projected an agricultural community of manors, much like those in England. He recruited 119 men, women, and children, members of the English middle class, and granted each person an estate of 500 acres. He also appointed as governor the artist John White, who brought along a suit of armor for ceremonial occasions.

White deplored Lane's treachery toward Wingina and hated the brazen, senseless violence that had characterized the entire endeavor. The artist had spent his time on Roanoke closely observing native peoples, their material cultures, and their customs. His sensitive watercolors, especially those featuring women and children, indicate a genuine respect and affection. White felt strongly that under prudent, moral leaders an English colony could indeed coexist peacefully with American Indians.

Despite his best intentions, everything went wrong. In July of 1587 the expedition's pilot, Simon Ferdinando, insisted on leaving the colonists at Roanoke Island rather than along Chesapeake Bay. Understandably, the Roanokes took no pleasure in seeing the English return, and even before Ferdinando weighed anchor the settlers began skirmishing with Indians. Sensing that the situation on Roanoke could quickly become desperate, the colonists

John White's sensitive watercolor Indian Elder *or* Chief *may well be of Wingina. The portrayal includes the copper ornament worn hanging from his neck, indicating high social status and the presence of an active trade network, since copper is not found on the island. Just as Raleigh had to gauge his strategy in dealing with the Indians, Wingina had to decide how to treat the strange newcomers from across the Atlantic.*

prevailed on White to sail back with Ferdinando and bring reinforcements.

But White returned home in 1588 just as the massive Spanish navy, the Armada, was marshaling for an assault on England. Elizabeth enlisted every seaworthy ship and able-bodied sailor in her realm to stave off invasion. The Armada was defeated, but Raleigh left the Roanoke colonists to fend for themselves. When White finally returned to Roanoke Island in 1590, he found only an empty fort and a few cottages in a clearing. The sole clue to the colony's fate was carved on a post: CROATOAN. It was the name of a nearby island off Cape Hatteras.

Had the Roanoke colonists fled to Croatoan for safety? Had they moved to the mainland and joined Indian communities? Had they been killed by Wingina's people?

The fate of the "lost colony" remains a mystery, though later rumors suggest that the missing colonists merged with native societies in the interior. His dream of a tolerant, cooperative colony dashed, White sailed back to England, leaving behind the little cluster of cottages, which would soon be overgrown with vines, and his suit of armor, which was already "almost eaten through with rust."

✓ **REVIEW**

Why did Elizabeth agree to charter a colony in America, and how successful were the first attempts?

CONCLUSION

THE WORLD AT LARGE

All the world lay before them. Or so it had seemed to the young men from England's West Country who dreamed of gold and glory, conquest and colonization. True, they lived on the fringe of the civilized world in the fifteenth and sixteenth centuries. China remained the distant, exotic kingdom of power and wealth, supplying silks and spices and other luxurious goods. Islamic empires stood astride the land routes from Europe to the east. Nations on the western edge of Europe thus took to the seas. Portugal sent slave and gold traders to Africa, as well as merchants to trade with the civilizations of the Indies. Spanish conquerors such as Cortés toppled Indian empires and brought home mountains of silver. But England's West Country sea dogs—would-be conquistadors—met only with frustration. In 1600, more than a century after Columbus's first crossing, not a single English settlement existed in the Americas. The Atlantic had devoured Humphrey Gilbert before he could establish an outpost; Raleigh's Roanoke ventures lay in ruins.

What was left of the freebooting world of West Country adventurers? Raleigh, his ambition unquenchable, sailed to South America in quest of a rich city named El Dorado. In 1603, however, Elizabeth's death brought to the English throne her cousin James I, the founder of the Stuart dynasty. The new king arrested the old queen's favorite for treason and imprisoned him for 15 years in the Tower of London. Set free in 1618 at the age of 64, Raleigh returned to South America, his lust for El Dorado undiminished. Along the way he plundered some Spanish silver ships, defying King James's orders. It was a fatal mistake, because England had made peace with Spain. Raleigh lost his head.

James I did not want to harass the king of Spain; he wanted to imitate him. The Stuarts were even more determined than the Tudors had been to enlarge the sphere of royal power. There would be no room in America for a warrior nobility of conquistadors, no room for a feudal fiefdom ruled by the likes of Raleigh or Gilbert. Instead, there would be English colonies in America like the new outpost of Jamestown, planted on the Chesapeake Bay in Virginia in 1607. There would be profitable plantations and other bold enterprises, enriching English royalty and managed by loyal, efficient bureaucrats. Colonizing America would strengthen English monarchs, paving their path to greater power, just as the dominions of Mexico and Peru had enlarged the authority of the Spanish Crown. America would be the making of kings and queens.

Or would it? For some Europeans, weary of freebooting conquistadors and sea rovers, the order and security that Crown rule and centralized states promoted in western Europe would be enough. But others, men and women who were often desperate and sometimes idealistic, would cast their eyes west across the Atlantic and want more. ∞∞∞

CHAPTER SUMMARY

DURING THE LATE FIFTEENTH CENTURY, Europeans and Africans made their first contact with the Americas.

- Western Europeans had lived on the fringes of an international economy drawn together by Chinese goods.

- Technological advances, the rise of new trade networks and techniques, and increased political centralization made Europe's expansion overseas possible.

- Led by Portugal, European expansion pushed south along the West African coast. Sugar plantations and a slave trade in Africans became critical to this expansive commerce.

- Spain led in exploring and colonizing the Americas, consolidating a vast and profitable empire. Divisions within Indian empires and the devastating effects of European diseases made Spanish conquest possible.

- The early conquistadors were replaced by a centralized royal bureaucracy. The discovery of vast silver deposits provided Spain with immense wealth, while leading to sharply increased mortality among the native population.

- Conquistadors also explored much of the present-day southeastern and southwestern United States. The native peoples they encountered thwarted their efforts.

- Martin Luther and later John Calvin spearheaded the Protestant Reformation, which spread to England, Scotland, the Netherlands, and the Huguenots in France.

- England did not turn to exploration and colonization until the 1570s and 1580s. By that time, European rivalries were heightened by splits arising out of the Protestant Reformation.

- England's merchants and gentry supported colonizing ventures, although early efforts, such as those at Roanoke, failed.

Additional Reading

FOR ORDINARY FOLK IN THE era of exploration, see Kenneth R. Andrews, *Trade, Plunder, and Settlement* (1985). For Portugal's initial expansion, see Malyn Newitt, *A History of Portuguese Overseas Expansion, 1400–1668* (2004). John Thornton's *Africa and Africans in the Making of the Atlantic World, 1400–1680* (1998) explores West Africa's role in the international economy. For sugar and expansion, see Philip D. Curtin, *The Rise and Fall of the Plantation Complex* (2nd ed., 1998). The demographic catastrophe that followed contact is explored in Massimo Livi-Bacci, *Conquest: The Destruction of American Indios* (2008). For European expansion in global perspective, see Jared Diamond, *Guns, Germs, and Steel* (1998).

For Spain in the Caribbean, see David Abulafia, *The Discovery of Mankind* (2008). For Indians in central Mexico after Cortés, see James Lockhart, *The Nahuas after Conquest* (1992).

For a magisterial narrative of Spain's activities in North America, see David J. Weber, *The Spanish Frontier in North America* (1992). Coronado's sojourn is the subject of the exacting work by Richard Flint, *No Settlement, No Conquest* (2008). For the Southeast, see Daniel S. Murphree, *Constructing Floridians* (2006).

For a good introduction to the Reformation in England, see Christopher Haigh, *English Revolutions* (1993); Eamon Duffy's *The Voices of Morebath* (2001) asks how the Reformation transformed the lives of ordinary people. For early English attempts at colonization, in both Ireland and the Americas, consult the works of Nicholas Canny in the Bibliography, as well as Michael Leroy Oberg, *The Head in Edward Nugent's Hand* (2007).

For a fuller list of readings, see the Bibliography at www.mhhe.com/eh8e.

Significant Events

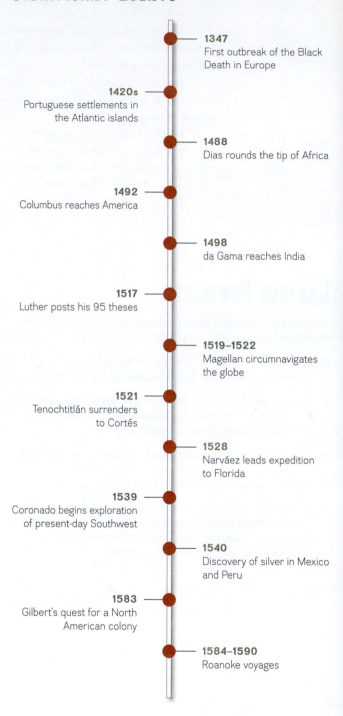

1347
First outbreak of the Black Death in Europe

1420s
Portuguese settlements in the Atlantic islands

1488
Dias rounds the tip of Africa

1492
Columbus reaches America

1498
da Gama reaches India

1517
Luther posts his 95 theses

1519–1522
Magellan circumnavigates the globe

1521
Tenochtitlán surrenders to Cortés

1528
Narváez leads expedition to Florida

1539
Coronado begins exploration of present-day Southwest

1540
Discovery of silver in Mexico and Peru

1583
Gilbert's quest for a North American colony

1584–1590
Roanoke voyages

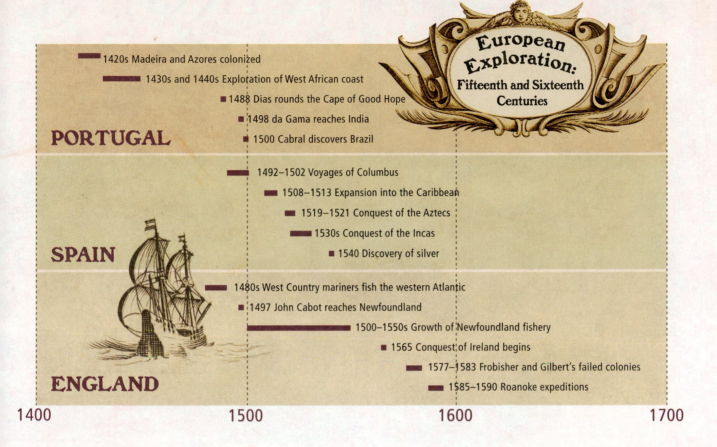

European Exploration: Fifteenth and Sixteenth Centuries

PORTUGAL

- 1420s Madeira and Azores colonized
- 1430s and 1440s Exploration of West African coast
- 1488 Dias rounds the Cape of Good Hope
- 1498 da Gama reaches India
- 1500 Cabral discovers Brazil

SPAIN

- 1492–1502 Voyages of Columbus
- 1508–1513 Expansion into the Caribbean
- 1519–1521 Conquest of the Aztecs
- 1530s Conquest of the Incas
- 1540 Discovery of silver

ENGLAND

- 1480s West Country mariners fish the western Atlantic
- 1497 John Cabot reaches Newfoundland
- 1500–1550s Growth of Newfoundland fishery
- 1565 Conquest of Ireland begins
- 1577–1583 Frobisher and Gilbert's failed colonies
- 1585–1590 Roanoke expeditions

1400   1500   1600   1700

In Jamestown's early years its military orientation was clear. The fort's heavy palisades and its strategic location upriver and some distance inland underscore the colonists' concern for defense—as does the imposing figure of Powhatan seated at the right.

CHAPTER 3

Colonization and Conflict in the South

1600–1750

What's to Come

∞∞∞∞ **AN AMERICAN STORY** ∞∞∞∞

OUTLANDISH STRANGERS

In the year 1617, European time, on a bay Europeans called the Chesapeake, in a land they named Virginia, the mighty weroance Powhatan surveyed his domain with satisfaction. While in his prime, the tall, robust man had drawn some 30 villages along the Virginia coast into a powerful confederacy. As tribute for his protection and leadership, Powhatan collected food, furs, and skins. He forged alliances with communities too distant or too powerful for him to dominate. He married the daughters of prominent men, dozens in all, to solidify his network of patronage and power. His confederacy numbered perhaps 20,000 souls. Some coastal villages had fiercely resisted Powhatan's efforts to incorporate them; some peoples to the west still threatened the security of his confederacy.

After 1607 Powhatan was forced to take into account yet another group. The English, as this new people called themselves, came by sea, crammed into three ships. They were 100 men and 4 boys, all clad in heavy, outlandish clothing, many dressed in gaudy colors. The ships followed a river deep into Powhatan's territory and built a fort on a swampy, mosquito-infested site that they called Jamestown.

Powhatan knew of these strangers from across the waters, who had larger boats and louder, more deadly weapons. But the Indians quickly learned how to use guns, and they vastly outnumbered the English, a clumsy and unprepared people who seemed unlikely to live long and prosper in Powhatan's land. Even amid the bounty of the Chesapeake they failed to feed themselves. With bows and arrows, spears and nets, Indian men brought in an abundance of meat and fish. Fields tended by Indian women yielded generous crops of corn, beans, squash, and melon, and edible nuts and fruits grew wild. Still, for several years the English starved. Powhatan could understand why the English refused to grow food. Cultivating crops was women's work—like building houses; or making clothing, pottery, and baskets; or caring for children. And the English settlement included no women until two arrived in the fall of 1608. Yet even after more women came, the English still starved, and they expected—no, they demanded—that Powhatan's people feed them.

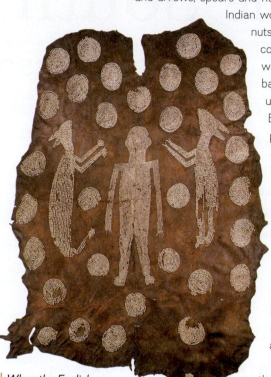

| When the English attempted to crown Powhatan as a subject king, he may have sent King James I this cloak as a reciprocal present. Made from four tanned deerskins, the mantle is decorated with many small marine shells sewn into designs. In addition to human and animal figures, the cloak has 34 roundlets that may represent the Indian districts under Powhatan's control.

Worse, these hapless folk put on such airs. They boasted about the power of their god—they had only one—and denounced the Indians' "devil-worship" of "false gods." They crowed endlessly about the power of their king, James I, who expected Powhatan to become his vassal. The English had even planned a "coronation" to crown Powhatan as a "subject king." He was unimpressed. "If your king has sent me presents," he responded, "I also am a king, and this is my land. . . . Your father is to come to me, not I to him." In the end the English did come to Powhatan, only to find what "a fowle trouble there was to make him kneele to receave his crowne. . . . [He] indured so many perswasions, examples and instructions as tired them all. At last by leaning hard on his shoulders, he a little stooped, and . . . put the Crowne on his head."

Inconceivable to Powhatan—that he should bow before this King James, the ruler of so small and savage a people! When the Indians made war, they killed the male warriors of rival communities but adopted their women and children. But when Powhatan's people defended their land from these invaders, the English retaliated by murdering Indian women and children. Worse, the English could not even keep order among themselves. Too many of them wanted to lead, and they squabbled constantly among themselves.

Only one man, a brash fellow called Captain John Smith, had briefly brought order to the English settlement. Powhatan granted him a grudging respect, though Smith bragged endlessly of his earlier exploits across the ocean, where he had fought as a soldier of fortune. He told fanciful tales of his irresistible appeal to beautiful women who had rescued him from harrowing perils. A rough man, he bullied the Indians for food and would have enslaved them if it had been in his power. Even so, Smith took a genuine interest in Indian ways. But the fellow returned to England in 1609 after being injured when some English gunpowder blew up by mistake. Thereafter the newcomers returned to squabbling and starving.

The temptation to wipe out the helpless, troublesome, arrogant tribe of English—or simply to let them starve to death—was almost overwhelming. But Powhatan had allowed the English to survive. Like Wingina before him, he decided that even these barbaric people had their uses. English labor, English trading goods, and, most important, English guns would help subdue his Indian rivals, within and beyond his confederacy. In 1614 Powhatan cemented his claim on the English and their weapons with the marriage between his favorite child, Pocahontas, and an ambitious Englishman, John Rolfe.

By 1617 events had vindicated Powhatan's strategy of tolerating the English. His chiefdom flourished, ready to be passed on to his brother. Powhatan's people still outnumbered the English, who seldom starved outright now but continued to fight among themselves and sicken and die.

Only one thing had changed in the Chesapeake by 1617: the English were clearing woodland along the rivers and planting tobacco.

That was the doing of Powhatan's son-in-law, Rolfe, a man as strange as the rest of the newcomers. Rolfe had been obsessed with finding a crop that could be grown in Virginia and then sold for gain across the sea. When he succeeded by growing tobacco, other English followed his lead. Odder still, not women but men tended the tobacco fields. Here was more evidence of English inferiority. Men wasted long hours laboring when they might supply their needs with far less effort.

In 1617 Powhatan, ruler of the Pamunkeys, surveyed his domain, and sometime in that year, he looked no longer. He had lived long enough to see the tobacco fields lining the riverbanks, straddling the charred stumps of felled trees. But perhaps he went to his grave believing that he had done what Wingina had failed to do: bend the English to his purposes. He died before those stinking tobacco weeds spread over the length of his land and sent his hard-won dominion up in smoke.

Wingina and Powhatan were not the only native leaders that dreamed of turning Europeans to their advantage. Across North America, the fleeting if destructive encounters of the sixteenth century gave way to sustained colonialism in the seventeenth. As Europeans began to settle the edges of North America in earnest, Indian peoples struggled not only to survive and adapt to new realities but also, when possible, to profit from the rapid changes swirling around them.

Those often dramatic changes reflected upheavals under way all across the globe. The tobacco John Rolfe had begun to cultivate was only one of several plantation **monocultures** that Europeans began to establish in their far-flung colonies. Sugar, already flourishing in the Atlantic islands off the coast of West Africa, was gaining a foothold in the islands of the Caribbean. Rice, long a staple in Asia and grown also in Africa, made its way into South Carolina toward the end of the seventeenth century. Because these crops were grown most efficiently on plantations and required intensive labor, African slavery spread during these years, fueled by an expanding international slave trade. Whites, blacks, and Indians were all, in different ways, caught up in the wrenching transformations. ∞∞∞∞

| No stranger to self-promotion, Captain John Smith included this portrait of himself and verses celebrating his ennobling exploits at the beginning of his Description of New England (1616).

SPAIN'S NORTH AMERICAN COLONIES

AND JUST AS SPAIN HAD been the first European power to explore North America's interior, so, too, it led the way in establishing lasting colonies north of Mexico. But while France and especially England would eventually colonize territory ideally suited to European-style agriculture, territory capable of sustaining large colonial populations, Spain confined its North American ventures to the ecologically challenging regions of the upper Rio Grande and coastal Florida. Because economic opportunities and quality farmland existed in abundance elsewhere in Spanish America, relatively few Spaniards chose to eke out an existence in distant and difficult northern outposts. Nonetheless, Spain's colonial endeavors would have tremendous implications for North America's native peoples and for the geopolitics of the continent as a whole.

The Founding of a "New" Mexico

By the 1590s Coronado's dismal expedition a half century earlier had been all but forgotten. Again, rumors were circulating in Mexico about great riches in the North. New Spain's viceroy began casting about for a champion of means to establish a "new" Mexico, one perhaps as magnificent and profitable as its namesake. He chose Juan de Oñate, son of one of New Spain's richest miners and husband to Isabel de Tolosa Cortés Moctezuma, granddaughter of Hernán Cortés and great-granddaughter of Moctezuma. Oñate needed wealthy connections. Colonizing New Mexico would eventually cost him and his backers more than half a million pesos. But the would-be conquistador expected to recoup the investment with ease. Ignorant of North America's geography and overestimating New Mexico's riches, Oñate even requested and received permission to sail ships up the Pacific to Pueblo country, so that twice a year he could resupply his would-be colony and export its expected treasures.

The magnitude of his mistaken assumptions began coming into focus in 1598, when he led 500 colonists, soldiers, and slaves to the Upper Rio Grande and, like Coronado before him, found modest villages, no ocean, and no evidence of significant mineral wealth. But, whatever the disappointments, Oñate had come with women and children, with livestock and tools, with artisans and tradesmen, with seeds and books and Bibles. He had come to stay. Eager to avoid the violence of earlier encounters, and perhaps hopeful of a mutually beneficial relationship, Tewa-speaking Pueblos evacuated a village for the newcomers to use. Many native leaders pledged Oñate their allegiance, Pueblo artisans labored on irrigation systems and other public works for the Spaniards, and Indian women (traditionally the builders in Pueblo society) constructed the region's first Catholic church.

THE ACOMA SIEGE

The colonizers mistook this cautious courtesy for subservience. Oñate's oldest nephew, Juan de Zaldívar, was bolder and cruder than most. At Acoma Pueblo, known today as "Sky City"

Like many other Pueblo peoples, the founders of Acoma built their village atop a sandstone mesa to gain protection from enemies. As punishment for resisting his troops, Juan de Oñate ordered that every surviving Acoma male have one foot cut off. Four hundred years later, when this statue of Oñate was erected, vandals attacked the statue with a saw. "We took the liberty of removing Oñate's right foot on behalf of our brothers and sisters of Acoma Pueblo," they announced. Monuments to and celebrations of the "distant past" often provoke passionate disagreements in the present. What other monuments or commemorations have provoked disagreements?

because of its position high atop a majestic mesa, he brazenly seized several sacred turkeys to kill and eat, answering Indian protests with insults. Outraged, Acoma's men fell upon Zaldívar, killing him and several of his companions. Oñate responded by putting Zaldívar's younger brother Vicente in command of a punitive expedition. Fueled by grief and rage, Vicente de Zaldívar and his men laid siege to the Pueblo, killed perhaps 800 of its people, and made slaves of several hundred more. Following up on these punishments, Oñate decreed that all adult male survivors were to have one foot chopped off, so that they might spend their lives as limping advertisements for Spanish power. Scholars now doubt that this sentence was actually carried out, but even today, many Pueblos still consider Oñate's harsh edict as emblematic of Spanish cruelty. Whether or not Oñate executed his cruel judgment, the savagery of the Acoma siege and the brutal repression of other acts of defiance educated all of the region's native communities about the risks of resistance.

IMPOVERISHED NEW MEXICO

But it was easier to instill terror than grow rich. Desperate to salvage their enterprise and turn their investments to account, Oñate and key followers toiled on long, fruitless expeditions in search of gold, silver, and cities, and a place to dock those biannual ships. Some more practical entrepreneurs decided to exploit the resources they could see. The younger Zaldívar, headstrong conquerer of Acoma, spent time with Apache hunters and decided it would be more efficient to domesticate bison than search for them on the plains. He and his men labored for three days to build a sprawling cottonwood corral, only to discover that bison were "stubborn animals, brave beyond praise," dangerous to catch, and virtually impossible to hold. With varying degrees of enthusiasm, most Spaniards had to turn to more mundane and less hazardous pursuits, to farming and husbandry, in order to support themselves and their families. Others despaired of even securing a living in arid New Mexico, let alone getting rich. The Spanish Crown had promised to make minor nobles of those who stayed at least five years, but many spurned even this incentive and fled back into New Spain.

They were not the only ones losing confidence. In 1606 royal authorities removed Oñate from his position, brought him up on charges of mismanagement, and, as they had with Coronado, accused him of abusing Indians. Ruined, the would-be conquerer spent the rest of his days struggling to rebuild his fortune and clear his name. Meanwhile, a new viceroy decided that the colonization of "worthless" New Mexico had been an expensive mistake and began planning for its evacuation. The colony would have been abandoned but for the Franciscan religious order. Arguing that it would be a crime and a sin to forsake the many thousands of Indians they claimed to have baptized since 1598, the Franciscans convinced a skeptical King Philip III to continue supporting his outpost on the Upper Rio Grande.

The Growth of Spanish Florida

FRANCISCANS RENEW SPAIN'S EFFORTS

Franciscans would become key actors in Spanish North America. Members of a medieval religious order founded by St. Francis of Assisi, Franciscan monks foreswore property, remained **celibate,** and survived by begging for alms or accepting donations from wealthy patrons. Like their peers and occasional rivals the Jesuits, Franciscans wore only sandals, simple robes, and a rope belt and took it as their charge to live with and minister to the poor. Contact with the Americas reinvigorated their mission. Franciscans accompanied Columbus on his second voyage, and they began ministering to the Indians of central Mexico soon after Tenochtitlán fell. By the 1570s Spanish authorities started secularizing central Mexico's missions, transforming them into self-supporting parishes, and the friars looked to the frontiers for new fields of conversion. Jesuits established several missions in present-day Arizona, and Franciscans went on to become powerful figures in colonial New Mexico.

FLORIDA'S STRATEGIC IMPORTANCE

The Crown needed them, nowhere more so than in Florida. Seventeenth-century New Mexico was a Catholic obligation for Spain's monarchs, but a small worry compared with the strategic importance of Florida. As long as pirates or rival colonies on the Atlantic seaboard threatened Spanish shipping, the king had to control Florida. Pedro Menéndez de Avilés did much to secure the peninsula in the 1560s when he destroyed France's Fort Caroline and established several Spanish posts on the coast (Chapter 2). By the 1580s, however, the energetic Menéndez was dead and nearly all his coastal establishments destroyed by Indians or privateers. Only St. Augustine endured, with a population of perhaps 500 in 1600. Spanish Florida needed something more than a beachhead along the coast if it was to survive.

FRANCISCAN FLORIDA

The king turned to the Franciscans, as part of a two-stage policy to consolidate his influence over Florida's interior. First, royal administrators enticed or menaced the peninsula's many native peoples into alliances. In return for trade privileges and regular diplomatic presents, native leaders promised to trade with no other European power, support the Spanish in war, and tax their people on behalf of the Spaniards. Second, allied Indian communities were made to accept Franciscan missions and a few resident soldiers, a policy that would be critical to molding and monitoring native villages. Franciscans set about their work with characteristic determination. By 1675, 40 missions were ministering to as many as 26,000 baptized Indians. That same year, the bishop of Cuba toured Florida and spoke enthusiastically of converts who embraced "with devotion the mysteries of our holy faith."

Spain's plan for Florida seemed to be working, barely. St. Augustine had grown to a settlement of 1,500 by the time of the bishop's tour. Still, Florida's mission system and network of Indian alliances convinced Spanish authorities that they could maintain their grip on this crucial peninsula.

Artist Jacques Le Moyne recorded this scene of Florida Indians holding council in the 1560s. Observers from Jean Ribaut's French expedition can be seen in the foreground.

Popé and the Pueblo Revolt

As the seventeenth century progressed, Spain's colony in New Mexico also seemed to stabilize. Although more than a few desperate colonists fled south, enough remained to establish a separate Spanish town, El Villa Real de Santa Fe, in 1610. Santa Fe (the second-oldest European town in the United States after St. Augustine) became the hub of Spanish life in New Mexico. The demands of agriculture and stock raising forced many families to settle elsewhere on the Rio Grande, on well-watered lands near Pueblo villages. Economic and political life revolved around a dozen prominent families. By 1675 New Mexico had a colonial population of perhaps 2,500. It was a diverse community, including Spaniards, Africans, Mexican Indians, mestizos (persons of mixed Spanish-Indian heritage), and mulattoes (of Spanish-African heritage).

INDIAN CAPTIVES This population of 2,500 also included large numbers of Indian captives. Occasionally captives came to Spanish households through war, as after the siege of Acoma. In addition, Spaniards purchased enslaved women and children from other Indians and regularly launched slave raids against so-called enemy Indians such as Utes, Apaches, and Navajos. By 1680 half of all New Mexican households included at least one Indian captive, someone who, depending on age, gender, and the master's disposition, could be treated affectionately as a low-status family member or terrorized and abused as disposable human property.

The colonists also extracted labor from Pueblo Indians. Officially Pueblo households had to surrender three bushels of corn and one processed hide or large cotton blanket each year. Pueblos were also sometimes made to labor on public works, and elite Spaniards often exploited their privileges by insisting on more tribute and labor than legally allowed. Still, the populous Pueblos would have been able to satisfy Spanish demands with little difficulty but for other changes in their world. First and most importantly, colonialism meant epidemics. Smallpox arrived in the early 1620s. In less than a generation the Pueblo population plumeted by 70 percent, to about 30,000. Whereas New Mexico had approximately 100 native villages at contact, by 1680 only 30 remained inhabited. Infestations of locusts, severe droughts, and crop failures compounded the crisis. By 1667 a distraught Franciscan reported widespread famine, with native men, women, and children "lying dead along the roads, in the ravines, and in their hovels." Mounted Utes, Apaches, and Navajos, embittered by New Mexican slaving and barred from their customary trade in the pueblos, launched punishing raids against the most vulnerable Pueblo villages.

PUEBLO SUFFERING In their deepening misery Pueblos turned to religion—their own. Since 1598 the Franciscans had worked tirelessly to supress the dances, idols, and ceremonies that long mediated Pueblo relationships with the divine. By the 1670s Pueblo elders could argue convincingly that the calamities of the past decades could be reversed only by a rejection of Christianity and a return to the old faith. Such revivalist sentiments threw the friars into a panic. Franciscans and civil authorities scrambled to extinguish the movement, arresting key Pueblo leaders, executing two and whipping 43 others in front of large crowds.

SPANISH MISSIONS IN NORTH AMERICA, CA. 1675

From St. Augustine, Spanish missionaries spread north into Guale Indian villages in present-day Georgia and westward among the Indians of Timucua, Apalachee, and Apalachicola. In New Mexico, missions radiated outward from the Rio Grande, as distant as Hopi Pueblos in the west.

One of the 43, a prominent Tewa man known to history as Popé, nursed his wounds in Taos and laid the groundwork for a general uprising against the Spaniards. Appealing to headmen throughout the Pueblo world, Popé called for a war to purify the land. Many individuals and some entire villages refused to participate. But on August 10, 1680, Indians from across New Mexico rose up and began killing Spaniards. Astonished survivors fled to Santa Fe, followed by Popé and his army, who put the town to siege. Weeks later the desperate Spanish governor, wounded by an arrow in the face and a gunshot to the chest, gathered the remainder of the colonial population and fled south out of New Mexico. The most successful pan-Indian uprising in North American history, the Pueblo Revolt sent shock waves throughout Spanish America, and left the Catholic devout agonizing over what they might have done to provoke God's wrath.

 **REVIEW**

Where and why did Spain establish colonies in North America, and how did native peoples resist colonization?

ENGLISH SOCIETY ON THE CHESAPEAKE

BY 1700, THEN, SPAIN VIEWED its situation in the Americas from a very different perspective than it had 100 years earlier. The Pueblo Revolt had checked its power at the northern reach of its American possessions. Equally disturbing was the progress of Spain's European rivals in the Americas during the seventeenth century. During the sixteenth, both France and England had envied the wealth Spain reaped from its American conquests. But neither nation did much to check Spain's power, beyond preying on Spanish ships and fishing for cod. During the seventeenth century, this would change.

MERCANTILISM In fact, by 1600 other European kingdoms were beginning to view overseas colonies as essential to a nation's power and prosperity. They did so in part because of an economic model known as **mercantilism,** which guided Europe's commercial expansion for 200 years. (The theory was so named by the eighteenth-century economist Adam Smith.) Mercantilists called for the state to regulate and protect industry and commerce. Their primary objective was to enrich the nation by fostering a favorable balance of trade. Once the value of exports exceeded the cost of imports, they theorized, gold and silver would flow into home ports.

If a nation could make do without any imports from other countries, so much the better. It was here that the idea of colonies entered the mercantilist scheme. Colonial producers would supply raw materials that the mother country could not produce, while colonial consumers swelled demand for the finished goods and financial services that the mother country could provide. Convinced that colonies would enhance national self-sufficiency, mercantilists urged states to sponsor overseas settlements.

Mercantilist notions appealed to Europe's monarchs. A thriving trade meant that more taxes and customs

What Caused the Pueblo Revolt?

In the chaotic days following the outbreak of the Pueblo Revolt, shocked Spanish authorities detained several Indians and interrogated them about the rebels' motives. The first informant, Pedro García, was a Spanish-speaking Indian who had been raised in a Spaniard's household. Don Pedro Nanboa, the second informant, was captured by the Spanish and gave his testimony through an interpreter. The final declaration comes from Juan, detained and interrogated more than a year after the rebellion.

DOCUMENT 1 Pedro García

The deponent said that he was in the service of Captain Joseph Nieto, because he was born and has been brought up in his house. . . . While weeding part of a corn field on his master's estancia, which is something like a league from the pueblo of Galisteo, [he] saw coming to the place where he was an Indian named Bartolomé, the cantor mayor of the Pueblo of Galisteo. He came up weeping and said to him, "What are you doing here? The Indians want to kill the custodian, the fathers, and the Spaniards, and have said that the Indian

who shall kill a Spaniard will get an Indian woman for a wife, and he who kills four will get four women, and he who kills ten or more will have a like number of women; and they have said that they are going to kill all the servants of the Spaniards and those who know how to speak Castilian, and they have also ordered that rosaries be taken away from everyone and burned. Hurry! Go! Perhaps you will be lucky enough to reach the place where the Spaniards are and will escape with your wife and an orphan girl that you have." Asked why they were plotting

such treason and rebellion, he said that the said cantor told him that they were tired of the work they had to do for the Spaniards and the religious, because they did not allow them to plant or do other things for their own needs; and that, being weary, they had rebelled.

Source: "Declaration of Pedro García, an Indian of the Tagno nation, a native of Las Salinas, August 25, 1680," in Charles Wilson Hackett, ed., and Charmion Clair Shelby, trans., *Revolt of the Pueblo Indians of New Mexico and Otermín's Attempted Reconquest, 1680–1682* (Albuquerque: University of New Mexico Press, 1943), 1:23–26.

DOCUMENT 2 Don Pedro Nanboa

Having been asked his name and of what place he is a native, his condition, and age, he said that his name is Don Pedro Nanboa, that he is a native of the pueblo of Alameda, a widower, and somewhat more than 80 years of age. Asked for what reason the Indians of this Kingdom have rebelled, forsaking their obedience to his Majesty and failing in their obligation as Christians, he said that for a long time, because the Spaniards punished sorcerers and idolaters, the nations of the

Teguas, Taos, Pecuríes, Pecos, and Jemez had been plotting to rebel and kill the Spaniards and religious, and that they have been planning constantly to carry it out, down to the present occasion. . . . He declared that the resentment which all the Indians have in their hearts has been so strong, from the time this kingdom was discovered, because the religious and the Spaniards took away their idols and forbade their sorceries and idolatries; that they have

inherited successively from their old men the things pertaining to their ancient customs; and that he has heard this resentment spoken of since he was of an age to understand. What he has said is the truth and what he knows, under the oath taken, and he ratifies it.

Source: "Declaration of one of the rebellious Christian Indians who was captured on the road, September 6, 1680," in Hackett, ed., *Revolt of the Pueblo Indians,* 1:60–62.

DOCUMENT 3 Juan, of the Tegua Nation

Asked for what reasons and causes all the Indians of the Kingdom in general rebelled . . . he said that what he knows concerning this question is that not all of them joined the said rebellion willingly; that the chief mover of it is an Indian who is a native of the Pueblo of San Juan, named El Popé, and that from fear of this Indian all of them joined in the plot that he made. Thus he replied. Asked why they held the said Popé in such fear and obeyed him, and whether he was the chief man of the pueblo, or a good Christian, or a sorcerer, he said that the common report that circulated and still is current among all the natives is that the said Indian Popé talks with the devil, and for this reason all held him in

terror, obeying his commands although they were contrary to the señores governors, the prelate and the religious, and the Spaniards, he giving them to understand that the word which he spoke was better than that of all the rest; and he states that it was a matter of common knowledge that the Indian Popé, talking with the devil, killed in his own house a son-in-law of his named Nicolás Bua, the governor of the pueblo of San Juan. On being asked why he killed him, he said that it was so that he might not warn the Spaniards of the rebellion, as he intended to do.

Source: "Declaration of the Indian, Juan, December 18, 1681," in Hackett, ed., *Revolt of the Pueblo Indians,* 2:232–238, 233–234.

Thinking Critically

Why does Pedro García say the Indians rebelled? Don Pedro Nanboa? Juan, the Tegua Indian? Can modern historians take these documents at face value? Why or why not? How might the circumstances of each informant have shaped his testimony?

duties would fill royal coffers, increasing royal power. That logic led England's King James I to approve a private venture to colonize the Chesapeake Bay, a sprawling inlet of the Atlantic Ocean fed by over 100 rivers and streams.

The Virginia Company

In 1606 the king granted a charter to a number of English merchants, gentlemen, and aristocrats, incorporating them as the Virginia Company of London. The members of the new **joint stock company** sold stock in their venture to English investors, as well as awarding a share to those willing to settle in Virginia at their own expense. With the proceeds from the sale of stock, the company planned to send to Virginia hundreds of poor and unemployed people as well as scores of skilled craftworkers. These laborers were to serve the company for seven years in return for their passage, pooling their efforts to produce any commodities that would return a profit to stockholders. If gold and silver could not be found, perhaps North America would yield other valuable commodities—furs, pitch, tar, or lumber. In the spring of 1607—nearly a decade after Oñate had launched Spain's colonies in New Mexico—the first expedition dispatched by the Virginia Company founded Jamestown.

 **JAMESTOWN'S PROBLEMS** Making the first of many mistakes, Jamestown's 104 men and boys pitched their fort on an inland peninsula in order to prevent a surprise attack from the Spanish. Unfortunately, the marshy, thickly wooded site served as an ideal breeding ground for malaria. The settlers, as well as those who followed them, were weakened by bouts of the disease and beset by dysentery, typhoid, and yellow fever. They died by the scores. During the summers, Indians familiar with the region's environment scattered beyond the estuary waters of the Chesapeake to find food. The English newcomers, by contrast, remained close to their fort, where the brackish waters became even more salty in the hot summer months. Salt poisoning in the wells left many colonists listless and apathetic.

Even before sickness took its toll, many of Jamestown's colonists had little taste for labor. The gentlemen of the expedition expected to lead rather than to work, and most of the other early settlers were gentlemen's servants and craftworkers who knew nothing about growing crops. As did the colonists on Roanoke, Jamestown's settlers resorted to bullying native people for food. Many colonists suffered from malnutrition, which heightened their susceptibility to disease. Only 60 of Jamestown's 500 inhabitants lived through the winter of 1609–1610, known as the "starving time." Some desperate colonists unearthed and ate corpses; one settler even butchered his wife. De facto martial law failed to turn the situation around, and skirmishes with the Indians became more brutal and frequent as rows of tobacco plants steadily invaded tribal lands.

Reform and a Boom in Tobacco

KEY REFORMS Determined to salvage their investment, Virginia Company managers in 1618 set in place sweeping reforms. To attract more capital and colonists, the company established a "headright" system for granting land to individuals. Those already settled in the colony received 100 acres apiece. New settlers each received 50 acres, and anyone who paid the passage of other immigrants to Virginia—either family members or servants—received 50 acres per "head." The company also abolished martial law, allowing the planters to elect a representative assembly. Along with a governor and an advisory council appointed by the company, the House of Burgesses had the authority to make laws for the colony. It met for the first time in 1619, beginning what would become a strong tradition of representative government in the English colonies.

The new measures met with immediate success. The free and unfree laborers who poured into Virginia during the 1620s made up the first wave of an English migration to the Chesapeake that numbered between 130,000 and 150,000 over the seventeenth century. Drawn from the ranks of ordinary English working people, the immigrants were largely men, outnumbering women by six to one. Most were young, ranging in age from 15 to 24. Because of their youth, most lacked skills or wealth. Some of those who came to the Chesapeake as free immigrants prospered as Virginia's tobacco economy took off. When in the 1620s demand soared and prices peaked in European markets, colonists with an eye for profit planted every inch of their farms in tobacco and reaped windfalls.

INDENTURED SERVANTS Indentured servants accounted for three-quarters of all immigrants to Virginia. For most of them, the crossing was simply the last of many moves made in the hope of finding work. Although England's population had been rising since the middle of the fifteenth century, the demand for farm laborers was falling because many landowners were converting croplands into pastures for sheep. The search for work pushed young men and women out of their villages, sending them through the countryside and then into the cities. Down and out in London, Bristol, or Liverpool, some decided to make their next move across the Atlantic and signed **indentures.** Pamphlets promoting immigration promised abundant land and quick riches once servants had finished their terms of four to seven years.

Even the most skeptical immigrants were shocked at what they found. The death rate in Virginia during the 1620s was higher than that of England during times of epidemic disease. The life expectancy for Chesapeake men who reached the age of 20 was a mere 48 years; for women it was lower still. Servants fared worst of all, because malnutrition, overwork, and abuse made them vulnerable to disease. As masters scrambled to make quick profits, they extracted the maximum amount of work before death carried off their laborers. An estimated 40 percent of servants did not survive to the end of their indentured terms.

WAR WITH THE CONFEDERACY The expanding cultivation of tobacco also claimed many lives by putting unbearable pressure on Indian land. After Powhatan's death in 1617 leadership of the confederacy passed to Opechancanough, who watched, year after year, as the tobacco mania grew. In March 1622 he coordinated a sweeping attack on white settlements that killed about a quarter of Virginia's colonial population. English retaliation over the next decade cut down an entire generation of young Indian men, drove the remaining Powhatans to the west, and won the colonists hundreds of thousands more acres for tobacco.

Tobacco plant

News of the ongoing Indian war jolted English investors into determining the true state of their Virginia venture. It came to light that, despite the tobacco boom, the Virginia Company was plunging toward bankruptcy. Nor was that the worst news. Stockholders discovered that more than 3,000 immigrants had succumbed to the brutal conditions of Chesapeake life. An investigation by James I revealed the grisly truth, causing the king to dissolve the Virginia Company and take control of the colony himself in 1624. Henceforth Virginia would be governed as a royal colony.

DECLINE IN MORTALITY RATES As the tobacco boom broke in the 1630s and 1640s, Virginians began producing more corn and cattle. Nutrition and overall health improved as a result. More and more poor colonists began surviving their indenture and establishing modest farms of their own. For women who survived servitude, prospects were even better. With wives at a premium, single women stood a good chance of improving their status by marriage. Even so, high mortality rates still fractured families: one out of every four children born in the Chesapeake did not survive to maturity, and among those children who reached their 18th birthday, one-third had lost both parents to death.

By 1650 Virginia could boast about 15,000 colonists, although much of that increase resulted from servants and free immigrants arriving in the colony every year. But Virginians looking to expand into more northerly bays of the Chesapeake found their way blocked by a newer English colony.

The Founding of Maryland and the Renewal of Indian Wars

Unlike Virginia, established by a private corporation and later converted into a royal colony, Maryland was founded in 1632 by a single aristocratic family, the Calverts. They held absolute authority to dispose of 10 million acres of land, administer justice, and establish a civil government. All these powers they exercised, granting estates, or "manors," to their friends and dividing other holdings into smaller farms for ordinary immigrants. From all these "tenants"—that is, every settler in the colony—the family collected "quitrents" every year, fees for use of the land. The Calverts appointed a governor and a council to oversee their own interests while allowing the largest landowners to dispense local justice in manorial courts and make laws for the entire colony in a representative assembly.

Virginians liked nothing about Maryland. To begin with, the Calvert family was Catholic and had extended complete religious freedom to all Christians, making Maryland a haven for Catholics. Worse still, the Marylanders were a source of economic competition. Two thousand inhabitants had settled on Calvert holdings by 1640, virtually all of them planting tobacco on land coveted by the Virginians.

Another obstacle to Virginia's expansion was the remnant of the Powhatan confederacy. Hounded for corn and supplies (most colonial fields grew tobacco rather than food), and constantly pressured by the expanding plantation economy, Virginia's native peoples became desperate and angry enough to risk yet another war. Aged Opechancanough led a new generation of Indians into battle in 1644 against the encroaching Virginia planters. Though his warriors killed several hundred English and brought the frontier to a standstill, Opechancanough was eventually captured and summarily shot through the head. The Powhatan confederacy died with him. Virginia's Indians would never again be in a position to resist the colony militarily. Over the next decades and centuries, many Indians fled the region altogether. But whole communities remained, quietly determined to continue their lives and traditions in their homeland.

Changes in English Policy in the Chesapeake

Throughout the 1630s and 1640s colonial affairs drew little concern from royal officials. England itself had become engulfed first by a political crisis and then by a civil war.

THE ENGLISH CIVIL WAR Outraged at the contempt that King Charles I had shown toward Parliament, disaffected **elites** and radical Puritans overthrew the king and executed him in 1649. When the "republic" of Oliver Cromwell turned out to be something closer to a military dictatorship, most English were happy to see their throne restored in 1660 to Charles II, the son of the beheaded king. The new monarch was determined to ensure that not only his subjects at home but also his American colonies abroad contributed to England's prosperity. His colonial policy was reflected in a series of regulations known as the Navigation Acts.

NAVIGATION ACTS The first, passed by Parliament in 1660, gave England and English colonial merchants a monopoly on the shipping and marketing of all colonial goods. It also ordered that the colonies could export certain "enumerated commodities" only to England

COLONIES OF THE CHESAPEAKE

Settlements in Virginia and Maryland spread out along the many bays of the Chesapeake, where tobacco could easily be loaded from plantation wharves. The "fall line" on rivers, dividing Tidewater and Piedmont regions, determined the extent of commercial agriculture, since ships could not pick up exports beyond that point.

or other British ports. These goods included sugar, tobacco, cotton, ginger, indigo (a blue dye), and eventually rice. In 1663 Parliament added another regulation, giving British merchants a virtual monopoly on the sale of European manufactured goods to Americans by requiring that most imports going to the colonies pass through England. In 1673 a third Navigation Act placed duties on the coastal trade of the American colonies and provided for customs officials to collect tariffs and enforce commercial regulations.

These acts were mercantilistic, insofar as they were designed to ensure that England—and no foreign nations or their merchants—would profit from colonial production and

trade. Chesapeake planters chafed under the Navigation Acts. They were used to conducting their affairs as they pleased—and they were often pleased to trade with the Dutch. What was worse, the new restrictions came at the same time as a downturn in tobacco prices. In the effort to consolidate its empire, England had unintentionally worsened the economic and social difficulties of Chesapeake society.

✓ **REVIEW**

How did the Chesapeake colonies support the aims of British mercantilism?

CHESAPEAKE SOCIETY IN CRISIS

BY THE 1660S OVERPRODUCTION WAS depressing tobacco prices, and wealthy planters reacted by putting even more prime coastal land into production. Newly freed servants had either to become tenants or try to establish farms to the west in Indian country. Meanwhile, export duties on tobacco paid under the Navigation Acts helped plunge many small planters into crushing debt, and some were forced back into servitude. By 1676 one-quarter of Virginia's free white men remained landless and frustrated.

DIMINISHING OPPORTUNITIES

Diminishing opportunities in the 1660s and 1670s provided the tinder for unrest in Virginia. As the discontent of the poor mounted, so did the worries of big planters. The assembly of the colony lengthened terms of servitude, hoping to limit the number of servants entering the free population. It curbed the political rights of landless men, hoping to stifle opposition by depriving them of the vote. But these measures only set off a spate of mutinies among servants and protests over rising taxes among small planters.

Bacon's Rebellion and Coode's Rebellion

NATHANIEL BACON

Those tensions came to a head in 1676. The rebellion was renewed fighting between desperate Indians and the expanding colonial population. Virginia's royal governor, William Berkeley, favored building forts to guard against Indians, but frontier farmers opposed his plan as an expensive and ineffective way to defend their scattered plantations. As they clamored for an expedition to punish the Indians, Nathaniel Bacon stepped forward to lead it.

Wealthy and well connected, Bacon had arrived recently from England, expecting to receive every favor from the governor—including permission to trade with the Indians from his frontier plantation. But Berkeley and a few select friends already held a monopoly on the Indian trade. When they declined to include Bacon, he took up the cause of his poorer frontier neighbors against their common enemy, the governor. Other recent, well-to-do immigrants who resented being excluded from Berkeley's circle of power and patronage also joined Bacon.

This ceramic pipe from the 1670s was probably used by an indentured servant or tenant farmer living near Jamestown. Its design, featuring an animal carved around the pipe bowl, combined features typical of pipes made by English colonists, Indians, and African Americans. Virginia during this period experienced unstable relations between the expanding English population, the declining Indian population (due to wars and enslavement), and the growing number of enslaved Africans taking a larger role in the colony.

In the summer of 1676 Bacon marched into Jamestown with a body of armed men and bullied the assembly into approving his expedition to kill Indians. While Bacon carried out that grisly business, slaughtering friendly as well as hostile Indians, Berkeley rallied his supporters and declared Bacon a rebel. Bacon retaliated by turning his forces against those led by the governor. Both sides sought allies by offering freedom to servants and slaves willing to join their ranks. Many were willing: for months the followers of Bacon and Berkeley plundered one another's plantations. In September 1676 Bacon reduced Jamestown to a mound of ashes. It was only his death from dysentery a month later that snuffed out the rebellion.

Political upheaval also shook Maryland, where colonists had long resented the sway of the Calvert family. As proprietors, the Calverts and their favorites monopolized political offices, just as Berkeley's circle had in Virginia. Well-to-do planters wanted a share of the Calverts' power. Smaller farmers, like those in Virginia, wanted a less expensive and more representative government. Compounding the tensions were religious differences: the Calverts and their friends were Catholic, but other colonists, including Maryland's most successful planters, were Protestant.

The unrest among Maryland's discontented planters peaked in July 1689. A former member of the assembly, John Coode, gathered an army, captured the proprietary governor, and then took grievances to authorities in England. There Coode received a sympathetic hearing. The Calverts' charter was revoked and not restored until 1715, by which time the family had become Protestant.

GROWING STABILITY

After 1690 rich planters in both Chesapeake colonies fought among themselves less and cooperated more. In Virginia older leaders and newer arrivals divided the spoils of political office. In Maryland Protestants and Catholics shared power and privilege. Those arrangements ensured that no future Bacon or Coode would mobilize restless gentlemen against the government. By acting together in legislative assemblies, the planter elite managed to curb the power of royal and proprietary governors for decades.

But the greater unity among the Chesapeake's leading families did little to ease that region's most fundamental problem—the sharp inequality of white society. The gulf between rich and poor planters, which had been etched ever more deeply by the troubled tobacco economy, persisted long after the rebellions of Bacon and Coode. All that saved white society in the Chesapeake from renewed crisis and conflict was the growth of black slavery.

From Servitude to Slavery

Like the tobacco plants that spread across Powhatan's land, a labor system based on African slavery was an on-the-ground innovation. Both early promoters and planters preferred paying for English servants to importing alien African slaves. Black slaves, because they served for life, were more expensive than white workers, who served only for several years. Because neither white nor black immigrants lived long, cheaper servant labor was the logical choice. The black population of the Chesapeake remained small for most of the seventeenth century, constituting just 5 percent of all inhabitants in 1675.

THE LIVES OF SERVANTS AND SLAVES

Africans had arrived in Virginia by 1619, most likely via the Dutch, who dominated the slave trade until the middle of the eighteenth century. The lives of those newcomers resembled the lot of white servants, with whom they shared harsh work routines and living conditions. White and black bound laborers socialized with one another and formed sexual liaisons. They conspired to steal from their masters and ran away together; if caught, they endured similar punishments. There was more common ground: many of the first black settlers did not arrive directly from Africa but came from the Caribbean, where some had learned English and had adopted Christian beliefs. And not all were slaves: some were indentured servants. A handful were free.

A number of changes after 1680 caused planters to invest more heavily in slaves than in servants. First, as death rates in the Chesapeake began to drop, slaves became a more profitable investment. Although they were more expensive to buy than servants, planters could now expect to get many years of work from their bondspeople. Equally important, masters would have title to the children that slaves were now living long enough to have. At the same time, the influx of white servants was falling off just as the pool of available black labor was expanding. When the Royal African Company lost its monopoly on the English slave trade in 1698, other merchants entered the market. The number of Africans sold by British dealers swelled to 20,000 annually.

Africa and the Atlantic Slave Trade

From 1492 to 1820, enslaved African migrants outnumbered European migrants to the New World by nearly five to one. Put differently, before the twentieth century, African workers did most of the heavy lifting in the economies of the Americas.

DIMENSIONS OF THE SLAVE TRADE

For a century after Columbus's arrival, the traffic in slaves to the Americas had numbered a few thousand annually. But as sugar cultivation steadily prospered after 1600, slave imports rose to 19,000 a year during the seventeenth century and mushroomed to 60,000 a year in the eighteenth century. All told, as many as 21 million people were captured in West Africa between 1700 and 1850: some 9 million among them entered the Americas as slaves, but millions died before or during the Atlantic crossing, and as many as 7 million remained slaves in Africa. Although slavery became indispensible to its economy, British North America played a relatively small role in the Atlantic slave trade.

Nine-tenths of all Africans brought to the New World landed in Brazil or the Caribbean islands.

 TRANSFORMATION OF WEST AFRICAN SOCIETY

The rapid growth of the trade transformed not only the Americas but also Africa. Slavery became more widespread within African society, and slave trading more central to its domestic and international commerce. Most important, the African merchants and political leaders most deeply invested in the slave trade used their profits for political advantage—to build new chiefdoms and states such as Dahomey, Asante, and the Lunda Empire. Their ambitions and the greed of European slave dealers drew an increasingly large number of Africans, particularly people living in the interior, into slavery's web. By the late seventeenth century, Africans being sold into slavery were no longer only those who had put themselves at risk by committing crimes, running into debt, or voicing unpopular political and religious views. The larger number were instead captives taken by soldiers or kidnappers in raids launched specifically to acquire prisoners for the slave trade, or else desperate refugees captured while fleeing war, famine, and disease. During the decades after 1680, captives coming directly from Africa made up more than 80 percent of all new slaves entering the Chesapeake and the rest of mainland North America. Many were shipped from the coast of Africa that Portuguese explorers had first probed, between the Senegal and Niger Rivers. Most of the rest came from Angola, farther south.

Seized by other Africans, captives were yoked together at the neck and marched hundreds of miles through the interior to coastal forts or other outposts along the Atlantic. There, they were penned in hundreds of prisons, in lots of anywhere from 20 or 30 to more than 1,000. They might be forced to wait for slaving vessels in French *captiveries* below the fine houses of traders on the island of Gorée, or herded into "outfactories" on the Banana Islands upstream on the Sierra Leone River, or perhaps marched into the dank underground slaveholds at the English fort at Cape Coast. Farther south, captives were held in marshy, fever-ridden lowlands along the Bight of Benin, waiting for a slaver to drop anchor. One African, Ottobah Cugoano, recalled finally being taken aboard ship:

There was nothing to be heard but the rattling of chains, smacking of whips, and the groans and cries of our fellow-men. Some would not stir from the ground, when they were lashed and beat in the most horrible manner. . . . And when we found ourselves at last taken away, death was more preferable than life, and a plan was concerted amongst us that we might burn and blow up the ship and to perish altogether in the flames.

THE MIDDLE PASSAGE

Worse than the imprisonment was the voyage itself: the so-called Middle Passage, a nightmarish journey across the Atlantic that could take anywhere between three weeks and three months, depending on currents, weather, and where ships

AFRICAN TRANSATLANTIC SLAVE TRADE, 1450–1760

Toward the end of the seventeenth century, Chesapeake and Carolina planters began importing increasing numbers of slaves. In Africa the center of that trade lay along a mountainous region known as the Gold Coast, where more than a hundred European trading posts and forts funneled the trade. Unlike most of the rest of West Africa's shoreline, the Gold Coast had very little dense rain forest. Despite the heavy trade, only about 4 percent of the total transatlantic slave trade went to North America.

Katharina, sketched by Albrecht Dürer in 1521, was a servant of a Portuguese diplomat living in Antwerp. She was probably one of the increasing number of Africans being brought to Europe owing to the growing slave trade along the West African coast.

Slaves captured in the African interior were marched out in slave "coffles," a forced march in which captives were linked either by chains or by wooden yoke restraints linking two slaves together as they walked.

Africans found themselves in a variety of conditions in the Americas. Most toiled on plantations. Some, however, like these "watermen" along the James River in Virginia (lower right), claimed more independence. Still others ran away to Maroon communities in the interior. This armed Maroon (a runaway slave; lower left) is from Dutch Guiana, where conditions on the plantations were particularly harsh.

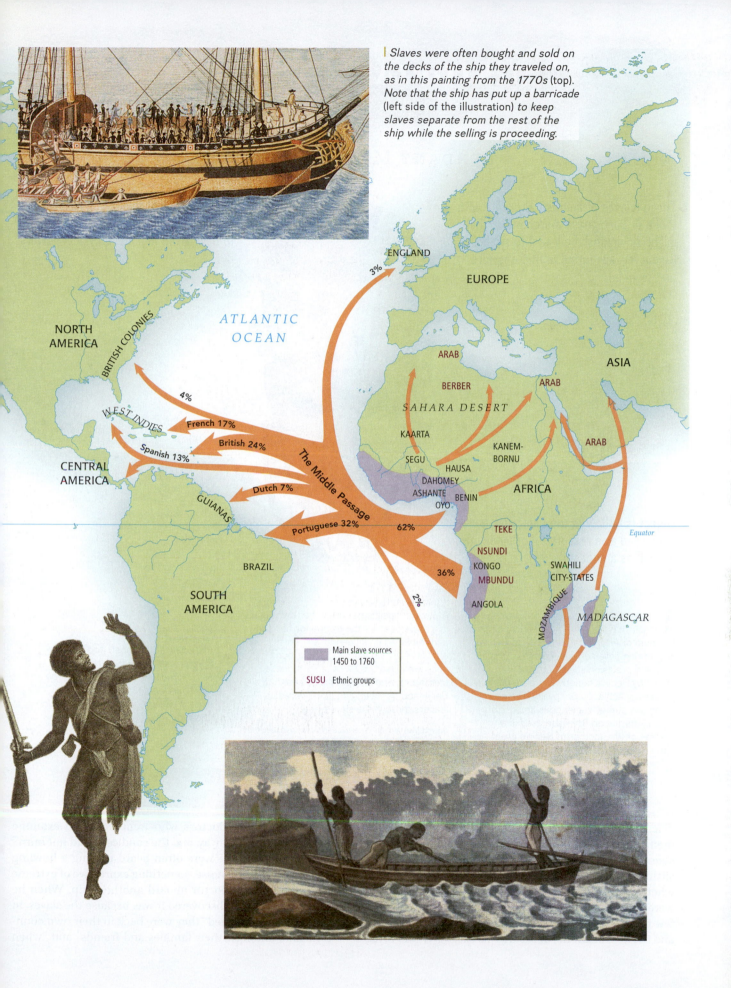

Slaves were often bought and sold on the decks of the ship they traveled on, as in this painting from the 1770s (top). Note that the ship has put up a barricade (left side of the illustration) to keep slaves separate from the rest of the ship while the selling is proceeding.

ENGLAND

EUROPE

3%

ATLANTIC
OCEAN

NORTH
AMERICA

BRITISH COLONIES

ASIA

ARAB

BERBER

ARAB

SAHARA DESERT

WEST INDIES

4%

KAARTA

French 17%

ARAB

Spanish 13%

British 24%

SEGU

KANEM-
BORNU

HAUSA

CENTRAL
AMERICA

The Middle Passage

DAHOMEY

ASHANTE

AFRICA

Dutch 7%

BENIN

OYO

GUIANAS

Portuguese 32%

62%

TEKE

Equator

BRAZIL

NSUNDI

KONGO

SWAHILI
CITY-STATES

MBUNDU

MOZAMBIQUE

SOUTH
AMERICA

36%

ANGOLA

MADAGASCAR

2%

Main slave sources
1450 to 1760

SUSU   Ethnic groups

PENDANT MASK FROM BENIN

These images of mudfish alternate with those of Portuguese merchants. What might the mudfish be meant to symbolize? (Use a few key terms to find answers on the web.)

These pieces of inlaid iron represent medicine-filled incisions that were said to have given Idia metaphysical powers.

Object is hollow at the back; may have been used as a receptacle for medicines, as well as a pendant.

This exquisite sixteenth-century ivory mask, now in New York's Metropolitan Museum of Art, graced the neck of Benin's king during ceremonial occasions. Its subtlety and precision suggest that it was produced by Benin's famed guild of royal ivory carvers, specifically for royalty. The object communicates a tremendous amount of visual information. The face itself is a portrait of Idia, mother of Benin's great early-sixteenth-century leader Esigie.

A powerful political figure in her own right, Idia helped secure the throne for her son and remained an influential adviser throughout his reign. On her head and around her neck are miniature faces of Portuguese merchants who brought great wealth to Benin and enriched and empowered its leaders through the slave trade.

Source: Metropolitan Museum of Art, www.metmuseum.org/toah/ho/08/sfg/ho_1978.412.323.htm.

Thinking Critically

Why pair the mudfish and the Portuguese? Do you think that the artist conceived of the Portuguese merchants as equals? Would you expect Benin's artistic sophistication to shape how the Portuguese regarded the kingdom?

disembarked and landed. Often several hundred black men, women, and children were packed below-decks, squeezed onto platforms built in tiers spaced so close that sitting upright was impossible. It was difficult to know whether the days or the nights were more hellish. Slaves were taken out and forced to exercise for their health for a few hours each day; the rest of the day, the sun beat down and the heat below the decks was "so excessive," one voyager recalled, that the doctors who went below to examine slaves "would faint away, and the candles would not burn." At night, the slaves "were often heard making a howling melancholy kind of noise, something expressive of extreme anguish," noted a doctor aboard another ship. When he made inquiries, he discovered it was because the slaves, in sleeping, had dreamed "they were back in their own country again, amongst their families and friends" and "when they woke up to find themselves in reality on a slave ship they began to bay and shriek." Historians estimate that for every 85 enslaved Africans that set foot in the Americas, 15 died during the middle passage.

"SEASONING" After the numb, exhausted survivors reached American ports, they faced more challenges to staying alive. The first year in the colonies was the most deadly for new, "unseasoned" slaves. The sickle-cell genetic trait gave them a greater immunity to malaria than Europeans, but Africans were highly susceptible to respiratory infections. One-quarter of all Africans died during their first year in the Chesapeake, and among Carolina and Caribbean slaves, mortality rates were far higher. In addition to the new disease environment, Africans had to adapt to lives without freedom in a wholly unfamiliar country and culture.

Exchanging a labor system based on servitude for one based on slavery transformed the character of Chesapeake society. Most obviously, the number of Afro-Virginians rose sharply. By 1740, 40 percent of all Virginians were black, and most of those were African-born. Unlike many African men and women who had arrived earlier from the Caribbean, these new inhabitants had little familiarity with English language and culture. This larger, more distinctively African community was also locked into a slave system that was becoming ever more rigid and demeaning. By the late decades of the seventeenth century, new laws made it more difficult for masters to free slaves. Other legislation systematically separated the races by prohibiting free black settlers from having white servants and outlawing interracial marriages and sexual relationships. The legal code encouraged white contempt for black Virginians in a variety of other ways. While masters were prohibited from whipping their white servants on the bare back, slaves had no such protection. And "any Negro that shall presume to strike any white" was to receive 30 lashes for that rash act.

GROWING RACISM The new laws both reflected and encouraged **racism** among white colonists of all classes. Deepening racial hatred, in turn, made it unlikely that poor white planters, tenants, and servants would ever join with poor black slaves to challenge the privilege of great planters. Instead of identifying with the plight of the slaves, the Chesapeake's poorer white residents considered black Virginians their natural inferiors. They could pride themselves on sharing with wealthy white gentlemen the same skin color and on being their equals in the eyes of the law.

OPPORTUNITIES FOR WHITE SETTLERS The leaders of the Chesapeake colonies cultivated unity among white inhabitants by improving economic prospects for freed servants and lesser planters. The Virginia assembly made provisions for freed servants to get a better start as independent farmers. It lowered taxes, allowing small planters to keep more of their earnings. New laws also gave most white male Virginians a vote in elections,

allowing them an outlet to express their grievances. Economic trends toward the end of the seventeenth century contributed to the greater prosperity of small planters, because tobacco prices rose slightly and then stabilized. As a result of Bacon's savage campaign against the Virginia Indians, new land on the frontier became available. Even the domestic lives of ordinary people became more secure as mortality rates declined and the numbers of men and women in the white population evened out. As a result, virtually all men were now able to marry, and families were fragmented less often by the premature deaths of spouses and parents.

After 1700 the Chesapeake evolved into a more stable society. Gone were the bands of wild, landless, young bachelors one step ahead of the law, the small body of struggling lesser planters one step ahead of ruin, and the great mass of exploited servants one step away from rebellion. Virginia and Maryland became colonies of farming families, most of them small planters who owned between 50 and 200 acres. These families held no slaves, or at most two or three. And they accepted, usually without question, the social and political leadership of their acknowledged "superiors," great planters who styled themselves the "gentry."

George Booth, the son of a wealthy planter family in Gloucester County, Virginia, was being raised for mastery. The young man's self-assured stance, the bow and arrows, the dog at his feet clutching the kill, the classical busts of women flanking his figure, and his family estate in the distance all suggest the gentry's concern for controlling the natural and social worlds.

The gentry's fortunes rested in part on the cultivation of tobacco on thousands of acres by hundreds of slaves. But the leading planters made even more money by marketing the tobacco of their humbler neighbors, selling them manufactured goods, supplying them with medical and legal services, lending money, and hiring out slaves. Unlike the rough-hewn barons of the early tobacco boom, the gentry did not owe their wealth to wringing work from poor whites. Instead, they amassed great estates by wringing work from black slaves while converting their white "inferiors" into modestly prosperous small planters and paying clients. But the gentry wanted more than money: they wanted the respect of lesser whites. And they received it. On court days, gentlemen served as justices of the peace, bedecked in wigs and robes and seated on raised benches. On Sundays, worshipers filed into the Anglican chapel in order of social rank, with gentlemen heading the procession. When the local militia trained, it did so at the head of gentlemen officers. The courthouse, the church, and the training field all served as theaters in which the new Chesapeake gentry dramatized their superiority and lesser men deferred.

✓ REVIEW
Why did slavery replace servitude as the dominant labor system in Virginia and Maryland?

FROM THE CARIBBEAN TO THE CAROLINAS

TRANSFORMATION OF THE CARIBBEAN

DURING THE SAME DECADE THAT the English invaded Powhatan's land, they began to colonize the Caribbean, whose islands extended north and west, like beads on a string, from the Lesser Antilles toward the more substantial lands of Puerto Rico, Hispaniola, Jamaica, and Cuba (map, page 72). At their long journey's end English sailors found what seemed a paradise: shores rimmed with white sand beaches that rose sharply to coral terraces, then to broad plateaus or mountain peaks shrouded in rain forests. The earliest arrivals came intending not to colonize but to steal from the Spanish. Even after 1604, when some English settled on the islands, few intended to stay.

Yet the English did establish permanent plantation colonies in the West Indies. Beyond that, their Caribbean settlements became the jumping-off points for a new colony on the North American mainland—South Carolina. Because of the strong West Indian influence, South Carolina developed a social order in some ways distinct from that of the Chesapeake colonies. In other ways, however, the development paralleled Virginia and Maryland's path. In both regions, extreme violence, high mortality,

and uncertainty gave way to relative stability only over the course of many decades.

Paradise Lost

The English had traded and battled with the Spanish in the Caribbean since the 1560s. From those island bases English buccaneers conducted an illegal trade with Spanish settlements, sacked the coastal towns, and plundered silver ships bound for Seville. Weakened by decades of warfare, Spain could not hold the West Indies. The Dutch drove a wedge into Caribbean trade routes, and the French and the English began to colonize the islands.

In the 40 years after 1604, some 30,000 immigrants from the British Isles planted crude frontier outposts on St. Kitts, Barbados, Nevis, Montserrat, and Antigua. The settlers—some free, many others indentured servants, and almost all young men—devoted themselves to working as little as possible, drinking as much as possible, and returning to England as soon as possible. They cultivated for export a poor quality of tobacco, which returned just enough profit to maintain straggling settlements of small farms.

 CARIBBEAN SUGAR Then, nearly overnight, sugar cultivation transformed the Caribbean. In the 1640s Barbados planters learned from the Dutch how to process sugarcane. The Dutch also supplied African slaves to work the cane fields and marketed the sugar for high prices in the Netherlands. Sugar plantations and slave labor rapidly spread to other English and French islands as Europeans developed an insatiable sweet tooth for the once scarce commodity. Caribbean sugar made more money for England than the total volume of commodities exported by all the mainland American colonies.

Even though its great planters became the richest people in English America, they could not have confused the West Indies with paradise. Throughout the seventeenth century, disease took a fearful toll, and island populations grew only because of immigration. In the scramble for land, small farmers were pushed onto tiny plots that barely allowed them to survive.

SLAVERY IN THE CARIBBEAN The desperation of bound laborers posed another threat. After the Caribbean's conversion to cultivating sugar, African slaves gradually replaced indentured servants in the cane fields. By the beginning of the eighteenth century resident Africans outnumbered English by four to one. Fear of servant mutinies and slave rebellions frayed the nerves of island masters. They tried to contain the danger by imposing harsh slave codes and inflicting brutal punishments on all laborers. But planters lived under a constant state of siege. One visitor to Barbados observed that whites fortified their homes with parapets from which they could pour scalding water on attacking servants and slaves. During the first century of settlement, seven major slave uprisings shook the English islands.

A Taste for Sugar

It is said that shortly before his death in 735 CE, the Venerable Bede, an English abbot, bequeathed a precious treasure to his brother monks. It consisted of a cache of spices, including a little stock of sugar. What separated Bede's world, in which sugar was a costly luxury, from twenty-first-century Americans' world of ever-present sweetness was the discovery of America and the establishment of plantation economies in the Caribbean and Brazil.

Until the fourteenth century, Europe's merchants imported only small quantities of sugar at great expense from North Africa as well as from distant Persia and India, countries that had produced sugar since 500 CE.

Throughout the Middle Ages and the early modern era, only the royal and the rich of Europe could indulge their desire for sugar, and even those classes partook sparingly. Europeans classified sugar as a spice, like the equally scarce and exotic pepper, nutmeg, ginger, and saffron. Nobility valued sugar as a medicine for sore throats, stomach disorders, and infertility. The cooks of castle kitchens seasoned food and sauces with a pinch of sugar or sprinkled it on meat, fish, fowl, and fruit to preserve freshness—or to conceal rot. Only on great occasions did the confectioners of noble families splurge, fashioning for courtly feasts great baked sugar sculptures of knights and kings, horses and apes, called "subtleties."

For the ordinary folk of Europe, life was not as sweet. Their diets consisted of bread, peas, beans, and, in good years, a little milk, butter, and cheese. The occasional pig slaughtered, rabbit trapped, or fish caught supplied stray protein for the poor.

That pattern of consumption changed as Europeans turned to African slave labor to grow sugar for them. The early sugar plantations of Madeira and the Canary Islands (Chapter 2) were a foretaste of veritable sugar factories created in the Caribbean colonies of England and France.

By the sixteenth and seventeenth centuries, Europe's merchant classes could imitate elite patterns of eating by pouring sugar into pastries and puddings. And by the middle of the eighteenth century, an increasingly large supply from the Caribbean was making sugar essential to the poorest Europeans. Among England's laboring classes, another colonial import—Indian tea, laced heavily with sugar—began to accompany an otherwise cold supper of bread. Cheaper, warmer, and more stimulating than milk or beer (its prime competitors), sugared tea won the loyalty of England's mass market and ranked as the nonalcoholic beverage of national choice. By the nineteenth century English working families were also combining sugar and starch by pouring treacle (molasses) over porridge and spreading jams or marmalades on their bread.

Europe and America affected each other in many ways, but diet figured among the more fundamental conditions of life altered by colonization. More than coffee, chocolate, rum, or tobacco—indeed, more than any of the other "drug foods" produced by the colonies except tea—sugar provided a major addition to the diet of the English and other Europeans.

Even though sugar became a mass-marketed basic foodstuff, its association with power persisted. But it was no longer the consumption of sugar that bestowed status. Instead, after 1700 it was the production of sugar that conferred power. Planters who grew it, merchants who shipped and sold it, industrialists who refined it, and politicians who taxed it discovered in sugar sources of profit and distinction less perishable than sweetness on the tongue.

Thinking Critically

How did the growth of sugar cultivation in the Americas change European diets for different social classes?

Once harvested, sugarcane in the West Indies was crushed, as in this sugar mill. The juice was collected and channeled to the sugar works, where it was concentrated through boiling and evaporation. This neat diagrammatic picture belies the harsh conditions of labor and the high mortality that slaves experienced: sweetness came at a steep price.

As more people, both white and black, squeezed onto the islands, some settlers looked for a way out. With all the land in use, the Caribbean no longer offered opportunity to freed servants or even planters' sons. It was then that the West Indies started to shape the history of the American South.

The Founding of the Carolinas

The colonization of the Carolinas began with the schemes of Virginia's royal governor, William Berkeley, and Sir John Colleton, a supporter of Charles I who had been exiled to the Caribbean at the end of England's civil war. Colleton saw that the Caribbean had a surplus of white settlers, and Berkeley knew that Virginians needed room to expand as well. Together the two men set their sights on the area south of Virginia. Along with a number of other aristocrats, they convinced Charles II to make them joint proprietors in 1663 of a place they called the Carolinas, in honor of the king.

NORTH CAROLINA A few hardy souls from Virginia had already squatted around Albemarle Sound in the northern part of the Carolina grant. The proprietors provided them with a governor and a representative assembly. About 40 years later, in 1701, they set off North Carolina as a separate colony. The desolate region quickly proved a disappointment. Lacking good harbors and navigable rivers, the colony had no convenient way of marketing its produce. North Carolina remained a poor colony, its sparse population engaged in general farming and the production of masts, pitch, tar, and turpentine.

SOUTH CAROLINA The southern portion of the Carolina grant held far more promise, especially in the eyes of one of its proprietors, Sir Anthony Ashley Cooper, Earl of Shaftesbury. In 1669 he sponsored an expedition of a few hundred English and Barbadian immigrants, who planted the first permanent settlement in South Carolina. By 1680 the colonists had established the center of economic, social, and political life at the confluence of the Ashley and Cooper Rivers, naming the site Charles Town (later Charleston) after the king. Like others before him, Cooper hoped to create an ideal society in America. His utopia was a place where a few landed aristocrats and gentlemen would rule with the consent of many smaller property holders. With his personal secretary, the renowned philosopher John Locke, Cooper drew up an intricate scheme of government, the Fundamental Constitutions. The design provided Carolina with a proprietary governor and a hereditary nobility who, as a Council of Lords, would recommend all laws to a Parliament elected by lesser landowners.

The Fundamental Constitutions met the same fate as other lordly dreams for America. Instead of peacefully observing its provisions, most of the Carolinians, emigrants from Barbados, plunged into the economic and political wrangling that had plagued Maryland's first government. They challenged proprietary rule, protested or

| With large majorities of their populations enslaved, the sugar-producing islands of the Caribbean were anxious, fearful places of brutal labor and gruesome discipline. But they were also sites of rich social life and cultural development, as this slave dance on the island of St. Vincent suggests.

ignored laws and regulations imposed on them, and rejected the proprietors' relatively benevolent vision of Indian relations. Instead of forging genuine alliances with regional Indians, Carolina's colonists fomented a series of Indian slave wars that would nearly destroy the colony altogether.

Carolina, Florida, and the Southeastern Slave Wars

Taking wealthy Barbados as the model, the colonists intended from the start to grow Carolina's economy around cash crops tended by African slaves. But before they could afford to establish such a regime, the newcomers needed to raise capital through trade with Indians. Colonists gave textiles, metal goods, guns, and alcohol in exchange for hundreds of thousands of deerskins, which they then exported.

GROWTH OF THE INDIAN SLAVE TRADE

But the trade soon came to revolve around a commodity dearer still. As did most peoples throughout history, southeastern Indians sometimes made slaves of their enemies. Carolina's traders vastly expanded this existing slave culture by turning captives into prized commodities. Convinced that local Indians were physically weaker than Africans and more likely to rebel or flee, colonial traders bought slaves from Indian allies and then exported them to other mainland colonies or to the Caribbean. They found eager native partners in this business. Contact with Europe had unleashed phenomenal changes in interior North America; epidemics ruined one people and gave advantage to another, new commercial opportunities sparked fierce wars over hunting and trading territories, and many thousands of Indian families became displaced and had to rebuild their lives somewhere new. The chaos, conflict, and movement gave enterprising Indians ample opportunity to enslave weak neighbors and stock Carolina's slave pens.

RAIDS INTO SPANISH FLORIDA

To ensure a steady supply of slaves and maximize profits, Carolinian merchants courted a variety of Indian allies during the late seventeenth and early eighteenth centuries and encouraged them to raid mission Indians in Spanish Florida. By 1700 Florida's Indian peoples were in sharp decline, and Charles Town's slave traders turned to the large and powerful Creek, Choctaw, Chickasaw, and Cherokee confederacies of the interior, encouraging them to raid one another. Before long the slave wars had a momentum all their own, extending as far west as the Mississippi River. Even native peoples who deplored the violence and despised the English felt compelled to participate, lest they, too, become victims. One small Indian community elected an elder representative to travel to Charles Town and discover what his people needed to do to stay safe. The town's traders seized the man and sold him into slavery. The trade had become central to Carolina's growing economy, and colonists high and low sought to profit from it. In 1702 Governor James Moore, one of the colony's chief slave traders, launched an audacious raid against Spanish St. Augustine and Florida's missions, returning with hundreds of Indian captives. His campaign inspired still more raids, and over the next few years Creeks, Yamasees, and Englishmen laid waste to 29 Spanish missions, shattering thousands of lives and destroying Spain's precarious system of Indian alliances in Florida. By 1706 Spanish authority was once again confined to St. Augustine and its immediate vicinity, and within another 10 years most of Florida had been depopulated of Indians.

It seemed a double victory from Charles Town's perspective. The English had bested a European rival for the Crown and had reaped enormous profits besides. The fragmentary evidence suggests that Carolinians had purchased or captured between 30,000 and 50,000 Indian slaves before 1715. Indeed, before that date South Carolina was a net exporter of slaves: it exported more slaves than it imported from Africa or the Caribbean. But in 1715 Carolina's merchants finally paid a price for the wars that they had cynically fomented for over 40 years.

YAMASEE WAR

With Florida virtually exhausted of slaves, the Yamasees grew nervous. Convinced that Carolina would soon turn on them as it had on other one-time allies, the Yamasees struck first. They attacked traders, posts, and plantations on the outskirts of Charles Town, killing hundreds of colonists and dragging scores more to Florida to sell as slaves in St. Augustine. Panicked authorities turned to other Indian peoples in the region but found most had either joined the Yamasee or were too hostile and suspicious to help. Though it lasted only a few months, the Yamasee War finally put an end to the destructive regional slave trade. Animal skins again dominated regional commerce. The powerful southern confederacies grew wary of aligning too closely with any single European power and henceforth sought to play colonies and empires off each other. It was a strategy that would bring them relative peace and prosperity for generations.

White, Red, and Black: The Search for Order

As for South Carolina, the Yamasee War set it back 20 years. In its aftermath, colonists invested more and more of their resources in African slaves and in the cultivation of rice, a crop that eventually made South Carolina's planters the richest social group in mainland North America. Unfortunately, South Carolina's swampy coast, so perfectly suited to growing rice, was less suited for human habitation. Weakened by chronic malaria, settlers died in epic numbers from yellow fever, smallpox, and respiratory infections. The white population grew slowly, through

THE CAROLINAS AND THE CARIBBEAN

The map underscores the geographic link between West Indian and Carolina settlements. Emigrants from Barbados dominated politics in early South Carolina, while Carolinians provided foodstuffs, grain, and cattle to the West Indies. As South Carolinians began growing rice, Caribbean slave ships found it an easy sail north and west to unload their cargoes in Charles Town. **The fall line is marked here and on the map of the Chesapeake region on page 61. What is the fall line? Why is it significant?**

immigration rather than natural increase, and numbered only 10,000 by 1730.

Early South Carolinians had little in common but the harsh conditions of frontier existence. Most colonists lived on isolated plantations; early deaths fragmented families and neighborhoods. Immigration after 1700 further intensified the colony's ethnic and religious diversity, adding Swiss and German Lutherans, Scots-Irish Presbyterians, Welsh Baptists, and Spanish Jews. The colony's only courts were in Charles Town; churches and clergy of any denomination were scarce. On those rare occasions when early Carolinians came together, they gathered at Charles Town to escape the pestilential air of their plantations, to sue one another for debt and haggle over prices, or to fight over religious differences and proprietary politics.

Finally, in 1729, the Crown formally established royal government; by 1730 economic recovery had done much to ease the strife. Even more important in bringing greater political stability, the white colonists of South Carolina came to realize that they must unite if they were to counter the Spanish in Florida and the French and their Indian allies on the Gulf Coast.

SLAVERY IN SOUTH CAROLINA

The growing black population gave white Carolinians another reason to maintain a united front. During the first decades of settlement, frontier conditions and the scarcity of labor had forced masters to allow enslaved Africans greater freedom within bondage. White and black laborers shared chores on small farms. On stock-raising plantations, called "cowpens," black cowboys ranged freely over the countryside. African contributions to the defense of the colony also reinforced racial interdependence and muted white domination. Whenever threats arose—during the Yamasee War, for example—black Carolinians were enlisted in the militia.

White Carolinians depended on black labor even more after turning to rice as their cash crop. In fact, planters began to import slaves in larger numbers partly because of West African skill in rice cultivation. But whites harbored deepening fears of the black workers whose labor built planter fortunes. As early as 1708 black men and women had become a majority in the colony, and by 1730 they outnumbered white settlers by two to one. As their colony recovered and began to prosper, white Carolinians put into effect strict slave codes like those in the Caribbean that converted their colony into an armed camp and snuffed out the marginal freedoms that African settlers once enjoyed.

The Founding of Georgia

After 1730 white South Carolinians could take comfort not only in newfound prosperity and new political harmony but also in the founding of a new colony on their southern border. South Carolinians liked Georgia a great deal more than the Virginians had liked Maryland, because the colony formed a buffer between British North America and Spanish Florida in much the same way that Yamasees and Shawnees had, before the war.

JAMES OGLETHORPE

Enhancing the military security of South Carolina was only one reason for the founding of Georgia. More important to General James Oglethorpe and other idealistic English gentlemen was the aim of aiding the "worthy poor" by providing them with land, employment, and a new start. They envisioned a colony of hardworking small farmers who would produce silk and wine, sparing England the need to import those commodities. That dream seemed within reach when George II made Oglethorpe and his friends the trustees of the new colony in 1732, granting them a charter for

The Yuchi were neighbors of one of Georgia's early settlements; one of the newly emigrated German colonists painted this watercolor of a Yuchi celebration. Judging from the guns hanging at the back of the shelter, these Indians were already trading with white colonists in the area.

21 years. At the end of that time Georgia would revert to royal control.

The trustees did not, as legend has it, empty England's debtors' prisons to populate Georgia. They freed few debtors but recruited from every country in Europe paupers who seemed willing to work hard—and who professed Protestantism. Trustees paid the paupers' passage and provided each with 50 acres of land, tools, and a year's worth of supplies. Settlers who could pay their own way were encouraged to come by being granted larger tracts of land. Much to the trustees' dismay, that generous offer was taken up not only by many hoped-for Protestants but also by several hundred Ashkenazim (German Jews) and Sephardim (Spanish and Portuguese Jews), who established a thriving community in early Savannah.

The trustees were determined to ensure that Georgia became a small farmers' utopia. Rather than selling land, the trustees gave it away, but none of the colony's settlers could own more than 500 acres. The trustees also outlawed slavery and hard liquor in order to cultivate habits of industry and sustain equality among whites. This design for a virtuous and egalitarian utopia was greeted with little enthusiasm by Georgians. They pressed for a free market in land and argued that the colony could never prosper until the trustees revoked their ban on slavery. Because the trustees had provided for no elective assembly, settlers could express their discontent only by moving to South Carolina—which many did during the early decades.

As mounting opposition threatened to depopulate the colony, the trustees caved in. They revoked their restrictions on land, slavery, and liquor a few years before the king assumed control of the colony in 1752. Under royal control, Georgia continued to develop an ethnically and religiously diverse society, akin to that of South Carolina. Similarly, its economy was based on rice cultivation and the Indian trade.

 **REVIEW**

How was the colonization of Carolina both distinct from and parallel to that of the Chesapeake?

CONCLUSION

THE WORLD AT LARGE

Empire . . . utopia . . . independence. . . . For more than a century after the founding of Oñate's colony on the upper Rio Grande in 1598, those dreams inspired residents of New Mexico, Florida, the Chesapeake, the English Caribbean, the Carolinas, and Georgia.

Although South Carolina and the English West Indies were more opulent and unstable societies than Virginia and Maryland, the colonies stretching from the Chesapeake to the Caribbean had much in common. So did the South American sugar and coffee plantations of the Guianas and the sugar plantations of Brazil. As Europeans put down colonies throughout the Americas, Indian farmers and hunters were enslaved or expelled. Planters depended on a single staple crop, which brought wealth and political power to those commanding the most land and the most labor. And the biggest planters relied for their success on the very people whom they most feared—enslaved African Americans. That fear was reflected in the development of repressive slave codes and the spread of racism throughout all classes of white society.

The dream of an expanding empire faltered for the Spanish, who discovered few riches in the Southwest and eventually found rebellion. The dream of empire failed, too, when James I and Charles I of England found their power checked by Parliament. And the dream foundered fatally for Indians, unable to resist Old World diseases and land-hungry colonists.

English lords dreamed of establishing feudal utopias in America. But proprietors in Maryland and the Carolinas were hounded by frontier planters and farmers looking for their own economic and political power. Georgia's trustees failed to erect their utopia for the poor. And Indian resistance dimmed the utopian dreams of Spanish Catholic missionaries in the American Southwest.

The dream of independence proved most deceptive, especially for English colonists. Almost half of white servant emigrants to the Chesapeake died from disease or were worn down by tobacco barons. And real independence eluded even English planters. The poorer ones depended on richer settlers for land and leadership, while even the richest needed English and Scottish merchants to supply credit and market their crops.

And everywhere in the American Southeast and Southwest, the dreams of Europeans depended on the labor of the least free members of colonial America. That stubborn reality would haunt Americans of all colors who continued to chase after freedom and independence. ∞∞∞

CHAPTER SUMMARY

DURING THE SEVENTEENTH CENTURY, SPAIN and England moved to colonize critical regions of southern North America.

- Native peoples everywhere in the American South resisted colonization, despite losses from warfare, disease, and enslavement.

- Spanish colonies in New Mexico and Florida grew slowly and faced a variety of threats. By the late seventeenth century, Spanish New Mexico had been lost to the Pueblo Revolt and Florida's delicate mission system was under siege from English Carolina and its Indian allies.

- Thriving monocultures were established in all of England's southern colonies—tobacco in the Chesapeake, rice in the Carolinas, and sugar in the Caribbean.

- Despite a period of intense enslavement of native peoples, African slavery emerged as the dominant labor system throughout these regions.

- Instability and conflict characterized both Spanish and English colonies in the South for most of the first century of their existence.

Additional Reading

David J. Weber's *Spanish Frontier in North America* (1992) remains indispensable. For New Mexico, see also John L. Kessell's *Spain in the Southwest* (2002) and James F. Brook's pathbreaking *Captives and Cousins* (2002). For Spain in the Southeast, see Paul E. Hoffman's *Florida's Frontiers* (2002) and Daniel S. Murphree's *Constructing Floridians* (2006).

For enduring treatments of early Virginia, see Edmund S. Morgan, *American Slavery, American Freedom* (1975), and Kathleen Brown, *Good Wives, Nasty Wenches, and Anxious Patriarchs* (1996). James D. Rice's *Tales from a Revolution* (2012) explores the multiple perspectives of Indians to Bacon's Rebellion.

For Indians in the colonial Southeast, see Gregory A. Waselkov, Peter Wood, and Tom Hatley, eds., *Powhatan's Mantle* (2006). For native Virginia, see also Hellen C. Rountree, *Pocahontas, Powhatan, Opechancanough* (2005).

In recent years there has been a surge in scholarship on African slavery in the New World. For a magisterial overview, see David Brion Davis, *Inhuman Bondage* (2006). For British North America, see Ira Berlin, *Many Thousands Gone* (1998), and Philip D. Morgan, *Slave Counterpoint* (1998). The classic account of the British Caribbean remains Richard Dunn's *Sugar and Slaves* (2000 [1972]). Vincent Brown's *Reaper's Garden* (2008) examines the brutalities of the Jamaican slave system. Stephanie Smallwood's *Saltwater Slavery* (2007) provides a haunting portrait of the Middle Passage.

The best overview of South Carolina's development remains Robert Weir, *Colonial South Carolina* (1982). The complexities of Carolina's slave wars are explored in Alan Gallay, *The Indian Slave Trade* (2002). For the topic more broadly, see Christina Snyder, *Slavery in Indian Country* (2010).

For a fuller list of readings, see the Bibliography at www.mhhe.com/eh8e.

Significant Events

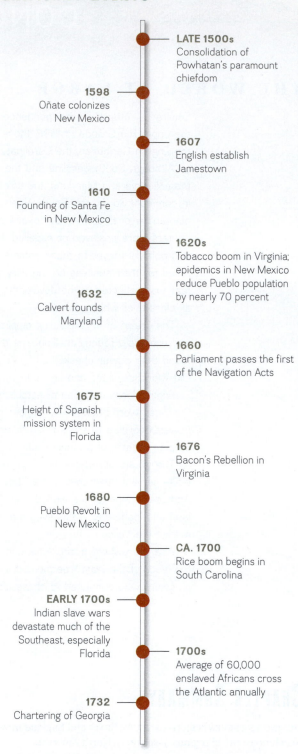

LATE 1500s
Consolidation of Powhatan's paramount chiefdom

1598
Oñate colonizes New Mexico

1607
English establish Jamestown

1610
Founding of Santa Fe in New Mexico

1620s
Tobacco boom in Virginia; epidemics in New Mexico reduce Pueblo population by nearly 70 percent

1632
Calvert founds Maryland

1660
Parliament passes the first of the Navigation Acts

1675
Height of Spanish mission system in Florida

1676
Bacon's Rebellion in Virginia

1680
Pueblo Revolt in New Mexico

CA. 1700
Rice boom begins in South Carolina

EARLY 1700s
Indian slave wars devastate much of the Southeast, especially Florida

1700s
Average of 60,000 enslaved Africans cross the Atlantic annually

1732
Chartering of Georgia

COLONY	FOUNDING/ SETTLEMENT	CHARACTER AND DEVELOPMENT	APPROXIMATE COLONIAL POPULATION
New Mexico	Oñate expedition 1598; Santa Fe 1610	Arid; few Spanish colonists; agriculture, stock raising, trade with Indians	2,500, including Indian slaves, in 1675
Florida	St. Augustine 1565	Spain uses as a buffer against English settlements to the north	40 Franciscan missions to c. 26,000 baptized Indians by 1675. 1,500 Spaniards in Florida by 1700.
Virginia	Jamestown 1607	Tobacco boom 1620s; population of young, single, indentured servants; Bacon's Rebellion 1676; slavery replaces servitude as the prevailing labor system, 1680s	72,000, including 56,000 white, 16,000 black, in 1700
Maryland	Founded by the Calverts as proprietors, 1632	Religious freedom for Christians; tobacco economy; Coode's Rebellion 1689	30,000, including 27,000 white, 3,000 black, in 1700
West Indies (British)	English settlements after 1604: islands of Barbados, Antigua, St. Kitts, Nevis, and Montserrat	Tobacco gives way to sugar boom, 1640s; African slaves become majority population on sugar islands	65,000, including 15,000 white, 50,000 black, in 1700
Carolinas	Charles Town established by colonists from England and Barbados, 1669	Trade in hides and Indian slaves; increased stability as rice cultivation established; made royal colony in 1729; North Carolina becomes separate colony in 1701	South Carolina: 6,000—3,500 white, 2,500 black; North Carolina: 10,700—10,300 white, 400 black, in 1700
Georgia	Chartered in 1732	Refuge for debtors; slavery not allowed until shortly before it becomes a royal colony in 1752	5,000, including 4,000 white, 1,000 black, in 1752

By **1664**, when this map of New Amsterdam was engraved, the town had grown
considerably from its origins as a fort and fur-trading outpost. (Compare the engraving
from **1626**, on page 95.) Behind the houses in the foreground, a palisade fence still
stands as a wall protecting against Indian attacks. A gallows stands in the foreground
and a windmill in the distance. The English renamed the city New York when they
pushed out the Dutch, in this year.

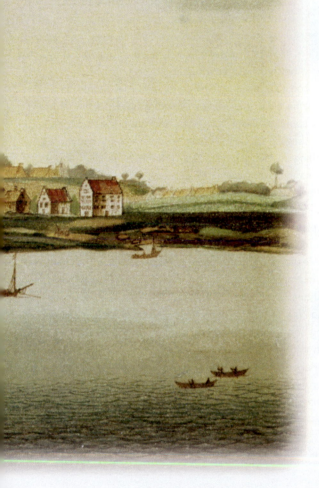

CHAPTER 4

Colonization and Conflict in the North

1600–1700

What's to Come

∞∞∞ AN AMERICAN STORY ∞∞∞

BEARS ON FLOATING ISLANDS

They came to her one night while she slept. Into her dreams drifted a small island, and on the island were tall trees and living creatures, one of them wearing the fur of a white rabbit. When she told of her vision, no one took her seriously, not even the wise men among her people, shamans and conjurers whose business it was to interpret dreams. No one, that is, until two days later, when the island appeared to all, floating toward shore. On the island, as she had seen, were tall trees, and on their branches—bears. Or creatures that looked so much like bears that the men grabbed their weapons and raced to the beach, eager for the good hunt sent by the gods. They were disappointed. The island was not an island at all but a strange wooden ship planted with the trunks of trees. And the bears were not bears at all but a strange sort of men whose bodies were covered with hair. Strangest among them, as she had somehow known, was a man dressed all in white. He commanded great respect among the bearlike men as their "shaman," or priest.

In that way, foretold by the dreams of a young woman, the Micmac Indians in 1869 recounted their people's first encounter with Europeans more than two centuries earlier. Uncannily, the traditions of other northern tribes record similar dreams predicting the European arrival: "large canoes with great white wings like those of a giant bird," filled with pale bearded men bearing "long black tubes."

Perhaps the dreamers gave shape in their sleep to stories heard from other peoples who had actually seen white strangers and ships. Or perhaps, long before they ever encountered the newcomers, these Indians imagined them, just as Europeans fantasized about a new world.

However Micmacs and other northern Indians first imagined and idealized Europeans, they quickly came to see them as fully human. Traders might bring seemingly wondrous goods, goods that could transform the way labor, commerce, politics, and war functioned in native communities. And yet the traders themselves hardly seemed magical. They could be by turns generous and miserly, brave and frightful, confident and confused, kind and cruel. Moreover, it soon became clear that these newcomers hailed from different nations, spoke different languages, and often seemed to have different goals. English colonists, it seemed, were every day more numerous and wanted nothing so much as land. The French, in contrast, were relatively few and seemed to care for nothing so much as trade—unless it was their Christian God they brought with them from across the waters. Strange to say, the Europeans argued over their deity as they did over so many other things. The English, the French, and the Dutch were all rivals, and the Micmacs and others who encountered these new peoples studied them closely and began to make alliances.

| Micmacs

As northern Indians became more and more aware of Europeans and their ways, they came also to realize that whatever their attitudes and intentions, the newcomers provoked dramatic changes everywhere they went. Thousands of English migrants coming into the land founded villages and towns that multiplied throughout the seventeenth century. They not only took up land but also brought animals and plants that changed the way Indians lived. The Dutch, Europe's most powerful commercial nation, established no more than a handful of trading settlements up and down the Hudson River, but they encouraged the Iroquois confederacy to push into rival Indian territories in a quest for furs to trade. Even the French, who styled themselves loyal allies to many Indian peoples and claimed to want little more than beaver pelts, brought with them profound, sometimes cataclysmic changes—changes that would upend the world that natives knew when Frenchmen were but bears on floating islands. ∞∞∞

France in North America

Cartier and Champlain

The first official expedition to the land the French would call Canada took place in 1535, when Jacques Cartier sailed through the Gulf of St. Lawrence. But not until 1605 did the French plant a permanent colony, at Port Royal in Acadia (Nova Scotia). Three years later, Samuel de Champlain established Quebec farther up the St. Lawrence valley, where he could pursue the fur trade with less competition from rival Europeans. Champlain soon aligned himself with local Montagnais, Algonquins, and, especially, the mighty Hurons—a confederacy of farmers 20,000 strong whose towns near the Georgian Bay straddled a vast trading network.

The Origins of New France

FRENCH-INDIAN ALLIANCES
These allied peoples had reason to embrace Champlain. Like Europeans elsewhere in North America, the Frenchman came with wondrous goods, such as textiles, glass, copper, and ironware. In the early years of contact such things would have been treated as exotic commodities rather than utilitarian items. Copper kettles, for instance, might be cut into strips for jewelry. But before long, metal tools, especially, began transforming native life. Metal knives made it far easier to butcher animals; trees could be felled and buildings built far more easily with iron than stone axes; cooking became more efficient with brass kettles that could be placed directly on the fire; flint strike-a-lights eliminated the cumbersome need for transporting hot coals in bounded shells; beads, cloth, needles, and thread made possible a new level of creative and visual expression; and, because metal arrowheads traveled farther and truer than stone, they would make hunters and warriors more deadly than they had ever been.

Champlain found a warm welcome for all these reasons. But native peoples in North America seldom viewed exchange as a simple market transaction. All exchanges were bound up in complex social relations, and the Montagnais, Algonquins, and Hurons wanted assurance that Champlain would be a good friend as well as a good merchant. To satisfy his hosts, he agreed to accompany them on a campaign against their mutual enemies the Mohawks, one of the five confederated tribes of the Iroquois. The Frenchman proved his friendship, and his worth, in the spring of 1609 when he and his Indian companions confronted 200 Mohawk warriors in what is now upstate New York. According to Champlain, he strode to the front as the battle was about to begin, raised his musket, and shot dead two Mohawk chiefs. Few if any of the assembled warriors had ever seen a gun fired in combat. Champlain's allies let out a joyous cry, so loud "one could not have heard it thunder," attacked the astonished Mohawks, and drove the survivors from the field. It was not the last time that European newcomers would alter the balance of power in North America.

THE FUR TRADE
Satisfied with their new ally, the Montagnais, Algonquins, and Hurons became eager trading partners over the next generation. In return for European goods, they provided tens of thousands of otter, raccoon, and especially beaver pelts. These furs went to make fashionable European hats, whereas mink and marten were sent to adorn the robes of high-ranking European officials and churchmen. Some in France derided the colonial endeavor, dismissing New France as a *comptoir*, a storehouse for the skins of

French women as well as men in religious orders dedicated their lives to missionary work in Canada. Marguerite Bourgeoys founded a religious community dedicated to the education of young girls.

dead animals. And yet Champlain wanted more. He struggled to encourage more immigration to Canada, to convince those who came to settle permanently, and, above all, to bind his native allies closer and closer to the colonial project. To that end, Champlain encouraged certain French men and boys to live with Indian families, to learn their language and become conversant in their customs.

JESUIT MISSIONS
Along with these *coureurs de bois*, or "runners in the woods," French authorities engaged Jesuits, members of the Society of Jesus, to establish missions among the region's Indians. Just as devout but often more culturally flexible than Franciscan missionaries, Jesuit friars came to New France in the 1610s determined to master Indian languages and make inroads into native culture. They were also fired with the passions of the **Counter-Reformation** in Europe, a movement by devout Catholics to correct those abuses that had prompted the Protestant Reformation. Initially, Jesuit missionaries were tolerated more than listened to. But by the 1630s Champlain began pressing the Indians, insisting that trading partners accept resident Jesuits. More importantly, Christianized Indians got better prices for furs than did their unconverted counterparts. Such policies helped the French pursue what they saw as interlocked economic, strategic, and religious objectives. French pressure also caused friction in native communities, among the Huron in particular. Should they accept European customs and religion? Converts remained relatively few into the 1640s, and the debate over Huron cultural identity provoked internal quarrels that eventually left the confederacy fragmented and vulnerable to enemies.

New Netherland, the Iroquois, and the Beaver Wars

THE DUTCH STRENGTH IN TRADE
If Canada was merely a *comptoir*, it was a profitable one. Potential revenues from the fur trade drew the attention of rival European powers, including the Dutch. By the beginning of the seventeenth century the Calvinist Dutch had finally freed their homeland from Spanish domination. Having won independence, they were equally determined to compete with Spanish merchants and to contain the spread of Spanish Catholicism. Along the Amazon River and the African coast, forts and trading posts of the Dutch West India Company protected and promoted Dutch commerce while harrying Spanish competitors.

Furthermore, by the early seventeenth century the Netherlands had the greatest manufacturing capacity in the world and had become the key economic power in Europe. Intent especially on trade, the Dutch had little desire to plant permanent colonies abroad because they enjoyed prosperity and religious freedom at home. But they did

This undated French engraving depicts something often overlooked or trivialized by European observers: native women's work. Two Iroquois women grind corn into meal while a swaddled infant rests in a backboard.

want to tap directly into the wealth flowing out of North America and therefore explored and laid claim to a number of sites around the Connecticut, Delaware, and Hudson Rivers (the last named for the Englishman Henry Hudson, who first explored it for the Dutch in 1609). Most of New Netherland's few settlers would cluster in the village of New Amsterdam on Manhattan Island at the mouth of the Hudson.

 **COLLAPSE OF THE BEAVER POPULATION** More important for the geopolitics of the continent, the Dutch West India Company also established a trading outpost 150 miles upriver known as Fort Orange (present-day Albany). Initially the traders at Fort Orange hoped to obtain cheap furs by fostering competition among rival Indian customers. But by 1630 the powerful Mohawks had displaced their competitors and come to dominate the fort's commerce. Ever since their encounter with Champlain's musket, the Mohawks and the other four members of the **Iroquois League** (the Oneidas, Onondagas, Cayugas, and Senecas) had suffered from their lack of direct access to European goods. With Mohawk ascendancy around Fort Orange, the Iroquois finally had reliable access to the tools and weapons necessary to go on the offensive against their northern enemies. They felt compelled to do so because the beaver population, always fragile, had collapsed within their own territory. To maintain their trading

position, they began preying on Huron convoys on their way to Quebec and then selling the plundered pelts to the Dutch.

SMALLPOX EPIDEMIC Just as this old rivalry revived, and soon after the aging Champlain died of a stroke, two things happened to help plunge the region into catastrophe. First, waves of disease afflicted the settlements in the Northeast in the 1630s and took a nightmarish toll on nearly all the region's native peoples, especially agricultural communities in their densely populated towns. Between 1634 and 1640 smallpox killed more than 10,000 Hurons, reducing their total population by half and precipitating a spate of conversions to Christianity that divided the community all the more. The Iroquois likewise suffered greatly, but, unlike the Hurons, they reacted by waging war in an effort to obtain captives that could formally replace dead kin. The second transformative event was a dramatic expansion in the regional arms trade. Initally reluctant to deal in guns, by the late 1630s the Dutch at Fort Orange relaxed their policy in order to obtain more furs. Before long the Iroquois had many times more muskets than the Hurons, whom the French had traditionally refused to arm so long as they remained unconverted.

Reeling from disease and internal division, the Hurons saw their world collapsing. In 1648 well-armed Iroquois warriors destroyed three Huron towns. The attacks continued into the next year. At one town under siege the Jesuit Paul Ragueneau saw desperate Hurons seek baptism and Christian consolation. "Never was their faith more alive, nor their love for their good fathers and pastors more keenly felt." The Hurons made the wrenching decision to burn their remaining towns and abandon their lands for good. As many as 2,000 became Iroquois, as either war captives or humble refugees. Others merged with neighboring peoples, while thousands more fled in desperation and starved to death or died of exposure in the harsh winter of 1649–1650.

The Hurons, who became infected with smallpox in the 1630s, would have experienced fevers, aches, and vomiting before the telltale spots emerged on their skin. Agonizing pustules would have soon covered them from head to toe, as in the picture here, and sometimes the pustules merged into oozing sheets that caused large sections of the victims' skin to peel away from their bodies. This horrible disease claimed millions of lives in the Americas after 1492.

A FRENCH MAP

Information on Pawnee Indians on Great Plains suggests the scope of French exploration—or at least French interests—by the late seventeenth century.

Mapmaker included population estimates for some native groups.

"There are a number of unknown savages and villages whose names are unknown," says the mapmaker. Why don't we see similar notations elsewhere?

Carte de Louisiane, by Jean Baptiste Louis Franquelin (1684)

Maps are and always have been far more than simple representations of physical or political space. Maps should also be seen as arguments. Consider the choices made by the cartographer who made the map above. Through the inclusion of certain physical, demographic, and geopolitical details, and through the exclusion of other information, this mapmaker sought to shape perceptions about North America. Choices about where to put boundaries, the relative size and boldness of the words used to identify different regions, the names applied to natural landmarks, and whether to even mention a given place or group all had political implications. The decisions Franquelin made along these lines would surely have been contested by mapmakers from rival empires and would likely have seemed bizarre and mostly useless to the continent's native peoples, who had their own methods for representing space through images.

Thinking Critically

Locate New Spain, New France, and Louisiana. Which English colonies does the map indicate? Could maps be used as tools in interimperial rivalries? Would Spain have agreed with France about the boundaries around Texas? Would England have agreed with France about the boundaries of New England or Virginia? What might native peoples have thought about any of these claims?

So began the Beaver Wars, a series of conflicts at least as profoundly transformative for the colonial north as the Indian slave wars were for the south. Seeking new hunting grounds and new captives to replenish their diminishing population, Iroquois raiders attacked peoples near and far. After the Hurons, they struck and scattered the nearby Petuns, Eries, and Neutrals—peoples who, like the Hurons, were all Iroquoian speakers and could thus be integrated into Iroquois communities with relative ease. Iroquois warriors next moved against non-Iroquoian groups, including Delawares and Shawnees in the Ohio valley, and even extended their raids south to the Carolinas. To the north they attacked Algonquins in the Canadian Shield, and Abenakis and others in New England.

The Lure of the Mississippi

The Beaver Wars continued in fits and starts for the rest of the seventeenth century, bringing dozens of Indian nations to grief and provoking a massive refugee crisis as families fled their traditional territories and tried to rebuild their lives in peace. The wars also very nearly led to the ruin of New France. About 300 Frenchmen were killed or captured in the wars, cutting the colony's meager population in half by 1666. The survivors saw Champlain's carefully managed trading system thrown into disarray. French authorities scrambled to find reliable new partners in the fur trade and henceforth were less reluctant to trade guns to Indian allies. More broadly, the scope of the conflict and the far-flung movement of refugees compelled the French to take a more expansive view of the continent and their place in it.

By the 1660s, French traders, priests, and officers were making inroads among diverse refugee villages in the Western Great Lakes, a region the French referred to as the *pays d'en haut.* These peoples sought trade, assistance against the Iroquois, and mediation of their own disputes. While the French set about building alliances in the *pays d'en haut,* they became aware of and began exploring the greatest watercourse in North America.

LA SALLE DESCENDS THE MISSISSIPPI

The Mississippi River travels nearly 2,500 miles from its source in present-day Minnesota to the Gulf of Mexico, carrying water from several other major rivers and dominating a drainage area larger than the Indian subcontinent in Asia. As the French began exploring the river in earnest in the 1670s, it dawned on them that the Mississippi valley could be the strategic key to success in North America. French officials set out courting Indian peoples along the river and its tributaries, employing their hard-won insights into native diplomatic culture along the way. The region's peoples—the Illinois, Shawnees, Quapaws, and others—expressed keen interest in French trade, as well as fear and hatred of their common Iroquois enemies. When René Robert Cavelier, Sieur de La Salle, became the first European to descend the river to the Gulf in 1682, he encountered the Natchez, Chickasaws, and others who had not seen Europeans since de Soto and his maniacal march

nearly a century and a half before. Other Frenchmen went further, erecting trading posts and simple missions, and even making contact and tentative alliances with Osages, Arkansas, Ottos, Pawnees, and others west of the great river.

By the early eighteenth century New France had helped broker an uneasy peace between the Iroquois and Indian nations to the west, extended its influence over a vast area, and fortified its colonial core along the St. Lawrence. In 1700 the colony had scores of simple missions and three modest towns—Quebec, Montreal, and Trois-Rivières—containing a population of approximately 15,000. Most immigrants to New France eventually returned to Europe, and shortsighted French monarchs insisted that Canada be a Catholic colony, off limits to France's most obvious emigrants, the Protestant Huguenots. But even with its small colonial population, New France emerged as a powerful player in North America, given its strategic and economic alliances with native peoples. The French had reason to hope that their native allies could help contain the Spanish to the west and limit English expansion from the east.

✓ REVIEW
What caused the Beaver Wars?

THE FOUNDING OF NEW ENGLAND

AT FIRST THE ENGLISH REGARDED the northern part of North America as a place in which only the mad French could see possibility. English fisherfolk who strayed from Newfoundland to the coast of Acadia and New England carried home descriptions of the long, lonely coast, rockbound and rugged. Long winters of numbing cold melted into short summers of steamy heat. There were no minerals to mine, no crops suitable for export, no large native population available for enslaving. The Chesapeake, with its temperate climate and long growing season, seemed a much likelier spot.

But by 1620 worsening conditions at home had instilled in some English men and women the mixture of desperation and idealism needed to settle an uninviting, unknown world. Religious differences among English Protestants became a matter of sharper controversy during the seventeenth century. Along with the religious crisis came mounting political tensions and continuing problems of unemployment and recession. Times were bad—so bad that the anticipation of worse times to come swept English men and women to the shores of New England.

The Puritan Movement

The colonization of New England started with a king who chose his enemies unwisely. James I, shortly after succeeding Elizabeth I in 1603, vowed to purge England of all radical Protestant reformers. The radicals James had in mind were the Puritans, most of whom were either Presbyterians or Congregationalists. Although both groups of Puritan reformers embraced Calvin's ideas, they differed on the best form of church organization. Individual **Presbyterian** churches (or congregations) were guided by higher governing bodies of ministers and laypersons. Those in the **Congregationalist** churches, in contrast, believed that each congregation should conduct its own affairs independently, answering to no other authority.

Like all Christians, Protestant and Catholic, the Puritans believed that God was all-knowing and all-powerful. And, like all Calvinists, the Puritans emphasized that idea of divine sovereignty known as **predestination.** At the center of their thinking was the belief that God had ordained the outcome of history, including the eternal fate of every human being. The Puritans found comfort in their belief in predestination because it provided their lives with meaning and purpose. They felt assured that a sovereign God was directing the fate of individuals, nations, and all of creation. The Puritans strove to play their parts in that divine drama of history and to discover in their performances some signs of personal salvation.

The divine plan, as the Puritans understood it, called for reforming both church and society along the lines laid down by John Calvin. It seemed to the Puritans that England's government hampered rather than promoted religious purity and social order. It tolerated drunkenness, theatergoing, gambling, extravagance, public swearing, and Sabbath-breaking. It permitted popular recreations rooted in pagan custom and superstition—sports such as bear baiting and maypole dancing and festivals such as the celebration of Christmas and saints' days.

PURITAN CALLS FOR REFORM

Even worse, the state had not done enough to purify the English church of the "corruptions" of Roman Catholicism. The Church of England counted as its members everyone in the nation, saint and sinner alike. To the Puritans, belonging to a church was no birthright. They wished to limit membership and the privileges of baptism and communion to godly men and women. The Puritans also deplored the hierarchy of bishops and archbishops in the Church of England, as well as its elaborate ceremonies in which priests wore ornate vestments. Too many Anglican clergy were "dumb dogges" in Puritan eyes, too poorly educated to instruct churchgoers in the truths of Scripture or to deliver a decent sermon. In reformer John Foxe's vision of good and evil (below), Anglican priests on the right side of the drawing are shown in vestments and headdresses worshiping Satan before an altar. Anglican worshipers (bottom right) superstitiously count rosary beads and follow a priestly procession like so many dumb sheep. In contrast, Puritan worshipers (bottom left) conspicuously hold their Bibles and attend only to the word of God.

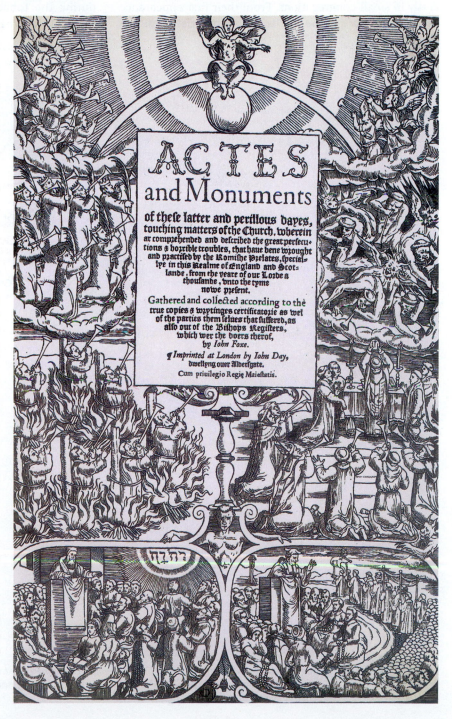

| John Foxe's Actes and Monuments *(1563)*, a book revered by the Puritan founders of New England, arrayed the forces of righteousness (left side of page) *against a host of devils, priests, and their sheeplike followers within the Church of England at right. Under the Catholic Queen Mary, Protestants were regarded as heretics and some were burned at the stake* (middle left).

Because English monarchs had refused to take stronger measures to reform church and society, the Puritans became their outspoken critics. Elizabeth I had tolerated this opposition, but James I would not endure it and intended to rid England of these radicals. With some of the Puritans, known as the Separatists, he seemed to succeed.

The Pilgrim Settlement at Plymouth Colony

The Separatists were devout Congregationalists who concluded that the Church of England was too corrupt to be reformed. They abandoned Anglican worship and met secretly in small congregations. From their first appearance in England during the 1570s, the Separatists suffered persecution from the government—fines, imprisonment, and, in a few cases, execution. Always a tiny minority within the Puritan movement, the Separatists were people from humble backgrounds: craftworkers and farmers without influence to challenge the state. By 1608 some had become so discouraged that they migrated to Holland, where the Dutch government permitted complete freedom of religion. But when their children began to adopt Dutch customs and other religions, some Separatists decided to move again, this time to Virginia.

EARLY DIFFICULTIES It can only be imagined what fate would have befallen the unworldly Separatists had they actually settled in the Chesapeake during the tobacco boom. But a series of mistakes—including an error in charting the course of their ship, the

EARLY NEW ENGLAND

Despite some variety among emigrants, New England's English settlements remained relatively homogeneous and stable. Over the years, groups of settlers "hived off" from the settlements around Massachusetts Bay, beginning new towns along the Connecticut River, southern and western Connecticut, Long Island, and East Jersey.

Mayflower—brought the little band far to the North, to a region Captain John Smith had earlier dubbed "New England." In November 1620 some 88 Separatist "Pilgrims" set anchor at a place they called Plymouth on the coast of present-day southeastern Massachusetts. They were sick with scurvy, weak from malnutrition, and shaken by a shipboard mutiny, and neither the site nor the season invited settlement. As one of their leaders, William Bradford, later remembered:

> For summer being done, all things stand upon them with a weather beaten face, and the whole country, full of woods and thickets represented a savage hue. If they looked behind them, there was the mighty ocean which they had passed and was now as a main bar and gulf to separate them from all the civil parts of the world.

For some, the shock was too great. Dorothy Bradford, William's wife, is said to have fallen overboard from the *Mayflower* as it lay anchored off Plymouth. It is more likely that she jumped to her death.

Few Pilgrims could have foreseen founding the first permanent European settlement in New England, and many did not live long enough to enjoy the distinction. They had arrived too late to plant crops and had failed to bring an adequate supply of food. By the spring of 1621 half the immigrants had died. English merchants who had financed the *Mayflower* voyage failed to send supplies to the struggling settlement. Plymouth might have become another doomed colony had the Pilgrims not received better treatment from native inhabitants than they did from their English backers.

EFFECT OF EPIDEMIC DISEASE
Though they understood it only dimly, the Pilgrims were, in one historian's memorable phrase, the "beneficiaries of catastrophe." Only four years before their arrival, coastal New England had been devastated by a massive epidemic, possibly the plague. Losses varied locally, but overall the native coastal population may have been reduced by as much as 90 percent. Abandoned villages lay in ruins up and down the coast, including the village of Patuxet, where the Pilgrims established Plymouth. Years later visitors would still marvel at heaps of unburied human remains dating from the epidemic.

The Wampanoags dominated the lands around Plymouth. Still reeling from loss in 1620 and eager to obtain trade goods and assistance against native enemies, Massasoit, their chief, agreed to help the starving colonists. Initially, the peoples communicated through a remarkable Wampanoag named Squanto, who had been kidnapped by English sailors before the epidemic. Taken to Europe, Squanto learned English and eventually returned to America in time to play a crucial intermediary role between Massasoit and the newcomers. The Pilgrims accepted Wampanoag hospitality and instruction and invited native leaders to a feast in honor of their first successful harvest in 1621 (the genesis of the "First Thanksgiving" story).

THE MAYFLOWER COMPACT
The Pilgrims set up a government for their colony, the framework of which was the Mayflower Compact, drawn up on board ship before landing. That agreement provided for a governor and several assistants to advise him, all to be elected annually by Plymouth's adult males. In the eyes of English law the Plymouth settlers had no clear basis for their land claims or their government, because they had neither a royal charter nor approval from the Crown. But English authorities, distracted by problems closer to home, left the tiny colony of farmers alone.

THE PURITAN SETTLEMENT AT MASSACHUSETTS BAY

AMONG THE CROWN'S DISTRACTIONS WERE two groups of Puritans more numerous and influential than the Pilgrims. They included both the Presbyterians and the majority of Congregationalists who, unlike the Pilgrim Separatists, still considered the Church of England capable of being reformed. But the 1620s brought these Puritans only fresh discouragements. In 1625 Charles I inherited his father's throne and all his enemies. When Parliament attempted to limit the king's power, Charles simply dissolved it, in 1629, and proceeded to rule without it. When Puritans pressed for reform, the king began to move against them.

This persecution swelled a second wave of Puritan migration that also drew from the ranks of Congregationalists. Unlike the humble Separatists, these emigrants included merchants, landed gentlemen, and lawyers who organized the Massachusetts Bay Company in 1629. Those able Puritan leaders aimed to build a better society in America, an example to the rest of the world. Unlike the Separatists, they had a strong sense of mission and destiny. They were not abandoning the English church, they insisted, but merely regrouping across the Atlantic for another assault on corruption.

Despite the company's Puritan leanings, it somehow obtained a royal charter confirming its title to most of present-day Massachusetts and New Hampshire. Advance parties in 1629 established the town of Salem on the coast well north of Plymouth. In 1630 the company's first governor, a tough-minded and visionary lawyer named John Winthrop, sailed from England with a dozen other company stockholders and a fleet of men and women to establish the town of Boston. The newcomers intended to build a godly "city on a hill" that would serve as an example to the world.

ESTABLISHING THE COLONY'S GOVERNMENT
Once established in the Bay Colony, Winthrop and the other stockholders transformed the charter for their trading company into the framework of government for a colony. The company's governor became the colony's chief executive, and the company's other officers became the governor's assistants. The charter provided for annual elections

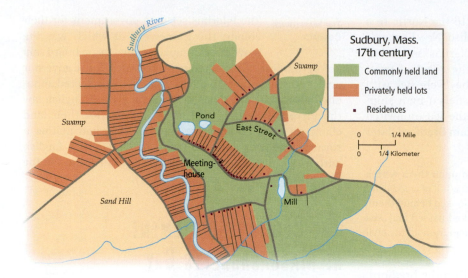

SUDBURY, MASSACHUSETTS

Sudbury, Mass. 17th century

- Commonly held land
- Privately held lots
- Residences

Everyday life in New England centered in small towns such as Sudbury, west of Boston. Families lived in houses clustered around the meetinghouse, in contrast to the decentralized plantations of the South. The privately held farm lots were mixed together as well, so that neighbors worked and lived in close contact with one another. **How does the pattern of settlement in Sudbury differ from the pattern of settlement in the Chesapeake region?**

of the governor and his assistants by company stockholders, known as the freemen. But to create a broad base of support for the new government, Winthrop and his assistants expanded the freemanship in 1631 to include every adult male church member.

The governor, his assistants, and the freemen together made up the General Court of the colony, which passed all laws, levied taxes, established courts, and made war and peace. In 1634 the whole body of the freemen stopped meeting, and instead each town elected representatives or deputies to the General Court. Ten years later, the deputies formed themselves into the lower house of the Bay Colony legislature, and the assistants formed the upper house. By refashioning a company charter into a civil constitution, Massachusetts Bay Puritans were well on the way to shaping society, church, and state to their liking.

Contrary to expectations, New England proved more hospitable to the English than did the Chesapeake. The character of the migration itself gave New England settlers an advantage, for most arrived in family groups—not as young, single, indentured servants of the sort whose discontents unsettled Virginia society. The heads of New England's first households were typically freemen—farmers, artisans, and merchants. Most were skilled and literate. Since husbands usually migrated with their wives and children, the ratio of men to women within the population was fairly evenly balanced.

THE "GREAT MIGRATION" Most of the immigrants, some 21,000, came in a cluster between 1630 and 1642. Thereafter new arrivals tapered off because of the outbreak of the English Civil War. This relatively rapid colonization fostered solidarity because immigrants shared a common past of persecution and a strong desire to create an ordered society modeled on Scripture.

✓ REVIEW

Who settled the earliest New England colonies?

STABILITY AND ORDER IN EARLY NEW ENGLAND

LONG-LIVED NEW ENGLANDERS PURITAN EMIGRANTS AND THEIR descendants thrived in New England's bracing but healthy climate. The first generation of colonists lived to an average age of 70, nearly twice as long as Virginians and 10 years longer than men and women living in England. With 90 percent of all children reaching adulthood, the typical family consisted of seven or eight children who came to maturity. Because of low death rates and high birthrates, the number of New Englanders doubled about every 27 years—while the populations of Europe and the Chesapeake barely reproduced

Susan Gill, an English maidservant from the 1670s.

themselves. By 1700 New England and the Chesapeake would both have populations of approximately 100,000. But, whereas the southern population grew because of continuing immigration and the importation of slaves, New England's expanded primarily through natural increase.

As immigrants arrived in the Bay Colony after 1630, they carved out an arc of villages around Massachusetts Bay. Within a decade settlers pressed into Connecticut, Rhode Island, and New Hampshire. Connecticut and Rhode Island received separate charters from Charles II in the 1660s, guaranteeing their residents the rights to land and government. New Hampshire, to which Massachusetts laid claim in the 1640s, did not become a separate colony until 1679. The handful of hardy souls settled along the coast of present-day Maine had also accepted the Massachusetts Bay Colony's authority.

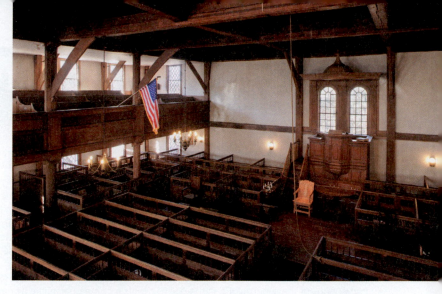

| The Old Ship Meetinghouse, built in Hingham, Massachusetts in 1681, expresses the importance of hierarchy among New England Puritans. Wealthy families enjoyed the enclosed wooden pews on the ground floor, whereas poorer folk sat on benches in the second-floor gallery. The raised pulpit (front) bespeaks the congregation's respect for the authority and learning of the clergy. The American flag, of course, is a modern addition.

PATTERNS OF SETTLEMENT Early New Englanders established most of their settlements with an eye to stability and order. Unlike the Virginians, who scattered across the Chesapeake to isolated plantations, most New Englanders established tightly knit communities like those they had left behind in England. Each family received a lot for a house along with about 150 acres of land in nearby fields. Farmers left many of their acres uncultivated as a legacy for future generations, for most had only the labor of their own families to work their land. While the Chesapeake abounded with servants, tenant farmers, and slaves, almost every adult male in rural New England owned property. With little hope of prospering through commercial agriculture, New England farmers also had no incentive to import large numbers of servants and slaves or to create large plantations.

Strong family institutions contributed to New England's order and stability. Although the early deaths of parents regularly splintered Chesapeake families, two adult generations were often on hand to encourage order within New England households. Husbands and fathers exacted submission from wives and strict obedience from children. Land gave New England's long-lived fathers great authority over even their grown children; sons and daughters relied on paternal legacies of farms in order to marry and establish their own families.

CHURCH MEMBERSHIP Whereas churches were few and far between in seventeenth-century Virginia, they constituted the center of community life in colonial New England. Individual congregations ran their own affairs and regulated their own membership. Those wishing to join had to convince ministers and church members that they had experienced a genuine spiritual rebirth or "conversion." Most New Englanders sought and won membership. As majority institutions supported by public taxes, churches had the reach and the resources to oversee public morality, often censuring or expelling wayward neighbors. Still, ministers enjoyed less public power in New England than in the old country. New England's ministers did not serve as officers in the civil government, and the Congregational churches owned no property. In contrast, Catholic and Anglican church officials wielded real temporal power in European states, and the churches held extensive tracts of land.

Finally, New Englanders governed themselves more democratically than did their counterparts in England.

HIERARCHY OF LEADERSHIP Communities throughout the region held regular town meetings of all resident white men. The town fathers generally set the meeting's agenda and offered advice, but the unanimous consent of townsmen determined all decisions. Colony governments in early New England also evolved into representative and responsive institutions. Typically the central government of each colony, such as the General Court of Massachusetts Bay, consisted of a governor and a bicameral legislature, including an upper house, or council, and a lower house, or assembly. All officials were elected annually by the freemen—white adult men entitled to vote in colony elections. Voting qualifications varied, but the number of men enfranchised made up a much broader segment of society than that in seventeenth-century England.

Communities in Conflict

Although most New Englanders called themselves Puritans and Congregationalists, the very fervency of their convictions often led them to disagree about how best to carry out the teachings of the Bible and the ideas of John Calvin. During the first decades of colonization, such disagreements led to the founding of breakaway colonies. In 1636 Thomas Hooker, the minister of Cambridge, Massachusetts, led part of his congregation to Connecticut, where they established the first English settlement. Somewhat more liberal than other Bay Puritans, Hooker favored more lenient standards

A WORLD OF WONDERS AND WITCHCRAFT

In 1684 the Reverend Increase Mather, a learned Boston minister, proudly issued a plump book titled *Remarkable Providence*. The work was packed with fantastic occurrences that had taken place during the first 50 years of New England's settlement. Those occurrences dealt with "wonders"—interventions of the supernatural in the normal order of things. Ministers throughout New England contributed marvels of all sorts: a "Conjuring Book" from Salem, which filled readers with "a strange kind of Horror" and caused their hair to stand on end; a house in Newbury inhabited by evil spirits and a "monstrous birth"; a phantom ship sighted sailing into New Haven harbor that suddenly disappeared.

Mather's book of wonders became one of many available to New England readers—a numerous group, for literacy was almost universal. Accounts of marvelous events poured from presses in England, the Continent, and the colonies. The authors drew their reports of visions and voices, untimely deaths and natural disasters from ancient and early Christian authors, medieval chronicles, the Bible, and local lore collected by contemporaries.

Most seventeenth-century New Englanders preferred to read religious books: the Bible, psalmbooks, sermons. Even so, authors such as Increase Mather recognized that a wider audience might be reached by volumes blending godly messages with sensational topics. Ministers recounted wonders to make the religious argument that the world was shot through with mystery and miracle and that men and women were at the mercy of God's will and the devil's wiles. At the same time, these books titillated readers with accounts of witches, apparitions, and freaks of nature. Published narratives of New Englanders taken captive by the Indians and the confessions of convicted murderers combined the same mixture of religion and sensationalism.

Knowing what early New Englanders liked to read offers a glimpse not only of their entertainments but of their inner world as well. Especially significant was their enduring fascination with wonders, which were believed to be true both by learned folks and by humble farmers and

their wives. The popularity of wonder lore is powerful proof that all New Englanders inhabited an enchanted universe. Their world brimmed with invisible forces and supernatural beings that could interrupt the order of nature.

That widely shared belief made witchcraft a crime punishable by death and allowed for the unfolding of the notorious witchcraft trials in Salem Village. There, in the early months of 1692, a group of adolescent girls used the white of a raw egg suspended in a glass of water as a kind of crude crystal ball to divine what sorts of men their future husbands might be. Somehow, the seance went sour, and the frightened adolescents began behaving in ways that other villagers took to be signs of bewitchment. Crying out in pain and terror, the afflicted girls claimed to see taunting specters of witches, whom they recognized as fellow villagers. In the hysteria that ensued, hundreds of accusations of witchcraft led to the trial and execution

Witchcraft trials and executions took place throughout Europe in the sixteenth and seventeenth centuries, occurring far more frequently and claiming many more victims than in colonial America. But, as this engraving of an English hanging of witches indicates, women composed a majority of those charged and executed on both sides of the Atlantic.

of 20 innocent women and men. Only when Increase Mather and 14 other Massachusetts ministers publicly warned against the trials' excesses did the killings stop.

Many historians have tried to explain the deeper causes behind the Salem episode. Some point to the Puritan mistrust of independent women, others to the bitter rivalries among Salem Village families. Still others have noted ties between accused witches and heretical groups such as the Quakers, or deep communal traumas stemming from conflicts with Indians and the French. Whatever the source of Salem's particular troubles, the witchcraft charges there and elsewhere in seventeenth-century New England were rooted in the widespread belief in a world of wonders, at once terrible and fascinating. Witchcraft trials and executions took place throughout Europe in the sixteenth and seventeenth centuries, occurring far more frequently and claiming many more victims than in colonial America. But, as this engraving (left) of an English hanging of witches indicates, women composed a majority of those charged and executed on both sides of the Atlantic.

The one arena in which women could attain something approaching equal standing with men was the churches. Puritan women could not become ministers, but after the 1660s they made up the majority of church members. In some churches membership enabled them to vote for ministerial candidates and to voice opinions about admitting and disciplining members. Puritan doctrine itself rejected the medieval Catholic suspicion of women as "a necessary evil," seeing them instead as "a necessary good." Even so, the Puritan ideal of the virtuous woman was a chaste, submissive "helpmeet," a wife and mother who served God by serving men.

Thinking Critically

What might account for the disproportionate number of women charged with witchcraft?

for church membership. He also opposed the Bay's policy of limiting voting in colony elections to church members. In contrast, New Haven (a separate colony until it became part of Connecticut in 1662) was begun in 1638 by strict Congregationalists who found Massachusetts too liberal.

ROGER WILLIAMS While Connecticut and New Haven emerged from voluntary migration, enforced exile filled Rhode Island with men and women whose radical ideas unsettled the rest of Massachusetts. Roger Williams, Rhode Island's founder, had come to New England in 1631, serving as a respected minister of Salem. But soon Williams announced that he was a Separatist, like the Pilgrims of Plymouth. He encouraged the Bay Colony to break all ties to the corrupt Church of England. He also urged a more complete **separation of church and state** than most New Englanders were prepared to accept, and later in his career he endorsed full religious toleration. Finally, Williams denounced the Bay's charter—the legal document that justified Massachusetts's existence—on the grounds that the king had no right to grant land that he had not purchased from the Indians. When Williams boldly suggested that Massachusetts actually inform the king of his mistake, angry authorities prepared to deport him. Instead, Williams fled the colony in the dead of winter to live with the Indians. In 1636 he became the founder and first citizen of Providence, later to be part of Rhode Island.

ANNE HUTCHINSON Another charismatic heretic from Massachusetts arrived soon after. Anne Hutchinson, a skilled midwife and the spouse of a wealthy merchant, came to Boston in 1634. Enthusiasm for her minister, John Cotton, started her on a course of explaining his sermons to gatherings of her neighbors—and then to elaborating ideas of her own. The fact that a woman would do such things made the authorities uneasy; but they became alarmed when they learned that Hutchinson embraced controversial positions on doctrine. Soon a majority of the Bay's ministers accused the troublesomely popular Hutchinson of holding heretical views. She in turn denounced her detractors, and the controversy escalated. In 1638 the Bay Colony government expelled Hutchinson and her followers for sedition. She settled briefly in Rhode Island before moving on to Long Island, where she died in an Indian attack.

Goodwives and Witches

If Anne Hutchinson had been a man, her ideas would still have been deemed heretical. However, if she had been a man, she might have found other ways to express her intelligence and magnetism. But life in colonial New England offered women, especially married women, little scope for their talents.

Most adult women were hardworking farm wives who cared for large households of children. Between marriage and middle age, most New England wives were pregnant except when breast-feeding. When they were not nursing or minding children, mothers were producing and preparing much of what was consumed and worn by their families. They planted vegetable gardens and pruned fruit trees, salted beef and pork and pressed cider, milked cows and churned butter, kept bees and tended poultry, cooked and baked, washed and ironed, spun, wove, and sewed. While husbands and sons engaged in farmwork that changed with the seasons, took trips to taverns and mills, and went off to hunt or fish, housebound wives and daughters were locked into a humdrum routine with little time for themselves.

WITCHCRAFT Communities sometimes responded to assertive women with accusations of witchcraft. Like most early modern Europeans, New Englanders believed in wizards and witches, men and women who

The artist who sketched this Quaker meeting called attention to one of that sect's most controversial practices by placing a woman at the center of his composition. Women were allowed to speak in Quaker worship services and to preach and proselytize at public gatherings of non-Quakers. The Puritans roundly condemned this liberty as contrary to the teachings of St. Paul.

DUELING DOCUMENTS

ACCUSATIONS AND DEFENSES IN THE SALEM WITCHCRAFT TRIALS

The Salem witchcraft trials of 1692 set neighbor against neighbor and resulted in the execution of 20 women and men. One of the accused was tavern owner John Proctor, on whom Arthur Miller loosely based the main protagonist in his famous play The Crucible. *The documents below include testimony of three witnesses against Proctor and his own remarkable response.*

DOCUMENT 1   The Accusations

Sarah Bibber

The Deposition of Sarah Bibber agged about 36 years who testifieth and saith that on the 3 june 1692. Jno: proctor. sen'r came to me and did most greviously torment me by pinching pricking and almost presing me to death urging me to drink: drink as Red as blood which I refusing he did tortor me with variety of tortors and immediatly he vanished away also on the same day I saw Jno: proctor most greviously tortor Susannah Shelden by claping his hands on hir throat and almost choaking hir. also severall times sence Jno: proctor sen'r has most greviously tortored me a grat many times with a variety of tortors

Sara vibber ownid this har testimony to be the truth on har oath before the Juriars of Inqwest this: 30. of June 1692.
   Jurat in Curia
   (Reverse) Sarah Bibber

Ann Putnam

The Deposistion of Ann putnam Jun'r who testifieth and saith I have often seen the Apperishtion of Jno procktor senr. amongst the wicthes but he did not doe me much hurt tell a little before his examination which was on the 11th of April 1692 and then he sett upon me most greviously and did tortor me most dreadfully also in the time of his examination he afflected

me very much: and severall times sence the Apperishtion of John prockter senr, has most greviously tortored me by pinching and allmost choaking me urging me vehemently to writ in his book also on the day of his examination I saw the Apperishtion of Jno: proctor senr goe and afflect and most greviously tortor the bodys of Mistris pope mary walcott Mircy lewes. Abigail williams and Jno: Indian. and he and his wife and Sarah Cloys keept Elizabeth Hubburd speachless all the time of their examination

(mark) Ann Putnam

---

were said to acquire supernatural powers by signing a compact with Satan. A total of 344 New Englanders were charged with witchcraft during the first colonial century, with the Salem Village episode of 1692 producing the largest outpouring of accusations and 20 executions. More than three-quarters of all accused witches were women, usually middle-aged and older, and most of those accused were regarded as unduly independent. Before they were charged with witchcraft, many had been suspected of heretical religious beliefs, others of sexual impropriety. Still others had inherited or stood to inherit property.

The People in the Way

SIMILARITIES BETWEEN PURITANS AND INDIANS

Whatever their political battles, doctrinal disputes, and inequalities, New Englanders were all participants in a colonial project that depended on taking land from other people. Perhaps 100,000 Algonquin men and women lived in the area reaching from the Kennebec River in Maine to Cape Cod at contact. Like the Puritans, they relied on fishing in spring and summer, hunting year-round, and cultivating and harvesting corn and other crops in spring and fall. And, to an even greater degree than among the colonists, Indian political authority was local. Within each village, a single leader known as the "sachem" or "sagamore" directed economic life, administered justice, and negotiated with other tribes and English settlers. As with New England's town fathers, a sachem's power was contingent on keeping the trust and consent of his people.

Thus the newcomers had more in common with their hosts than they cared to admit. But English expansion in the region had to come at someone's expense, and colonists obtained Indian lands in one of three ways. Sometimes they purchased it. Sales varied—they might be free and fair, fraudulent, subtly coerced, or forced through intimidation and violence. Second, colonists eagerly expanded into lands emptied by epidemics. The English often saw God's hand in such events. Following a terrible smallpox epidemic in 1633–1634, for example, one observer exclaimed that "without this remarkable and terrible stroke of God upon the natives, [we] would with much more difficulty have found room, and at far greater charge have obtained and purchased land."

Ann Putman owned what is above written upon oath before and unto the Grand inquest on the 30'th Day of June 1692

(Reverse) Ann puttnam ag't John procter

Mary Warren

The deposition of mary warrin aged 20 y'rs ho testifieth I have seen the apparition of John procter sen'r among the wiches and he hath often tortored me by penching me and biting me and Choakeing me and presing me one my Stomack tell the blood came out of my mouth and all so I saw him tortor Mes poap and marcey lues and John Indian a pon the day of his examination and he hath allso temted me to right in his book and to eat bread which he brought to me which I Refuseing to doe: Jno proctor did most greviously tortor me with variety of torturs all most Redy to kill me.

Mary Warren owned the above written upon her oath before & unto the Grand inquest on the 30'th Day of June 1692

DOCUMENT 2 **The Defense**

SALEM-PRISON, July 23, 1692. *Mr. Mather, Mr. Allen, Mr. Moody, Mr. Willard, and Mr. Bailey. Reverend Gentlemen.*

The innocency of our Case with the Enmity of our Accusers and our Judges, and Jury, whom nothing but our Innocent Blood will serve their turn, having Condemned us already before our Tryals, being so much incensed and engaged against us by the Devil, makes us bold to Beg and Implore your Favourable Assistance of this our Humble Petition to his Excellency, That if it be possible our Innocent Blood may be spared, which undoubtedly otherwise will be shed, if the Lord doth not mercifully step in. The Magistrates, Ministers, Jewries, and all the People in general, being so much inraged and incensed against us by the Delusion of the Devil, which we can term no other, by reason we know in our own Consciences, we are all Innocent Persons. Here are five Persons who have lately confessed themselves to be Witches, and do accuse some of us, of being along with them at a Sacrament, since we were committed into close Prison, which we know to be Lies. Two of the 5 are (Carriers Sons) Youngmen, who would not confess any thing till they tyed them Neck and Heels till the Blood was ready to come out of their Noses, and 'tis credibly believed and reported this was the occasion of making them confess that they never did, by reason they said one had been a Witch a Month, and another five Weeks, and that their Mother had made them so, who has been confined here this nine Weeks. My son William Procter, when he was examin'd, because he would not confess that he was Guilty, when he was Innocent, they tyed him Neck and Heels till the Blood gushed out at his Nose, and would have kept him so 24 Hours, if one more Merciful than the rest, had not taken pity on him, and caused him to be unbound. These actions are very like the Popish Cruelties. They have already undone us in our Estates, and that will not serve their turns, without our Innocent Bloods. If it cannot be granted that we can have our Trials at Boston, we humbly beg that you would endeavour to have these Magistrates changed, and others in their rooms, begging also and beseeching you would be pleased to be here, if not all, some of you at our Trials, hoping thereby you may be the means of saving the sheeding our Innocent Bloods, desiring your Prayers to the Lord in our behalf, we rest your Poor Afflicted Servants,

JOHN PROCTER, etc.

Source: http://etext.virginia.edu/etcbin/salembrowse?id=684 (Click through to "next page" to see all the relevant documents.)

Thinking Critically

What patterns do you see in the accusations? What does the language in all four pieces tell you about how members of this community conceived of Satan? How does Proctor try to defend himself? What do you think he was trying to accomplish by comparing the interrogations his son and others faced to "Popish Cruelties"?

Third and finally, colonists commonly encouraged and participated in regional wars to obtain native lands. This proved easy enough to do, because, like Europeans, the Indians of New England quarreled frequently with neighboring nations. The antagonism among the English, Spanish, Dutch, and French was matched by the hostilities among the Abenakis, Pawtuckets, Massachusetts, Narragansetts, and Wampanoags of the north Atlantic coast. Epidemics often intensified existing rivalries. Affecting some villages and nations more than others, outbreaks of Old World disease opened up new opportunities for stronger neighbors to press the advantage. New England settlers, like those in the Chesapeake, studied Indian feuds to better exploit them.

The English began by aligning with Massasoit and his Wampanoags against other coastal peoples in New England. In 1637 colonial forces joined the Narragansetts in a campaign against the formidable Pequots, who controlled coveted territory in present-day Connecticut. The colonists shocked even their Indian allies when they set fire to the main Pequot village, killing hundreds of men, women, and children. Plymouth's William Bradford recalled that "it was a fearful sight to see them thus frying in the fire, and the streams of blood quenching the same, and horrible was the stink and scent thereof; but the victory seemed a sweet sacrifice, and they gave the praise thereof to God, who had wrought so wonderfully for them." Several years later the colonists turned against their former allies, joining forces with the Mohegans to intimidate the Narragansetts into ceding much of their territory. Only a few colonists objected to those ruthless policies, among them Roger Williams. "God Land," he warned one Connecticut leader, "will be (as it now is) as great a God with us English as God Gold was with the Spainards."

 REVIEW

What were the sources of stability and conflict in early New England?

Metacom's War

Throughout these wars, the colonists more or less nurtured their original alliance with Massasoit and his Wampanoags. As long as regional enemies bore the brunt of English expansion, Massasoit and his people could live in relative safety. Indeed, certain colonists tried to bring the two societies closer together. While the impulse to convert was not nearly as strong in New England as in New Spain or New France, a few Englishmen worked tirelessly to bring the word of their God to Indians.

MISSIONS TO THE INDIANS Most famously, Puritan minister John Eliot began preaching in Algonquian in the 1640s. Over the next two decades he oversaw a project to publish the scriptures in Algonquian using the Latin alphabet. He also trained scores of native ministers (many of whom became literate) and established seven villages or "praying towns" exclusively for Christian Indians. Eliot was not alone. According to its charter of 1650, for example, Harvard College defined its mission as "the education of English & Indian youth of this Country in knowledge and godliness." In 1655 Harvard established an Indian college and dormitory on campus specifically to instruct Wampanoag youth in the English language and in Protestantism. None of these efforts embodied respect for Indian culture or religion. But some in New England, at least, wanted to assimilate Indians rather than drive them away.

And yet the colony always grasped for more land. By the time Massasoit died and was succeeded by his son in the 1660s, the partnership had become a relationship of subordination and suspicion. Colonial authorities reacted to rumors of pending native rebellion with humiliating interrogations and increasingly severe rules and restrictions. The colonists' cows and pigs invaded and destroyed Indian fields, provoking innumerable conflicts as white pressures on Indian lands increased. When Indians tried to adapt by raising their own cows and pigs, colonial authorities barred them from using common pasture or selling meat in Boston. At the same time, as many as half the dwindling Wampanoags had followed Eliot into the praying towns, threatening tribal unity in a time of mounting crisis.

By 1675 these and other pressures convinced Massasoit's son, Metacom, whom the English called King Philip, that his nation could be preserved only by chancing war. Complaining that the English were plotting to kill him and other sachems and replace them with Christian Indians more willing to sell land, Metacom rallied most of southern New England's native peoples and laid waste to Plymouth Colony. Metacom's forces destroyed more than two dozen colonial towns. By the spring of 1676 they were closing in on the coast, raiding settlements within 20 miles of Boston.

But the momentum could not be sustained. Faced with shortages of food and ammunition, Metacom called for assistance from the Abenakis of Maine and the Mahicans of

Though no images of Metacom survive from his time, in later years artists frequently portrayed him. This image is based on an engraving by Paul Revere.

New York. Both refused his plea, and the English even recruited the powerful Mohawks to their cause. In the summer of 1676 Metacom met his death in battle; colonial forces dismembered his body and brought his severed head to Boston and his hands to Plymouth as trophies. The Indian offensive collapsed but not before threatening New England's very existence. In proportion to population, "King Philip's War" inflicted twice the casualties on New England that the United States as a whole would suffer in the American Civil War. And Metacom's desperate gamble exhausted native military power in southern New England, virtually destroyed the Wampanoags as a coherent people, and consigned the region's surviving Indians, Christian or not, to quiet and often desperate lives on the margins of colonial life.

THE MID-ATLANTIC COLONIES

THE INHABITANTS OF THE MID-ATLANTIC colonies—New York, New Jersey, Pennsylvania, and Delaware—enjoyed more secure lives than most southern colonials. But they lacked the common bonds that lent stability to early New England. Instead, throughout the mid-Atlantic region a variety of ethnic and religious groups vied for wealth from farming and the fur trade and contended bitterly against governments that commanded little popular support.

English Rule in New York

By the 1660s the Dutch experiment on the mid-Atlantic coast was faltering. While Fort Orange continued to secure furs for the Dutch West India company, the colonial population remained small and fractious. The company made matters worse by appointing corrupt, dictatorial governors who ruled without an elective assembly. It also provided little protection for outlying Dutch settlements; when it did attack neighboring Indian nations, it did so savagely, triggering terrible retaliations. By the time the company went bankrupt in 1654, it had virtually abandoned its American colony.

Taking advantage of the disarray in New Netherland, Charles II ignored Dutch claims in North America and granted his brother, James, the Duke of York, a proprietary charter there. The charter granted James all of New Netherland to Delaware Bay as well as Maine, Martha's Vineyard, and Nantucket Island. In 1664 James sent an

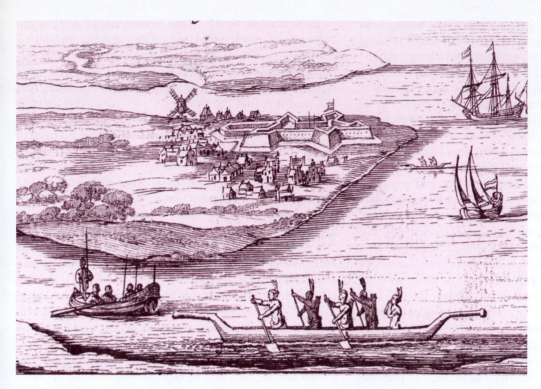

New Amsterdam (later New York City) in about 1626. Despite having this outpost in New Netherland, the Dutch had far more interest in vying with the Portuguese for control of commerce with the Far East than in competing with the English for the fur trade in North America.

invading fleet, whose mere arrival caused the Dutch to surrender.

ETHNIC AND RELIGIOUS DIVERSITY New York's dizzying diversity would make it difficult to govern. The Duke inherited 9,000 or so colonists: Dutch, Belgians, French, English, Portuguese, Swedes, Finns, and Africans—some enslaved, others free. The colony's ethnic diversity ensured a variety of religions. Although the Dutch Reformed church predominated, other early New Netherlanders included Lutherans, Quakers, and Catholics. There were Jews as well, refugees from Portuguese Brazil, who were required by law to live in a ghetto in New Amsterdam. The Dutch resented English rule, and only after a generation of intermarriage and acculturation did that resentment fade. James also failed to win friends among New Englanders who had come to Long Island seeking autonomy and cheap land during the 1640s. He grudgingly gave in to their demand for an elective assembly in 1683 but rejected its first act, the Charter of Liberties, which would have guaranteed basic political rights. The chronic political strife discouraged prospective settlers. By 1698 the colony numbered only 18,000 inhabitants, and New York City, the former New Amsterdam, was an overgrown village of a few thousand.

The Founding of New Jersey

Confusion attended New Jersey's beginnings. The lands lying west of the Hudson and east of the Delaware River had been part of the Duke of York's proprietary grant. But in 1664 he gave about 5 million of these acres to Lord Berkeley and Sir George Carteret, two of his favorites who were already involved in the proprietary colonies of the Carolinas. New Jersey's new owners guaranteed settlers land, religious freedom, and a representative assembly in exchange for a small quitrent, an annual fee for the use of the land. The proprietors' terms promptly drew Puritan settlers from New Haven, Connecticut. At the same time, unaware that James had already given New Jersey to Berkeley and Carteret, New York's Governor Richard Nicolls granted Long Island Puritans land there.

More complications ensued when Berkeley and Carteret decided to divide New Jersey into east and west and sell both halves to **Quaker** investors—a prospect that outraged New Jersey's Puritans. Although some English Quakers migrated to West Jersey, the investors quickly decided that two Jerseys were less desirable than one Pennsylvania and resold both East and West Jersey to speculators. In the end the Jerseys became a patchwork of religious and ethnic groups. Settlers who shared a common religion or national origin formed communities and established small family farms. When the Crown finally reunited East and West as a single royal colony in 1702, New Jersey was overshadowed by settlements not only to the north but now, also, to the south and west.

Quaker Odysseys

Religious and political idealism similar to that of the Puritans inspired the colonization of Pennsylvania, making it an oddity among the mid-Atlantic colonies. The oddity began with an improbable founder, William Penn. Young Penn devoted his early years to disappointing his distinguished father, Sir William Penn, an admiral in the Royal Navy.

Several years after being expelled from college, young Penn finally chose a career that may have made the admiral yearn for mere disappointment: he undertook a lifelong commitment to put into practice Quaker teachings. By the 1670s he had emerged as an acknowledged leader of the Society of Friends, as the Quakers formally called themselves.

QUAKER BELIEFS The Quakers behaved in ways and believed in ideas that most people regarded as odd. They dressed in a deliberately plain and severe manner. They withheld from their social superiors the customary marks of respect, such as bowing, kneeling, and removing their hats. They refused to swear oaths or to make war. They allowed women public roles of religious leadership. That pattern of behavior reflected their egalitarian ideals, the belief that all men and women shared equally in the "Light Within." Some 40,000 English merchants, artisans, and farmers embraced Quakerism by 1660, and many suffered fines, imprisonment, and corporal punishment.

PENNSYLVANIA ESTABLISHED Since the English upper class has always prized eccentricity among its members, it is not surprising that Penn, despite his Quakerism, remained a favorite of Charles II. More surprising is that the king's favor took the extravagant form of presenting Penn in 1681 with all the land between New Jersey and Maryland. Perhaps the king was repaying Penn for the large sum that his father had lent the Stuarts. Or perhaps the king was hoping to export England's Quakers to an American colony governed by his trusted personal friend.

Penn envisioned that his proprietary colony would provide a refuge for Quakers while producing quitrents for himself. To publicize his colony, he distributed pamphlets praising its attractions throughout the British Isles and Europe. The response was overwhelming: by 1700 its population stood at 21,000. The only early migration of equal magnitude was the Puritan colonization of New England.

Patterns of Growth

Perhaps half of Pennsylvania's settlers arrived as indentured servants; the families of free farmers and artisans made up the rest. The majority were Quakers from Britain, Holland, and Germany, but the colonists also included Catholics, Lutherans, Baptists, Anglicans, and Presbyterians. In 1682, when Penn purchased and annexed the Three Lower Counties (later the colony of Delaware), his colony included the 1,000 or so Dutch, Swedes, and Finns living there.

Quakers from other colonies—West Jersey, Maryland, and New England—also flocked to the new homeland. Those experienced settlers brought skills and connections that contributed to Pennsylvania's rapid economic growth. Farmers sowed their rich lands into a sea of wheat, which merchants exported to the Caribbean. The center of the colony's trade was Philadelphia, a superb natural harbor situated at the confluence of the Delaware and Schuylkill Rivers.

In contrast to New England's landscape of villages, the Pennsylvania countryside beyond Philadelphia was dotted with dispersed farmsteads. Commercial agriculture required larger farms, which kept settlers at greater distances from one another. As a result, the county rather than the town became the basic unit of local government in Pennsylvania.

QUAKERS AND INDIANS Another reason that farmers did not need to cluster their homes within a central village was that they were at peace with the coastal Indians, the Lenni Lenapes (also called Delawares by the English). Thanks to two Quaker beliefs—their commitment to pacifism and their conviction that the Indians rightfully owned their land—peace prevailed between native inhabitants and newcomers. Before Penn sold any land to colonists, he purchased it from the Indians. He also prohibited the sale of alcohol to the tribe, strictly regulated the fur trade, and learned the language of the Lenni Lenapes. "Not a language spoken in Europe," he remarked, "hath words of more sweetness in Accent and Emphasis than theirs."

"Our Wildernesse flourishes as a Garden," Penn declared late in 1683, and in fact, his colony lived up to its promises. New arrivals readily acquired good land on liberal terms, while Penn's Frame of Government instituted a representative assembly and guaranteed all inhabitants the basic English civil liberties and complete freedom of worship.

Quakers and Politics

Even so, Penn's colony suffered constant political strife. Rich investors whom he had rewarded with large tracts of land and trade monopolies dominated the council, which held the sole power to initiate legislation. That power and Penn's own claims as proprietor set the stage for controversy. Members of the representative assembly battled for the right to initiate legislation. Farmers opposed Penn's efforts to collect quitrents. The Three Lower Counties agitated for separation, their inhabitants feeling no loyalty to Penn or Quakerism.

PENN'S COMPROMISES Penn finally bought peace at the price of approving a complete revision of his original Frame of Government. In 1701 the Charter of Privileges, Pennsylvania's new constitution, stripped the council of its legislative power, leaving it only the role of advising the governor. The charter also limited Penn's privileges as proprietor to the ownership of ungranted land and the power to veto legislation. Thereafter an elective unicameral assembly, the only single-house legislature in the colonies, dominated Pennsylvania's government.

As Pennsylvania prospered, Philadelphia became the commercial and cultural center of England's North American empire. Gradually the interior of Pennsylvania filled with immigrants—mainly Germans and Scots-Irish—who harbored no "odd" ideas about Indian rights, and the Lenni Lenapes and other native peoples were bullied into moving farther west. As for William Penn, he returned to England and spent time in a debtors' prison after being defrauded by his unscrupulous colonial agents. He died in 1718, an ocean away from his American utopia.

✓ **REVIEW**
In what ways were the mid-Atlantic colonies more diverse than the other colonies of the period?

ADJUSTMENT TO EMPIRE

WHATEVER HIS PERSONAL DISAPPOINTMENTS, PENN'S colony had enjoyed spectacular growth—as indeed had British North America more generally. And yet by the 1680s England's king had reason to complain. Although North America now abounded in places named in honor of English monarchs, the colonies themselves lacked any strong ties to the English state. Until Parliament passed the first Navigation Acts in 1660, England had not even set in place a coherent policy for regulating colonial trade. And the acts had not produced the desired sense of patriotism in the colonies. While Chesapeake planters grumbled over the customs duties levied on tobacco, New Englanders, the worst of the lot, ignored the Navigation Acts altogether and traded openly with the Dutch. Royally appointed proprietors increasingly met defiance in New York, New Jersey, the Carolinas, and Pennsylvania. If England were to prosper from colonies as Spain's monarchs had, the Crown needed to take matters in hand.

The Dominion of New England

And the Crown did so in 1686. At the urging of the new King James II (formerly the Duke of York), the Lords of Trade consolidated the colonies of Connecticut, Plymouth, Massachusetts Bay, Rhode Island, and New Hampshire into a single entity to be ruled by a royal governor and a royally appointed council. By 1688 James had added New York and New Jersey to that domain, now called the Dominion of New England. Showing the typical Stuart distaste for representative government, James also abolished all northern colonial assemblies. The king's aim to centralize authority over such a large territory made the Dominion not only a

The tidy, productive farmsteads of the Pennsylvania countryside were the basis of that colony's prosperity during the eighteenth century. Their produce fueled the growth of Philadelphia and sustained the expansion of sugar plantations on England's Caribbean islands.

royal dream but also a radical experiment in English colonial administration.

The experiment proved to be short-lived. In England James II had revealed himself to be yet another Stuart who tried to dispense with Parliament and who had embraced Catholicism besides. Parliament dispensed with the king just as it had with Charles I during the English Civil War of the 1640s. In a quick, bloodless coup d'état known as the Glorious Revolution, Parliament forced James into exile in 1688. In his place it elevated to the throne his daughter, Mary, and her Dutch husband, William of Orange. Mary was a distinctly better sort of Stuart—a staunch Protestant—and she agreed to rule with Parliament.

THE GLORIOUS REVOLUTION William and Mary officially dismembered the Dominion of New England and reinstated representative assemblies everywhere in the northern colonies. Connecticut and Rhode Island were restored their old charters, but Massachusetts received a new charter in 1691. Under its terms Massachusetts, Plymouth, and present-day Maine were combined into a single royal colony headed by a governor appointed by the Crown rather than elected by the people. The charter also imposed religious toleration and made property ownership rather than church membership the basis of voting rights.

| *England, in an effort to regulate colonial trade, required all ships bound from America to pass through British ports and pay customs duties. Places such as Plymouth, Liverpool, and Bristol (shown here) thrived as a result. Contrast this large, bustling commercial center with the modest size of Plymouth 200 years earlier (illustration, page 28).*

Royal Authority in America in 1700

CLOSER REGULATION OF TRADE William and Mary were more politic than James II but no less interested in revenue. In 1696 Parliament enlarged the number of customs officials stationed in each colony to enforce the Navigation Acts. To help prosecute smugglers, Parliament established colonial vice-admiralty courts, tribunals without juries presided over by royally appointed justices. To keep current on all colonial matters, the king appointed a new Board of Trade to replace the old Lords of Trade. The new enforcement procedures generally succeeded in discouraging smuggling and channeling colonial trade through England.

These changes were enough for England and its monarchs for half a century thereafter. English kings and queens gave up any dreams of imposing the kind of centralized administration of colonial life represented by the Dominion of New England. Clearly, royal control had increased over the previous half century. By 1700 royal governments had been established in Virginia, New York, Massachusetts, and New Hampshire. New Jersey, the Carolinas, and Georgia would shortly be added to the list. Royal rule meant that the monarch appointed governors and (everywhere except Massachusetts) also appointed their councils. Royally appointed councils could veto any law passed by a colony's representative assembly, royally appointed governors could veto any law passed by both houses, and the Crown could veto any law passed by both houses and approved by the governor.

THE LIMITS OF ROYAL POWER Nonetheless, the sway of royal power remained more apparent than real after 1700. The Glorious Revolution asserted once and for all that Parliament's authority—rule by the legislative

branch of government—would be supreme in the governing of England. In the colonies members of representative assemblies grew more skilled at dealing with royal governors and more protective of their rights. They guarded most jealously their strongest lever of power—the right of the lower houses to levy taxes.

The political reality of the assemblies' power reflected a social reality as well. No longer mere outposts along the Atlantic, the colonies of 1700 were becoming more firmly rooted societies. Their laws and traditions were based not only on what they had brought from England but also on the conditions of life in America. That social reality had already blocked Stuart ambitions to shape the future of North America, just as it had thwarted the designs of lordly proprietors and the dreams of religious reformers.

> ✅ **REVIEW**
>
> How did William and Mary try to increase colonial revenues?

CONCLUSION

THE WORLD AT LARGE

The dream of empire would revive among England's rulers in the middle of the eighteenth century—in part because the rulers of France had never abandoned their own imperial visions. France had long been Europe's largest kingdom in terms of land and overall population. By the 1660s, bureaucratic, financial, and political reforms had left the French with the mightiest military as well. Determined to have more territory, France's ambitious king, Louis XIV, unleashed this titanic war machine against his neighbors on four different occasions between 1667 and 1714.

Even after 1714, France, England and, to a lesser extent, Spain waged a kind of cold war for a quarter of a century, jockeying for position and influence. Western European monarchs had come to realize that confrontations in North America's vast and distant interior could influence the outcome of their feuds closer to home. In this global chess game, the British had the advantage of numbers: nearly 400,000 subjects in the colonies in 1720, compared with only about 25,000 French spread along a thin line of fishing stations and fur-trading posts, and a meager 5,000 or so Spaniards in New Mexico, Texas, and Florida combined. But by a considerable margin, native peoples still represented the majority population in North America. Moreover, they still controlled more than 90 percent of its territory. If events in North America could affect the balance of power in Europe, then French and Spanish administrators could still believe and hope that their Indian alliances might yet help them prevail against each other, especially against Britain's booming colonies. ∞∞∞∞

CHAPTER SUMMARY

WHILE THE FRENCH COLONIZED CANADA, the Protestant Reformation in England spurred the colonization of New England and Pennsylvania.

- During the seventeenth century, the French slowly established a fur trade, agricultural communities, and religious institutions in Canada while building Indian alliances throughout the Mississippi drainage.

- Competition over the fur trade in New France and New Netherland contributed to a devastating series of wars between Iroquois, Hurons, and dozens of other Indian groups.

- Over the same period, English Puritans planted more populous settlements between Maine and Long Island.

- The migration of family groups and a rough equality of wealth lent stability to early New England society, reinforced by the settlers' shared commitment to Puritanism and a strong tradition of self-government.

- The mid-Atlantic colonies also enjoyed a rapid growth of people and wealth, but political wrangling as well as ethnic and religious diversity made for a higher level of social conflict.

- Whereas New Englanders attempted to subdue native peoples, colonists in the mid-Atlantic enjoyed more harmonious relations with the region's original inhabitants.

- The efforts of the later Stuart kings to centralize England's empire ended with the Glorious Revolution in 1688, which greatly reduced tensions between the colonies and the parent country.

Additional Reading

For introductions to French and Indian encounters, see Olive Patricia Dickason, *Canada's First Nations* (1992), and Bruce G. Trigger, *Natives and Newcomers* (1995). Colin G. Calloway's *One Vast Winter Count* (2003) masterfully synthesizes the history of natives and Europeans in early North America west of the Appalachians, and Daniel K. Richter does the same for eastern North America in *Facing East from Indian Country* (2001). For a history of Dutch America, see Jaap Jacobs, *New Netherland* (2005). Jenny Hale Pulsipher's *Subjects unto the Same King* (2005) illuminates the complex tale of Indian-English relations in the Northeast by focusing on notions of authority. To understand the appeal of Puritanism, the best book to read is Charles Cohen, *God's Caress* (1986). To learn more about how English influences shaped the evolution of Puritanism in New England, read Stephen Foster's masterly study, *The Long Argument* (1991). And to learn more about the diversity of religious and super-natural views in New England, consult Philip Gura, *A Glimpse of Sion's Glory* (1984), and David Hall, *Worlds of Wonder, Days of Judgment* (1989).

For the everyday lives of northern colonists in New England and New York, rely on Virginia Dejohn Anderson's *New England's Generation* (1991) and Joyce Goodfriend's *Before the Melting Pot* (1991). The best assessment of British imperial policy in the late seventeenth century is Richard R. Johnson, *Adjustment to Empire* (1981). For the complex interplay among English colonialism, environmental change, and Indian power in the Northeast, see William Cronon's classic *Changes in the Land* (1983). The event and memory of "King Philip's War" is the subject of Jill Lepore's *The Name of War* (1998).

For a fuller list of readings, see the Bibliography at www.mhhe.com/eh8e.

Significant Events

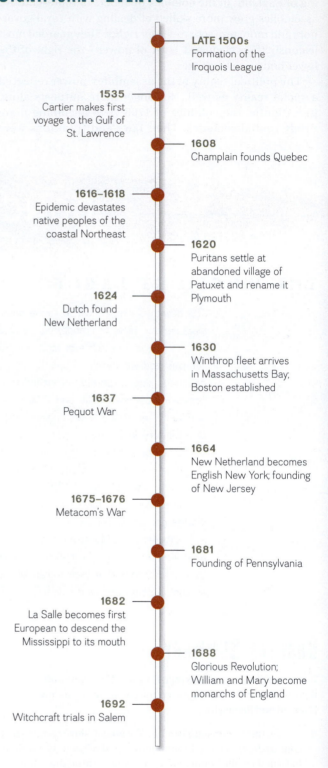

LATE 1500s
Formation of the Iroquois League

1535
Cartier makes first voyage to the Gulf of St. Lawrence

1608
Champlain founds Quebec

1616–1618
Epidemic devastates native peoples of the coastal Northeast

1620
Puritans settle at abandoned village of Patuxet and rename it Plymouth

1624
Dutch found New Netherland

1630
Winthrop fleet arrives in Massachusetts Bay; Boston established

1637
Pequot War

1664
New Netherland becomes English New York; founding of New Jersey

1675–1676
Metacom's War

1681
Founding of Pennsylvania

1682
La Salle becomes first European to descend the Mississippi to its mouth

1688
Glorious Revolution; William and Mary become monarchs of England

1692
Witchcraft trials in Salem

COLONY	FOUNDING/ SETTLEMENT	CHARACTER AND DEVELOPMENT	APPROXIMATE POPULATION (1700)
New France	1605 Port Royal (Acadia); 1608 Quebec	Fur-traders and Jesuit missionaries; small number of farmers in 1660s; French into western Great Lakes in 1670s; Mississippi valley in 1680s	15,000
Massachusetts (including Maine)	Plymouth 1620; Massachusetts Bay 1629	Separatist and Puritan settlements; most colonists arrive in family groups; village-centered agricultural settlements	56,000
Connecticut	Thomas Hooker leads congregation to Connecticut 1636	New Haven, a separate, stricter settlement, joins Connecticut in 1662	26,000
Rhode Island	Roger Williams 1636	Williams champions separation of church and state, respect for Indian land claims	6,000
New Hampshire	Portsmouth 1631	Allied with Massachusetts for several decades; becomes royal colony 1680	5,000
New Netherland/ New York	Dutch settle 1624; England takes possession 1664	Dutch at Fort Orange (later Albany) ally with Iroquois to vie for furs; Dutch arms trade helps fuel Beaver Wars	9,000 by 1664 under Dutch; 18,000 in 1700
New Jersey	Duke of York grants lands out of New York holdings 1664	Patchwork of ethnic groups; small family farms; becomes royal colony 1702	14,000
Pennsylvania/Delaware (separates in 1703)	Penn receives lands in 1681 from Charles II; Philadelphia principal town	Penn recruits colonists from across Britain and Europe; dispersed farms the norm rather than village settlements; Penn pledges to deal fairly with Indians	20,000

In this detail from a remarkable painting, Don Pedro de Villasur lies dead, hands extended in the air as he is being dragged by the legs outside his blue tent. Just below, the Spanish (wearing hats) form a circle to fend off the attack of Pawnee warriors. Jean L'Archevêque stands bareheaded on the right side of the circle, wearing blue clothing. The shadow across his face likely represents his tattoos.

CHAPTER 5

The Mosaic of Eighteenth-Century America

∞

1689–1768

What's to Come

∞∞∞∞ **AN AMERICAN STORY** ∞∞∞∞

THE TALE OF A TATTOOED TRAVELER

August 13, 1720: morning sunlight breaks over the confluence of the Platte and Loup Rivers in what today is Nebraska. Jean L'Archevêque rises stiffly from where he slept and looks about camp. A few dozen Spanish soldiers huddle in the early light, donning their long, leather vests and their wide-brimmed hats. At another end of the encampment the Pueblo Indian men who have accompanied the expedition speak softly to one another, making less noise than the soldiers, though double their number. A friar in his habit passes among

17 feet long by 4½ feet high, this painting on bison or elk hide was likely made by a mission-trained Indian, after Villasur's debacle.

the tents. Don Pedro de Villasur, lieutenant governor of New Mexico and leader of the party, threads his arms through a bright, red officer's coat and orders the soldiers to bring in their horses.

Most of these men had known L'Archevêque for years—had come to appreciate his sly humor and grown accustomed to his thick French accent. But on this morning, as they set about the king's business some 600 miles from their homes and families, there must have been something unnerving about the dark, swirling tattoos that covered the Frenchman's face. They had been put there years earlier by Indians who had captured L'Archevêque in the aftermath of a Texas expedition that had ended in calamity. One had only to look at those tattoos to be reminded that things sometimes go badly for both kings and their servants.

Born in 1672 in Bayonne, France, L'Archevêque was only a boy when he boarded ship to the French Caribbean, fleeing his family's financial troubles. Then in 1684 he joined an expedition led by the French explorer René Robert Cavelier, Sieur de La Salle. Three years earlier La Salle had been the first to navigate the immense Mississippi River from the Great Lakes to the Gulf of Mexico. He was famous and respected. Now he was set to plant a permanent settlement near the Mississippi's mouth, as a strategic foothold for France. Yet try as he might, La Salle could not find the mouth of the Mississippi when he approached this time from the Gulf of Mexico. Instead, he landed on the coast of present-day Texas and threw up some ramshackle buildings. As months stretched into years, the expedition lost its ships, while the nearly 300 colonists sickened, starved, and died. The survivors blamed their leader and hatched a plan to be rid of him. Young L'Archevêque played a part, distracting the great explorer while an accomplice blew his head apart with a musket shot.

As the colony spiraled into ruin, L'Archevêque and a few desperate companions eventually found themselves unhappy guests among Caddo Indians in east Texas. These were the people who tattooed the young man's face, carefully inserting a dye made from walnuts into countless tiny cuts. Spanish explorers, determined to root out La Salle's French colony, stumbled across L'Archevêque in 1690, ransomed him from the Caddos, and imprisoned him—first in Mexico City and then for two and a half years in Spain. Finally he was freed and returned to Mexico City.

Meanwhile, news of La Salle's stillborn colony convinced Spanish officials to take more energetic measures to secure their claims on the North American West. A permanent French settlement could be used all too easily as a base to threaten New Spain and its famous silver mines. Crucially, Spain had to reconquer New Mexico, from which it had been driven out by Popé's Pueblo Revolt of 1680 (Chapter 3). When Spanish colonists returned in earnest in 1692, they met only fragmented resistance from the Pueblo villages.

It was in reconquered New Mexico that Jean L'Archevêque found his first real home since boyhood. Sent north perhaps because of his facility with not only French but also Indian languages, L'Archevêque quickly became a fixture in Santa Fe, prospering, marrying well, and gaining the trust of his neighbors. The Spanish had not long returned to New Mexico before they began hearing complaints from the plains Apaches about Pawnee raiders armed with French guns and mocking the Spanish, calling them "women." In 1720, with Spain and France at war in Europe, New Mexico's governor ordered his lieutenant Villasur to take L'Archevêque and a group of Indian and Spanish fighters to confront the French—hence the long trek to the Platte River, where the men awoke at daybreak on August 13 to do the king's business.

But things sometimes go badly for kings and their servants. Moments after ordering his men to bring in their horses, Villasur heard wild screams and saw dozens of painted Pawnee warriors rush the camp. The lieutenant governor was one of the first to die, killed with mouth agape just outside his tent; L'Archevêque fell soon after, his death demonstrating how unsettled the North American continent had become in the eighteenth century. The young Frenchman from Bayonne had been shipwrecked, recruited to murder, and tattooed in Texas, imprisoned in Mexico and Spain, married and made respectable on the upper Rio Grande, and finally shot dead and buried alongside Spanish and Indian companions somewhere in Nebraska. It was a remarkable and turbulent odyssey. ∞∞∞∞

CRISIS AND TRANSFORMATION IN NORTHERN NEW SPAIN

JEAN L'ARCHEVÊQUE'S LIFE TESTIFIES IN a very personal way to the unpredictable changes unleashed by contact between European and American civilizations. As Europeans established colonies and began competing with one another across the far reaches of the continent, individuals throughout North America, especially native peoples, found life changing at astonishing speed. Europeans, with their animals, plants, technologies, diseases, and designs, drove the existing dynamism in the Americas to a fever pitch of transformation. But Europeans could not predict and did not control the process. Despite their grand ambitions, colonial newcomers often found their

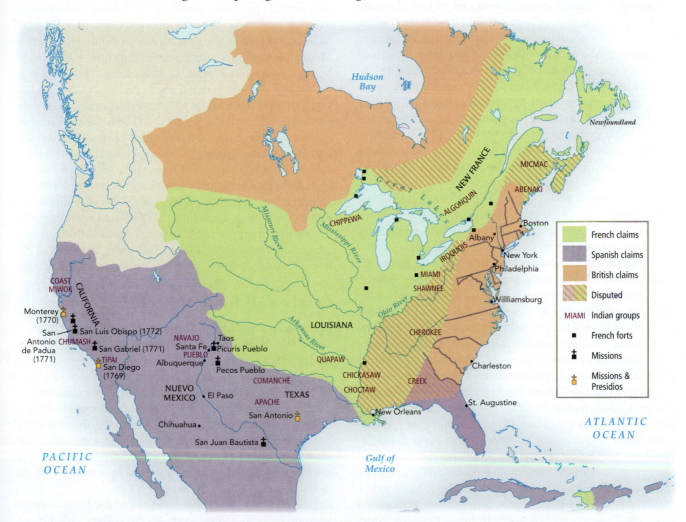

EUROPEAN TERRITORIAL CLAIMS IN THE EIGHTEENTH CENTURY

The French, English, and Indian nations all jockeyed for power and position across North America during the eighteenth century. The French expanded their fur trade through the interior, while the English at midcentury began to press the barrier of the Appalachians. But native peoples still controlled the vast majority of the continent and often held the balance of power in interimperial struggles. **What geographic advantages did the French enjoy? And the English?**

own plans upended and their lives reordered by the same forces reworking native life.

Defensive Expansion into Texas

As European rivals laid claim to more and more of North America, nervous Spanish officials stared at their maps. Around the region that had been the Aztec Empire, Spain controlled enormous cities, booming towns, and agricultural villages—a region still populated by millions despite waves of epidemic disease. Though drier and home to far fewer people, the lands hundreds of miles north of Mexico City were of special concern because of their remarkable silver mines. To protect these lands from French designs, Spain had to start paying more attention to the blank spaces still farther north on their maps—spaces entirely controlled by Indians.

TEXAS AS A BUFFER AGAINST THE FRENCH — Nowhere did the French seem more menacing than in Texas, one of the most important blank spots on Spanish maps. La Salle's catastrophic adventure could have turned out differently: before his grisly death, the Frenchman pledged to invade northern New Spain with an army of thousands of Indians, who, he believed, had "a deadly hatred of the Spaniards." Fearful that another French expedition might actually acquire such an army, in 1690 Spain began establishing missions among the native peoples of Texas. The project started haltingly, but by the early 1720s the Spanish had fortified their claim on Texas with 10 Franciscan missions, 4 presidios (military garrisons), and the beginnings of a civilian settlement on the San Antonio River.

Still, missions disappointed Franciscans and natives alike. Missionaries hoped to create orderly, regimented communities where Indians could be shielded from outside influence and taught to be industrious and devout. The friars did baptize natives by the thousands in Texas. But Indians insisted on coming and going when they pleased. Many nonsedentary peoples sought the food and sanctuary missions offered, only to leave periodically to rendezvous with kin, hunt, and harvest wild plant foods. Their comings and goings confounded the missionaries. Matters were even worse for Franciscans in east Texas, where sedentary Caddos barely tolerated the missions. Farmers themselves, and relatively secure in their fixed villages of beehive-shaped homes, Caddos had no need for the missionaries' crops or protection. Just as important, they could and did trade with Frenchmen from Louisiana, who offered more manufactured goods at better prices than Spaniards did.

INDIANS AND MISSIONS — However successful they were at retaining autonomy, Indians throughout Texas paid a steep price for any benefits they wrung from missions. Those compelled inside by hunger and insecurity often endured harsh discipline and corporal punishment for disobeying orders. Even worse, missions proved ideal vectors for epidemic disease. In the 1730s alone, smallpox killed more than 1,000 mission Indians near San Antonio. Other illnesses became commonplace as nomadic peoples

Comanche power derived in part from French guns, which they often obtained from Wichita Indians like these painted by Lino Sanchez y Tapia.

with sanitary practices suitable for life on the move crowded together in filthy, cramped buildings. Children were especially vulnerable to the new regime. In eighteenth-century Mission San Antonio, for example, only one in three newborns survived to his or her third birthday.

While friars and Indians negotiated their complex and tragic relationship, Spanish administrators struggled to foster civilian communities in Texas. The Crown tried to convince Spanish subjects to move to the infant colony and even sent agents to recruit among the impoverished families on the Canary Islands. These efforts met with only token success. In 1731 Texas's nonnative population barely amounted to 500 men, women, and children; by 1760 that figure had slightly more than doubled. In 1778 a Franciscan inspector described San Antonio as "a town so miserable that it resembles a most wretched village." The town consisted of "59 houses of stone and mud, and 79 of wood, but all poorly built."

Crisis and Rebirth in New Mexico

Spain had pushed into the blank space on the map that was Texas, but after generations into the project it still controlled only an archipelago of missions, presidios, and a few towns—surrounded on all sides by unconquered Indians, whose power in the region was, if anything, expanding. At first Apaches posed the greatest threat to Spain's ambitions in Texas. Their raids thinned Spanish herds, prevented ranching and farming communities from expanding outward, and threatened missions with destruction. Spaniards responded with slave raids on Apache camps, and the violence escalated.

COMANCHE NEWCOMERS — By the 1730s, however, a new force emerged to eclipse even Apaches. They called themselves Numunuu "the People." Their enemies came to call them Comanches. Emerging from the foothills of the Rockies in the late sixteenth century, Comanches integrated European horses into their lives, moved permanently onto the plains, and quickly became some of the most formidable equestrian warriors in history. They allied with Indians who could provide them French guns and ammunition from Louisiana and embarked on a program of territorial expansion. By the mid-eighteenth century Comanches drove most Apaches from the plains and took over their rich bison-hunting territories in what is today southern Colorado, eastern New Mexico, and west Texas. Without bison, Apaches turned more and more to stealing Spanish animals to survive. Spaniards from Santa Fe to San Antonio soon found themselves at war with Apaches and Comanches both; New Mexico often came into conflict with Navajos and Utes as well. Much of northern New Spain became a theater of desolation; abandoned villages up and down the Rio Grande testified to the limits of Spanish power.

Spaniards accused the "barbarians" of animalistic savagery, but all sides inflicted horrors on their enemies. Outside the little besieged town of Tucson, for example, Lieutenant Colonel Pedro de Allende boasted that he had decapitated a fallen Apache in front of the dead man's comrades and "charged the Apache line single-handed, with the head stuck on his lance." Away from the din of battle, a prominent Spaniard noted that his people accuse the Indians of cruelty but added, "I do not know what opinion they would have of us."

A Brokered Peace
By the 1780s nearly everyone had had enough of war. A farsighted Comanche leader named Ecueracapa helped broker peace with Spanish authorities in 1786, after which the new allies cooperated to entice or threaten Utes, Navajos, and Apaches into peace as well. Northern New Spain entered a period of relative calm, expansion, and economic growth. Changes were most dramatic in New Mexico, where Spanish subjects opened up new farms and ranches, enlarged their flocks and herds, and devoted new energy to local manufacturing. As New Mexico's non-Indian population grew (20,000 by the close of the eighteenth century), new roads funded by the Crown helped ease the province's isolation. Finally, peace meant that *nuevo mexicanos* could accumulate wealth by trading more with their Indian neighbors and with merchants in Chihuahua, Durango, and Mexico City. Trade and supply caravans began setting out from Santa Fe for Chihuahua once or even twice a year.

Distinctive New Mexican Culture
Some of the New Mexicans who profited most from the newfound opportunities began to patronize artists and skilled craftsmen. By the late eighteenth century a distinctive New Mexican culture started to emerge, one marked by new traditions in such crafts as woodworking and weaving, as well as in religious art and practice. A master craftsman known only as the Laguna Santero helped define this movement by training local apprentices in his workshop and making pieces for wealthy patrons. The Laguna Santero, his apprentices, and others he inspired began making exquisite portraits of saints on pine boards (*retablos*), hide paintings, elaborate altar screens for churches, and wooden statues of saints (*bultos*)—all art forms still associated with New Mexican folk culture today.

Spanish California

Spanish California was the empire's last major colonial project in North America. Like the colonies in Texas and Florida, settlement was sparked by a fear of foreign competition, this time from Russians moving south from Alaska. Though Spaniards first explored the California coast in 1542, not until 1768 did the Crown authorize permanent colonization. A joint expedition of military men and Franciscans led by the pragmatic Gaspar de Portolá and the iron-willed Fray (Friar) Junípero Serra, braved shipwrecks, scurvy, and earthquakes to establish ramshackle **presidios** (military garrisons) and missions at San Diego and Monterey.

This *retablo, or alterpiece, of San Jose (Saint Joseph) is typical of the work produced by the Laguna Santero and his workshop.*

DUELING DOCUMENTS

The Founders of Spanish California

Historians often turn to census data for insights into people's lives that are difficult to come by in other records. Often scholars analyze masses of historic census data with the help of computers. But these censuses from early colonial California survey households in what were then the tiny villages of Los Angeles and San José, making it relatively easy for us to look for patterns. For example, these documents reveal the striking heterogeneity of the "Spanish" colonization of California. Preoccupied with blood and birthright, officials throughout Spanish America routinely labeled people according to their supposed heritage. Mestizo/a referred to children of a Spaniard and an Indian; mulato/a to a child of a Spaniard and an African; coyote to a child of a mestizo/a and an Indian; chino/a to a child of a Spaniard and a salta-atras (a person with African features born of white parents); and pardo/a (child of an African and Indian). The second census, from San José, includes occupation and birthplace information for the head of house.

Census of Los Angeles, 1781

NAME	AGE		NAME	AGE
(1) Lara, Josef de; español	50		(6) Vanegas, Josef; indio	28
Maria Antonio Campos, india sabina	23		Maria Maxima Aguilar; India	20
Josef Julian	4		Cosme Damien	1
Juana de Jesus	6			
Maria Faustina	2		(7) Rosas, Alejandro; indio	19
			Juana Rodriguez; coyote india	20
(2) Navarro, Josef Antonio; mestizo	42			
Maria Rufina Dorotea; mulata	47		(8) Rodriguez, Pablo; indio	25
Josef Maria	10		Maria Rosalia Noriega; india	26
Josef Clemente	9		Maria Antonia	1
Maria Josefa	4			
			(9) Camero, Manuel; mulatto	30
(3) Rosas, Basillio; indio	67		Maria Tomasa; mulata	24
Maria Manuela Calixtra; mulata	43			
Jose Maximo	15		(10) Quintero, Luis; negro	55
Carlos	12		Maria Petra Rubio; Mulata	40
Antonio Rosalino	7		Josef Clemente	3
Josef Marcelino	4		Maria Gertrudis	16
Juan Esteban	2		Maria Concepcion	9
Maria Josefa	8		Tomasa	7
			Rafaela	6
(4) Mesa, Antonio; negro	38			
Ana Gertrudis Lopez; mulata	27		(11) Moreno, Jose; mulato	22
Antonio Maria	8		Maria Guadalupe Gertrudis	19
Maria Paula	10			
			(12) Rodriguez, Antonio Miranda; chino	50
(5) Villavicencio, Antonio; español	30		Juana Maria	11
Maria de los Santos Seferina; india	26			
Maria Antonio Josefa	8			

Source: David Weber, *Foreigners in Their Native Land: Historical Roots of the Mexican Americans,* 30th Anniversary ed. (Albuquerque: University of New Mexico Press, 2003), 33–35.

Census of San José, 1790

NAME	AGE		NAME	AGE
(1) Romero, Antonio, farmworker, pardo, from Guadalajara	40		(2) Archuleta, Ignacio; farmworker, Spaniard, from Horcasitas [Sonora]	36
Petra Aceves; parda	28		Gertrudis Pacheco; Spaniard	36
[Antonio]	14		[Petra]	9

NAME	AGE		NAME	AGE
[Miguel]	11	(10)	Lugo, Serafino; farmworker, español, from Villa Sinaloa	50
[Gregorio]	8		Gertrudis Pacheco, española	50
[Florentino]	6		[Juan]	19
[Juan José]	5		[Nicolas]	13
(3) Alvírez, Claudio; farmworker, coyote, from Tetuache [Sonora]	48		[Rafael]	11
Ana María Gonzales; india	30	(11)	Castro, Joaquín; farmworker, español, from Villa Sinaloa	50
[José]	8		Martina Botiller, española	50
[Brígida]	5		[Francisco María]	18
[Juan]	2		[Carlos]	15
[Jacoba]	baby		[unnamed orphan]	?
(4) Gonzales, Manuel; farmworker, indio, from San Bartolomé [Chihuahua]	70		[unnamed orphan]	?
Gertrudis Aceves; parda	20	(12)	Alegre, Antonio; farmworker, español, from	
[Francisco]	18		Genoa [Italy]	50
[Romualdo]	13		Catarina; India	28
(5) Rosales, Bernardo; farmworker, mulato, from Terrenate [Sonora]	?		[Vicenta Anastacia]	6
Mónica; india, from Mission San Antonio	28	(13)	Bojórquez, Pedro; cowboy, español, from Villa Sinaloa	36
[Josefa]	14		Angela Trejo; española	43
[Cornelio]	12		[Hermenegildo Ignacio]	12
[Petra]	10		[Bartolomé Francisco]	10
[María Antonia]	7		[Juan José]	6
(6) Amézquita, Manuel; farmworker, mulato, from Terrenate [Sonora]	?	(14)	Aceves, Antonio; farmworker, mulato, from San Bartolomé [Chihuahua]	50
Graciana Arroyo, mulata	26		Feliciana Cortés, mestiza	50
[Gabriel]	14		[José Antonio]	18
[Serafín]	10		[José Maria]	11
[Ventura]	6	(15)	Sáez, Nazario; cowboy, español, from San Bartolomé [Chihuahua]	48
[Augustina]	4		Micaela Sotelo, españa	40
[Salvador]	2		[Juana]	16
(7) Vásquez, Tiburcio; farmworker, mestizo, from Ahualulco [Jalisco]	35		[Juan María]	12
María Bojórquez, española	30		[María Benita]	10
[Francisco]	12		[María Felipa]	8
[Felipe]	10	(16)	Cagüelas, Pedro; cowboy, indio, from San Luis Obispo	20
[Resurección]	8		Secundina, India	18
[Hermenegildo]	6	(17)	Osuna, Miguel; tailor, español, from Real de San Francisco [Sonora], single	52
[Rosalía]	4			
[Faustino]	2	(18)	Nervo, Pedro Ruiz; español, from San Blas [Nayarit], single	
[Féliz]	1			21
(8) Avila, Francisco; farmworker, español, from El Fuerte [Sinaloa], widower	46			
Francisco Xavier	16			
(9) Mesa, Valerio; farmworker, español, from San Juan Bautista [Sonora]	60			
Leonor Borboa, española	50			
[Juan]	19			
[Nicolas]	13			
[Rafael]	11			

Source: William M. Mason, *The Census of 1790: A Demographic History of Colonial California,* Ballena Press anthropological papers no. 45 (Menlo Park, Calif.: Ballena Press, 1998), 98–100.

Thinking Critically

Other than individual ethnic heritage, what sorts of information or patterns can you find in these censuses? Can you spot any familial connections? What can these documents tell us about family size, marriage age, naming customs, or prevailing norms regarding interethnic unions? What sorts of cautions do historians need to keep in mind when working with documents such as these?

Officials found it difficult to recruit colonists for California and even turned to orphanages and prisons in New Spain, with little success. Moreover, it seemed nearly impossible to get colonists to California alive. The sea route along the Pacific coast proved costly and often deadly, and the backbreaking overland route from northwestern New Spain had to be abandoned after 1781, when an uprising of Yuma Indians shut down the crossing at the Colorado River. Still, the colony enjoyed steady if modest growth. By 1800 California had two more presidios (at San Francisco and Santa Barbara), three Spanish towns (San José, Los Angeles, and Branciforte, near present-day Santa Cruz), and a total of 18 Franciscan missions, ministering to 13,000 Indian converts.

THE CHANGING CALIFORNIA ENVIRONMENT

Like their colleagues in Texas and Florida, Franciscans tried to entice Indians into missions with promises of food, shelter, instruction, and protection. As time went on, missions became self-sufficient and more effective at both attracting Indians and policing those who came in. All the while, Indians saw the world changing around them. In Monterey, for example, imported pigs, sheep, mules, horses, and cows multiplied at astonishing speed. These animals radiated out from the mission and presidio, overgrazing and annihilating native plants. Soon weeds and plants that Spaniards had unwittingly brought with them began to spread throughout the region, outcompeting the disturbed native vegetation.

By 1800 the lands around Monterey had been thoroughly transformed. Pollen analysis of the vegetable matter in adobe from the early nineteenth century indicates that by the time the bricks were made, alien weeds had all but displaced native plants. With their lands transformed by overgrazing and invasive plant species, and their populations diminished by epidemics, native families around Monterey abandoned their villages and either fled to the interior or surrendered to the discipline and danger of mission life.

California's three colonial towns depended on missions for food and labor. Given the difficulties of immigrating to California, the colonial population grew mainly through natural increase. By 1800 California was home to only 1,800 Hispanic residents. Despite their relative poverty and isolation, these men, women, and children maintained distinctive traditions. An English visitor to Monterey savored local parties, bullfights, and hunts in the countryside. Most of all, he marveled at the "exhilarating" fandango, a dance that "requires no little elasticity of limbs as well as nimbleness of capers & gestures." The whirling men and women moved "with such wanton attitudes & motions, such leering looks, sparkling eyes and trembling limbs, as would decompose the gravity of a stoic."

Like most English-speaking visitors to California, this excitable traveler found Hispanic women both alluring and improper. Proper women knew their

Dame de Monterey

place, and, while delightful to watch, fandango seemed a good deal too joyous and suggestive to be proper. Had the Englishman probed deeper, he would have learned of other, far more consequential differences between Spanish and English women than the former's love of bold and beautiful dance.

Women and the Law in New Spain and British North America

Women in California and throughout the Spanish world had a host of important legal rights denied to women in English-speaking realms. For comparison's sake, consider a few critical moments in the lives of two imaginary women: Soledad Martínez, of Los Angeles, California; and Constance Snowling, of Albany, New York.

SPANISH LEGAL ADVANTAGES FOR WOMEN

When Soledad's parents passed away, Spanish law ensured that she would inherit their property on an equal footing with her brothers. English law, in contrast, allowed fathers to craft wills however they wished. Constance could theoretically receive nothing upon her parents' deaths. If, as was usually the case, Constance's father died without a will, by law his eldest son inherited all his land and any buildings on it. Constance and any other sisters or brothers would receive only a share of the remaining personal property (money, tools, furniture, clothing, and so on).

The legal advantages enjoyed by women in the Spanish Empire become even more apparent in marriage. Suppose that both Soledad and Constance were fortunate enough to come into their marriages with some personal property of their own and with modest dowries—sums of money meant to help the young couple get established. After her wedding, Soledad retained complete legal control over her personal property and could dispose of it however she wished (with or without her husband's blessing). Moreover, although her husband had the right to manage the dowry and invest it as he saw fit, it still belonged to Soledad. Once death or divorce ended the marriage, he was legally obliged to return its full value to her or her family. Finally, as a married woman Soledad retained the right to buy and sell land in her own name and could legally represent herself in court.

Wives in the English-speaking world had no such rights in the colonial era. Upon marriage, Constance surrendered her dowry and even her personal property to her new husband, who could dispose of all of it however he wished. As a married woman, Constance had virtually no control over property of any kind, could not write a will, and could initiate no legal actions without her husband's consent.

Finally, if our two imaginary colonial women had outlived their husbands, they would have experienced widowhood very differently. In addition to the full value of her dowry, Soledad was legally entitled to at least one-half of all property she and her deceased husband had accumulated in marriage. Upon Soledad's death, this property would pass to her own children or to her other family members. Constance had no claim on her dowry following her husband's death. She would have entered widowhood with her personal "paraphernalia" (clothes, jewelry, and similar items), any land she had been fortunate enough to inherit during marriage, and control over a third of her dead husband's property. Crucially, however, Constance could use this property only to support herself in life. Upon her death, it would pass into the hands of her husband's family.

Not all Spanish and English women would have felt these legal differences as keenly as Soledad and Constance. Poor women who inherited little, came into marriages with paltry dowries, and lived hand to mouth as adults endured poverty whether they lived under English or Spanish law. But for those who did have some property or wealth, it mattered a great deal whether they lived in New Spain or British North America.

WOMEN'S LEGAL RIGHTS IN NEW FRANCE
France's legal traditions descended from the same Roman sources as Spain's, so women in New France enjoyed legal protections similar to women in Florida, Texas, New Mexico, and California. And France and Spain's colonies in North America had other, less happy things in common. Like northern New Spain, New France generally cost the Crown more money than it brought in. Like their Spanish counterparts, French administrators found it all but impossible to convince or compel large numbers of their fellow subjects to move to the colonies. As in Florida, Texas, New Mexico, and California, the colonial population of New France struck many well-heeled observers as degraded, insolent, lazy, and ignorant. And, as with all Spanish colonies north of the Rio Grande, New France remained dependent on Indians generations after its founding.

✓ REVIEW

Why did Spain establish colonies in Texas and California, and what role did missions play in establishing the Spanish presence?

EIGHTEENTH-CENTURY NEW FRANCE

LIKE THE SPRAWLING VASTNESS OF Spain's territorial claims in North America, France's imperial reach was nothing if not ambitious. French colonial maps laid claim to the heart of the continent, a massive imperial wedge stretching from Newfoundland southwest to the Mississippi delta, then northwest across the Great Plains and into the cold north woods, and east again through Upper Canada to the North Atlantic. Of course it was one thing to draw an empire on a map, another to make the empire a reality.

Colonial Compromises

Despite their grand claims, most eighteenth-century French Americans continued to live along the St. Lawrence River.

Most dwelt in farming communities up and down the river valley between the small cities of Montreal and Quebec, capital of New France. Jesuit missions also lined the river, ministering to native converts. The Crown had given the valley a boost with an energetic colonization program in the 1660s and 1670s, but thereafter the French population grew almost totally through natural increase. Fortunately for France, the colonists excelled at natural increase—nurturing large, thriving families and basically doubling their own population every generation.

GROWTH ALONG THE ST. LAWRENCE RIVER
Those determined enough to endure darkness, isolation, and numbing cold in winter, then heat, humidity, and swarming mosquitoes in summer, found life in Canada considerably easier than life in France. Colonists were healthier and lived longer, were much more likely to own their own land, and enjoyed significantly more autonomy over their lives than rural peasants across the Atlantic. By 1760 the valley was home to around 75,000 French colonists, soldiers, and priests. Many Canadian households also included Indian slaves: women and children, mostly, who had been captured by other Indians in places as faraway as the Arkansas valley and sold into trade networks that eventually brought them to New France. Though modest by Anglo-American standards, by the mid-eighteenth century the colonial project along the St. Lawrence River had nonetheless put an unmistakable French stamp upon the land.

FRENCH AND INDIANS IN THE PAYS D'EN HAUT
To the west and north in the country known as the *pays d'en haut* ("upper country"), France's eighteenth-century venture took on a very different look. Around the Great Lakes, north around Lakes Manitoba and Winnipeg, and south along the Mississippi River basin, forts and missions rather than farms or towns anchored French ambition. More exactly, the goodwill of Indian peoples provided the anchor. Though as quick as other Europeans to use violence to get what they wanted, the French in North America recognized that they were too few to secure their interests through force alone. France gained an edge over its rivals in the interior by being useful to Indians, primarily the Algonquian-speaking nations who spread across eastern Canada and the upper Mississippi. French merchants brought coveted European presents and trade goods, while military men, administrators, and Jesuits often mediated in conflicts between native groups. Vastly outnumbered by Indians throughout most of the territory that it claimed in North America, France remained deeply dependent on native peoples.

Dependence meant compromise. Cultural differences between the French and their Indian allies often seemed vast and irreconcilable. The two peoples had radically divergent expectations about warfare, trade, marriage, child rearing, religion, food, beauty, and many other areas of life. Few cultural differences seemed as difficult to bridge as those concerning law. In 1706, for example, men associated with a prominent Ottawa leader known as Le Pesant killed a priest and a French soldier outside of Fort Detroit. Enraged French authorities demanded that Le Pesant be delivered to them so that he could be tried and, once found guilty, executed for murder. Ottawa leaders countered by offering to replace the dead Frenchmen with Indian slaves. "Raising" the dead this way was a common Ottawa remedy in cases of murder between allies, because it helped avoid a potentially disastrous cycle of blood revenge. Moreover, Le Pesant was a powerful man. His execution would have political consequences dangerous to the broader French alliance.

Neither side surrendered to the other. Instead, they crafted a novel solution that exemplified the pattern of creative, mutual compromises typical of what one scholar has called the "middle ground" characterizing French-Indian relations in the *pays d'en haut*. On a snowy morning, grim Ottawa leaders turned over Le Pesant to the French commander at Fort Detroit who then quickly condemned the man to death. But before the execution could be carried out, Le Pesant escaped to freedom. It is exceedingly difficult to believe that French authorities would have been careless enough to allow this most wanted of men to slip away. Moreover, Le Pesant was elderly and obese—hardly a nimble

escape artist. Clearly the French and their Ottawa allies came to an understanding. Le Pesant would be surrendered and, once condemned, quietly allowed to escape. This new compromise more or less satisfied both sides and became a model solution to later French-Indian murder cases.

Necessary and inevitable, such compromises nonetheless rankled authorities in Paris. In 1731 one such official bemoaned the fact that after more than a century, colonial administrators in New France had failed to make the "savages" obedient to the Crown. The colony's governor-general dashed off a terse reply: "If this has not been done, it is because we have found the task to be an impossible one. Kindly apprise me of any means you should conceive of for securing such obedience."

France on the Gulf Coast

Forced into uncomfortable compromises in the north, authorities in Paris hoped to establish a colony on the Gulf Coast that could be more profitable and more French. When shipwreck

Algonquin and French Views Regarding Trade and Justice

	ALGONQUIN VALUES	FRENCH VALUES
Trade	Trade embedded in personal relationships. Expectation that exchanges will be relatively uniform and consistent season to season. Negative changes in trade terms attributed to decay of personal relationship.	Trade structured mostly by markets, and only marginally by personal relationships. Trade terms will naturally change as market conditions change. Nothing inherently personal about fluctuations in prices or trade terms.
Justice	Upon a murder, most urgent question was "To what group did the killer belong?" Response to the murder would be determined and pursued by family of the victim. Families could (a) seek another death in revenge—especially if the killer belonged to an enemy people; (b) accept presents to "cover" the death; or (c) take an Indian slave in compensation and thereby "raise" the victim.	Upon a murder, most urgent question was "Who was the killer?" Response to the murder would be determined and pursued by state authorities. State authorities held that the only legitimate remedy for a murder was the apprehension, trial, and execution of the killer.

on the Texas coast sealed La Salle's doom, it fell to Pierre Le Moyne d'Iberville to establish French Louisiana. A veteran sailor and soldier, d'Iberville spent much of the 1690s destroying British settlements in Newfoundland and the North Atlantic. Sent to the Gulf in 1698, he inaugurated the new colony of Louisiana with a post at Biloxi Bay. D'Iberville's successors established settlements at Mobile Bay and, in 1718, the town of New Orleans. Crown officers and entrepreneurs envisioned an agricultural bonanza, expecting Louisiana to have far more in common with the Caribbean's lucrative sugar islands than with the maddening *pays d'en haut.*

Nothing went according to plan. Here, too, Indians forced the French into painful concessions. While disease and aggression devastated the smaller Indian communities along the coast, more powerful peoples in the interior endured and protected their interests. Louisiana came into conflict with the mighty Chickasaws, and in 1729 the Natchez Indians rose up against French encroachment, killing or capturing some 500 colonists. Underfunded and usually neglected by the Crown, Louisiana's officials became notoriously corrupt and arbitrary. The colony was, according to one observer, a place "without religion, without justice, without discipline, without order, and without police."

DIFFICULTIES IN FRENCH LOUISIANA More to the point, the Gulf Coast was without many French colonists. The region quickly acquired a reputation among would-be French migrants as unattractive and unhealthy. When colonists were not fighting Indians, they contended with heat, humidity, hurricanes, droughts and crop failures, with never-ending battles to turn swamps and forests into farmland, and with the scourges of malaria and yellow fever. One despairing official lamented that "death and disease are disrupting and suspending all operations . . . the best workers are dead." By 1731, two-thirds of the French who had chanced the journey to Louisiana had died or fled. Still, like New Mexico, Canada, California, and Texas, colonial Louisiana persevered to become more populous and more prosperous. Nearly 4,000 French men, women, and children called the colony home by 1746. Their fortunes had in large part come to depend on another, even larger group of newcomers: French Louisiana's African slaves.

Slavery and Colonial Society in French Louisiana

When the first colonists founded New Orleans in 1718, they immediately clamored for bound laborers. Their goal was to create prosperous plantations in the surrounding Mississippi delta. A year later the Company of the Indies, which managed France's slave trade, brought nearly 6,000 slaves, overwhelmingly men, directly from Africa to Louisiana. Unfortunately for white planters, Louisiana tobacco and, later, indigo proved inferior to the varieties exported from Britain's colonies. Instead of providing the formula for economic success, the sudden influx of Africans challenged French control. In 1729 some newly arrived slaves joined forces with the Natchez Indians in their rebellion. The alliance sent waves of panic through the colony, whose population by then had more slaves than free French. The French retaliated in a devastating counterattack, enlisting both the Choctaw Indians, rivals of the Natchez, and other enslaved blacks, who were promised freedom in return for their support.

The planters' costly victory persuaded French authorities to stop importing slaves into Louisiana. Thus the colony did not develop a plantation economy until the end of the eighteenth century, when the cotton boom transformed its culture. In the meantime, blacks continued to make up a majority of all Louisianans, and by the middle of the eighteenth century, nearly all were native-born. The vast majority were slaves, but their work routines—tending cattle, cutting timber, producing naval stores, manning boats—allowed them greater freedom of movement than most slaves enjoyed elsewhere in the American South. They were also encouraged to market the produce of their gardens, hunts, and handicrafts, which became the basis of a thriving trade with both white settlers and the dwindling numbers of coastal Native Americans. But the greatest prize—freedom—was awarded those black men who served in the French militia, defending the colony from the English and Indians as well as capturing slave runaways. The descendants of these black militiamen would become the core of Louisiana's free black community.

Male subjects throughout French America stood ready to perform militia duty, formally or informally. They had to. While the French struggled to sustain peaceful relations with key Indian allies, they turned to violent coercion when they thought it would work. Though not as devastating as the Beaver Wars (Chapter 3), conflicts with Indians proved to be common enough to require a ready defense.

 IMPERIAL RIVALRIES More fundamentally, France found itself in conflict with the English in the backcountry beyond the Appalachian Mountains. The rivalries had their beginnings in Europe

---

| Louisiana's socially mixed society is evident from this market scene: the buyers and sellers include Indians as well as colonials of French, Spanish, and African descent.

and flared regularly throughout the late seventeenth century and into the eighteenth. In 1689 England joined the Netherlands and the League of Augsburg (several German-speaking states) in a war against France. While the main struggle raged in Europe, French and English colonials, joined by their Indian allies, skirmished in what was known as King William's War. Peace returned in 1697, but only until the Anglo-French struggle resumed with Queen Anne's War, from 1702 to 1713.

For a quarter of a century thereafter, the two nations waged a kind of cold war, competing for advantage. At stake was not so much control over people or even territory as control over trade. In North America, France and England vied for access to the sugar islands of the Caribbean, a monopoly on supplying manufactured goods to Spanish America, and dominance of the fur trade. The British had the advantage of numbers: nearly 400,000 subjects in the colonies in 1720, the year of L'Archevêque's death, compared with only about 25,000 French. But this is precisely where France's many compromises paid dividends. So long as the French maintained their network of alliances with powerful native peoples, British colonies had little chance of expanding west of the Appalachian Mountains.

 **REVIEW**

How did Louisiana differ from French Canada?

FORCES OF DIVISION IN BRITISH NORTH AMERICA

BRITISH COLONIALS FROM MAINE TO the Carolinas distrusted the French and resented their empire of fish and furs. But the English were preoccupied with their own affairs and, by and large, uninterested in uniting against New France. Indeed a traveler during the first half of the eighteenth century would have been struck by how hopelessly divided and disunited England's mainland colonies were, split by ethnicity, race, region, wealth, and religion. The British colonies were a diverse and fragmented lot.

Immigration and Natural Increase

One of the largest immigrant groups—250,000 black men, women, and children—had come to the colonies from Africa in chains. White arrivals included many English immigrants but also a quarter of a million Scots-Irish, the descendants of seventeenth-century Scots who had regretted settling in northern Ireland; perhaps 135,000 Germans; and a sprinkling of Swiss, Swedes, Highland Scots, and Spanish Jews. Most non-English white immigrants were fleeing lives torn by famine, warfare, and religious persecution. All the voyagers, English and non-English, risked the hazardous Atlantic crossing (Daily Lives, page 115). Many had paid for passage by signing indentures to work as servants in America. The immigrants and slaves who arrived in

the colonies between 1700 and 1775 swelled an American population that was already growing dramatically from natural increase. The birthrate in eighteenth-century America was triple what it is today. Most women bore between five and eight children, and most children survived to maturity.

 NORTH AMERICA LEADS A GLOBAL RISE IN POPULATION

This astonishing population explosion was quite possibly the fastest in the world at the time. Even so, the surge was merely one part of a more general global acceleration of population in the second half of the eighteenth century. China's population of 150 million in 1700 had doubled to more than 313 million by century's end. Europe's total rose from about 118 million to 187 million over the same period. The unprecedented global population explosion had several causes. Europe's climate, for one, had become warmer and drier, allowing for generally better harvests. Health and nutrition improved globally with the worldwide spread of Native American crops. Irish farmers discovered that a single acre planted with the American potato could support an entire family. The tomato added crucial vitamins to the Mediterranean diet, and in China the American sweet potato thrived in hilly regions where rice would not grow.

Dramatic population increase in the British colonies, fed by the importation of slaves, immigration, and natural increase, made it hard for colonials to share any common identity. Far from fostering political unity, almost every aspect of social development set Americans at odds with one another. And that process of division and disunity was reflected in the outpouring of new settlers into the backcountry.

Moving into the Backcountry

To immigrants from Europe weary of war or worn by want, the seaboard's established communities must have seemed havens of order and stability. But by the beginning of the eighteenth century, Anglo-America's colonists had to look farther and farther west to obtain farmland. With older rural communities offering bleak prospects to either native-born or newly arrived families, both groups turned westward in search of new opportunities. The founding of frontier communities in New England was left mainly to the descendants of old Yankee families. Immigrants from Europe had more luck obtaining land south of New York. By the 1720s German and Scots-Irish immigrants as well as native-born colonists were pouring into western Pennsylvania. Some settled permanently, but others streamed southward into the backcountry of Virginia and the Carolinas, where they encountered native-born southerners pressing westward.

ISOLATION OF THE BACKCOUNTRY Living in the West could be profoundly isolating. From many farmsteads it was a day's ride to the nearest courthouse, tavern, or church. Often lacking decent roads or navigable rivers, frontier families had no means of sending crops to market and aimed for self-sufficiency instead. Distance inhibited the formation of strong social bonds, as did the rapid turnover in western communities. Many families pulled up

DAILY LIVES

TRANSATLANTIC TRIALS

A mountain of water swelled from the Atlantic, towered over the *Jamaica Packet,* then toppled onto the small wooden passenger ship. The impact hurled Janet Schaw and her maid about their cabin like rag dolls. As seawater surged in, the ship pitched wildly, "one moment mounted to the clouds and whirled on the pointed wave," the next plunging into the heaving ocean. The ship's provisions—hogsheads of water, coops of chickens, and barrels of salted meat—snapped from their fastenings and careened across the deck before bouncing overboard.

For more than two days the *Jamaica Packet* hurtled in the gale's grip. Then its foremast splintered, and the ship flipped onto its side. Schaw found herself "swimming amongst joint-stools, chests, [and] tables" in her cabin and listening to the sound of "our sails fluttering into rags." It would have been the end of the *Jamaica Packet* if, at that moment, its masts had not washed overboard. With the weight of the masts gone, the ship righted itself.

Schaw, "a lady of quality," as she described herself, was traveling by the finest accommodations from Great Britain to America in the age of sail. For passengers who could not pay for a private cabin, the storm was worse. Twenty-two or more indentured servants from Scotland in that year of 1774 were bound aboard ship for the West Indies. Like thousands of others who came to America in the eighteenth century, they were consigned to steerage, the between-decks area or "upper hold."

Perhaps 4 to 5 feet high, that space was crowded with narrow wooden bunks arranged in tiers about 2 feet apart. It was impossible for most people to stand in steerage or to sit up in a bunk, where as many as four people huddled together at night. Sanitary facilities consisted of a few wooden buckets filled with seawater; candles and fish-oil lanterns supplied the only light. The sole source of air was the hatch opening onto the deck.

When the storm struck, the hatch was fastened tightly to keep the holds from filling with water. But as waves dashed over the decks, water streamed into steerage, forcing its occupants to stand, clutching their children to keep them from being crushed, drowned, or suffocated. For nine days they stood in water, without a fire or any food except raw potatoes and moldy biscuits. And they were without light or fresh air, except for one young man and his pregnant wife. During the storm the woman miscarried, and her "absolutely distracted" husband, Schaw reported, somehow forced open the hatch and carried her up to the deck, reviving the unconscious woman and saving her life.

Luckily, the *Jamaica Packet* escaped not only shipwreck but epidemic disease. Passengers on other transatlantic voyages were not so fortunate. Outbreaks of epidemic disease—smallpox, influenza, typhus, and diphtheria—were common. Although there are no reliable statistics for shipboard mortality during the eighteenth century, estimates range from 3 percent of all passengers to as

high as 10 to 15 percent, a rate nearly comparable to that for slave ships during the Middle Passage across the Atlantic.

For all who ventured abroad, transatlantic travel was tedious and dirty at best, hazardous and horrific at worst. With good reason, those who risked the crossing routinely made out wills and sought the prayers of loved ones. On the high seas, disease and misfortune took a heavy toll.

Thinking Critically

In what ways did the hazards of transatlantic travel shape the profile of people who willingly undertook these journeys?

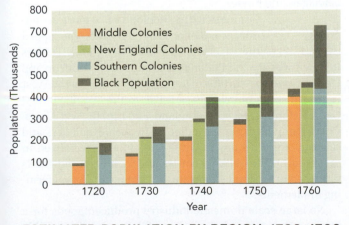

ESTIMATED POPULATION BY REGION, 1720–1760

(Chart legend: Middle Colonies, New England Colonies, Southern Colonies, Black Population. Y-axis: Population (Thousands), 0–800. X-axis: Year, 1720, 1730, 1740, 1750, 1760.)

stakes three or four times before settling permanently. Most backcountry inhabitants could not afford to invest in a slave or even a servant. Those conditions made the frontier, more than anywhere else in America, a society of equals. Most families crowded into one-room shacks walled with mud, turf, or crude logs. And everyone worked hard.

FRONTIER WOMEN

Hard work dominated the lives of backcountry settlers. Besides doing the usual chores of farm women, western wives and daughters joined male family members in the fields. One traveler from the East expressed his astonishment at seeing German women in western Pennsylvania "at work abroad on the Farm mowing, Hoeing Loading Dung into a Cart." Perhaps even more difficult to endure than the hard labor was the loneliness of many women's lives. The reactions of women to being resettled on the frontier can be imagined from the promise that one Scottish husband offered his wife: "We would get all these trees cut down . . . [so] that we would see from house to house."

Social Conflict on the Frontier

Despite the discomforts of frontier life, cheap land lured many families to the West. Benjamin Franklin, Pennsylvania's most successful entrepreneur, inventor, and politician, had observed the hordes of Scots-Irish and German immigrants lingering in Philadelphia just long enough to scrape together the purchase price of a frontier farm. From Franklin's point of view, the backcountry performed a valuable service by siphoning off surplus people from congested eastern settlements. But he knew, too, that the opened frontier unleashed discord, especially between the Eastern Seaboard and the backcountry.

Ethnic differences heightened sectional tensions between East and West. People of English descent predominated along the Atlantic coast, whereas Germans, Scots-Irish, and other white minorities were concentrated in the interior. Many English colonials regarded these new immigrants as culturally inferior and politically subversive. Charles Woodmason, an Anglican missionary in the Carolina backcountry, lamented the arrival of "5 or 6,000 Ignorant, mean, worthless, beggarly Irish Presbyterians, the Scum of the Earth, the Refuse of Mankind," who "delighted in a low, lazy, sluttish, heathenish, hellish life."

German immigrants were generally credited with steadier work habits, as well as higher standards of sexual morality and personal hygiene. But like the clannish Scots-Irish, the Germans preferred to live, trade, and worship among themselves. By 1751 Franklin was warning that the Germans would retain their separate language and customs: the Pennsylvania English would be overrun by "the Palatine Boors."

| This log cabin, built in the North Carolina backcountry in 1782, would have been dark inside, given its lack of windows. The spaces between the logs in such cabins were usually chinked with thin stones or wedges of wood and then daubed with mortar.

Ethnic prejudices only aggravated clashes between wealthy landlords and backcountry tenants. In eastern New Jersey, landed proprietors insisted that squatters pay rent on land that had become increasingly valuable. When the squatters, many of them migrants from New England, refused to pay rents, the proprietors began evictions, touching off riots in the 1740s. Tenant unrest also raged in New York's Hudson River valley, where about 30 manors around New York City and Albany dominated the region. The estates encompassed some 2 million acres and were worked by several thousand tenants. Newcomers from New England, however, demanded to own land and preached their ideas to Dutch and German tenants. Armed insurrection exploded in 1757 and again, more violently, in 1766. Tenants refused to pay rents, formed mobs, and stormed the homes of landlords.

Eighteenth-Century Seaports

While most Americans on the move flocked to the frontier, others swelled the populations of colonial cities. By present-day standards such cities were small, harboring from 8,000 to 22,000 citizens by 1750. The scale of seaports remained intimate, too: all of New York City was clustered at the southern tip of Manhattan island, and the length of Boston or Charleston could be walked in less than half an hour.

All major colonial cities were seaports, their waterfronts fringed with wharves and shipyards. A jumble of shops, taverns, and homes crowded their streets; the spires of churches studded their skylines. By the 1750s the grandest and most populous was Philadelphia, which boasted straight, neatly paved streets, flagstone sidewalks, and three-story brick buildings. Older cities such as Boston and New York had a medieval aspect: most of their dwellings and shops were wooden structures with tiny windows and low ceilings, rising no higher than two stories to steeply pitched roofs. The narrow cobblestone streets of Boston and New York City also challenged pedestrians, who competed for space with livestock being driven to the butcher, roaming herds of swine and packs of dogs, clattering carts, carriages, and horses.

THE COMMERCIAL CLASSES Commerce, the lifeblood of seaport economies, was managed by merchants who tapped the wealth of surrounding regions. Traders in New York City and Philadelphia shipped the Hudson and Delaware valleys' surplus of grain and livestock to the West Indies. Boston's merchants sent fish to the Caribbean and Catholic Europe, masts to England, and rum to West Africa. Charlestonians exported indigo to English dyemakers and rice to southern Europe. Other merchants specialized in the import trade, selling luxuries and manufactured goods produced in England—fine fabrics, ceramics, tea, and farming implements.

No large-scale domestic industry produced goods for a mass market: instead, craft shops filled orders for specific items placed by individual purchasers. Some **artisans** specialized in the maritime trades as shipbuilders, blacksmiths, and sailmakers. Others, such as butchers, millers, and distillers, processed and packed raw materials for export. Still others served the basic needs of city dwellers—the men and, occasionally, women who baked bread, mended shoes, combed and powdered wigs, and tended shops and taverns.

On the lowest rung of a seaport's social hierarchy were free and bound workers. Free laborers were mainly young white men and women—journeyman artisans, sailors, fishermen, domestic workers, seamstresses, and prostitutes. The ranks of unfree workers included apprentices and indentured servants doing menial labor in shops and on the docks.

INCREASE OF AFRICANS IN NORTHERN SEAPORTS — Black men and women also made up a substantial part of the bound labor force of colonial seaports, but the character of slavery in northern seaports changed decisively during the mid-eighteenth century. When wars raging in Europe reduced the supply of white indentured servants, colonial cities imported a larger number of Africans. In the two decades after 1730, one-third of all immigrants arriving in New York harbor were black; by 1760 blacks constituted more than three-quarters of all bound laborers in Philadelphia.

High death rates and a preference for importing African males inhibited the growth of slave families. Even so, city-dwelling African Americans forged an urban black culture exhibiting a new awareness of a common West African past. The influence of African traditions appeared most vividly in an annual event known as "Negro election day," celebrated in northern seaports. During the festival, similar to ones held in West Africa, some black men and women paraded in their masters' clothes or mounted on their horses. An election followed to choose black kings, governors, and judges who then held court and settled minor disputes among black and white members of the community. Negro election day did not challenge the established racial order with its temporary reversal of roles. But it did allow the black communities of seaports to honor their own leaders.

WOMEN IN CITIES — Working women found a number of opportunities in port cities. Young single women from poor families worked in wealthier households as maids, cooks, laundresses, seamstresses, or nurses. The highest-paying occupations for women were midwifery and dressmaking, and both required long apprenticeships and expert skills. The wives of artisans and traders sometimes assisted their husbands and, as widows, often continued to manage groceries, taverns, and print shops. But less than 10 percent of women in seaports worked outside their own homes. Most women spent their workday caring for households: seeing to the needs of husbands and children, tending to gardens and domestic animals, and engaged in spinning and weaving—activities crucial to the household economy.

NON-ENGLISH SETTLEMENTS IN EIGHTEENTH-CENTURY BRITISH NORTH AMERICA

Many non-English settlers spilled into the backcountry: the Scots-Irish and Germans followed the Great Wagon Road through the western parts of the middle colonies and southern colonies; the Dutch and other Germans moved up the Hudson River valley. **In what ways did the concentration of non-English immigrants in the backcountry influence the development of that region?**

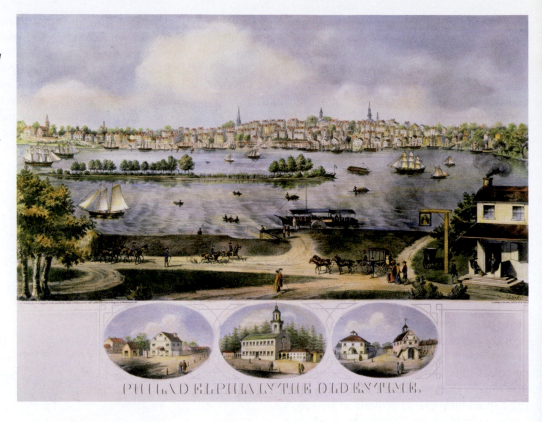

In the mid-eighteenth century, Philadelphia became the largest city in the colonies and the second largest in all the British Empire. Its busy harbor served not only as a commercial hub but also as the disembarkation point for thousands of immigrants.

PHILADELPHIA IN THE OLDEN TIME.

URBAN DIVERSIONS AND HAZARDS All seaport dwellers—perhaps 1 out of every 20 Americans—enjoyed a more stimulating environment than other colonials did. Plays, balls, and concerts for the wealthiest; taverns, clubs, celebrations, and church services for everyone. Men of every class found diversion in drink and cockfighting. Crowds of men, women, and children swarmed to tavern exhibitions of trained dogs and horses or the spectacular

waxworks of one John Dyer, featuring "a lively Representation of Margaret, Countess of Herrinburg, who had 365 Children at one Birth."

Then as now, cities were also places of economic insecurity. In seaports throughout British North America, poverty became increasingly apparent as the eighteenth century wore on. Although the major seaports established workhouses to employ the able-bodied poor, city governments continued to aid most of the dependent with small subsidies of money, food, and firewood. Furthermore, epidemics and catastrophic fires occurred with greater frequency and produced higher mortality rates in congested seaports than in the countryside.

Social Tension in Seaports

The swelling of seaport populations, like the westward movement of whites, often churned up trouble. English, Scots-Irish, Germans, Swiss, Dutch, French, and Spanish jostled uneasily against one another in the close quarters of Philadelphia and New York City. To make matters worse, religious differences heightened ethnic divisions. Jewish funerals in New York City, for example, drew crowds of hostile and curious Protestants, who heckled mourners.

Class resentment also stirred unrest. Some merchant families flaunted their wealth, building imposing town mansions and dressing in the finest imported fashions. During hard times, symbols of merchant wealth such as expensive coaches and full warehouses became targets of

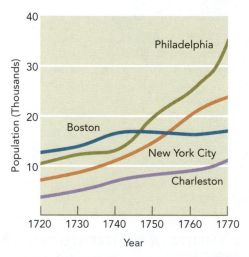

ESTIMATED POPULATION OF COLONIAL CITIES, 1720–1770

Although Boston's population remained stable after 1740, it was surpassed owing to the sharp growth of New York City and, especially, Philadelphia.

A Woman's Cupboard

Using a technique known as polarized light microscopy, researchers determined that the paint on the columns combined white lead with a shade of blue first synthesized in Berlin in 1704.

Eighteenth-century Americans spelled names, even their own, inconsistently. Beneath the first 'A' in 'Barnard' curators found a faint 'E' for 'Bernard.'

What sorts of possessions do you think Hannah might have kept in these drawers?

Objects can help historians appreciate complex connections. For example, the owner of this exuberantly designed cupboard lived in western Massachusetts in the late seventeenth and early eighteenth centuries, a time of chronic warfare between the English and the French and their Indian allies. Hannah's husband John had been captured in a well-known Indian raid on Deerfield, Massachusetts, in 1704. Perhaps the cupboard can be seen as a defiant assertion of normality in a violent and insecure world. The imagery on the cupboard echoes patterns found on European manufactures from the time, illustrating transatlantic cultural connections even as the piece itself represents a distinct local craft tradition. Finally, the cupboard and the textiles it probably contained open a window into the sorts of property Anglo-American women retained in marriage and passed down to their descendants. According to historian Laurel Thatcher Ulrich, the cupboard's history "teaches us that material objects were not only markers of wealth but devices for building relationships and lineages over time, and it helps us to understand the cultural framework within which ordinary women became creators as well as custodians of household goods."

Source: Henry Ford Museum, www.thehenryford.org/exhibits/pic/1997/hannah.asp.

Thinking Critically

Why did the owner have her name emblazoned on the cupboard? Might it have something to do with restrictive English laws about what women could own in marriage? Do you think women in New Spain or New France would have done the same? What might objects such as these tell us about how women viewed property and identity in British North America?

mob vandalism. Crowds also gathered to intimidate and punish other groups who provoked popular hostility—politicians, prostitutes, and "press gangs." Impressment, attempts to force colonials to serve in the British navy, triggered some of the most violent urban riots.

✓ REVIEW

What kinds of divisions led to social tensions and conflicts in British North America?

SLAVE SOCIETIES IN THE EIGHTEENTH-CENTURY SOUTH

INEQUALITIES AND DIVISIONS BETWEEN SLAVE and free in the South dwarfed those between seaport dwellers. By 1775 one out of every five Americans was of African ancestry, and more than 90 percent of all black Americans lived in the South, most along the seaboard. Here, on tobacco and rice plantations, slaves fashioned a distinctive African

American society and culture. But they were able to build stable families and communities only late in the eighteenth century and against enormous odds.

THE CHESAPEAKE AND THE LOWER SOUTH

The character of a slave's life depended to a great extent on whether he or she lived in the Chesapeake or the Lower South. Slaves in the low country of South Carolina and Georgia lived on large plantations with as many as 50 other black workers, about half African-born. They had infrequent contact with whites. "They are as 'twere, a Nation within a Nation," observed Francis LeJau, an Anglican priest in the low country. And their work was arduous, because rice required constant cultivation. Black laborers tended young plants and hoed fields in the sweltering summer heat of the mosquito-infested lowlands. During the winter and early spring, they built dams and canals to regulate the flow of water into the rice fields. But the use of the **"task system"** rather than gang labor widened the window of freedom within slavery. When a slave had completed his assigned task for the day, one planter explained, "his master feels no right to call upon him."

Most Africans and African Americans in the Chesapeake lived on plantations with fewer than 20 fellow slaves. Less densely concentrated than in the low country, Chesapeake slaves also had more contact with whites. Unlike Carolina's absentee owners, who left white overseers and black drivers to run their plantations, Chesapeake masters actively managed their estates and subjected their slaves to closer scrutiny.

The Slave Family and Community

The four decades following 1700 marked the heaviest years of slave importation into the Chesapeake and Carolina regions. Those Africans had survived the trauma of captivity, the Middle Passage, and sale at slave auctions only to be thrust into a bewildering new world: a sea of unfamiliar faces, a clamor of different languages, a host of demands and threats from men and women who called themselves masters.

AFRICAN SLAVES VS. AMERICAN-BORN SLAVES

The newcomers also had to adjust to their fellow slaves. The "new Negroes" hailed from a number of diverse West African peoples, each with a separate language or dialect and distinctive cultures and kinship systems. Often, they had little in common with one another and even less in common with the American-born black minority. Native-born African Americans enjoyed better health, command of English, and experience in dealing with whites. They were also more likely to enjoy a family life, because their advantages probably made the men the preferred partners of black women, who were outnumbered two to one by black

DISTRIBUTION OF THE AMERICAN POPULATION, 1775

The African American population expanded dramatically during the eighteenth century, especially in the southern colonies. The high volume of slave imports accounts for most of the growth in the first half of the century, but natural increase was responsible for the rising black population during later decades.

Persons Per County/Parish

- 30,001 to 55,000
- 15,001 to 30,000
- 5001 to 15,000
- 2000 to 5000
- Fewer than 2000

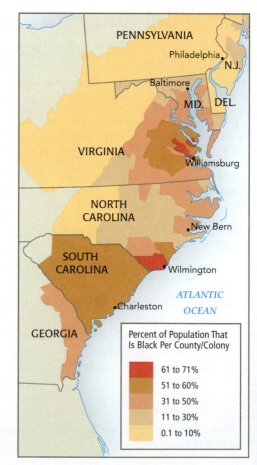

Percent of Population That Is Black Per County/Colony

- 61 to 71%
- 51 to 60%
- 31 to 50%
- 11 to 30%
- 0.1 to 10%

men. And, since immigrant women waited two or three years before marrying, some immigrant men died before they could find a wife. Competition for wives often bred conflict and division.

After the middle of the eighteenth century a number of changes fostered the growth of black families and the vitality of slave communities. At the same time that slave importations began to taper off, the rate of natural reproduction among blacks started to climb. Gender ratios became more equal. These changes, along with the rise of larger plantations throughout the South, made it easier for black men and women to find partners and start families. Elaborate kinship networks gradually developed, often extending over several plantations in a single neighborhood. And, as the immigrant generations were replaced by native-born offspring, earlier sources of tension and division within the slave community disappeared.

Even so, black families remained vulnerable. If a planter fell on hard times, members of black families might be sold off to different buyers to meet his debts. When an owner died, black spouses, parents, and children might be divided among surviving heirs. Even under the best circumstances, fathers might be hired out to other planters for long periods or sent to work in distant quarters. The migration of slaveholders from the coast to the interior also disrupted black efforts to fashion domestic and communal bonds. Between 1755 and 1782, masters on the move resettled fully one-third of all adult African Americans living in Tidewater, Virginia. Most slaves forced to journey west were men and women in their teens and early 20s, who had to begin again the long process of establishing families and neighborhood networks far from kin and friends.

Black families struggling with terrible uncertainties were sustained by the distinctive African American culture evolving in the slave community. The high percentage of native Africans among the eighteenth-century American black population made it easier for slaves to retain the ways of their lost homeland. Christianity won few converts, in part because white masters feared that baptizing slaves might make them more rebellious but also because African Americans preferred their traditional religions. African influence appeared as well in the slaves' agricultural skills and practices, folktales, music, and dances.

Slave Resistance in Eighteenth-Century British North America

British North America had no shortage of African Americans who both resisted captivity and developed strategies for survival. Collective attempts at escape were most common among recently arrived Africans. Groups of slaves, often made up of newcomers from the same region, fled inland and formed **"Maroon" communities** of runaways. These efforts were rarely successful, because the Maroon settlements were too large to go undetected for long.

More-acculturated blacks turned to subtler subversions, employing what one scholar has called "weapons of the weak." Domestics and field hands alike faked illness, feigned stupidity and laziness, broke tools, pilfered from storehouses, hid in the woods for weeks at a time, or simply took off to visit other plantations. Other slaves, usually escaping bondage as solitary individuals, found a new life as craftworkers, dock laborers, or sailors in the relative anonymity of colonial seaports.

The Old Plantation *affords a rare glimpse of life in the slave quarters. At this festive gathering, both men and women dance to the music of a molo (a stringed instrument similar to a banjo) and drums. The gudugudu drum is an instrument common throughout West Africa and similar to the drum depicted* (far right) *in the painting.*

Sometimes slaves rebelled openly. Whites in communities with large numbers of blacks lived in gnawing dread of arson, poisoning, and insurrection. Four slave conspiracies were reported in Virginia during the first half of the eighteenth century. In South Carolina more than two decades of abortive uprisings and insurrection scares culminated in the Stono Rebellion of 1739, the largest slave revolt of the colonial period. Nearly 100 Africans, led by a slave named Jemmy, seized arms from a store in the coastal district of Stono and killed several white neighbors before they were caught and killed by the colonial militia. But throughout the eighteenth century, slave rebellions occurred far less frequently on the mainland of North America than in the Caribbean or Brazil. Whites outnumbered blacks in all of Britain's mainland colonies except South Carolina, and only there did rebels have a haven for a quick escape—Spanish Florida. Faced with those odds, most slaves reasoned that the risks of rebellion outweighed the prospects for success—and most sought opportunities for greater personal freedom within the slave system itself.

 REVIEW

How did African American culture evolve in the slave community, and what form did resistance to captivity take?

ENLIGHTENMENT AND AWAKENING IN AMERICA

WHERE COLONISTS LIVED, HOW WELL they lived, whether they were male or female, native-born or immigrant, slave or free—all these variables fostered distinctive worldviews, differing attitudes and assumptions about the individual's relationship to nature, society, and God. The diversity of colonials' inner lives became even more pronounced during the eighteenth century because of the **Enlightenment,** an intellectual movement that started in Europe during the seventeenth century.

The Enlightenment in America

The leading figures of the Enlightenment, the *philosophes,* stressed the power of human reason to promote progress by revealing the laws that governed both nature and society. Like many devotees of the Enlightenment, Benjamin Franklin of Philadelphia was most impressed by its emphasis on useful knowledge and experimentation. He pondered air currents and then invented a stove that heated houses more efficiently. He toyed with electricity and then invented lightning rods to protect buildings in thunderstorms. Other amateur colonial scientists constructed simple telescopes, classified animal species native to North America, and sought to explain epidemics in terms of natural causes.

American colleges helped promote Enlightenment thinking. Although institutions such as Harvard (founded 1636) and Yale (1701) initially focused on training ministers, by the eighteenth century their graduates included lawyers, merchants, doctors, and scientists. Most offered courses in mathematics and the natural sciences that taught students algebra and such advanced theories as Copernican astronomy and Newtonian physics.

By the middle of the eighteenth century, Enlightenment ideals had given rise to "rational Christianity," which commanded a small but influential following among Anglicans or liberal **Congregationalists** in the colonies. Their God was not the Calvinists' awesome deity but a benevolent creator who offered salvation not to a small, predestined elite, but to everyone. They believed that God's greatest gift to humankind was reason, which enabled all human beings to follow the moral teachings of Jesus. They muted the Calvinist emphasis on human sinfulness and the need for a soul-shattering conversion. An even smaller number of Americans steeped in the Enlightenment embraced deism, which rejected the divinity of Jesus and looked to nature rather than the Bible for proof of God's existence. In the magnificent design of creation, deists detected a Supreme Architect who had wrought the world and then withdrew to let events unfold through natural law.

Enlightenment philosophy and rational Christianity did little to change the lives of most colonials. French and Spanish authorities suppressed Enlightenment literature in their colonies. Likewise, innovations in Protestant doctrine were meaningless in New Spain and New France, where Catholicism was the only European religion tolerated. Eighteenth-century British North Americans suffered from fewer restrictions, and more than half of all white men (and a smaller percentage of white women) could read. But few colonial readers had the interest or the background necessary to tackle the learned writings of Enlightenment *philosophes.* The great majority still looked for ultimate truth in biblical revelation rather than human reason and explained the workings of the world in terms of divine providence rather than natural law.

Widespread attachment to traditional Christian beliefs was strengthened by the hundreds of new churches built during the first half of the eighteenth century. Church attendance ran highest in the northern colonies, where some 80 percent of the population turned out for public worship on the Sabbath. In the South, because of the greater distances involved and the shortage of clergy, about half of all colonials regularly attended Sunday services.

Despite the prevalence of traditional religious beliefs, many ministers grew alarmed over the dangerous influence of rational Christianity. They also worried that the lack of churches might tempt many frontier families to abandon Christianity altogether. Exaggerated as these fears may have been, they gave rise to a major religious revival that swept the colonies during the middle decades of the eighteenth century.

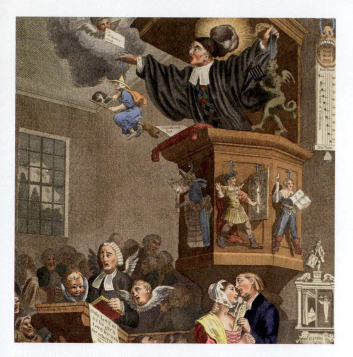

A sharp critic of the evangelical revivals that swept both sides of the Atlantic, the English artist William Hogarth satirized preaching in the style of George Whitefield. In this detail from an engraving of 1762 titled "Credulity, Superstition, and Fanaticism," the minister wears a clown's jacket under his gown and plays upon the superstitious beliefs of his congregation by dangling a witch from one hand, a devil from the other. The page before him reads, "I speak as a fool"; the ribbon to his right shows a scale of "vociferation" that runs from a "Natural Tone" of speaking all the way up to "Bull Roar." Hogarth did not think critical thinking was incompatible with biblical teachings, for below the engraving he included a bit of scripture: "Believe not every Spirit, but try the Spirits whether they are of God: because many false Prophets are gone out into the World."

The First Great Awakening

The **Great Awakening,** as the revival came to be called, first appeared in the 1730s among Presbyterians and Congregationalists in the middle colonies and New England. Many ministers in these churches preached an "evangelical" message, emphasizing the need for individuals to experience "a new birth" through religious conversion. Among them was Jonathan Edwards, the pastor of a Congregational church in Northampton, Massachusetts. Edwards's Calvinist preaching combined moving descriptions of God's grace with terrifying portrayals of eternal damnation. "The God that holds you over the pit of hell, much as one holds a spider or some loathsome insect over the fire, abhors you and is dreadfully provoked," he declaimed to one congregation. "There is no other reason to be given, why you have not dropped into hell since you arise in the morning, but that God's hand has held you up."

These local revivals of the 1730s were mere tremors compared to the earthquake of religious enthusiasm that shook the colonies with the arrival in the fall of 1739 of George Whitefield. This handsome (though cross-eyed) "boy preacher" from England electrified crowds from Georgia to New Hampshire during his two-year tour of the colonies. He and his many imitators among colonial ministers turned the church into a theater, enlivening sermons with dramatic gestures, flowing tears, and gruesome depictions of hell. The drama of such performances appealed to people of all classes, ethnic groups, and races. By the time Whitefield sailed back to England in 1741, thousands of awakened souls were joining older churches or forming new ones.

The Aftermath of the Great Awakening

Whitefield also left behind a raging storm of controversy. Many "awakened" church members now openly criticized their ministers as cold, unconverted, and uninspiring. To supply the missing fire, some laymen—"and even Women and Common Negroes"—took to "exhorting" any audience willing to listen. The most popular ministers became **itinerants,** traveling as Whitefield did from one town to another.

RELIGIOUS DIVISIONS

Although Americans had been fighting over religion well before the Great Awakening, the new revivals left colonials even more divided along religious lines. The largest single group of churchgoers in the northern colonies remained within the Congregational and Presbyterian denominations. But both of these groups split into factions over the revivals. Quakers and Anglicans shunned them. In contrast, the most radical converts joined forces with the warmest champions of the Awakening, the Baptists.

While northern churches splintered and bickered, the fires of revivalism spread to the South and its backcountry. From the mid-1740s until the 1770s scores of new Presbyterian and Baptist churches formed, sparking controversy. Ardent Presbyterians disrupted Anglican worship by loosing packs of dogs in local chapels. County officials, prodded by resentful Anglican parsons, harassed, fined, and imprisoned Baptist ministers.

And so a diverse lot of Americans found themselves continually at odds with one another: arguing over religion and the Enlightenment, conflicted over racial and ethnic tensions, and divided between coastal and backcountry cultures. Benjamin Franklin, a man who made it his business to know, surely understood the depth of those divisions. Even he had brooded over the boatloads of non-English newcomers. He had lived in two booming seaports and felt the explosive force of the frontier. He personified the Enlightenment—and yet looked on in admiration at a George Whitefield sermon on the steps of the Philadelphia courthouse.

Franklin recognized these divisions. Yet oddly enough, even though he knew how little held colonials together, he still harbored hopes for their political unity. After all, most were English. That much they had in common.

REVIEW

Describe the different outlooks of Enlightenment and evangelical Christians.

Anglo-American Worlds of the Eighteenth Century

Most colonists in British North America prided themselves on being English. Colonial towns bore English names; colonial governments drew on English precedents; colonial diets, dress, architecture, furniture, and literature all followed English models. And yet there were important differences. Some differences made colonials feel inferior, ashamed of their simplicity when compared with London's sophistication. But they also came to appreciate the greater equality of their society and the more representative character of their governments. If it was good to be English, it was better still to be English in America.

English Economic and Social Development

The differences between England and America began with their economies. Large financial institutions such as the Bank of England and influential corporations such as the East India Company were driving England's commercial development. A growing number of textile factories and mines were deepening its industrial development. Although most English men and women worked at agriculture, it, too, had become a business. Gentry rented their estates to tenants, the rural middle class. In turn, these tenants hired men and women from the swollen ranks of England's landless to perform the farm labor. In contrast, most colonial farmers owned their land, and most family farms were a few hundred acres. The scale of commerce and manufacturing was equally modest, limited by the preference of colonials to farm instead.

England's more developed economy fostered the growth of cities, especially London, a teeming colossus of 675,000 in 1750. In contrast, 90 percent of all eighteenth-century colonials lived in towns of fewer than 2,000.

The Consumer Revolution

But in another respect, England's more advanced economy drew the colonies and the parent country together. Americans were so eager to acquire British-made commodities that their per capita consumption of imported manufactures rose 120 percent between 1750 and 1773. People of all classes demanded and indulged in small luxuries such as a tin of tea, a pair of gloves, and a bar of Irish soap. In both England and its colonies, the spare and simple material life of earlier centuries was giving way to a new order in which even people of ordinary means owned a wider variety of things.

Inequality in England and America

Then there were people of no means. In England they were legion. London seethed with filth, crime, and desperate poverty. The poor and the unemployed as well as pickpockets and prostitutes crowded into its gin-soaked slums, taverns, and brothels. The contrast between the luxuries enjoyed by a wealthy few Londoners and the misery of the many disquieted colonial observers. Ebenezer Hazard, an American Quaker visiting London, knew for certain he was in "a Sink of Sin."

CLASS DISTINCTIONS

New wealth and the inherited privileges of England's landed aristocracy made for deepening class divisions. Two percent of England's population owned 70 percent of its land. By right of birth, English aristocrats claimed membership in the House of Lords; by custom, certain powerful gentry families dominated the other branch of Parliament, the House of Commons.

The colonies had their own prominent families, but no titled ruling class holding political privilege by hereditary right. And even the wealthiest colonial families lived far more humbly than their English counterparts. Probably the finest mansion in eighteenth-century America, William Byrd's plantation at Westover, Virginia, was scarcely a tenth the size of the Marquis of Rockingham's country house, a sprawling edifice longer than two football fields.

If England's upper classes lived more splendidly, its lower classes were larger and worse off than those in the colonies. Less than a third of England's inhabitants belonged to the "middling sort" of traders, professionals, artisans, and tenant farmers. More than two-thirds struggled for survival at the bottom of society. In contrast, the colonial middle class counted for nearly three-quarters of the white population. With land cheap, labor scarce, and wages for both urban and rural workers 100 percent higher in America than in England, it was much easier for colonials to accumulate savings and farms of their own.

Colonials were both fascinated and repelled by English society. Benjamin Rush, a Philadelphia physician, felt in the House of Lords as if he "walked on sacred ground." He begged his guide for permission to sit on the throne therein and then sat "for a considerable time." Other colonials gushed over the grandeur of aristocratic estates and imported suits of livery for their servants, tea services for their wives, and wallpaper for their drawing rooms.

But colonials recognized that England's ruling classes purchased their luxury and leisure at the cost of the rest of the nation. In his autobiography, Benjamin Franklin painted a devastating portrait of the degraded lives of his fellow workers in a London print shop, who drowned their disappointments by drinking throughout the workday, even more excessively on the Sabbath, and then faithfully observing the holiday of "St. Monday" to nurse their hangovers. Like Franklin, many colonials regarded the idle among England's rich and poor alike as ominous signs of a degenerate nation.

Politics in England and America

ENGLAND'S BALANCED CONSTITUTION

Colonials were also of two minds about England's government. While they praised the English constitution as the basis of all liberties, they were alarmed by the actual workings of English politics. In theory, England's "**balanced constitution**" gave every order of society a voice in government. Whereas the Crown represented the monarchy and the House of Lords the aristocracy, the House of Commons represented the democracy, the people of England.

In fact, webs of patronage and outright bribery compromised the whole system. The monarch and his ministers had the power to appoint legions of bureaucrats to administer the growing state and empire. By the middle of the eighteenth century, almost half of all members of Parliament held such Crown offices or government contracts. Many had won their seats in corrupt elections, where the small electorate (perhaps a quarter of all adult males) were bought off with money or liquor.

COLONIAL GOVERNMENTS Americans liked to think that their colonial governments mirrored the ideal English constitution. Most colonies had a royal governor who represented the monarch in America and a bicameral (two-house) legislature made up of a lower house (the assembly) and an upper house (or council). The democratically elected assemblies, like the House of Commons, stood for popular interests, whereas the councils, some of which were elected and others appointed, more roughly approximated the House of Lords.

But these formal similarities masked real differences between English and colonial governments. On the face of it, royal governors had much more power than the English Crown. Unlike kings and queens, royal governors could veto laws passed by assemblies; they could dissolve those bodies at will; they could create courts and dismiss judges. However, governors who asserted their full powers quickly met opposition from their assemblies, who objected that such overwhelming authority endangered popular liberty. In any showdown with their assemblies, most royal governors had to give way, because they lacked the government offices and contracts that bought loyalty. The colonial legislatures possessed additional leverage, since all of them retained the sole authority to levy taxes.

At the same time, widespread ownership of land meant that more than half of the colonies' white adult male population could vote. The larger electorate made it more difficult to buy votes. The colonial electorate was also more watchful. Representatives had to reside in the districts that they served, and a few even received binding instructions from their constituents about how to vote.

Most Americans were as pleased with their inexpensive and representative colonial governments as they were

Coffeehouses such as this establishment in London were favorite gathering places for eighteenth-century Americans visiting Britain. Here merchants and mariners, ministers and students, lobbyists and tourists warmed themselves, read newspapers, and exchanged gossip about commerce, politics, and social life.

John Stuart, the third Earl of Bute (1713–1792), in the ceremonial robes of the House of Lords. The lavish style epitomizes the opulence of Britain's ruling class in the eighteenth century.

things. Those few Britons who thought about America at all believed that colonials resembled the "savage" Indians more than the "civilized" English. As a London acquaintance remarked to the Boston merchant Thomas Hancock, it was a pity Mrs. Hancock had to remain in Boston when he could "take her to England and make her happy with Christians."

The same indifference contributed to England's haphazard administration of its colonies. Aside from passing an occasional law to regulate trade, restrict manufacturing, or direct monetary policy, Parliament made no effort to assert its authority in America. Its members assumed that Parliament's sovereignty extended over the entire empire, and nothing had occurred to make them think otherwise.

BENEFITS OF BENIGN NEGLECT

For the colonies, this chaotic and inefficient system of colonial administration left them a great deal of freedom. Even England's regulation of trade rested lightly on the shoulders of most Americans. Southern planters were obliged to send their rice, indigo, and tobacco to Britain only, but they enjoyed favorable credit terms and knowledgeable marketing from English merchants. Colonials were prohibited from finishing iron products and exporting hats and textiles, but they had scant interest in developing domestic industries. Americans were required to import all manufactured goods through England, but by doing so, they acquired high-quality goods at low prices. At little sacrifice, most Americans obeyed imperial regulations. Only sugar, molasses, and tea were routinely smuggled.

Following this policy of **benign neglect,** the British Empire muddled on to the satisfaction of most people on both sides of the Atlantic. Economic growth and political **autonomy** allowed most Americans to like being English, despite their misgivings about their parent nation. The beauty of it was that Americans could be English in America, enjoying greater economic opportunity and political equality. If imperial arrangements had remained as they were in 1754, the empire might have muddled on indefinitely.

horrified by the conduct of politics in England. John Dickinson, a young Pennsylvanian training as a lawyer in London, was scandalized by a parliamentary election he witnessed in 1754. The king and his ministers had spent over 100,000 pounds sterling to buy support for their candidates, he wrote his father, and "if a man cannot be brought to vote as he is desired, he is made dead drunk and kept in that state, never heard of by his family and friends, till all is over and he can do no harm."

This tea caddy, owned by a Massachusetts colonial, was a new consumer luxury, as was the tea it held.

The Imperial System before 1760

Few Britons gave the colonists as much thought as the colonists gave them. It would be hard to overstate just how insignificant North America was in the English scheme of

REVIEW

What were the similarities, differences, and connections between England and America?

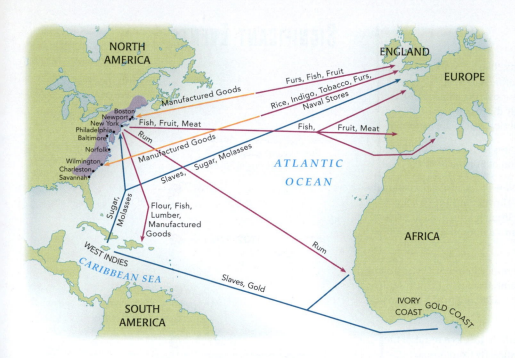

Commercial ties to Spain and Portugal, Africa, and the Caribbean sustained the growth of both seaports and commercial farming regions on the British North American mainland and enabled colonials to purchase an increasing volume of finished goods from England. The proceeds from exports in foodstuffs and lumber to the West Indies and trade in fish to Spain and Portugal enabled northern merchants and farmers to buy hardware and clothing from the mother country. Southern planters financed their consumption of English imports and their investment in African slaves with the profits from the sale of tobacco, rice, and indigo abroad.

CONCLUSION

THE WORLD AT LARGE

By the 1750s North America was changing, both within the British world and in relation to the international order. For decades, Europe's imperial wars found their way to America almost as an afterthought. Colonial officials, traders, land speculators, and would-be pioneers regularly seized on news of the latest European conflict as an excuse to attack their Spanish or French or British counterparts in the North American borderlands. The interests of kings and queens had to be served, of course. And yet it was easier to exploit war for local or personal purposes out on the far margins of Europe's empires. Eastern North America's native peoples likewise sought advantage in these interimperial flare-ups. But for them the stakes were higher. When chiefs joined in a fight for profit or revenge, or to please one or another colonial ally, they also put their own people at risk.

However the various players positioned themselves, they often found that the outcome of their struggles could be determined by men they would never see: well-heeled diplomats sipping drinks around mahogany tables in European capitals. Victories, defeats, territories won or lost—all this could be and often was undone in Paris, Madrid, or London, where negotiators casually agreed to ignore territorial gains and losses in the colonies and return everything as it was before the fighting broke out. The message was clear: great imperial struggles began in Europe and ended in Europe. America followed.

Though few recognized it in 1754, this older model was about to be swept away. That year marked the beginning of yet another imperial war, one begun not in Europe but in the American borderlands. Rather than following events, this time Indians proved decisive to the war's origins, course, and outcome. And rather than the conflict ending with a return to the status quo, this time war would produce changes greater than anyone could have anticipated. In waging the war and managing its aftermath, London would pursue policies that made it difficult—and ultimately impossible—for its American subjects to remain within the empire. ∞∞∞

Chapter Summary

During the eighteenth century, Spain, France, and Great Britain competed for power and influence in North America. Native peoples, too, played off these shifting alliances. British North Americans grew increasingly diverse, which made the prospect of any future colonial political union appear remote.

- Spain established mission systems in Texas and California, largely to preempt the expansion of European rivals.

- Low immigration compelled New France to seek sustainable alliances with Indian peoples throughout the Far North and the Mississippi drainage. French Louisiana grew very slowly and failed to develop into a booming plantation colony.

- Differences became more pronounced among whites because of the immigration of larger numbers of non-English settlers, the spread of settlement to the backcountry, and the growth of major seaports.

- The South became more embattled, too, as a result of the massive importation of slaves directly from Africa.

- Religious conflict among colonials was intensified by Enlightenment ideas and the first Great Awakening.

- Still, a majority of white colonials took pride in their common English ancestry.

Additional Reading

For a richly textured history of early Texas, see Juliana Barr, *Peace Came in the Form of a Woman* (2007). H. Ross Frank's *From Settler to Citizen* (2000) recovers the economic and social changes that came to New Mexico with peace in the late eighteenth century. Steven Hackel's *Children of Coyote, Missionaries of St. Francis* (2005) has set a new standard for scholarship on colonial California. For France in America, see *The People of New France* by Allan Greer (2000). Alan Taylor's *American Colonies* (2001) takes a sweeping, continental perspective. For women's rights in comparison, see Deborah A. Rosen, "Women and Property across Colonial America," *William and Mary Quarterly* 60: 2(2003), 355–382.

On ethnic and racial diversity, see Bernard Bailyn, *Voyagers to the West* (1986), and Peter Silver, *Our Savage Neighbors* (2007). Philip Morgan's *Slave Counterpoint* (1998) offers an overview of African American cultures in the early South. For mounting tensions in American seaports, consult Jill Lepore, *New York Burning* (2005), and Gary Nash, *The Urban Crucible* (1979).

Nancy Shoemaker, *A Strange Likeness* (2004), and James M. Merrell, *Into the American Woods* (1999), are two compelling accounts of how Indians and white Americans came to perceive one another as different peoples. For the expansion of colonial settlement into the backcountry, begin with Eric Hinderaker and Peter C. Mancall, *At the Edge of Empire* (2003). On religion in eighteenth-century society, see Patricia Bonomi, *Under the Cope of Heaven* (1986), and George Marsden, *Jonathan Edwards* (2003).

For a fuller list of readings, see the Bibliography at www.mhhe.com/eh8e.

Significant Events

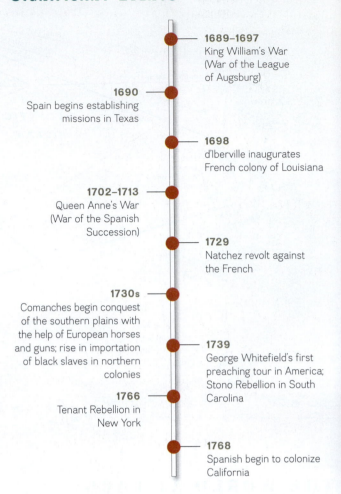

1689–1697
King William's War (War of the League of Augsburg)

1690
Spain begins establishing missions in Texas

1698
d'Iberville inaugurates French colony of Louisiana

1702–1713
Queen Anne's War (War of the Spanish Succession)

1729
Natchez revolt against the French

1730s
Comanches begin conquest of the southern plains with the help of European horses and guns; rise in importation of black slaves in northern colonies

1739
George Whitefield's first preaching tour in America; Stono Rebellion in South Carolina

1766
Tenant Rebellion in New York

1768
Spanish begin to colonize California

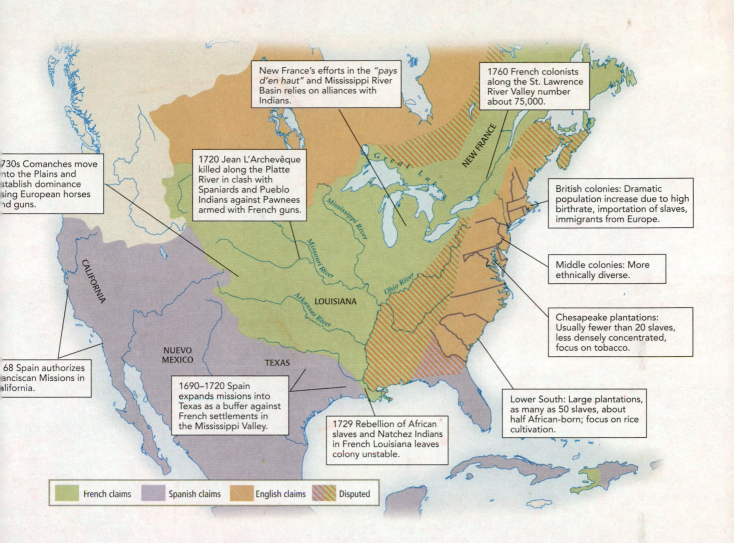

New France's efforts in the *"pays d'en haut"* and Mississippi River Basin relies on alliances with Indians.

1760 French colonists along the St. Lawrence River Valley number about 75,000.

1720 Jean L'Archevêque killed along the Platte River in clash with Spaniards and Pueblo Indians against Pawnees armed with French guns.

730s Comanches move nto the Plains and stablish dominance sing European horses nd guns.

British colonies: Dramatic population increase due to high birthrate, importation of slaves, immigrants from Europe.

Middle colonies: More ethnically diverse.

Chesapeake plantations: Usually fewer than 20 slaves, less densely concentrated, focus on tobacco.

68 Spain authorizes anciscan Missions in alifornia.

1690–1720 Spain expands missions into Texas as a buffer against French settlements in the Mississippi Valley.

1729 Rebellion of African slaves and Natchez Indians in French Louisiana leaves colony unstable.

Lower South: Large plantations, as many as 50 slaves, about half African-born; focus on rice cultivation.

CALIFORNIA

NUEVO MEXICO

TEXAS

LOUISIANA

NEW FRANCE

Great Lakes

Mississippi River

Missouri River

Ohio River

Arkansas River

French claims   Spanish claims   English claims   Disputed

George Washington was only 22 when he led 200 militiamen and a party of Indians to confront French forces in the Ohio Country in the spring of 1754. He came upon a French detachment at what is now called Jumonville Glen, shown in this 2007 photograph. By the time the encounter had ended, Washington's smart Virginia militia uniform was badly worn and most of his troops, he noted, were "almost naked, and scarcely a man has either Shoes, Stockings, or Hat."

CHAPTER 6

Imperial Triumph, Imperial Crisis

1754–1776

What's to Come

∞∞∞ AN AMERICAN STORY ∞∞∞

GEORGE WASHINGTON AND THE HALF KING

Everyone seemed to want something from the Ohio Country. And when so many rivals—assertive, anxious, and aggressive—assembled in one location, it was a situation made for disaster. Young George Washington, deep in the forests of the Ohio Country, learned this lesson in the spring of 1754.

The region north of the Ohio River had been a no-man's-land for decades following the Beaver Wars (Chapter 4). Though the mighty Iroquois had no interest in occupying the territory, they claimed sovereignty over it into the 1750s by right of conquest. By then, however, Delawares, Shawnees, Mingos, and other native peoples had established villages in the territory. If they looked to the Iroquois it was for advice, not orders. Who, then, could claim dominion over the Ohio Country?

European rivalries compounded these uncertainties. By the 1750s both Britain and France saw the lands as vital to their strategic interests. Pennsylvania traders had wandered the territory for years, their reports drawing the interest of land speculators. The Ohio Country boasted forests of white oak, plentiful game, and grassy meadows, ideally suited for farming. Chunks of black coal thrust from the ground, hinting at mineral riches. Wealthy Virginians and Pennsylvanians envisioned colonies in the Ohio Country—schemes London happily encouraged in hopes of weakening New France. In 1745 the Virginia House of Burgesses granted 300,000 acres of land to a newly formed enterprise called the Ohio Company. For their part, the French in Quebec relied on the Ohio lands as a buffer between their own relatively small settlements and the populous British settlements to the east. Anxious, the French built new forts and shored up their Indian alliances.

The British countered. In 1754 Virginia's governor (a major investor in the Ohio Company) ordered 200 militiamen under 22-year-old Lieutenant Colonel George Washington (another investor) to assert British interests in the Ohio Country. Washington's militia marched west with the help of several Indians under the "Half King" Tanaghrisson, the Iroquois representative for the Ohio Country. Tanaghrisson had grown up near the important forks of the Ohio River (present-day Pittsburgh)

Indians and Europeans negotiate in the Ohio Country, an area coveted by the English, French, Delawares, Shawnees, and Mingos.

and advised the British to build a "strong house" at this key position. He had even laid down the fort's first log in a ceremony. Washington, who was intelligent, able, and disciplined but inexperienced and badly out of his depth, soon discovered how little control he had over the circumstances—or even over his own expedition.

To begin with, the French had beaten the Virginians to the forks of the Ohio, where they erected Fort Duquesne. On hearing of the approaching British militia, the French commander there dispatched 35 men under an ensign named Jumonville to advise Washington to withdraw. The Virginians learned of the approaching party and marched to intercept it, following Tanaghrisson's lead, "in a heavy rain and a night as dark as pitch," as Washington recalled. At dawn, just as the French were crawling out from under their bark lean-tos to make breakfast, the British and their Indian companions opened fire. Badly wounded along with nearly half of his men, the ensign cried out to stop shooting, that he had come only to talk. Once Washington had gotten control of his force, Jumonville handed him a letter from the French commander. But it was in French,

which Washington did not read. He turned to fetch his translator. Just then Tanaghrisson stepped in front of the wounded Jumonville. The grave Iroquois representative was older and far more experienced than Washington, and he had his own agenda. Unhappy with the emboldened French posture in the region and convinced that Iroquois interests would be best served if the French and British were at each other's throats, he did something neither Washington nor his French counterpart could have possibly expected. "You're not dead yet, my father," he told Jumonville; and then sank a hatchet into the officer's head, ripped his skull apart, and pulled out his brains. Washington staggered back dumbstruck as Tanaghrisson's Indians set about killing the other wounded soldiers.

This was not how it was supposed to happen. Washington hastily retreated some way, threw up a makeshift structure, aptly named "Fort Necessity," and waited for reinforcements from Virginia. About a month later a formidable French force (led by Jumonville's grieving brother) laid siege and quickly compelled Washington's surrender. The Virginians returned home in defeat, bearing the news that the Shawnees, Delawares, and Mingos had either sided with the French or refused to fight at all. "The chief part" of his men, Washington wrote in dismay, "are almost naked, and scarcely a man has either Shoes, Stockings or Hat." It was an ignominious beginning to a long, exhausting war that would eventually spread across the entire globe. ∞∞∞

THE SEVEN YEARS' WAR

THE SEVEN YEARS' WAR, WHICH actually lasted nine years, pitted Britain and its ally, Prussia, against France, in league with Austria and Spain. The conflict raged from 1754 until 1763 and deserves to be called the first global war. Because the contending powers had colonial possessions and economic interests around the world, the fight spanned the continent of Europe, the coast of West Africa, India, the Philippines, the Caribbean, and North America. The spark that started this worldwide conflagration came from the Ohio Country.

Britain and France had come to blows in the backcountry before. And Indian peoples had long sought to profit from their interimperial rivalry and turn it to their own ends. But for the first time, bloodshed in the forests of North America would lead Europe into war, rather than the other way around. And Washington's misadventure at Fort Necessity set the pattern for the early years of the conflict more broadly, years marked by British missteps and British defeats.

Years of Defeat

Washington's surrender only stiffened Britain's resolve to assert its claims to the Ohio Country: hence its decision to send two divisions under General Braddock to wrest the region from France. France responded by sending the equivalent of eight divisions to Canada. There was therefore great anticipation surrounding Braddock's campaign. Unfortunately for the English, General Braddock had all but sealed his doom before even marching into the backcountry. Ignoring American advisers who insisted that Indian alliances would be key to victory, Braddock alienated native leaders and refused to acknowledge their claims to land. "The English should inhabit and inherit the land . . . no savage should inherit the land," he insisted. In 1755 Braddock's divisions pushed into the Ohio Country with fewer than 10 Indians along. After five weeks of agonizing progress through dense woods and over rough terrain, the troops were ambushed by French and Indian sharpshooters firing into the British column from the cover of trees. As his men fell around him, Braddock calmly rode back and forth on horseback and ordered the troops to remain or get back in formation and return fire as they had been trained. But none had been trained for this kind of fighting, and gathering together only made them easier to shoot. The smoke and gunfire, the screams of dying men and horses, and—perhaps most memorably—the haunting cries of the attacking Indians gradually overcame British discipline. Three hours into the battle Braddock still sat atop his horse, as brave as he was unimaginative, yelling at his men to fight as if they were on a European battlefield. Finally, the general lurched up in his saddle and collapsed, a musket ball buried deep in his back. The British troops still able to walk or run fled the scene.

The monumental defeat sent shock waves throughout the empire, emboldened the French, and convinced many wavering Indian peoples that the French were the people to back. Raiding parties began striking backcountry settlements from New York to Virginia, and terrified refugees fled east.

ALBANY PLAN OF UNION — Britain's war went from bad to worse in North America. British colonists generally saw the French and their Indian allies as a common threat but found cooperation among colonies elusive. At the start of the war, representatives from throughout the colonies came to the so-called Albany Congress, designed in part to repair the "Covenant Chain," the long-standing alliance between Britain and the Iroquois that had been badly damaged by British missteps and French victories in the Ohio Country. More broadly, Benjamin Franklin presented the other colonial delegates with a plan for colonial cooperation, in which a federal council made up of representatives from each colony would assume responsibility for a united colonial defense. The Albany delegates were alarmed enough by the wavering Iroquois and the threatening French to accept the idea. But when they brought the proposal home to their respective legislatures, not a single one approved the Albany Plan of Union. "Everyone cries, a union is necessary," Franklin complained, "but when they come to the manner and form of the union, their weak noodles are perfectly distracted."

London did little to encourage collective self-sacrifice. When England and France formally declared war in May 1756, John Campbell, the Earl of Loudoun, took command of the North American theater. American soldiers and colonial assemblies alike despised Lord Loudoun. They balked at his efforts to take command over colonial troops and dragged their heels at his high-handed demands for men and supplies. Meanwhile, the French appointed an effective new commanding general of their forces in Canada, Louis Joseph, the marquis de Montcalm. Montcalm drove southward, capturing key British forts and threatening the security of both New York and New England.

 THE WAR WIDENS — France decided to press its advantage in Europe as well. In addition to threatening England itself, French ships began attacking British holdings throughout the Mediterranean. Meanwhile, the complex system of alliances that was supposed to keep continental Europe at peace began to fail. In August of 1756 Prussia, an English ally, invaded Austria, a French ally. France went to Austria's aid and Prussia suddenly found itself on the defensive, begging London for salvation. The war seemed to be spreading in all directions, and none of the changes seemed to bode well for the British Empire.

A Shift in Policy

WILLIAM PITT TURNS THE TIDE — British fortunes rebounded only when the veteran English politician William Pitt came out of retirement to direct the war.

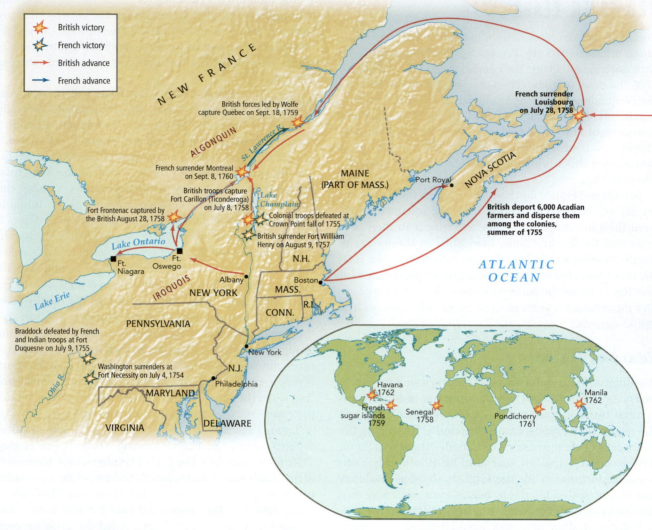

THE SEVEN YEARS' WAR

*After Washington's surrender and Braddock's defeat in the Pennsylvania backcountry, the British and French waged their final contest for supremacy in North America in northern New York and Canada. But the rivalry for empire between France and Britain was worldwide, with naval superiority providing the needed edge to Britain. The British navy isolated French forces in India, winning a victory at Pondicherry, while English offensives captured the French sugar islands in the Caribbean and French trading posts along the West African coast. When Spain entered the war on the side of France, British fleets captured both Havana and the strategic port of Manila in the Philippines. **Which victory sealed the British triumph over New France? Why was the win geographically important?***

Pitt was an odd character. Subject to bouts of depression and loathed for his opportunism and egotism, he was nonetheless buoyed by a strong sense of destiny—his own and that of England. He believed Great Britain must seize the world's trade, because trade meant wealth and wealth meant power. France seemed to him the greatest obstacle to this British destiny—and Pitt returned to the political fray charged with energy. "I know that I can save this country," he declared with typical confidence, "and that no one else can."

Pitt's strategy was bold. He would leave the fighting in Europe to the Prussians but support them with massive infusions of cash with which they could buy supplies and recruit men. France was strongest in Europe, he reasoned, so Britain ought to focus its military energies elsewhere. Better to attack France around the world—in the Caribbean, in West Africa, and in the Indian Ocean. Most especially, Pitt would attack them in North America. He audaciously pledged to drive France out of the continent altogether. To do so he would have to convince the colonists who had been alienated by Braddock's arrogance and Loudoun's harsh policies that they would be treated as equals. Pitt recalled Loudoun, put limits on the powers enjoyed by his successor, pledged to respect the officers in colonial militias, and, crucially, promised that London—not the colonies—would bear the financial burden of the war.

| John Campbell | William Pitt

INDIANS AND THE WAR EFFORT

Last but certainly not least, the new government acknowledged the centrality of Indians to the war effort. The officers Pitt sent to execute the new approach listened to colonial Indian agents and go-betweens, authorized new, high-level conferences, and approved the distribution of presents to key leaders. These conciliatory gestures and more accommodating policies were well timed, because by then, the Indian peoples of the Ohio Country and the *pays d'en haut* had increasingly come to question the French alliance.

Though French authorities often took Indians more seriously than their English counterparts, they, too, struggled to reconcile cultural difference. In the aftermath of joint victories, for example, French officers sometimes felt obliged by European military protocol to deny their Indian allies customary war spoils—captives, plunder, and scalps. Disgruntled native warriors generally took them anyway and often refused to fight for France again. More critical than even such cultural differences, the economic toll of the war damaged French-Indian alliances. By 1757 Britain's unsurpassed navy had instituted a formidable blockade on the St. Lawrence that cut off supplies to Canada. Without arms, ammunition, and metal goods, French authorities found it more and more difficult to maintain their Indian alliances. More and more withdrew from the conflict or sided with Britain.

Years of Victory

The reforms galvanized the colonies. Most British North Americans were proud to be part of the empire and welcomed the chance to help fight for it so long as they would be treated as equals. With Pitt's reforms in place, the tide of the war finally began to turn. In July of 1758 the British gained control of the St. Lawrence River when the French fortress at Louisbourg fell before the combined force of the Royal Navy and British and colonial troops. In August a force of New Englanders strangled France's frontier defenses by capturing Fort Frontenac, thereby isolating French forts lining the Great Lakes and the Ohio valley. More and more Indians, seeing the French routed from the interior, switched their allegiance to the English.

WOLFE AND MONTCALM BATTLE FOR QUEBEC

The British succeeded even more brilliantly in 1759. In Canada, Brigadier General James Wolfe gambled on a daring stratagem and won Quebec from Montcalm. Under the cover of darkness, naval squadrons landed Wolfe's men beneath the city's steep bluffs, where they scaled the heights to a plateau known as the Plains of Abraham. Montcalm might have won by holding out behind the walls of his fortress and awaiting reinforcements. Instead, he matched Wolfe's recklessness and offered battle. Five days later both Wolfe and Montcalm lay dead, along with 1,400 French soldiers and 600 British and American troops. Quebec had fallen to the British. A year later the French surrender of Montreal ended the imperial war in North America, although it continued elsewhere around the world for another two years.

 TREATY OF PARIS

The Treaty of Paris, signed in February 1763, ended the French presence on the continent of North America. The terms confirmed British title to all French territory east of the Mississippi. Spain had foolishly entered the war on France's side in 1762 and quickly lost Havana to British warships. The treaty restored Cuba to Spain, but at a high price: the Spanish relinquished Florida to Britain. With France driven from the continent, something had to be done with the vast and ill-defined territory of Louisiana, west of the Mississippi. Spain did not want the trouble and expense of administering this sprawling region, but it did not want Britain to have it. Somewhat reluctantly, then, Spain accepted nominal dominion over all land west of the great river, as well as the port of New Orleans, in the separate Treaty of San Ildefonso. In addition to its North America spoils, Britain won several Caribbean islands in the war, as well as Senegal in West Africa.

After generations of inconclusive imperial wars, British North Americans found the victory almost impossibly grand. Towns up and down the Atlantic coast glowed bright with celebratory bonfires and rang with the sounds of clanking tankards and jolly song. How good it was to be British!

Postwar Expectations

Grand expectations came hot on the heels of joyful celebration. The end of the war, Americans felt sure, meant the end of high taxes. The terms of the peace, they were confident, meant that the fertile lands of the Ohio valley would be thrown open to English settlement. The prosperity of the war years alone made for a mood of optimism. British military spending and William Pitt's subsidies had made money for farmers, merchants, artisans, and anyone else who had anything to do with supplying the army or navy. Colonials also took pride in their contributions of troops and money to the winning of the war. In view of

that support, Americans expected to be given more consideration within the British Empire. Now, as one anonymous pamphleteer put it, Americans would "not be thought presumptuous, if they consider[ed] themselves upon an equal footing" with English in the parent country.

ENGLISH RESENTMENTS

But most imperial officials in America thought that if Americans took pride in being English, they had done a poor job of showing it. British statesmen grumbled that colonial assemblies had been tightfisted when it came to supplying the army. British commanders charged that colonial troops had been lily-livered when it came to fighting the French. Such accusations were unjust, but they stuck in the minds of many Britons at home. The nation had accumulated a huge debt that would saddle it with high taxes for years to come. To make matters worse, some Britons suspected that, with the French removed from North America, the colonies would move toward independence. As early as 1755 Josiah Tucker, a respected English economist, had warned that "to drive the French out of all North America would be the most fatal step we could take."

Americans in 1763 were not, in truth, revolutionaries in the making. They were loyal British subjects in the flush of postwar patriotism. Americans in 1763, deeply divided,

| The British navy bombarded Quebec, reducing many of the city's buildings to smoldering ruins. The devastation presaged the end of France's empire in North America.

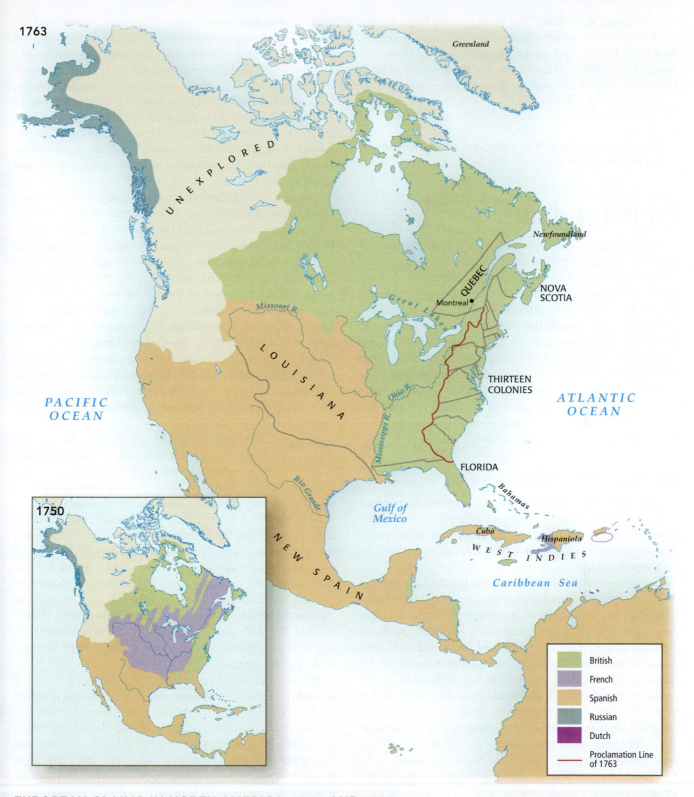

1763

Greenland

U N E X P L O R E D

Newfoundland

QUEBEC

Montreal •

NOVA SCOTIA

L O U I S I A N A

Missouri R.

Great Lakes

THIRTEEN COLONIES

Ohio R.

Mississippi R.

PACIFIC OCEAN

ATLANTIC OCEAN

FLORIDA

Rio Grande

N E W   S P A I N

Gulf of Mexico

Bahamas

Cuba

Hispaniola

W E S T   I N D I E S

Caribbean Sea

1750

	British
	French
	Spanish
	Russian
	Dutch
	Proclamation Line of 1763

EUROPEAN CLAIMS IN NORTH AMERICA, 1750 AND 1763

The British victory in the Seven Years' War secured Great Britain's title to a large portion of present-day United States and Canada. Colonials hoped to settle the newly won territory, but politicians in London intended to restrict westward movement with the Proclamation of 1763.

were not even "Americans." But most postwar English colonials did expect to enjoy a more equal status in the empire. And most Britons had no inclination to accord them that equality. The differing expectations of the colonies' place in the empire poised the postwar generation for crisis.

 **REVIEW**

What started the Seven Years' War, and how did Britain emerge victorious?

THE IMPERIAL CRISIS

IT WAS COMMON SENSE. Great Britain had waged a costly war to secure its empire in America; now it needed to consolidate those gains. The empire's North American territory needed to be protected, its administration tightened, and its colonies made as profitable as possible to the parent nation. In other words, the empire needed to be centralized. That conclusion dictated Britain's decision to leave a standing army of several thousand troops in America after the Seven Years' War. And, of course, armies needed to be paid for; that would mean taxes. That the colonists, who benefited most from the great victory, ought to pull out their purses for king and country—well, Britain's political leaders thought that, too, was common sense.

Pontiac's Rebellion

British authorities justified the army's continued presence in part by pointing to the various foreign peoples that the Crown now had to administer. The army must be prepared to police French colonists in Canada, Spaniards in Florida, and, especially, dozens of native peoples west of the Appalachians. General Jeffery Amherst, the top British officer in North America, believed Indian troubles could be avoided if military and civil authorities simply projected strength. Now that French power had been expelled, Amherst thought, Britain need not purchase Indian friendship with presents, and subsidize trade, and sponsor tiresome diplomatic ceremonies. All this was to cease. Knowledgeable colonists saw too much of Edward Braddock in all of this. When they insisted that presents, favorable trade, and diplomacy were the indispensable elements of Indian relations, Amherst would have none of it. "When men of what race soever behave ill," the general insisted, "they must be punished but not bribed." Indians had to learn that the English now were masters of the land.

NEOLIN   Britain's new attitude of triumph provoked great anxiety within Indian communities that had troubles enough to contend with. Many had lost men in the war, crops had been destroyed or had failed, and whole villages and towns had been put to the torch. British traders, now untroubled by French competition, bartered eagerly but charged far more for their goods than previously. Finally, the end of the war brought a surge of speculators and colonists eager to claim land beyond the mountains. These interlocked crises prompted calls for a return to tradition—for a revival that would empower resistance movements across tribal lines. Such was the message of a Delaware holy man named Neolin, who told followers he spoke for God, or the Master of Life. The Master of Life commanded his Indian children to "drive [the British] out, make war on them. I do not love them at all; they know me not, and are my enemies. Send them back to the lands I have created for them and let them stay there."

Pontiac, a charismatic and tactically gifted Ottawa chief, embraced Neolin's message of renaissance and rebellion. In the summer of 1763 he organized attacks against British forts. Shawnees, Mingos, Potawatomis, Wyandots, and other Indian peoples in the Ohio Country, or the *pays d'en haut,* working with Pontiac or independently, captured every British fort west of Detroit by early July. Colonial settlements in the backcountry came under attack from Pennsylvania to Virginia, leaving hundreds of colonists dead and hundreds more fleeing east. Enraged and determined to assert British rule, Amherst organized troops to march west and attack Indian forces and native villages. He also authorized the commander at Fort Pitt to give Indians blankets from the forts' infirmary, where several men had been stricken with smallpox.

THE PAXTON Hatreds mounted on all sides. In western
BOYS   Pennsylvania, where Indian raids had taken
            an especially grim toll, a number of Scots-Irishmen calling themselves the "Paxton Boys" set out to purge the colony of Indians altogether. In December of 1763 they burst into a small village of Christian Indians, killed the six people they found there, and burned it to the ground. Fourteen others who had been absent fled to the town of Lancaster. Learning that Lancaster's officials had put the survivors into protective custody, the Paxton Boys organized a mob, forced their way into the safe house, and massacred all 14 men, women, and children with broadswords. Colonists and natives alike were increasingly willing to simplify difference and see all "Indians" or all "whites" as despicable enemies.

When officials in London learned of Pontiac's Rebellion and all the violence it occasioned, they attributed it to bad leadership and immediately replaced Amherst. More important, the Crown issued the Proclamation of 1763, which transformed colonial policy in critical ways. Presents and respectful diplomacy were to resume, and the Crown put two Indian superintendents in place (one in South Carolina and one in New York) to help oversee good relations. Most critical, colonial settlement west of the Appalachians was to cease immediately. The so-called proclamation line designated all western territories as Indian territory and strictly off limits to colonization. (Quebec and Florida were the exceptions, divided into eastern and western halves, for colonials and Indians.) Restricting westward movement might ease Indian fears, the British hoped, and so stave off future conflicts.

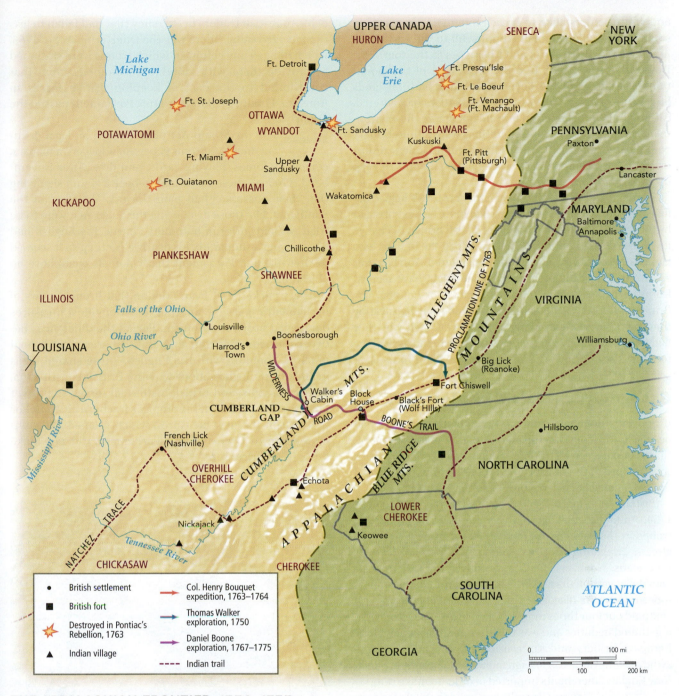

THE APPALACHIAN FRONTIER, 1750–1775

Made bold by the presence of British forts and soldiers, land-hungry colonials spilled into the West through the Cumberland Gap, a notch in the chain of mountains stretching the length of the North American interior. Only Indians and some white hunters knew of the Cumberland Gap before it was scouted in 1750 by Dr. Thomas Walker and a party of Virginians on behalf of a company of land speculators. In 1763 Indians led by Pontiac seized eight British forts before troops under Colonel Henry Bouquet stopped the offensive at Bushy Run, Pennsylvania. In 1775 Daniel Boone took the first large party of pioneers through the Cumberland Gap and established a fort at Boonesborough in present-day Kentucky.

THE PROCLAMATION VS. THE ENVIRONMENT ON THE GROUND

In drawing their proclamation line, British officials in London adopted what they thought would be a commonsense boundary rooted in the environment on the ground. The Appalachian Mountains, after all, provided a natural barrier, and the line forbidding settlement could be defined in reference to physical features: "any lands beyond the heads or sources of any of the rivers which fall into the Atlantic Ocean from the west or northwest." Yet the real environment was more ambiguous and diverse. Rivers (and their valleys) often acted as pathways into the interior, beckoning Indians and white settlers alike to breach mountain "barriers." In some areas, Indians remained powerful to the east of the Appalachians (the Creeks and Cherokees to the south, the Iroquois to the north). In other areas west of the mountains, the chaos of the Seven Years' War had left lands largely unoccupied, into which white settlers had entered. Although the proclamation line did not ignore the environment on the ground, actual conditions were infinitely more complicated, and the British Indian commissioners almost immediately began redrawing the line in an effort to keep up with the realities.

Amherst's recall and the conciliatory measures helped defuse the conflict, and the violence had more or less subsided by the fall of 1764. Insofar as it helped push Britain to change its Indian policy, Pontiac's Rebellion helped the Indians who launched it. But the war's animosities endured. And however sensible and just the proclamation line might have seemed from the perspective of the Ohio Country or London, few British colonists would see it as anything but betrayal by their own government. Many of them wondered why they had fought and sacrificed in the war against France, if all the territory they helped win was to be set aside for Indians.

George Grenville's New Measures

If Pontiac's Rebellion and the Proclamation of 1763 had been the only postwar disappointments colonists faced, that would have been trouble enough. But George Grenville, the first lord of the treasury, had yet to confront the dismal financial consequences of the Seven Years' War.

Britain's national debt had doubled in the decade after 1754. Adding to that burden was the drain of supporting troops in the colonies. As matters stood, heavy taxes were already triggering protests among hard-pressed Britons. Americans, in contrast, paid comparatively low taxes to their colonial governments and little in trade duties to the empire. Indeed, Grenville discovered that the colonial customs service paid out four times more in salaries to its collectors than it gathered in duties and was thereby operating at a net loss. Rampant bribery and tax evasion allowed merchants to avoid existing duties on foreign molasses, for example, which New England merchants imported in order to make rum.

SUGAR ACT George Grenville reasoned that if Americans could pay out a little under the table to protect an illegal trade, they would willingly pay a little more to go legitimate. Parliament agreed. In April 1764 it passed the Revenue Act, commonly called the Sugar Act. This **tariff** actually lowered the duty on foreign molasses from six to three pence a gallon. This time, however, the tax would be scrupulously collected, ships would be tightly monitored for compliance, and violators would be tried in admiralty courts, far harsher than typical colonial courts.

CURRENCY AND QUARTERING ACTS Grenville made other, similar proposals, all approved by Parliament. There was the Currency Act of 1764, which prohibited the colonies from making their paper money legal tender. That prevented Americans from paying their debts to British traders in currency that had fallen to less than its face value. There was the Quartering Act of 1765, which obliged any colony in which troops were stationed to provide them with suitable accommodations. That contributed to the cost of keeping British forces in America. Finally, in March of 1765, Parliament passed the Stamp Act.

STAMP ACT The Stamp Act placed **taxes** on legal documents, customs papers, newspapers, almanacs, college diplomas, playing cards, and dice. After November 1, 1765, all these items had to bear a stamp signifying that their possessor had paid the tax. Violators of the Stamp Act, like those disobeying the Sugar Act, were to be tried without juries in admiralty courts. The English had been paying a similar tax for nearly a century, so it seemed to Grenville and Parliament that colonials could have no objections.

Every packet boat from London that brought news of Parliament's passing another of Grenville's measures dampened postwar optimism. For all the differences between the colonies and England, Americans still held much in common with the English. Those shared ideas included firm beliefs about why the British constitution, British customs, and British history all served to protect liberty and the rights of the empire's freeborn citizens. For that reason the new measures, which seemed like common sense to Grenville and Parliament, did not make sense to Americans.

Visual imagery brought home the urgency of resistance to Americans who could not read political pamphlets or radical newspapers. This detail from an engraving by Paul Revere includes a liberty tree, from which is hung an effigy of the Boston stamp distributor, and a beast busily destroying the Magna Carta while trampling American colonials. The date on the tree, August 14, 1765, marked the first Stamp Act riot in Boston.

The Beginning of Colonial Resistance

LOCKE ON PROPERTY AND LIBERTY

Like other Britons, colonials in America accepted a maxim laid down by the English philosopher John Locke: property guaranteed liberty. Property, in this view, was not merely real estate, or wealth, or material possessions. It was the source of strength for every individual, providing the freedom to think and act independently. Protecting the individual's right to own property was the main responsibility of government, because if personal property was not sacred, then neither was personal liberty.

It followed from this close connection between property, power, and liberty that no people should be taxed without consenting—either personally or through elected representatives. The power to tax was the power to destroy by depriving a person of property. Yet both the Sugar Act and the Stamp Act were taxes passed by members of Parliament, none of whom had been elected by colonials.

Like the English, colonials also prized the right of trial by jury as one of their basic constitutional liberties. Yet both the Sugar Act and the Stamp Act would prosecute offenders in the admiralty courts, not in local courts, thus depriving colonials of the freedom claimed by all other English men and women.

The concern for protecting individual liberties was only one of the convictions shaping the colonies' response to Britain's new policies. Equally important was their deep suspicion of power itself, a preoccupation that colonials shared with a minority of radical English thinkers. These radicals were known by a variety of names: the Country Party, the Commonwealthmen, and the **Opposition.** They drew their inspiration from the ancient tradition of classical **republicanism,** which held that representative government safeguarded liberty more reliably than either monarchy or oligarchy did. Underlying that judgment was the belief that human beings were driven by passion and insatiable ambition. One person (a monarch), or even a few people (an oligarchy), could not be entrusted with governing, because they would inevitably become corrupted by power and turn into despots. Even in representative governments, the people were obliged to watch those in power at all times. The price of liberty was eternal vigilance.

The Opposition believed that the people of England were not watching their rulers closely enough. During the first half of the eighteenth century, they argued, the entire executive branch of England's government—monarchs and their ministers—had been corrupted by their appetite for power. Proof of their ambition was the executive bureaucracy of civil officials and standing armies that steadily grew larger, interfered more with citizens' lives, and drained increasing amounts of money from taxpayers. Even more alarming, in the Opposition's view, the executive branch's bribery of members of Parliament was corrupting the representative branch of England's government. They warned that a sinister conspiracy originating in the executive branch of government threatened English liberty.

Opposition thinkers commanded little attention in England, where they were dismissed as a discontented radical fringe. But they were revered by political leaders in the American colonies. The Opposition's view of politics confirmed colonial anxieties about England, doubts that ran deeper after 1763. Parliament's attempt to tax the colonies and the quartering of a standing army on the frontier confirmed all too well the Opposition's description of how powerful rulers turned themselves into tyrants and reduced the people whom they ruled to slaves. In sum, Grenville's new measures led some colonials to suspect that ambitious men ruling England might be conspiring against American liberties.

IMPACT OF POSTWAR RECESSION

Britain's attempt to raise revenue after 1763 was a disaster of timing, not just psychologically but also economically. By then, the colonies were in the throes of a recession. The boom produced in America by government spending during the war had collapsed once subsidies were withdrawn. Colonial merchants were left with stocks full of imported goods gathering dust on their shelves. Farmers lost the brisk and profitable market of the army.

Colonial response to the Sugar Act reflected the painful postwar readjustments. New England merchants led the opposition, objecting to the Sugar Act principally on economic grounds. But with the passage of the Stamp Act, the terms of the imperial debate widened. The Stamp Act hit all colonials, not just New England merchants. It took money from the pockets of anyone who made a will, filed a deed, traded out of a colonial port, bought a newspaper, consulted an almanac, graduated from college, took a chance at dice, or played cards. More important, the Stamp Act served notice that Parliament claimed the authority to tax the colonies directly and for the sole purpose of raising revenue.

Riots and Resolves

That unprecedented assertion provoked an unprecedented development: the first display of colonial unity. During the spring and summer of 1765 American assemblies passed resolves denying that Parliament could tax the colonies. The right to tax Americans belonged to colonial assemblies alone, they argued, by the law of nature and by the liberties guaranteed in colonial charters and in the British constitution.

PATRICK HENRY'S RESOLVES

Virginia's assembly, the House of Burgesses, took the lead in protesting the Stamp Act, prodded by Patrick Henry. Just 29 years old in 1765, Henry had tried his hand at planting in western Virginia before recognizing his real talent—demagoguery. Blessed with the eloquence of an evangelical preacher, the dashing charm of a southern gentleman, and a mind uncluttered by much learning, Henry parlayed his popularity as a smooth-talking lawyer into a place among the Burgesses. He took his seat just 10 days before introducing the Virginia Resolves against the Stamp Act.

The Burgesses passed Henry's resolutions upholding their exclusive right to tax Virginians. They stopped short of adopting those resolves that called for outright resistance. When news of Virginia's stand spread to the rest of the colonies, other assemblies followed suit, affirming that the sole right to tax Americans resided in their elected representatives. But some colonial newspapers deliberately printed a different story—that the Burgesses had approved all of Henry's resolves, including one that sanctioned disobedience to any parliamentary tax. That prompted a few assemblies to endorse resistance. In October 1765, delegates from nine colonies convened in New York, where they prepared a joint statement of the American position and petitioned the king and Parliament to repeal both the Sugar Act and the Stamp Act.

Meanwhile, colonial leaders turned to the press to arouse popular opposition to the Stamp Act. Disposed by the writings of the English Opposition to think of politics in conspiratorial terms, they warned that Grenville and the king's other ministers schemed to deprive the colonies of their liberties by unlawfully taxing their property. The Stamp Act was only the first step in a sinister plan to enslave Americans.

Whether or not fears of a dark conspiracy haunted most colonials in 1765, many resisted the Stamp Act. The merchants of Boston, New York, and Philadelphia agreed to stop importing English goods in order to pressure British traders to lobby for repeal. In every colony, organizations emerged to ensure that the Stamp Act, if not repealed, would never be enforced.

SONS OF LIBERTY The new resistance groups, which styled themselves the "Sons of Liberty," consisted of traders, lawyers, and prosperous artisans. With great success, they organized the lower classes of seaports in opposition to the Stamp Act. The sailors, dockworkers, poor artisans, apprentices, and servants who poured into the streets resembled mobs that had been organized from time to time earlier in the century. Previous riots against houses of prostitution, merchants who hoarded goods, or supporters of smallpox inoculation had not been spontaneous, uncontrolled outbursts. Crowds chose their targets and their tactics carefully and then carried out the communal will with little violence.

In every colonial city, the mobs of 1765 burnt the stamp distributors in effigy, insulted them on the streets, demolished their offices, and attacked their homes. One hot night in August 1765 a mob went further than the Sons of Liberty

This idealized likeness of Patrick Henry, by the American artist Thomas Sully, conveys the subject's intensity. Henry's eloquence and passion as an orator made a vivid impression on his contemporaries.

had planned. They all but leveled the stately mansion of Thomas Hutchinson, the unpopular lieutenant governor of Massachusetts and the brother-in-law of the colony's stamp distributor. The destruction stunned Bostonians, especially the Sons of Liberty, who resisted Britain in the name of protecting private property. Thereafter they took care to keep crowds under tighter control. By the first of November, the day that the Stamp Act took effect, most of the stamp distributors had resigned.

Repeal of the Stamp Act

Meanwhile, the repeal of the Stamp Act was already in the works back in England. The man who came—unintentionally—to America's relief was George III. The young king was a good man, industrious and devoted to the empire, but he was also immature and not particularly bright. Insecurity made him an irksome master, and he ran through ministers rapidly. By the end of 1765 George had replaced Grenville with a new first minister, the Marquis of Rockingham. Rockingham had opposed the Stamp Act from the outset, and he had no desire to enforce it. He received support from London merchants, who were beginning to feel the pinch of the American nonimportation campaign, and secured repeal of the Stamp Act in March 1766.

VIRTUAL VS. ACTUAL The Stamp Act controversy demonstrated to colonials how similar in political outlook they were to one another and how different they were from the British. Americans found that they shared the same assumptions about the meaning of representation. To counter colonial objections to the Stamp Act, Grenville and his supporters had claimed that Americans *were* represented in Parliament, even though they had elected none of its members. Americans were virtually represented, Grenville insisted, for each member of Parliament stood for the interests of the whole empire, not just those of the particular constituency that had elected him.

Colonials could see no virtue in the theory of **virtual representation.** After all, the circumstances and interests of colonials, living an ocean away, were significantly different from those of Britons. The newly recognized consensus among Americans was that colonials could be truly represented only by those whom they had elected. Their view, known as **actual representation,** emphasized that elected officials were directly accountable to their constituents.

Americans also had discovered that they agreed about the extent of Parliament's authority over the colonies: it did not include the right to tax. Colonials conceded Parliament's right to legislate and to regulate trade for the good of the whole empire. But taxation, in their view, was the free

LORD CHATHAM AND AMERICA

Note Pitt's stance, typical of portraits of European aristocrats in the eighteenth century.

Why is the woman's dress slipping from her shoulder?

The British lion, celebrating Pitt's long service to the British Empire

What's this animal? What meaning is conveyed by the woman kneeling on it? Why is it juxtaposed to the book next to Pitt?

This 1766 porcelain attests to the great popularity of William Pitt, earl of Chatham, among Americans who resisted the Stamp Act. Almost alone among British politicians, Pitt had grasped and approved the colonists' objections to taxation. During Parliament's debate over the repeal of the Stamp Act, Grenville asked sarcastically: "Tell me when the colonies were emancipated?" Pitt shot back, "I desire to know when they were made slaves." The porcelain's representation of "America" as an enslaved African American woman kneeling before him, her face raised in gratitude, references Pitt's celebrated remark and echoes the colonists' association of taxation with slavery

Thinking Critically

What is the significance of the feather headdress worn by the "America" figure? Why choose a black woman to represent "America"? What do those choices suggest about the ways in which colonials disaffected with Britain regarded themselves and their place within the British Empire? Why is Pitt represented extending his hand to the kneeling woman but not meeting her gaze?

gift of the people through their representatives—who were not sitting in Parliament.

DECLARATORY ACT

Members of Parliament brushed aside colonial petitions and resolves, all but ignoring these constitutional arguments. To make its own authority clear, Parliament accompanied the repeal of the Stamp Act with a Declaratory Act, asserting that it had the power to make laws for the colonies "in all cases whatsoever." In fact, the Declaratory Act clarified nothing. Did Parliament understand the power of legislation to include the power of taxation?

The Townshend Acts

In the summer of 1766 George III—again inadvertently—gave the colonies what should have been an advantage by changing ministers again. The king replaced Rockingham with William Pitt, who enjoyed great favor among colonials for his leadership during the Seven Years' War and for his opposition to the Stamp Act. If the man who believed that Americans were "the sons not the bastards of England" had been well enough to govern, matters between Great Britain and the colonies might have turned out differently. But almost immediately after Pitt took office, his health collapsed, and power passed into the hands of Charles Townshend, the chancellor of the exchequer, who wished only to raise more revenue. In 1767 he persuaded Parliament to tax the lead, paint, paper, glass, and tea that Americans imported from Britain.

In addition, Townshend was determined to curb the power of the upstart American assemblies. To set a bold example, he singled out for punishment the New York legislature, which was refusing to comply with provisions of the Quartering Act of 1765. The troops that were left on the western frontier after the Seven Years' War had been pulled back into colonial seaports in 1766. In part their movement was meant to economize on costs, but royal officials also hoped the troops' presence would help quiet agitation over the Stamp Act. When the largest contingent came to New York, that colony's assembly protested, claiming that the cost of quartering the troops constituted a form of indirect taxation. But Townshend held firm, and Parliament backed him, suspending the New York assembly in 1767 until it agreed to obey the Quartering Act.

Townshend also dipped into the revenue from his new tariffs in order to make royal officials less dependent on the assemblies. Governors and other officers such as customs collectors and judges had previously received their salaries from colonial legislatures. The assemblies lost that crucial leverage when Townshend used the revenues to pay those bureaucrats directly. Finally, in order to ensure more effective enforcement of all the duties on imports, Townshend created an American Board of Customs Commissioners, who appointed a small army of new customs collectors. He also established three new vice-admiralty courts in Boston, New York City, and Charleston to bring smugglers to justice.

The Resistance Organizes

JOHN DICKINSON AND SAMUEL ADAMS

In Townshend's efforts to centralize the administration of the empire, Americans saw new evidence that they were not being treated like the English. A host of newspapers and pamphlets took up the cry against taxation. The most widely read publication, "A Letter from a Farmer in Pennsylvania," was the work of John Dickinson—who was, in fact, a Philadelphia lawyer. He urged Americans to protest the Townshend duties by consuming fewer imported English luxuries. The virtues of hard work, thrift, and home manufacturing, Dickinson argued, would bring about repeal.

As Dickinson's star rose over Philadelphia, the Townshend Acts also shaped the destiny of another man, farther north. By the 1760s Samuel Adams was a leader in the Massachusetts assembly. In some ways his rise had been unlikely. Adams's earlier ventures as a merchant ended in bankruptcy; his stint as a tax collector left all of Boston

in the red. But he proved a consummate political organizer and agitator. First his enemies and later his friends claimed that Adams had decided on independence for America as early as 1768. In that year he persuaded the assembly to send to other colonial legislatures a circular letter condemning the Townshend Acts and calling for a united American resistance.

As John Dickinson and Samuel Adams whipped up public outrage, the Sons of Liberty again organized the opposition in the streets. Customs officials, like the stamp distributors before them, became targets of popular hatred. But the customs collectors gave as good as they got. Using the flimsiest excuses, they seized American vessels for violating royal regulations. With cold insolence they shook down American merchants for what amounted to protection money. The racketeering in the customs service brought tensions in Boston to a flash point in June 1768 after officials seized and condemned the *Liberty,* a sloop belonging to one of the city's biggest merchants, John Hancock. Several thousand Bostonians vented their anger in a night of rioting, searching out and roughing up customs officials.

The new secretary of state for the colonies, Lord Hillsborough, responded to the *Liberty* riot by sending two regiments of troops to Boston. In the fall of 1768 the redcoats, like a conquering army, paraded into town under the cover of warships lying off the harbor. In the months that followed, citizens bristled when challenged on the streets by armed soldiers. Even more disturbing to Bostonians was the execution of British military justice on the Common, an open field on the outskirts of the city. British soldiers were whipped savagely for breaking military discipline, and desertion was punished by execution.

The *Liberty* riot and the arrival of British troops in Boston pushed colonial assemblies to coordinate their resistance more closely. Most legislatures endorsed the Massachusetts circular letter sent to them by Samuel Adams. They promptly adopted agreements not to import or to consume British goods. The reluctance among some merchants to revive nonimportation in 1767 gave way to greater enthusiasm by 1768, and by early 1769 such agreements were in effect throughout the colonies.

The Stamp Act crisis had also called forth intercolonial cooperation and tactics such as nonimportation. But the protests against the Townshend Acts raised the stakes by creating new institutions to carry forward the resistance. Subscribers to the nonimportation agreements established "committees of inspection" to enforce the ban on trade with Britain. The committees publicly denounced merchants who continued to import, vandalized their warehouses, forced them to stand under the gallows, and sometimes resorted to tar and feathers.

After 1768 the resistance also brought a broader range of colonials into the politics of protest. Artisans, who recognized that nonimportation would spur domestic manufacturing, began to organize as independent political groups. In many towns, women took an active part in opposing the Townshend duties. The "Daughters of Liberty" took to heart John Dickinson's advice: they wore homespun clothing instead of English finery, served coffee instead of tea, and boycotted shops selling British goods.

Liberty's Other Sons

The resistance after 1768 grew broader in another sense as well. Many of its supporters in the colonies felt a new sense of kinship with freedom fighters throughout Europe. Eagerly they read about the doings of men such as Charles Lucas, an Irish newspaper editor and member of the Irish Parliament, and John Wilkes, a London journalist and a leading politician of the Opposition. Both men charged the king's ministers with corrupting the political life of the British Isles. The doings of political rebels even in distant Poland and Turkey engaged colonial sympathies, too. But perhaps the international cause that proved dearest to American lovers of liberty was the fate of Corsica.

COLONIALS FOLLOW PAOLI'S STRUGGLE For years, this tiny island off the coast of Italy had fought for its independence, first from the Italian state of Genoa and then from France, which bought the island in 1768. The leader of the Corsican rebellion, Pascal Paoli, led what one New York newspaper touted as a "glorious struggle." Many in the British Empire hoped that England would rally to defend Corsica's freedom, if only to keep France from seizing this strategic point in the Mediterranean. But British statesmen had no intention of going to war with France over mere Corsica, and when French troops routed his rebel army, Paoli fled to exile in England in 1769. Adding insult to injury, this "greatest man of earth," as he was lionized, began to hobnob with British nobles. He even accepted a pension of 1,000 pounds sterling a year from George III. The moral of the sad story, according to more than one colonial newspaper, was that British corruption pervaded not only the empire but all of Europe as well. Paoli had been "bought"—and if the Corsican sons of liberty could not survive, would their American counterparts manage to remain virtuous for very long?

The Boston Massacre

Meanwhile, the situation in Boston deteriorated steadily. British troops found themselves regularly cursed by citizens and occasionally pelted with stones, dirt, and human excrement. The British regulars were particularly unpopular among Boston's laboring classes because they competed with them for jobs. Off-duty soldiers moonlighted as maritime laborers, and they sold their services at rates cheaper than the wages paid to locals. By 1769 brawls between British regulars and waterfront workers broke out frequently.

With some 4,000 redcoats enduring daily contact with some 15,000 Bostonians under the sway of Samuel Adams, what happened on the night of March 5, 1770, was nearly

John Wilkes, an English journalist and member of the Opposition.

inevitable. A crowd gathered around the customshouse for the sport of heckling the 10 soldiers who guarded it. The redcoats panicked and fended off insults and snowballs with live fire, hitting 11 rioters and killing 5. Adams and other propagandists seized on the incident. Labeling the bloodshed "the Boston Massacre," they publicized that "atrocity" throughout the colonies. The radical *Boston Gazette* framed its account in an eye-catching black-bordered edition headed with a drawing of five coffins.

While Townshend's policies spurred the resistance in America, the obvious finally dawned on Parliament. It recognized that Townshend's duties on imported English goods only discouraged sales to colonials and encouraged them to manufacture at home. The argument for repeal was overwhelming, and the way had been cleared by the unexpected death of Townshend. In 1770 his successor, Lord North, convinced Parliament to repeal all the Townshend duties except the one on tea, allowing that tax to stand as a source of revenue and as a symbol of Parliament's authority.

Resistance Revived

Repeal of the Townshend duties took the wind from the sails of American resistance for more than two years. But the controversy between England and the colonies had not been resolved. Colonials still paid taxes on molasses and tea, taxes to which they had not consented. They were still

STREET THEATER

On the first night of November 1765 the narrow, winding streets of New York glowed with unaccustomed light. The Stamp Act was to have taken effect on that date, but the colony's stampmaster had long since resigned his office. What had frightened him into resignation could be seen in the moving shadows of men, women, and children, hundreds of them. The flaring torches and flickering candles that they carried aloft through the city's crooked byways cast on storefronts and doorways dark images of a crowd protesting the "death of Liberty."

Bringing up the rear of the procession was a seaman, bearing atop his head an old chair in which was seated a paper effigy. It represented Cadwallader Colden, "the most hated man in the province" and, as New York's temporary governor, the local representative of British authority. The crowd marched to the center of town, shouting insults at Colden's figure and peppering it with pistol shots. When some of the marchers decided that their effigy should evoke the Roman Catholic pope, the chief symbol of tyrannical power to colonial Americans, they broke into Colden's stable and stole his fine coach for a proper papal throne. A second group joined the crowd, bearing its own piece of portable political theater—a gallows illuminated with two lanterns. Hanging from the gallows were effigies of Colden and the devil, the "grand Deceiver of Mankind." The entire assembly climaxed the evening by burning the effigies in a bonfire and then vandalizing the homes of several Stamp Act supporters.

Similar protests were staged in seaports all over the colonies. Some crowds held mock trials of unpopular British officials and then tarred and feathered, beat, hung, or burned their effigies. Other crowds enacted mock funerals, parading effigies in carts or coffins as church bells tolled. Certain symbols appeared repeatedly: devils and gallows, lanterns and the paraphernalia of papal authority. The "people-out-of-doors," as such crowds were called in the eighteenth century, were making their views known—and their collective power felt.

A Pope's Day parade in mid-eighteenth-century Boston. Dressed as the devil's imps, boys accompany a cart bearing an effigy of the pope.

The frequency and the political focus of street protests were new, the actions taken after 1765 drew on rituals and symbols surrounding traditional forms of protest, punishment, and celebration. For centuries before the Revolution, crowds on both sides of the Atlantic had meted out to prostitutes, adulterers, and henpecked husbands punishments known in England as "rough music." After being tarred and feathered, the targets of rough music were often ridden "skimmington": placed on the back of a donkey, pelted with mud and dung, and driven through the streets to the accompaniment of hooting laughter and beating drums.

An even more important inspiration for resistance rituals came from Pope's Day, an elaborate annual outdoor celebration of anti-Catholic sentiment that started in Boston early in the eighteenth century. Craftworkers and apprentices from both the North End and the South End of town fashioned a cart bearing a lantern, effigies of the pope and the devil, and signs reading "The devil take the pope." Local boys with blackened faces and jester's caps played the part of the "devil's imps," taunting the pope's effigy as laboring people from both ends of town paraded their carts through the streets. Each group tried to destroy the other's creation before the final bonfire at the end of the evening.

It was not so great a leap, then, to jump from mocking a pope to vilifying a king. Beginning in 1776, Americans celebrated public readings of the Declaration by parading, burning, and burying effigies of George III. Strangely enough, Americans had converted symbols and ceremonies designed to honor monarchy to represent the killing of a king.

Thinking Critically

What explains the hostility to Roman Catholicism expressed by so many American colonials? Why did they identify the pope with tyranny?

subject to trial in admiralty courts, which operated without juries. They still lived with a standing army in their midst. Beneath the banked fires of protest smoldered the live embers of Americans' political inequality. Any shift in the wind could fan those embers into flames.

The wind did shift, quite literally, on Narragansett Bay in 1772, running aground the *Gaspee,* a British naval schooner in hot pursuit of Rhode Island smugglers. Residents of nearby Providence quickly celebrated the *Gaspee*'s misfortune by burning it down to the waterline. Outraged British officials sent a special commission to look into the matter, intending once again to bypass the established colonial court system. The arrival of the Gaspee Commission reignited the imperial crisis, and in America, once again, resistance flared.

COMMITTEES OF CORRESPONDENCE

It did so through an ingenious mechanism, the **committees of correspondence.** Established in all the colonies by their assemblies, the committees drew up statements of American rights and grievances, distributed those documents within and among the colonies, and solicited responses from towns and counties. The brainchild of Samuel Adams, the committee structure formed a new communications network, one that fostered an intercolonial agreement on resistance to British measures. The strategy succeeded, and not only among colonies. The committees spread the scope of the resistance from colonial seaports into rural areas, engaging farmers and other country folk in the opposition to Britain.

The committees had much to talk about when Parliament passed the Tea Act in 1773. The law was an effort to bail out the bankrupt East India Company by granting that corporation a monopoly on the tea trade to Americans. Because the company could use agents to sell its product directly, cutting out the middlemen, it could offer a lower price than that charged by colonial merchants. Thus, although the Tea Act would hurt American merchants, it promised to make tea cheaper for ordinary Americans. Still, many colonials saw the act as Parliament's attempt to trick them into accepting its authority to tax the colonies. They set out to deny that power once and for all.

In the early winter of 1773 popular leaders in Boston called for the tea cargoes to be returned immediately to England. On the evening of December 16, thousands of Bostonians, as well as farmers from the surrounding countryside, packed into the Old South Meetinghouse. Some members of the audience knew what Samuel Adams had on the evening's agenda, and they awaited their cue. It came when Adams told the meeting that they could do nothing more to save their country. War whoops rang through the meetinghouse, the crowd spilled onto the streets and out to the waterfront, and the Boston Tea Party commenced. From the throng emerged 50 men dressed as

Like a swarm of angry bees, British troops disembark on one of Boston's long wharves in 1768. American colonials who had cheered the triumphs of British soldiers only a few years earlier now complained bitterly at the presence of a standing army designed to intimidate them.

DUELING DOCUMENTS

WHO WAS TO BLAME FOR THE BOSTON MASSACRE?

Following the shootings in King Street, Captain Thomas Preston and six of his men stood trial for murder. Two radical patriot lawyers, Josiah Quincy Jr. and future President John Adams, served as defense council. Convinced that Boston must prove itself fair and faithful to the rule of law, both lawyers performed brilliantly. The jury acquitted Preston and four of the soldiers, and convicted two others of manslaughter. The depositions from the trial provide some of our best evidence for how soldiers and Bostonians viewed the standoff differently.

DOCUMENT 1   Deposition of Captain Thomas Preston, March 12, 1770

The mob still increased and were more outrageous, striking their clubs or bludgeons one against another, and calling out, come on you rascals, you bloody backs, you lobster scoundrels, fire if you dare, G-d damn you, fire and be damned, we know you dare not, and much more such language was used. At this time I was between the soldiers and the mob, parleying with, and endeavouring all in my power to persuade them to retire peaceably, but to no purpose. They advanced to the points of the bayonets, struck some of them and even the muzzles of the pieces, and seemed to be endeavouring to close with the soldiers. On which some well-behaved persons asked me if the guns were charged. I replied yes. They then asked me if I intended to order the men to fire. I answered no, by no means, observing to them that I was advanced before the muzzles of the men's pieces, and must fall a sacrifice if they fired; that the soldiers were upon the half cock and charged bayonets, and my giving the word fire under those circumstances would prove me to be no officer. While I was thus speaking, one of the soldiers having received a severe blow with a stick, stepped a little on one side and instantly fired, on which turning to and asking him why he fired without orders, I was struck with a club on my arm, which for some time deprived me of the use of it, which blow had it been placed on my head, most probably would have destroyed me. On this a general attack was made on the men by a great number of heavy clubs and snowballs being thrown at them, by which all our lives were in imminent danger, some persons at the same time from behind calling out, damn your bloods—why don't you fire. Instantly three or four of the soldiers fired, one after another, and directly after three more in the same confusion and hurry. The mob then ran away, except three unhappy men who instantly expired, in which number was Mr. Gray at whose rope-walk the prior quarrels took place; one more is since dead, three others are dangerously, and four slightly wounded. The whole of this melancholy affair was transacted in almost 20 minutes. On my asking the soldiers why they fired without orders, they said they heard the word fire and supposed it came from me. This might be the case as many of the mob called out fire, fire, but I assured the men that I gave no such order; that my words were, don't fire, stop your firing. In short, it was scarcely possible for the soldiers to know who said fire, or don't fire, or stop your firing.

DOCUMENT 2   Deposition of Robert Goddard

The Soldiers came up to the Centinel and the Officer told them to place themselves and they formed a half moon. The Captain told the Boys to go home least there should be murder done. They were throwing Snow balls. Did not go off but threw more Snow balls. The Capt. was behind the Soldiers. The Captain told them to fire. One Gun went off. A Sailor or Townsman struck the Captain. He thereupon said damn your bloods fire think I'll be treated in this manner. This Man that struck the Captain came from among the People who were 7 feet off and were round on one wing. I saw no person speak to him. I was so near I should have seen it. After the Capt. said Damn your bloods fire they all fired one after another about 7 or 8 in all, and then the officer bid Prime and load again. He stood behind all the time. Mr. Lee went up to the officer and called the officer by name Capt. Preston. I saw him coming down from the Guard behind the Party. I went to Gaol the next day being sworn for the Grand Jury to see the Captain. Then said pointing to him that's the person who gave the word to fire. He said if you swear that you will ruin me everlastingly. I was so near the officer when he gave the word fire that I could touch him. His face was towards me. He stood in the middle behind the Men. I looked him in the face. He then stood within the circle. When he told 'em to fire he turned about to me. I looked him in the face.

Source: http://law2.umkc.edu/faculty/projects/ftrials/bostonmassacre/prestontrialexcerpts.html.

Thinking Critically

Preston and Goddard come to different conclusions about the shootings but describe similar details (the snowballs, the man who struck Preston). Can details from these two accounts be reconciled? Do they simply have different perspectives on the same event, or do you think one of the depositions must be misleading? Given the tensions these accounts relate, do you think that a violent confrontation between soldiers and Bostonians was inevitable?

Indians to disguise their identities. The party boarded three vessels docked off Griffin's Wharf, broke open casks containing 90,000 pounds of tea, and brewed a beverage worth 10,000 pounds sterling in Boston harbor.

The Empire Strikes Back

COERCIVE ACTS The Boston Tea Party proved to British satisfaction that the colonies aimed at independence. Lord North's assessment was grim: "We are now to dispute whether we have, or have not, any authority in that country." To reassert its authority, Parliament passed the Coercive Acts, dubbed in the colonies the "Intolerable Acts." The first of these came in March 1774, two months after hearing of the Tea Party, when Parliament passed the Boston Port Bill, closing that harbor to all oceangoing traffic until such time as the king saw fit to reopen it. And George, Parliament announced, would not see fit until colonials paid the East India Company for its losses.

During the next three months, Parliament approved three other "intolerable" laws designed to punish Massachusetts. The Massachusetts Government Act handed over the colony's government to royal officials. Even convening town meetings would require royal permission. The Impartial Administration of Justice Act permitted any royal official accused of a crime in Massachusetts to be tried in England or in another colony. The Quartering Act allowed the housing of British troops in uninhabited private homes, outlying buildings, and barns—not only in Massachusetts but in all the other colonies as well.

| While the new political activism of some American women merely amused male leaders of the resistance, it inspired the scorn of some partisans of British authority. When the women of Edenton, North Carolina, renounced imported tea, this British cartoon mocked them. Can you find at least five details in the painting used by the artist to insult the Americans?

FEAR OF CONSPIRACY Many colonials saw the Coercive Acts as proof of a plot to enslave the colonies. In truth, the taxes and duties, laws and regulations of the past decade *were* part of a deliberate design—a plan to centralize the administration of the British Empire that seemed only common sense to British officials. But those efforts by the king's ministers and Parliament to run the colonies more efficiently and profitably were viewed by more and more Americans as a sinister conspiracy against their liberties.

For colonials, the study of history confirmed that interpretation, especially their reading of the histories written by the English Opposition. The Opposition's favorite historical subject was the downfall of republics, whether those of ancient Greece and Rome or more recent republican governments in Venice and Denmark. The lesson of their histories was always the same: power overwhelmed liberty, unless the people remained vigilant. The pattern, argued radicals, had been repeated in America over the previous dozen years: costly wars waged; oppressive taxes levied to pay for them; standing armies sent to overawe citizens; corrupt governors, customs collectors, and judges appointed to enrich themselves by enforcing the measures. Everything seemed to fit.

QUEBEC ACT Week after week in the spring of 1774, reports of legislative outrages came across the waters. Shortly after approving the Coercive Acts, Parliament passed the Quebec Act, which established a permanent government in what had been French Canada. Ominously, it included no representative assembly. Equally ominous to Protestant colonials, the Quebec Act officially recognized the Roman Catholic church and extended the bounds of the province to include all land between the Mississippi and Ohio Rivers. Suddenly New York, Pennsylvania, and Virginia found themselves bordering a British colony whose subjects had no voice in their own government.

With the passage of the Coercive Acts, many more colonials came to believe not only that ambitious men plotted to enslave the colonies but also that those conspirators included almost all British political leaders. At the time of the Stamp Act and again during the agitation against the Townshend Acts, most colonials had confined their suspicions to the king's ministers. By 1774 members of Parliament were also implicated in that conspiracy—and a few radicals were wondering aloud about George III.

FIRST CONTINENTAL CONGRESS CALLED As alarm deepened in the wake of the Coercive Acts, one colony after another called for an intercolonial congress—like the one that had met during the Stamp Act crisis—to determine the best way to defend their freedom. But many also remained unsettled about where the logic of their actions seemed to be taking them: toward a denial that they were any longer English.

✓ REVIEW

How did British colonial policy change after the Seven Years' War, and what was the colonial response?

TOWARD THE REVOLUTION

BY THE BEGINNING OF SEPTEMBER 1774, when 55 delegates to the First Continental Congress gathered in Philadelphia, the news from Massachusetts was grim. The colony verged on anarchy, it was reported, as its inhabitants resisted the enforcement of the Massachusetts Government Act.

In the midst of this atmosphere of crisis, the members of Congress also had to take one another's measure. Many of the delegates had not traveled outside their own colonies. (All but Georgia sent representatives.) Although the delegates encountered a great deal of diversity, they quickly discovered that they esteemed the same traits of character, attributes that they called "civic virtue." These traits included simplicity and—self-reliance, industry and thrift, and above all, an unselfish commitment to the public good. Most members of the Congress also shared a common mistrust of England, associating the mother country with vice, extravagance, and corruption.

Still, the delegates had some misgivings about those from other colonies. Massachusetts in particular brought with it a reputation—well deserved, considering that Samuel Adams was along—for radical action and a willingness to use force to accomplish its ends.

The First Continental Congress

As the delegates settled down to business, their aim was to reach agreement on three key points: How were they to justify the rights they claimed as American colonials? What were the limits of Parliament's power? And what were the proper tactics for resisting the Coercive Acts? Congress quickly agreed on the first point. The delegates affirmed that the law of nature, the colonial charters, and the British constitution provided the foundations of American liberties. This position was what most colonials had argued since 1765. On the two other issues, Congress charted a middle course between the demands of radicals and the reservations of conservatives.

Since the time of the Stamp Act, most colonials had insisted that Parliament had no authority to tax the colonies. But later events had demonstrated that Parliament could undermine colonial liberties by legislation as well as by taxation. The suspension of the New York legislature, the Gaspee Commission, and the Coercive Acts all fell into this category. Given those experiences, the delegates adopted a Declaration of Rights and Grievances on October 14, 1774, asserting the right of the colonies to tax and legislate for themselves. The Declaration of Rights thus limited Parliament's power over Americans more strictly than colonials had a decade earlier.

JOSEPH GALLOWAY'S PLAN By denying Parliament's power to make laws for the colonies, the Continental Congress blocked efforts of the most conservative delegates to reach an accommodation with England. Their leading advocate, Joseph Galloway of Pennsylvania, proposed a plan of union with Britain similar to the one set forth by the Albany Congress in 1754. Under it, a grand council of the colonies would handle all common concerns, with any laws it passed subject to review and veto by Parliament. For its part, Parliament would have to submit for the grand council's approval any acts it passed affecting America. A majority of delegates judged that Galloway's proposal left Parliament too much leeway in legislating for colonials, and they rejected his plan.

Although the Congress denied Parliament the right to impose taxes or to make laws, delegates stopped short of declaring that it had no authority at all in the colonies. They approved Parliament's regulation of trade, but only because of the interdependent economy of the empire. And although some radical pamphleteers were attacking the king for plotting against American liberties, Congress acknowledged the continuing allegiance of the colonies to George III. In other words, the delegates called for a return to the situation that had existed in the empire before 1763, with Parliament regulating trade and the colonies exercising all powers of taxation and legislation.

THE ASSOCIATION On the question of resistance, the Congress satisfied the desires of its most radical delegates by drawing up the Continental Association, an agreement to cease all trade with Britain until the Coercive Acts were repealed. They agreed that their fellow citizens would immediately stop drinking East India Company tea and that by December 1, 1774, merchants would no longer import goods of any sort from Britain. A ban on the export of American produce to Britain and the West Indies would go into effect a year later, during September 1775—the lag being a concession to southern rice and tobacco planters, who wanted to market crops already planted.

REVERE AND THE SUFFOLK RESOLVES The Association provided for the total cessation of trade, but Samuel Adams and other radicals wanted bolder action. They received help from Paul Revere, a Boston silversmith who had long provided newspapers with many lurid engravings showing British abuses. On September 16, Revere galloped into Philadelphia bearing a copy of resolves drawn up by Bostonians and other residents of Suffolk County. The Suffolk Resolves, as they were called, branded the Coercive Acts as unconstitutional and called for civil disobedience to protest them. Congress endorsed the resolves, as Adams had hoped. But it would not approve another part of the radicals' agenda—preparing for war by authorizing proposals to strengthen and arm colonial militias.

Thus the First Continental Congress steered a middle course. Although determined to bring about repeal of the Coercive Acts, it held firm in resisting any revolutionary

Samuel Adams, a radical who masterminded colonial resistance tactics.

course of action. If British officials had responded to its recommendations and restored the status quo of 1763, the war for independence might have been postponed—perhaps indefinitely. However, even though the Congress did not go to the extremes urged by the radicals, its decisions drew colonials farther down the road to independence.

The Last Days of the British Empire in America

Most colonials applauded the achievements of the First Continental Congress. They expected that the Association would bring about a speedy repeal of the Coercive Acts. But fear that the colonies were moving toward a break with Britain led others to denounce the doings of the Congress. Conservatives were convinced that if independence were declared, chaos would ensue. Colonials, they argued, would quarrel over land claims and sectional tensions and religious differences, as they had so often in the recent past. Without Britain to referee such disputes, they feared, the result would be civil war, followed by anarchy.

THOMAS GAGE IN BOSTON The man in America with the least liking for the Continental Congress sat in the hottest seat in the colonies, that of the governor of Massachusetts. General Thomas Gage now watched as royal authority crumbled in Massachusetts and the rebellion spread to other colonies. In June 1774 a desperate Gage dissolved the Massachusetts legislature, only to see it reform, on its own, into a Provincial Congress. That new body assumed the government of the colony in October and began arming the militia. Gage then started to fortify Boston and pleaded for more troops—only to find his fortifications damaged by saboteurs and his requests for reinforcements ignored by Britain.

COLLAPSE OF ROYAL AUTHORITY Outside Boston, royal authority fared no better. Farmers in western Massachusetts forcibly closed the county courts, turning out royally appointed justices and establishing their own tribunals. Popularly elected committees of inspection charged with enforcing the Association took over towns everywhere in Massachusetts, not only restricting trade but also regulating every aspect of local life. The committees called on townspeople to display civic virtue by renouncing "effeminate" English luxuries such as tea and fine clothing and "corrupt" leisure activities such as dancing, gambling, and racing. The committees also assigned spies to report on any citizen unfriendly to the resistance. "Enemies of American liberty" risked being roundly condemned in public or beaten and pelted with mud and dung by hooting, raucous mobs.

Throughout the other colonies a similar process was under way. During the winter

and early spring of 1775 provincial congresses, county conventions, and local committees of inspection were emerging as revolutionary governments, replacing royal authority at every level. As the spectacle unfolded before General Gage, he concluded that only force could subdue the colonies. It would take more than he had at his command, but reinforcements might be on the way. In February of 1775 Parliament had approved an address to the king declaring that the colonies were in rebellion.

The Fighting Begins

As spring came to Boston, the city waited. A band of artisans, organized as spies and express riders by Paul Revere, watched General Gage and waited for him to act. On April 14 word from Lord North finally arrived: Gage was to seize the leaders of the Provincial Congress, an action that would behead the rebellion, North said. Gage knew better than to believe North—but he also knew that he had to do something.

LEXINGTON AND CONCORD On the night of April 18 the sexton of Boston's Christ Church hung two lamps from its steeple. It was a signal that British troops had moved out of Boston and were marching toward the arms and ammunition stored by the Provincial Congress in Concord. As the lamps flashed the signal, Revere and a comrade, William Dawes, rode out to arouse the countryside.

| A British grenadier

When the news of a British march reached Lexington, its Minuteman militia of about 70 farmers, chilled and sleepy, mustered on the Green at the center of the small rural town. Lexington Green lay directly on the road to Concord. About four in the morning 700 British troops massed on the Green, and their commander, Major John Pitcairn, ordered the Lexington militia to disperse. The townsmen, outnumbered and overawed, began to obey. Then a shot rang out—whether the British or the Americans fired first is unknown—and then two volleys burst from the ranks of the redcoats. With a cheer the British set off for Concord, 5 miles distant, leaving eight Americans dead on Lexington Green.

By dawn, hundreds of Minutemen from nearby towns were surging into Concord. The British entered at about seven in the morning and moved, unopposed, toward their target, a house lying across the bridge that spanned the Concord River. While three companies of British soldiers searched for American guns and ammunition, three others, posted on the bridge itself, had the misfortune to find those American arms—borne by the rebels and being fired with deadly accuracy. By noon, the British were retreating to Boston.

The narrow road from Concord to Boston's outskirts became a corridor of carnage. Pursuing Americans fired on the column of fleeing redcoats from the cover of fences and forests. By the end of

April 19, the British had sustained 273 casualties; the Americans, 95. It was only the beginning. By evening of the next day, some 20,000 New England militia had converged on Boston for a long siege.

Common Sense

The bloodshed at Lexington Green and Concord's North Bridge committed colonials to a course of rebellion—and independence. That was the conclusion drawn by Thomas Paine, who urged other Americans to join the rebels.

Paine himself was hardly an American at all. He was born in England, first apprenticed as a corsetmaker, appointed later a tax collector, and fated finally to become midwife to the age of republican revolutions. Paine came to Philadelphia late in 1774, set up as a journalist, and made the American cause his own. "Where liberty is, there is my country," he declared. In January 1776 he wrote a pamphlet to inform colonials of their identity as a distinct people and their destiny as a nation. *Common Sense* enjoyed tremendous popularity and wide circulation, selling 120,000 copies.

After Lexington and Concord, Paine wrote, as the imperial crisis passed "from argument to arms, a new era for

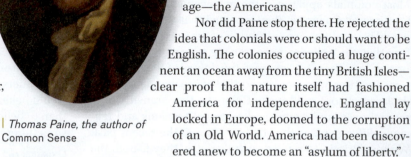

| Thomas Paine, the author of Common Sense

politics is struck—a new method of thinking has arisen." That new era of politics for Paine was the age of republicanism. He denounced monarchy as a foolish and dangerous form of government, one that violated the dictates of reason as well as the word of the Bible. By ridicule and remorseless argument, he severed the ties of colonial allegiance to the king. *Common Sense* scorned George III as "the Royal Brute of Britain," who had enslaved the chosen people of the new age—the Americans.

Nor did Paine stop there. He rejected the idea that colonials were or should want to be English. The colonies occupied a huge continent an ocean away from the tiny British Isles—clear proof that nature itself had fashioned America for independence. England lay locked in Europe, doomed to the corruption of an Old World. America had been discovered anew to become an "asylum of liberty."

✓ **REVIEW**

What had happened by the mid-1770s to transform nonimportation and political protest into organized rebellion?

| The Irish artist John Dixon created this mezzotint, The Oracle, in 1774. In it, Father Time puts on a magic-lantern show for an audience of women who represent Britain, Scotland, Ireland, and America. The image projected on the wall conjures up a brilliant future for the British Empire, in which protest and discord give way to freedom and unity—wishful thinking, since little more than a year later American rebels fired the first shots at Lexington. Note that America, who sits in the shadows apart from the three other women, is a tawny Indian princess, her face hidden, a weapon at her side. What does this representation suggest about the ways that Britons viewed Americans?

CONCLUSION

THE WORLD AT LARGE

Many Americans had liked being English, but being English hadn't worked. Perhaps that is another way of saying that over the course of nearly two centuries, colonial society and politics had evolved in such a way that for Americans an English identity no longer fit.

The radicals in America viewed this change in identity in terms of age-old conspiracies that repeated themselves throughout history. First, the people of a republic were impoverished by costly wars—as the colonists could well appreciate after the Seven Years' War. Then the government burdened the people with taxes to pay for those wars—as in the case of the Sugar Act or the Stamp Act or the Townshend duties. Next, those in power stationed a standing army in the country, pretending to protect the people but actually lending military force to their rulers. The rhetoric of the Opposition about ministerial conspiracies gave such talk a fervid quality that, to some modern ears, may seem an exaggeration.

Take away the rhetoric, however, and the argument makes uncomfortable sense. The British administration began its "backwoods" war with France, intending to limit it to the interior of North America. But the war aims of William Pitt—the leader Americans counted as their friend—grew with every victory, and he urged war with Spain even as France was looking for peace. Britain had already taken its war in Europe farther afield, driving France out of India. When it declared war against Spain, British naval forces in India sailed farther east, in a surprise attack on Spain's colony in the Philippines. At the same time, another fleet raced toward Spanish Cuba. Peace came only once Britain and the major powers had bankrupted their treasuries. Conspiracy may not have been at the heart of the plan. But wars must be paid for. And the prevailing assumptions in a monarchy about who should pay led to the effort to regulate and bring order to Britain's "ungrateful" colonies.

In America, colonists were ungrateful precisely because they had established political institutions that made the rights of "freeborn Britons" more available to ordinary citizens than they were in the nation that had created those liberties. Perhaps, in other words, most Americans had succeeded *too* well at becoming English, regarding themselves as political equals entitled to basic constitutional freedoms. In the space of less than a generation, the logic of events made clear that despite all that the English and Americans shared, in the distribution of political power they were fundamentally at odds. And the call to arms at Lexington and Concord made retreat impossible.

On that point Paine was clear. It was the destiny of Americans to be republicans, not monarchists. It was the destiny of Americans to be independent, not subject to British dominion. It was the destiny of Americans to be American, not English. That, according to Thomas Paine, was common sense. ∞∞∞

CHAPTER SUMMARY

BRITAIN'S STUNNING VICTORY IN THE Seven Years' War prompted it to embrace policies designed to administer new territories and boost revenue. These policies provoked a backlash in the colonies that would ultimately lead to the Revolutionary War.

- French and Indian forces inflicted major defeats on the British during the mid-1750s, in large part thanks to British policies that had alienated colonists and Indians alike.

- Starting in 1757, William Pitt's reforms galvanized the colonies, secured Indian allies, and salvaged the war. By 1760 the French had been defeated throughout the continent.

- Partly thanks to Pontiac's Rebellion, the British prohibited colonial settlement west of the Appalachians.

- The acts by Parliament in the early 1760s—the Proclamation of 1763, the Sugar Act, the Stamp Act, the Currency Act, and the Quartering Act—were all designed to generate revenue and bind the colonies to the empire.

- These new measures violated what Americans understood to be their constitutional and political liberties.

- Although Parliament repealed the Stamp Act in the face of colonial protests, it reasserted its authority to tax Americans by passing the Townshend Acts in 1767.

- With the passage of the Coercive Acts in 1774, many Americans concluded that all British actions in the past decade were part of a deliberate plot to enslave Americans by depriving them of property and liberty.

- The First Continental Congress denied Parliament any authority in the colonies except regulating trade; it also prohibited trade with Britain until the Coercive Acts were repealed.

- When in April 1775 British troops tried to seize arms at Concord, the first battle of the Revolution took place

ADDITIONAL READING

FOR COMPREHENSIVE OVERVIEWS OF THE revolutionary era, consult Edward Countryman, *The American Revolution* (1985), and Robert Middlekauff, *The Glorious Cause* (rev. ed., 2007). Fred Anderson, *Crucible of War* (2000), offers a magisterial account of the Seven Years' War. *The Stamp Act Crisis* (1953) by Edmund S. Morgan and Helen M. Morgan remains the clearest and most vivid portrayal of the issues, events, and people involved in that defining moment of the imperial crisis. To understand that struggle as lived and recalled by a Boston artisan, read Alfred F. Young's engaging book, *The Shoemaker and the Tea Party* (1999). Two important interpretations of how the logic of resistance took shape among colonials in Massachusetts and Virginia are Robert Gross, *The Minutemen and Their World* (1976), and Timothy Breen, *Tobacco Culture* (1985). A more recent study by Breen, *The Marketplace Revolution* (2005), sheds new light on the role of a transatlantic consumer culture in fueling tensions within the British Empire.

Bernard Bailyn, *The Ideological Origins of the American Revolution* (1967), remains the classic study of the English Opposition's influence on the evolution of republican political thought in the American colonies. Many fine biographies chronicle the careers of eighteenth-century Americans who led—or opposed—the resistance to Britain and also shed light on the times in which they lived. Of particular interest are Jack Rakove, *Revolutionaries* (2010), Gordon Wood, *Revolutionary Characters,* and two biographies of Thomas Paine (both published in 2006) by Harvey Kaye and Craig Nelson.

For a fuller list of readings, see the Bibliography at www.mhhe.com/eh8e.

SIGNIFICANT EVENTS

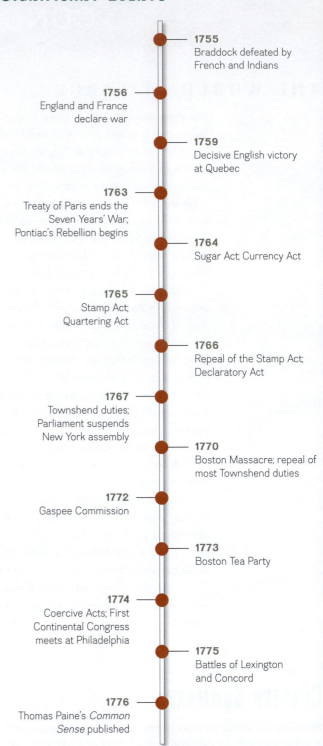

1755
Braddock defeated by French and Indians

1756
England and France declare war

1759
Decisive English victory at Quebec

1763
Treaty of Paris ends the Seven Years' War; Pontiac's Rebellion begins

1764
Sugar Act; Currency Act

1765
Stamp Act; Quartering Act

1766
Repeal of the Stamp Act; Declaratory Act

1767
Townshend duties; Parliament suspends New York assembly

1770
Boston Massacre; repeal of most Townshend duties

1772
Gaspee Commission

1773
Boston Tea Party

1774
Coercive Acts; First Continental Congress meets at Philadelphia

1775
Battles of Lexington and Concord

1776
Thomas Paine's *Common Sense* published

Parliament and the Road to Revolution

DATE	ACT	DETAILS	REACTION
1764	Sugar Act	Decreased existing tax on molasses but increased policing and punishment for violation	Angry protests by New England merchants
1764	Currency Act	Prohibited colonies making paper bills legal tender	
1765	Quartering Act	Compelled colonies to house army troops	New York refuses to comply
1765	Stamp Act	Taxed legal documents, various paper products, and dice	Assemblies deny Parliament's right to tax colonies; nonimportation campaign; mobs intimidate stamp distributors
1766	Declaratory Act	Though Stamp Act repealed, Parliament insists on power to tax colonies	Patriot writing flourishes; crowds attack customs agents; nonimportation more sophisticated
1767	Townshend Acts	Taxed lead, paper, paint, glass, and tea	Riots; propaganda; Townshend duties repealed except for tea
1770	Boston Massacre	5 men shot dead by British troops in Boston	Refusal to let the tea shipments land; destruction of tea in Boston Harbor and elsewhere
1773	Tea Act	Allowed East India Company to sell tea in colonies at discount, but tea would still be taxed	First Continental Congress meets in Philadelphia
1774	Coercive Acts	Closed Boston's port; placed Massachusetts government under royal control	

BOSTON

CHARLE

On June 17, 1775, thousands of colonials flocked to the rooftops and upper windows of their Boston homes to witness the British attack on Breed's Hill across the water on nearby Charlestown peninsula. As the British artillery sent shells into the peninsula, houses there caught fire and burst into flames. Then the redcoats, unloaded from their ships, launched their assault on the hill.

CHAPTER 7

The American People and the American Revolution

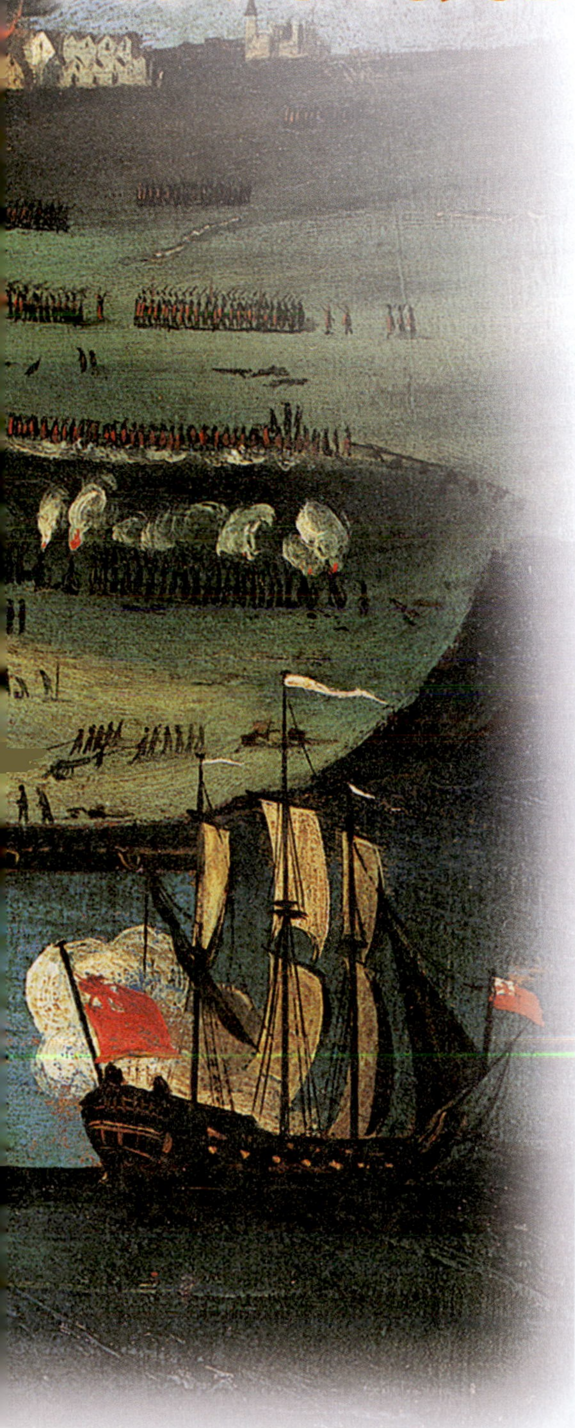

1775–1783

What's to Come

AN AMERICAN STORY

"Will He Fight?"

From a high place somewhere in the city—Beacon Hill, perhaps, or Copse Hill—General Thomas Gage looked down on Boston. Through a spyglass his gaze traveled over the church belfries and steeples, the roofs of brick and white frame houses. Finally he fixed his sights on a figure far in the distance across the Charles River. The man was perched atop a crude fortification on Breed's Hill, an elevation lying just below Bunker Hill on the Charlestown peninsula. Gage took the measure of his enemy: an older man, past middle age, a sword swinging beneath his homespun coat, a broad-brimmed hat shading his eyes. As he passed the spyglass to his ally, an American loyalist, Gage asked Abijah Willard if he knew the man on the fort. Willard peered across the Charles and identified his own brother-in-law, Colonel William Prescott. A veteran of the Seven Years' War, Prescott was now a leader in the rebel army laying siege to Boston.

"Will he fight?" Gage wondered aloud.

"I cannot answer for his men," Willard replied, "but Prescott will fight you to the gates of hell."

Fight they did on June 17, 1775, both William Prescott and his men. The evening before, three regiments had followed the colonel from Cambridge to Breed's Hill—soldiers drawn from the thousands of militia who had swarmed to surround British-occupied Boston after the bloodshed at Lexington and Concord. All through the night, they dug deep trenches and built up high earthen walls atop the hill. At the first light of day, a British warship spotted the new rebel outpost and opened fire. By noon barges were ferrying British troops under Major General William Howe across the half mile of river that separated Boston from Charlestown. The 1,600 raw rebel troops tensed at the sight of scarlet-coated soldiers streaming ashore, glittering bayonets grasped at the ready. The rebels were farmers and artisans, not professional soldiers, and they were frightened out of their wits.

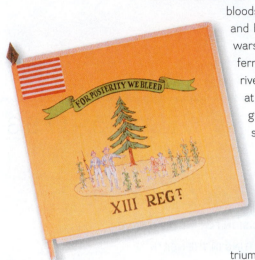

| Will they fight? This Pennsylvania regimental flag gives one reason why some did.

But Prescott and his men held their ground. The British charged Breed's Hill twice, and Howe watched in horror as streams of fire felled his troops. Finally, during the third British frontal assault, the rebels ran out of ammunition and were forced to withdraw. Redcoats poured into the rebel fort, bayoneting its handful of remaining defenders. By nightfall the British had taken Breed's Hill and the rest of the Charlestown peninsula. They had bought a dark triumph at the cost of 228 dead and 800 wounded.

The cost came high in loyalties as well. The fighting on Breed's Hill fed the hatred of Britain that had been building since April. Throughout America, preparations for war intensified: militia in every colony mustered; communities stockpiled arms and ammunition. Around Charlestown civilians fled the countryside, abandoning homes and shops set afire by the British shelling of Breed's Hill. "The roads filled with frightened women and children, some in carts with their tattered furniture, others on foot fleeing into the woods," recalled Hannah Winthrop, one of their number.

The bloody, indecisive fight on the Charlestown peninsula known as the Battle of Bunker Hill actually took place on Breed's Hill. And the exchange between Thomas Gage and Abijah Willard that is said to have preceded the battle may not have taken place. But the story has persisted in the folklore of the American Revolution. Whether it really happened or not, the conversation between Gage and Willard raised the question that both sides wanted answered. Were Americans willing to fight for independence from British rule? It was one thing, after all, to oppose the British ministry's policy of taxation. It was another to support a rebellion for which the ultimate price of failure was hanging for treason. And it was another matter entirely for men to wait nervously atop a hill as the seasoned troops of their own "mother country" marched toward them with the intent to kill.

Indeed, the question "Will they fight?" was revolutionary shorthand for a host of other questions concerning how ordinary Americans would react to the tug of loyalties between long-established colonial governments and a long-revered parent nation and monarch. For slaves, the question revolved around their allegiance to masters who spoke of liberty or to their masters' enemies who promised liberation. For those who led the rebels, it was a question of strengthening the resolve of the undecided, coordinating resistance, instilling discipline—translating the *will* to fight into the *ability* to do so. And for those who believed the rebellion was a madness whipped up by artful politicians, it was a question of whether to remain silent or risk speaking out, whether to take up arms for the king or flee. All these questions were raised, of necessity, by the act of revolution. But the barrel of a rifle shortened them to a single, pointed question: Will you fight? ∞∞∞

The Decision for Independence

The delegates to the Second Continental Congress gathered at Philadelphia on May 10, 1775, just one month after the battles at Lexington and Concord. They had to determine whether independence or reconciliation offered the best way to protect the liberties of their colonies.

For a brash, ambitious lawyer from Braintree, Massachusetts, British abuses dictated only one course. "The Cancer [of official corruption] is too deeply rooted," wrote John Adams, "and too far spread to be cured by anything short of cutting it out entire." Yet, during the spring and summer of 1775, even strong advocates of independence did not openly seek a separation from Britain. If the radicals' objective of independence was ever to be achieved, greater agreement among Americans had to be attained. Moderates and conservatives harbored deep misgivings about independence: they had to be brought along slowly.

The Second Continental Congress

To bring them along, Congress adopted the "Olive Branch Petition" in July 1775. Drawn up by Pennsylvania's John Dickinson, the document affirmed American loyalty to George III and asked the king to disavow the policies of his principal ministers. At the same time, Congress issued a declaration denying that the colonies aimed at independence. Yet, less than a month earlier, Congress had authorized the creation of a rebel military force, the **Continental Army,** and had issued paper money to pay for the troops.

AGGRESSIVE BRITISH RESPONSE

A Congress that sued for peace while preparing for war was a puzzle that British politicians—least of all, Lord George Germain—did not even try to understand. A tough-minded statesman now charged with overseeing colonial affairs, Germain was determined to subdue the rebellion by force. George III proved just as stubborn: he refused to receive the Olive Branch Petition. By the end of that year, Parliament had shut down all trade with the colonies and had ordered the Royal Navy to seize colonial merchant ships on the high seas. In November 1775 Virginia's royal governor, Lord Dunmore, offered freedom to any slaves who would join the British. During January of the next year, he ordered the shelling of Norfolk, Virginia, reducing that town to smoldering rubble.

British belligerence withered the cause of reconciliation within Congress and the colonies. Support for independence gained more momentum from the overwhelming reception of Paine's *Common Sense* in January 1776. Radicals in Congress realized that the future was theirs and were ready to act. In April 1776 the delegates opened American trade to every nation in the world except Great Britain; a month later Congress advised the colonies to establish new state governments. And on June 7 Virginia's Richard Henry Lee offered the motion "that these United Colonies are, and of right ought to be, free and independent States . . . and that all political connection between them and the State of Great Britain is, and ought to be, totally dissolved."

The Declaration

Congress postponed a final vote on Lee's motion until July. Some opposition still lingered among delegates from the middle colonies, and a committee appointed to write a declaration of independence needed time to complete its work. That committee included some of the leading delegates in Congress: John Adams, Benjamin Franklin, Connecticut's Roger Sherman, and New York's Robert Livingston. But the man who did most of the drafting was a young planter and lawyer from western Virginia.

THOMAS JEFFERSON

Thomas Jefferson was just 33 years old in the summer of 1776 when he withdrew to his lodgings on the outskirts of Philadelphia, pulled a portable writing desk onto his lap, and wrote the statement that would explain American independence to a "candid world." In the document's brief opening section, Jefferson set forth a general justification of revolution that invoked the "self-evident truths" of human equality and "unalienable rights" to "life, liberty, and the pursuit of happiness." These natural rights had been "endowed" to all persons "by their Creator," the Declaration pointed out; thus there was no need to appeal to the narrower claim of the "rights of Englishmen."

BLAMING GEORGE III

While the first part of the Declaration served notice that Americans no longer considered themselves English, its second and longer section denied England any authority in the colonies. In its

| *Rough draft of the Declaration of Independence*

detailed history of American grievances against the British Empire, the Declaration referred only once to Parliament. Instead, it blamed George III for a "long train of abuses and usurpations" designed to achieve "absolute despotism." Unlike *Common Sense*, the Declaration denounced only the reigning king of England; it did not attack the institution of monarchy itself. But like *Common Sense*, the Declaration affirmed that government originated in the consent of the governed and upheld the right of the people to overthrow oppressive rule.

Later generations have debated what Jefferson meant by the "pursuit of happiness" and whether he had either women or black Americans in mind when he wrote the famous phrase "all men are created equal." His own contemporaries in Congress did not pause to consider those questions and surely would have found themselves divided if they had. No matter. By firmly grounding the Declaration on the natural rights due all people, Jefferson placed equality at the center of the new nation's identity, setting the framework for a debate that would continue over the next two centuries. Congress adopted the Declaration of Independence on July 4, 1776.

 THE BRITISH PERSPECTIVE The colonies thus followed the course set by common sense into the storms of independence. To those Britons who took a wide view of their empire, it made no sense whatsoever, and their perplexity is understandable. Since the end of the Seven Years' War, Britain had added to its overseas dominion a vast and diverse number of subjects formerly under French rule—Native Americans, French Catholic Canadians, peoples of African descent in the Caribbean. And then there was India, part Hindu, part Muslim, most of it ruled by the East India Company. What better, more efficient way to regulate this sprawling empire than to bring all of its parts under the rule of a sovereign Parliament? What other way could the empire endure and prosper—and fend off future challenges from Catholic, monarchical France? Of course, it was impossible to grant colonials the same rights as Britons: it would require an empire firmly based on hierarchy to hold chaos at bay. Most colonial elites assented to the logic of that position—East India Company officials, Bengal nabobs, Canadian traders and landlords. Only the leading men in Britain's original 13 colonies would not go along.

American Loyalists

But the sentiment for independence was not universal. Americans who would not back the rebellion, supporters of the king and Parliament, numbered perhaps one-fifth of the population in 1775. While they proclaimed themselves **loyalists,** their rebel opponents dubbed them "tories"—"a thing whose head is in England, whose body is in America, and whose neck ought to be stretched." That division made the Revolution a conflict pitting Americans against one another as well as the British. In truth, the war for independence was the first American civil war.

This detail from a painting, commemorating the signing of the Declaration of Independence, shows Benjamin Franklin (seated center) weighing the consequences of the decisions he and his colleagues are about to undertake. John Hancock, the president of the Congress, is reported to have remarked, "We must be unanimous; there must be no pulling different ways; we must all hang together." Franklin is said to have rejoined, "Yes, we must indeed all hang together, or most assuredly, we shall all hang separately."

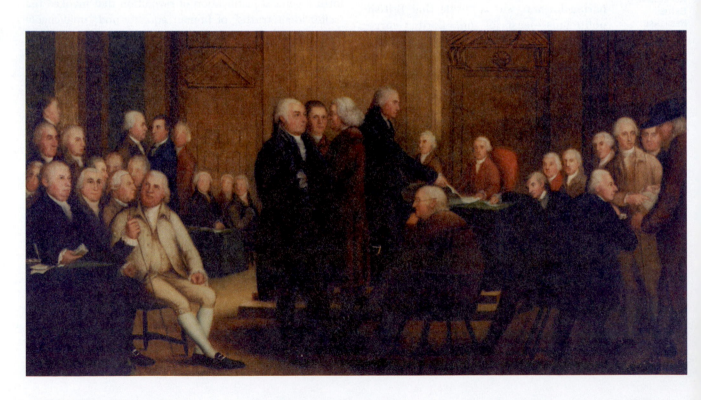

DUELING DOCUMENTS

ABIGAIL AND JOHN ADAMS SPAR ON WOMEN'S RIGHTS AND THE AMERICAN REVOLUTION

While she managed the family farm in Braintree, Massachusetts, he served as a delegate to the Continental Congress at Philadelphia, running the war and framing a new national government. She had concerns about the war and advice about the future government:

DOCUMENT 1   Abigail Adams to John Adams, March 31, 1776

I wish you would ever write me a Letter half as long as I write you; and tell me if you may where your Fleet are gone? What sort of Defence Virginia can make against our common Enemy . . . ? Whether it is so situated as to make an able Defence? Are not the Gentery Lords and the common people vassals . . . ?

I have sometimes been ready to think that the passion for Liberty cannot be Eaquelly Strong in the Breasts of those who have been accustomed to deprive their fellow Creatures of theirs. . . .

I long to hear that you have declared an independency—and by the way in the new Code of Laws which I suppose it will be necessary for you to make I desire you would Remember the Ladies, and be more generous and favourable to them than your ancestors. Do not put such unlimited power into the hands of the Husbands. Remember all Men would be tyrants if they could. If perticuliar care and attention is not paid to the Ladies we are determined to foment a Rebellion, and will not hold ourselves bound by any Laws in which we have no voice, or Representation.

That our Sex are Naturally Tyrannical is a Truth so thoroughly established as to admit of no dispute, but such of you as wish to be happy willingly give up the harsh title of Master for the more tender and endearing one of Friend. Why then, not put it out of the power of the vicious and the Lawless to use us with cruelty and indignity with impunity. Men of Sense in all Ages abhor those customs which treat us only as the vassals of your Sex. Regard us then as Beings placed by providence under your protection and in imitation of the Supreem Being make use of the power only for our happiness.

DOCUMENT 2   John Adams to Abigail Adams, April 14, 1776

You justly complain of my short Letters, but the critical State of Things and the Multiplicity of Avocations must plead my Excuse. . . . You ask what Sort of Defence Virginia can make. I believe they will make an able Defence. Their Militia and minute Men have been some time employed in training them selves. . . . Their neighbouring Sister or rather Daughter Colony of North Carolina, which is a warlike Colony, and has several Battalions at the Continental Expence, as well as a pretty good Militia, are ready to assist them. . . . The Gentry are very rich, and the common People very poor.

This Inequality of Property, gives an Aristocratical Turn to all their Proceedings, and occasions a strong Aversion in their Patricians, to Common Sense. But the Spirit of these Barons, is coming down, and it must submit. . . .

As to your extraordinary Code of Laws, I cannot but laugh. We have been told that our Struggle has loosened the bands of Government every where. That Children and Apprentices were disobedient—that schools and Colledges were grown turbulent—that Indians slighted their Guardians and Negroes grew insolent to their Masters. But your Letter was the first Intimation that another

Tribe more numerous and powerfull than the rest were grown discontented. —This is rather too coarse a Complement but you are so saucy I wont blot it out.

Depend upon it, We know better than to repeal our Masculine systems. Altho they are in full Force, you know they are little more than Theory. We dare not exert our Power in its full Latitude. We are obliged to go fair, and softly, and in Practice you know We are the subjects. We have only the Name of Masters, and rather than give up this, which would completely subject Us to the Despotism of the Peticoat, I hope General Washington, and all our brave Heroes would fight.

DOCUMENT 3   Abigail Adams to John Adams, May 7, 1776

I can not say that I think you very generous to the Ladies, for whilst you are proclaiming peace and good will to Men, Emancipating all Nations, you insist on retaining an absolute power over Wives, But you must remember that Arbitrary power is like most other things which are very hard, very liable to be broken—and notwithstanding all your wise Laws and Maxims we have it in our power not only to free ourselves but to

subdue our Masters, and without violence throw both your natural and legal authority at our feet

> Charm by accepting, by submitting sway
> Yet have our Humour most when we obey.

Source: Adams Family Papers, Massachusetts Historical Society.

Thinking Critically

What rights for women did Abigail Adams advocate? What rights receive no mention in her March 31st letter? What did John Adams mean by "another tribe"? How did he respond to his wife's advice? Both Adamses were keenly aware of class and racial inequalities. How did that awareness shape their respective views of gender inequality?

Predictably, the king and Parliament commanded the strongest support in colonies that had been wracked by internal strife earlier in the eighteenth century. In New York, New Jersey, Pennsylvania, and the Carolinas, not only did memories of old struggles sharpen worries of future upheaval, but old enemies often took different sides in the Revolution. The Carolina backcountry emerged as a stronghold of loyalist sentiment because of influential local men who cast their lot with Britain. To win support against Carolina's rebels, whose ranks included most wealthy coastal planters, western loyalist leaders played on ordinary settlers' resentments of privileged easterners. Grievances dating back to the 1760s also influenced the revolutionary allegiances of former land rioters of New York and New Jersey. If their old landlord opponents opted for the rebel cause, the tenants took up loyalism.

Other influences also fostered allegiance to Britain. Government officials who owed their jobs to the empire, major city merchants who depended on British trade, and Anglicans living outside the South retained strong ties to the parent country. Loyalists were also disproportionately represented among recent emigrants from the British Isles. The inhabitants of Georgia, the newest colony, inclined toward the king, as did the Highland Scots, many of whom had arrived in the colonies as soldiers during the Seven Years' War or had worked for a short time in the southern backcountry as tobacco merchants and Indian traders.

Although a substantial minority, loyalists never became numerous enough anywhere to pose a serious menace to the Revolution. A more formidable threat was posed by the British army. And the greatest threat of all was posed by those very Americans who claimed that they wanted independence. For the question remained: Would they fight?

> ### ✓ REVIEW
> What were the arguments for and against independence, and how did the advocates for independence prevail?

THE FIGHTING IN THE NORTH

IN THE SUMMER OF 1775 Americans who wished to remain neutral probably outnumbered either loyalists or rebels. From the standpoint of mere survival, staying neutral made more sense than fighting for independence. Even the most ardent advocates of American rights had reason to harbor doubts, given the odds against the rebel colonists defeating the armed forces of the British Empire.

GEORGE
WASHINGTON,
GENERAL

Perhaps no friend of American liberty saw more clearly how slim the chances of a rebel victory were than George Washington. But Washington's principles, and his sense of honor, prevailed. June of 1775 found him, then 43 years old, attending the deliberations of the Second Continental Congress and dressed—a bit conspicuously—in his officer's uniform. The other delegates listened closely to his opinions on military matters, because Washington was the most celebrated American veteran of the Seven Years' War who remained young enough to lead a campaign. Better still, as a southerner he could bring his region into what thus far had remained mostly New England's fight. Congress readily appointed him commander-in-chief of a newly created Continental Army.

The Two Armies at Bay

Thus did Washington find himself, only a month later, looking to bring some order to the rebel forces massing around Boston. He knew he faced a formidable foe.

Highly trained, ably led, and efficiently equipped, the king's troops were seasoned professionals. Rigorous drills and often severe discipline welded rank-and-file soldiers, men drawn mostly from the bottom of British society, into a savage fighting machine. At the height of the campaign in America, reinforcements brought the number of British troops to 50,000, strengthened by some 30,000 **Hessian** mercenaries from Germany and the support of half the ships in the British navy, the largest in the world.

"REGULARS" VS.
THE MILITIA

Washington was more modest about the army under his command, and he had much to be modest about. At first Congress recruited his fighting force of 16,600 rebel "regulars," the Continental Army, from the ranks of local New England militia bands. Although enlistments swelled briefly during the patriotic enthusiasm of 1775, for the rest of the war Washington's Continentals suffered chronic shortages of men and supplies. Even strong supporters of the Revolution hesitated to join the regular army, with its low pay and strict discipline and the constant threat of disease and danger. Most men preferred to fight instead as members of local **militia** units, the "irregular" troops who turned out to support the regular army whenever British forces came close to their neighborhoods.

The general reluctance to join the Continental Army created a host of difficulties for its commander and for Congress. Washington wanted and needed an army whose size and military capability could be counted on in long campaigns. He could not create an effective fighting force out of militias that mustered occasionally or men who enlisted for short stints in the Continental Army. In contrast, most republican leaders feared standing armies and idealized "citizen-soldiers"—men of civic virtue who volunteered whenever needed—as the backbone of the common defense. "Oh, that I was a soldier," chubby John Adams fantasized in 1775. "Everyone must and will and shall be a soldier."

But everyone did not become a soldier, and the dwindling number of volunteers gradually overcame republican fears of standing armies. In September 1776 Congress set terms in the Continental Army at a minimum of three years or for the duration of the war and assigned each state to

*Although most New Englanders
rallied behind the rebel cause,
support for the Revolution was
not as widespread in the middle
colonies and southern colonies.*

🟥	Strongly loyalist
🟧	Loyalist or neutral Indians
🟨	Strongly neutralist
🟩	Strong support for rebels
🟪	Other British territory

raise a certain number of troops. They offered every man who enlisted in the army a cash bounty and a yearly clothing issue; enlistees for the duration were offered 100 acres of land as well. Still the problem of recruitment persisted. Less than a year later, Congress recommended that the states adopt a draft, but Congress had no authority to compel the states to meet their troop quotas.

Even in the summer of 1775, before enlistments fell off, Washington was worried. As his inexperienced Continentals laid siege to British-occupied Boston, most officers provided no real leadership, and the men under their command shirked their duties. They slipped away from camp at night; they left sentry duty before being relieved; they took potshots at the British; they tolerated filthy conditions in their camps.

WOMEN OF THE ARMY   While Washington strove to impose discipline on his Continentals, he also attempted, without success, to rid himself of "the Women of the Army." When American men went off to fight,

DAILY LIVES

RADICAL CHIC AND REVOLUTIONARY WOMEN

Women and men of revolutionary America sought to invest themselves with virtue as they escaped British "corruption." The most zealous partisans of colonial rights took that "investiture" to a literal extreme: they made and wore particular clothing as an emblem of political commitment. In the 1760s "homespun," any coarse cloth made in America, became a badge of opposition to British colonial policy.

Clothes sewn from domestic textiles identified the men and women who wore them as friends of liberty, freed from the vanity of British fashion and the humiliating dependence on British imports. As early as 1766 the radical press called for increased domestic industry to offset American reliance on English cloth. It aimed its pleas particularly at the women who managed colonial households.

By 1769 radical propaganda had produced a new ritual of American resistance, the patriotic spinning competition. Wives and daughters from some of the wealthiest and most prominent families, women who had earlier vied to outdo one another in acquiring the latest English finery, were the featured players in this new form of political theater. Its setting was usually the home of a local minister, where, early in the morning, "respectable" young ladies, all dressed in homespun, assembled with their spinning wheels. They spent the day spinning furiously, stopping only to sustain themselves with "American produce . . . which was more agreeable to them than any foreign Dainties and Delicacies" and to drink herbal tea. At

A wheel for spinning flax, made around 1775.

the end of the day the minister accepted their homespun and delivered an edifying sermon to all present. That was a large group, often including from 20 to 100 "respectable" female spinners as well as hundreds of other townsfolk who had come to watch the competition or to provide food and entertainment.

Women reveled in the new attention and value that the male resistance movement and the radical press now attached to a common and humdrum domestic task. By the beginning of 1769 New England newspapers were highlighting spinning bees and their female participants, sometimes termed the "Daughters of Liberty." Wives and daughters from families of every rank were made to feel that they could play an important role in the resistance by imitating the elite women showcased in public spinning spectacles.

Spinning bees and "dressing down" in homespun thus contributed to the solidarity of the resistance by narrowing the visible distance between rich and poor Americans. In accounts of spinning competitions, the radical press emphasized that even the daughters of the elite sacrificed for the cause of resistance by embracing domestic economy and simplicity.

American women took pride in the new political importance that radical propaganda attributed to domestic pursuits. Writing to her English cousin, Charity Clarke of New York City cast herself as one of America's "fighting army of amazones . . . armed with spinning wheels."

Thinking Critically

What are some other historical examples of people using dress or other visible emblems to express their political opinions?

---

their wives usually stayed at home. To women then fell the sole responsibility for running farms and businesses, raising children, and keeping households together. They helped to supply the troops by sewing clothing, making blankets, and saving rags and lead weights for bandages and bullets. Other women on the home front organized relief for the widows and orphans of soldiers and protests against merchants who hoarded scarce commodities.

But the wives of poor men who joined the army were often left with no means to support their families. Thousands of such women—1 for every 15 soldiers—drifted after the troops. In return for half-rations, they cooked and washed for the soldiers; and after battles, they nursed the wounded, buried the dead, and scavenged the field for clothing and

equipment. An even larger number of women accompanied the redcoats: their presence was the only thing that Washington did not admire about the British army and could barely tolerate in his own. But the services that they performed were indispensable, and women followed the troops throughout the war.

Laying Strategies

At the same time that he tried to discipline the Continentals, Washington designed a defensive strategy to compensate for their weakness. To avoid exposing raw rebel troops on "open ground against their Superiors in number and Discipline," he planned to fight the British from strong fortifications. With that aim in mind, in March 1776, Washington barricaded his army on Dorchester Heights, an elevation commanding Boston harbor from the south. That maneuver, which allowed American artillery to fire on enemy warships, confirmed a decision already made by the British to evacuate their entire army from Boston and sail for Halifax, Nova Scotia.

THE BRITISH CHOOSE CONVENTIONAL WAR

Britain had hoped to reclaim its colonies with a strategy of strangling the resistance in Massachusetts. But by the spring of 1776 it saw clearly that more was required than a show of force against New England. Instead, Britain's leaders chose to wage a conventional war in America, capturing major cities and crushing the Continental forces in a decisive battle. Military victory, the British believed, would enable them to restore political control and reestablish imperial authority.

The first target was New York City. General William Howe and Lord George Germain, the British officials now charged with overseeing the war, chose that seaport for its central location and—they hoped—its large loyalist population. Howe's army intended to move from New York City up the Hudson River, meeting with British troops under General Sir Guy Carleton coming south from Canada. Either the British drive would lure Washington into a major engagement, crushing the Continentals, or, if unopposed, the British offensive would cut America in two, smothering resistance to the south by isolating New England.

HOWE BROTHERS

The strategy was sounder than the men placed in charge of executing it. Concern for preserving troops addicted General Howe to caution, when daring more would have carried the day. Howe's brother, Admiral Lord Richard Howe, the head of naval operations in America, also stopped short of pressing the British advantage, owing to his personal desire for reconciliation. The reluctance of the Howe brothers to fight became the formula for British frustration in the two years that followed.

THE CAMPAIGNS IN NEW YORK AND NEW JERSEY

By mid-August, 32,000 British troops, including 8,000 Hessians, the largest expeditionary force of the eighteenth century, faced Washington's army of 23,000, which had marched down from Boston to take up positions on Long Island. At dawn on August 22 the Howe brothers launched their offense, easily pushing the rebel army back across the East River to Manhattan. After lingering on Long Island for a month, the Howes again lurched into action, ferrying their forces to Kip's Bay, just a few miles south of Harlem. When the British landed, the handful of rebel defenders at Kip's Bay fled—straight into the towering wrath of Washington, who happened on the scene during the rout. For once the general lost his habitual self-restraint, flogged both officers and men with his riding crop, and came close to being captured himself. But the Howes remained reluctant to hit hard, letting Washington's army escape from Manhattan to Westchester County.

At the Battle of Princeton, British troops bayoneted the rebel general Hugh Mercer, an assault later memorialized in this painting by George Washington Parke Custis, the adopted step-grandson of George Washington. This rendering focuses attention not only on Mercer's courage but also on the savagery of the redcoats, both of which helped the rebels gain civilian support.

BRITISH CAPTURE NEW YORK CITY

Throughout the fall of 1776 General Howe's forces followed as Washington's fled southward across New Jersey. On December 7, with the British nipping at their heels, the rebels crossed the Delaware River into Pennsylvania. There Howe stopped, pulling back most of his army to winter in New York City and leaving the Hessians to hold the British line of advance along the New Jersey side of the Delaware River.

REBEL VICTORIES AT TRENTON AND PRINCETON

Although the retreat had shriveled rebel strength to only 3,000 men, Washington decided that the campaign of 1776 was not over. On a snowy Christmas night, the Continentals floated back across the Delaware, picked their way over roads iced with sleet, and finally slid into Hessian-held Trenton at eight in the morning. One thousand German soldiers, still recovering from their spirited Christmas celebration and caught completely by surprise, quickly surrendered. Washington's luck held when, on January 3, 1777, the Continentals defeated British troops on the outskirts of Princeton, New Jersey.

During the winter of 1776–1777 the British lost more than battles: they alienated the very civilians whose loyalties they had hoped to maintain. In New York City the presence of the main body of the British army brought shortages of food and housing and caused constant friction between soldiers and city dwellers. In the New Jersey countryside still held by the Hessians, the situation was more desperate. Forced to live off the land, the Germans aroused resentment among local

THE FIGHTING IN THE NORTH, 1775–1777

After the British withdrew from Boston in 1775, they launched an attack on New York City the following year. Washington was forced to retreat northward, then across the Hudson and south into New Jersey and Pennsylvania, before surprising the British at Trenton and Princeton. Burgoyne's surrender at Saratoga in 1777 marked a turning point in the war. **If General Howe had moved forces toward Albany, could he and General Burgoyne have split rebel New England from the rest of the former colonies? How?**

farmers by seizing "hay, oats, Indian corn, cattle, and horses, which were never or but very seldom paid for," as one loyalist admitted. The Hessians ransacked and destroyed homes and churches; they kidnapped and raped young women.

Many repulsed neutrals and loyalists now took their allegiance elsewhere. Bands of militia on Long Island, along the Hudson River, and all over New Jersey rallied to support the Continentals.

Capturing Philadelphia

BRANDYWINE AND GERMANTOWN In the summer of 1777 General Howe still hoped to entice the Continentals into a decisive engagement. But he had now decided

to goad the Americans into battle by capturing Philadelphia. Rather than risk a march through hostile New Jersey, he sailed his army to Maryland and began a march to Philadelphia, 50 miles away. Washington had hoped to stay on the strategic defensive, holding his smaller army together and harassing the enemy but avoiding full-scale battles. Howe's march on the new nation's capital made that impossible. Washington engaged Howe twice—in September at Brandywine Creek and in October in an early dawn attack at Germantown—but both times the rebels were beaten back. He had been unable to prevent the British occupation of Philadelphia.

But in Philadelphia, as in New York, British occupation created hostile feelings, as the flood of troops drove up the price of food, fuel, and housing. While inflation hit hardest at the poor, the wealthy resented British officers who became their uninvited house guests. Philadelphians complained of redcoats looting their shops, trampling their gardens, and harassing them on the streets. Elizabeth Drinker, the wife of a Quaker merchant, confided in her diary that "I often feel afraid to go to bed."

Even worse, the British march through Maryland and Pennsylvania had outraged civilians, who fled before the army and then returned to find their homes and barns bare, their crops and livestock gone. Everywhere Howe's men went in the mid-Atlantic, they left in their wake Americans with compelling reasons to support the rebels. Worst of all, just days after Howe marched his occupying army into Philadelphia in the fall of 1777, another British commander in North America was surrendering his entire army to rebel forces at Saratoga, New York.

Disaster at Saratoga

The calamity that befell the British at Saratoga was the doing of a glory-mongering general, John "Gentleman Johnny" Burgoyne. After his superior officer, Sir Guy Carleton, bungled a drive into New York in 1776, Burgoyne won approval to command another attack from Canada. The following summer he set out from Quebec with a force of 9,500 redcoats, 2,000 women and children, and a baggage train that included the commander's silver dining service, his dress uniforms, and numerous cases of his favorite champagne. As Burgoyne's entourage lumbered southward, it was slowed by a winding road that was broken by boulders, felled trees, and ramshackle bridges. Meanwhile, a handful of Continentals and a horde of New England militia assembled several miles below Saratoga at Bemis Heights under the command of General Horatio Gates.

BURGOYNE SURRENDERS AT SARATOGA On September 19 Gates's rebel scouts, nested high in the trees, spied the glittering bayonets of Burgoyne's approaching force. Benedict Arnold, a brave young officer, led several thousand rebels into battle at a clearing at Freeman's Farm. At the end of the day British reinforcements finally pushed the rebels back from a battlefield piled high with the bodies of soldiers from both sides. Burgoyne tried to flee to Canada but got no farther than Saratoga, where he surrendered his army to Gates on October 17.

Saratoga changed everything. Burgoyne had not just been nipped in a skirmish; he had lost his entire army. The triumph was enough to convince Britain's old rival France that, with a little help, the Americans might well reap the fruits of victory.

REVIEW
What challenges did the Continental Army face between 1775 and 1777?

THE TURNING POINT

FRANCE HAD BEEN WAITING FOR revenge against Britain since its humiliating defeat in the Seven Years' War. And for some years a scheme for evening the score had been taking shape in the mind of the French foreign minister, Charles Gravier de Vergennes. He reckoned that France might turn discontented colonials into willing allies against Britain.

The American Revolution Becomes a Global War

Vergennes approached the Americans cautiously. He wanted to make certain that the rift between Britain and its colonies would not be reconciled and that the rebels in America stood a fighting chance. Although France had been secretly supplying the Continental Army with guns and ammunition since the spring of 1776, Vergennes would go no further than covert assistance.

Congress approached its former French enemies with equal caution. Would France, the leading Catholic monarchy in Europe, make common cause with the republican rebels? A few years earlier American colonials had fought against the French in Canada. Only recently they had renounced a king. For centuries they had overwhelmingly adhered to Protestantism.

The string of defeats dealt the Continental Army during 1776 convinced Congress that they needed the French. In November Congress appointed a three-member commission to negotiate not only aid from France but also a formal alliance. Its senior member was Benjamin Franklin, who enchanted all of Paris when he arrived sporting a simple fur cap and a pair of spectacles (something no fashionable Frenchman wore in public). Hailed as a homespun sage,

The French public's infatuation with Benjamin Franklin knew no bounds. They particularly delighted in his rustic dress and styled him a representative of "frontier" America. He appears in this guise on a snuffbox along with two revered French philosophers, Voltaire and Rousseau.

Franklin played the role of American innocent to the hilt and watched as admiring Parisians stamped his face on everything from the top of snuffboxes to the bottom of porcelain chamber pots.

Still, Franklin understood that mere popularity could not produce the alliance sought by Congress. It was only news that Britain had surrendered an entire army at Saratoga that convinced Vergennes that the rebels could actually win. In February 1778 France signed a treaty of commerce and friendship and a treaty of alliance, which Congress approved in May. Under the terms of the treaties, both parties agreed to accept nothing short of independence for America. The alliance left the British no choice other than to declare war on France. Less than a year later Spain joined France, hoping to recover territory lost to England in earlier wars.

Winding Down the War in the North

The Revolution widened into a global war after 1778. Preparing to fight France and Spain dictated a new British strategy in America. No longer could the British concentrate on crushing the Continental Army. Instead, they would disperse their forces to fend off challenges all over the world. In May Sir Henry Clinton replaced William Howe as commander-in-chief and received orders to withdraw from Philadelphia to New York City.

Only 18 miles outside Philadelphia, at Valley Forge, Washington and his Continentals were assessing their own situation. Some 11,000 rebel soldiers had passed a harrowing winter in that isolated spot, starving for want of food, freezing for lack of clothing, huddling in miserable huts, and hating the British who lay so close and yet so comfortably in Philadelphia. Both officers and rank-and-file cursed their fellow citizens, blaming their suffering on congressional disorganization and civilian indifference. Congress lacked both money to pay and maintain the army and an efficient system for dispensing provisions to the troops. Most farmers and merchants preferred to supply the British, who could pay handsomely, than to do business with a financially strapped Congress. What little did reach the army often was food too rancid to eat or clothing too rotten to wear. Perhaps 2,500 perished at Valley Forge, the victims of cold, hunger, and disease.

Why did civilians who supported the rebel cause allow the army to suffer? Probably because by the winter of 1777, the Continentals came mainly from social classes that received little consideration at any time. The respectable, propertied farmers and artisans who had laid siege to Boston in 1775 had stopped enlisting. Serving in their stead were single men in their teens and early 20s, some who joined the army out of desperation, others who were drafted, still others who were hired as substitutes for the more affluent. The landless sons of farmers, unemployed laborers, drifters, petty criminals, vagrants, indentured servants, slaves, even captured British and Hessian soldiers—all men with no other means and no other choice—were swept into the Continental Army. The social composition of

A member of the Continental Congress (center) refuses to look at the sufferings of cold, poorly clad white soldiers and a wounded African American fallen to the ground. Why would the British have published such a cartoon in 1778? What messages are conveyed?

the rebel rank and file had come to resemble that of the British army. It is the great irony of the Revolution: a war to protect liberty and property was waged by those Americans who were poorest and least free.

The beginning of spring in 1778 brought a reprieve. Supplies arrived at Valley Forge, and so did a fellow calling himself Baron von Steuben, a penniless Prussian soldier of fortune. Although Washington's men had shown spirit and resilience ever since Trenton, they still lacked discipline and training. Those defects and more von Steuben began to remedy. Barking orders and spewing curses in German and French, the baron (and his translators) drilled the rebel regiments to march in formation and to handle their bayonets like proper Prussian soldiers. By the summer of 1778 morale had rebounded.

Spoiling for action after their long winter, Washington's army, now numbering nearly 13,500, harassed Clinton's army as it marched overland from Philadelphia to New York City. On June 28 at Monmouth Courthouse a long, confused battle ended in a draw. After both armies retired for the night, Clinton's forces slipped away to safety in New York City. Washington pursued, but he lacked the numbers to launch an all-out assault on New York City.

While both sides in the Revolution sought Indian allies, the American rebels spread sensationalized stories of British and Indian cruelties. This London cartoon shows the prime minister, Lord North, joining with Indians to feast on a child, an act of cannibalism that revolts even a dog. The archbishop of York promises to walk in God's ways, but is followed by his porter, who professes that "we are hellish good Christians" and carries boxes of scalping knives, tomahawks, and crucifixes. Such propaganda fueled Americans' hatred of Indians as they pushed westward.

ARMY UPRISINGS During the two hard winters that followed, resentments mounted among the rank and file over spoiled food, inadequate clothing, and arrears in pay. The army retaliated with mutinies. Between 1779 and 1780, officers managed to quell uprisings in three New England regiments. But in January 1781 both the Pennsylvania and New Jersey lines in an outright **mutiny** marched on Philadelphia, where Congress had reconvened. Order returned only after Congress promised back pay and provisions and Washington put two ringleaders in front of a firing squad.

War in the West

The battles between Washington's Continentals and the British made the war in the West seem, by comparison, a sideshow of attacks and counterattacks that settled little. American fighters such as George Rogers Clark, with great daring, captured outposts such as Kaskaskia and Vincennes, without materially affecting the outcome of the war. Yet the conflict sparked a tremendous upheaval in the West, both from the dislocations of war and from the disease that spread in war's wake.

INDIANS CAUGHT IN A CROSSFIRE The disruptions were so widespread because the "War for Independence" had also become a war involving the imperial powers of Britain, France, and Spain. The same jockeying for advantage went on in the West as had occurred in previous imperial wars. The United States as well as the European powers pressed Indian tribes to become allies and attacked them when they did not. Caught in the crossfire, some Indian nations were pushed to the brink of their own civil war, splitting into pro-American or pro-British factions. None suffered more than the mighty Iroquois. When days of impassioned speeches failed to secure a unified Iroquois policy regarding the Revolution, the six confederated tribes went their own ways. Most Tuscaroras and Oneidas remained neutral or joined the Americans, whereas Mohawk, Onondaga, Seneca, and Cayuga warriors aided the British by attacking frontier settlements. This pro-British faction rallied around the remarkable Mohawk leader Joseph Brant. Bilingual, literate, and formidable in war, Brant helped lead devastating raids across the frontiers of New York and Pennsylvania. In response Washington dispatched troops into Iroquois country, where they put the torch to 40 towns and destroyed fields and orchards everywhere they went. Many Iroquois perished the following winter—whichever side they had supported in the war—and the confederacy emerged from the Revolution with but a shadow of its former power.

Other native peoples switched allegiances more than once. Near St. Louis, a young Kaskaskia chief, Jean Baptiste de Coigne, allied first with the French, then joined the British and briefly threw in his lot with the Spanish, before finally joining the Virginians. Indians understood well that the pressures of war always threatened to deprive them of their homelands. "You are drawing so close to us that we can almost hear the noise of your axes felling our Trees," one Shawnee told the Americans. Another group of Indians concluded in 1784 that the Revolutionary War had been "the greatest blow that could have been dealt us, unless it had been our total destruction." Thousands fled the

THE SMALLPOX PANDEMIC, 1775–1782

Smallpox spread across North America beginning late in 1775 as American forces launched an unsuccessful attack on the city of Quebec in Canada. The routes of transmission give only a rough idea of the disease's spread and impact, as it moved down the Eastern Seaboard and around the Gulf of Mexico, and then penetrated the interior, where the scattered surviving data make the pandemic's progress much harder to track. But the ravages of smallpox, combined with the disruptions sparked by the western raids of the Revolutionary War, placed severe stress on Indian peoples all across the continent. The disruption continued through the end of the eighteenth century.

→ Known transmission route
→ Probable transmission route

raids and counter-raids, while whole villages relocated. Hundreds made their way even beyond the Mississippi, to seek shelter in territory claimed by Spain. The aftershocks and dislocations continued for the next two decades; an entire generation of Native Americans grew up with war as a constant companion.

SMALLPOX PANDEMIC The political instability was vastly compounded by a smallpox epidemic that broke out first among American troops besieging Quebec in 1775. The disease soon spread to Continentals in New England, and Washington was obliged to inoculate them—secretly, for the vaccination left many soldiers temporarily weakened. From New England, the pox spread south along the coast, eventually reached New Orleans and next leapt to Mexico City by the autumn of 1779. From New Orleans it spread via fur traders up the Mississippi River and across the central plains, and from New Spain northward as well. By the time the pandemic burned out in 1782, it had felled over 130,000. By contrast, the Revolutionary War caused the deaths of some 8,000 soldiers while fighting in battle and another 13,000 from disease, including the mortality from smallpox.

The Home Front in the North

Although in 1779 most northern civilians on the Eastern Seaboard enjoyed a respite from the war, the devastation lingered. Refugees on foot and in hastily packed carts filled the roads, fleeing the advancing armies. Those who remained to protect their homes and property might be caught in the crossfire of contending forces or cut off from supplies of food and firewood. Loyalists who remained in areas occupied by rebel troops faced harassment, imprisonment, or the confiscation of their property. Rebel sympathizers met similar fates in regions held by the British.

WOMEN AND THE WAR The demands of war also disrupted family economies throughout the northern countryside. The seasons of intense fighting drew men off into military service just when their labor was most needed on family farms. Wives and daughters were left to assume the work of husbands and sons while coping with loneliness, anxiety, and grief. Two years after she fled before Burgoyne's advance into upstate New York, Ann Eliza Bleecker confessed to a friend, "Alas! the wilderness is within: I muse so long on the dead until I am unfit for the company of the living."

Despite these hardships, many women vigorously supported the revolutionary cause in a variety of ways. The Daughters of Liberty joined in harassing opponents to the rebel cause. One outspoken loyalist found himself surrounded by angry women who stripped off his shirt, covered him with molasses, and plastered him with flower petals. In more genteel fashion, groups of well-to-do women collected not only money but also medicines, food, and pewter to melt for bullets.

✔ REVIEW

How did the Revolution become a global war, and what were conditions like for both soldiers and civilians?

THE STRUGGLE IN THE SOUTH

DESPITE THEIR ARMED PRESENCE IN the North, the British had come to believe by the autumn of 1778 that their most vital aim was to regain their colonies in the mainland South. The Chesapeake and the Carolinas were more profitable to the empire and more strategically important, being so much closer to rich British sugar islands in the West Indies. Inspired by this new "southern strategy," Clinton dispatched forces to the Caribbean and Florida. In addition, the British laid plans for a new offensive drive into the Carolinas and Virginia.

BRITAIN'S SOUTHERN STRATEGY

English politicians and generals believed that the war could be won in the South. Loyalists were numerous, they believed, especially in the backcountry, where resentment of the patriot seaboard would encourage frontier folk to take up arms for the king at the first show of British force. And southern rebels—especially the vulnerable planters along the coast—could not afford to turn their guns away from their slaves. So, at least, the British theorized. All that was needed, they concluded, was that the British army establish a beachhead in the South and then, in league with loyalists, drive northward, up the coast.

The Siege of Charleston

The southern strategy worked well for a short time in a small place. In November 1778 Clinton sent 3,500 troops to Savannah, Georgia. The resistance in the tiny colony quickly collapsed, and a large number of loyalists turned out to help the British. Encouraged, the army moved on to South Carolina.

During the last days of 1779 an expedition under Clinton himself set sail from New York City. Landing off the Georgia coast, his troops mucked through malarial swamps to the peninsula lying between the Ashley and Cooper Rivers. At the tip of that neck of land stood Charleston, and the British began to lay siege. By then, an unseasonably warm spring had set in, making the area a heaven for

mosquitoes and a hell for human beings. Sweltering and swatting, redcoats weighted down in their woolen uniforms inched their siege works toward the city. By early May Clinton's army had closed in, and British shelling was setting fire to houses within the city. On May 12 Charleston surrendered.

Clinton sailed back to New York at the end of June 1780, leaving behind 8,300 redcoats to carry the British offensive northward to Virginia. The man charged with leading that campaign was his ambitious and able subordinate, Charles, Lord Cornwallis.

The Partisan Struggle in the South

Cornwallis's task in the Carolinas was complicated by the bitter animosity between rebels and loyalists there. Many Carolinians had taken sides years before Clinton's conquest of Charleston. In the summer and fall of 1775 the supporters of Congress and the new South Carolina revolutionary government mobbed, tortured, and imprisoned supporters of the king in the backcountry. These attacks only hardened loyalist resolve: roving bands seized ammunition, broke their leaders out of jail, and besieged rebel outposts. But within a matter of months, a combined force of rebel militias from the coast and the frontier managed to defeat loyalist forces in the backcountry.

REBELS AND LOYALISTS BATTLE FOR THE BACKCOUNTRY

With the fall of Charleston in 1780, the loyalist movement on the frontier returned to life. Out of loyalist vengefulness and rebel desperation issued the brutal civil war that seared the southern backcountry after 1780. Neighbors and even families fought and killed each other as members of roaming rebel and tory militias. The intensity of **partisan warfare** in the backcountry produced unprecedented destruction. Loyalist militia plundered plantations and assaulted local women; rebel militias whipped suspected British supporters and burned their farms; both sides committed brutal assassinations and tortured prisoners. All of society, observed one minister, "seems to be at an end. Every person keeps close on his own plantation. Robberies and murders are often committed on the public roads. . . . Poverty, want, and hardship appear in almost every countenance."

Cornwallis, when confronted with the chaos, erred fatally. He did nothing to stop his loyalist allies or his own troops from mistreating civilians. A Carolina loyalist admitted that "the lower sort of People, who were in many parts originally attached to the British Government, have suffered so severely . . . that Great Britain has now a hundred enemies, where it had one before." Although rebels and loyalists alike plundered and terrorized the backcountry, Cornwallis's forces bore more of the blame and suffered the consequences.

A growing number of civilians outraged by the behavior of the king's troops cast their lot with the rebels. That upsurge of popular support enabled Francis Marion, the

"Swamp Fox," and his band of white and black raiders to cut British lines of communication between Charleston and the interior. It swelled another rebel militia led by "the Gamecock," Thomas Sumter, who bloodied loyalist forces throughout the central part of South Carolina. It mobilized the "over-the-mountain men," a rebel militia in western Carolina who claimed victory at the Battle of Kings Mountain in October 1780. By the end of 1780 these successes had persuaded most civilians that only the rebels could restore order.

BRITISH VICTORY AT CAMDEN

If rebel fortunes prospered in the partisan struggle, they faltered in the conventional warfare being waged at the same time in the South. In August of 1780 the Continentals commanded by Horatio Gates lost a major engagement to the British force at Camden, South Carolina. In the fall of 1780 Congress replaced Gates with Washington's candidate for the southern command, Nathanael Greene, an energetic 38-year-old Rhode Islander and a veteran of the northern campaigns.

Greene Takes Command

Greene bore out Washington's confidence by grasping the military situation in the South. He understood the needs of

General Nathanael Greene

his 1,400 hungry, ragged, and demoralized troops and instructed von Steuben to lobby Virginia for food and clothing. He understood the importance of the rebel militias and sent Lieutenant Colonel Henry "Lighthorse Harry" Lee to assist Marion's raids. He understood the weariness of southern civilians and prevented his men from plundering the countryside.

Above all, Greene understood that his forces could never hold the field against the whole British army, a decision that led him to break the first rule of conventional warfare: he divided his army. In December 1780 he dispatched to western South Carolina a detachment of 600 men under the command of Brigadier General Daniel Morgan of Virginia.

COWPENS

Back at the British camp, Cornwallis worried that Morgan and his rebels, if left unchecked, might rally the entire backcountry against the British. However, Cornwallis reckoned that he could not commit his entire army to the pursuit of Morgan's men, because then Greene and his troops might retake Charleston. The only solution, unconventional to be sure, was that Cornwallis divide *his* army. That he did, sending Lieutenant Colonel Banastre Tarleton and 1,100 men west after Morgan. Cornwallis had played right into Greene's hands: the rebel troops

THE FIGHTING IN THE SOUTH, 1780–1781

In December 1780 Nathanael Greene made the crucial decision to split his army, sending Daniel Morgan west, where he defeated the pursuing Banastre Tarleton at Cowpens. Meanwhile, Greene regrouped and replenished at Cheraw, keeping Cornwallis off balance with a raid (dotted line) toward Charleston and the coast. Then, with Cornwallis in hot pursuit, Greene and Morgan rejoined at Salisbury, retreating into Virginia. Cornwallis was worn down in this vain pursuit and lost three-quarters of the troops he began with before finally abandoning the Carolina campaign.

In 1845 painter William Ranney re-created a traditional retelling or account of the Battle of Cowpens recorded in John Marshall's biography of George Washington. According to Marshall, "a waiter, too small to wield a sword" saved the life of a relative of George Washington during the battle. Just as Lieutenant Colonel William Washington, leader of the patriot cavalry, was about to be cut down by a sword, the black man "saved him by wounding the officer with a ball from a pistol." Ranney depicts the unnamed man as a bugler astride a horse, as Morgan and Washington battle three British soldiers.

might be able to defeat a British army split into two pieces. For two weeks Morgan led Tarleton's troops on a breakneck chase across the Carolina countryside. In January 1781 at an open meadow called Cowpens, Morgan routed Tarleton's force.

Now Cornwallis took up the chase. Morgan and Greene joined forces and kept going north until the British army wore out. Cornwallis finally stopped at Hillsboro, North Carolina, but few local loyalists responded to his call for reinforcements. Greene decided to make a show of force near the tiny village of Guilford Courthouse. On a brisk March day the two sides joined battle, each sustaining severe casualties before Greene was forced to retreat. But the high cost of victory convinced Cornwallis that he could not put down the rebellion in the Carolinas. "I am quite tired of marching about the country in quest of adventures," he informed Clinton.

VALUE OF THE MILITIA
Although Nathanael Greene's command provided the Continentals with effective leadership in the South, it was the resilience of rebel militia that thwarted the British offensive in the Carolinas. Many Continental Army officers complained about the militia's lack of discipline, its habit of melting away when homesickness set in or harvest approached, and its cowardice under fire in conventional engagements. But when set the task of ambushing supply trains, harrying bands of local loyalists, or raiding isolated British outposts, the militia came through. Many southern civilians refused to join the British or to provide the redcoats with food and information, because they knew that once the British army left their neighborhoods, the rebel militia would be back. The Continental Army in the South lost many conventional battles, but the militia kept the British from restoring political control over the backcountry.

African Americans in the Age of Revolution

The British also lost in the Carolinas because they did not seek greater support from those southerners who would have fought for liberty *with* the British—African American slaves.

Black Americans, virtually all in bondage, made up one-third of the population between Delaware and Georgia. Since the beginning of the resistance to Britain, white southerners had worried that the watchwords of *liberty* and *equality* would spread to the slave quarters. Gripped by the fear of slave rebellion, southern revolutionaries began to take precautions. Marylanders disarmed black inhabitants and issued extra guns to the white militia. Charlestonians hanged and then burned the body of Thomas Jeremiah, a free black who was convicted of spreading the word to others that the British "were come to help the poor Negroes."

WHITE FEARS OF REBELLION
Southern whites fully expected the British to turn slave rebelliousness to their strategic advantage. As early as 1775 Virginia's royal governor, Lord Dunmore, confirmed white fears by offering to free any slave who joined the British. When Clinton invaded the South in 1779 he renewed that offer. One North Carolina planter heard that loyalists were "promising every Negro that would murder his master and family he should have his Master's plantation" and that "the Negroes have got it amongst them and believe it to be true."

HISTORIAN'S TOOLBOX

RUNAWAYS

What is implied by the tallying of children ["girls" and "boys"] with slave women?

What is the significance of the list specifyir occupations for some of the slave men?

A List of Negroes that went off to Dunmore April 14 1776.

Women	Ages	Girls	Boys	Negro Men	Ages
Pleasant	55	1		Sawney a Sawyer	60
Nancy	46	4		Tobey Do	54
Marcy	30	2	2	Ned	44
Judey	28	3	2	Peter a house Carpenter	37
Lucey	25	1	3	James a Shoemaker	35
Keziah	23		3	Robin a Sawyer	25
Cate	30	2	1	Bob	30
Rachel	25		4	Charles	24
Easter	27		3	Glascow	21
Betsey	23	1		Will	21
Jeney	42			Anthony	19
Linah	27	2	2	George	18
Manda	25		3	Jacob	20
Dynah	26	2		Isaack	16
Lidia	26	2	1		
Aby	27		3	Total 87	
Bess	23	1			
Jeney	30				
Josse	16			Entailed.	
Nell	25	2		Brister a Sawyer	25
Pegg	18	Nell's		Moses a house Carp	25

Fee Simple

Women	Girls	Boys	Men
21	23	27	16

Jno Willoughby

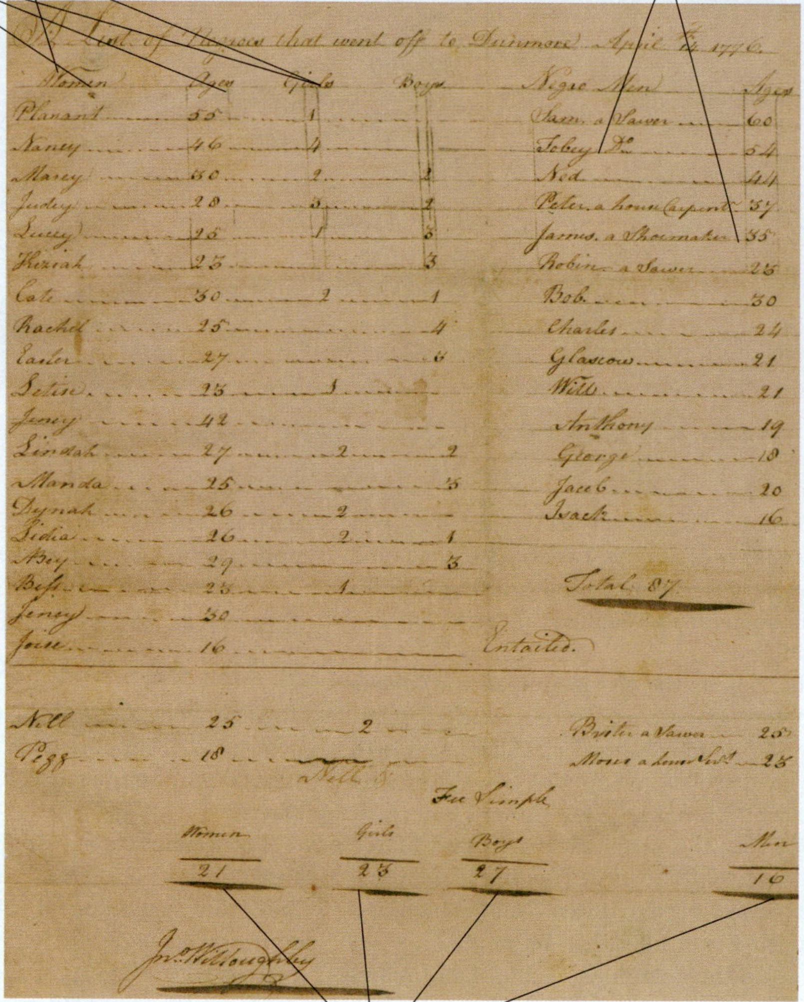

How does the number of female runaways compare with that of males? Children with adults?

"A List of Negroes That Went Off to Dunmore," dated April 14, 1776, Library of Virginia, Richmond.

Americans in earlier centuries were inveterate listmakers, providing present-day historians with a rich trove of evidence. College students recorded the titles of books they read; ministers noted the Bible passages on which they preached; clerks kept count of church members; tax assessors enumerated household members and the rates owed and paid; probate court officers inventoried the possessions of the dead, often down to chipped crockery and broken tools. But the roster of slaves shown above is an extraordinary list, drawn up not on account of their master's death but because these 87 men, women, and children had fled their Virginia plantation, emboldened by Lord Dunmore's promise of freedom. It is impossible to know whether they ran away in small groups, stealing off over a period of several months between 1775 and 1776, or whether they ran away in larger companies within the space of a few days. But we do know that throughout Virginia, as on this plantation, women and children made up a significant percentage of the runaways.

Thinking Critically

For what purposes might the Virginia master have composed this list? Why are slave artisans so well represented among the men on this list? Why were slave women and their children willing to risk escape in such large numbers?

But in Britain there was overwhelming opposition to organizing support among African Americans. British leaders dismissed Dunmore's ambitious scheme to raise a black army of 10,000 and another plan to create a sanctuary for black loyalists on the southeastern coast. Turning slaves against masters, they recognized, was not the way to conciliate southern whites.

Even so, southern fears of insurrection made the rebels reluctant to enlist black Americans as soldiers. At first, Congress barred African Americans from the Continental Army. But as the rebels became more desperate for manpower, policy changed. Northern states actively encouraged black enlistments, and in the Upper South, some states allowed free men of color to join the army or permitted slaves to substitute for their masters.

AFRICAN AMERICAN QUESTS FOR LIBERTY

Slaves themselves sought freedom from whichever side seemed most likely to grant it. Perhaps 10,000 slaves took up Dunmore's offer in 1775 and deserted their masters, and thousands more flocked to Clinton's forces after the fall of Charleston. For many runaways the hope of liberation proved an illusion. Although some served the British army as laborers, spies, and soldiers, many died of disease in army camps (upward of 27,000 by one estimate) or were sold back into slavery in the West Indies. About 5,000 black soldiers served in the revolutionary army in the hope of gaining freedom. In addition, the number of runaways to the North soared during the Revolution. In total, perhaps 100,000 men and women—nearly a fifth of the total slave population—attempted to escape bondage. Their odysseys to freedom took some to far-flung destinations: loyalist communities in Nova Scotia, a settlement established by the British in Sierra Leone on the West African coast, even the Botany Bay penal colony in Australia.

The slave revolts so dreaded by southern whites never materialized. Possibly the boldest slaves were drawn off into the armies; possibly greater white precautions discouraged schemes for black rebellions. In South Carolina, where the potential for revolt was greatest, most slaves chose to remain on plantations rather than risk a collective resistance and escape in the midst of the fierce partisan warfare.

✓ **REVIEW**

Why did the British fail to achieve their military and political goals in the South?

THE WORLD TURNED UPSIDE DOWN

DESPITE HIS LOSSES IN THE Carolinas, Cornwallis still believed that he could score a decisive victory against the Continental Army. The theater he chose for that showdown was the Chesapeake. During the spring of 1781 he had marched his army to the Virginia coast and joined forces with the hero of Saratoga and newly turned loyalist, Benedict Arnold. Embarrassed by debt and disgusted by Congress's shabby treatment of the Continental Army, Arnold had started exchanging rebel secrets for British money in 1779 before defecting outright in the fall of 1780. By June of 1781 Arnold and Cornwallis were fortifying a site on the tip of the peninsula formed by the York and James Rivers, a place called Yorktown.

Meanwhile, Washington and his French ally, the comte de Rochambeau, met in Connecticut to plan a major attack. Rochambeau urged a coordinated land-sea assault on the Virginia coast. Washington insisted instead on a full-scale offensive against New York City. Just when the rebel commander was about to have his way, word arrived that a French fleet under the comte de Grasse was sailing for the Chesapeake to blockade Cornwallis by sea. Washington's Continentals headed south.

Surrender at Yorktown

By the end of September, 7,800 Frenchmen, 5,700 Continentals, and 3,200 militia had sandwiched Yorktown between the devil of an allied army and the deep blue sea of French warships. "If you cannot relieve me very soon," Cornwallis wrote to Clinton, "you must expect to hear the worst." The British navy did arrive—but seven days after Cornwallis surrendered to the rebels on October 19, 1781. When Germain carried the news from Yorktown to the king's first minister, Lord North replied, "Oh, God, it is over." Then North resigned, Germain resigned, and even George III murmured something about abdicating.

It need not have ended at Yorktown, but timing made all the difference. At the end of 1781 and early in 1782, the British army received setbacks in the other theaters of the war: India, the West Indies, and Florida. The French and the Spanish were everywhere in Europe as well, gathering in the English Channel, planning a major offensive against Gibraltar. The cost of the fighting was already enormous. British leaders recognized that the rest of the empire was at stake and set about cutting their losses in America.

The Treaty of Paris, signed on September 3, 1783, was a diplomatic triumph for the American negotiators: Benjamin Franklin, John Adams, and John Jay. They dangled before Britain the possibility that a generous settlement might weaken American ties to France. The British jumped at the bait. They recognized the independence of the United States and agreed to ample boundaries for the new nation: the Mississippi River on the west, the 31st parallel on the south, and the present border of Canada on the north. American negotiators then persuaded a skeptical France to approve the treaty by arguing that, as allies, they were bound to present a united front to the British. Spain, the third member of the alliance, settled for retaining Florida and Minorca, an island in the Mediterranean.

On September 30, 1780, a wagon bearing this two-faced effigy was drawn through the streets of Philadelphia. The effigy represents Benedict Arnold, who sits between a gallows and the devil. Note the similarities between this piece of street theater and the demonstrations mounted on Pope's Day several decades earlier, shown on page 146.

If the Treaty of Paris marked both the end of a war and the recognition of a new nation, the surrender at Yorktown captured the significance of a revolution. Those present at Yorktown on that clear autumn afternoon in 1781 watched as the British second in command to Cornwallis (who had sent word that he was "indisposed") surrendered his superior's sword. He offered the sword first, in a face-saving gesture, to the French commander, Rochambeau, who politely refused and pointed to Washington. But the American commander-in-chief, out of a mixture of military protocol, nationalistic pride, and perhaps even wit, pointed to *his* second in command, Benjamin Lincoln.

Some witnesses recalled that British musicians arrayed on the Yorktown green played "The World Turned Upside Down." Their recollections may have been faulty, but the story has persisted as part of the folklore of the American Revolution—and for good reasons. The world had, it seemed, turned upside down with the coming of American independence.

✔ REVIEW

How did the United States manage to prevail in the war and in the treaty negotiations?

CONCLUSION

THE WORLD AT LARGE

The colonial rebels shocked the British with their answer to the question "Would they fight?" The answer had been yes—but on their own terms. By 1777 most propertied Americans avoided fighting in the Continental Army. Yet whenever the war reached their homes, farms, and businesses, many Americans gave their allegiance to the new nation by turning out with rifles or supplying homespun clothing, food, or ammunition. They rallied around Washington in New Jersey, Gates in upstate New York, Greene in the Carolinas. Middle-class American men fought, some from idealism, others out of self-interest, but always on their own terms, as members of the militia. These citizen-soldiers turned the world upside down by defeating professional armies.

Of course, the militia did not bear the brunt of the fighting. That responsibility fell to the Continental Army, which by 1777 drew its strength from the poorest ranks of American society. Yet even the Continentals, for all their desperation, managed to fight on their own terms. Some asserted their rights by raising mutinies, until Congress redressed their grievances. All of them, as the Baron von Steuben observed, behaved differently than European soldiers did. Americans followed orders only if the logic of commands was explained to them. The Continentals, held in contempt by most Americans, turned the world upside down by sensing their power and asserting their measure of personal independence.

Americans of African descent dared as much and more in their quests for liberty. Whether they chose to escape slavery by fighting for the British or the Continentals or by striking out on their own as runaways, their defiance, too, turned the world upside down. Among the tens of thousands of slaves who would not be mastered was one Henry Washington, a native of Africa who became the slave of George Washington in 1763. But Henry Washington made his own declaration of independence in 1776, slipping behind British lines and serving as a corporal in a black unit. Thereafter, like thousands of former slaves, he sought to build a new life elsewhere in the Atlantic world, settling first in Nova Scotia and finally in Sierra Leone. By 1800 he headed a community of former slaves who were exiled to the outskirts of that colony for their determined efforts to win republican self-government from Sierra Leone's white British rulers. Like Thomas Paine, Henry Washington believed that freedom was his only country.

In all those ways, a revolutionary generation turned the world upside down. They were a diverse lot—descended from Indians, Europeans, and Africans, driven by desperation or idealism or greed—but joined, even if they did not recognize it, by their common struggle to break free from the rule of monarchs or masters. What now awaited them in the world of the new United States? ∞∞∞

CHAPTER SUMMARY

THE AMERICAN REVOLUTION BROUGHT INDEPENDENCE to Britain's former colonies after an armed struggle that began in 1775 and concluded with the Treaty of Paris in 1783.

- When the Second Continental Congress first convened, many delegates still hoped for reconciliation—even as they created the Continental Army.

- The Second Continental Congress adopted the Declaration of Independence on July 4, 1776.

- British victories in the North throughout 1776 and 1777 secured both New York City and Philadelphia. But harsh tactics alienated much of the populace.

- The British suffered a disastrous defeat at the Battle of Saratoga in early 1778, which prompted France to openly ally with the American rebels soon thereafter.

- By 1780 Britain aimed to win the war by claiming the South, and captured both Savannah, Georgia, and Charleston, South Carolina.

- Although the war in the West contributed little to the outcome of the Revolution, the competition for Indian allies among the United States, Britain, France, and Spain sparked two decades of dislocation and conflict across the continent, a situation made worse by a smallpox pandemic.

- The Continental Army in the South, led by Nathanael Greene and aided by guerrilla fighters in the partisan struggle, foiled the British strategy, and Cornwallis surrendered at the Battle of Yorktown in 1781.

- Except during the first year of fighting, the rank and file of the Continental Army were drawn from the poorest Americans, whose needs for food, clothing, and shelter were neglected by the Continental Congress.

ADDITIONAL READING

THE OUTSTANDING MILITARY HISTORIES OF the American Revolution are Don Higginbotham, *The War for American Independence* (1971), and Robert Middlekauff, *The Glorious Cause,* 1763 to 1789 (1982). For a compelling treatment of the lives of soldiers in the Continental Army, read Caroline Cox, *A Proper Sense of Honor* (2004), and to become better acquainted with their commander-in-chief, turn to *His Excellency: George Washington* (2004) by Joseph Ellis. Colin Calloway, *The American Revolution in Indian Country* (1995), probes the role of American Indians in that conflict, and Peter Silver explores the Revolution's spur to Indian-hating in *Our Savage Neighbors* (2008). Benjamin Franklin's efforts to secure an alliance with France are vividly told in Stacy Schiff, *A Great Improvisation* (2005), and the best introductions to the global context of the American Revolution are David Armitage, *The Declaration of Independence* (2007), and P. J. Marshall, *The Making and Unmaking of Empires* (2005).

Impressive interpretations of the war's impact on American society include Alfred Young, *Liberty Tree* (2006), Charles Royster, *A Revolutionary People at War* (1979), and John Shy, *A People Numerous and Armed* (1976). Sylvia Frey offers a thoughtful history of African Americans during this era in *Water from the Rock* (1991), and Cassandra Pybus, *Epic Journeys of Freedom* (2006), recounts the experiences of runaway slaves who seized on the wartime crisis to gain liberty. The role of women in revolutionary America receives excellent coverage in Carol Berkin, *Revolutionary Mothers* (2005), and in Mary Beth Norton's classic study, *Liberty's Daughters* (1980).

For a fuller list of readings, see the Bibliography at www.mhhe.com/eh8e.

SIGNIFICANT EVENTS

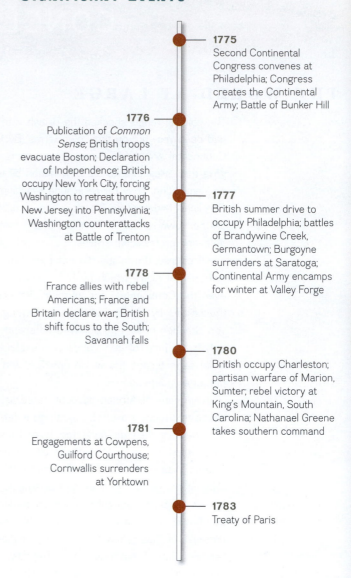

1775
Second Continental Congress convenes at Philadelphia; Congress creates the Continental Army; Battle of Bunker Hill

1776
Publication of *Common Sense;* British troops evacuate Boston; Declaration of Independence; British occupy New York City, forcing Washington to retreat through New Jersey into Pennsylvania; Washington counterattacks at Battle of Trenton

1777
British summer drive to occupy Philadelphia; battles of Brandywine Creek, Germantown; Burgoyne surrenders at Saratoga; Continental Army encamps for winter at Valley Forge

1778
France allies with rebel Americans; France and Britain declare war; British shift focus to the South; Savannah falls

1780
British occupy Charleston; partisan warfare of Marion, Sumter; rebel victory at King's Mountain, South Carolina; Nathanael Greene takes southern command

1781
Engagements at Cowpens, Guilford Courthouse; Cornwallis surrenders at Yorktown

1783
Treaty of Paris

British and American Forces in the Revolutionary War Compared

	IN THEORY	ON THE GROUND
British	Advantage: superior army	Advantage: training paid off in winning many major battles and controlling cities
		Disadvantage: but formal training left British forces vulnerable to guerrilla attacks
	Advantage: superior navy	Advantage neutralized by French navy at Cornwallis's surrender
		Disadvantage: entry of France into the war in 1778 obliged the British to divide their forces
		Disadvantage: British troops alienated rather than conciliated civilians
American	Disadvantage: badly trained, supplied, and equipped	Disadvantage: took years for the Continentals to gain training, discipline, and experience
	Advantage: militias turned out to defend home territories	Disadvantage: militias tended to disappear when the immediate threat passed
	Advantage: French alliance	Disadvantage: took Franklin's diplomacy nearly 3 years to secure alliance
	Disadvantage: slaves running for freedom undermined rebel resolve	Disadvantage neutralized: except for Dunmore, British were reluctant to enlist African Americans

South Carolina's low country supplies the background for this portrait of a wealthy Charleston couple, John Purves and his wife, Anne Pritchard Purves. John saw military service in both the state militia and the Continental Army; Anne, with her classically draped dress, evokes the goddess of Liberty. What do you make of the expressions on their faces?

CHAPTER 8

Crisis and Constitution

1776–1789

What's to Come

∞∞∞ AN AMERICAN STORY ∞∞∞

"*THESE* UNITED STATES"

"I am not a Virginian, but an American," Patrick Henry declared in the Virginia House of Burgesses. Most likely he was lying. Certainly no one listening took him seriously, for the newly independent colonists did not identify themselves as members of a nation. They would have said, as did Thomas Jefferson, "Virginia, Sir, is my country." Or as John Adams wrote to another native son, "Massachusetts is our country." Jefferson and Adams were men of wide political vision and experience: both were leaders in the Continental Congress and more inclined than most to think nationally. But like other members of the revolutionary generation, they identified deeply with their home states and even more deeply with their home counties and towns.

It followed that allegiance to the states, not the Union, determined the shape of the first republican political experiments. For a decade after independence, the revolutionaries were less committed to creating an American nation than to organizing 13 separate state republics. The Declaration of Independence referred explicitly not to *the* United States but to *these* United States. It envisioned not one republic so much as a federation of 13.

Only when peace was restored during the decade of the 1780s were Americans forced to face some unanswered questions raised by their revolution. The Declaration proclaimed that these "free and independent states" had "full power to levy war, conclude peace, contract alliances, establish commerce." Did that mean that New Jersey, as a free and independent state, could sign a trade agreement with France, excluding the other states? If the United States were to be more than a loose federation, how could it assert power on a national scale? Similarly, American borderlands to the west presented problems. If these territories were settled by Americans, would they eventually join the United States? Go their own ways as independent nations? Become new colonies of Spain or England?

Such problems were more than political; they were rooted in social realities. For a political union to succeed, the inhabitants of 13 separate states had to start thinking of themselves as Americans. When it came right down to it, what united a Vermont farmer working his rocky fields and a South Carolina gentleman presiding over a vast rice plantation? What bonds existed between a Kentuckian rafting the Ohio River and a Salem merchant sailing to China for porcelain?

And in a society in which all citizens were said to be "created equal," the inevitable social inequalities had to be confronted. How could women participate in the Revolution's bid for freedom if they were not free to vote or to hold property? How would free or enslaved African Americans live in a republic based on equality? As the British began leaving Yorktown, Charleston, and other ports, they transferred thousands of slaves who had been in their charge to New York City. Southern slaveholders followed, looking to reclaim their bondspeople. "The dreadful rumor" that slave masters were searching for their property "filled us all with inexpressible anguish and horror," reported Boston King, an escaped slave who had fought for the British; ". . . for some days we lost our appetite for food and sleep from our eyes." Repossessing such slaves could be perilous. One master was murdered by "about 12 or 15 of the Ward's blacks" when he came looking. How could black Americans feel a bond with white Americans when so often the only existing bonds had been forged with chains?

The Revolution provided many humble folk a new sense of pride and potential. These men, who manufactured pewter mugs and teapots, gave their support to the new Constitution: a "Federal Plan most solid and secure."

To such questions there were no final answers in 1781. There was ferment, excitement, and experimentation as 13 states each sought to create their governments anew; as Americans—or rather, Virginians and New Yorkers and Georgians and citizens of other countries—began to imagine how the revolutionary virtue of equality might transform their societies. But as the decade progressed, the sense of crisis deepened. ∞

REPUBLICAN EXPERIMENTS

AFTER INDEPENDENCE WAS DECLARED IN July 1776, many of America's best political minds turned to drawing up **constitutions** for their individual states. Thomas Jefferson deserted the Continental Congress, leaving the conduct of the war and national affairs to other men, for the more important business of creating Virginia's new government.

BELIEF IN THE
NEED FOR SMALL
REPUBLICS

In truth, the state constitutions were crucial republican experiments, the first efforts at establishing a government of and by the people. All the revolutionaries agreed that the people—not a king or a few privileged aristocrats—should rule. Yet they were equally certain that republican governments were best suited to small territories. They believed that the new United States was too sprawling and its people too diverse to be safely consolidated into a single national republic. They feared, too, that the government of a large republic would inevitably grow indifferent to popular concerns, being distant from many of its citizens. Without being under the watchful eye of the people, representatives would become less accountable to the electorate and turn tyrannical. A federation of small state republics, they reasoned, would stand a far better chance of enduring.

The State Constitutions

The new state constitutions retained the basic form of their old colonial governments, all except Georgia and Pennsylvania providing for a governor and a bicameral legislature. But although most states did not alter the basic structure of their governments, they changed dramatically the balance of power among the different branches of government.

CURBING EXECUTIVE POWER From the republican perspective in 1776, the greatest problem of any government lay in curbing executive power. What had driven Americans into rebellion was the abuse of authority by the king and his appointed officials. To ensure that the executive could never again threaten popular liberty, the new states either accorded almost no power to their governors or abolished that office entirely. The governors had no authority to convene or dissolve the legislatures. They could not veto the legislatures' laws, grant land, or erect courts. Most important from the republican point of view, governors had few powers to appoint other state officials. All these limits were designed to deprive the executive of any patronage or other form of influence over the legislature. By reducing the governors' power, Americans hoped to preserve their states from the corruption that they deplored in British political life.

STRENGTHENING LEGISLATIVE POWERS What the state governors lost, the legislatures gained. Sam Adams, the Boston rebel leader, expressed the political consensus when he declared that "every legislature of every colony ought to be the sovereign and uncontrollable Power within its own limits of territory." To ensure that those powerful legislatures truly represented the will of the people, the new state constitutions called for annual elections and required candidates for the legislature to live in the districts they represented. Many states even asserted the right of voters to instruct the men elected to office about how to vote on specific issues. Although no state granted universal manhood suffrage, most reduced the amount of property required of qualified voters. Finally, state supreme courts were also either elected by the legislatures or appointed by elected governors.

By investing all power in popular assemblies, Americans abandoned the British system of mixed government. In one sense, that change was fairly democratic. A majority of voters within a state could do whatever they wanted, unchecked by governors or courts. On the other hand, the arrangement opened the door for legislatures to turn as tyrannical as governors. The revolutionaries brushed that prospect aside: republican theory assured them that the people possessed a generous share of civic virtue, the capacity for selfless pursuit of the general welfare.

WRITTEN CONSTITUTIONS In an equally momentous change, the revolutionaries insisted on written state constitutions. Whenever government appeared to exceed the limits of its authority, Americans wanted to have at hand the written contract between rulers and ruled. When eighteenth-century Britons used the word *constitution,* they meant the existing arrangement of government—not an actual document but a collection of parliamentary laws, customs, and precedents. But Americans believed that a constitution should be a written code that stood

Americans responded to independence with rituals of "killing the king," like the one enacted by this New York crowd in 1776 as it pulls down a statue of George III. Americans also expressed their mistrust of monarchs and their ministers by establishing new state governments with weak executive branches.

First Seal of the United States

apart from and above government, a yardstick against which the people measured the performance of their rulers. After all, they reasoned, if Britain's constitution had been written down, available for all to consult, would American rights have been violated?

From Congress to Confederation

While Americans lavished attention on their state constitutions, the national government nearly languished during the decade after 1776. With the coming of independence, the Second Continental Congress conducted the common business of the federated states. It created and maintained the Continental Army, issued currency, and negotiated with foreign powers.

But while Congress acted as a central government by common consent, it lacked any legal basis for its authority. To redress that need, in July 1776 Congress appointed a committee to draft a constitution for a national government. The urgent business of waging the war made for delay, but Congress approved the first national constitution in November 1777. It took four more years—until February 1781—for all the states to ratify these Articles of Confederation.

ARTICLES OF CONFEDERATION The Articles of Confederation provided for a government by a national legislature—essentially a continuation of the Second Continental Congress. That body had the authority to declare war and make peace, conduct diplomacy, regulate Indian affairs, appoint military and naval officers, and requisition men from the states. In affairs of finance it could coin money and issue paper currency. Extensive as these responsibilities were, Congress could not levy taxes or even regulate trade. The crucial power of the purse rested entirely with the states, as did the final power to make and

execute laws. Even worse, the national government had no distinct executive branch. Congressional committees, constantly changing in their membership, not only had to make laws but had to administer and enforce them as well. With no executive to carry out the policies of finance, war, and foreign policy, the federal government's influence was extremely limited.

Those weaknesses appear more evident in hindsight. For Congress in 1777 it was no easy task to frame a new government in the midst of a war. And most American leaders of the 1770s had given little thought to federalism, the means by which political power could be divided among the states and the national government. In any case, to have given significant powers to the national government would have aroused only opposition among the states, each jealous of its independence. Creating a strong national government would also have antagonized many Americans, who after all had just rebelled against the distant, centralized authority of Britain's king and Parliament.

Guided by republican political theory and by their colonial experience, American revolutionaries created a loose confederation of 13 independent state republics under a nearly powerless national government. They succeeded so well that the United States almost failed to survive the first decade of its independence. The problem was that republican theory and lessons from the colonial past were not always useful guides to postwar realities. Only when events forced Americans to think nationally did they begin to consider the possibility of reinventing "these United States"—this time under the yoke of a truly federal republic.

 **REVIEW**

What political concerns shaped the first constitutions?

THE TEMPTATIONS OF PEACE

THE SURRENDER OF CORNWALLIS AT Yorktown in 1781 marked the end of military crisis in America. But as the threat from Britain receded, so did the source of American unity. The many differences among Americans, most of which lay submerged during the struggle for independence, surfaced in full force. Those domestic divisions, combined with challenges to the new nation from Britain and Spain, created conflicts that neither the states nor the national government proved equal to handling.

The Temptations of the West

The greatest opportunities and the greatest problems for postwar Americans awaited in the rapidly expanding West. With the boundary of the new United States now set at the Mississippi River, more settlers spilled across the Appalachians, planting farmsteads and raw frontier towns throughout Ohio, Kentucky, and Tennessee. By 1790 places that had been almost uninhabited by whites in 1760 held more than 2.25 million people, one-third of the nation's population.

After the Revolution, as before, western settlement fostered intense conflict. American claims that its territory stretched all the way to the Mississippi were by no means taken for granted by European and Indian powers. The West also confronted Americans with questions about their own national identity: Would the newly settled territories enter the nation as states on an equal footing with the original 13 states? Would they be ruled as dependent colonies? Could the federal government reconcile conflicting interests, cultures, and traditions over so great an area? The fate of the West, in other words, constituted a crucial test of whether "these" United States could grow and still remain united.

Foreign Intrigues

Both the British from their base in Canada and the Spanish in Florida and Louisiana hoped to chisel away at American borders. Their considerable success in the 1780s exposed the weakness of Confederation diplomacy.

Before the ink was dry on the Treaty of Paris, Britain's ministers were secretly instructing Canadians to maintain their forts and trading posts inside the United States' northwestern frontier. They reckoned—correctly—that with the Continental Army disbanded, the Confederation could not force the British to withdraw.

The British also made mischief along the Confederation's northern borders, mainly with Vermont. For decades, Ethan Allen and his Green Mountain Boys had waged a war of nerves with neighboring New York, which claimed Vermont as part of its territory. After the Revolution the Vermonters petitioned Congress for statehood, demanding independence from both New York and New Hampshire. When Congress dragged its feet, the British tried to woo Vermont into their empire as a province of Canada. That flirtation with the British pressured Congress into granting Vermont statehood in 1791.

SPANISH DESIGNS ON THE SOUTHWEST The loyalty of the southwestern frontier was even less certain. By 1790 more than 100,000 settlers had poured through the Cumberland Gap to reach Kentucky and Tennessee. Along with the farmers came speculators, who bought up large tracts of land from the Indians. But the commercial possibilities of the region depended entirely on access to the Mississippi and the port of New Orleans, since it was far too

Rivalries flared along the southwestern frontier of the United States as Spain vied to win the allegiance of Indians by supplying them with British trade goods. The Indians welcomed such goods (note the shovel, at left, the plow, center, and European clothing worn by some of the Indians). Here a white man, probably the American Indian agent Benjamin Hawkins, visits an Indian village during the 1790s.

WESTERN LAND CLAIMS, 1782–1802

The Confederation's settlement of conflicting western land claims was an achievement essential to the consolidation of political union. Some states asserted that their original charters extended their western borders to the Mississippi River. A few states, such as Virginia, claimed western borders on the Pacific Ocean. **Which states claimed western lands that they eventually ceded to the Confederation?**

BRITISH CANADA

L. Superior

L. Michigan

L. Huron

Ceded by Virginia' 1784

Ceded by MASS., 1785 and VA., 1784

Ceded by CONN., 1786 and VA., 1784

L. Ontario

L. Erie

VERMONT (1791)

MAINE (MASS.)

NEW HAMPSHIRE

MASSACHUSETTS

NEW YORK

Ceded by MASS., 1786

Ceded by CONN., 1782

RHODE ISLAND

CONNECTICUT

PENNSYLVANIA

NEW JERSEY

Ceded by CONN., 1800

DELAWARE

MARYLAND

Ceded by Virginia, 1784

Ohio R.

VIRGINIA

ATLANTIC OCEAN

SPANISH LOUISIANA

Ceded by Virginia, 1792

Ceded by North Carolina 1790

NORTH CAROLINA

Mississippi R.

Ceded by S.C., 1787

SOUTH CAROLINA

Ceded by Georgia, 1802

GEORGIA

Ceded by Spain, 1795
Ceded by Georgia, 1802

SPANISH FLORIDA

Gulf of Mexico

▨	States after land cessions
▨	Ceded territory
▬	Territory ceded by New York, 1782

---

costly to ship southwestern produce over the rough trails east across the Appalachians. And the Mississippi route was still dominated by the Spanish, who controlled Louisiana as well as forts along western Mississippi shores as far north as St. Louis. The Spanish, seeing their opportunity, closed the Mississippi to American navigation in 1784. That action prompted serious talk among southwesterners about seceding from the United States and joining Spain's empire.

The Spanish also tried to strengthen their hold on North America by making common cause with the Indians. Of particular concern to both groups was protecting Spanish Florida from the encroachment of American settlers filtering south from Georgia—backwoods folk, Florida's governor complained, who were "nomadic like Arabs and . . . distinguished from savages only in their color, language, and the superiority of their depraved cunning and untrustworthiness." So Spanish colonial officials responded eagerly to the overtures of Alexander McGillivray, a young Indian leader whose mother was of French-Creek descent and whose father was a Scots trader. His efforts brought about a treaty of alliance between the Creeks and the Spanish in 1784, quickly followed by similar alliances with the Choctaws and the Chickasaws. What cemented such treaties were the trade

goods that the Spanish agreed to supply the tribes, for, as McGillivray explained, "Indians will attach themselves to and serve them best who supply their necessities." Securing European gunpowder and guns had become essential to southeastern Indians, because their entire economies now revolved around hunting and selling deerskins to white traders. So eager were the Spanish to "serve" the Indians in that matter that they even permitted British merchants, who could command a steady supply of manufactured goods, to monopolize the Indian trade. The largest dealers developed a trading network that reached all the way to the Mississippi by the 1790s. This flood of British merchandise sustained the alliance between the Spanish and the Indians, while British guns enabled the Creeks to defend their hunting territory from American invaders.

Disputes among the States

LANDED VS. LANDLESS STATES

As if foreign intrigues were not divisive enough, the states continued to argue among themselves over western land claims. The old royal charters for some colonies had extended their boundaries all the way to the Mississippi and beyond. But the charters were often vague, granting both Massachusetts and Virginia, for example, undisputed possession of present-day Wisconsin. In contrast, other charters limited state boundaries to within a few hundred miles of the Atlantic coast. **Landed states** such as Virginia wanted to secure control over the large territory granted them by their charters. **Landless states** (which included Maryland, Delaware, Pennsylvania, Rhode Island, and New Jersey) called on Congress to restrict the boundaries of landed states and to convert western lands into a domain administered by the Confederation.

The landless states argued that the landed states enjoyed an unfair advantage from the money they could raise selling their western claims. That revenue would allow landed states to reduce taxes, and lower taxes would lure settlers from the landless states. Meanwhile, landless states would have to raise taxes to make up for the departed taxpayers, causing even more residents to leave. Speculators were also eager to see Congress control the western lands. Before the Revolution, many prominent citizens of landless Pennsylvania, Maryland, and New Jersey had purchased tracts in the West from Indians. These speculators now also lobbied for congressional ownership of all western lands—except those tracts that they had already purchased from the Indians.

The landless states lost the opening round in the contest over ownership of the West. The Articles of Confederation acknowledged the old charter claims of the landed states. Then Maryland, one of the smallest landless states, retaliated by refusing to ratify the Articles. Since every state had to approve the Articles before they were formally accepted, the fate of the United States hung in the balance. One by one the landed states relented, Virginia being the last. Only then did Maryland ratify the Articles, in February 1781.

The More Democratic West

An even greater bone of contention concerned the sort of men westerners elected to political office. The state legislatures of the 1780s were both larger and more democratic in their membership than the old colonial assemblies. Before the Revolution no more than a fifth of the men serving in the assemblies were middle-class farmers or artisans. Government was almost exclusively the domain of the wealthiest merchants, lawyers, and planters. After the Revolution twice as many state legislators were men of moderate wealth. The shift was more marked in the North, where middle-class men predominated among representatives. But in every state, some men of modest means, humble background, and little formal education attained political power.

CHANGING COMPOSITION OF STATE LEGISLATURES

State legislatures became more democratic in their membership mainly because as backcountry districts grew, so too did the number of their representatives. Since western districts tended to be less developed economically and culturally, their leading men were less rich and cultivated than the Eastern Seaboard elite. But many of these eastern republican gentlemen, while endorsing government by popular consent, doubted whether ordinary people were fit to rule. The problem, they contended, was that the new western legislators concerned themselves only with the narrow interests of their constituents, not with the good of the whole state. As Ezra Stiles, the president of Yale College, observed, the new breed of politicians was those with "the all-prevailing popular talent of coaxing and flattering," who "whenever a bill is read in the legislature . . . instantly thinks how it will affect his constituents." And if state legislatures could not rise above narrow self-interest, how long would it be before a concern for the general welfare simply withered away?

This sketch of a new cleared farm idealizes many aspects of life on the late-eighteenth-century frontier. Although western farmers first sought to "improve" their acreage by felling trees, as the stumps dotting the landscape indicate, their dwellings were far less substantial than those depicted in the background above. And although Indians sometimes guided parties of white surveyors and settlers into the West, as shown in the foreground, Indians more often resisted white encroachment. For that reason, dogs, here perched placidly in a canoe, were trained to alert their white masters to the approach of Indians.

The Northwest Territory

Such fears of "democratic excess" also influenced policy when Congress finally came to decide what to do with the **Northwest Territory.** Carved out of the land ceded by the states to the national government, the Northwest Territory comprised the present-day states of Ohio, Indiana, Illinois, Michigan, and Wisconsin. With so many white settlers moving into these lands, Congress was faced with a crucial test of its federal system. If an orderly way could not be devised to expand the confederation of states beyond the original 13 colonies, the new territories might well become independent countries or even colonies of Spain or Britain. Congress dealt with the issue of expansion by adopting three ordinances.

JEFFERSON'S PLAN FOR THE NORTHWEST — The first ordinance, drafted by Thomas Jefferson in 1784, divided the Northwest Territory into 10 states, each to be admitted to the Union on equal terms as soon as its population equaled that in any of the existing states. In the meantime, Jefferson provided for democratic self-government of the territory by all free adult males. A second ordinance of 1785 set up an efficient mechanism for dividing and selling public lands. The Northwest Territory was surveyed into townships 6 miles square. Each township was then divided into 36 lots of 1 square mile, or 640 acres.

Congress waited in vain for buyers to flock to the land offices it established. The cost of even a single lot—$640—was too steep for most farmers. Disappointed by the shortage of buyers and desperate for money, Congress finally accepted a proposition submitted by a private company of land speculators who offered to buy some 6 million acres in present-day southeastern Ohio. That several members of Congress numbered among the company's stockholders no doubt added to enthusiasm for the deal.

NORTHWEST ORDINANCE — The transaction concluded, Congress calmed the speculators' worries that incoming settlers might enjoy too much self-government by scrapping Jefferson's democratic design and substituting the Northwest Ordinance of 1787. That ordinance provided for a period in which Congress held sway in the territory through its appointees—a governor, a secretary, and three judges. When the population reached 5,000 free adult males, a legislature was to be established, although its laws required the governor's approval. A

THE ORDINANCE OF 1785

Surveyors entered the Northwest Territory in September of 1785, imposing on the land regular grids of 6 square miles to define new townships, as shown on this range map of a portion of Ohio. Farmers purchased blocks of land within townships, each 1 mile square, from the federal government or from land speculators. This pattern was followed in mapping and settling public lands all the way to the Pacific coast.

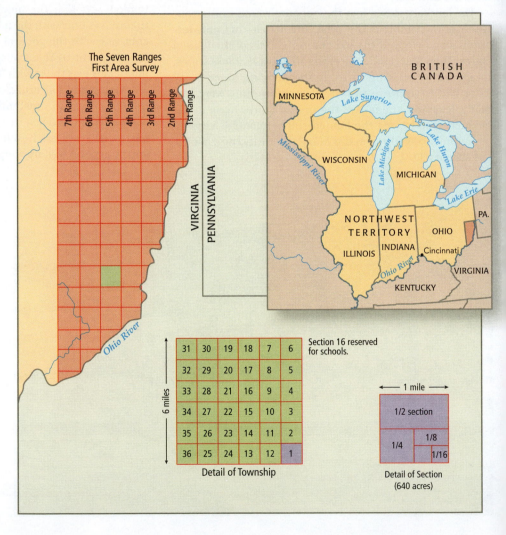

The Seven Ranges
First Area Survey

7th Range, 6th Range, 5th Range, 4th Range, 3rd Range, 2nd Range, 1st Range

VIRGINIA
PENNSYLVANIA

Ohio River

BRITISH CANADA

MINNESOTA

Lake Superior

WISCONSIN

Lake Michigan

Lake Huron

MICHIGAN

Lake Erie

NORTHWEST TERRITORY

OHIO

PA.

ILLINOIS

INDIANA

Cincinnati

Ohio River

VIRGINIA

KENTUCKY

6 miles

31	30	19	18	7	6
32	29	20	17	8	5
33	28	21	16	9	4
34	27	22	15	10	3
35	26	23	14	11	2
36	25	24	13	12	1

Section 16 reserved for schools.

Detail of Township

1 mile

1/2 section

1/4

1/8

1/16

Detail of Section
(640 acres)

representative could sit in Congress but had no vote. When the population reached 60,000, the inhabitants might apply for statehood, and the whole Northwest Territory was to be divided into not less than three or more than five states. The ordinance also guaranteed basic rights—freedom of religion and trial by jury—and provided for the support of public education. Equally significant, it also outlawed slavery throughout the territory.

With the Northwest Ordinance in place, Congress had succeeded in extending republican government to the West and incorporating the frontier into the new nation. The Republic now had an orderly way to expand its federation of states in a way that minimized the tensions between the genteel East and the democratic West that had plagued the colonies and the Confederation throughout much of the eighteenth century. Yet ironically, the new ordinance served to heighten tensions in a different way. By limiting the spread of slavery in the northern states, Congress deepened the critical social and economic differences between the North and the South, evident already in the 1780s.

THE TERRITORIAL SYSTEM AND NATIVE AMERICANS

The consequences of the new territorial system were also significant for hundreds of thousands of the continent's other inhabitants. In the short term, the ordinance ignored completely the rights of the Shawnee, Chippewa, and other Indian peoples who lived in the region. In the long term, the system "laid the blueprint," as one historian noted, for bringing new lands into the United States. The ordinance thus accelerated the pressures on Indian lands and aggravated the social and geographic dislocations already set in motion by disease and the western conflicts of the Revolutionary War.

Branding irons like these were sometimes used to burn a slaveholder's initials into the skin of his property to make running away more difficult.

Slavery and Sectionalism

When white Americans declared their independence, they owned nearly half a million black Americans. African Americans of the revolutionary generation, most of them enslaved, constituted 20 percent of the total population of the colonies in 1775, and nearly 90 percent of them lived in the South. Yet few political leaders directly confronted the issue of whether slavery should be permitted to exist in a truly republican society.

REPUBLICANISM AND SLAVERY

When political discussion did stray toward the subject of slavery, southerners—especially ardent republicans—bristled defensively. Theirs was a difficult position, riddled with contradictions.

On the one hand, they had condemned parliamentary taxation as tantamount to political "slavery" and had rebelled, declaring that all men were "created equal." On the other hand, enslaved African Americans formed the basis of the South's plantation economy. To surrender slavery, southerners believed, would be to usher in economic ruin. Some planters in the Upper South resolved the dilemma by freeing their slaves. Such decisions were made easier by changing economic conditions in the Chesapeake. As planters shifted from tobacco toward wheat, a crop demanding a good deal less labor, Virginia and Maryland liberalized their manumission statutes, laws providing for freeing slaves. Between 1776 and 1789, most southern states also joined the North in prohibiting the importation of slaves, and a few antislavery societies appeared in the Upper South. But no southern state legally abolished slavery. Masters defended their right to hold human property in the name of republicanism.

REPUBLICANISM AND PROPERTY

Eighteenth-century republicans regarded property as crucial, for it provided a man and his family with security, status, and wealth. More important, it provided a measure of independence: to be able to act freely, without fear or favor of others. People without property were dangerous, republicans believed, because the poor could never be politically independent. Southern defenders of slavery thus argued that free, propertyless black people would pose a political threat to the liberty of propertied white citizens. Subordinating the human rights of blacks to the property rights of whites, southern republicans reached the paradoxical conclusion that their freedom depended on keeping African Americans in bondage.

The North followed a different course. Because its economy depended far less on slave labor, black emancipation did not run counter to powerful economic interests. Antislavery societies, the first founded by the Quakers in 1775, spread throughout the northern states during the next quarter century. Over the same period the legislatures of most northern states provided for the immediate or gradual abolition of slavery. Freedom for most northern African Americans came slowly, but by 1830 there were fewer than 3,000 slaves out of a total northern black population of 125,000.

The Revolution, which had been fought for liberty and equality, did little to change the status of most black Americans. By 1800 more enslaved African Americans lived in the United States than had lived there in 1776. Slavery continued to grow in the Lower South as the rice culture of the Carolinas and Georgia expanded and as the new cotton culture spread westward.

In 1787 in Philadelphia, the year delegates to the Constitutional Convention met, Richard Allen and Absalom Jones founded Bethel African Methodist Episcopal Church. The first church was a former blacksmith's shop that the members hauled to a site they purchased on Sixth Street. By the time this illustration was created in 1829, a more spacious building had replaced the first church.

Still, a larger number of slaves than ever before became free during the war and in the following decades, whether through military service, successful escape, manumission, or gradual emancipation. All these developments fostered the growth of free black communities, especially in the Upper South and in northern cities. By 1810 free African Americans made up 10 percent of the total population of Maryland and Virginia.

GROWTH OF THE FREE BLACK COMMUNITY The composition of the postwar free community changed as well. Before independence most free blacks had been either mulattoes—the offspring of interracial unions—or former slaves too sick or aged to have value as laborers. In contrast, a larger proportion of the free population of the 1780s were darker skinned, younger, and healthier. This group injected new vitality into black communal life, organizing independent schools, churches, and mutual benefit societies for the growing number of "free people of color." Richard Allen and Absalom Jones led the way in these efforts after being ejected from their pews in the midst of prayers one Sunday at St. George **Methodist** Episcopal Church in Philadelphia. Both men ended up founding independent black churches.

After the Revolution, slavery ceased to be a national institution. It became the **peculiar institution** of a single region, the American South. The isolation of slavery in one section set North and South on radically different courses of social development, sharpening economic and political divisions.

Wartime Economic Disruption

With the outbreak of the Revolution, Americans had suffered an immediate economic loss. Formerly, Britain had supplied manufactured goods, markets for American exports, and credit that enabled commerce to flourish. No longer. Hardest hit were southern planters, who had to seek new customers for their tobacco, cotton, and rice as well as find new sources of capital to finance production. Northerners too faced difficulties, for their major seaports were occupied for a time by British troops, whose presence disrupted commercial activity.

PUBLIC AND PRIVATE DEBT Matters did not improve with the coming of peace. France and Britain flooded the new states with their manufactures, and postwar Americans, eager for luxuries, indulged in a most unrepublican spending spree. The flurry of buying left some American merchants and consumers as deeply in debt as their governments. When loans from private citizens and foreign creditors like France proved insufficient to finance the fighting, both Congress and the states printed paper money—a whopping total of $400 million. The paper currency was backed only by the government's promise to redeem the bills with money from future taxes, because legislatures balked at the unpopular alternative of levying taxes during the war. For the bills to be redeemed, the United States had to survive, so by the end of 1776, when Continental forces sustained a series of defeats, paper money started to depreciate dramatically. By 1781 it was virtually without value, and Americans coined the expression "not worth a Continental."

POSTWAR INFLATION The printing of paper money, combined with a wartime shortage of goods, triggered an inflationary spiral. As goods became scarcer and scarcer, they cost more and more worthless dollars. In this spiral, creditors were gouged by debtors, who paid them back with depreciated currency. At the same time, soaring prices for food and manufactured goods eroded the buying power of wage earners and small farmers. And the end of the war brought on demands for prompt repayment from the new nation's foreign creditors as well as from soldiers seeking back pay and pensions.

Congress could do nothing. With no power to regulate trade, it could neither dam the stream of imported goods rushing into the states nor stanch the flow of gold and silver to Europe to pay for these items. With no power to prohibit the states from issuing paper money, it could not halt depreciation. With no power to regulate wages or prices, it could not curb inflation. With no power to tax, it could not reduce the public debt. Efforts to grant Congress greater powers met with determined resistance from the states. They refused Congress any revenue of its own, fearing the first steps toward "arbitrary" government.

POLITICAL DIVISIONS OVER ECONOMIC POLICY

Within states, too, economic problems aroused discord. Some major merchants and large commercial farmers had profited handsomely during the war by selling supplies to the American, British, and French armies at high prices. Eager to protect their windfall, they lobbied state legislatures for an end to inflationary monetary policies. They pushed for the passage of high taxes to pay wartime debts, a paper currency that was backed by gold and silver, and an active policy to encourage foreign trade.

Less affluent men fought back, pressing legislatures for programs that met their needs. Western farmers, often in debt, urged the states to print more paper money and to pass laws lowering taxes and postponing the foreclosure of mortgages. Artisans opposed merchants by calling for protection from low-priced foreign imports that competed with the goods they produced. They set themselves against farmers as well by demanding price regulation of the farm products they consumed. In the continuing struggle, the state legislatures became the battleground of competing economic factions, each bent on gaining its own particular advantage.

As the 1780s wore on, conflicts mounted. As long as the individual states remained sovereign, the Confederation was crippled—unable to conduct foreign affairs effectively, unable to set coherent economic policy, unable to deal with discontent in the West. Equally dismaying was the discovery that many Americans, instead of being selflessly concerned for the public good, selfishly pursued their private interests.

✔ REVIEW

What challenges did the West pose for the new republic?

REPUBLICAN SOCIETY

THE WAR FOR INDEPENDENCE TRANSFORMED not only America's government and economy but also its society and culture. Inspired by the Declaration's ideal of equality, some Americans rejected the subordinate position assigned to them under the old colonial order. Westerners, newly wealthy entrepreneurs, urban artisans, and women all claimed greater freedom, power, and recognition. The authority of the traditional leaders of government, society, and the family came under a new scrutiny; the impulse to defer to social superiors became less automatic. The new assertiveness demonstrated how deeply egalitarian assumptions were taking root in American culture.

The New Men of the Revolution

The Revolution gave rise to a new sense of social identity and a new set of ambitions among several groups of men who had once accepted a humbler status. The more democratic society of the frontier emboldened westerners to believe themselves the equals of easterners. One Kentuckian explained that the western migrants "must make a very different mass from one which is composed of men born and raised on the same spot. . . . They see none about them to whom or to whose families they have been accustomed to think themselves inferior."

The war also offered opportunities to aspiring entrepreneurs everywhere, and often they were not the same men who had prospered before the war. At a stroke, independence swept away the political prominence of loyalists, whose ranks included an especially high number of government officials, large landowners, and major merchants. And while loyalists found their properties confiscated by revolutionary governments, other Americans grew rich. Many northern merchants gained newfound wealth from privateering or military contracts. Commercial farmers in the mid-Atlantic states prospered from the high food prices caused by wartime scarcity and army demand.

URBAN ARTISANS

The Revolution effected no dramatic redistribution of wealth. Indeed, the gap between rich and poor increased during the 1780s. But the republican ideal of equality emboldened city artisans to demand a more prominent role in politics. Calls for men of their own kind to represent them in government came as a rude shock to such gentlemen as South Carolina's William Henry Drayton, who balked at sharing power with men "who were never in a way to study" anything except "how to cut up a beast in the market to best advantage, to cobble an old shoe in the neatest manner, or to build a necessary house." The journeymen who worked for master craftsmen also exhibited a new sense of independence, forming new organizations to secure higher wages.

| *Gilbert Stuart's The Skater captures one American gentleman's characteristic sense of mastery over himself, nature, and society. But the Revolution gave other republican men a sense of power, too, including western backcountry farmers, aspiring entrepreneurs, and urban artisans such as the pewterers.*

TRANSFORMING THE FRONTIER

But the greatest gains accrued to those men newly enriched by the war and by the opportunities of independence. Representative of this aspiring group was William Cooper, a Pennsylvania Quaker who did not support the Revolution but in its aftermath strove to transform himself from a wheelwright into a gentleman. He hoped to become a gentleman by transforming thousands of acres of hilly, heavily forested land around Otsego Lake in upstate New York into wheat-producing farms clustered around a market village called Cooperstown. Yankee emigrants fleeing the shrinking farms of long-settled New England made Cooper's vision a reality and made him the leading land developer of the 1790s. But the influx of white settlement radically altered the environment of what had once been part of Iroquoia. Farmers killed off panthers, bears, and wolves to protect their livestock. Grains farming leeched nutrients from the thin topsoil, forcing farmers to clear more trees, and as the forest barrier fell, weeds and insects invaded. By the beginning of the nineteenth century, the children of many small farmers were migrating even farther west, to western New York and northern Ohio.

Similar scenarios played out on frontiers throughout the new United States. And everywhere, too, men like William Cooper demanded and received social recognition and political influence. Even though some, like Cooper, never lost the crude manners that betrayed humble origins, they styled themselves as the "aristocracy of merit" enshrined by republican ideals.

The New Women of the Revolution

Not long after the fighting with Britain had broken out, Margaret Livingston of New York wrote to her sister Catherine, "You know that our Sex are doomed to be obedient in every stage of life so that we shant be great gainers by this contest." By war's end, however, Eliza Wilkinson from rural South Carolina was complaining boldly to a woman friend: "The men say we have no business with political matters . . . it's not our sphere. . . . [But] I won't have it thought that because we are the weaker Sex (as to bodily strength my dear) we are Capable of nothing more, than minding the Dairy . . . surely we may have enough sense to give our Opinions."

What separated Margaret Livingston's resignation from Eliza Wilkinson's assertion of personal worth and independence was the Revolution. Eliza Wilkinson had managed her parents' plantation during the war and defended it from British marauders. Other women discovered similar reserves of skill and resourcefulness. When soldiers returned home, some were surprised to find their wives and daughters, who had been running family farms and businesses, less submissive and more self-confident.

EXCLUSION OF WOMEN FROM POLITICS

But American men had not fought a revolution for the equality of American women. In fact, male revolutionaries gave no thought whatsoever to the role of women in the new nation, assuming that those of the "weaker sex" were incapable of making informed and independent political deci-

sions. Most women of the revolutionary generation agreed that the proper female domain was the home, not the public arena of politics. Still, the currents of the Revolution occasionally left gaps that allowed women to display their keen political interests. When a loosely worded provision in the New Jersey state constitution gave the vote to "all free inhabitants" owning a specified amount of property, white widows and single women went to the polls. Only in 1807 did the state legislature close the loophole.

Mary Wollstonecraft's Vindication

In the wake of the Revolution there also appeared in England a book that would become a classic text of modern feminism, Mary Wollstonecraft's *A Vindication of the Rights of Women* (1792). Attracting a wide, if not widely approving, readership in America as well, it called not only for laws to guarantee women civil and political equality but also for educational reforms to ensure their social and economic equality.

EDUCATION AS A ROUTE TO EQUALITY

Like many young, single English women with more wit than fortune, Wollstonecraft started her working life as a governess and a school's headmistress. Then she turned to writing for her livelihood, producing book reviews, translations, a novel, and a treatise on women's education before dashing off *Vindication* in only six months. She charged that men deliberately conspired to keep women in "a state of perpetual childhood" by giving them inferior, frivolous educations. That encouraged young girls to fixate on fashion and flirtation and made them "only anxious to inspire love, when they ought to cherish a nobler ambition, and by their abilities and virtues exact respect." Girls, she proposed, should receive the same education as boys, including

A devoted mother with her daughter from the 1790s: but note the generation gap. While the mother holds fancy needlework in her lap, her daughter looks up from an opened book. Many women—especially younger women—in the decades around 1800 chose to include books in their portraits, indicating that literacy and education were becoming essential to their identity and self-esteem.

A WOMAN'S COMPASS

A woman drinking spirits as her baby tumbles from her lap.

A woman crying, pointing to letters on a table. Was she jilted by a lover? Other possibilities?

A woman at hard labor in prison.

A woman being apprehended by the authorities. For prostitution? Drunkenness? Debt?

Keep Within Compass, illustration, ca. 1785–1805, Winterthur Museum.

Could there be any more eloquent testimony to the anxieties aroused by the newly confident (and sometimes outspoken) women of postrevolutionary America? Much like jokes, idealized images (for example, the smiling woman within the compass) can point historians toward areas of tension and conflict in the past. In this illustration, the four scenes displayed outside the compass send even clearer signals. Published sometime between 1785 and 1805 and titled *Keep Within Compass*, the illustration celebrates domesticity and wifely devotion while also warning women tempted to stray from that straight and narrow path. It promises a contented and prosperous life—lovely home, thriving garden, swishy silk dress, killer hat, and even a pet squirrel—to the woman "whose bosom no passion knows." But woe betide her erring sisters who strayed from the path of virtue, disgracing themselves as well as the men in their lives! Those twin themes proved equally popular in American novels published during the decades after the American Revolution.

Thinking Critically

Is the kind of virtue promoted by the illustration similar to or different from the republican understanding of virtue? What accounts for the concern about the virtue of women in the decades after the American Revolution? Why did the virtue of women loom so large, since they had few legal or political rights?

Contrast the portrait of Mary Wollstonecraft rendered just before her death in 1797 (left) with a strikingly masculinized rendering in a book published in the United States in 1809 (right), which placed her in the company of "actresses, adventurers, authoresses, fortunetellers, gipsies, dwarfs, swindlers, and vagrants."

training that would prepare them for careers in medicine, politics, and business. No woman should have to pin her hopes for financial security on making a good marriage, Wollstonecraft argued. On the contrary, well-educated and resourceful women capable of supporting themselves would make the best wives and mothers, assets to the family and the nation.

Vindication might have been written in gunpowder rather than ink, given the reaction it aroused on both sides of the Atlantic. At first, Wollstonecraft won more than a few defenders among both men and women. This favorable reception ended abruptly after her death in childbirth in 1797, when a memoir written by her husband revealed that she had lived out of wedlock with him—and before him, with another lover. Even so, some of her readers continued to admire her views. The Philadelphia Quaker Elizabeth Drinker confided to her diary that "In very many of her sentiments, [Wollstonecraft] . . . *speaks my mind.*"

Republican Motherhood and Education

Wollstonecraft's ideas also lent support to the leading educational reformers in the revolutionary generation. Her sentiments echo in the writings of Judith Sargent Murray, a New Englander who urged the cultivation of women's minds to encourage self-respect and celebrated "excellency in our sex." Her fellow reformer, the Philadelphian Benjamin Rush, agreed that only educated and independent-minded women could raise the informed and self-reliant citizens that a republican government required.

The Revolution also prompted some states to reform their marriage laws, making divorce somewhat easier, although it remained extremely rare. But while women won greater freedom to divorce, courts became less concerned with enforcing a widow's traditional legal claim to one-third of her spouse's real estate. And married women still could not sue or be sued, make wills or contracts, or buy and sell property. Any wages that they earned went to their husbands; so did all personal property that wives brought into a marriage; so did the rents and profits of any real estate they owned. Despite the high ideals of **republican motherhood,** most women remained confined to the domestic sphere of the home and deprived of the most basic legal and political rights.

The Attack on Aristocracy

Why wasn't the American Revolution more revolutionary? Independence secured the full political equality of white men who owned property, but women were still deprived of political rights, African Americans of human rights. Why did the revolutionaries stop short of extending equality to the most unequal groups in American society—and with so little sense that they were being inconsistent?

REPUBLICAN VIEW OF EQUALITY

In part, the lack of concern was rooted in republican ideas themselves. Republican ideology viewed property as the key to independence and power. Lacking property, women and black Americans were easily consigned to the custody of husbands and masters. Then, too, prejudice played its part: the perception of women and blacks as naturally inferior beings.

But revolutionary leaders also failed to press for greater equality because they conceived their crusade in terms of eliminating the evils of a European past dominated by kings and aristocrats. They believed that the great obstacle to equality was monarchy—kings and queens who bestowed hereditary honors and political office on favored individuals and granted legal privileges and monopolies to favored churches and businesses. These artificial inequalities posed the real threat to liberty, most republicans concluded. In other words, the men of the Revolution were intent on attaining equality by leveling off the top of society. It did not occur to most republicans that the cause of equality could also be served by raising up the bottom—by attacking the laws and prejudices that kept African Americans enslaved and women dependent.

DISESTABLISHMENT OF STATE-SUPPORTED CHURCHES

The most significant reform of the republican campaign against artificial privilege was the dismantling of state-supported churches. Most states had a religious establishment. In New York and the South, it was the Anglican church; in New England, the Congregational church. Since the 1740s, dissenters who did not worship at state churches had protested laws that taxed all citizens to support the clergy of established denominations. After the Revolution, dissenters argued that equality required ending such privileges. As more dissenters became voters, state legislators gradually abolished state support for Anglican and Congregational churches.

SOCIETY OF CINCINNATI

In the same anti-aristocratic spirit, reformers attacked the Society of Cincinnati, a group organized by former officers of the Continental Army in 1783. The society, which was merely a social club for veterans, was forced to disband for its policy of passing on its membership rights to eldest sons.

| *A medal of the Society of the Cincinnati*

In this way, critics charged, the Cincinnati was creating artificial distinctions and perpetuating a hereditary warrior nobility.

Today, many of the republican efforts at reform seem misdirected. While only a handful of revolutionaries worked for the education of women and the emancipation of slaves, enormous zeal went into fighting threats from a monarchical past that had never existed in America. Yet the threat from kings and aristocrats was real to the revolutionaries—and indeed remained real in many parts of Europe. Their determination to sweep away every shred of formal privilege ensured that these forms of inequality never took root in America. And if eighteenth-century Americans did not extend equality to women and racial minorities, it was a failure they shared with later revolutionary movements that promised more.

 **REVIEW**

How did the Revolution alter American society?

FROM CONFEDERATION TO CONSTITUTION

WHILE AMERICANS IN MANY WALKS of life sought to realize the republican commitment to equality, Congress wrestled with the problem of preserving the nation itself. With the new republic slowly rending itself to pieces, some political leaders concluded that neither the Confederation nor the state legislatures were able to remedy the basic difficulties facing the nation. But how could the states be convinced to surrender their sovereign powers? The answer came in the wake of two events—one foreign, one domestic—that lent momentum to the cause of strengthening the central government.

The Jay-Gardoqui Treaty

The international episode was a debate over a proposed treaty with Spain. In 1785 southwesterners still could not legally navigate the Mississippi and still were threatening to secede from the union and annex their territory to Spain's American empire. To shore up southwestern loyalties, Congress instructed its secretary of foreign affairs, John Jay, to negotiate an agreement with Spain preserving American rights to navigate the Mississippi River. But the Spanish emissary, Don Diego de Gardoqui, sweet-talked Jay into accepting a treaty by which the United States would give up all rights to the Mississippi for 25 years. In return, Spain agreed to grant trading privileges to American merchants.

Jay, a New Yorker, knew more than a few northern merchants who were eager to open new markets. But when the proposed treaty became public knowledge, southwesterners denounced it as nothing short of betrayal. The treaty

THE SPIRITS OF INDEPENDENCE

If God had intended man to drink water, Ben Franklin remarked, he would not have made him with an elbow capable of raising a wineglass. Colonials from all across America agreed with Franklin on the virtues of drink. The ruddy glow of colonial cheeks (still visible in the portraits in museums) reflected not only good health but also substantial daily doses of alcohol. Colonials consumed about twice as much alcohol as Americans today, though in different forms. Beer was not popular, the only sort consumed being a weak, homemade "small beer" containing about 1 percent alcohol. Only the wealthy, like Franklin, could afford imported Madeira and port wines, but the produce of apple orchards allowed Americans northward from Virginia to drink their fill of hard cider. Far and away the most popular distilled liquor was rum, a potent 90 proof beverage (45 percent alcohol) that they sipped straight or mixed with water and sugar to make "toddies."

The liquor flowed freely at special occasions: ministerial ordinations in New England towns, court days in the South, house-raisings, corn-huskings, and quilting bees on the frontier, and weddings, elections, and militia musters everywhere in the colonies. But Americans did not confine their drinking to occasional celebrations. Some, like John Adams, started the day with a tankard of hard cider. Laborers in seaport docks and shipyards, fishermen and sailors at sea, and farmworkers in the countryside commonly received a daily allotment of liquor as part of their wages.

Women drank, too, although they sometimes explained their use of distilled liquor as serving some "medicinal" purpose. Slaves got around laws restricting their consumption of alcohol by stealing from masters or bartering with white peddlers.

Until the middle of the eighteenth century, most colonials (and Europeans) considered spirits an essential supplement to their diet. They did not condone public drunkenness, but they saw nothing amiss in the regular use of alcohol or even in occasional intoxication.

This easy acceptance of drinking prevailed for two reasons. First, until about the 1760s, frequent access to the strongest spirits, rum, lay beyond the means of most Americans. Second, the leaders of local communities were able to oversee most public drinking and to keep disorder to a minimum. But by the middle of the eighteenth century, some Americans developed misgivings about the drinking culture. Increased production and importation made rum so cheap that an ordinary laborer could earn enough in a day to stay "drunk as a lord" for the rest of the week. Taverns spread, making it impossible for community leaders to monitor the popular consumption of alcohol.

The new concern that the drinking of rum fostered crime and social disruption prompted the first steps toward temperance reform. By the 1770s Quakers such as Anthony Benezet were urging that alcohol, like slavery, was an "unrepublican vice," for both forms of bondage deprived their victims of liberty and the capacity for rationality and self-control. Some members of the medical profession, most notably Benjamin Rush, also joined early temperance ranks.

Although the advocates of more moderate consumption won some support, most Americans altered their drinking habits by consuming *more* hard liquor, as rum lost much of its ground to a new rival, whiskey. Whiskey was democratic and cheap, for it could be made in the lowliest backcountry farmhouse. It was patriotic, since it did not

New England sea captains in Surinam drink rum the two-handed way—out of a silver bowl.

depend on imports from the Caribbean. Gradually these "spirits of independence" supplanted rum not only in the frontier West but also in the urban East. Consumption of alcohol was on a steady rise that would finally result, half a century after the Revolution, in louder calls for temperance reform.

Thinking Critically

What factors besides the availability of inexpensive whiskey might account for the increased consumption of alcohol in the decades after the American Revolution?

---

was never ratified, but the hostility stirred up during the debate revealed the strength of sectional feelings. Only a decade later, when the Senate ratified a treaty negotiated with Spain by Thomas Pinckney in 1796, did Americans gain full access to the Mississippi.

Shays's Rebellion

On the heels of this humiliation by Spain came an internal conflict that challenged the notion that individual states could maintain order in their own territories. The trouble erupted in western Massachusetts, where many small farmers were close to ruin. By 1786 farm wages and prices had fallen sharply and farmers were selling little produce. Yet they still had to pay mortgages on their farms and other debts. In 1786 the lower house of the Massachusetts legislature obliged the farmers with a package of relief measures. But creditors in eastern Massachusetts, determined to safeguard their own investments, persuaded the upper house to defeat the measures.

In the summer of 1786 western farmers responded, demanding that the upper house of the legislature be abolished and that the relief measures go into effect. That autumn 2,000 farmers rose in armed rebellion, led by Captain Daniel Shays, a veteran of the Revolution. They closed the county courts to halt creditors from foreclosing on their farms and marched on the federal arsenal at Springfield. The state militia quelled the uprising by February 1787, but the insurrection left many in Massachusetts and the rest of the country thoroughly shaken.

RESPONSE TO AGRARIAN UNREST Alarmed conservatives saw Shays's Rebellion as the consequence of radical democracy. "The natural effects of pure democracy are already produced among us," lamented one republican gentleman; "it is a war against virtue, talents, and property carried on by the dregs and scum of mankind." He was wrong. The rebels with Daniel Shays were no impoverished rabble. They were reputable members of western communities who wanted their property protected and believed that government existed to provide that protection. The Massachusetts state legislature had been unable to safeguard the property of farmers from the inroads of recession or to protect the property of creditors from the armed debtors who closed the courts. It had failed, in other words, to fulfill the most basic aim of republican government.

What if such violent tactics spread? Other states with discontented debtors feared what the example of western Massachusetts might mean for the future of the Confederation itself. But by 1786 Shays's Rebellion supplied only the sharpest jolt to a movement for reform that was already under way. Even before the rebellion, a group of Virginians had proposed a meeting of the states to adopt a uniform system of commercial regulations. Once assembled at Annapolis in September 1786, the delegates from five states agreed to a more ambitious undertaking. They called for a second, broader meeting in Philadelphia, which Congress approved, for the "express purpose of revising the Articles of Confederation."

Framing a Federal Constitution

SOCIAL PROFILE OF THE DELEGATES It was the wettest spring anyone could remember. The 55 men who traveled over muddy roads to Philadelphia in May 1787 arrived drenched and bespattered. Fortunately, most of the travelers were men in their 30s and 40s, young enough to survive a good soaking. Since most were gentlemen of some means—planters, merchants, and lawyers with powdered wigs and prosperous paunches—they could recover from the rigors of their journey in the best accommodations offered by America's largest city.

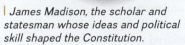

James Madison, the scholar and statesman whose ideas and political skill shaped the Constitution.

The delegates came from all the states except Rhode Island. The rest of New England supplied shrewd backroom politicians—Roger Sherman and Oliver Ellsworth from Connecticut and Rufus King and Elbridge Gerry, Massachusetts men who had learned a trick or two from Sam Adams. The middle states marshaled much of the intellectual might: two Philadelphia lawyers, John Dickinson and James Wilson; one Philadelphia financier, Robert Morris; and the aristocratic Gouverneur Morris. From New York there was Alexander Hamilton, the mercurial and ambitious young protégé of Washington. South Carolina provided fiery orators Charles Pinckney and John Rutledge.

It was "an assembly of the demi-gods," gushed Thomas Jefferson, who, along with John Adams, was serving as a diplomat in Europe when the convention met. In fact, the only delegate who looked even remotely divine was the convention's presiding deity. Towering a full half foot taller than most of his colleagues, George Washington displayed his usual self-possession from a chair elevated on the speaker's platform in the Pennsylvania State House, where the delegates met. At first glance, the delegate of least commanding presence was Washington's fellow Virginian, James Madison. Short and slightly built, the 36-year-old Madison had no profession except hypochondria; he read a great deal and dressed in black. But he was an astute politician and a brilliant political thinker who, more than anyone else, shaped the framing of the federal Constitution.

The delegates from 12 different states had two things in common. They were all men of considerable political experience, and they all recognized the need for a stronger national union. So, when the Virginia delegation introduced Madison's outline for a new central government, the convention was ready to listen.

The Virginia and New Jersey Plans

What Madison had in mind was a truly national republic, not a confederation of independent states. His "Virginia Plan" proposed a central government with three branches: legislative, executive, and judicial. Furthermore, the legislative branch, Congress, would possess the power to veto all state legislation. In place of the Confederation's single assembly, Madison substituted a bicameral legislature, with a lower house elected directly by the people and an upper house chosen by the lower, from nominations made by state legislatures. Representatives to both houses would be apportioned according to population—a change from practice under the Articles, in which each state had a single vote in Congress. Madison also revised the structure of government that had existed under the Articles by adding an executive, who would be elected by Congress, and an independent federal judiciary.

PATERSON'S NEW JERSEY PLAN

After two weeks of debate over the Virginia Plan, William Paterson, a lawyer from New Jersey, presented a less radical counterproposal. Although his "New Jersey Plan" increased Congress's power to tax and to regulate trade, it kept the national government as a unicameral assembly, with each state receiving one vote in Congress under the policy of equal representation. The delegates took just four days to reject Paterson's plan. Most endorsed Madison's design for a stronger central government.

Even so, the issue of apportioning representation continued to divide the delegates. While smaller states pressed for each state's having an equal vote in Congress, larger states backed Madison's provision for basing representation on population. Underlying the dispute over representation was an even deeper rivalry between southern and northern states. While northern and southern populations were nearly equal in the 1780s, and the South's population was growing more rapidly, the northern states were more numerous. Giving the states equal votes would put the South at a disadvantage. Southerners feared being outvoted in Congress by the northern states and felt that only proportional representation would protect the interests of their section.

That division turned into a deadlock as the wet spring burned off into a blazing summer. Delegates suffered the daily torture of staring at a large sun painted on the speaker's chair occupied by Washington. The stifling heat was made even worse because the windows remained shut to keep any news of the proceedings from drifting out into the Philadelphia streets.

The Deadlock Broken

COMPROMISE OVER REPRESENTATION

Finally, as the heat wave broke, so did the political stalemate. On July 2nd a committee headed by Benjamin Franklin suggested a compromise. States would be equally represented in the upper house of Congress, each state legislature appointing two senators to six-year terms. That satisfied the smaller states. In the lower house of Congress, which alone could initiate money bills, representation was to be apportioned according to population. Every 30,000 inhabitants would elect one representative for a two-year term. A slave was to count as three-fifths of a free person in the calculation of population, and the slave trade was to continue until 1808. That satisfied the larger states and the South.

ELECTORAL COLLEGE

By the end of August the convention was prepared to approve the final draft of the Constitution. The delegates agreed that the executive, now called the president, would be chosen every four years. Direct election seemed out of the question—after all, how could citizens in South Carolina know anything about a presidential candidate who happened to live in distant Massachusetts, or vice versa? But if voters instead chose presidential electors, those eminent men would likely have been involved in national politics, have known the candidates personally, and be prepared to vote wisely. Thus the Electoral College was established, with each state's total number of senators and representatives determining its share of electoral votes.

SEPARATION OF POWERS

An array of other powers ensured that the executive would remain independent and strong. He would have command over the armed forces, authority to conduct diplomatic relations, responsibility to nominate judges and officials in the executive branch, and the power to veto congressional legislation. Just as the executive branch was made independent, so too the federal judiciary was separated from the other two branches of government. Madison believed that this clear **separation of powers** was essential to a balanced republican government.

AMENDING THE CONSTITUTION

Madison's only real defeat came when the convention refused to give Congress veto power over state legislation. Still, the new bicameral national legislature enjoyed much broader authority than Congress had under the Confederation, including the power to tax and to regulate commerce. The Constitution also limited the powers of state legislatures, prohibiting them from levying duties on trade, coining money or issuing paper currency, and conducting foreign relations. The Constitution and the acts passed by Congress were declared the supreme law of the land, taking precedence over any legislation passed by the states. And changing the Constitution would not be easy. Amendments could be proposed only by a two-thirds vote of both houses of Congress or in a convention requested by two-thirds of the state legislatures. Ratification of amendments required approval by three-quarters of the states.

A REPUBLIC OF THE PEOPLE, NOT A CONFEDERATION OF STATES

On September 17, 1787, 39 of the 42 delegates remaining in Philadelphia signed the Constitution. It was fortunate that the signatories included so many lawyers, because the summer's proceedings had been of such dubious legality that many skilled attorneys would be needed to make them seem otherwise. Charged only to revise the Articles, the delegates had instead written a completely new frame of government. And to speed up ratification, the convention decided that the Constitution would go into effect after only nine states had approved it, overlooking the fact that even a revision of the Articles would have required the assent of all state legislatures. They further declared that the people themselves—not the state legislatures—would pass judgment on the Constitution in special ratifying conventions. To serve final notice that the new central government was a republic of the people and not merely another confederation of states, Gouverneur Morris of Pennsylvania hit on a happy turn of phrase to introduce the Constitution. "We the People," the document begins, "in Order to form a more perfect Union . . ."

Ratification

THE ANTI-FEDERALISTS

With grave misgivings on the part of many, the states called for conventions to decide whether to ratify the new Constitution.

Those Americans with the gravest misgivings—the Anti-Federalists as they came to be called—voiced familiar republican fears. Older and less cosmopolitan than their **Federalist** opponents, the Anti-Federalists drew on their memories of the struggle with England to frame their criticisms of the Constitution. Expanding the power of the central government at the expense of the states, they warned, would lead to corrupt and arbitrary rule by new aristocrats. Extending a republic over a large territory, they cautioned, would separate national legislators from the interests and close oversight of their constituents.

THE FEDERALIST PAPERS — Madison responded to these objections in *The Federalist Papers,* a series of 85 essays written with Alexander Hamilton and John Jay during the winter of 1787–1788. He countered Anti-Federalist concerns over the centralization of power by pointing out that each separate branch of the national government would keep the others within the limits of their legal authority. That mechanism of **checks and balances** would prevent the executive from oppressing the people while preventing the people from oppressing themselves.

To answer Anti-Federalist objections to a national republic, Madison drew on the ideas of an English philosopher, David Hume. In his famous tenth essay in *The Federalist Papers,* Madison argued that in a great republic, "the Society becomes broken into a greater variety of interests, of pursuits, of passions, which check each other." The larger the territory, the more likely it was to contain multiple political interests and parties, so that no single faction could dominate. Instead, each would cancel out the others.

BILL OF RIGHTS — The one Anti-Federalist criticism Madison could not get around was the absence of a national bill of rights. Opponents insisted on an explicit statement of rights to secure the freedoms of individuals and minorities from being violated by the federal government. Madison finally promised to place a bill of rights before Congress immediately after the Constitution was ratified.

Throughout the early months of 1788, Anti-Federalists continued their opposition. But they lacked the articulate and influential leadership that rallied behind the Constitution and commanded greater access to the public press. In the end, too, Anti-Federalist fears of centralized power proved less compelling than Federalist prophecies of the chaos that would follow if the Constitution were not adopted.

BILL OF RIGHTS RATIFIED — By the end of July 1788 all but two states had voted in favor of ratification. The last holdout—Rhode Island, to no one's surprise—finally came aboard in May 1790, after Madison had carried through on his pledge to submit a bill of rights to the new Congress. Indeed, these 10 amendments—ratified by enough states to become part of the Constitution by the end of 1791—proved to be the Anti-Federalists' most impressive

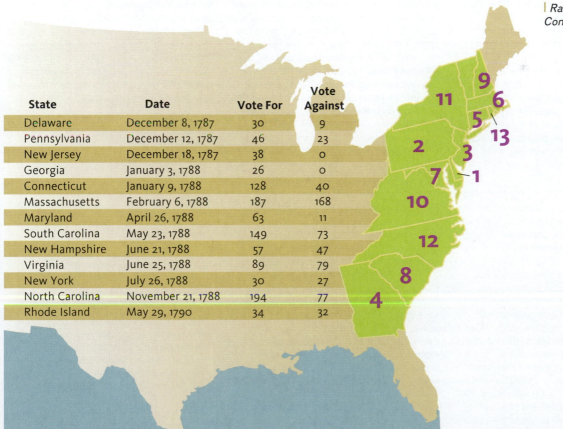

| Ratification of the Constitution

State	Date	Vote For	Vote Against
Delaware	December 8, 1787	30	9
Pennsylvania	December 12, 1787	46	23
New Jersey	December 18, 1787	38	0
Georgia	January 3, 1788	26	0
Connecticut	January 9, 1788	128	40
Massachusetts	February 6, 1788	187	168
Maryland	April 26, 1788	63	11
South Carolina	May 23, 1788	149	73
New Hampshire	June 21, 1788	57	47
Virginia	June 25, 1788	89	79
New York	July 26, 1788	30	27
North Carolina	November 21, 1788	194	77
Rhode Island	May 29, 1790	34	32

DUELING DOCUMENTS

REPUBLICAN REMEDY?

James Madison and "Brutus"—perhaps the Anti-Federalist judge Robert Yates—debated the proposed Constitution in the New York newspapers during 1787. One of the most contentious issues was whether a republic could effectively govern a territory as extensive as the United States.

DOCUMENT 1 James Madison

The two great points of difference between a democracy and a republic are: first, the delegation of the government in the latter, to a small number of citizens elected by the rest; secondly, the great number of citizens and greater sphere of country over which the latter may be extended.

The effect of the first difference is, on the one hand, to refine and enlarge the public views by passing them through the medium of a chosen body of citizens, whose wisdom may best discern the true interest of their country and whose patriotism and love of justice will be least likely to sacrifice it to temporary or partial considerations. Under such a regulation it may well happen that the public voice, pronounced by the representatives of the people, will be more consonant to the public good than if pronounced by the people themselves, convened for the purpose. On the other hand . . . men of factious tempers, of local prejudices, or of sinister designs, may, by intrigue, by corruption, or by other means, first obtain the suffrages, and then betray the interests of the people. The question resulting is, whether small or extensive republics are more favorable to the election of proper guardians of the public weal; and

it is clearly decided in favor of the latter by two obvious considerations.

In the first place . . . if the proportion of fit characters be not less in the large than in the small republic, the former will present a greater option, and consequently a greater probability of a fit choice.

In the next place, as each representative will be chosen by a greater number of citizens in the large than in the small republic, it will be more difficult for unworthy candidates to practice with success the vicious arts by which elections are too often carried. . . .

The other point of difference is the greater number of citizen and extent of territory which may be brought within the compass of republican than democratic government; and it is this circumstance principally which render factious combinations less to be dreaded in the former than in the latter. The smaller the society, the fewer probably will be the distinct parties and interests composing it; the fewer the distinct parties and interests, the more frequently will a majority be found of the same party; and the smaller the number of individuals compassing a majority . . . the more easily will they concert and execute their plans of oppression. Extend the sphere and you take in a

greater variety of parties and interests; you make it less probable that a majority of the whole will have a common motive to invade the rights of other citizens; or if such a common motive exists, it will be more difficult for all who feel it to discover their own strength and to act in unison with each other.

The influence of factious leaders may kindle a flame within their particular States but will be unable to spread a general conflagration through the other States. A religious sect may degenerate into a political faction in a part of the Confederacy; but the variety of sects dispersed over the entire face of it must secure the national councils against any danger from that source. A rage for paper money, for an abolition of debts, for an equal division of property, or for any other improper or wicked project, will be less apt to pervade the whole body of the Union than a particular member of it. . . .

In the extent and proper structure of the Union, therefore, we behold a republican remedy for diseases most incident to republican government.

Source: James Madison, Federalist No. 10, The Federalist: A Collection of Essays, Written in Favour of the New Constitution (New York, 1788).

DOCUMENT 2 "Brutus"

A free republic cannot succeed over a country of such immense extent, containing such a number of inhabitants, and these increasing in such rapid progression as that of the whole United States. . . .

Now, in a large extended country, it is impossible to have a representation, possessing the sentiments and of integrity, to declare the minds of the people, without having it so numerous and unwieldly, as to be subject in great measure to the inconveniency of a democratic government. . . .

In a republic, the manners, sentiments, and interest of the people should be similar. If this be not the case . . . [it] will retard the operations of government, and prevent such conclusions as will promote the public good. . . . The productions of the different

parts of the union are very variant, and their interests, of consequence, diverse. Their manners and habits differ as much as their climates and production; and their sentiments are by no means coincident.

The confidence which people have in their rulers, in a free republic, arises from their knowing them, from their being responsible to them for their conduct, and from the power they have of displacing them when they misbehave: but in a republic of the extent of this continent, the people in general would be acquainted with few of their rulers. . . . The consequence will be, they will have no confidence in their legislature, suspect them of ambitious views, be jealous of every measure they adopt, and will not support the laws they pass . . . no way will be

left to render it otherwise, but by establishing an armed force to execute laws at the point of a bayonet.

Source: "Brutus," in the New York Journal, October 18, 1787.

Thinking Critically

How did Madison define the differences between a democracy and a republic? What did he regard as the chief advantage of a large republic? On what grounds did "Brutus" argue against large republics? Has our republican form of government been successful in avoiding the kinds of oppression and "improper projects" that Madison describes?

legacy. The bill of rights set the most basic terms for defining personal liberty in the United States. Among the rights guaranteed were freedom of religion, the press, and speech, as well as the right to assemble and petition and the right to bear arms. The amendments also established clear procedural safeguards, including the right to a trial by jury and protection against illegal searches and seizures. They pro- hibited excessive bail, cruel and unusual punishment, and the quartering of troops in private homes.

✓ **REVIEW**

What short-term crises precipitated the Constitutional Convention, and what were the main points of debate at that meeting?

CONCLUSION

THE WORLD AT LARGE

Within the span of a single generation, Americans had declared their independence twice. In many ways the political freedom claimed from Britain in 1776 was less remarkable than the intellectual freedom from the Old World that Americans achieved by agreeing to the Constitution. The Constitution represented a triumph of the imagination—a challenge to many beliefs long cherished by western Europe's republican thinkers.

Revolutionary ideals had been deeply influenced by the conflicts of British politics, in particular the Opposition's warnings about the dangers of executive power. Those concerns at first committed the revolutionaries to making legislatures supreme. In the end, though, Americans ratified a constitution that provided for an independent executive and a balanced government. The Opposition's fears of distant, centralized power had at first prompted the revolutionaries to embrace state sovereignty. But in the Constitution Americans established a national government with authority independent of the states. Finally, the common sense among all of western Europe's republican theorists—that large national republics were an impossibility—was rejected by Americans, making the United States an impossibility that still endures.

What, then, became of the last tenet of the old republican creed—the belief that civic virtue would sustain popular liberty? The hard lessons of the war and the crises of the 1780s withered confidence in the capacity of Americans to sacrifice their private interests for the public welfare. The Constitution reflected the view that interest rather than virtue shaped the behavior of most people most of the time and that the clash of diverse interest groups would remain a constant of public life.

Yet Madison and many other Federalists did not believe that the competition between private interests would always foster the public welfare. That goal would be met instead by the new national government acting as "a disinterested and dispassionate umpire in disputes between different passions and interests in the State." A large republic, Federalists believed, with its millions of citizens, would yield more of that scarce resource—disinterested gentlemen dedicated to serving the public good. Such gentlemen, in Madison's words, "whose enlightened views and virtuous sentiments render them superior to local prejudices," would fill the small number of national offices.

Not all the old revolutionaries agreed. Anti-Federalists drawn from the ranks of ordinary Americans still believed that the national government should be composed of representations from every social class and occupational group, not dominated by "enlightened" gentlemen. "These lawyers and men of learning, and moneyed men, that talk so finely," complained one Anti-Federalist, would "get all the power and all of the money into their own hands, and then they will swallow up all us little folks."

That fear made Patrick Henry so ardent an Anti-Federalist that he refused to attend the Constitutional Convention in 1787, saying that he "smelt a rat." "I am not a Virginian, but an American," Henry had once declared. Most likely he was lying. Or perhaps Patrick Henry, a southerner and a slaveholder, could see himself as an "American" only so long as sovereignty remained firmly in the hands of the individual states. Henry's convictions, 70 years later, would rise again to haunt the Union. ∞∞∞

Chapter Summary

LEADING AMERICANS GAVE MORE THOUGHT to federalism, the organization of a United States, as events in the 1780s revealed the weaknesses of the state and national governments.

■ For a decade after independence, the revolutionaries were less committed to creating a single national republic than to organizing 13 separate state republics, each dominated by popularly elected legislatures.

■ The Articles of Confederation's national legislature left the crucial power of the purse, as well as all final power to make and execute laws, entirely to the states.

■ Many conflicts in the new republic were occasioned by westward expansion, which created both international difficulties with Britain and Spain and internal tensions over the democratization of state legislatures.

■ After the Revolution, Americans struggled to define republican society; workers began to organize, some women claimed a right to greater political, legal, and educational opportunities, and religious dissenters called for disestablishment.

■ The Revolution's egalitarian principles sparked a debate over slavery that increased the split between northern and southern states. Antislavery societies appeared in the North; some planters in the Upper South freed their slaves, but no southern state abolished slavery.

■ In the mid-1780s the political crisis of the Confederation came to a head, prompted by the controversy over the Jay-Gardoqui Treaty and Shays's Rebellion.

■ The Constitutional Convention of 1787 produced an entirely new frame of government that established a truly national republic and provided for a separation of powers among a judiciary, a bicameral legislature, and a strong executive.

■ The Anti-Federalists, opponents of the Constitution, pushed for a bill of rights, which was incorporated into the Constitution by 1791.

Additional Reading

THE WORK OF GORDON WOOD is indispensable for understanding the transformation of American politics and culture during the 1780s and thereafter; see especially *The Creation of the American Republic* (1969) and *The Radicalism of the American Revolution* (1992). Other good accounts of the Confederation period and the framing of the Constitution include Forrest MacDonald, *E Pluribus Unum* (1965) and *Novus Ordo Seclorum* (1985), and Woody Holton's *Unruly Americans* (2007). To understand the arguments in favor of the Constitution, consult Garry Wills, *Explaining America* (1981), and to appreciate the contributions of its opponents, read Saul Cornell, *The Other Founders* (1999), and Cecilia Kenyon's *Men of Little Faith* (2003). The proceedings of the Constitutional Convention receive full coverage in Christopher Collier and James Lincoln Collier, *Decision in Philadelphia* (1987), and Clinton Rossiter, *1787: The Grand Convention* (1973).

To explore the meaning of republicanism for American women, see two fine studies by Linda Kerber, *Women of the Republic* (1980) and *No Constitutional Right to Be Ladies* (1998), as well as Rosemarie Zagarri's provocative *Revolutionary Backlash* (2007). For a vivid sense of how the 1780s transformed one Massachusetts county, read John Brooke, *The Heart of the Commonwealth* (1991), and for a fascinating tale of how the Revolution made one ordinary man's life extraordinary, enjoy Alan Taylor, *William Cooper's Town* (1995). For the effects of the Revolution on African Americans in the North, see Joan Pope Melish, *Disowning Slavery* (1998), and James Sidbury, *Becoming African in America* (2007).

For a fuller list of readings, see the Bibliography at www.mhhe.com/eh8e.

Significant Events

1777
Continental Congress approves the Articles of Confederation

1781
Articles of Confederation ratified

1784
Spain closes the Mississippi River to American navigation

1785
Jay-Gardoqui Treaty negotiated but not ratified

1786
Shays's Rebellion; Annapolis convention calls for revising the Articles

1787
Congress adopts the Northwest Ordinance; Constitutional Convention

1787–1788
Publication of *The Federalist Papers*

1788
New Hampshire becomes ninth state to ratify Constitution

1791
Bill of Rights adopted

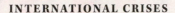

Crises of the 1780s—and Consequences

INTERNATIONAL CRISES

British efforts to annex Vermont to Canada

Spanish efforts to ally with Indians in the
Southeast and with white settlers
in the Ohio valley

↓

Culminated in debate over the Jay-Gardoqui
Treaty, 1785

EXPOSED

Weakness of confederation diplomacy;
consequences of having no national army

Weakness of confederation diplomacy
and Indian policy; consequences of
having no national army

Simmering tensions between East and West,
North and South; potential of sectional
conflict to threaten national union

DOMESTIC CRISES

Postwar inflationary spiral

Debtor vs. creditor interests producing
political divisions and deadlock in
state legislatures

↓

Culminated in Shays's Rebellion (1786)

EXPOSED

Confederation Congress's lack of power to set
national economic policy, tax, regulate trade

Inability of sovereign states to solve
economic conflicts

Potential for future agrarian violence;
failure of state governments to
protect property

White and Black Southerners Worshiping Together

Religious beliefs, gatherings, and rituals reflect some of the deepest human emotions. Often they also lay bare some of society's deepest divisions. For both these reasons and more, historians often study religious institutions and practices to understand how a society functions.

During the 50 years before 1800, **evangelicals** introduced southerners to new ways of being religious. Those attending their worship services were drawn into the earliest southern Baptist, Methodist, and Presbyterian churches by the First Great Awakening and other revivals that followed. Some of these early services were held in private homes, others in crudely constructed churches, and still others in open fields. As evangelical preachers stressed the importance of being "reborn" by faith in Jesus Christ, some southerners wept, confessed their sins, and encouraged one another with hopeful words and warm embraces. Those who came to such gatherings engaged in the most intimate kind of sharing and self-revelation.

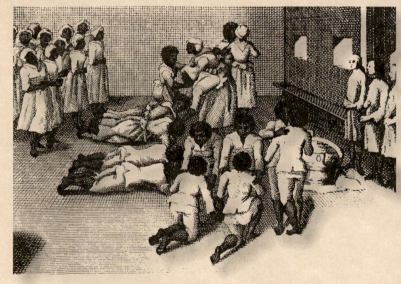

What made the services even more extraordinary is that some participants were white and some black. These religious fellowships were truly biracial and remained so until after the Civil War. That remarkable fact has intrigued historians. In a society increasingly shaped by the institution of slavery, evangelical churches were one of the few southern institutions that brought blacks and whites together rather than keeping them apart. How did members behave toward one another daily? Were born-again converts from both races treated equally? How was authority within such churches distributed among black and white members?

The questions are tantalizing, but the answers by no means easy to come by. Some letters and diaries survive from the last half of the eighteenth century, among them the daily journals and correspondence of ministers. A few preachers even published autobiographies

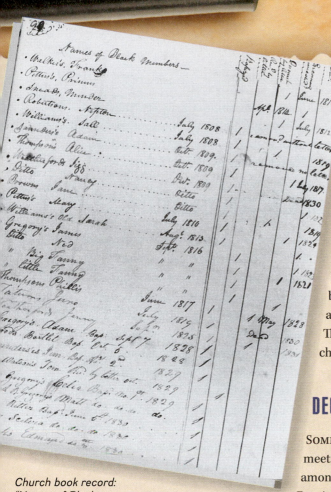

Church book record: "Names of Black Members." Note the treatment of black names.

of their experiences. But even more valuable information can be gathered from what might seem at first a rather drab source. There are scores of church records dating from this period, most kept by Virginia Baptists. The members of each Baptist church elected a clerk, always a white male "brother," whose duty it was to record all the business transacted at their monthly meetings, often in a ledger-sized bound volume called the "church book." Church books provide an insight into relations between whites and blacks in part because their clerks are not consciously trying to write about race relations. They are simply recording the everyday business of churches, week in, week out.

DECODING THE CHURCH BOOKS

SOMETIMES PRACTICAL CONCERNS DOMINATED THE meeting. Should the church building be repaired? Who among the brethren will be permitted to preach? (Many Baptist churches boasted several preachers besides the pastor.) On other occasions, members debated what, according to the Bible, was the holiest way to govern their churches. But at most meetings, members fixed their attention on admitting new converts to their fellowship and "disciplining" older members suspected of sexual misconduct or theft, slander or swearing, drinking or fighting. Church clerks duly noted all those accepted as new members, as well as the names of wayward brothers and sisters—and whether they were merely scolded for their faults or expelled.

Such records offer the most direct and vivid sense of African Americans' presence and participation in early evangelical churches. First, historians can start by doing a little counting. How many members are white and how many black? The records show that blacks made up a substantial minority—perhaps one-fifth to one-quarter—of the members in most churches. In a few, they constituted a majority. Many churches, too, authorized at least one African American brother to preach, sometimes permitting him that "liberty" only among other blacks but in other instances allowing him to address racially mixed gatherings. There were even a few predominantly white churches in early Virginia that black preachers served as pastors.

What about voting? In some churches, too, black men and, more rarely, black women were permitted to vote in meetings. In all, African American members could participate in deliberations and give testimony in discipline cases. Indeed, there are several instances of masters being disciplined after slave members complained of being abused. Black members, too, were sometimes charged with wrongdoing, but white men were far more likely than any other group of members to be hauled before the church for reported misdeeds. In short, evangelical churches like these Baptist fellowships were among the most racially egalitarian

"Uncle Jack," shown in this 1849 engraving, preaches informally to a white congregation. He began his career as a minister in the 1790s and continued until 1832.

institutions in early southern society. They offered African Americans unusual opportunities to hold positions of authority, to voice their opinions, and to gain leverage over their masters.

LIMITS OF RACIAL EQUALITY

YET THESE SAME CHURCH RECORDS also reveal the limits of racial equality among early evangelicals. Like all evidence mined by historians, the sources yield data that are sometimes complex and contradictory.

Records of those meetings at which members discussed the mundane matter of church repair reveal, for example, that the Baptists segregated seating at public worship. African Americans were consigned to the least choice spots at the back of the church or in "sheds" attached to the side. Moreover, when white members filled every available seat, black members were ordered outdoors to listen from underneath open windows. The attitude that such practices convey— that whites regarded African Americans as "second-class" members—is also suggested by the manner in which many clerks recorded new church members. They always entered the full names of white converts; however, new African American members were usually listed last and often collectively as "several Negroes."

Church discussions about who might preach also show a growing concern on the part of white members to restrict the activities of black preachers. Increasingly after 1750, those allowed that "liberty" were given ever stricter instructions about whom they might preach to, at which times, and from what texts of the Bible. At meetings in which the rules of conducting church business were discussed, white members also began to express concern about whether African American members should be allowed to vote. Most churches revoked that right before the end of the eighteenth century. Tracing how churches dealt with black members accused of misbehavior suggests a similar anxiety among white members, which increased over time. Although African Americans continued to make up only a tiny minority of church members suspected of misbehavior, those convicted of wrongdoing were far more likely than white members to be expelled rather than to receive a milder punishment.

In other words, a closer inspection of church records suggests that white evangelicals drifted toward more racially restrictive policies over the latter half of the eighteenth century. Why? The numbers in the church books are suggestive. After the Revolution, increasing numbers of African Americans were entering Baptist (and other evangelical) churches.

As the percentage of black members rose, white evangelicals feared that the "freedoms" given to black worshipers might detract from the church's ability to win converts among slaveholders.

SEEKING A SEPARATE WAY

CLEARLY, EVANGELICALS WERE WINNING CONVERTS among African Americans. Yet other evidence suggests that black members were left unsatisfied by their treatment in white churches. The diaries and letters of white evangelicals reveal that many black members of biracial churches had also begun conducting their own separate devotions. Even by the 1790s, African American Christians were meeting nightly in the slave quarters to pray, sing, and hear the sermons of black preachers. Such "shadow churches" served as the crucible of Afro-Christianity, a melding of evangelical Protestant and West African religious traditions. John Antrobus's painting *Plantation Burial* (in a detail shown above) reflects the situation that prevailed by the mid-nineteenth century. Although blacks attended white services in greater numbers, their most vital worship often took place elsewhere. White masters and preachers were like the shadowy couple Antrobus painted on the right: divorced from the Christian worship of their slaves.

Citizens staged Fourth of July parades as one way to define the identity of their young republic. This New York parade in 1812 was led by the Tammany Society, whose members rejected the aristocratic inclinations of the Federalist Party. The society was named to honor a Delaware Indian chief; its members often marched wearing Indian style garb, as seen here. But by 1812 the patriotic associations of Indian dress (recall the Boston Tea Party disguises) were less popular due to increased clashes with Indians on the frontier.

The Early Republic

1789–1824

What's to Come

∞∞∞ AN AMERICAN STORY ∞∞∞

"I FELT MY BLOOD BOIL"

One spring evening in 1794 General John Neville rode home from Pittsburgh with his wife and granddaughter. As they went up a hill, his wife's saddle started to slip, so Neville dismounted. As he adjusted the strap, a rider galloped up and in a gruff voice asked, "Are you Neville the excise officer?"

"Yes," Neville replied, without turning around.

"Then I must give you a whipping!" cried the rider and leapt from his horse. He grabbed Neville by the hair and lunged at his throat. Breaking free, Neville finally managed to knock the man down, after which he fled. But Neville could not help but be shaken as he resumed his journey. The general was not accustomed to such treatment. As one of the wealthiest men in the area, he expected respect from those of lower social rank. And he had received it—until becoming embroiled in a controversy over the new "whiskey tax" on distilled spirits. In a frontier district like western Pennsylvania, farmers regularly distilled their grain into whiskey for barter and sale. Not surprisingly, the **excise tax,** passed by Congress in 1791, was notoriously unpopular. Still, Neville had accepted an appointment to be one of the tax's regional inspectors. For three years he had endured the occasional threat, but this roadside assault showed that popular hostility was rising.

As spring turned to summer the grain ripened, and so did the people's anger. In mid-July a federal marshal arrived to serve summonses to a number of farmer-distillers who had not paid taxes. One, William Miller, squinted at the paper and was amazed to find the government ordering him to appear in court—hundreds of miles away in Philadelphia—in little more than a month. Worse, the papers claimed he owed $250.

And there, next to this unknown federal marshal, stood John Neville.

"I thought $250 would ruin me," recalled Miller; "and I felt my blood boil at seeing General Neville along to pilot the sheriff to my very door." Within minutes 30 or 40 laborers had swarmed from a nearby field. Armed with muskets and pitchforks, they forced Neville and the marshal to beat a hasty retreat. Next morning, the local militia company marched to Neville's estate. A battle ensued, and the general, aided by his slaves, beat back the attackers. A larger group, numbering 500 to 700, returned the following day to find Neville fled and his home garrisoned by a group of soldiers from nearby Fort Pitt. The mob burned down most of the outbuildings and, after the soldiers surrendered, torched Neville's elegantly furnished home.

A tax collector in league with the devil.

That summer, marauding bands roamed the countryside, burning homes and attacking tax collectors. Western Pennsylvania experienced the greatest unrest, but farmers in the western districts of several other states also defied federal officials, thus launching a full-scale "Whiskey Rebellion" in the summer of 1794.

Alexander Hamilton, a principal architect of the strong federal government established by the Constitution, knew a challenge to authority when he saw one: "Shall there be a government, or no government?" So did an alarmed George Washington, now president and commander-in-chief of the new republic, who led an army of 13,000 men—larger than that he had commanded at Yorktown against the British—into the Pennsylvania countryside. That show of force cowed the Pennsylvania protesters, snuffing out the Whiskey Rebellion.

Federalists such as Washington and Hamilton—supporters of a powerful national government—had high hopes for their newly created republic. But the riots and rebellion deepened fears for its future. The nation's founders recognized all too well how risky it was to unite such a vast territory. Yankee merchants living along Boston wharves had economic interests and cultural traditions distinct from those of backcountry farmers who raised hogs, tended a few acres of corn, and distilled whiskey. Even among farmers there was a world of difference between a South Carolina planter who shipped tons of rice to European markets and a New Hampshire family whose stony fields yielded barely enough to survive. Could the new government established by the Constitution provide a framework strong enough to unite such a patchwork of peoples, cultures, and classes? These newly united states were a fragile creation, buffeted by changes beyond their borders and struggling to create a stable government at home. During the nation's first three decades, the republic's survival depended on balancing the interests of a socially and economically diverse population. ◦◦◦◦◦

A Social and Political Portrait of the New Republic

WHEN THE CONSTITUTION WENT INTO effect, the United States stretched from the Atlantic Ocean to the Mississippi River. Comprising some 840,000 square miles in 1789, it was approximately four times the size of France, five times the size of Spain, ten times the size of Great Britain. The first federal census, compiled in 1790, counted approximately 4 million people, divided about evenly between the northern and southern states. Only about 100,000 settlers lived beyond the Appalachians in the Tennessee and Kentucky territories, which were soon to become states.

Within the Republic's boundaries were two major groups that lacked effective political influence: African Americans and Indians. In 1790 black Americans numbered 750,000, almost one-fifth the total population. More than 90 percent lived in the southern states from Maryland to Georgia; most were slaves who worked on tobacco and rice plantations, but there were free blacks as well. The census did not count the number of Indians living east of the Mississippi. North of the Ohio, the powerful Miami Confederacy discouraged settlement, while to the south, five strong, well-organized tribes—the Creeks, Cherokees, Chickasaws, Choctaws, and Seminoles—dominated the region from the Appalachians to the Mississippi River.

POPULATION GROWTH That composition would change as the white population continued to double about every 22 years. Immigration contributed only a small part to this astonishing growth. On average, fewer than 10,000 Europeans arrived annually between 1790 and 1820. The primary cause was natural increase, since, on average, American white women gave birth to nearly eight children each. As a result, the United States had an unusually youthful population: in 1790 almost half of all white Americans were under 16 years old. The age at first marriage was about 25 for men, 24 for women—and three or four years younger in newly settled areas—which contributed to the high birthrate.

This youthful, growing population remained overwhelmingly rural. Only 24 towns and cities boasted 2,500 or more residents, and 19 out of 20 Americans lived outside them. In fact, more than 80 percent of American families in 1800 were engaged in agriculture. In such a rural environment the movement of people, goods, and information was slow. Few individuals used the expensive postal system, and most roads were still little more than dirt paths hacked through the forest. In 1790 the country had 92 newspapers, but they were published mostly in towns and cities along major avenues of transportation.

Life in isolated regions contrasted markedly with that in bustling urban centers like New York City and Philadelphia. But the most basic division in American society was not between the cities and the countryside, important as that was. What would divide Americans most broadly over the coming decades was the contrast between semisubsistence and commercial ways of life. Semisubsistence farmers lived on the produce of their own land and labor. Americans in the commercial economy were tied more closely to the larger markets of a far-flung world.

Semisubsistence and Commercial Economies

Most rural white Americans in the interior of the northern states and the backcountry of the South lived off the produce of their own land. Wealth in those areas, although not distributed equally, was spread fairly broadly. And subsistence remained the goal of most white families. "The great effort was for every farmer to produce anything he required within his own family," one European visitor noted. In such an economy women played a key role. Wives and daughters had to be skilled in making articles such as candles, soap, clothing, and hats, since the cost of buying such items was steep.

With labor scarce and expensive, farmers also depended on their neighbors to help clear fields, build homes, and harvest crops. If a farm family produced a small surplus, it usually exchanged it locally rather than selling it for cash in a distant market. In this barter economy, money was seldom seen and was used primarily to pay taxes and purchase imported goods.

INDIAN ECONOMIES Indian economies were also based primarily on subsistence. In the division of labor women raised crops, while men fished or hunted—not only for meat but also for skins to make clothing. Because Indians followed game more seasonally than did white settlers, they moved their villages to several different locations over the course of a year. But both whites and Indians in a **semisubsistence economy** moved periodically to new fields after they had exhausted the old ones. Indians exhausted agricultural lands less quickly because they planted beans, corn, and squash in the same field, a technique that better conserved soil nutrients.

Despite the image of both the independent "noble savage" and the self-reliant yeoman farmer, virtually no one in the backcountry operated within a truly self-sufficient economy. Although farmers tried to grow most of the food their families ate, they normally bought salt, sugar, and coffee, and they often traded with their neighbors for food and other items. In addition, necessities such as iron, glass, lead, and gunpowder had to be purchased, and many farmers hired artisans to make shoes and weave cloth. Similarly, Indians were enmeshed in the wider world of European commerce, exchanging furs for iron tools or clothing and ornamental materials.

Outside the backcountry, Americans were tied much more closely to a **commercial economy.** Here, merchants, artisans, and even farmers did not subsist on what they produced but instead sold goods or services in a wider market and lived on their earnings. Cities and towns, of

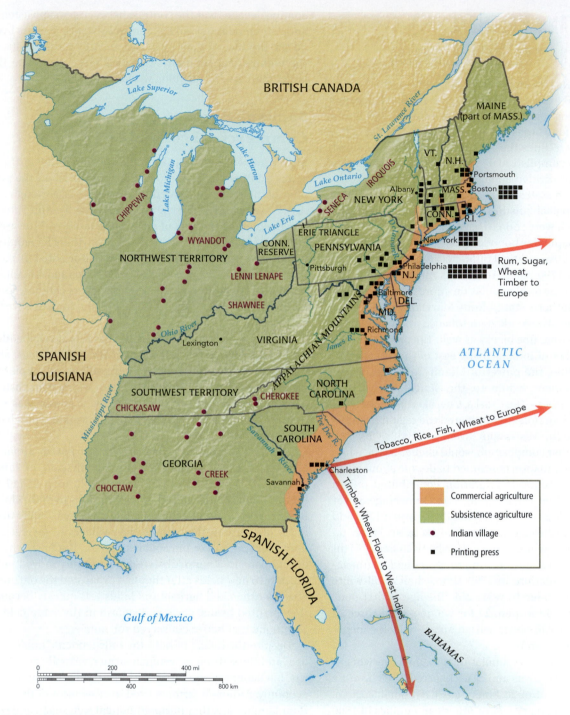

SEMISUBSISTENCE AND COMMERCIAL AMERICA, 1790

To prosper, a commercial economy demanded relatively cheap transportation to move goods. Thus in 1790 American commerce was confined largely to settled areas along the coast and to navigable rivers below the fall line. Because commerce depended on an efficient flow of information and goods, newspapers flourished in these areas. **Did the split between commercial and semisubsistence ways of life reflect a division more between east and west or north and south? Why?**

course, played a key part in the commercial economy. But so did the agricultural regions near the seaboard and along navigable rivers.

For commerce to flourish, goods had to move from producers to market cheaply enough to reap profits. Water

offered the only cost-effective transportation over any distance; indeed, it cost as much to ship goods a mere 30 miles over primitive roads as to ship by boat 3,000 miles across the Atlantic to London. Cost-effective transportation was available to the planters of the Tidewater South, and city merchants used their access to the sea to establish trading ties to the West Indies and Europe. But urban artisans and workers were also linked to this market economy, as were many farm families in the Hudson valley, southeastern Pennsylvania, and southern New England.

In commercial economies wealth was less equally distributed. By 1790 the richest 10 percent of Americans living in cities and in the plantation districts of the Tidewater South owned about 50 percent of the wealth. In the backcountry the top 10 percent was likely to own 25 to 35 percent of the wealth.

The Constitution and Commerce

In many ways the fight over ratification of the Constitution represented a struggle between the commercial and the subsistence-oriented elements of American society. Urban merchants and workers as well as commercial farmers and planters generally rallied behind the Constitution. They took a broader, more cosmopolitan view of the nation's future, and they had a more favorable view of government power than did subsistence farmers.

Americans who remained a part of the semisubsistence **barter economy** tended to oppose the Constitution. More provincial in outlook, they feared concentrated power, were suspicious of cities and commercial institutions, opposed aristocracy and special privilege, and in general just wanted to be left alone.

And so in 1789 the United States embarked on its new national course, with two rival visions of the direction that the fledgling Republic should take. Which vision would prevail—a question that was as much social as it was political—increasingly divided the generation of revolutionary leaders in the early republic.

Washington Organizes the Government

Whatever the Republic was to become, Americans agreed that George Washington personified it. When the first Electoral College cast its votes, Washington was unanimously elected, the only president in history so honored. John Adams became vice president. Loyalty to the new Republic, with its untried form of government and diversity of peoples and interests, rested to a great degree on the trust and respect Americans gave Washington.

George Washington realized that as the first occupant of the executive office, everything he did was fraught with significance. "I walk on untrodden ground," he commented. "There is scarcely any part of my conduct which may not hereafter be drawn into precedent."

THE CABINET The Constitution made no mention of a cabinet. Yet the drafters of the Constitution, aware of the experience of the Continental Congress under the Articles of Confederation, clearly assumed that the president would have some system of advisers. Congress authorized the creation of four departments—War, Treasury, State, and Attorney General—whose heads were to be appointed with the consent of the Senate. Washington's most important choices were Alexander Hamilton as secretary of the treasury and Thomas Jefferson to head the State Department. Washington gradually excluded Adams from cabinet discussions, and any meaningful role for the vice president, whose duties were largely undefined by the Constitution, soon disappeared.

The Constitution created a federal Supreme Court but beyond that was silent about the court system. The Judiciary Act of 1789 set the size of the Supreme Court at 6 members; it also established 13 federal district courts and 3 circuit courts of appeal. Supreme Court justices spent much of their time serving on these circuit courts, a distasteful duty whose long hours "riding the circuit" caused one justice to grumble that Congress had made him a "traveling postboy." The Judiciary Act made it clear that federal courts had the right to review decisions of the state courts and specified cases over which the Supreme Court would have original jurisdiction. Washington appointed John Jay of New York, a staunch Federalist, as the first chief justice.

Hamilton's Financial Program

HAMILTON'S TWO GOALS When Congress called on Alexander Hamilton to prepare a report on the nation's finances, the new secretary of the treasury undertook the assignment eagerly. A brilliant thinker and an ambitious politician, he did not intend to be a minor figure in the new administration. Convinced that human nature was fundamentally selfish, Hamilton was determined to link the interests of the wealthy with those of the new government. He also intended to use federal power to encourage manufacturing and commerce in order to make the United States economically strong and independent of Europe.

FUNDING AND ASSUMPTION Neither goal could be achieved until the federal government solved its two most pressing financial problems: revenue and credit. Without revenue it could not be effective. Without credit—the faith of merchants and other nations that the government would repay its debts—it would lack the ability to borrow. Hamilton proposed that all $52 million of the federal debt, much of it generated by the Revolutionary War, be paid in full (or funded). He also recommended that the federal government assume responsibility for the remaining $25 million in debts that individual states owed—a policy of "assumption." He intended with these twin policies to put the new federal government on a sound financial footing and enhance its power by increasing its need for revenue and making the wealthy look to the national government, not the states. Hamilton also proposed a series of excise taxes, including a controversial 25 percent levy on whiskey, to help meet government expenses.

Philadelphia was the largest and most prosperous city in the country in 1789. In this scene, young men wolf down fresh oysters after enjoying a play at Philadelphia's Chestnut Theater (background).

BANK OF THE UNITED STATES

After heated debate, Congress deadlocked over funding and assumption. Finally, at a dinner with Hamilton, Jefferson and James Madison of Virginia agreed to support his proposal if, after 10 years in Philadelphia, the permanent seat of government would be located in the South, on the Potomac River between Virginia and Maryland. Aided by this understanding, funding and assumption passed Congress. In 1791 Congress also approved a 20-year charter for the first Bank of the United States. The bank would hold government deposits and issue banknotes that would be received in payment of all debts owed the federal government. Congress proved less receptive to the rest of Hamilton's program, although a limited tariff to encourage manufacturing and several excise taxes, including the one on whiskey, won approval.

The passage of Hamilton's program caused a permanent rupture among supporters of the Constitution. Madison, who had collaborated closely with Hamilton in the 1780s, broke with his former ally over funding and assumption. Jefferson finally went over to the opposition when Hamilton announced plans for a national bank. Eventually the two warring factions organized themselves into political

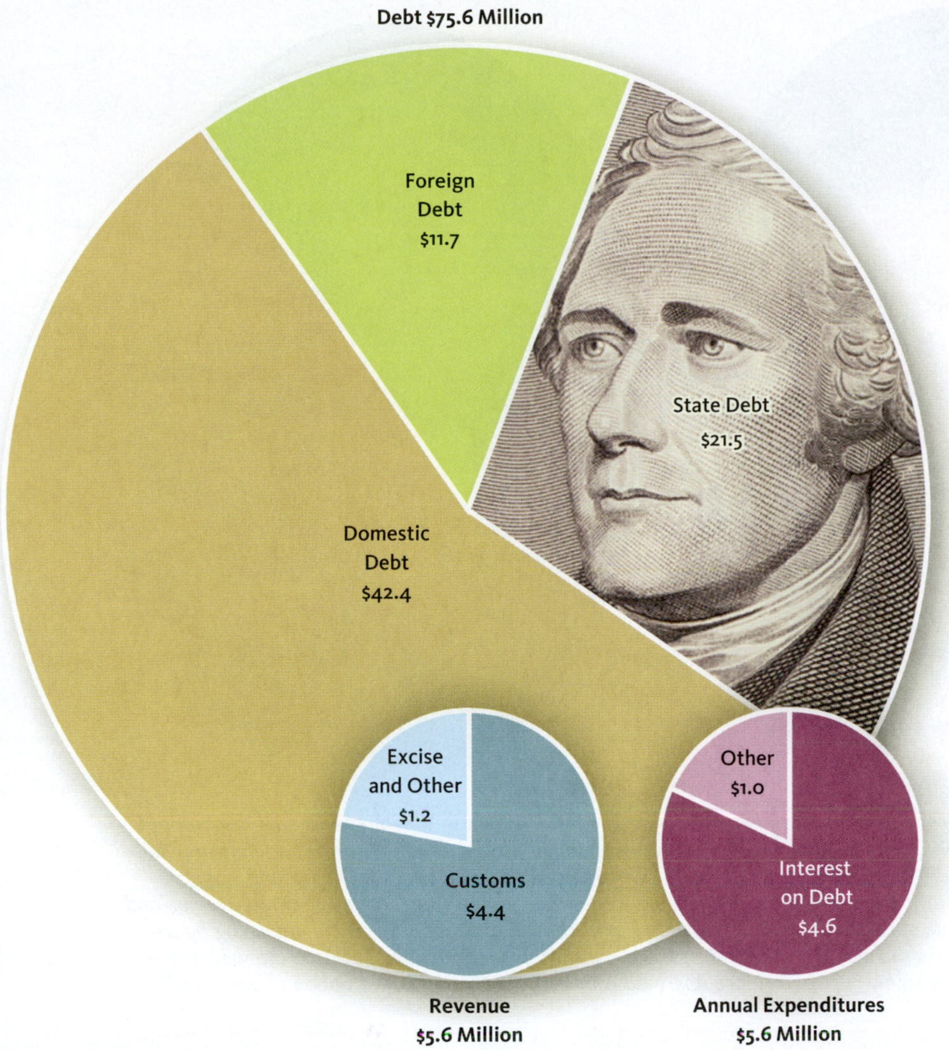

Debt $75.6 Million

Foreign
Debt
$11.7

State Debt
$21.5

Domestic
Debt
$42.4

Excise
and Other
$1.2

Customs
$4.4

Other
$1.0

Interest
on Debt
$4.6

Revenue
$5.6 Million

Annual Expenditures
$5.6 Million

Under Hamilton's financial system, more than 80 percent of federal revenues went to pay the interest on the national debt. Note that most of the revenue came from tariff duties (customs).

parties: the Republicans, led by Jefferson and Madison, and the Federalists, led by Hamilton and Adams.* But the division emerged slowly over several years.

FEARS OF A FINANCIAL ARISTOCRACY Hamilton's program promoted the commercial sector at the expense of semisubsistence farmers. Thus it rekindled many of the concerns that had surfaced during the struggle over ratification of the Constitution. The ideology of the Revolution had stressed that republics inevitably contained groups who sought power in order to destroy popular liberties and overthrow the republic. To some Americans, Hamilton's program seemed a clear threat to establish a privileged and powerful financial aristocracy—perhaps even a monarchy.

SYSTEMS OF CORRUPTION Who, after all, would benefit from the funding proposal? During and after the Revolution, the value of notes issued by the Continental Congress dropped sharply. Speculators had bought up most

of these notes for a fraction of their face value from small farmers and workers. If the government finally paid back the debt, speculators would profit accordingly. Equally disturbing, members of Congress had been purchasing the notes before the adoption of Hamilton's program. Nearly half the members of the House of Representatives owned U.S. securities, a dangerous mimicking of Britain, where the Bank of England's loans to many members of Parliament gave it great political influence.

Fears were heightened because Americans had little experience with banks: only three existed in the country when the Bank of the United States was chartered. One member of Congress expressed a common attitude when he said that he would no more be caught entering a bank than a house of prostitution. Then, too, banks and commerce were a part of the urban environment that rural Americans so distrusted. Although Hamilton's opponents admitted that a certain amount of commerce was necessary, they believed that it should remain subordinate. Hamilton's program, in contrast, encouraged manufacturing and urbanization, developments that history suggested were incompatible with liberty and equality.

---

*The Republican Party of the 1790s, sometimes referred to as the Jeffersonian Republicans, is not to be confused with the modern-day Republican Party, which originated in the 1850s.

A study in contrasts, Jefferson and Hamilton increasingly came into conflict in Washington's administration. Despite his aristocratic upbringing, Jefferson (left) was awkward, loose-jointed, reserved, and ill at ease in public. Testifying before a congressional committee, he casually lounged in a chair and spoke in a rambling, nonstop manner. "Yet he scattered information wherever he went," conceded Senator William Maclay of Pennsylvania, "and some even brilliant sentiments sparkled from him." Hamilton (right), though short of stature, cut a dashing figure with his erect bearing, strutting manner, meticulous dress, and carefully powdered hair. Declared the wife of the British ambassador: "I have scarcely ever been more charmed with the vivacity and conversation of any man."

STRICT CONSTRUCTION OF THE CONSTITUTION

After Congress approved the bank bill, Washington hesitated to sign it. When he consulted his cabinet, Jefferson stressed that the Constitution did not specifically authorize Congress to charter a bank. Both he and Madison upheld the idea of strict construction—that the Constitution should be interpreted narrowly and the federal government restricted to powers expressly delegated to it. Otherwise, the federal government would be the judge of its own powers, and there would be no safeguard against the abuse of power.

Hamilton countered that the Constitution contained implied as well as enumerated powers. He particularly emphasized the clause that permitted Congress to make all laws "necessary and proper" to carry out its duties. A bank would be useful in carrying out the enumerated powers of regulating commerce and maintaining the public credit; Congress thus had a right to decide whether to establish one. In the end Washington accepted Hamilton's arguments and signed the bill.

Economically Hamilton's program was a success. The government's credit was restored, and the national bank ended the inflation of the previous two decades and created a sound currency. In addition, Hamilton's theory of implied powers and broad construction gave the nation the flexibility necessary to respond to unanticipated crises.

REVIEW

Analyze the relationship between economic interests and politics in the 1790s.

THE EMERGENCE OF POLITICAL PARTIES

MEMBERS OF THE REVOLUTIONARY GENERATION fervently hoped that political parties would not take root in the United States. "If I could not go to heaven but with a party, I would not go at all," remarked Jefferson. Influenced by radical English republican thought, American critics condemned parties as narrow interest groups that placed selfishness and party loyalty above a concern for the public good. Despite Americans' distrust of such institutions, however, the United States became the first nation to establish truly popular parties.

SOCIAL CONDITIONS ENCOURAGING POLITICAL PARTIES

Social conditions encouraged the rise of parties. Because property ownership was widespread, the nation had a broad **suffrage.** During the American Revolution legislatures lowered property requirements in many states, increasing the number of voters still further. If party members hoped to hold office, they had to offer a program attractive to the broader voting public. When parties acted as representatives of economic and social interest groups, they became one means by which a large electorate could make its feelings known. In addition, the United States had the highest literacy rate in the world and the largest number of newspapers, further encouraging political interest and participation. Finally, the fact that well-known patriots of the Revolution headed both the Federalists and the Republicans helped defuse the charge that either party was hostile to the Revolution or the Constitution.

 ## Americans and the French Revolution

Although domestic issues first split the supporters of the Constitution, it was a crisis in Europe that pushed the nation toward political parties. Americans had hoped that their revolution would spark similar movements for liberty on the European continent, and in fact the American Revolution was only one of a series of revolutions in the late eighteenth century that shook the Western world, the most important of which began in France in 1789. There a rising population and the collapse of government finances sparked a challenge to royal authority that became a mass revolution. The French revolutionary ideals of "liberty, equality, and fraternity" eventually spilled across Europe.

DIFFERING VIEWS OF THE FRENCH REVOLUTION

Americans first hailed the Revolution. Many rejoiced to learn that the Bastille prison had been stormed and that a new National Assembly had abolished feudal privileges and adopted the Declaration of the Rights of Man. But by 1793, American enthusiasm for the Revolution had cooled after radical elements instituted a reign of terror, executing the king and queen and many of the nobility. The French Republic even outlawed Christianity and substituted the worship of Reason. Finally, in 1793 republican France and monarchical England went to war. Americans were deeply divided over whether the United States should continue its old alliance with France or support Great Britain.

Hamilton and his allies viewed the French Revolution as sheer anarchy. French radicals seemed to be destroying the very institutions that held civilization together: the church, social classes, property, law and order. The United States, Hamilton argued, should renounce the 1778 treaty of alliance with France and side with Britain. By contrast, Jefferson and his followers supported the treaty and

The execution of King Louis XVI by guillotine left Americans divided over the French Revolution.

regarded France as a sister republic. They believed that despite deplorable excesses, its revolution was spreading the doctrine of liberty.

Washington's Neutral Course

Washington, for his part, was convinced that in order to prosper, the United States must remain independent of European quarrels and wars. Thus he issued a proclamation of American neutrality and tempered Jefferson's efforts to support France.

NEUTRAL RIGHTS

Under international law, neutrals could trade with belligerents—nations at war—as long as the trade had existed before the outbreak of hostilities and did not involve war supplies. But both France and Great Britain refused to respect the rights of neutrals in the midst of their desperate struggle. They began intercepting American ships and confiscating cargoes. In addition, Britain, which badly needed manpower to maintain its powerful navy, impressed into service American sailors it suspected of being British subjects. Britain also continued to maintain the western forts it had promised to evacuate in 1783, and it closed the West Indies, a traditional source of trade, to American ships.

JAY'S TREATY

Recognizing that the United States was not strong enough to challenge Britain militarily, Washington sent John Jay to negotiate the differences between the two countries. Although Jay did persuade the British to withdraw their troops from the Northwest, he could gain no other concessions. Disappointed, Washington nonetheless submitted Jay's Treaty to the Senate. After a bitter debate, the Senate narrowly ratified it in June of 1795.

The Federalists and the Republicans Organize

Thus events in Europe contributed directly to the rise of parties in the United States by stimulating fears over the course of American development. By the mid-1790s both sides were organizing on a national basis. Hamilton took the lead in coordinating the Federalist party, which grew out of the voting bloc in Congress that had enacted his economic program. Increasingly, Washington drew closer to Federalist advisers and policies and became the symbol of the party, although he clung to the vision of a nonpartisan administration.

REPUBLICANS IN OPPOSITION
The guiding genius of the opposition movement was Hamilton's onetime colleague James Madison. Jefferson, who resigned as secretary of state at the end of 1793, became the symbolic head of the party, much as Washington reluctantly headed the Federalists. But it was Madison who orchestrated the Republican strategy and lined up their voting bloc in the House. The disputes over Jay's Treaty and over the whiskey tax in 1794 and 1795 gave the Republicans popular issues, and they began organizing on the state and local levels. Republican leaders had to be careful to distinguish between opposing the administration and opposing the Constitution. And they had to overcome the ingrained idea that an opposition party was seditious.

As more and more members of Congress allied themselves with one faction or the other, voting became increasingly partisan. By 1796 even minor matters were decided by partisan votes. Gradually, party organization filtered downward to local communities.

The 1796 Election

As long as Washington remained head of the Federalists, they enjoyed a huge advantage. But in 1796 the weary president, stung by the abuse heaped on him by the opposition press, announced that he would not accept a third term. In doing so, he set a two-term precedent that future presidents followed until Franklin Roosevelt. In his Farewell Address, Washington warned against the dangers of parties and urged a return to the earlier nonpartisan system. That vision, however, had become obsolete: parties were an effective way of expressing the interests of different social and economic groups within the nation. When the Republicans chose Thomas Jefferson to oppose John

| John Adams

Adams, the possibility of a constitutional system without parties ended.

The framers of the Constitution did not anticipate that political parties would run competing candidates for both the presidency and the vice presidency. Thus they provided that, of the candidates running for president, the one with the most electoral votes would win and the one with the second highest number would become vice president. But Hamilton strongly disliked both Adams and Jefferson. Ever the intriguer, he tried to manipulate the electoral vote so that the Federalist vice presidential candidate, Thomas Pinckney of South Carolina, would be elected president. In the ensuing confusion, Adams won with 71 electoral votes, and his rival, Jefferson, gained the vice presidency with 68 votes.

Federalist and Republican Ideologies

The fault line between Federalists and Republicans reflected basic divisions in American life. Geographically, the Federalists were strongest in New England, with its commercial ties to Great Britain and its powerful tradition of hierarchy and order. Moving farther south, the party became progressively weaker. Of the southernmost states, the Federalists enjoyed significant strength only in aristocratic South Carolina. The Republicans won solid support in semisubsistence areas such as the West, where farmers were only weakly involved with commerce. The middle states were closely contested, although the most cosmopolitan and commercially oriented elements remained the core of Federalist strength.

In other ways, each party looked both forward and backward: toward certain traditions of the past as well as toward newer social currents that would shape America in the nineteenth century.

FEDERALIST IDEAS
Most Federalists viewed themselves as a kind of natural aristocracy making a last desperate stand against the excesses of democracy. They clung to the notion that the upper class should rule over its social and economic inferiors. In supporting the established social order, most Federalists opposed unbridled individualism. In their view, government should regulate individual behavior for the good of society and protect property from the violent and unruly.

Yet the Federalists were remarkably forward-looking in their economic ideas. They sensed that the United States would become a major economic and military power only by government encouragement of economic development.

REPUBLICAN IDEAS
The Republicans, in contrast, looked backward to the traditional Revolutionary fear that government power threatened liberty. The Treasury, they warned, was corrupting Congress, the army would enslave the people, and interpreting the Constitution broadly would make the federal government all-powerful. Nor

did Republican economic ideals anticipate future American development. For the followers of Madison and Jefferson, agriculture—not commerce or manufacturing—was the foundation of American liberty and virtue. Republicans also failed to appreciate the role of financial institutions in promoting economic growth, condemning speculators, bank directors, and holders of the public debt.

Yet the Jeffersonians were more farsighted in matters of equality and personal liberty. Their faith in the people put them in tune with the emerging egalitarian temper of society. They embraced the virtues of individualism, hoping to reduce government to the bare essentials. And they looked to the West—the land of small farms and a more equal society—as the means to preserve opportunity and American values.

The Presidency of John Adams

As president, John Adams became the head of the Federalists, although in many ways he was out of step with his party. Unlike Hamilton, Adams felt no pressing need to aid the wealthy, nor was he fully committed to Hamilton's commercial-industrial vision. As a revolutionary leader who in the 1780s had served as American minister to England, Adams also opposed any alliance with Britain.

Increasingly, Adams and Hamilton clashed over policies and party leadership. Part of the problem stemmed from personalities. Adams was so thin-skinned that it was difficult for anyone to get along with him, and Hamilton's intrigues in the 1796 election had not improved relations between the two men. Although Hamilton had resigned from the Treasury Department in 1795, key members of Adams's cabinet regularly turned to the former secretary for advice. Indeed, they opposed Adams so often that the frustrated president sometimes dealt with them, according to Jefferson, "by dashing and trampling his wig on the floor."

NAVAL WAR WITH FRANCE — Adams began his term trying to balance relations with both Great Britain and France. Because the terms of Jay's Treaty were so favorable to the British, the French in retaliation set their navy and privateers to raiding American shipping. To resolve the conflict, Adams dispatched three envoys to France in 1797, but the French foreign minister demanded a bribe before negotiations could even begin. The American representatives refused, and when news of these discussions became public, the situation became known as the XYZ Affair.

In the public's outrage over French bribery, Federalist leaders saw a chance to retain power by going to war. In 1798 Congress repudiated the French alliance of 1778 and enlarged the army and navy. Republicans suspected that the real purpose of the army was not to fight the French army—none existed in North America—but to crush the opposition party and establish a military despotism. All that remained was for Adams to whip up popular feeling and lead the nation into war.

But Adams feared he would become a scapegoat if his policies failed. Furthermore, he distrusted standing armies and preferred the navy as the nation's primary defense. So an unofficial naval war broke out between the United States and France as ships in each navy raided the fleets of the other, while Britain continued to impress American sailors and seize ships suspected of trading with France.

Suppression at Home

ALIEN AND SEDITION ACTS — Meanwhile, Federalist leaders attempted to suppress disloyalty at home. In the summer of 1798 Congress passed several measures known together as the Alien and Sedition Acts. The Alien Act authorized the president to arrest and deport aliens suspected of "treasonable" leanings. Although never used, the act directly threatened immigrants who had not yet become citizens, many of whom were prominent Jeffersonians. To limit the number of immigrant voters—again, most of them Republicans—Congress increased the period of residence required to become a **naturalized** citizen from 5 to 14 years. But the most controversial law was the Sedition Act, which established heavy fines and even imprisonment for writing, speaking, or publishing anything of "a false, scandalous and malicious" nature against the government or any officer of the government.

Because of the partisan way it was enforced, the Sedition Act quickly became a symbol of tyranny. Federalists convicted and imprisoned a number of prominent Republican editors, and several Republican papers ceased publication. In all, 25 people were arrested under the law and 10 convicted and imprisoned.

The crisis over the Sedition Act forced Republicans to develop a broader conception of freedom of the press. Previously, most Americans had agreed that newspapers should not be restrained before publication but that they could be punished afterward for sedition. Jefferson and others now argued that the American government was uniquely based on the free expression of public opinion, and thus criticism of the government was not a sign of criminal intent. Only overtly seditious acts, not opinions, should be subject to prosecution. The courts eventually endorsed this view, adopting a new, more absolute view of freedom of speech guaranteed by the First Amendment.

VIRGINIA AND KENTUCKY RESOLUTIONS — The Republican-controlled legislatures of Virginia and Kentucky each responded to the crisis of 1798 by passing a set of resolutions. Madison secretly wrote those for Virginia, and Jefferson those for Kentucky. These resolutions proclaimed that the Constitution was a compact among sovereign states that delegated strictly limited powers to the federal government. When the government exceeded those limits and threatened the liberties of citizens, states had the right to interpose their authority. In the 1830s the two resolutions would serve as the precedent for state efforts to nullify federal laws.

But Jefferson and Madison were not ready to rend a union that had so recently been forged. The two men intended for the Virginia and Kentucky resolutions only to rally public opinion to the Republican cause. They opposed any effort to resist federal authority by force.

The Election of 1800

With a naval war raging on the high seas and the Alien and Sedition Acts sparking debate at home, Adams shocked his party by negotiating a peace treaty with France. It was a courageous act, for Adams not only split his party in two but also ruined his own chances for reelection by driving Hamilton's pro-British wing of the party into open opposition. But the nation benefited, as peace returned.

With the Federalist Party split, Republican prospects in 1800 were bright. Again the party chose Jefferson to run against Adams, along with Aaron Burr for vice president. Sweeping to victory, the Republicans won the presidency, as well as control of both houses of Congress for the first time. Yet the election again demonstrated the fragility of the fledgling political system. Jefferson and Burr received an equal number of votes, but the Constitution did not distinguish between the votes for president and vice president. With the election tied, the decision lay with the House of Representatives, where each state was allotted one vote. Because Burr refused to step aside for Jefferson, the election remained deadlocked for almost a week, until the Federalists decided that Jefferson represented the lesser of two evils. They allowed his election on the 36th ballot. In 1804 the Twelfth Amendment corrected the problem, specifying that electors were to vote separately for president and vice president.

John Marshall and Judicial Review

Having lost both the presidency and control of Congress in 1800, the Federalists took steps to shore up their power before Jefferson took office. They did so by expanding the size of the federal court system, the one branch of the federal government that they still controlled. The Judiciary Act of 1801 created 6 circuit courts and 16 new judgeships. Federalists justified these "midnight appointments" (executed by Adams in the last weeks of his term) on the grounds that the expanding nation required a larger judiciary.

MARBURY V. MADISON

Among Adams's last-minute appointments was that of William Marbury as justice of the peace for the District of Columbia. When James Madison assumed the office of secretary of state under the new administration, he found a batch of undelivered commissions, including Marbury's. Wishing to appoint loyal Republicans to these posts, Jefferson instructed Madison not to hand over the commissions, whereupon Marbury sued. The case of *Marbury v. Madison* went directly to the Supreme Court in 1803.

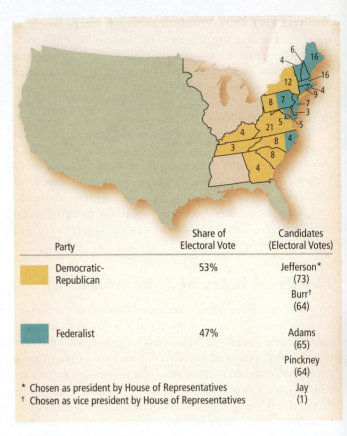

| John Marshall

Party		Share of Electoral Vote	Candidates (Electoral Votes)
	Democratic-Republican	53%	Jefferson* (73)
			Burr† (64)
	Federalist	47%	Adams (65)
			Pinckney (64)
			Jay (1)

* Chosen as president by House of Representatives
† Chosen as vice president by House of Representatives

ELECTION OF 1800

Chief Justice John Marshall, a Federalist and one of Adams's late-term appointments, actually ruled in favor of Madison—but in a way that strengthened the power of the federal courts. Marshall affirmed the right of the Supreme Court to review statutes and interpret the meaning of the Constitution. "It is emphatically the province of and duty of the judicial department to say what the law is," he wrote in upholding the doctrine of **judicial review.** In Marshall's view, the Court "must of necessity expound and interpret" the Constitution and the laws when one statute conflicted with another or when a law violated the framework of the Constitution.

Marshall and his colleagues later asserted the power of the Court to review the constitutionality not only of federal but also of state laws. In fact, during his long tenure as chief justice (over 30 years), John Marshall extended judicial review to all acts of government.

FEDERALIST ACHIEVEMENTS AND DISAPPOINTMENTS

As John Adams left office, he looked back with mixed feelings on the 12 years that the Federalist Party had held power. Under Washington's firm leadership and his own, his party had made the Constitution a workable instrument of government. The Federalists had proved that a republican form of government was compatible with stability and order. They had established economic policies that brought a return of prosperity. Washington had established the principle of American neutrality in foreign affairs, which became an accepted ideal by both parties for decades to come.

But most Federalists took no solace in such reflections, because the forces of history seemed to be running against them. In the election of 1800 they stood as the champions of order and hierarchy, of government by the wellborn, of a society in which social betters guided their respectful inferiors. They had waged one last desperate battle to save their disintegrating world—and had lost. Power had fallen into the hands of the ignorant rabble, led by that demagogue Thomas Jefferson.

This festive gathering of frontier Pennsylvanians depicted in a painting of 1813 illustrates the access among middle-class Americans to an expanding array of consumer goods. Gone were the sparsely furnished interiors of the colonial era; the owners of this dwelling have purchased a tall clock, a hutch filled with pewter and glassware, a quilting frame, framed pictures, a tea service, even a pet bird. What is the significance of the two African Americans in this scene?

The Political Culture of the Early Republic

Such extreme views poisoned the political atmosphere of the early republic. Two distinct parties had emerged during the 1790s, but both longed to reestablish a one-party system. Neither Federalists nor Republicans could accept the novel idea that political parties might peacefully resolve differences among competing social, geographic, and economic interests. Instead, each party regarded its opponents as a dangerous faction of ambitious men striving to increase their wealth and power at the expense of republican liberty.

What resulted was a **political culture** marked by verbal and, at times, physical violence. Republicans accused Washington and Hamilton of being British agents and monarchists; Federalists denounced Jefferson as an atheist and his partisans as a pack of "blood-drinking cannibals." The leading Republican newspaper editor in Philadelphia plunged into a street brawl with his Federalist rival; two members of Congress slugged it out on the floor of the House of Representatives. Mobs threatened the leaders of both parties, and at the height of the crisis of 1798–1799, Adams smuggled guns into his home for protection.

The deepening divisions among national leaders also encouraged ordinary Americans to take an interest in politics. Beginning in the 1790s and for decades thereafter, activists in cities and villages everywhere in the new republic organized grand festivals to celebrate American patriotism and the glories of the Republicans or the Federalists. That grassroots movement democratized the conduct of politics by educating men and women, white and black, voters and nonvoters alike, about the issues of the day. In doing so, such activities encouraged strong partisan loyalties.

PARADES AND CELEBRATIONS Holidays such as the Fourth of July or Washington's Birthday became prime occasions for local party leaders to rally their fellow citizens. They hosted celebrations that began with parades in which marchers, hoisting banners to identify their particular trade, militia company, or social club, processed through the main street to a church, meeting hall, or public square. There the assembled throng of marchers and onlookers sang patriotic songs, recited prayers, and listened to the reading of the Declaration of Independence, all capped by a rousing sermon or political oration. Then the party started: in the North, taverns and hotels hosted community banquets; in the South, the crowds flocked to outdoor barbecues. Everywhere the feasts ended with many toasts to the glories of republican liberty and, of course, to the superiority of Federalists or Republicans.

These local celebrations not only made an impact on those who were able to attend the festivities but also reached a wider audience through newspaper accounts. During the 1790s and beyond, the number of local or regional newspapers in the new republic mushroomed, but their coverage was far from objective. Most editors were either staunch Federalists or ardent Republicans who could be counted on to publish glowing accounts of the festivities sponsored by their party and to instruct a much wider audience about party policies and values.

African American Celebrations

African Americans, too, were drawn to political festivals, but only to discover that party organizers were determined to keep them away. In the years after 1800, bullies often drove black men and women from Fourth of July celebrations with taunts, threats, and assaults. James Forten, a leading citizen of Philadelphia's African American community, complained that because of the hostility of drunken whites, "black people, upon certain days of public jubilee, dare not to be seen" on the streets after noon.

The growing free black population of northern cities countered that opposition by organizing celebrations to express their own political convictions. They established annual holidays to celebrate the abolition of the slave trade in Britain and the United States as well as the successful slave revolt in the Caribbean led by Toussaint L'Ouverture, that resulted in the founding of Haiti in 1804. Those acts of defiance—the spectacle of blacks marching down the main streets with banners flying and bands of music playing, and of black audiences cheering orators who publicly condemned slavery—only inflamed racial hatred and opposition among many whites.

CALLING FOR FULL CITIZENSHIP

But African Americans continued to press for full citizenship by persuading sympathetic white printers to publish poetry, slave narratives, and pamphlets composed by black authors. The strategy of those writings was to refute racist notions by drawing attention to the intelligence, virtue, and patriotism of black American women and men, both free and enslaved. Typical was the autobiography of Venture Smith, the first slave narrative published in the United States (1798), which followed his captivity as a young boy in West Africa through his lifelong struggle in New England to purchase his own freedom and that of his wife and children. Hardworking and thrifty, resourceful and determined to better himself and his family, Venture Smith's story invited white readers to conclude that he was as true a republican and a self-made man as Benjamin Franklin.

| The artist used watercolor and ink to draw this scene on silk cloth. Young women were no longer being educated merely in the polite arts of dancing, sewing, and embroidery. An increasing number were taking such academic subjects as algebra, history, and geography (note the young woman making measurements on the globe).

Women's Education and Civic Participation

The new republic's political festivals and partisan newspapers aimed to woo the loyalty of white adult males who held enough property to vote. But they also sought the support of white women, some of whom joined in the crowds and even took part in the parades. In one New Jersey village the folks lining the parade route cheered as "16 young ladies uniformed in white with garlands in their hats" marched past, playing a patriotic anthem on their flutes. Federalists and Republicans alike encouraged women's involvement on those occasions, hoping that displays of approval from "the American Fair" would encourage husbands and male admirers to support their parties.

Many women seized on such opportunities for greater civic involvement. True, the law excluded most from taking direct part in voting and governing, but those prohibitions did not prevent women from taking an active interest in politics and voicing their opinions. When a female guest in a best-selling novel of the 1790s (the first by an American woman) "simpered" that their sex should not meddle with politics, her hostess shot back, "Why then should the love of our country be a masculine passion only? Why should government, which involves the peace and order of society, of which we are a part, be wholly excluded from our observation?"

WOMEN'S ACADEMIES

What contributed to women's interest in the wider world was the formal education that increasing numbers of elite and middle-class girls received. By the 1790s the number of seminaries and academies for female students was skyrocketing, encouraged by a new ideal of republican motherhood (see Chapter 8). Although the curricula of those schools still included "ornamental" training in dancing, needlework, penmanship, and music, their offerings increasingly emphasized history, geography, geometry, algebra, chemistry, botany, and geology—even Greek and Latin. In the course of this solid academic training, students also spoke at school exhibitions and published school newspapers. Such activities encouraged young women to imagine themselves as independent citizens—not simply as republican mothers. And, after graduation, many women continued to cultivate their intellects in reading circles, literary societies, and mutual improvement associations. Those experiences habituated women to presenting their views before an audience in an articulate and self-possessed manner.

RISING FEMALE LITERACY

Even young women unable to attend the new academies benefited from access to an increasing number of books and magazines, many of them aimed at a female audience. The new importance of reading to the identity of women appears in a striking number of portraits depicting young girls, middle-aged matrons, and elderly dowagers with books in hand. By 1850,

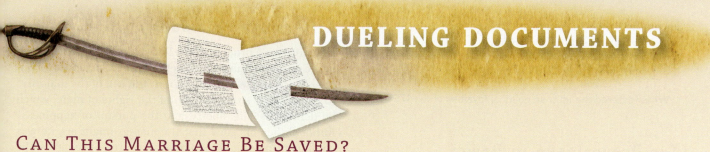

DUELING DOCUMENTS

CAN THIS MARRIAGE BE SAVED?

Proponents of providing women with greater educational opportunities—here identified as "The Female Advocate"—often held ideals of marriage that differed dramatically from those embraced by more conservative Americans such as Samuel Jennings, a Methodist minister and the founder of a medical college in Baltimore.

DOCUMENT 1   "The Female Advocate" on the Virtues of an Educated Wife

How greatly doth a man of science [knowledge] misjudge in choosing a companion for life, if he selects one from the class of ignorant and untaught, that he may, by this mean, the more securely retain his favorite supremacy. Is it not a total blindness to the ideas of refined happiness, arising from a reciprocity of sentiments and the exchange of rational felicity, as well as an illiberal prejudice, thus to conduct? Shall a woman be kept ignorant, to render her more docile in the management of domestic concerns? How illy capable is such a person of being a companion for a man of refinement? How miserably capable of augmenting his social joys, or managing prudently the concerns of a family, or educating his children? Is it not of the utmost consequence, that the tender mind of the youth receive an early direction for future usefulness? And is it not equally true, that the first direction of a child

necessarily becomes the immediate and peculiar province of the woman? And may I not add, is not a woman of capacious and well stored mind, a better wife, a better widow, a better mother, and a better neighbor; and shall I add, a better friend in every respect. . . .

When women, no longer the humble dependent, or the obsequious slave, but the companion and friend, is party to an attachment founded on mutual esteem, then, and not till then, does man assume his intended rank in the scale of creation. . . .

Suppose one who has from her youth been indoctrinated and habituated to sentiments of female inferiority, one who has never been suffered to have an opinion of her own, but on the reverse, has been taught, and accustomed to rely, and implicitly believe, right or wrong, on her parents, guardians, or husband. What will be the

consequence of this, in a situation when deprived of the counsel of either or all of them, she is necessitated to act for herself, or be exposed to the fraudulence of an unfriendly world? Perhaps she is left a widow with a large property and a flock of small dependent children? But where have they to look for protection, or on whom to rely, but on their insufficient, helpless mother? How poorly capable is she to fill the vacancy, and act to her tender babes and orphans, in their bereaved situation, as is absolutely necessary, both father and mother? How incapable also is she of assisting in the settlement and adjustment of the estate; how liable to fraud, and how probable to be injured by unreal or exaggerated debts.

Source: The Female Advocate, Written by a Lady (New Haven, Conn., 1801).

DOCUMENT 2   Samuel K. Jennings on the Virtues of a Submissive Wife

As it is your great wish and interest, to enjoy much of your husband's company and conversation, it will be important to acquaint yourself with his temper, his inclination, and his manner, that you may render your house, your person, and your disposition quite agreeable to him. . . .

Your choice in forming the connexion [marriage], was at best a passive one. Could you have acted the part of a courtier and made choice of a man whose disposition might have corresponded precisely with yours, there would have been less to do afterwards. But under present circumstances, it is your interest to adapt yourself to your husband, whatever may be his peculiarities. Again, nature has made man the stronger, the consent of mankind has given him superiority over his wife, his inclination is, to claim his natural and acquired rights. He

of course expects from you a degree of condescension, and he feels himself the more confident of the propriety of his claim, when he is formed, that St. Paul adds to his authority its support. "Wives submit to your own husbands, as unto the Lord, for the husband is the head of his wife."

In obedience then to this precept of the gospel, to the laws of custom and of nature, you ought to cultivate a cheerful and happy submission. . . .

Do not suppose, that my plan implies that the husband has nothing to do. So far from this he is bound "To love and cherish his wife, as his own flesh." But I repeat, this obligation seems, in a great degree, to rest on the condition of a loving and cheerful submission on the part of the wife. Here again perhaps you object and say, "Why not the husband, first shew a

little condescension as well as the wife?" I answer for these plain reasons. It is not his disposition; it is not the custom but with the henpecked; it is not his duty; it is not implied in the marriage contract; it is not required by law or the gospel.

Source: Samuel K. Jennings, The Married Lady's Companion, or Poor Man's Friend (revised 2nd ed., New York, 1808).

Thinking Critically

How did "The Female Advocate" advise men to choose their wives? How to behave as husbands? Why did she believe that her advice served the best interests of men? On what grounds did Samuel Jennings argue that women should submit to their husbands?

for the first time in American history, there were as many literate women as there were men.

 **REVIEW**

What fostered the intense political loyalties of the 1790s?

THE REPUBLICANS IN POWER

THE GROWING POLITICAL ENGAGEMENT OF ordinary white Americans played an important role in electing Thomas Jefferson to the presidency. He later referred to his election as "the Revolution of 1800," asserting that it "was as real a revolution in the principles of our government as that of 1776 was in its form." That claim exaggerates: Jefferson's presidency did little to enhance political rights or social opportunities of white women or African Americans. Even so, during the following two decades Republicans did set the United States on a more democratic course. And in their dealings with Britain and France, as well as with the Indian tribes of the West, Republican administrations defined, for better and worse, a fuller sense of American nationality.

The New Capital City

Thomas Jefferson was the first president to be inaugurated in the new capital, Washington, D.C. In 1791 George Washington had commissioned Pierre Charles L'Enfant, a French architect and engineer who had served in the American Revolution, to draw up plans for the new seat of government. L'Enfant designed a city with broad avenues, statues and fountains, parks and plazas, and a central mall. Because the Federalists believed that government was the paramount power in a nation, they had intended that the city would be a new Rome—a cultural, intellectual, and commercial center of the Republic.

The new city fell far short of this grandiose dream. It was located in a swampy river bottom near the head of the Potomac, and the surrounding hills rendered the spot oppressively hot and muggy during the summer. The streets were filled with tree stumps and became seas of mud after a rain. Much of the District was wooded, and virtually all of it remained unoccupied. When the government moved to its new residence in 1800, the Senate chamber, where Jefferson took the oath of office, was the only part of the Capitol that had been completed.

This isolated and unimpressive capital reflected the new president's attitude toward government. Distrustful of centralized power of any kind, Jefferson deliberately set out to remake the national government into one of limited scope that touched few people's daily lives. The states rather than the federal government were "the most competent administrators for our domestic concerns," he asserted in his inaugural address. Ever the individualist, he recommended a government that left people "free to regulate their own pursuits of industry and improvement."

Jefferson's Philosophy

Jefferson was a product of the Enlightenment, with its faith in the power of human reason to improve society and decipher the universe. He considered "the will of the majority" to be "the only sure guardian of the rights of man," which he defined as "life, liberty, and the pursuit of happiness." Although he conceded that the masses might err, he was confident they would soon return to correct principles. His faith in human virtue exceeded that of most of the founding generation, yet in good republican fashion, he feared those in power, even if they had been elected by the people. Government seemed to Jefferson a necessary evil at best.

AGRARIAN VALUES   To Jefferson, agriculture was a morally superior way of life. "Those who labour in the earth are the chosen people of God, if ever he had a chosen people," he wrote in *Notes on the State of Virginia* (1787). Jefferson praised rural life for nourishing the honesty, independence, and virtue so essential in a republic.

Although Jefferson asserted that "the tree of liberty must be refreshed from time to time by the blood of patriots and tyrants," his reputation as a radical was undeserved. While he wanted to extend the suffrage to a greater number of Americans, he clung to the traditional republican idea that voters should own property and thus be economically independent. One of the largest slaveholders in the country, he increasingly muffled his once-bold condemnation of slavery, and in the last years of his life he reproached critics of the institution who sought to prevent it from expanding westward.

Slaveholding aristocrat and apostle of democracy, lofty theorist and pragmatic politician, Jefferson was a complex, at times contradictory, personality. But like most politicians, he was flexible in his approach to problems and tried to balance means and ends. And like most leaders, he quickly discovered that he confronted very different problems in power than he had in opposition.

Jefferson's Economic Policies

The new president quickly proceeded to cut spending and to reduce the size of the government. He also abolished the internal taxes enacted by the Federalists, including the controversial excise on whiskey, and thus was able to get rid of all tax collectors and inspectors. Land sales and the tariff duties would supply the funds needed to run the scaled-down government.

The most serious spending cuts were made in the military branches. Jefferson slashed the army budget in half, decreasing the army to 3,000 men. In a national emergency, he reasoned, the militia could defend the country. Jefferson reduced the navy even more, halting work on powerful frigates authorized during the naval war with France.

COMING TO ACCEPT HAMILTON'S POLICIES   By such steps, Jefferson made significant progress toward paying off Hamilton's national debt. Still, he did not entirely dismantle the Federalists' economic program. Funding and assumption could not be reversed—the nation's honor was pledged to paying these debts, and Jefferson understood the importance of maintaining the nation's credit. More surprising, Jefferson argued that the national bank should be left to run its course until 1811, when its charter would expire. In reality, he expanded the bank's operations and, in words reminiscent of Hamilton, advocated tying banks and members of the business class to the government by rewarding those who supported the Republican Party. In effect, practical politics had triumphed over agrarian economics.

The Miami Confederacy Resists

For all his pragmatism, Jefferson still viewed the lands stretching from the Appalachians to the Pacific through the perspective of his agrarian ideals. America's vast spaces provided enough land to last for a thousand generations, he predicted in his inaugural address, enough to transform the United States into "an empire of liberty."

That optimistic vision contrasted sharply with the views of most Federalists, who feared the West as a threat to social order and stability. In the 1790s they had good reason to fear. British troops refused to leave their forts in the Northwest, and Indian nations still controlled most of the region. Recognizing that fact, the United States conceded that Indian nations had the right to negotiate as sovereign powers. North of the Ohio, leaders of the Miami Confederacy, composed of eight tribes, stoutly refused to sell their homelands without "the united voice of the confederacy."

VICTORIES OF LITTLE TURTLE AND BLUE JACKET In response the Washington administration sent 1,500 soldiers in 1790 under General Josiah Harmar to force the Indians to leave by burning their homes and fields. The Miami Confederacy, led by Blue Jacket and Little Turtle, roundly defeated the whites. Harmar was court-martialed, the nation embarrassed, and a second expedition organized the following year under General Arthur St. Clair. This force of over 2,000 was again routed by Little Turtle, whose warriors killed 600 and wounded another 300. The defeat was the worst in the history of Indian wars undertaken by the United States. (In contrast, Custer's defeat in 1876 counted 264 fatalities.)

TREATY OF GREENVILLE President Washington dispatched yet another army of 2,000 to the Ohio valley, commanded by "Mad Anthony" Wayne, an accomplished general. At the Battle of Fallen Timbers in August 1794, Wayne won a decisive victory, breaking the Indians' hold on the Northwest. In the Treaty of Greenville (1795), the tribes **ceded** the southern two-thirds of the area between Lake Erie and the Ohio River, opening it up to white families. Federalists were still not eager to see the land settled. Although they allowed the sale of federal land, they kept the price high, with a required purchase of at least 640 acres—more than four times the size of most American farms.

Once in power, Jefferson and the Republicans encouraged settlement by reducing the minimum tract that buyers could purchase (to 320 acres) and by offering land on credit. Sales boomed. By 1820 more than 2 million whites lived in a region they had first entered only 50 years earlier. From Jefferson's perspective, western expansion was a blessing economically, socially, and even politically, because most of the new westerners were Republican.

Doubling the Size of the Nation

LOUISIANA PURCHASE With Spain's colonial empire weakening, Americans were confident that before long they would gain control of Florida and the rest of the Mississippi, either through purchase or by military occupation. Spain had already agreed, in Pinckney's Treaty (see page 196), to allow Americans to navigate the lower Mississippi River. But in 1802 Spain suddenly retracted this right. More alarming, word came that France was about to take control of Louisiana—the territory lying between the Mississippi River and the Rocky Mountains—after a secret agreement with Spain. Under the leadership of Napoleon Bonaparte, France had become the most powerful nation on the European continent, with the military might to protect its new colony and to block American expansion.

Jefferson dispatched James Monroe to Paris to join Robert Livingston, the American minister, in negotiating the purchase of New Orleans and West Florida from the French and thus securing control of the Mississippi. The timing was fortunate: with war looming again in Europe, Napoleon lost interest in Louisiana. He needed money, and in April 1803 he offered to sell not just New Orleans but all of Louisiana to the United States. This proposal flabbergasted Livingston and Monroe. Their instructions said nothing about acquiring all of Louisiana, and they had not been authorized to spend what the French demanded. But here was an opportunity to expand dramatically the boundaries of the United States. Pressed for an immediate answer, Livingston and Monroe took a deep breath and, after haggling over a few details, agreed to purchase Louisiana for approximately $15 million. In one fell swoop, the American negotiators had doubled the country's size by adding some 830,000 square miles.

While Jefferson was pleased at the prospect of acquiring so much territory, he found the legality of the act troubling. The Constitution, after all, did not authorize the acquisition of territory by treaty. In the end, the president sent the treaty to the Senate for ratification, noting privately, "The less we say about constitutional difficulties the better." Once again pragmatism triumphed over theory.

LEWIS AND CLARK Even before the Louisiana Purchase was completed, Congress secretly funded an expedition up the Missouri River to the Pacific. Leading that party were Meriwether Lewis, Jefferson's secretary, and William Clark, a younger brother of George Rogers Clark. Jefferson instructed them to make detailed

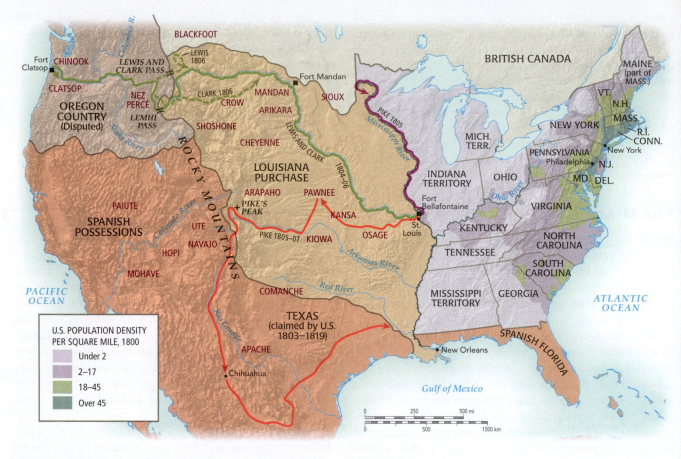

EXPLORATION AND EXPANSION: THE LOUISIANA PURCHASE

The vast, largely uncharted Louisiana Purchase lay well beyond the most densely populated areas of the United States. The Lewis and Clark expedition, along with Lieutenant Zebulon Pike's exploration of the upper Mississippi River and the Southwest, opened the way for westward expansion. **What geographic factors helped to determine Lewis and Clark's route across North America?**

observations of the soil, climate, rivers, minerals, and plant and animal life. They were also to investigate the practicability of an overland route to the Pacific and engage in diplomacy with the Indians along the way. By pushing onward to the Pacific, Lewis and Clark would strengthen the American title to Oregon, which several nations claimed but none effectively occupied.

In the spring of 1804 Lewis and Clark left St. Louis and headed up the Missouri River with 48 men. They laboriously hauled their boats upstream to present-day North Dakota, where they spent the winter with the Mandan Indians. The next spring, they headed west again. Only with great difficulty did the expedition pass the rugged mountains ahead of the winter snows and then float down first the Snake and then the Columbia River to the Pacific.

A LAND TRANSFORMED BY CHANGE The western country Lewis and Clark traversed had been shaken by momentous changes over the previous quarter of a century. The trade routes across the plains and through the mountains circulated goods in greater quantities than ever before. Horses and guns in particular upset older Indian ways, making tribes more mobile and more dangerous. Lewis and Clark's expedition

spotted Spanish horse gear from Mexico in villages along the upper Missouri River, guns from French traders to the northeast, and British teapots along the Columbia River. In one example of these trading networks at work, members of Lewis and Clark's expedition sold war hatchets to Indians during their winter stay at Fort Mandan. The expedition ran into the same hatchets the following summer in distant Idaho, the trade goods having made their trip across the plains faster than the expedition.

Most disruptive to these western lands was smallpox, which had made its way along the same trade routes ever since the pandemic of the 1780s (see Chapter 7). The disease decimated Indian populations and forced many tribes to resettle. The Arikaras, who before 1780 had numbered perhaps 24,000, had dwindled to about 2,000 by the time Lewis and Clark passed through. Portions of tribes to the east had migrated westward, including the Delawares, Shawnees, Miamis, Chickasaws, and Cherokees. Captain Clark, who was present when the Treaty of Greenville was signed in 1795, discovered a Delaware chief he had seen there, along the Missouri, 500 miles west of his earlier home.

After a bleak winter in Oregon, the expedition returned home over the Rockies in 1806. It brought back thousands of plant and animal specimens and produced a remarkably accurate map of its journey. Lewis and Clark had crossed a continent disrupted by change. In the century to come the changes would only accelerate.

Pressure on Indian Lands and Culture

East of the Mississippi, white settlers continued to flood into the backcountry. Jefferson endorsed the policy that Indian tribes either would have to assimilate into American culture by becoming farmers and abandoning their semi-nomadic hunting or would have to move west. Jefferson defended these alternatives as in the best interests of the Indians, because he believed that otherwise they faced extermination. But he also recognized that by becoming farmers they would need less land. He encouraged the policy of selling goods on credit in order to lure Indians into debt. "When these debts get beyond what the individuals can pay," the president observed, "they become willing to lop them off by a cession of lands."

Between 1800 and 1810, whites pressed Indians into ceding more than 100 million acres in the Ohio River valley. The loss of so much land devastated Indian cultures and transformed their environment by reducing hunting grounds and making game and food scarce. "Stop your people from killing our game," the Shawnees complained in 1802 to federal Indian agents. "They would be angry if we were to kill a cow or hog of theirs, the little game that remains is very dear to us." Tribes also became dependent on white trade to obtain blankets, guns, metal utensils, alcohol, and decorative beads. To pay for these goods with furs, Indians often overtrapped, which forced them to invade the lands of neighboring tribes, provoking wars.

The strain produced by white expansion led to alcoholism, growing violence among tribe members, family disintegration, and the collapse of the clan system designed to regulate relations among different villages. The question of how to deal with white culture became a matter of anguished debate. Although some Native Americans attempted to take up farming and accommodate to white ways, for most the course of assimilation proved unappealing and fraught with risk.

White Frontier Society

Whites faced their own problems on the frontier. In the first wave of settlement came backwoods families who cleared a few acres of forest by girdling the trees, removing the brush, and planting corn between the dead trunks. Such settlers were mostly squatters without legal title to their land. As a region filled up, these pioneers usually sold their improvements and headed west again.

| The Prophet

Taking their place, typically, were young single men from the East, who married and started families. These pioneers, too, engaged in semisubsistence agriculture, save for the lucky few whose prime locations allowed them to transport their crops down the Ohio and Mississippi Rivers to New Orleans for shipment to distant markets. But many frontier families struggled, moving several times but never managing to rise from the ranks of squatters or tenant farmers to become independent landowners. Fledgling western communities lacked schools, churches, and courts, and inhabitants often lived miles distant from even their nearest neighbors.

The Beginnings of the Second Great Awakening

This hardscrabble frontier proved the perfect tinder for sparking a series of dramatic religious revivals in the decades surrounding 1800. What lit the fire were missionary efforts by major Protestant churches—particularly the Baptists and the Methodists—who sent their ministers to travel the countryside on horseback and to preach wherever they could gather a crowd. Often those religious meetings took place outdoors and drew eager hearers from as far as 100 miles away, who camped for several days in makeshift tents to listen to sermons and to share in praying and singing hymns.

CANE RIDGE Thus was born a new form of Protestant worship, the camp meeting, which drew national notice after a mammoth gathering at Cane Ridge, Kentucky, in August of 1801. At a time when the largest city in the state had only 2,000 people, more than 10,000 men, women, and children, white and black, flocked there to hear dozens of ministers preaching the gospel. Many in the crowd were overwhelmed by powerful religious feelings, some shrieking and shaking over guilt for their sins, others laughing and dancing from their high hopes of eternal salvation.

Some Protestant ministers denounced the "revival" at Cane Ridge and elsewhere as yet another instance of the ignorance and savagery of westerners. Other ministers were more optimistic: they saw frontier camp meetings as the first sign of a Protestant Christian renewal that would sweep the new republic. Their hopes set the stage for what would come to be called the Second Great Awakening, a wave of religious revivals that swept throughout the nation after 1800 (see Chapter 12).

The Prophet, Tecumseh, and the Pan-Indian Movement

Native peoples also turned to religion to meet the challenges of the early national frontier. Indeed, in traditional Indian religions, they found the resource to revitalize their cultures by severing all ties with the white

THE FRONTIER CAMP MEETING

The Cane Ridge revival, one of the earliest along the frontier, was a chaotic, disorganized affair. But as western clergy became more experienced with outdoor camp meetings, they standardized the format. About a week in advance, organizers chose a forest clearing, removed nearby underbrush, erected pulpits, and constructed benches. Usually the camp went up near an established church, which provided lodging for the ministers. Since a water supply was essential, camps were located near springs, creeks, or rivers. A good site needed dry ground, shade so worshipers could escape the blazing sun, and pasturage for the horses.

The tents of the worshipers formed a ring around the outdoor auditorium where services were held. At large meetings as many as 200 tents were set up in rows with streets in between to allow easy access. To help people find their lodgings, the streets were sometimes even named. This outer perimeter constituted the meeting's private space. Here, beneath tents of sailcloth or even shelters patched together from old blankets and sheets, individuals could withdraw from the larger group to find relative solitude, cook meals in front of campfires, and sleep on rude beds of straw or simply on the ground.

Worshipers filled bench after bench in the central public space at the periodic call of a bugle. Rising above the listeners stood the preachers' pulpit. Sometimes it was merely a 10-foot-square platform on stilts; other times it was more elaborate, with several levels and a roof. Services were held in the open, and neither rain nor thunderstorms would interrupt them. At night, the dancing light and shadows produced by the candles, torches, campfires, and fire altars heightened the feeling of awe.

The democracy of the frontier did not automatically break down customary social constraints. For reasons of authority as well as practicality, the ministers' pulpit rose above the congregation. And the audience itself was segregated: women on one side of the clearing, men on the other. In the South black worshipers were seated in an area behind the pulpit, where they set up their own camp and conducted separate services.

Since the purpose of camp meetings was to "revive" religion and stir listeners'

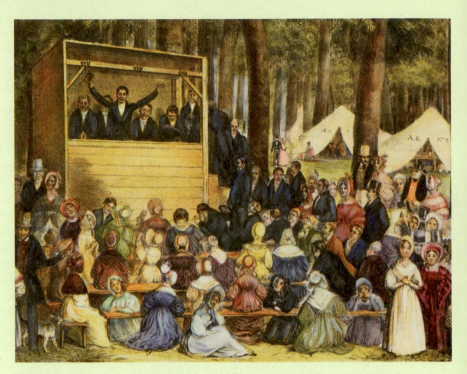

Tents ringed the central area of a camp meeting where benches faced the preachers' platform. What does this illustration of an 1837 camp meeting suggest about gender relations and religious experience?

hearts, several rows of planks were set aside directly in front of the pulpit as an "anxious bench," for those whose souls struggled in the agony of conversion. The design of the space thus focused the attention of both congregation and ministers on the "mourners," who were prayed over in hopes that they would receive a new birth in Christ.

But the social boundaries between public and private, male and female, and even black and white could be broken down. As excitement grew, several services might be held at once, some people praying, others singing, shouting, or listening to ministers who stood on wagons. And when formal services ended, men and women often continued in small groups, searching one another's souls by campfires late into the night. Indeed, the spontaneous excitement was great enough that meeting sponsors quickly learned that supervision was necessary to prevent unseemly activities. The nearby forest and the numerous tents at nightfall all

offered temptations for drinking, carousing, or lovemaking. Official patrols regularly investigated suspicious activities.

On the final day, white and black worshipers joined in a singing and marching festival before disbanding to their humdrum daily routines. Successful camp meetings depended on more than the talents of the clergy and the enthusiasm of participants. In their layout they were carefully planned and regulated communities in the forest, designed to reduce the distance between public and private space and thereby instill a sense of religion into all the activities that took place in the meeting as well as those that would be resumed in the regular world.

Thinking Critically

Why does this portrayal of a camp meeting focus on the emotional responses of women?

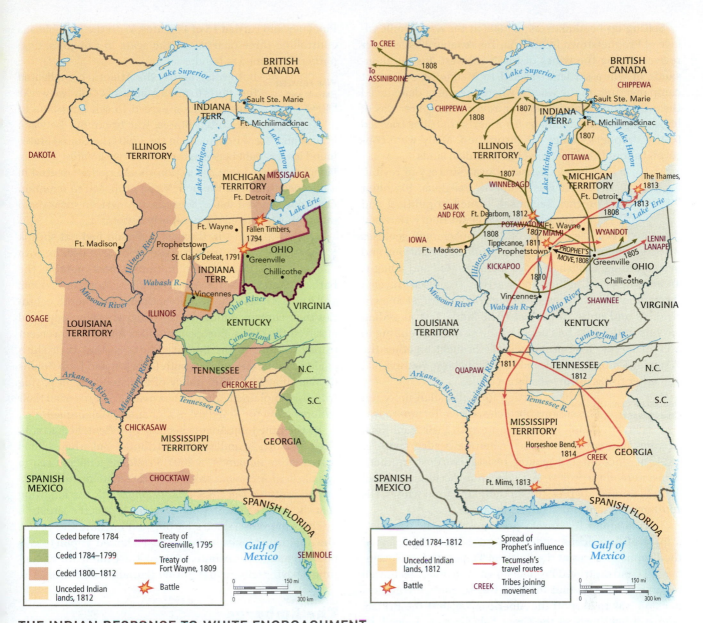

THE INDIAN RESPONSE TO WHITE ENCROACHMENT

With land cessions and white western migration placing increased pressure on Indian cultures after 1790, news of the Prophet's revival fell on eager ears. It spread especially quickly northward along the shores of Lake Michigan and westward along Lake Superior and the interior of Wisconsin. Following the Battle of Tippecanoe, Tecumseh eclipsed the Prophet as the major leader of Indian resistance, but his trips south to forge political alliances met with less success. **How far south did Tecumseh travel in his attempt to unite Indian resistance?**

world. During the 1790s a revival led by Handsome Lake took hold among the Iroquois, following the loss of most of the Iroquois lands and the collapse of their military power in western New York. Later, Lalawethika, also known as the Prophet, sparked a religious renewal among the Shawnees. The Prophet's early life was bleak: he was a poor hunter and as a child accidentally blinded himself in the right eye with an arrow; the ridicule of his fellow tribe members drove him to alcoholism. Suddenly, in April 1805 he lapsed into a trance so deep that he was given up for dead. When he revived he spoke of being reborn. From this vision and others he outlined a new creed for the Shawnees.

INDEPENDENCE FROM WHITE SOCIETY

Taking a new name—Tenskwatawa (Open Door)—the Prophet urged the Shawnees to renounce whiskey and white goods and return to their old ways of hunting with bows and arrows, eating customary foods such as corn and beans, and wearing traditional garb. The Shawnees could revitalize their culture, he insisted, by condemning intertribal violence, embracing monogamous marriage, and rejecting the idea of private instead of communal property. Except for guns, which could be used in self-defense, his followers were to discard all items made by whites. Intermarriage with white settlers was forbidden.

Setting up headquarters in 1808 at the newly built village of Prophetstown in Indiana, Tenskwatawa led a wider revival among the tribes of the Northwest. Just as thousands of white settlers traveled to Methodist or Baptist camp meetings in the woods, where preachers denounced the evils of liquor and called for a return to a purer way of life, so thousands of Indians from northern tribes traveled to the Prophet's village for inspiration. Many were concerned about the threatened loss of Indian lands.

TECUMSEH'S POLITICAL STRATEGY Whereas Tenskwatawa's strategy of revitalization was primarily religious, his older brother Tecumseh turned to political and military solutions. William Henry Harrison described Tecumseh as "one of those uncommon geniuses which spring up occasionally to produce revolutions and overturn the established order of things." Tall and athletic, an accomplished hunter and warrior, Tecumseh traveled throughout the Northwest, urging tribes to forget ancient rivalries and unite to protect their lands. Just as Indian nations in the past had adopted the strategy of uniting in a confederacy, Tecumseh's alliance brought together the Wyandot, Chippewa, Sauk and Fox, Winnebago, Potawatomi, and other tribes on an even larger scale.

OBSTACLES TO A CONFEDERACY But the campaign for pan-Indian unity ran into serious obstacles. Often, Tecumseh was asking tribes to unite with their traditional enemies in a common cause. When he headed south in 1811, he encountered greater resistance. Most southern tribes were more prosperous, were more acculturated, and felt less immediate pressure on their land from whites. His southern mission ended largely in failure.

To compound Tecumseh's problems, while he was away a force of Americans under Governor Harrison defeated the Prophet's forces at the Battle of Tippecanoe in November 1811 and destroyed Prophetstown. As a result, Tecumseh became convinced that the best way to contain white expansion was to play off the Americans against the British, who still held forts in the Great Lakes region. Indeed, by 1811, the United States and Great Britain were on the brink of war.

✓ REVIEW

How did Jefferson's presidency shape the settlement of the West?

THE SECOND WAR FOR AMERICAN INDEPENDENCE

AS TECUMSEH WORKED TO ACHIEVE a pan-Indian alliance, Jefferson encountered his own difficulties in trying to achieve American political unity. The president hoped to woo all but the most extreme Federalists into the Republican camp. His reelection in 1804 showed how much progress he had made, as he defeated Federalist Charles Cotesworth

Pinckney and carried 15 of 17 states. With the Republicans controlling three-quarters of the seats in Congress, one-party rule seemed at hand.

WAR BETWEEN BRITAIN AND FRANCE But events across the Atlantic complicated the efforts to unite Americans. Only two weeks after Napoleon agreed to sell Louisiana to the United States, war broke out between France and Great Britain. As in the 1790s the United States found itself caught between the world's two greatest powers. Jefferson insisted that the nation should remain neutral in a European war. But the policies he proposed to maintain neutrality sparked sharp divisions in American society and momentarily revived the two-party system.

THE BARBARY PIRATES In the past, Jefferson had not shrunk from the use of force in dealing with foreign nations—most notably the Barbary States of North Africa—Algiers, Morocco, Tripoli, and Tunis. During the seventeenth and eighteenth centuries their corsairs plundered the cargo of enemy ships and enslaved the crews. European nations found it convenient to pay tributes to the Barbary States so that their ships could sail unmolested. But both Jefferson and John Adams disliked that idea. The "policy of Christendom" of paying tribute, complained Adams, "has made Cowards of all their Sailors before the Standard of Mahomet [Mohammed]."

By the time John Adams became president, he had subdued his outrage and agreed to tributes. But when Tripoli increased its demands in 1801, President Jefferson sent a squadron of American ships to force a settlement. In 1803 Tripoli captured the U.S.S. *Philadelphia*. Only the following year did Lieutenant Stephen Decatur repair the situation by sneaking into Tripoli's harbor and burning the vessel. The American blockade that followed forced Tripoli to give up its demands for tribute. Even so, the United States continued paying tribute to the other Barbary states until 1816.

The Embargo

Jefferson was willing to fight the Barbary States, but he drew back from declaring war against Britain or France. Between 1803 and 1807, Britain seized more than 500 American ships; France more than 300. The British navy also impressed into service thousands of sailors, some of whom were deserters from England's fleet but others, native-born Americans. Despite such harassment, Jefferson pursued a program of "peaceable coercion" designed to protect neutral rights without war. His proposed **embargo** not only prohibited American ships from trading with foreign ports but also stopped the export of all American goods. The president was confident that American exports were so essential to the two belligerents that they would quickly agree to respect American neutral rights. In December 1807 Congress passed the Embargo Act.

Jefferson had seriously miscalculated. France did not depend on American trade and so managed well enough, while British ships quickly took over the carrying trade as American vessels lay idle. Under the embargo, both

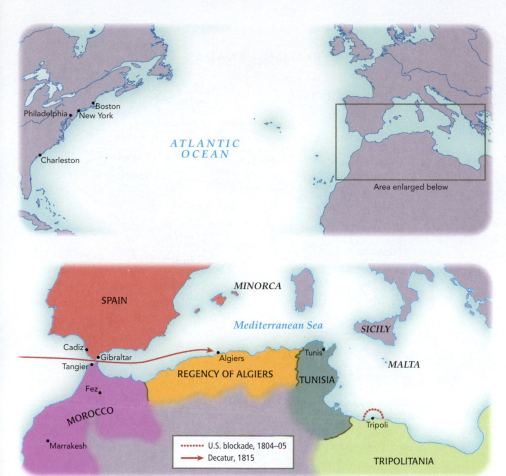

THE UNITED STATES AND THE BARBARY STATES, 1801–1815

The young United States, like many European powers, found its trading vessels challenged by the Barbary states of Morocco, Algiers, Tunisia, and Tripoli. When the pasha of Tripoli declared war on the United States in 1801, Jefferson dispatched a force that blockaded Tripoli to bring the war to an end in 1805. Tribute paid to the other Barbary States continued until 1816, after a new naval force, led by Captain Stephen Decatur, forced the ruler of Algiers to end the practice.

American imports and exports plunged. As the center of American shipping, New England port cities protested the loudest, and their merchants smuggled behind officials' backs.

Madison and the Young Republicans

Following Washington's example, Jefferson did not seek a third term. A caucus of Republican members of Congress selected James Madison to run against Federalist Charles Cotesworth Pinckney. Madison triumphed easily, although in discontented New England, the Federalists picked up 24 seats in Congress.

MADISON'S CHARACTER Few men have assumed the presidency with more experience than James Madison, yet his tenure as president proved disappointing. Despite his intellectual brilliance, he lacked the force of leadership and the inner strength to impose his will on less capable men.

WAR HAWKS With a president reluctant to fight for what he wanted, leadership passed to Congress. The elections of 1810 swept in a new generation of Republicans, led by the magnetic 34-year-old Henry Clay of Kentucky, who gained the rare distinction of being elected Speaker of the House in his first term. These younger Republicans were more nationalistic than the generation led by Jefferson and Madison. They sought an ambitious program of economic development and were aggressive expansionists, especially those from frontier districts. Their willingness to go to war earned them the name of War Hawks. Though they numbered fewer than 30 in Congress, they quickly became the driving force in the Republican Party.

The Decision for War

REPEAL OF THE EMBARGO During Jefferson's final week in office in early 1809, Congress repealed the Embargo Act. The following year Congress authorized trade with France and England but decreed that if one of the two belligerents agreed to stop interfering with American shipping, trade with the other would be prohibited.

Given these circumstances, Napoleon outmaneuvered the British by announcing that he would put aside the French trade regulations. Madison took the French emperor at his word and reimposed a ban on trade with England. French raiders continued to seize American ships, but American anger focused on the British, who then seized many more ships and continued to impress American sailors. Finally, on June 16, 1812, the British ministry suspended the searches and seizures of American ships.

THE WAR OF 1812

After the American victory on Lake Erie and the defeat of the western Indians at the Battle of the Thames, the British adopted a three-pronged strategy to invade the United States, climaxing with an attempt on New Orleans. But they met their match in Andrew Jackson, whose troops marched to New Orleans after fighting a series of battles against the Creeks and forcing them to cede a massive tract of land.

The concession came too late. Two days earlier, unaware of the change in policy, Congress granted Madison's request for a declaration of war against Britain. The vote was mostly along party lines, with every Federalist voting against war. By contrast, members of Congress from the South and the West clamored most strongly for war. Their constituents were consumed with a desire to seize additional territory in Canada or in Florida (owned by Britain's ally Spain). In addition, they accused the British of stirring up hostility among the Indian tribes.

Perhaps most important, the War Hawks were convinced that Britain had never truly accepted the verdict of the American Revolution. To them, American independence—

and with it republicanism—hung in the balance. For Americans hungering to be accepted in the community of nations, nothing rankled more than still being treated by the British as colonials.

With Britain preoccupied by Napoleon, the War Hawks expected an easy victory. In truth, the United States was totally unprepared for war. Crippled by Jefferson's cutbacks, the navy was unable to lift the British blockade of the American coast, which bottled up the country's merchant marine and most of its navy. As for the U.S. Army, it was small and poorly led. When Congress moved to increase its size to 75,000, even the most hawkish states failed to meet their quotas. Congress was also reluctant to levy taxes to finance the war.

BATTLE OF LAKE ERIE

A three-pronged American invasion of Canada from Detroit, Niagara, and Lake Champlain failed dismally in 1812. Americans fared better the following year, as both sides raced to build a navy on the strategically located Lake Erie. Led by Commander Oliver Hazard Perry, American forces won a decisive victory at Put-In Bay in 1813.

As the United States struggled to organize its forces, Tecumseh sensed that his long-awaited opportunity had come to drive Americans out of the western territories. "Here is a chance . . . such as will never occur again," he told a war council, "for us Indians of North America to form ourselves into one great combination." Allying with the British, Tecumseh traveled south in the fall to talk again with his Creek allies. To coordinate an Indian offensive for the following summer, he left a bundle of red sticks with eager Creek soldiers. They were to remove one stick each day from the bundle and attack when the sticks had run out.

JACKSON DEFEATS THE CREEK INDIANS

Some of the older Creeks were more acculturated and preferred an American alliance. But about 2,000 younger "Red Stick" Creeks launched a series of attacks, climaxed by the destruction of Fort Mims along the Alabama River in August 1813. Once again, the Indians' lack of unity was a serious handicap, as warriors from the Cherokee, Choctaw, and Chickasaw tribes, traditional Creek enemies, allied with the Americans. At the Battle of Horseshoe Bend in March 1814, General Andrew Jackson and his Tennessee militia soundly defeated the Red Stick Creeks. Jackson promptly dictated a peace treaty under which the Creeks ceded 22 million acres of land in the Mississippi Territory. They and the other southern tribes still retained significant landholdings, but Indian military power had been broken in the South, east of the Mississippi.

DEATH OF TECUMSEH

Farther north, in October 1813, American forces under General William Henry Harrison defeated the British and their Indian allies at the Battle of the Thames. In the midst of heavy fighting Tecumseh was killed. With him died any hope of a pan-Indian movement.

The British Invasion

As long as the war against Napoleon continued, the British were unwilling to divert army units to North America. But in 1814 Napoleon was at last defeated. Free to concentrate on America, the British devised a coordinated strategy to invade the United States in the northern, central, and

The Hartford Convention or *LEAP NO LEAP*.

After Andrew Jackson's victory at New Orleans, the Hartford Convention looked to many like a traitorous leap into the arms of the British king.

HISTORIAN'S TOOLBOX

REMEMBERING LAFAYETTE

Men's kid leather gloves, showing images of Washington and Lafayette, ca. 1824–1825

What might have prompted the maker of this platter to inscribe it with Lafayette's name? What was the likely social status of the owner?

On what occasions would a man wear gloves like these? What was the likely social status of the owner?

Events that were commemorated even as they unfolded hold a special fascination for historians. Just as the celebration of Franklin's arrival in Paris tells us much about the French in the 1770s, the hoopla in the United States over the return of the Marquis de Lafayette reveals a great deal about early national Americans. A major general in the Continental Army, a comrade-in-arms of Washington, and a lifelong defender of liberal values and human rights, Lafayette made his second voyage from France to the United States in 1824 at the invitation of President James Monroe. A triumphal 13-month tour of all 24 states followed, the Marquis traveling by stagecoach and steamboat and drawing crowds that numbered in the tens of thousands. While only a lucky few Americans basked in the 67-year-old hero's presence at dinners and balls, nearly all could afford to purchase one of the souvenirs produced by artisans of both humble and fine crafts.

Thinking Critically

Consider the challenges confronting President Monroe's administration. What might he have hoped to accomplish by inviting Lafayette to the United States? What do the two objects suggest about Lafayette's popularity as a public figure?

southern parts of the country. The main army headed south from Montreal but was checked when Americans destroyed the British fleet on Lake Champlain.

Meanwhile, a smaller British force captured Washington and burned several public buildings, including the Capitol and the president's home. To cover the scars of this destruction, the executive mansion was painted with whitewash and became known as the White House. The burning of the capital was a humiliating event: President Madison and his wife, Dolley, were forced to flee. But the defeat had little military significance. The principal British objective was Baltimore, where for 25 hours their fleet bombarded Fort McHenry in the city's harbor. When Francis Scott Key saw the American flag still flying above the fort at dawn, he hurriedly composed the verses of "The Star Spangled Banner," which was eventually adopted as the national anthem.

The third British target was New Orleans, where a formidable army of 7,500 British troops was opposed by a hastily assembled force commanded by Major General Andrew Jackson. The Americans included regular soldiers; frontiersmen from Kentucky and Tennessee; citizens of New Orleans, including several companies of free African Americans; Choctaw Indians; and a group of pirates. Jackson's outnumbered and ill-equipped forces won a stunning victory, which made the general an overnight hero.

HARTFORD CONVENTION

In December 1814, while Jackson was organizing the defense of New Orleans, New England Federalists met in Hartford to map strategy against the war. Angry as they were, the delegates still rejected calls for secession. Instead, they proposed a series of amendments to the Constitution that showed their displeasure with the government's economic policies and their resentment of the South's national political power.

JACKSON'S VICTORY AT NEW ORLEANS

To the convention's dismay, its representatives arrived in Washington to present their demands just as news of Andrew Jackson's victory was being trumpeted on the streets. The celebrations badly undercut the Hartford Convention, as did news from across the Atlantic that American negotiators in Ghent, Belgium, had signed a treaty ending the war. Hostilities had ceased, technically, on Christmas Eve 1814, two weeks before the Battle of New Orleans. Both sides were relieved to end the conflict, even though the Treaty of Ghent left unresolved the issues of impressment, neutral rights, or trade.

COLLAPSE OF THE FEDERALIST PARTY

The return of peace hard on the heels of Jackson's victory sparked a new confidence in many Americans. The new nationalism sounded the death knell of the Federalist Party, for even talk of secession at the Hartford Convention had tainted the party with disunion and treason. In the 1816 election Madison's secretary of state, James Monroe, resoundingly defeated Federalist Rufus King of New York. Four years later Monroe ran for reelection unopposed.

Monroe's Presidency

The major domestic challenge that Monroe faced was the renewal of sectional rivalries in 1819, when the Missouri Territory applied for admission as a slave state. Before the controversy over Missouri erupted, slavery had not been a major issue in American politics. Congress had debated the institution when it prohibited the African slave trade in 1808, the earliest year this step could be taken under the Constitution. But lacking any specific federal legislation to stop it, slavery had crossed the Mississippi River into the Louisiana Purchase. Louisiana entered the Union in 1812 as a slave state, and in 1818 Missouri, which had about 10,000 slaves in its population, asked permission to come in, too.

In 1818 the Union contained 11 free and 11 slave states. As the federal government became stronger and more active, both the North and the South worried about maintaining their political power. The North's greater population gave it a majority in the House of Representatives, 105 to 81. The Senate, of course, was evenly balanced, because each state had two senators regardless of population. But Maine, which previously had been part of Massachusetts, requested admission as a free state. That would upset the balance unless Missouri came in as a slave state.

MISSOURI COMPROMISE

Representative James Tallmadge of New York disturbed this delicate state of affairs when in 1819 he introduced an amendment that would establish a program of gradual emancipation in Missouri. For the first time Congress directly debated the morality of slavery, often bitterly. The House approved the Tallmadge amendment, but the Senate refused to accept it, and the two houses deadlocked.

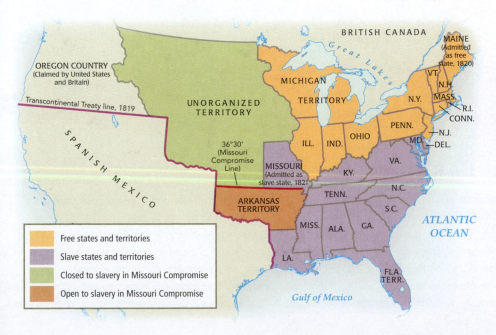

THE MISSOURI COMPROMISE AND THE UNION'S BOUNDARIES IN 1820

When Congress reconvened in 1820, Henry Clay of Kentucky promoted what came to be known as the Missouri Compromise. Under its terms Missouri was admitted as a slave state and Maine as a free state. In addition, slavery was forever prohibited in the remainder of the Louisiana Purchase north of 36°30′ (the southern boundary of Missouri). Clay's proposal, the first of several sectional compromises he would engineer in his long career, won congressional approval and Monroe signed the measure, ending the crisis. But southern fears for the security of slavery and northern fears about its spread remained.

Monroe's greatest achievements were diplomatic, accomplished largely by his talented secretary of state, John Quincy Adams, the son of President John Adams. An experienced diplomat, Adams thought of the Republic in continental terms and was intent on promoting expansion to the Pacific. Such a vision required dealing with Spain, which had never recognized the legality of the Louisiana Purchase. In addition, between 1810 and 1813 the United States had occupied and unilaterally annexed Spanish West Florida.

But Spain was preoccupied with events farther south in the Americas. In the first quarter of the nineteenth century, its colonies one after another revolted and established themselves as independent nations. These revolutions increased the pressure on the Spanish minister to America, Luis de Onís, to come to terms with the United States. So, too, did Andrew Jackson, who marched into East Florida and captured several Spanish forts in 1818. Jackson had exceeded his instructions, but Adams understood the additional pressure this aggression put on Onís and refused to disavow it.

TRANSCONTINENTAL TREATY

Fearful that the United States might next invade Texas or other Spanish territory, Spain agreed to the Transcontinental Treaty in February 1819. Its terms set the boundary between American and Spanish territory all the way to the Pacific. Spain not only gave up its claims to the Pacific Northwest but also ceded Florida. To obtain the line to the Pacific, the United States abandoned its contention that Texas was part of the Louisiana Purchase.

More importantly, the United States also came to terms with Great Britain. Following the War of 1812, the British abandoned their connections with the western Indian tribes and no longer attempted to block American expansion to the Rocky Mountains. In a growing spirit of cooperation, the countries agreed in 1818 to the 49th parallel as the northern boundary of the Louisiana Purchase and also to joint control of the Oregon Territory for 10 years, subject to renewal.

In his annual message to Congress, on December 2, 1823, Monroe also announced that the United States would not interfere with already established European colonies in the Western Hemisphere. But any intervention in the new republics of Latin America, he warned, would be considered a hostile act: "The American continents . . . are henceforth not to be considered as subjects for future colonization by any European powers." The essence of this policy was the concept of two worlds, one old and one new, each refraining from interfering in the other's affairs. American public opinion hailed Monroe's statement and then promptly forgot it. Only years later would it be referred to as the Monroe Doctrine.

MONROE DOCTRINE

✓ **REVIEW**

What were the causes of the War of 1812?

CONCLUSION

THE WORLD AT LARGE

The three decades after 1789 demonstrated how profoundly events in the wider world could affect life within the United States, shaping its politics, its boundaries, its economy—its future.

The French Revolution contributed to splintering the once-united leaders of the American Revolution into two rival parties. The wars that followed, between France and England, deepened the divisions between Federalists and Republicans and prompted both parties to mobilize the political loyalties of ordinary white American men and women. Napoleon's ambitions to conquer Europe handed Jefferson the Louisiana Territory, while British efforts to reclaim its American empire tempted some New Englanders to secede from the Union and encouraged Tecumseh's hopes of mounting a pan-Indian resistance on the frontier. The Haitian Revolution in the Caribbean prompted free blacks in northern cities to protest racial inequalities and slavery within the United States.

But by the 1820s most white Americans paid less attention to events abroad than to expanding across the vast North American continent. Jefferson had dreamed of an "empire of liberty," delighting in expansion as the means to preserve a nation of small farmers. But younger, more nationalistic Republicans had a different vision of expansion. They spoke of internal improvements, protective tariffs to foster American industries, roads and canals to link farmers with towns, cities, and wider markets. These new Republicans were not aristocratic, like the Federalists of old. Still, their dream of a national, commercial republic resembled Franklin's and Hamilton's more than Jefferson's. They had seen how handsomely American merchants and commercial farmers profited when European wars swelled demand for American wheat and cotton. They looked to profit from speculation in land, the growth of commercial agriculture, and new methods of industrial manufacturing. If they represented the rising generation, what would be the fate of semisubsistence farm communities? The answer was not yet clear. ∞∞∞

CHAPTER SUMMARY

BASIC SOCIAL DIVISIONS BETWEEN THE commercial and semisubsistence regions shaped the politics of the new United States. Between 1789 and the 1820s the first parties emerged and, along with them, a more popular and participatory political culture. Over the same decades, Indian confederacies mounted a sustained resistance to westward expansion, while events in Europe deepened divisions among Federalists and Republicans and threatened the very existence of the fledgling American republic.

- The first party to organize in the 1790s was the Federalists, led by Alexander Hamilton and George Washington.

- Divisions over Hamilton's policies as secretary of the treasury led to the formation of the Republicans, led by James Madison and Thomas Jefferson.

- The commercially minded Federalists believed in order and hierarchy, supported loose construction of the Constitution, and wanted a powerful central government to promote economic growth.

- The Republican Party, with its sympathy for agrarian ideals, endorsed strict construction of the Constitution, wanted a less active federal government, and harbored a strong fear of aristocracy.

- The French Revolution, the XYZ Affair, the naval war, and the Alien and Sedition Acts also deepened the partisan division between Federalists and Republicans during the 1790s. The Federalists demonstrated that the new government could be a more active force in American society, but their controversial domestic and foreign policies, internal divisions, and open hostility to the masses led to their downfall.

- Before becoming president, Jefferson advocated the principles of agrarianism, limited government, and strict construction of the Constitution. But once in power, he failed to dismantle Hamilton's economic program and promoted western expansion by acquiring Louisiana from France.

- Chief Justice John Marshall proclaimed that the courts were to interpret the meaning of the Constitution (judicial review), a move that helped the judiciary emerge as an equal branch of government.

- Lewis and Clark produced the first reliable information and maps of the Louisiana territory. The lands they passed through had been transformed over the previous 25 years by disease, dislocation, and the arrival of horses and guns.

- The Shawnee prophet Tenskwatawa and his brother Tecumseh organized the most important Indian resistance to the expansion of the new republic, but the movement collapsed with the death of Tecumseh during the War of 1812.

- France and Britain both interfered with neutral rights, and the United States went to war against Britain in 1812.

- In the years after 1815 there was a surge in American nationalism, reinforced by Britain's recognition of American sovereignty and the Monroe Doctrine's prohibition of European intervention in the Western Hemisphere. But the Missouri crisis was an early indication of growing sectional rivalries.

ADDITIONAL READING

TWO GOOD OVERVIEWS OF EARLY national politics are Stanley Elkins and Eric McKitrick's *The Age of Federalism* (1993) and James Roger Sharp's *American Politics in the Early Republic* (1993). For a fuller understanding of Federalist political thought, consult Linda Kerber, *Federalists in Dissent* (1970), and David Hackett Fischer, *The Revolution of American Conservatism* (1965); for the Republicans, read Lance Banning, *The Jeffersonian Persuasion* (1978), and Drew R. McCoy, *The Elusive Republic* (1980). Another approach to understanding the politics of this period is to read about the lives of leading political figures: among the best are Joseph Ellis's biographies of John Adams (*Passionate Sage*, 1993) and Thomas Jefferson (*American Sphinx,* rev. ed., 1998) and two biographies of Alexander Hamilton by Ron Chernow and Gerald Stourzh (all cited in the full bibliography). To become better acquainted with the popular political culture of the early republic, consult *Beyond the Founders* (2004), a superb collection of essays edited by Jeffrey Pasley, Andrew W. Robertson, and David Waldstreicher. For an engaging narrative about the political influence exerted by white women, see Catherine Allgor, *Parlor Politics* (2000), and for an outstanding analysis of women's education and their civic participation, read Mary Kelley, *Learning to Stand and Speak* (2006). Rich descriptions of the social and political interactions among whites, African Americans, and Indians in the new republic include Joshua-Rothman, *Notorious in the Neighborhood* (2003), and John Wood Sweet, *Bodies Politic* (2003). To gain a fuller understanding of the lives of both Indians and western frontier settlers, rely on Gregory Evans Dowd, *A Spirited Resistance* (1993); Roger Kennedy, *Mr. Jefferson's Lost Cause* (2003); John Mack Faragher, *Sugar Creek* (1986); Adam Rothman, *Slave Country* (2005); and R. David Edmunds, *The Shawnee Prophet* (1983) and *Tecumseh and the Quest for Indian Leadership* (1984).

For a fuller list of readings, see the Bibliography at www.mhhe.com/eh8e.

SIGNIFICANT EVENTS

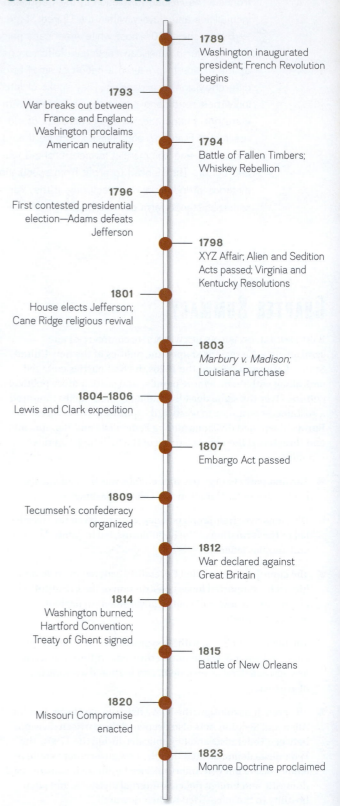

1789
Washington inaugurated president; French Revolution begins

1793
War breaks out between France and England; Washington proclaims American neutrality

1794
Battle of Fallen Timbers; Whiskey Rebellion

1796
First contested presidential election—Adams defeats Jefferson

1798
XYZ Affair; Alien and Sedition Acts passed; Virginia and Kentucky Resolutions

1801
House elects Jefferson; Cane Ridge religious revival

1803
Marbury v. Madison; Louisiana Purchase

1804–1806
Lewis and Clark expedition

1807
Embargo Act passed

1809
Tecumseh's confederacy organized

1812
War declared against Great Britain

1814
Washington burned; Hartford Convention; Treaty of Ghent signed

1815
Battle of New Orleans

1820
Missouri Compromise enacted

1823
Monroe Doctrine proclaimed

FEDERALIST POSITIONS

Rejection of political parties

Encouragement of commerce, manufacturing, urbanization

Importance of funding the national debt

Condemnation of the French Revolution as anarchy; support for British ties

Importance of order, hierarchy, curbing democratic excess and unbridled individualism

FEDERALIST ACHIEVEMENTS

Restored credit of national government

Ended postwar inflation and created sound currency

Instituted policy of neutrality (Washington)

Negotiated peace with France (Adams)

Established Supreme Court's right of judicial review (Marshall)

Proved republican government compatible with stability and order; peaceful transition to Republican power in 1800

DUBIOUS ACHIEVEMENTS

Alien and Sedition Acts

Forcible efforts to push Indian nations from the Ohio valley

REPUBLICAN POSITIONS

Rejection of political parties

Encouragement of agriculture as the basis of liberty and virtue

Suspicion of banks, speculators, public debt, taxation, government spending

Celebration of France as a fellow republic; suspicion of Britain as former foe

Support for the values of individualism, egalitarianism, limited government

REPUBLICAN ACHIEVEMENTS

Endorsed a broad conception of freedom of the press in response to Alien and Sedition Acts

Made significant progress in paying off the national debt; expanded the national bank

Dispatched Louis and Clark expedition (Jefferson)

Negotiated the Louisiana Purchase (Jefferson)

Proclaimed the Monroe Doctrine

Proved republican government compatible with stability and order; peaceful transition to power in 1800

DUBIOUS ACHIEVEMENTS

Virginia and Kentucky Resolutions

Forced cessions of Indians lands in the Ohio valley and the South

Embargo of 1807

Missouri Compromise

After the Fact

Historians Reconstruct the Past

Sally Hemings and Thomas Jefferson

So much goes into the weighing of historical evidence: not only the application of logic and reason, and the use of large theories and small inferences, but also the influence of emotion and a culture's prevailing myths. The distortions created by the latter pair come into play especially when topics like race and sex are involved—as can be seen by following the trail of a story first made public more than two centuries ago.

SOME RUMORS—AND SOME FACTS

THE RUMORS BEGAN IN ALBEMARLE County, Virginia, more than 200 years ago; they came to the notice of a contemporary journalist by the name of James Callender. A writer for hire, Callender had once lent his pen to the Republicans but turned from friend into foe when the party failed to reward him with a political appointment. When his story splashed onto the pages of the *Recorder,* a Richmond newspaper, the trickle of rumor turned into a torrent of scandal. Callender alleged that Thomas Jefferson, during his years in Paris as the American minister, had contracted a liaison with one of his own slaves. The woman was the president's mistress even now, he insisted, in 1802. She was kept at Monticello, Jefferson's plantation, and Jefferson had fathered children with her. Her name was Sally Hemings.

Solid information about Sally Hemings is scarce. She was one of six children, we know, born to Betty Hemings and her white master, John Wayles, a Virginia planter whose white daughter, Martha Wayles Skelton, married Jefferson in 1772. We know that Betty Hemings was the child of an African woman and an English sailor, which means Betty's children with Wayles, Sally among them, were quadroons—light-skinned and one-quarter African. We know that Sally accompanied one of Jefferson's daughters to Paris as her maid in 1787 and that, on returning to Virginia a few years later, she performed domestic work at Monticello. We know that she had six children and that the four who survived to adulthood escaped from slavery into freedom: Jefferson assisted her two eldest children, Beverly and Harriet, in leaving Monticello in 1822, and her two youngest children, Madison and Eston, were freed by Jefferson's will in 1827. We know that shortly after Jefferson's death, his daughter, Martha Jefferson Randolph, freed Sally Hemings and that she lived with her two sons in Charlottesville until her death in 1835.

DUELING ORAL TRADITIONS

This view of Monticello was painted shortly after Jefferson's death. It portrays his white descendants surrounded by a serene landscape.

WE KNOW, TOO, THAT JEFFERSON'S white descendants stoutly denied (and, to this day, some still deny) any familial connection with the descendants of Sally Hemings. Even though Callender's scandal quickly subsided, doing Jefferson no lasting political damage, Jefferson's white grandchildren were still explaining away the accusations half a century later. In the 1850s Jefferson's granddaughter, Ellen Coolidge Randolph, claimed that her brother, Thomas Jefferson Randolph, had told her that one of Jefferson's nephews, Samuel Carr, fathered Hemings's children. In the 1860s Henry Randall, an early biographer of Jefferson, recalled a conversation with Thomas Jefferson Randolph in the 1850s in which he attributed paternity to another nephew, Samuel's brother Peter Carr.

Until the end of the twentieth century most scholars resolved the discrepancy of this dual claim by suggesting that one of the Carr nephews had fathered Sally Hemings's children. And all of Jefferson's most eminent twentieth-century biographers—Douglass Adair, Dumas Malone, John Chester Miller, and Joseph J. Ellis—contended that a man of Jefferson's character and convictions could not have engaged in a liaison with a slave woman. After all, Jefferson was a Virginia gentleman and an American *philosophe* who believed that reason should rule over passion; he was also an eloquent apostle of equality and democracy and an outspoken critic of the tyrannical power of masters over slaves. And, despite his opposition to slavery, Jefferson argued in his *Notes on the State of Virginia* (1785) for the likelihood that peoples of African descent were inferior intellectually and artistically to those of European descent. Because of that conviction he warned of the dire consequences that would attend the mixing of the races.

The official version of events did not go unchallenged. Madison Hemings, a skilled carpenter, in 1873 told an Ohio newspaper reporter of an oral tradition, long repeated among his family, that his mother had been Thomas Jefferson's "concubine" and that Jefferson had fathered all her children. Even so, nearly a century passed before Madison Hemings's claims won wider attention. In 1968 the historian Winthrop Jordan noted that Sally Hemings's pregnancies coincided with Jefferson's stays at Monticello. In 1975 Fawn Brodie's best-selling "intimate history" of Jefferson portrayed his relationship with Sally Hemings as an enduring love affair; four years later, Barbara Chase-Rimboud set Brodie's findings to fiction.

OVERTURNING CULTURAL ASSUMPTIONS

AN EVEN MORE POWERFUL CASE for Jefferson's paternity of all of Hemings's children was made in 1997 by Annette Gordon-Reed. She drew on her legal training to subject the handling of the evidence by Jefferson's biographers to a close and telling cross-examination. Although they had dismissed Madison Hemings's recollections as mere family lore and wishful thinking, Gordon-Reed argued that such oral testimony was, in fact, no more or less reliable than the oral testimony of Jefferson's white Randolph descendants.

One year later Gordon-Reed's arguments crested on a tidal wave of new revelations: a team of DNA research scientists headed by Eugene A. Foster discovered an exact match on the Y-chromosome markers between Thomas Jefferson's line and the descendants of Eston Hemings. (Eston was Sally's youngest child and the only one who left male-line descendants whose DNA could be tested.) Since the chance of such a match occurring randomly was less than 1 in 1,000, the DNA evidence made it highly probable that Thomas Jefferson fathered at least one of Sally Hemings's children. In addition, Foster's team found no DNA match between the Hemings line and the Carr family, thus discrediting the assertions of Jefferson's white descendants. Intrigued by these findings, historian Fraser D. Neiman undertook a sophisticated statistical analysis of Hemings's conceptions and Jefferson's returns to Monticello (where he spent about half his time), which established a 99 percent probability that he had fathered all of Hemings's children.

This new evidence has persuaded most historians that Thomas Jefferson conducted a monogamous liaison with Sally Hemings over 38 years and that their union produced at least one and most likely all six of her children. As a result, the debate among historians has moved on to explore questions left unresolved by the new scientific findings.

UNRESOLVED QUESTIONS

ONE SUCH QUESTION BEARS ON how historians should assess the credibility of their sources. Specifically, how reliable are the oral traditions passed down through families? Both the DNA and the statistical evidence bear out Madison Hemings's recollections. Surely that outcome, as Annette Gordon-Reed has urged, should prompt future historians to scrutinize the oral testimonies of white masters such as the Jeffersons and the Randolphs as closely as they do the narratives of slaves and the oral traditions of their descendants. But does it follow that historians should regard the recollections of nonliterate peoples as possessing a superior claim to being accurate recoveries of the past? Gordon-Reed and a host of other historians warn against that conclusion, arguing that all oral testimony must be tested against the findings yielded by the documentary record and scientific research. Their caution is warranted by the fact that the DNA findings to date have failed to show a match between the Jefferson line and that of Thomas Woodson, another Monticello slave whose African

The names of Sally Hemings and her sons appear on this list of Thomas Jefferson's slaves.

American descendants have long cited their own family's oral tradition as evidence of a biological connection to Jefferson.

An equally intriguing question concerns the character of the relationship between Sally Hemings and Thomas Jefferson. Was it forced and exploitative or consensual and even affectionate? On the one hand, the long duration of their liaison suggests that it may have been based on a shared emotional intimacy. (If Jefferson fathered all of Hemings's children, their involvement began in Paris during the late 1780s and endured at least until the birth of Eston Hemings in 1808.) As Annette Gordon-Reed points out, even stronger support for this interpretation is that Sally Hemings and all her children were the only nuclear slave family at Monticello who finally attained their freedom. Furthermore, biographers have never doubted Jefferson's affection for his first wife, Martha Wayles Skelton, before she died in 1782. Is it not likely that Jefferson felt similarly toward Sally, who was in fact Martha's unacknowledged half-sister?

This bell once belonged to Martha Wayles Jefferson, the wife of Thomas Jefferson. According to Hemings family tradition, she gave the bell to Sally Hemings, who was her half-sister.

On the other hand, the sexual exploitation of black women was common among white masters in the Chesapeake, the Carolinas, and the Caribbean. Like them, Jefferson may have availed himself of the privileges of ownership to compel sexual favors over many years from a slave whom he fancied. Or perhaps Sally Hemings submitted to Jefferson's sexual demands because she hoped to win better treatment—and, in the end, freedom—for herself and her children. Many bondswomen (among them, possibly, Sally's mother, Betty Hemings, and her grandmother) used that strategy to protect their children from the ravages of slavery. What lends added support to either of those interpretations is the testimony of Madison Hemings, who recalled that although Jefferson was affectionate with his white Randolph grandchildren, he was "not in the habit of showing partiality or fatherly affection" to his children with Sally Hemings.

RGINIAN LUXURIES.

This painting was discovered on the reverse side of a portrait of a Virginia gentleman. Experts believe that it dates from the early republic, and the artist, still unknown, evidently shared Jefferson's criticisms of slavery.

In the last analysis, the significance of Sally Hemings's relationship with Thomas Jefferson may reside in its power to reveal the complexity of southern plantation societies between the American Revolution and the Civil War. In that place and time the American South was not starkly divided into whites and blacks; instead, it was a culture in which the races had been mingling for generations, yielding many people of mixed ancestry, such as Sally Hemings. Israel Jefferson, who passed part of his life in slavery at Monticello, remembered her as being "mighty near white," with "long straight hair down her back." Because of their shared bonds of blood, such light-skinned slaves sometimes enjoyed greater privileges and freedoms from their masters, but they also had to negotiate more complicated relationships with them and with less favored members of the slave community.

The Erie Canal was pivotal in transforming many inland settlements from semi-subsistance economies into commercial ones. This canal boat is named after the first inland boomtown in America, Rochester.

The Opening of America

1815–1850

What's to Come

∞∞∞ **AN AMERICAN STORY** ∞∞∞

FROM BOOM TO BUST WITH ONE-DAY CLOCKS

In the years before the Civil War, the name of Chauncey Jerome could be found traced in neat, sharp letters in a thousand different places across the globe: everywhere from the fireplace mantels of southern planters to the log cabins of Illinois prairie farmers and even in Chinese trading houses in Canton. Chauncey Jerome was a New England clockmaker whose clever, inexpensive, and addictive machines had conquered the markets of the world.

Jerome, the son of a Connecticut blacksmith, at first barely made a living peddling his clocks from farmhouse to farmhouse.

Then in 1824 his career took off thanks to a "very showy" bronze looking-glass clock. Between 1827 and 1837 Jerome's factory produced more clocks than any other in the country. But when the Panic of 1837 struck, the entrepreneur had to scramble to avoid financial ruin.

Looking for a new opportunity, he set out to produce an inexpensive brass "one-day" clock—so called because its winding mechanism kept it running that long. Traditionally, the works of these clocks were made of wood, and the wheels and teeth had to be painstakingly cut by hand. Furthermore, wooden clocks could not be exported overseas because the humidity on board ship swelled the wood and ruined them. Jerome's brass version proved more accurate than earlier types and cheaper to boot. Costs came down further when he began to use interchangeable parts and combined his operations for making cases and movements within a single factory in New Haven, Connecticut. By organizing the production process, Jerome brought the price of a good clock within the reach of ordinary people. So popular were the new models that desperate competitors began attaching Jerome labels to their own inferior imitations.

Disaster struck again in 1855, when Jerome went into partnership with several unreliable associates. Within a few years his business faltered, then failed. At the age of 62, the once-prominent business leader found himself working again in a clock factory as an ordinary mechanic. He lived his last years in poverty.

| *Like this peddler, young Chauncey Jerome sold his clocks from farmhouse to farmhouse.*

Jerome rose higher than most Americans of his generation, and he fell farther. Yet his fellow citizens shared his dreams of success, just as they were haunted by the fear of losing everything. For Jerome, it wasn't only material comforts that vanished; so did respect. "One of the most trying things to me now," he confessed in his autobiography, "is to see how I am looked upon by the community since I lost my property. I never was any better when I owned it than I am now, and never behaved any better. But how different is the feeling towards you, when your neighbors can make nothing more out of you. . . . You are passed by without notice."

As the **boom-and-bust economy** swirled around him, Jerome sensed that society had taken on a different tone—that the marketplace and its ethos had become dominant. "It is all money and business, business and money which make the man now-a-days," he complained. "Success is every thing, and it makes very little difference how, or what means he uses to obtain it." The United States, according to one foreign traveler, had become "one gigantic workshop, over the entrance of which there is the blazing inscription *'No admission here except on business.'*"

During the life of Chauncey Jerome, the United States became a commercial republic dominated by a national market. Americans from different regions tied themselves to one another eagerly, even aggressively, through the mechanism of the free market. They sold cotton or wheat and bought manufactured cloth or brass one-day clocks. They borrowed money not merely to buy a house or farm but also to speculate and profit. They relied, even in many rural villages, on cash and paper money instead of bartering for goods and services. Manufacturing changed as well, shifting from the master-apprentice system of production set in urban and rural workshops toward mechanization and the rise of the factory system.

Those economic developments reshaped the lives and values of many Americans. They moved from face-to-face dealings with neighbors to impersonal transactions with distant buyers and sellers. They shifted from performing mechanically simple tasks to tackling the more technologically complex, and growing numbers moved from sparsely settled rural areas to densely populated cities and towns. Equally important, they came to regard free market capitalism, upward mobility, and conspicuous consumption as integral to the emerging American national identity.

Such were the changes Chauncey Jerome witnessed—indeed, changes he helped to bring about himself, with his clocks that divided the working days of Americans into more disciplined, orderly segments. ∞∞∞

THE NATIONAL MARKET ECONOMY

IN 1844 JOHN BURROWS HEARD that potatoes were selling for $2 a bushel in New Orleans. Potatoes fetched less than 50 cents a bushel in Davenport in the Iowa Territory where Burrows was a small merchant, so he loaded 2,500 bushels on a flatboat and started down the Mississippi River. Along the way he learned that other merchants, acting on the same information, had done the same and that the market in New Orleans was now glutted with potatoes. When he reached his destination 6 weeks later, he could not sell his load. Desperate, he finally swapped his potatoes at 8 cents a bushel, taking a load of coffee in return. He made nothing on the transaction, since it had cost him that much to ship the load to New Orleans.

Burrows's experience demonstrated that a national market economy required not just the efficient movement of goods but also rapid communications. Looking back many years later on the amazing transformation that had occurred in his lifetime, Burrows commented, "No one can realize the difficulties of doing a produce business in those days."

A truly national system of markets began to grow following the War of 1812, when the United States entered a period of unprecedented economic expansion. As it grew, the economy became varied enough to sustain and even accelerate its growth. Before the war it had been tied largely to international trade. The United States exported staples such as cotton, wheat, tobacco, and timber; if the nations that bought these commodities suddenly stopped doing so, the domestic economy suffered. That happened during the European wars of the 1790s and again after 1803. Because so many Americans remained rural and primarily self-sufficient, they could not absorb any increase in goods produced by American manufacturers.

GROWTH OF A DOMESTIC MARKET

But the War of 1812 marked the turning point in the creation and expansion of a domestic market. First the embargo and then the war itself stimulated the growth of manufacturing, particularly in textiles. In 1808 the United States had 8,000 spindles spinning cotton thread; by the end of the war the number had jumped to around 130,000. In addition, war had also bottled up capital in Europe. When peace was restored, this capital flowed into the United States, seeking investments. Finally, the war experience led the federal government to adopt policies designed to spur economic expansion.

The New Nationalism

After the war with Britain, leadership passed to a new generation of the Republic—younger men such as Henry Clay, John C. Calhoun, and John Quincy Adams. All were ardent nationalists eager to use federal power to promote rapid development of the nation. Increasingly dominant within the Republican Party, they advocated the "New Nationalism," a set of economic policies designed to foster the prosperity of all regions of the country and bind the nation more tightly together.

NATIONAL BANK

Even James Madison saw the need for increased federal activity, given the problems the government experienced during the war. The national bank had closed its doors in 1811 when its charter expired. Without it the country had fallen into financial chaos. Madison had opposed Hamilton's national bank in 1791, but now, with his approval, Congress in 1816 chartered the Second Bank of the United States for a period of 20 years. Madison also agreed to a mildly protective tariff to aid budding American industries by raising the price of competing foreign goods. Passed in 1816, it set an average duty of 20 percent on imported woolen and cotton cloth, iron, and sugar. The measure enjoyed wide support in the North and the West, but a number of southern representatives voted against it because most of its benefits went to northern manufacturers.

Madison also recommended that the government promote internal improvements such as roads, canals, and bridges. The war had demonstrated how cumbersome it was to move troops or supplies overland. Although Madison did not believe that federal funds could be used merely for local projects, he was willing to support projects broader in scope. His successor, James Monroe, approved additional ones.

The Cotton Trade

WHITNEY'S COTTON GIN

Cotton proved to be the key to American economic development after 1815. By the end of the eighteenth century, southern planters had discovered that short-fiber cotton would grow in the lower part of the South. But the cotton contained sticky green seeds that could not be easily separated from the lint by hand. The needed breakthrough came in 1793 when Eli Whitney invented the cotton gin, a mechanical device that removed the seeds from the lint. The gin allowed a laborer to clean 50 pounds of cotton a day, compared with only 1 pound by hand. With prices high on the world market, cotton production in the Lower South soared. By 1840 the South produced more than 60 percent of the world supply, which accounted for almost two-thirds of all American exports.

The cotton trade was the major expansive force in the economy until the depression of 1839. Northern factories increasingly made money by turning raw cotton into cloth, while northern merchants reaped profits from shipping

| *Whitney's cotton gin*

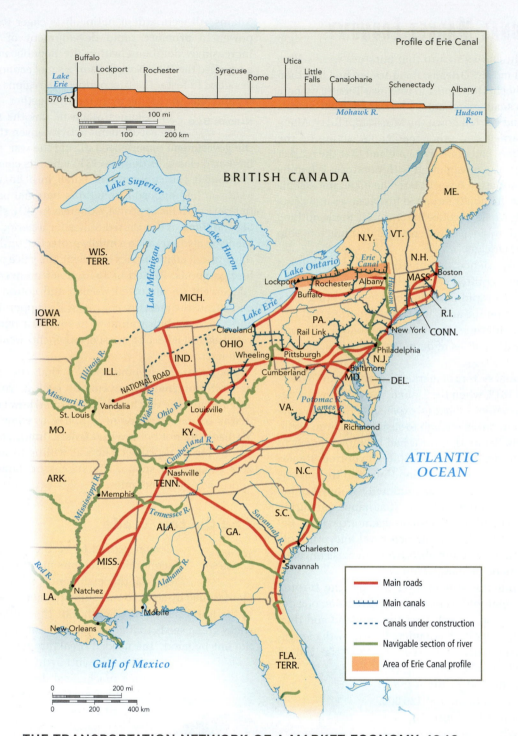

Profile of Erie Canal

Buffalo · Lockport · Rochester · Syracuse · Rome · Utica · Little Falls · Canajoharie · Schenectady · Albany

Lake Erie 570 ft.

Mohawk R. · Hudson R.

0 — 100 mi

0 — 100 — 200 km

THE TRANSPORTATION NETWORK OF A MARKET ECONOMY, 1840

Canals played their most important role in the Northeast, where they linked eastern cities to western rivers and the Great Lakes. On the Erie Canal a system of locks raised and lowered boats in a series of steps along the route. Steamboats were most crucial in the extensive river systems in the South and the West. **What accounts for the concentration of canals in the northern states?**

the cotton and then reshipping the textiles. Planters used the income they earned to purchase foodstuffs from the West and goods and services from the Northeast.

The Transportation Revolution

To become truly national, a market economy needed an efficient transportation network linking various regions of the nation. The economy had not become self-sustaining earlier partly because the only means of transporting goods cheaply was by water. That limited trade largely to coastal and international markets, because even on rivers, bulky goods moved easily in only one direction—downstream.

But dramatic change came after 1815, drawing new regions into the market. From 1825 to 1855—the span of a single generation—the cost of transportation on land fell 95 percent while its speed increased five-fold.

THE CANAL AGE Canals attracted considerable investment capital, especially after the success of the wondrous Erie Canal. Built between 1818 and 1825 the canal stretched 364 miles from Albany on the Hudson River to Buffalo on Lake Erie. Its construction by the state was an act of faith; in 1816 the United States had only 100 miles of canals, none longer than 28 miles. Then, too, the proposed route ran through forests, disease-ridden swamps, and unsettled wilderness. The canal's engineers lacked experience, but they made up for that by sheer ingenuity. Improving on European tools, they devised a cable and screw that allowed one man to pull down even the largest trees and a stump-puller that removed up to 40 stumps a day.

The project paid for itself within a few years. The Erie Canal reduced the cost of shipping a ton of goods from Buffalo to New York City from more than 19 cents a mile to less than 3 cents a mile. By 1860 the cost had fallen to less than a penny a mile. Where its busy traffic passed, settlers flocked, and towns like Rochester and Lockport sprang up and thrived by moving goods and serving markets. "Everything in this bustling place appears to be in motion," wrote one English traveler about Rochester in 1827. The steady flow of goods eastward gave New York City the dominant position in the scramble for control of western trade. New York's commercial rivals, such as Philadelphia and Baltimore, were soon frantically trying to build their own canals to the West. Western states such as Ohio and Indiana, convinced that prosperity depended on cheap transportation, constructed canals to link interior regions with the Great Lakes. By 1840 the nation had completed more than 3,300 miles of canals—a length greater than the distance from New York City to Seattle—at a cost of about $125 million. Almost half that amount came from state governments.

By 1850 the canal era was over. The depression of 1839 caused several states to halt or slow their construction, especially since many poorly planned canals lost money. Still, whether profitable or not, canals sharply reduced transportation costs and stimulated economic development in a broad belt along their routes.

STEAMBOATS AND RAILROADS Because of its vast expanse, the United States was particularly dependent on river transportation. But shipping goods downstream from Pittsburgh to New Orleans took 6 weeks, and

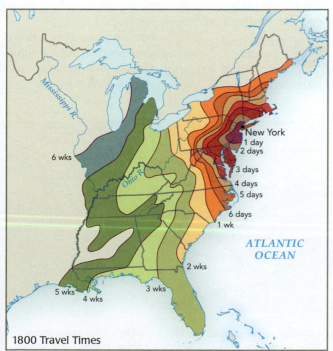

1800 Travel Times

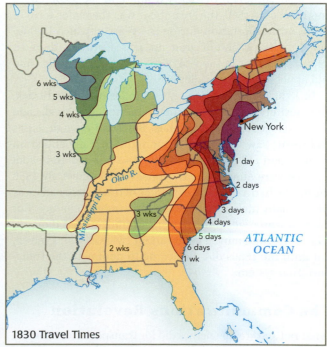

1830 Travel Times

Travel times, 1800 and 1830

A far cry from the sleek trains of today, the earliest railroad cars looked more like horse-drawn conveyances.

the return journey required 17 weeks or more. Steamboats reduced the time of a trip from New Orleans to Louisville from 90 to 8 days while cutting upstream costs by 90 percent.

Robert Fulton demonstrated the commercial possibilities of propelling a boat with steam when his ship, the *Clermont*, traveled in 1807 from New York City to Albany on the Hudson River. But steamboats had the greatest effect on transportation on western rivers, where the flat-bottomed boats could haul heavy loads even when the water level was low. The number of steamboats operating in those waters jumped from 17 in 1817 to 727 in 1855. Since steamboats could make many more voyages annually, the carrying capacity on western rivers increased 100-fold between 1820 and 1860. Although railroads would end the steamboat's dominance by 1860, the steamboat was the major form of western transportation during the years in which the national market economy grew up, and it proved the most important factor in the rise of manufacturing in the Ohio and upper Mississippi valleys.

In 1830 the nation had only 13 miles of railroad track, and most of the lines constructed in the following decade served as feeder lines to canals. But soon enough, cities and towns saw that their economic future depended on having good rail links, so that by 1840 railroad and canal mileage were almost exactly equal (3,325 miles). By 1850 the nation had a total of 8,879 miles of track. Railroad rates were usually higher than canal or steamboat charges, but the new iron roads operated year-round, offered more direct routes, and moved goods about twice as fast. Even so, not until the 1850s did they come to dominate the transportation system.

The Communications Revolution

What rail and steam engines did for transportation, Samuel F. B. Morse's telegraph did for communications. Morse patented a device that sent electrical pulses over a wire in 1837, and before long, telegraph lines fanned out in all directions, linking various parts of the country instantaneously. By 1860 more than 50,000 miles of telegraph lines had been laid. The new telegraph sped business information, helped link the transportation network, and allowed newspapers to provide readers with up-to-date news.

The invention of the telegraph and the perfection of a power press (1847) by Robert Hoe and his son Richard revolutionized journalism. The mechanical press greatly increased the speed with which sheets could be printed over the old hand method. Mass-produced newspapers, often selling for only a penny, gained huge circulations, since ordinary families could afford them. Hoe's press had a similar impact on book publishing, since thousands of copies could be printed at affordable prices.

 **POSTAL SYSTEMS COMPARED** The development of a national market economy depended on mass communications that transmitted commercial information and connected producers and sellers separated

A hotel scene somewhere along the Ohio River reflects the Information Age of the 1830s. In a market economy the flow of information was as crucial as the movement of goods, so guests were asked not to steal the newspapers.

by great distances. Although postage was relatively expensive, the American postal system subsidized the distribution of newspapers and spread other information widely. Indeed, in the years before the Civil War, the postal system had more employees than any other enterprise in the country. Although the postal system's primary purpose was to promote commerce, it made a profound social impact by accustoming people to long-range and even impersonal communication. By 1840 the post office was handling almost 41 million letters and 39 million newspapers a year.

Alexis de Tocqueville, a French political philosopher on a visit to the United States, was amazed at the scope of the postal system by the 1830s. "There is an astonishing circulation of letters and newspapers among these savage woods," he reported from the Michigan frontier. There was hardly a village or town in the country, no matter how remote, that was not connected with the rest of the country through the postal system. While the British and French post offices handled a greater volume of mail, he noted, the United States throughout these years had a much more extensive postal system. In 1828 there were almost twice as many post offices in the United States as in Great Britain, and over five times as many as in France.

In the Americas, the Canadian postal system was so limited that merchants and even government officials routinely used the United States postal system to get mail to other provinces, and by midcentury Mexico had no regularized mail service for the whole country. In China the government maintained a very efficient military-courier system for official communications, but foreigners developed the first private postal system, mainly for business correspondence. Most countries had no true postal system in these years, since literacy was so limited.

The Transformation of Agriculture

The new forms of transportation and communication had a remarkable effect on farm families: they became linked ever more tightly to a national market system. Before the canal era, wheat could be shipped at a profit no farther than 50 miles. But given cheap transportation, farmers eagerly grew more grain and sold the surplus in distant markets.

COMMERCIAL AGRICULTURE

In this shift toward commercial agriculture, farmers began cultivating more acres, working longer hours, and adopting scientific farming methods, including crop rotation and the use of manures as fertilizer. Instead of bartering goods with friends and neighbors, they more often paid cash or depended on banks to extend them credit. Instead of taking the crops to market themselves, they began to rely on regional merchants, intermediaries in a far-flung distribution system. Like southern planters, western wheat farmers increasingly sold in a world market. Banks and distributors advanced credit to farmers, who more and more competed in a market controlled by impersonal forces centered in distant locations.

As transportation and market networks connected more areas of the nation, they encouraged regional specialization. The South increasingly concentrated on staple crops for export, and the West grew foodstuffs, particularly grain. By 1850 Wisconsin and Illinois were major wheat-producing states. Eastern farmers, unable to compete with wheat yields from fertile western farms, shifted to grazing sheep or producing fruits, vegetables, and dairy products for rapidly growing urban areas. Although foreign commerce expanded, too, the dramatic growth in domestic markets far outstripped the volume of trade abroad. The cities of the East looked primarily to southern and western markets.

John Marshall and the Promotion of Enterprise

For a national market system to flourish, a climate favorable to investment had to exist. Under the leadership of Chief Justice John Marshall, the Supreme Court became the branch of the federal government most aggressive in protecting the new forms of business central to the growing market economy.

Marshall, who presided over the Court from 1801 to 1835, at first glance seemed an unlikely leader. Informal in manners and almost sloppy in dress, he was nonetheless a commanding figure, combining a forceful intellect with a genial ability to persuade. Time after time he convinced his colleagues to uphold the sanctity of private property and the power of the federal government to promote economic growth.

CONSTITUTIONALITY OF THE NATIONAL BANK

In the case of *McCulloch v. Maryland* (1819) the Court upheld the constitutionality of the Second Bank of the United States. Just as Alexander Hamilton had argued in the debate over the first national bank, Marshall emphasized that the Constitution gave Congress the power to make all "necessary and proper" laws to carry out its delegated powers. If Congress believed that a bank would help it meet its responsibilities, such as maintaining the public credit and regulating the currency, then it was constitutional. The bank had to be only useful, not essential. "Let the end be legitimate," Marshall wrote, "let it be within the scope of the Constitution, and all means which are appropriate, which are plainly adapted to that end, which are not prohibited . . . are constitutional." By upholding Hamilton's doctrine of implied powers, Marshall enlarged federal power to an extraordinary degree.

INTERSTATE COMMERCE

Marshall also encouraged a more freewheeling commerce in *Gibbons v. Ogden* (1824). The case gave Marshall a chance to define the greatest power of the federal government in peacetime: the right to regulate interstate commerce. In striking down a steamboat monopoly granted by the state of New York, the chief justice gave the term commerce the broadest possible definition, declaring that it covered all commercial dealings and that Congress's power over interstate commerce

Floating Palaces of the West

Plying the Mississippi River and its tributaries, the steamboat carried both freight and passengers, but it won its greatest fame as a mode of travel. The most luxurious boats, dubbed floating palaces, offered accommodations far beyond the experience of the average American. Steamboats also provided the cheapest form of inland transportation up to the Civil War. By midcentury, cabin passage for the 1,400-mile trip from Louisville to New Orleans was only $12 to $15.

On the earliest steamboats passengers were housed on the main deck along with the cargo, but as the boats became larger, designers added a second, or boiler, deck (which, despite its name, was not where the boilers were located). Eventually a third level was added, the hurricane or texas, with additional accommodations. The boiler deck's saloon was the center of society, with the ladies' parlor at one end and the barroom at the other. Besides serving as a dining room and lounge, the saloon sometimes provided the sleeping quarters for men. Berths were arranged in two tiers on both sides and, at least on the better boats, contained bedding and a mattress. Women entered the saloon only for meals.

Steamboats also offered passage on the main deck for about one-fifth the price of a regular ticket. These passengers received no living quarters or toilet facilities and had to provide their own food. Then, too, boiler explosions, collisions, and sinkings from a snag took a much higher loss of life among lower-deck passengers, who were primarily the poor, immigrants, and African Americans. Between 1811 and 1851, 44 steamboats collided, 166 burned, 209 exploded, and 576 hit obstructions and sank, costing thousands of lives.

The steamboat was, as many travelers remarked, a "world in miniature," conveying slaves and planters, farmers and manufacturers, merchants and frontier families, soldiers and Indians, ministers and professional gamblers. As fares steadily dropped, people of widely different wealth and position were thrown together in the main cabin and mingled with democratic familiarity. Women spent their time talking, sewing, caring for children, and strolling the deck. Men passed the time in conversation about politics, the weather, business, and crops. The bar was the center of their social world, and gambling was rife.

The most famous vessels on the rivers boasted intricately carved gingerbread facings, painted a glistening white and trimmed in gold leaf—an architectural style known as "Steamboat Gothic." For all their luxurious veneer, however, steamboats lacked many amenities. Most 6-by-6 staterooms had two narrow shelves to sleep on and no lighting or heat. The washrooms in the main cabin contained tin basins and pitchers of cold water, a comb and brush, and a communal toothbrush. One traveler complained that there were only two towels for 70 men on one boat. Water, for both drinking and washing, came directly from the river and was laden with silt.

Steamboat food came saturated with grease.

Despite the discomforts of swarming mosquitoes, heat from the boilers, and noisy engines at all hours of the night, observers agreed that journeying by steamboat was far more pleasant than taking a stagecoach, the principal alternative in the West before 1850. With their churning paddlewheels, gingerbread decks, and belching smokestacks, these gaudy vessels became the grandest showpieces of life along the commercial waterways of the Mississippi.

Thinking Critically

Why didn't steamboats offer more amenities to travelers?

Although a steamboat's furnishings in the main saloon often boasted fancy gingerbread trimmings, travelers usually had to make do with primitive facilities.

could be "exercised to its utmost extent." The result was increased business competition throughout society.

PROTECTION OF CONTRACTS

In the case of *Fletcher v. Peck* (1810), Marshall took an active role in defining contract law, then in its infancy, and showed how far he was willing to go to protect private property. The Supreme Court unanimously struck down a Georgia law taking back a land grant that a group of speculators had obtained by bribing members of the legislature. A grant was a contract, Marshall declared, and because the Constitution forbade states to impair "the obligation of contracts," the legislature could not interfere with the grant once it had been made. Although the framers of the Constitution probably meant contracts to refer only to agreements between private parties, Marshall made no distinction between public and private agreements, thereby greatly expanding the meaning of the contract clause.

Marshall's most celebrated decision on the contract clause came in *Dartmouth College v. Woodward,* decided in 1819. The case arose out of the attempt by New Hampshire to alter the college's charter granted by George III in 1769. The Court overturned the state law on the grounds that state charters were also contracts and could not be altered by later legislatures. By this ruling Marshall intended to protect **corporations,** which conducted business under charters granted by individual states. Thus the Marshall Court encouraged economic risk taking. Its decisions protected property and contracts, limited state interference in business affairs, and created a climate of confidence.

IMPORTANCE OF CORPORATIONS

State laws also fostered economic development by encouraging banks, insurance companies, railroads, and manufacturing firms to form as corporations. By pooling investors' resources, corporations provided a way to raise capital for large-scale undertakings while limiting the financial liability of individual investors. Originally, state legislatures were required to approve a special charter for each new corporation, but in the 1830s states began to adopt general incorporation laws that automatically granted a charter to any applicant who met certain minimum qualifications. That change further stimulated organization of the national market.

✓ REVIEW

In what ways were the transportation and communication revolutions essential to a national market economy? How did the Marshall Court's decisions encourage the new markets?

A PEOPLE IN MOTION

"EATING ON THE FIRST OF MAY," commented one New York City resident, "is entirely out of the question." That day was "moving day," when all the leases in the city expired. On that date nearly everyone, it seemed, moved to a new residence or place of business. Bedlam prevailed as furniture and personal belongings cluttered the sidewalks and people, movers, and horses crowded the streets. Whereas in Europe millions of ordinary folk had never ventured beyond their local village, a Boston paper commented in 1828, "here, the whole population is in motion."

This restless mobility affected nearly every aspect of American life. Americans ate so quickly that one disgusted European visitor described food being "pitchforked down" by his fellow diners. Steamboat captains risked boiler explosions for the honor of having the fastest boat on the river. Unlike Europe's trains, lightweight and hastily built railroads in the United States offered little safety or comfort of passengers. Even so, Americans quickly embraced this new mode of transportation because of its speed. Eighteen-year-old Caroline Fitch of Boston likened her first ride on a

| *Europeans were shocked that Americans bolted their food or gorged themselves on anything within reach, as this English drawing indicates. Such habits reflected both the indifferent preparation of food and the frenetic tempo of American life.*

railroad to a "lightning flash": "It was 'whew!' and we were there, and 'whew!' and we were back again." Even within railroad cars Americans were too fidgety to adapt to the European system of individual passenger compartments. Instead, American cars had a center aisle, allowing passengers to wander the length of the train.

Horatio Greenough, a sculptor who returned to the United States in 1836 after an extended stay abroad, was amazed and a bit frightened by the pace he witnessed. "Go ahead! is the order of the day," he observed. "The whole continent presents a scene of scrambling and roars with greedy hurry." Not only the growth of a national market but also population growth, geographic mobility, and urbanization increased the sense of perpetual motion in a high-speed society.

Population Growth

The American population continued to double about every 22 years—more than twice the birthrate of Great Britain. The number of Americans—fewer than 4 million in 1790—surpassed 23 million in 1850. During the 1840s, as urban areas grew rapidly, the birthrate dipped about 10 percent, the first significant decrease in American history. In cities, families were smaller, in part because the labor of children was not as critical to the family's economic welfare. Life expectancy did not improve significantly during the first half of the nineteenth century, the population remained quite young, and early marriage remained the norm, especially in rural areas.

IMMIGRATION RISES AFTER 1830 From 1790 to 1820 natural increase accounted for virtually all the country's population growth. But immigration, which had been disrupted by the Napoleonic Wars in Europe, revived after 1815. By 1820, 20 percent of New York City's inhabitants were foreign-born; by the 1830s some 600,000 immigrants had arrived in the United States, more than double the number in the quarter century after 1790. Those newcomers were a harbinger of the flood of immigrants that reached America beginning in the late 1840s: by 1850 half of all New Yorkers had been born outside the United States.

Geographic Mobility

The vast areas of land available for settlement absorbed much of the growing population. By 1850 almost half of all Americans lived outside the original 13 states. Well over 2 million lived beyond the Mississippi River. As settlers streamed west, speculation in western lands reached frenzied proportions. In the single year of 1818, at the peak of land-buying fever, the United States sold 3,500,000 million acres of its public domain. (In contrast, the government sold only 68,000 acres in 1800.) And by the 1820s, Congress had reduced the minimum tract offered for sale to 80 acres, which meant that an ordinary farm could be purchased for $100.

SPECULATORS HELP SETTLE WESTERN LANDS Even so, speculators purchased most of the public lands sold, since the law put no limit on how many acres an individual or a land company could buy. These land speculators played a leading role in settlement of the West. To hasten sales, they usually sold land partially on credit—a vital aid to poorer farmers. They also provided loans to purchase needed tools and supplies, since the cost of establishing a farm was beyond the means of many young men. Many farmers became speculators themselves, buying up property in the neighborhood and selling it to latecomers at a tidy profit. "Speculation in real estate has been the ruling idea and occupation of the Western mind," one Englishman reported in the 1840s. "Clerks, labourers, farmers, storekeepers merely followed their callings for a living while they were speculating for their fortunes."

ON THE ROAD AGAIN Given such rapid settlement, geographic mobility became one of the most striking characteristics of the American people. The 1850 census revealed that nearly half of all native-born free Americans lived outside the state where they had been born. Often, too, the influence of the market uprooted Americans. In 1851 a new railroad line bypassed the village of Auburn, Illinois, on the way to Springfield. "It seemed a pity," wrote one resident, "that so pretty a site as that of the old town should be abandoned for so unpromising a one . . . much of it mere swamp—but railroad corporations possess no bowels of compassion, the practical more than the beautiful being their object." After residents quickly moved to the new town that sprang up around the depot, a neighboring farmer purchased the site and plowed up the streets, and Auburn reverted to a cornfield.

Urbanization

Although the United States remained a rural nation, the four decades after 1820 witnessed the fastest rate of urbanization in American history. In 1820 there were only 12 cities with a population of more than 5,000; by 1850 there were nearly 150. The 1820 census showed that only about 9 percent of the population lived in towns with a population of 2,500 or more. Forty years later the number had risen to 20 percent. As a result, the ratio of farmers to city dwellers steadily dropped from 15-to-1 in 1800 to 5.5-to-1 in 1850. Improved transportation and the productivity of midwestern farms made it possible to feed urban populations being swelled by the beginnings of industrialization and migration from both rural areas of the United States and Europe.

URBAN CENTERS, OLD AND NEW The most heavily urbanized area of the country was the Northeast.* The nation's largest city was New York, with more than half a million people, and older cities such as Philadelphia, Boston, Baltimore, and New Orleans continued to be major

---

*The Northeast included New England and the mid-Atlantic states (New York, Pennsylvania, and New Jersey). The South comprised the slave states plus the District of Columbia.

urban centers. In the West, strategically located cities such as Albany and Rochester in New York, Erie and Pittsburgh in Pennsylvania, Cincinnati and Cleveland in Ohio, and St. Louis, Missouri, sprang up primarily to provide provisions and transportation for migrants settling newly opened land. By the century's midpoint, 40 percent of the nation's total urban population resided in such interior cities. The South, with only 10 percent of its people living in cities, was the least urbanized region.

Cities grew far more rapidly than did the ability of local authorities to make them clean, healthy, and safe. A haze always hung in their air from the combined pollution of fires for cooking and heating, tobacco smoke from pipes and stogies, and the steam and coal dust belched by factories. Deadlier still was the water, which city dwellers drank from backyard wells dug next to outhouses—privies that often overflowed in rainy weather. Horse manure piled up in the streets, and when garbage choked the alleys, city fathers attacked the problem by sending geese and hogs to eat whatever the dogs, rats, and vultures had left. Small wonder, then, that city-bred boys were not as tall and strapping as farm boys, that the life expectancy of city-born babies was six years less than that of newborn southern slaves, and that the urban death rate was higher than the birthrate.

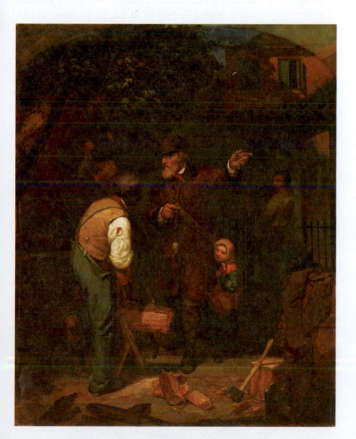

| In antebellum New York City a newly arrived German immigrant asks directions from a free black man cutting wood as two white laborers look on. What do you think was the artist's intention in framing this scene with the German and the African American in the foreground?

CRIME AND URBAN POVERTY Crime, too, posed a daily risk. Theft and assault were the most common, and gangs frequently launched attacks against their political and ethnic rivals, rioted to intimidate African Americans, and raped working-class women of both races. Small, ineffective police forces could do little to curb the disorder, and fire companies arriving at the scene of a blaze were more likely to fight one another than to contain the flames.

Desperate poverty posed an abiding—and worsening—problem. By the 1830s New York City had thousands of prostitutes, because the sex trade was one of the few well-paying occupations for women. In the 1850s nearly 2,000 vagrant children roamed Philadelphia's streets. Winter was the worst season for those living on the margins: the newspaper editor Horace Greeley commented that as Manhattan's rivers and canals froze up and the cost of food and fuel mounted, "mechanics and laborers lived awhile on the scanty savings of the preceding Summer and Autumn; then on such credit as they could wring from grocers and landlords, till milder weather brought them work again."

Yet migration into antebellum cities did not slacken. Indeed, the influx of foreign-born and rural migrants was all that kept city populations rising. Even young men without skills readily found work in the commercial, maritime, and construction businesses. Once employed, they earned higher wages doing less arduous labor than farmworkers. And then there was the lure of theaters, taverns, shops, public markets, and the endless variety of the passing scene. Far more beckoning, for many, than the sleepy farming villages that they had left behind.

✓ **REVIEW**

What motives led Americans to move about so frequently, and how did that mobility affect cities?

THE RISE OF FACTORIES

IT WAS AN ISOLATED LIFE, growing up in rural, hilly Vermont. But stories of the textile factories that had sprung up in Lowell and other towns in Massachusetts reached even small villages such as Barnard. Fifteen-year-old Mary Paul was working there as a domestic servant when she asked her father for permission to move to Lowell. "I am in need of clothes which I cannot get about here," she explained. In 1845 two friends from Barnard helped her find a job at the Lowell mills, from which she earned $128 in 11 months. After four years she returned home but now found "countryfied" life too confining. This time she left her rural hometown for good. She moved about and supported herself at several occupations before finally marrying and settling down in nearby Lynn.

The market economy fundamentally transformed Mary Paul's life—and the lives of thousands of other rural

Americans. The new factories and industries needed more than technological innovation to run smoothly: they also reorganized the labor employed in manufacturing.

Technological Advances

SMALL-SCALE MANUFACTURING Before 1815 the main setting for manufacturing had been the workshops of skilled artisans, where masters taught their trades to apprentices and **journeymen.** And in rural areas, some men engaged in part-time manufacturing in farm workshops, turning out articles such as tools, chairs, and wagons, while farm women and children worked in their homes during the winter months, fashioning items such as brooms and fans. By the beginning of the nineteenth century, New England merchants had devised a way to tap the labor of these rural workers; it was known as the putting-out system. Supplied with tools and materials by the merchants, farm families spun wool into thread or stitched the parts of shoes requiring the least skilled labor. These older forms of manufacturing persisted and even dominated production until the Civil War. But after 1815, factories with machinery tended by unskilled or semiskilled laborers were becoming increasingly important in many industries.

From England came many of the earliest technological innovations, machines that Americans often improved or adapted to more extensive uses. "Everything new is quickly introduced here," one European visitor commented in 1820. "There is no clinging to old ways; the moment an American hears the word 'invention' he pricks up his ears." From 1790 to 1860 the United States Patent Office granted more patents than England and France combined.

To protect their economic advantage, the British forbade the export of any textile machinery or emigration of anyone trained in their construction. But in 1790 a mill worker named Samuel Slater slipped past English authorities and built the first textile mill in America. Two decades later, the Boston merchant Francis Cabot Lowell imitated British designs for a power loom and then improved on them.

INTERCHANGEABLE PARTS The hearth of this early national culture of invention was southern New England. Home manufacturing in countless farm workshops had honed the mechanical skills of many Yankees who, thanks to the region's strong system of public education, also enjoyed almost universal literacy. One of the sharpest minds among these tinkerers belonged to Connecticut's Eli Whitney. Having won a contract to produce 10,000 muskets for the government, Whitney developed machinery that would mass-produce parts that were interchangeable from one gun to another. Once the process was perfected, a worker could assemble a musket quickly with only a few tools. Chauncey Jerome applied the same principle to the production of clocks.

But the production of cloth became the first manufacturing process to make significant use of machines on a large scale, both in England and in the United States. Eventually all the processes of manufacturing cloth took place in a single location, from opening the cotton bales to weaving the cloth, and machines did virtually all the work.

Textile Factories

LOWELL The factory system originated in the Northeast, where capital, water power, and transportation facilities were available. In 1820 a group of wealthy Boston merchants known as the Boston Associates set up operations at Lowell, Massachusetts. Intended as a model community, Lowell soon became the nation's most famous center of textile manufacturing. Its founders sought to avoid the exploitation and misery that characterized the factory system in England by combining **paternalism** with high profits. Instead of relying primarily on child labor or a permanent working class, the Lowell mills employed daughters of New England farm families, who became the first factory workers in the United States. They lived in company boardinghouses under the watchful eye of a matron. To its many visitors Lowell presented an impressive sight: huge factories, well-kept houses, bustling shops. Their employers encouraged women workers to attend lectures and to use the library. The mill employees even published their own magazine, the *Lowell Offering*.

HARD WORK IN THE MILLS But factory life involved strict rules and long hours of tedious, repetitive work. At Lowell work typically began at 7 a.m. (earlier in the summer) and continued until 7 at night, six days a week. With only 30 minutes for the noon meal, many workers had to run to the boardinghouse and back to avoid being late.

| Mill workers, Lowell

Winter was the "lighting up" season, when work began before daylight and ended after dark. The only light after sunset came from whale oil lamps that filled the long rooms with smoke.

Employers also closely monitored the behavior of their labor force. Mill workers paid fines for lateness or misconduct, including talking on the job, and rules also forbade alcohol, cards, and gambling in the shop or yard. Boardinghouse matrons strictly guarded women's morals, supervised male visitors, and enforced a 10 p.m. curfew.

Although the labor was hard, the female operators earned from $2.40 to $3.20 a week, wages that were considered good at the time. (Domestic servants and seamstresses, two of the most common jobs women held, earned less than a dollar a week.) The average "mill girl," as they were called, was between 16 and 30 years old. Most were not working to support their families back home on the farm; instead, they wanted to save some money for perhaps the first time in their lives and sample some of life's pleasures. "I must . . . have something of my own before many more years have passed," Sally Rice wrote in rejecting her parents' request that she return home to Somerset, Vermont. "And where is that something coming from if I go home and earn nothing?"

The sense of sisterhood that united women in the boardinghouses made it easier for farm daughters to adjust to the stress and regimen the factory imposed on them. So did their view of the situation as temporary rather than permanent, because most women worked in the mills no more than five years before getting married.

But in the 1830s, as competition in the textile industry intensified, factory managers sought ways to raise productivity by increasing workloads and speeding up the machinery. When even those changes failed to maintain previous profits, factories cut wages. The ever-quickening pace of work finally provoked resistance among the mill workers, sparking several strikes in which some workers walked out. Management retaliated by firing strike leaders, hiring new workers, and blacklisting women who refused to return. In the 1840s workers' protests focused on the demand for a 10-hour day.

TRANSFORMATION OF LOWELL The quest for profits also undercut the owners' paternalism. As the mills expanded, a smaller proportion of the workers lived in company boardinghouses, and moral regulations were relaxed. But the greatest change was a shift in the workforce from native-born women to Irish immigrants, including men and children. In 1845 the Irish made up only 8 percent of the Lowell workforce; by 1860 they amounted to almost half. Because these new workers were poor and desperate for work, wages went into an even steeper decline, and a permanent working class began to take shape.

Lowell and the Environment

Lowell was a city built on water power. Early settlers had used the power of the Merrimack River to run mills, but never on the scale used by the new textile factories. As the market spread, Americans came to link progress with the fullest use of the natural resources of the environment. Just as they had done in Lowell itself, the Boston Associates sought to impose a sense of order and regularity on the surrounding physical environment in order to efficiently use its natural resources. In the process, they fundamentally reshaped the area's waterscape.

RESHAPING THE AREA'S WATERSCAPE As more and more mills were built, the Boston Associates sought to harness water for energy. By 1836 Lowell had seven canals, with a supporting network of locks and dams, to govern the Merrimack's flow and distribute water to the city's 26 mills. At Lawrence they constructed the largest dam in the world at the time, a 32-foot-high granite structure that spanned 1,600 feet across the river. But, even dammed, the Merrimack's waters proved insufficient. So the Associates gained control of a series of lakes in New Hampshire covering more than 100 square miles that fed into the river system. By damming these lakes, they could provide a regular flow of water down the river, especially in the drier summer months. In the course of establishing this elaborate water-control system, they came to see water as a form of property, divorced from the ownership of land along the river. Water became a commodity that was measured in terms of its power to operate a certain number of spindles and looms.

By regulating the river's waters, the Boston Associates made the Merrimack valley the greatest industrial center in the country in the first half of the nineteenth century. But not all who lived in the valley benefited. By raising water levels, the dams flooded farmlands, blocked the transportation of logs downstream, and damaged mills upstream by reducing the current that powered waterwheels. The dams also devastated the fish population by preventing upstream spawning, and factories routinely dumped their wastes into the river. These wastes, combined with sewage from the growing population, eventually contaminated water supplies. Epidemics of typhoid, cholera, and dysentery broke out with increasing frequency.

In the end, the factory system fundamentally transformed the environment. Far from existing in harmony with its rural surroundings, Lowell, with its clattering machines and dammed rivers, presented a glaring contrast to rural life. The founding vision of Lowell had disappeared.

Industrial Work

ARTISAN SYSTEM Most workers did not easily adapt to the disciplined work routine of the factory. Master artisans had worked in shops within their homes, treating journeymen and apprentices as members of the family. Journeymen took pride in their work, knowing that if they perfected their skill, they could become respected master artisans with their own shops. Apprentices not only learned a trade but also received some education and moral supervision from their masters. And in artisans'

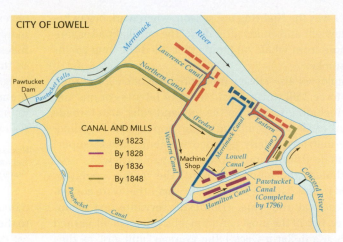

DEVELOPMENT OF THE LOWELL MILLS

As more mills were built at Lowell, the demand increased for water to power them. By 1859 the mills drew water from lakes 80 to 100 miles upstream, including Winnipesaukee, Squam, and Newfound. The map at left shows the affected watersheds. In the city of Lowell, a system of canals was enlarged over several decades. The photograph shows Pawtucket Canal as it has been preserved at Lowell National Historical Park.

shops, all employees worked not by the clock, at a steady pace, but rather in bursts of intense labor alternating with more leisurely time.

TRANSFORMATION OF WORK — The factory changed that. Its discipline required workers to discard old habits, because industrialism demanded a worker who was sober, dependable, and self-disciplined. The machines, whirring and clacking away, set a strict schedule that had to be followed. Absenteeism, lateness, and drunkenness hurt productivity and disrupted the regular factory routine. Thus industrialization not only changed the way work was organized but also made work alienating rather than fulfilling.

The factory regimen was dehumanizing. One mill worker who finally quit complained of "obedience to the ding-dong of the bell—just as though we are so many living machines." And factory work was debasing: whereas the master-apprentice relationship was a close, personal bond, factories sharply separated workers from management. Few workers rose through the ranks to supervisory positions, and even

fewer could achieve the artisan's dream of setting up one's own business. Even well-paid workers sensed their decline in status.

THE DECLINE OF THE CRAFTS — The craft of manufacturing goods declined as well. Factory-produced goods were not as finished or elegant as those done by hand, and the demands of productivity eroded both skills and pride in craftsmanship.

The career of Micajah Pratt, a shoemaker from Lynn, Massachusetts, illustrates the process. Pratt's father, also a skilled cobbler, knew how to judge the quality of leather, to cut out the various parts of a shoe, and to stitch and glue the parts together. He then sold the shoes in the shop where he and his apprentices made them. Following in his father's footsteps, Micajah began selling shoes in 1812 to customers in New England, but he discovered that there were ready markets in the South and the West for cheaply made shoes. So he hired workers to produce shoes in larger and larger central shops. Pratt cut costs further by using new production techniques, such as standardized patterns and

| Set in a carpenter's shop, this painting titled The Young Mechanic celebrates American ingenuity and skill by drawing the eye to the barefoot boy who is whittling a mast for the wooden boat held by its owner on the other side of the counter. Are there other ways of interpreting this scene?

sole-cutting machines. He eventually employed as many as 500 men and women.

So great was the national market that other shoe manufacturers in Lynn could not keep pace with demand. Increasingly they hired nearby farmers, fishermen, and their families to do part-time work at home. Women and girls sewed the upper parts of a shoe, men and boys attached the bottoms. This use of the putting-out system allowed wages to be reduced still further. A few highly paid workers performed such skilled tasks as cutting leather, but most work was done either in large central shops or in homes. With workers no longer able to make an entire shoe, in little more than a generation shoemaking ceased to be a craft. Though still not organized in a factory setting, shoe manufacture had become essentially an assembly-line process.

ECONOMIC SPECIALIZATION

Similarly, for those industries now conducted within factories, the division of labor broke down the manufacture of an item into smaller, more specialized (and less skilled) tasks. Although large factories were the exception rather than the rule during the first half of the nineteenth century, the tendency in manufacturing was toward more technology, greater efficiency, and increasing specialization. The division of labor accompanying early industrialization was only one way in which the national market economy promoted economic specialization. Just as the new transportation and communication networks allowed factories to focus on making a single item such as cloth or shoes, they also permitted farmers to concentrate on producing certain crops.

The Labor Movement

In this newly emerging economic order, workers sometimes organized to protect their rights. Craftworkers, such as carpenters, printers, and tailors, formed unions, and in 1834 individual unions came together in the National Trades' Union.

Union leaders argued that labor was degraded in America: workers endured long hours, low pay, and low status. Unlike most American social thinkers of the day, a number of labor leaders accepted the idea of conflict between different classes. They did not believe that the interests of workers and employers could be reconciled, and they blamed the plight of labor on monopolies, especially banking and paper money, and on machines and the factory system.

EMERGENCE OF UNIONS

If the unions' rhetoric sounded radical, the solutions they proposed were moderate. Reformers agitated for public education and abolition of imprisonment for debt to provide better opportunities for workers. Leaders saw effective unions and political action as the means to restore labor to its former honored position. Proclaiming the republican virtues of freedom and equality, they attacked special privilege and decried workers' loss of independence.

The labor movement gathered some momentum in the decade before the Panic of 1837, but in the depression that followed, its strength collapsed. During hard times, few workers were willing to strike or engage in collective action. Nor did skilled artisans, who spearheaded the union movement, feel a particularly strong bond with semiskilled factory workers and unskilled laborers. More than a decade of agitation did finally gain the 10-hour day for some workers by the 1850s, and the courts also recognized workers' right to strike, but these gains had little immediate impact.

Workers were united in resenting the industrial system and their loss of status. But they found themselves divided by a host of other factors: ethnic and racial antagonisms, gender, conflicting religious perspectives, occupational differences, party loyalties, and disagreements over tactics.

For most workers, the factory and industrialism were not agents of opportunity but reminders of their loss of independence and a measure of control over their lives.

Sam Patch and a Worker's "Art"

Some workers fought against the loss of independence in unusual ways. The waterfalls that attracted capitalists looking to build mills also attracted workers in their off-hours, coming to picnic, swim, or fish. For those with nerve, the falls provided also a place to show off their skills as waterfall jumpers. Sam Patch was such a young man, known for his daring leaps into the Passaic River at the mills around Paterson, New Jersey.

In 1827 Patch became disgusted by a sawmill owner who was set to open a private park, "Forest Gardens," close to Passaic Falls. The owner said he would charge admission in order to keep out "the lazy, idle, rascally, drunken vagabonds" who might spoil the pleasure of more refined folk come to enjoy the view. Workers who resented this fencing out rejoiced when Patch vowed to spoil Forest Garden's opening-day party. As gentlefolk gathered, thousands of ordinary laborers crowded along the opposite bank and cheered as Patch leapt 70 feet straight into the foaming water.

Sam Patch's fame led him eventually to the biggest challenge of all: Niagara Falls. Twice he jumped more than 80 feet into the cascade's churning waters. But he drowned a month later when he dared the Genesee Falls in another mill town along the Erie Canal—Rochester, New York. Still, his fame persisted for decades. Leaping waterfalls was "an art which I have knowledge of and courage to perform," he

Waterfalls at mill towns, like this one in Pawtucket, Rhode Island, were places to swim, fish, and relax, as the people do in the foreground. Jumpers like Sam Patch leaped off the Pawtucket bridge and also off the roof of a nearby building into the foamy froth.

had insisted. In a market economy in which skilled "arts" were being replaced by machine labor, Patch's acts were a defiant protest against the changing times.

✓ REVIEW
How did the rise of factories affect the making of clothing? habits of work? the lives of farm girls? the waterscape of Lowell? handcrafted labor?

SOCIAL STRUCTURES OF THE MARKET SOCIETY

THE NEW DOMINATION OF THE market had a profound impact on American society as a whole. It greatly diminished the importance of women's contributions to household production, while placing a greater emphasis on the acquisition of material goods. It also restructured American society, widening the gulf between rich and poor and contributing to the growth of a middle class. It even changed the way Americans thought about time.

Household Production and Consumption

The average eighteenth-century American woman produced thread, cloth, clothing, and candles in the home for family use. But with the growth of factories, household manufacturing all but disappeared. As a result, women lost many of the economic functions they had once performed at home. Again, textiles are a striking example. Between 1815 and 1860 the price of cotton cloth fell from 18 to 2 cents a yard. Because manufactured cloth was also smoother and more brightly colored than homespun, most women purchased cloth rather than making it themselves. The new ready-made men's clothing also reduced the amount of sewing women did, especially in cities, where more men purchased clothing from retail stores.

Farm wives and daughters still contributed to the income of their households by stitching shoes or covering buttons, crafting straw bonnets and palm-leaf hats, or selling their produce of butter, eggs, and chickens. Working-class women in cities, both whites and blacks, also earned money through the putting-out system, doing piecework for the garment industry, while others boarded lodgers, took in laundry, and worked as domestic servants. But the new ideal for middle-class women was to restrict their labor to performing unpaid duties in their homes—what was now called "housework." For women of middling means or better and their families, households had become places of consumption rather than production.

DUELING DOCUMENTS

The Market and Equality: She Said, He Said

Frances Wright, a Scotswoman who would later make her career in America as an advocate of slaves, workers, and women, made her first trip in 1819 at the age of 23 and found much to celebrate. Alexis de Tocqueville, 25 when he arrived in the United States in 1831, agreed that white Americans were the freest people in the world, but he described their pursuit of equality as elusive and paradoxical.

DOCUMENT 1   Equality Secures Liberty: Frances Wright

The universal spread of useful and practical knowledge, the exercise of great political rights, the ease and, comparatively, the equality of condition give to this people [Americans] a quality peculiar to themselves. Every hand is occupied, and every head is thinking, not only of the active business of human life (which usually sits lighter upon this people than many others), but of matters touching the general weal of a vast empire. Each man being one of a sovereign people is not only a politician but a legislator—a partner, in short, in the grand concern of the state . . . one engaged in narrowly inspecting its operations, balancing its accounts, guarding its authority, and judging of its interests. A people so engaged are

not those with whom a lounger might find it agreeable to associate: he seeks amusement, and he finds business. . . .

It is not very apparent that public virtue is peculiarly requisite for the preservation of political equality; envy might suffice for this: You shall not be greater than I. Political equality is, perhaps, yet more indispensable to preserve public virtue than public virtue to preserve it; wherever an exclusive principle is admitted, baleful passions are excited. Divide a community into classes, and insolence is entailed upon the higher, servility or envy, and often both united, upon the lower. . . .

In all republics, ancient or modern, there has been a leaven of aristocracy. America

fortunately had, in her first youth, virtue sufficient to repel the introduction of hereditary honors. . . .

Liberty is here secure, because it is equally the portion of all. The state is liable to no convulsions, because there is nowhere any usurpations to maintain, while every individual has an equal sovereignty to lose.* No king will voluntarily lay down his scepter, and in a democracy all men are kings.

---

*"A grievous exception to this rule is found in the black slavery of the commonwealths of the South . . ."

Source: Frances Wright, *Views of Society and Manners in America* (London, 1821).

DOCUMENT 2   Equality Promotes Anxiety: Alexis de Tocqueville

In America I saw the freest and most enlightened men, placed in the happiest circumstances which the world affords; it seemed to me as if a cloud habitually hung upon their brow, and I thought them serious and almost sad even in their pleasures.

It is strange to see with what feverish ardor the Americans pursue their own welfare; and to watch the vague dread that constantly torments them lest they should not have chosen the shortest path which may lead to it.

A native of the United States clings to this world's goods as if he were certain never to die; and he is so hasty in grasping at all within his reach, that one would suppose he was constantly afraid of not living long enough to enjoy them. He clutches everything, he holds nothing fast, but soon loosens his grasp to pursue fresh gratifications.

In the United States a man builds a house to spend his latter years in it, and he sells it before the roof is on; he plants a garden, and lets it [rents it] just as the trees are coming into bearing; he brings a field into tillage, and leaves other men to gather the crops; he embraces a profession, and gives it up; he settles in a place, which he soon afterward leaves, to carry his changeable longings elsewhere. If his private affairs leave him any leisure, he instantly plunges into the vortex of

politics; and if at the end of a year of unremitting labor he finds he has a few days' vacation, his eager curiosity whirls him over the vast extent of the United States, and he will travel fifteen hundred miles in a few days, to shake off his happiness. Death at length overtakes him, but it is before he is weary of his bootless chase of that complete felicity which is for ever on the wing.

At first sight there is something surprising in this strange unrest of so many happy men, restless in the midst of abundance. The spectacle itself is, however, as old as the world; the novelty is to see a whole people furnish an exemplification of it. . . .

The equality of conditions leads by a still straighter road to several of the effects which I have here described. When all the privileges of birth and fortune are abolished, when all professions are accessible to all, and a man's own energies may place him at the top of any one of them, an easy and unbounded career seems open to his ambition, and he will readily persuade himself that he is born to no vulgar destinies. But this is an erroneous notion, which is corrected by daily experience. The same equality which allows every citizen to conceive these lofty hopes, renders all the citizens less able to realize them; it circumscribes their powers on every

side, while it gives freer scope to their desires. Not only are they themselves powerless, but they are met at every step by immense obstacles, which they did not at first perceive. They have swept away the privileges of some of their fellow-creatures which stood in their way, but they have opened the door to universal competition. . . .

Among democratic nations men easily attain a certain equality of conditions; they can never attain the equality they desire. It perpetually retires from before them, yet without hiding itself from their sight, and in retiring draws them on. At every moment they think they are about to grasp it; it escapes at every moment from their hold. . . .

Source: Alexis de Tocqueville, *Democracy in America* (1835, 1840).

> ### Thinking Critically
>
> *What did Frances Wright admire about Americans? How does she think political equality will help preserve public virtue? How did Alexis de Tocqueville account for the restless ambition of Americans? According to Tocqueville, what was the paradox of pursuing equality?*

MATERIALISM Even as household production diminished, Americans' demand for consumer goods skyrocketed. Europeans who visited the United States during these years remarked on how hard Americans worked and how preoccupied they were with material goods and achievements. The new generation did not invent materialism, but the spread of the market after 1815 made it much more evident. And in 1836 the American writer Washington Irving coined the classic phrase that captured the spirit of the age when he spoke, in one of his stories, of "the almighty dollar, that great object of universal devotion throughout the land."

WEALTH AND STATUS In a nation that had no legally recognized aristocracy and class lines that were only informally drawn, wealth and its trappings became the most obvious symbols of status. Dismissing birth as "a mere idea," one magazine explained, "Wealth is something substantial. Everybody knows that and feels it." Materialism reflected more than a desire for goods and physical comfort. It represented a quest for respect and recognition. "Americans boast of their skill in money making," one contemporary observed, "and as it is the only standard of dignity and nobility and worth, they endeavor to obtain it by every possible means." Families were rated by the size, not the source, of their fortunes. Americans also emphasized practicality over theory. The esteem of the founding generation for intellectual achievement sank from sight in the scramble for wealth that consumed the new generation.

The Emerging Middle Class

SEPARATION OF MIDDLE CLASS FROM MANUAL LABORERS In the years after 1815 a new middle class took shape in American society. A small class of shopkeepers, professionals, and master artisans had existed earlier, but the creation of a national market economy greatly expanded its size and influence. The growing number of mercantile firms, brokerage houses, insurance businesses, and banks created thousands of new positions for clerks, bookkeepers, and traveling salesmen (known as "drummers"). New factories needed managers and accountants, and the burgeoning railroad industry required superintendents, station agents, and conductors. These new occupations offered the salaries and steady employment that boosted many white men, typically native-born, into the emerging middle class.

This traffic jam in New York City conveys the rapid pace and impatient quality of American life in the first half of the nineteenth century. "In the streets all is hurry and bustle," one European visitor to the city reported. "Carts, instead of being drawn by horses at a walking pace, are often met at a gallop, and always in a brisk trot. . . . The whole population seen in the streets seem to enjoy this bustle and add to it by their own rapid pace, as if they were all going to some place of appointment, and were hurrying on under the apprehension of being too late."

THE CLOCK'S TWO FACES

A table clock made in Wilmington, Delaware, ca. 1790–1805. What is being depicted at the top of the clock face?

This dial of an 8-day tall clock shows the phases of the moon. Is the moon waxing or waning?

Which of these two clocks would be more helpful if you were wondering whether to travel at night?

Clocks such as those crafted by Chauncey Jerome became fixtures in private homes, offices, factories, and schoolhouses throughout the United States during the first half of the nineteenth century. And their widespread adoption seems to hold a single, unmistakable meaning: everyday life in the new republic was becoming more regimented. But is the significance of clocks that simple? True, men and women increasingly regulated their lives by machines that ticked and chimed. Some clocks even showed the day of the month and the phases of the moon (the better to plan for travel at night). But historians who take an interest in material culture (the

study of objects, buildings, and landscapes) believe that the popularity of clocks had two faces—one looking toward a fast-paced, industrialized future but another gazing nostalgically backward at a past that prized leisure and gentility. The clocks that a steadily growing number of Americans coveted and purchased for their halls, walls, shelves, tables, and mantels often featured faces adorned with flowers, fruit, and images of gracious homes or cozy cottages set in idyllic rural landscapes. (Washington's Mount Vernon was a patriotic favorite.) Even if a clock's owner could not yet afford a bountiful country estate, the painted scene

proclaimed that he had at least taken a first step to fulfilling his aspirations by investing in that genteel possession, a timepiece.

Thinking Critically

A paradox?—Why would Americans decorate objects intended to encourage punctuality, efficiency, and diligence at work with tranquil images of the natural world and domesticity? How are clocks looking forward, reflecting new developments in American society? How do they provide reminders of older traditions?

Since their office work and selling increasingly took place away from where goods were actually produced, these middle-class men were all the more inclined to think of themselves as a distinct social group. "In America it is customary to denominate as 'clerk' all young men engaged in commercial pursuits," wrote one observer at midcentury. "Of course, the term is not applied to those

engaged in mechanical trades." Members of the growing middle class had access to more education and enjoyed greater **social mobility.** They were paid not only more but differently. A manual worker might earn $300 a year, paid as wages computed on an hourly basis. White-collar employees received a yearly salary and might make $1,000 a year or more.

Middle-class neighborhoods, segregated along income and occupational lines, began to develop in towns and cities. And in large urban areas, the separation of work from place of residence combined with improvements in transportation made it possible for many middle-class residents to live in surrounding suburbs and travel to work. Leisure also became segregated as separate working-class and middle-class social organizations and institutions emerged.

MATERIAL GOODS AS EMBLEMS OF SUCCESS During these years, a distinct middle-class way of life evolved based in part on levels of consumption. Greater wealth meant the ability to consume more. Someone like Joseph Engles, a Philadelphia publishing agent, might boast a house furnished with not one but two sofas, a looking glass, thirteen chairs, five yards of carpet on the floors, and even a piano. Material goods became emblems of success and status—as clockmaker Chauncey Jerome sadly discovered when his business failed and his wealth vanished. This materialistic ethos was most apparent in the middle class, as they strove to set themselves apart from other groups in society.

The rise of a middle class would soon launch far-reaching changes in American society. The middle class came to embrace a new concept of marriage, the family, and the home. Along with occupation and income, moral outlook also marked class boundaries during this period, as described in Chapter 12.

The Distribution of Wealth

As American society became more specialized and differentiated, greater extremes of wealth appeared. The concentration of wealth was greatest in large eastern cities and in the cotton kingdom of the South, but everywhere the tendency was for the rich to get richer. In New York City, Brooklyn, Boston, and Philadelphia, the top 1 percent of the wealth holders owned a quarter of the total wealth in 1825; by 1850 they owned half. By 1860, 5 percent of American families owned more than 50 percent of the nation's wealth. Not surprisingly, it was around 1840 that the term "millionaire" first appeared.

In contrast, those at the bottom of society held a smaller percentage of a community's wealth. In Connecticut towns between 1831 and 1851, the number of inhabitants listed as having no property increased by 33 percent. In Cincinnati the lower half of the city's taxpayers held 10 percent of the wealth in 1817; in 1860 their share had dropped to less than 3 percent.

In a market society, the rich were able to build up their assets, because those with capital were in a position to increase it dramatically by taking advantage of new investment opportunities. Although a few men, such as Cornelius Vanderbilt and John Jacob Astor, vaulted from the bottom ranks of society to the top, most of the nation's richest individuals came from wealthy families.

Social Mobility

The existence of great fortunes is not necessarily inconsistent with opportunities for social mobility or property accumulation. Although the gap between the rich and the poor widened after 1820, even the incomes of most poor Americans rose, because the total amount of wealth produced in America had become much larger. From about 1825 to 1860 the average per capita income almost doubled to $300. Voicing the popular belief, a New York judge proclaimed, "In this favored land of liberty, the road to advancement is open to all."

LIMITS OF SOCIAL MOBILITY True, social mobility existed in these years— but not as much as contemporaries boasted. Most laborers—or more often their sons— did manage to move up the social ladder, but only a rung or two. Few unskilled workers rose higher than to a semi-skilled occupation. Even the children of skilled workers normally did not escape the laboring classes and enter the middle-class ranks of clerks, managers, or lawyers. For most workers, improved status came in the form of a savings account or homeownership, which gave them some security during economic downswings and in old age.

A New Sensitivity to Time

It was no accident that Chauncey Jerome's clocks spread throughout the nation along with the market economy. The new methods of doing business involved a new and stricter sense of time. Factory life required a regimented schedule in which work began at the sound of a bell, workers kept machines going at a constant pace, and the day was divided into hours and even minutes.

Clocks began to invade private as well as public space. Before Jerome and his competitors began using standardized parts, only the wealthy owned clocks, but with mass production ordinary families could afford them. Even farmers became more sensitive to time as they became integrated into the marketplace. As one frontier traveler reported in 1844, "In Kentucky, in Indiana, in Illinois, in Missouri, and here in every dale in Arkansas, and in cabins where there was not a chair to sit on, there was sure to be a Connecticut clock."

The Market at Work: Three Examples

The scope and sweep of the national market economy transformed American lives from the towns of the East Coast to prairies of the Midwest to the distant frontier of the Rocky Mountains.

THE MARKET TRANSFORMS KINGSTON, NEW YORK In 1820 Kingston, New York, was a rural community of only 1,000 people, located along the Hudson River. But in 1828 the Delaware and Hudson Canal linked Kingston with the Pennsylvania coalfields, jolting the town's economy. The coal trade stimulated commerce and greatly increased the number of banks and the variety of

| Indians and fur traders mixed at Fort Laramie, Wyoming, maintained by the government as a way station for the burgeoning fur trade of the 1830s. The scene looks exotic, but the fur trade was a serious and extensive business that stretched from the Rocky Mountains to eastern cities and to Europe beyond.

businesses. Life in Kingston now focused on the docks, stores, and canal boats rather than on planting and harvest. By 1850 Kingston had a population of 10,000.

Its landscape had changed, too. In 1820 most storekeepers and artisans conducted business from their homes. By 1850 a commercial district boasted specialized stores, some handling china and glassware, others dry goods, clothing, or jewelry and watches. Separated from both the commercial center and the manufacturing facilities, which now hugged the city's outskirts, residential neighborhoods had become segregated along class lines. By midcentury, street signs and gas lamps were going up. Kingston had become a city.

SUGAR CREEK, ILLINOIS — A thousand miles west lay the small prairie settlement of Sugar Creek, Illinois. The first white settlers had moved to Sugar Creek in 1817, and their primary concern was simply surviving. The land they plowed was on the edge of the forest, where girdled trees often remained standing among the crops until they could be cleared. The roads to larger towns such as Springfield were mere cart paths, winding among the trees.

But by the 1840s and 1850s the market economy had made inroads at Sugar Creek. True, a farmer like Eddin Lewis might still keep an account book noting that James Wilson came by for "six days work planting corn [$]3.00." That was the traditional barter system in action, for no cash actually changed hands. Lewis was simply keeping tabs, noting also when he helped Wilson, so that eventually the account could be balanced. But Lewis had begun to drive hogs to St. Louis, where he received cash in return. By 1848 he was shipping south 6,000 pounds of barreled pork, as well as lard and 350 bushels of corn. Sugar Creek, in other words, was becoming more specialized, more stratified in its wealth, and more tied into regional and national markets.

MOUNTAIN MEN AND THE FUR TRADE — Another thousand miles west a different sort of American roamed, who might at first seem unconnected to the bustle of urban markets. These were the legendary mountain men. Traveling across the Great Plains, along upland streams, and over the passes of the Rockies, hard-bitten outdoorsmen such as Jim Bridger, Jedediah Smith, and James Walker wore buckskin hunting shirts, let their unkempt hair grow to their shoulders, and stuck pistols and tomahawks in their belts. In good times they feasted on raw buffalo liver and roasted hump; when game was scarce, some were not above holding their hands "in an anthill until they were covered with ants, then greedily [licking] them off," as one trapper recalled. Wild and exotic, the mountain men quickly became romantic symbols of the American quest for individual freedom.

Yet these wanderers were tied to the market. During their heyday, from the mid-1820s to the early 1840s, they trapped beaver, whose pelts were shipped east and turned into fancy hats for gentlemen. The fur trade was not a sporting pursuit but a business, dominated by organizations such as John Jacob Astor's American Fur Company, and the trapper was part of a vast economic structure that stretched from the mountains to the eastern cities and on to Europe. The majority of these men went into the wilderness not to flee civilization but to make money. Of those who survived the fur trade, most returned from the wild and took up new careers. They, like farmers, were expectant capitalists for whom the West was a land of opportunity.

 REVIEW

Why did the middle class become larger and more distinct during the first half of the nineteenth century?

PROSPERITY AND ANXIETY

AS AMERICANS SAW THEIR NATION'S frontiers expand and its market economy grow, many began to view history in terms of an inevitable and continuous improvement. But the path of commerce was not steadily upward. Instead, it advanced in a series of wrenching boom-and-bust cycles: accelerating growth and overheated expansion, followed by a crash and then depression.

BOOM-AND-BUST CYCLES The country remained extraordinarily prosperous from 1815 until 1819, only to sink into a depression that lasted from 1819 to 1823. During the next cycle, slow economic expansion in the 1820s gave way to almost frenzied speculation and investment in the 1830s. Then came the inevitable contraction in 1837, and the country suffered an even more severe depression from 1839 to 1843. The third cycle followed the same pattern: growth during the 1840s, frantic expansion in the 1850s, and a third depression that began in 1857 and lasted until the Civil War. In each "panic," thousands of workers lost their jobs, overextended farmers lost their farms, and many businesses closed their doors.

In such an environment, prosperity and personal success seemed all too fleeting. Because Americans believed that the good times would not last—that the bubble would burst and another "panic" would set in—their optimism was often tinged by insecurity and anxiety. They knew too many individuals like Chauncey Jerome, who had been rich and then lost all their wealth in a downturn.

The Panic of 1819

The initial shock of this boom-and-bust psychology came with the Panic of 1819, the first major depression in the nation's history. From 1815 to 1818 cotton had commanded fabulous prices on the Liverpool market, reaching 32.5 cents a pound in 1818. In this heady prosperity, the federal government extended liberal credit for land purchases, and the new national bank encouraged merchants and farmers to expand their operations by borrowing in order to catch the rising tide.

NATIONAL DEPRESSION But in 1819 the price of cotton collapsed and took the rest of the economy with it. Once the inflationary bubble burst, land values, which had been driven to new heights by the speculative fever, plummeted 50 to 75 percent almost overnight. As the economy went slack, so did the demand for western foodstuffs and eastern manufactured goods and services, pushing the nation into a severe depression. Because the market economy had spread to new areas, the downturn affected not only city folk but rural Americans as well. Especially hard hit were the new cotton planters in the Southwest, who were most vulnerable to the ups and downs of the world market.

This mock banknote illustrates the anxieties often felt in times of "bust," when the value of currencies plummeted and it was difficult to tell whether the banks that issued paper money were solvent.

CONCLUSION

THE WORLD AT LARGE

As depression spread in the years following 1819, most Americans could not guess that the ups and downs of the boom-and-bust cycle would continue through the next three decades, their swings made sharper by the growing networks of the market economy. But the interconnections between buyers and sellers did feed both prosperity and panic. Farmers and factories specialized in order to sell goods to distant buyers. Canals and railroads widened the network, speeding products, information, and profits.

As markets tied distant lands more tightly together, international events contributed to the business cycles. It was the Liverpool market in England that bid the price of American cotton to its high at over 32 cents; then in 1816 and 1817 English textile manufacturers, looking for cheaper cotton, began to import more of it from India, sending the price of cotton in New Orleans plummeting to 14 cents. Broader changes also hurt American markets. The French and the British had been at war with one another for decades—more than 100 years, if the imperial wars of the seventeenth and eighteenth centuries were counted. In 1814 and 1815 the major powers of Europe hammered out a peace at the Congress of Vienna, one that lasted, with only minor interruptions, until the coming of World War I in 1914. When Europe had been at war, American farmers found a ready market abroad. With thousands of European soldiers returning to their usual work as farmers, demand for American goods dropped.

The stresses of the Panic of 1819 shook the political system at home, too. As the depression deepened and hardship spread, Americans viewed government policies as at least partly to blame. The postwar nationalism, after all, had been based on the belief that government should stimulate economic development through a national bank and protective tariff, by improving transportation, and by opening up new lands. As Americans struggled to make sense of their new economic order, they looked to take more direct control of the government that was so actively shaping their lives. During the 1820s the popular response to the market and the Panic of 1819 produced a strikingly new kind of politics in the United States. ∞∞∞

CHAPTER SUMMARY

BY UNITING THE COUNTRY IN a single market, the market revolution transformed the United States during the quarter century after 1815.

- The federal government promoted the creation of a market through a protective tariff, a national bank, and internal improvements.

- The development of new forms of transportation, including canals, steamboats, and eventually railroads, allowed goods to be transported cheaply on land.

- The Supreme Court adopted a pro-business stance that encouraged investment and risk taking.

- Economic expansion generated greater national wealth, but it also brought social and intellectual change.

Additional Reading

THE OUTSTANDING SYNTHESIS OF AMERICAN development during the first half of the nineteenth century is Daniel Walker Howe, *What Hath God Wrought* (2007). Also worth consulting is Christopher Clark, *Social Change in America* (2006). The most provocative analysis of economic development and its impact remains Charles Sellers, *The Market Revolution* (1991). The best recent book on the transportation revolution is John Larson, *Internal Improvements* (2001), and for a fascinating study of the role played by the postal system in linking Americans, see Richard John, *Spreading the News* (1995). There are many fine studies of urban social classes during the first half of the nineteenth century, and among the best are Sean Wilentz, *Chants Democratic* (1984), which traces the formation of New York City's working class, and Stuart Blumin, *The Emergence of the Middle Class* (1989). To understand the market economy's effect on rural society, read John Mack Faragher's vivid account of the transformation of a farming community in frontier Illinois, *Sugar Creek* (1986), and Robert Shalhope, *A Tale of New England* (2003), which traces the fortunes of a Vermont farmer and his family.

There is also no shortage of excellent books exploring the relationship between the market revolution and antebellum American culture. Begin with Karen Halttunen's classic study of middle-class culture, *Confidence Men and Painted Women* (1982), and a more recent study, Thomas Augst, *The Clerk's Tale* (2003), and then turn to Paul Johnson's lively exploration of working-class culture, *Sam Patch, the Famous Jumper* (2003). To celebrate any occasion, treat yourself to Stephen Nissenbaum, *The Battle for Christmas* (1996). And to console yourself in between celebrations, turn to Scott Sandage, *Born Losers: A History of Failure in America* (2005).

For a fuller list of readings, see the Bibliography at www.mhhe.com/eh8e.

Significant Events

1793
Eli Whitney invents the cotton gin

1810
Fletcher v. Peck

1810–1820
Cotton boom begins in the South

1811
First steamboat trip from Pittsburgh to New Orleans

1816
Second Bank of the United States chartered; protective tariff enacted

1819
Dartmouth College v. Woodward; McCulloch v. Maryland

1819–1823
Panic and depression

1820
Lowell mills established

1824
Gibbons v. Ogden

1825
Erie Canal opened

1834
National Trades' Union founded

1837
Panic

1839–1843
Depression

1844
Samuel F. B. Morse sends first intercity telegraphic message

	LOCATION OF MANUFACTURE	LABOR FORCE	GOALS OF MANUFACTURE
Before 1815	Shops, private homes, family farms	Master craftsman supervising the education and behavior of journeymen and apprentices; some rural women and children employed part-time in the putting-out system	Filling orders for individual customers, pride in craftsmanship; for putting-out system, doing piecework consigned by merchants
1815–1830	First factories	Young women from New England farm families, most employed no longer than 5 years	Successful competition with British manufacturers, recruiting a stable workforce
1830s–1860	Factories with steadily increasing workloads, speeded-up machinery, greater regimentation to encourage sobriety, punctuality, efficiency	Steadily growing numbers of Irish immigrants—men, women, and children; declining status of workers; sharp separation of workers and management; beginnings of the labor movement	Highest possible rate of mass production

By **1837** the new style of democratic politics was in full swing. This state election in Detroit shows the usual bustle of election day. Look at the make-up of the crowd: what does this indicate about the vote during the Jacksonian era?

The Rise of Democracy

1824–1840

Whats to Come

○○○○ **AN AMERICAN STORY** ○○○○

"WANTED: CURLING TONGS, COLOGNE, AND SILK-STOCKINGS . . ."

The notice, printed in a local paper, made the rounds in the rural Pearl River district of Mississippi. A traveler, the advertisement announced, had lost a suitcase while fording the Tallahala River. The contents included "6 ruffled shirts, 6 cambric handkerchiefs, 1 hair-brush, 1 tooth-brush, 1 nail-brush, . . ." And as the list went on, the popular reaction inevitably shifted from amusement to disdain: "1 pair curling tongs, . . . 1 bottle Cologne, 1 [bottle] rose-water, 4 pairs silk stockings, and 2 pairs kid gloves." The howls of laughter that filled the air could only have increased on learning that anyone finding said trunk was begged to contact the owner— Mr. Powhatan Ellis of Natchez.

Powhatan Ellis was no ordinary backcountry traveler. Born into a genteel Virginia family, Ellis had moved to the raw Southwest to increase his fortune. With his cultivated tastes and careful dress, he upheld the tradition of the gentleman politician. In Virginia he would have commanded respect: indeed, in Mississippi he had been appointed district judge and U.S. senator. But for the voters along the Pearl River, the advertisement for his trunk of ruffled shirts, hair oils, and fancy "skunkwater" proved to be the political kiss of death. His opponents branded him an aristocrat and a dandy, and his support among the piney woods farmers evaporated faster than a morning mist along Old Muddy.

No one was happier with this outcome than the resourceful Franklin E. Plummer, one of Ellis's political enemies. In truth, although Judge Ellis *had* lost a trunk, he had never placed the advertisement trying to locate it. That was Plummer's doing, a man who well understood the new playing field of politics in the 1820s. If Powhatan Ellis typified the passing political world of the Revolutionary era, Plummer was a product of the raucous democratic system emerging in its place. A New Englander, Plummer had worked his way south to bustling New Orleans, and then inland to Mississippi, where he hung out his shingle as an attorney. His shrewdness made up for any lack of legal training, and he was quickly elected to the legislature.

ELECTIONEERING IN MISSISSIPPI.

| Franklin Plummer campaigning

In 1830 Plummer ran for Congress against a wealthy Natchez merchant, military hero, and member of the state's political elite. The uncouth candidate seemed overmatched at first, but Plummer portrayed himself as the champion of the people battling against the aristocrats of Natchez. Contrasting his humble background with that of his wealthy opponent, Plummer proclaimed: "We are taught that the highway to office, distinction and honor, is as free to the *meritorious poor* man, as to the *rich*." Taking as his slogan "Plummer for the People, and the People for Plummer," he was easily elected.

On the campaign trail he knew how to affect the common touch. Once, while canvassing the district with his opponent, the pair stopped at a farmhouse. When his opponent, seeking the farmer's vote, kissed the daughter, Plummer lifted up a toddling boy and began picking red bugs off him, telling the enchanted mother: "They are powerful bad, and mighty hard on babies." On another occasion, while his opponent slept, Plummer rose at dawn to help milk the family's cow—and won another vote. He was a master at secretly planting false stories attacking himself in the press, and then bringing out the sworn personal testimonials of well-known men defending his character and denouncing the charges against him.

As long as Plummer maintained this democratic style, he remained invincible. But running for Senate in 1835, his touch deserted him. Borrowing money from a Natchez bank, he purchased a stylish coach, put his servant in a uniform, and campaigned across the state. Aghast at such pretensions, his followers promptly abandoned him. He died in 1852 in obscurity and poverty. Ah, Plummer! Even the boldest of nature's noblemen may stumble, prey to the temptations of power and commerce!

The forces transforming American society after 1815 pulled Franklin Plummer in two ways. On the one hand, the growth of new markets opened up opportunities for more and more Americans. Through his connections with bankers and the well-to-do, Plummer saw the chance to gain status, wealth, and respect. Yet as new markets were producing a more **stratified,** unequal society, the nation's politics were becoming more democratic. These politics involved more voters than ever before and created a new class of politicians. And the system's central feature—a byword on everyone's lips—was equality. But the relation between the new equalities of politics and the new opportunities of the market was a most uneasy one. ∞∞∞

Equality, Opportunity, and the New Political Culture of Democracy

Coming from the more stratified society of Europe, middle- and upper-class European visitors to the United States were struck by the "democratic spirit" that had become "infused into all the national habits and all the customs of society" during the 1820s and 1830s.

To begin with, they discovered that only one class of seats was available on stagecoaches and railcars. These were filled according to the rough-and-ready rule of first come, first served. In steamboat dining rooms or at country taverns, everyone ate at a common table, sharing food from the same serving plates. As one upper-class gentleman complained: "The rich and the poor, the educated and the ignorant, the polite and the vulgar, all herd on the cabin floor, feed at the same table, sit in each others laps, as it were." Being ushered to bed at an inn, visitors found themselves lodged 10 to 12 people a room, often with several bodies occupying a single bed. Fastidious Europeans were horrified at the thought of sleeping with unwashed representatives of American democracy.

Indeed, the democratic "manners" of Americans seemed positively shocking. In Europe social inferiors would speak only if spoken to. But Americans felt free to strike up a conversation with anyone, including total strangers. The British author Frances Trollope was offended by the "coarse familiarity of address" between classes, while another visitor complained that in a nation where every citizen felt free to shake the hand of another, it was impossible to know anyone's social station. This informality—a forward, even *rude* attitude—was not limited to shaking hands. At theaters, it was hard to get patrons to remove their hats so that those behind them could see. Still worse, men chewed tobacco and spit everywhere: in the national Capitol, in taverns, courts, and hospitals, even in private homes. Fanny Kemble, an English actress, reported that on an American steamboat "it was a perfect shower of saliva all the time."

Americans were self-consciously proud of such democratic behavior, which they viewed as a valued heritage of the Revolution. The keelboaters who carried the future King Louis-Philippe of France on a trip down the Mississippi made their republican feelings plain when the keelboat ran aground. "You kings down there!" bellowed the captain. "Show yourselves and do a man's work, and help us three-spots pull off this bar!" The ideology of the Revolution made it clear that, in the American deck of cards, "three-spots" counted as much as jacks, kings, and queens. Kings were not allowed to forget that—and neither was Franklin Plummer.

The Tension between Equality and Opportunity

Although Americans praised both opportunity and equality, a fundamental tension existed between the two values.

Inevitably, widespread opportunity would produce inequality of wealth. In the 1790s less pronounced inequalities of wealth and status had prevailed because of the lack of access to markets. Shoemakers in Lynn, with no way to ship large quantities of shoes across the country, could not become wealthy. Without steamboats or canals, farmers could not market surplus grain for profit. But by the 1820s and 1830s, as the opportunities of the market expanded, wealth became much more unevenly distributed. Thus the new generation had to confront contradictions in the American creed that their parents had been able to conveniently ignore.

MEANING OF EQUALITY

By equality, Americans did not mean equality of wealth or property. "I know of no country where profounder contempt is expressed for the theory of permanent equality of property," Alexis de Tocqueville wrote. Nor did equality mean that all citizens had equal talent or capacity. Americans realized that individuals possessed widely differing abilities, which inevitably produced differences in wealth. "Distinctions in society will always exist under every just government," Andrew Jackson declared. "Equality of talents, or education, or of wealth cannot be produced by human institutions."

In the end, Americans embraced the equality of opportunity, not equality of condition. "True republicanism requires that every man shall have an equal chance—that every man shall be free to become as unequal as he can," one American commented. In an economy that could go bust as well as boom, Americans agreed that one primary objective of government was to safeguard opportunity. Thus the new politics of democracy walked hand in hand with the new opportunities of the market.

The New Political Culture of Democracy

DEATH OF THE CAUCUS SYSTEM

The stately James Monroe, with his powdered hair and buckled shoes and breeches, was not part of the new politics. In 1824 as he neared the end of his second term, a host of new leaders in the Republican Party looked to succeed him. Traditionally, a congressional caucus selected the party's presidential nominee, and the Republican caucus finally settled on Secretary of Treasury William H. Crawford of Georgia. Condemning "King Caucus" as undemocratic, three other Republicans, all ardent nationalists, refused to withdraw from the race: Secretary of State John Quincy Adams; John C. Calhoun, Monroe's secretary of war; and Henry Clay, the Speaker of the House.

None of these men bargained on the sudden rise of another Republican candidate, Andrew Jackson, the hero of the Battle of New Orleans. Because of his limited political experience, no one took Jackson's candidacy seriously at first, including Jackson himself. But soon the general's supporters and rivals began receiving reports of his unusual popularity. From Cincinnati an observer wrote: "Strange!

DAILY LIVES

THE PLAIN DARK DEMOCRACY OF BROADCLOTH

The emergence of democracy in American life was accompanied by a dramatic change in men's clothing. In the eighteenth century clothing was a prime indicator of social rank and set members of the upper class apart from ordinary citizens. Only a gentleman could afford ruffled shirts, lace cuffs, silk stockings, decorative garters, and buckled shoes. Because of the cost and extensive labor involved, most Americans owned only a few clothes, and these usually were made out of homespun—cloth woven from thread spun in the household. With a quick glance an observer could tell a person's social rank.

In the Jacksonian era, however, fashionable clothing made from textile mill fabrics became cheaper and much more widely available. As a result, dress no longer revealed social standing. "All sorts of cotton fabrics are now so cheap that there is no excuse of any person's not being well provided," commented *The Young Lady's Friend* in 1836.

The colorful shirts, rude trousers, leather aprons, frocks, and heavy boots and shoes worn by farmers and mechanics while working were readily distinguishable from the coats and trousers of middle-class merchants, professionals, managers, and clerks. But outside the workplace, differences in clothing style, if not tailoring quality, largely disappeared. British traveler John Fowler in 1831 was amazed to see American workers, decked out in their Sunday best, walking the streets wearing "sleek coats, glossy hats, watchguards, and deerskin gloves!" Unlike men in the eighteenth century, these Americans dressed in somber colors. By the 1830s "black was the prevailing color," one New Yorker recalled. "It was worn for promenade, parlor, church, ball, [or] business."

The emergence after 1840 of the ready-made clothing industry also affected men's fashions. Many men in middle-class positions were anxious to create a proper image but could not afford the expert tailoring required to make a business suit. So tailors developed standardized patterns and a proportional sizing system and began mass-producing affordable ready-made clothing. Decently made suits could be purchased off the rack, and thus clerks began wearing clothing identical in style to that worn by their employer. By eliminating the distinction between home-made apparel and that sewed by a tailor, ready-made clothing further democratized men's attire.

Rather than distinguishing one class from another, democratic fashions increasingly set men apart from women. Fashion came to be considered a female concern, and ornamentation and bright colors now were associated with women's clothing. Ready-made clothing was not available for women, because female apparel required a close fit in the bodice. But the style of women's clothing also became standardized. American women strove to imitate the latest in Paris fashions, and if they could not afford a dressmaker's fitting, they sewed their own clothing. Illustrated magazines such as *Godey's Lady's Book* publicized the latest fashions, and even young women working in the mills at Lowell joined together to buy a subscription.

New ways of dressing began with the urban middle class and gradually spread throughout most of society. As one newspaper commented, Americans in the Jacksonian era were citizens of the "plain dark democracy of broadcloth."

As this nattily dressed butcher suggests, clothes were not much help in sorting out social status in America. Although the clothing of the upper class was often made of finer material and was more skillfully tailored, by the 1820s less-prosperous Americans wore similar styles.

Thinking Critically

What economic and social changes might account for the concern with fashion and brightly colored clothing becoming restricted to women?

Wild! Infatuated! All for Jackson!" Savvy politicians flocked to his standard, but it was the people who first made Jackson a serious candidate.

The Election of 1824

Calhoun dropped out of the race, but that still left four candidates, none of whom received a majority of the popular vote. Jackson led the field and finished first in the Electoral College with 99 votes. Adams had 84, Crawford 41, and Clay 37. Under the Twelfth Amendment, the House was to select a president from the top three candidates. Clay, though himself eliminated, held enough influence as Speaker of the House to name the winner. After he met privately with Adams, he rallied the votes in the House needed to put Adams over the top.

CORRUPT BARGAIN? Two days later Adams announced that Clay would be his new secretary of state, the usual stepping-stone to the presidency. Jackson and his supporters promptly charged that there had been a "corrupt bargain" between Adams and Clay. Before Adams had even assumed office, the 1828 race was under way.

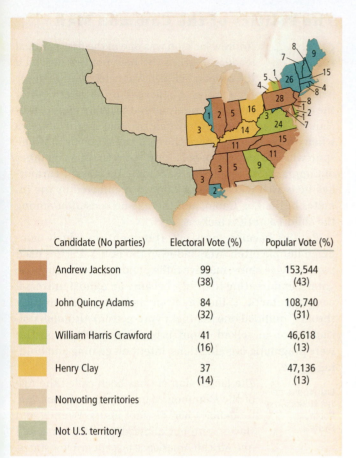

Candidate (No parties)	Electoral Vote (%)	Popular Vote (%)
Andrew Jackson	99 (38)	153,544 (43)
John Quincy Adams	84 (32)	108,740 (31)
William Harris Crawford	41 (16)	46,618 (13)
Henry Clay	37 (14)	47,136 (13)
Nonvoting territories		
Not U.S. territory		

ELECTION OF 1824

The election of 1824 shattered the old party system. Henry Clay and John Quincy Adams began to organize a new party, known as the National Republicans, to distinguish it from Jefferson's old party. Jackson's disappointed supporters eventually called themselves Democrats. By the mid-1830s, the National Republicans had given way to the Whigs, a political party that also drew members from another party that flourished briefly, the Anti-Masons. (The Anti-Masons had led a campaign against the Freemasons, or Masons, a fraternal order whose members—including George Washington and Benjamin Franklin—shared the Enlightenment belief in the power of reason but whose secret meetings and rituals seemed aristocratic and undemocratic to many Americans.) The Democrats, as the other major party, came together under the leadership of Andrew Jackson. Once established, this second American party system dominated the nation's politics until the 1850s.

Social Sources of the New Politics

NEW ATTITUDES TOWARD GOVERNMENT Why was it that a new **political culture** emerged in the 1820s? Both the revolution in markets and the Panic of 1819 played key roles. The ensuing depression convinced many Americans that government policy had aggravated, if not actually produced, hard times. As a result, they decided that the government had a responsibility to relieve distress and promote prosperity.

For the first time, large numbers of Americans saw politics as relevant to their daily lives. Agitation mounted, especially at the state level, for government to enact relief for those in debt and provide other forms of assistance. Elections soon became the means through which the majority expressed its policy preferences by voting for candidates pledged to specific programs. The older idea that representatives should be independent and vote according to their best judgment gave way to the notion that representatives were to carry out the will of the people, as expressed in the outcomes of elections.

DEMOCRATIC REFORMS With more citizens championing the "will of the people," pressure mounted to open up the political process. Most states eliminated property qualifications for voting in favor of white manhood suffrage, under which all adult white males were allowed to vote. Similarly, property requirements for officeholders were reduced or dropped.

Presidential elections became more democratic as well. By 1832 South Carolina was the only state in which the legislature rather than the voters still chose presidential electors. The Anti-Masons pioneered the convention as a more democratic method of nominating party candidates and approving a platform, and the other parties soon followed suit. Furthermore, because a presidential candidate had to carry a number of states in different sections of the country, the backing of a national party, with effective state and local organizations, became essential.

 MALE SUFFRAGE IN EUROPE AND LATIN AMERICA These democratic winds of change affected European societies and eventually other areas of the world, but in no other major country were such reforms achieved as early, and with as little resistance, as in the United States. Suffrage provides a good example. In Britain, in response to growing demonstrations and the cautionary example of the French monarchy's overthrow in 1830, Parliament approved the Reform Bill of 1832, which enfranchised a number of property holders and gave Britain the broadest electorate in Europe. Yet in fact, only about 15 percent of the adult males in Britain enjoyed the right of suffrage after the bill's passage. In France the figure was less than 1 percent.

The democratic revolutions of 1848 championed universal male suffrage in France and Prussia. Yet this ideal soon suffered setbacks. By 1852 the French Republic had been replaced by a monarchy under the emperor Louis Napoléon. And in Prussia, the new constitution essentially negated universal male suffrage by dividing the electorate into three classes according to wealth, a formula that enabled 5 percent of the voters to elect one-third of parliament. Belgium, which had the most liberal constitution in Europe, did not approximate manhood suffrage until 1848. Even the second Reform Act (1867) in Britain enfranchised only about one-third of the adult males.

Likewise, the Latin American republics established in the 1820s and 1830s imposed property requirements on voting or, as Uruguay did, excluded certain occupational groups such as servants and peasants from the suffrage. One exception was Mexico, where a number of states adopted an extremely broad suffrage, but even there a new constitution in 1836 established a much more centralized state and sharply limited voting rights. The most restricted suffrage existed in the Republic of Haiti, where only army officers and a few other privileged individuals enjoyed the franchise. When the Revolution of 1843 brought a new constitution with mass-based suffrage, it met widespread resistance among elites, and the government quickly failed.

VOTER TURNOUT As the new reforms in the United States went into effect, voter turnout soared. Whereas in the 1824 presidential election only 27 percent of eligible voters bothered to go to the polls, four years later the proportion had more than doubled to 56 percent. In 1840, 78 percent of eligible voters cast ballots, probably the highest turnout in American history.

The Acceptance of Parties

RISE OF THE PROFESSIONAL POLITICIAN All these developments worked to favor the rise of a new type of politician: one whose life was devoted to party service and who often depended for his living on public office. As the number of state-sponsored internal improvement projects increased during the 1820s, so did the number of government jobs that could support party workers. No longer was politics primarily the province of the wealthy, who spent only part of their time on public affairs. Instead, political leaders were more likely to come from the middle ranks of society, especially those outside the South. Many became economically established after entering politics, but as Franklin Plummer demonstrated, large sums of money were not required to conduct a campaign. Indeed, a successful politician now had to mingle with the masses and voice their feelings—requirements that put the wealthy elite at a disadvantage.

VAN BUREN In many ways, Martin Van Buren epitomized the new breed of politician. The son of a New York tavern keeper, Van Buren lacked great oratorical skills or a magnetic personality. But he was a master organizer and tactician, highly skilled at using the new party system. His abilities eventually carried him to the White House. Unlike the Revolutionary generation, who had regarded political parties as dangerous and destructive, Van Buren argued that they were not only "inseparable from free governments" but "in many and material respects . . . highly useful to the country." While conceding that political parties were subject to abuse, he stressed that competing parties would watch one another and check abuses at the same time that they kept the masses informed.

The Politics of the Common Man

NEW STYLE OF POLITICS Andrew Jackson was one of the first political leaders to grasp the new politics in which the ordinary citizen was celebrated as never before. "Never for a moment believe that the great body of the citizens . . . can deliberately intend to do wrong," he proclaimed. Party leaders everywhere avoided aristocratic airs when on the stump. "I have always dressed chiefly in Home spun when among the people," one North Carolina member of Congress explained. "If a Candidate be dressed Farmerlike he is well received and kindly remembered by the inmates of the Log Cabin, and there is no sensation among the children or the chickens."

Politics became mass entertainment, in which campaign hoopla often overshadowed the issues. Parties used parades, glee clubs, massive rallies, and barbecues to rouse voters, and treating to drinks became an almost universal campaign tactic. ("The way to men's hearts is down their throats," quipped one Kentucky vote-getter.) Although politicians often talked about principles, political parties were pragmatic organizations, intent on gaining and holding power.

LIMITATIONS OF THE DEMOCRATIC POLITICAL SYSTEM The Jacksonian era has been called the Age of the Common Man, but such democratic tendencies had distinct limits. Women and slaves were not allowed to vote, nor could free African Americans (except in a few states, primarily in the Northeast) and Indians. Nor did the parties always deal effectively with (or even address) basic problems in society. Still, Van Buren's insight was perceptive. Popular political parties provided an essential mechanism for peacefully resolving differences among competing interest groups, regions, and social classes.

✔ **REVIEW**

In what ways did the political culture of the 1820s and 1830s differ from that of the 1780s and 1790s?

JACKSON'S RISE TO POWER

THE NEW DEMOCRATIC STYLE OF politics first appeared on the state and local levels: Van Buren deftly working behind the scenes in New York; Amos Kendall of Kentucky campaigning in favor of debtor relief; Davy Crockett of Tennessee carefully dressed in frontier garb and offering voters a drink from a jug of whiskey and a chew from a large plug of tobacco. The national implications of these changes were not immediately clear.

John Quincy Adams's Presidency

When he assumed the presidency in 1825, John Quincy Adams might have worked to create a mass-based party. But Adams, a talented diplomat and a great secretary of

Oyster houses were the sports bars of antebellum America, and the preferred sport was politics. Newspapers expressed strong party loyalties, inspiring the man at the right to harangue his friend, who seems unpersuaded.

state, possessed hardly a political bone in his body. Cold and tactless, he could build no popular support for the ambitious and often farsighted programs he proposed. His plans for the federal government to promote not only manufacturing and agriculture but also the arts, literature, and science left his opponents aghast.

Nor would Adams take any steps to gain reelection, though he earnestly desired it. Despite urgent pleas from Henry Clay and other advisers, he declined to remove from federal office men who actively opposed him. Since Adams refused to be a party leader, Clay undertook to organize the National Republicans. But with a reluctant candidate at the top of the ticket, Clay labored under serious handicaps. The new style of politics came into its own nationally only when Andrew Jackson swept to power at the head of a new party, the Democrats.

JACKSON'S
ELECTION
Building a new party was a tricky business. Because Jackson's coalition was made up of conflicting interests, "Old Hickory" remained vague about his own position on many issues. Thus the campaign of 1828 soon degenerated into a series of personal attacks, splattering mud on all involved. Aided by enormous majorities in the South, Jackson won handily.

In one sense the significance of the election was clear. It marked the beginning of politics as Americans have practiced it ever since, with two disciplined national parties actively competing for votes, an emphasis on personalities over issues, and the resort to mass electioneering techniques. Yet in terms of public policy, the meaning of the election was anything but clear. The people had voted for Jackson as a national hero without any real sense of what he would do with his newly won power.

President of the People

Certainly the people looked for change. "I never saw such a crowd here before," Daniel Webster wrote as inauguration day approached. "Persons have come 500 miles to see General Jackson, and they really seem to think that the country is rescued from some dreadful danger!" Some 15,000 supporters cheered wildly after Jackson was sworn in.

At the White House reception, pandemonium reigned as thousands of ordinary citizens pushed inside to catch a glimpse of their idol. The new president had to flee after being nearly crushed to death by well-wishers. The crowd trampled on the furniture, broke glass, smashed mirrors, and ruined carpets and draperies. "It was a proud day for the people," boasted Amos Kendall, one of the new president's advisers. Supreme Court Justice Joseph Story was less thrilled: "I never saw such a mixture. The reign of King Mob seemed triumphant."

JACKSON'S
CHARACTER
Whether loved as a man of the people or hated as a demagogue leading the mob, Jackson was the representative of the new democracy. The first president from west of the Appalachians, he moved as a young lawyer to the Tennessee frontier. He had a quick mind but limited schooling and little use for learning; after his death a family friend acknowledged that the general had never believed that the Earth was round. A man of action, his decisiveness served him well as a soldier and also in the booming economy around Nashville, where he established himself as a large landowner and slaveholder. Tall and wiry, with flowing white hair, Jackson carried himself with a soldier's bearing. His troops had nicknamed him Old Hickory out of respect for his toughness, but that strength sometimes became arrogance, and he could be vindictive and a bully. He was not a man to provoke, as his reputation for dueling demonstrated.

For all these flaws, Jackson was a shrewd politician. He knew how to manipulate men and could be affable or abusive as the occasion demanded. He would sometimes burst into a rage to get his way with a hostile delegation, only to chuckle afterward, "They thought I was mad." He also displayed a keen sense of public opinion, skillfully reading the shifting national mood.

SPOILS SYSTEM
As the nation's chief executive, Jackson defended the **spoils system,** under which public offices were awarded to political supporters, as a democratic reform. Rotation in office, he declared, would guard against insensitive bureaucrats who presumed that they held their positions by right. The cabinet, he believed, existed more to carry out his will than to offer counsel, and

| "The Will of the People the Supreme Law" reads the banner at this county election. One of the few occasions when most of the men would assemble at the village, Election Day remained an all-male event as well as a time of excitement, heated debate, and boisterous celebration. As citizens give their oath to an election judge, diligent party workers dispense free drinks, solicit support, offer party tickets, and keep a careful tally of who has voted. Liquor and drinking are prominently featured: one elector enjoys another round, a prospective voter who is too drunk to stand is held up by a faithful party member, and on the right a groggy partisan sports a bandage as a result of a political brawl.

throughout his term he remained a strong executive who insisted on his way—and usually got it.

The Political Agenda in the Market Economy

Jackson took office at a time when the market economy was spreading through America and the nation's borders were expanding geographically. The three major problems his administration faced were directly caused by the resulting growing pains.

First, the demand for new lands put continuing pressure on Indians, whose valuable cornfields and hunting grounds could produce marketable commodities like cotton and wheat.

Second, as the economies of the North, South, and West became more specialized, their rival interests forced a confrontation over the tariff and whether South Carolina could nullify that federal law. And finally, the booming economy focused attention on the role of credit and banking in society and on the new

| Jackson's stubborn determination shows clearly in this portrait by Asher Durand, painted in 1835. "His passions are terrible," Jefferson noted. "When I was President of the Senate, he was Senator, and he could never speak on account of the rashness of his feelings. I have seen him attempt it repeatedly, and as often choke with rage. His passions are, no doubt, cooler now; he has been much tried since I knew him, but he is a dangerous man."

Democratic reforms of the 1820s and 1830s brought a new sort of politician to prominence, one whose life was devoted to party service and whose living often depended on public office. This cartoon from 1834 shows the downside of the new situation. Andrew Jackson sports the wings, horns, and tail of a devil as he dangles the rewards of various political offices above a clamoring group of eager job-seekers.

commercial attitudes that were a central part of the developing market economy. The president attacked all three issues in his characteristically combative style.

 **REVIEW**

What were the most pressing problems faced by President Andrew Jackson?

DEMOCRACY AND RACE

AS A PLANTER, JACKSON BENEFITED from the international demand for cotton that was drawing new lands into the market. He had gone off to the Tennessee frontier in 1788, a rowdy, ambitious young man who could afford to purchase only one slave. Caught up in the get-rich-quick mania of the frontier, he became a prominent land speculator, established himself as a planter, and by the time he became president owned nearly 100 slaves. His popularity derived not only from defeating the British but also from opening extensive tracts of valuable Indian lands to white settlement. Through military fighting and treaty negotiating, he was personally responsible for obtaining about a third of Tennessee for the United States, three-quarters of Florida and Alabama, a fifth of Georgia and Mississippi, and a tenth of Kentucky and North Carolina.

Even so, in 1820 an estimated 125,000 Indians remained east of the Mississippi River. In the Southwest the Choctaws, Creeks, Cherokees, Chickasaws, and Seminoles retained millions of acres of prime agricultural land in the heart of the cotton kingdom. Led by Georgia, southern states demanded that the federal government clear these titles. In response Monroe in 1824 proposed to Congress that the remaining eastern tribes be relocated west of the Mississippi River.

NEW ATTITUDES TOWARD RACE As white pressure for removal intensified, a shift in the attitude toward Indians and race increasingly occurred. Previously most whites had attributed cultural differences among whites, blacks, and Indians to the environment. After 1815 the dominant white culture stressed "innate" racial differences that could never be erased. A growing number of Americans began to argue that Indians were by nature inferior savages, obstacles to progress because they were incapable of adopting white ways.

Accommodate or Resist?

That argument placed Indians and other minorities in the Old Southwest in a difficult position. During the seventeenth and eighteenth centuries the region reflected a multiracial character, because Indians, Spanish, French, and Africans had all settled there. The intermixture of cultures could be seen in the garb of the Creek Indian chief William McIntosh, who adopted a style of dress that reflected both his Indian and white heritage. McIntosh's father was a Scot, his mother a Creek, his wife a Cherokee—and McIntosh himself had allied his people with Andrew Jackson's forces during the War of 1812. But not long after he signed a treaty for the cession of Creek lands in 1825, Creeks who believed that McIntosh had betrayed the tribe's interest murdered him. As southern whites increased their clamor for Indian removal, similar tensions among various tribal factions increased.

Among the Seminoles, mixed-bloods (those with white as well as Indian ancestry) took the lead in urging military resistance to any attempt to expel them. By contrast, mixed-bloods in the Cherokee Nation led by John Ross advocated a program of accommodation by adopting white ways to prevent removal. After a bitter struggle Ross prevailed, and in 1827 the Cherokees adopted a written constitution modeled after that of the United States. They also enacted the death penalty for any member who sold tribal lands to whites without consent of the governing general council. Developing their own alphabet, they published a bilingual newspaper, the *Cherokee Phoenix*. Similarly, the neighboring Creeks moved to centralize authority by strengthening the power of the governing council at the expense of local towns. They, too, made it illegal for individual chiefs to sell any more land to whites.

CHANGING NATURE OF CHEROKEE SOCIETY

The division between traditionalists and those favoring accommodation reflected the fact that Indians, too, had been drawn into a web of market relationships. As more Cherokee families began to sell their surplus crops, they ceased to share property communally as in the past. Cherokee society became more stratified and unequal, just as white society had, and economic elites dominated the tribal government. Women's traditional economic role was transformed as well, as men now took over farming operations, previously a female responsibility. As the cotton boom spread, some Cherokees became substantial planters who owned large numbers of black slaves and thousands of acres of cotton land. Largely of mixed ancestry, slaveholders were wealthier, had investments in other enterprises such as gristmills and ferries, raised crops for market, were more

| A southern belle whose father owned a cotton plantation? Perhaps, but this was a Chickasaw Indian girl. Her elegant hair and fashionable dress suggest the complexity of cultural relations in the Old Southwest, where some Indians had acculturated to white ways, owned plantations and even slaves. This young woman was among the thousands of Indians removed to territory west of the Mississippi during the first half of the nineteenth century.

likely to read English, and were the driving force behind acculturation.

As cotton cultivation expanded among the Cherokees, slavery became harsher and a primary means of determining status, just as in southern white society. The general council passed several laws forbidding intermarriage with African Americans and excluding African Americans and mulattoes from voting or holding office. Ironically, at the same time that white racial attitudes toward Indians were deteriorating, the Cherokees' racial attitudes toward blacks were also hardening, paralleling the increased racism among white Americans.

Trail of Tears

PRESSURE FOR INDIAN REMOVAL

As western land fever increased and racial attitudes sharpened, Jackson prodded Congress to provide funds for Indian removal. He watched sympathetically as the Georgia legislature overturned the Cherokee constitution, declared Cherokee laws null and void, and decreed that tribal members would be tried in state courts. In 1830 Congress finally passed a removal bill.

But the Cherokees brought suit in federal court against Georgia's actions. In 1832 in the case of *Worcester v. Georgia,* the Supreme Court sided with the Cherokees. Indian tribes had full authority over their lands, wrote Chief Justice John Marshall in the opinion. Thus Georgia had no right to extend its laws over Cherokee territory. Pronouncing Marshall's decision "stillborn," Jackson ignored the Court's edict and went ahead with plans for removal.

Although Jackson assured Indians that they could be removed only voluntarily, he paid no heed when state governments harassed tribes into surrendering lands. Under the threat of coercion, the Choctaws, Chickasaws, and Creeks reluctantly agreed to move to tracts in present-day Oklahoma. In the process, land-hungry schemers cheated tribal members out of as much as 90 percent of their land.

REMOVAL OF THE CHEROKEES

The Cherokees held out longest, but to no avail. To deal with more pliant leaders of the tribe, Georgia authorities kidnapped Chief John Ross, who led the resistance to relocation, and threw him into jail. Ross was finally released but not allowed to negotiate the treaty, which stipulated that the Cherokees leave their lands no later than 1838. When that time came, most refused to go. In response, President Martin Van Buren had the U.S. Army round up resistant members and force them, at bayonet point, to join the westward march. Of the 15,000 who traveled this Trail of Tears, approximately one-quarter died along the way of exposure, disease, and exhaustion, including Ross's wife. As for the western tracts awaiting the survivors, they were smaller and generally inferior to the rich lands that had been taken from the Cherokees.

MILITARY RESISTANCE   Some Indians chose resistance. In the Old Northwest a group of the Sauk and Fox led by Black Hawk recrossed the Mississippi into Illinois in 1832, only to be crushed by federal troops and the militia. More successful was the military resistance of a minority of Seminoles led by Osceola. Despite his death, they held out until 1842 in the Florida Everglades before being subdued and removed. In the end only a small number of southern tribe members were able to escape removal.

In his Farewell Address in 1837 Jackson defended his policy by piously asserting that the eastern tribes had been finally "placed beyond the reach of injury or oppression, and that [the] paternal care of the General Government will hereafter watch over them and protect them." But Indians knew the bitter truth of the matter. Without effective political power, they found themselves at the mercy of the pressures of the marketplace and the hardening racial attitudes of white Americans.

 ## Removal and Epidemics in the West

As the Indian nations east of the Mississippi battled racism and removal, disease stalked those in the West. Smallpox, measles, cholera, and influenza followed in the wake of white traders and settlers, triggering at least 27 epidemics—more recorded than in any preceding century of contact—among Indians living west of the Mississippi. One such scourge came on the heels of removal in 1837, when an American Fur Company steamer unwittingly carried smallpox to trading posts along the upper Missouri. It spread like wildfire across the Great Plains, and within a year the epidemic had leapt the Rockies and headed south

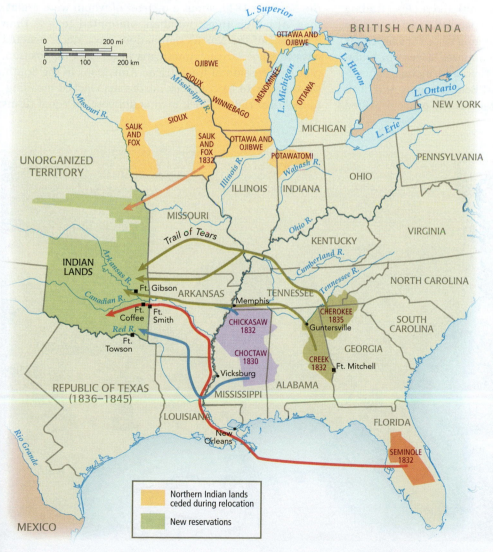

INDIAN REMOVAL

During Jackson's presidency, the federal government concluded nearly 70 treaties with Indian tribes, in the Old Northwest as well as in the South. Under their terms, the United States acquired approximately 100 million acres of Indian land. **Which Indian nation was the latest to be removed to western lands? Why?**

to Texas. All told, 50–95 percent of those infected lost their lives, shattering families, disrupting native economies, and demoralizing cultures during the same years that eastern nations were being forced into the West. Indeed, the massive forced migration of eastern Indians had profound consequences for plains peoples, who suddenly faced increased competition for resources and often came to blows with Cheyennes, Creeks, Chickasaws, Choctaws, and other formable newcomers.

The region's challenges and misfortunes did not affect native peoples equally. Some found their communities all but destroyed. Around 2,000 sedentary Mandans lived on the upper Missouri when smallpox arrived in 1837; before year's end fewer than 150 remained alive. Other agriculturalists such as the Wichitas, Omahas, and Pawnees endured their bouts with disease but increasingly found themselves hemmed in and weakened by immigrating peoples from the east and by the expansionist Sioux.

Still others reacted to the threats of the 1830s through creative diplomacy. Most important, in the summer of 1840 the Comanches and Kiowas of the southern plains and the Southern Cheyennes and Arapahoes of the central plains laid aside a long-standing and bloody feud and made peace. The "Great Peace" initiated a close trading relationship and allowed all four peoples to safely pursue economic opportunities in a changing West. For Cheyennes and Arapahos this meant unhampered access to buffalo-rich territory in present-day Colorado, increasingly important as they sold hides at Fort Bent to supply American markets. For Comanches and Kiowas the peace provided the security necessary for their men to embark on long-distance raiding expeditions deep into Mexico, expeditions at once dangerous and profitable. Despite a series of calamities, then, Indian peoples continued to be the masters of western North America well into the second half of the nineteenth century.

Free Blacks in the North

Unlike Indian removal, the rising discrimination against free African Americans during this period did not depend directly on presidential action. Still, it was Jackson's Democratic Party, which was in the vanguard of promoting white equality, that was also the most strongly proslavery and the most hostile to black rights. The intensifying racism that accompanied the emergence of democracy in American life bore down with particular force on free African Americans. "The policy and power of the national and state governments are against them," commented one northerner. "The popular feeling is against them—the interests of our citizens are against them."

DISCRIMINATION   Before the Civil War the free black population remained small: only about 171,000 in the North in 1840, about a quarter of whom were mulattoes. Although those numbers amounted to less than 2 percent of the North's population, most states enacted laws to keep African Americans in an inferior position. (For a discussion of free African Americans in the South, see Chapter 13.) Most black northerners lacked meaningful political rights. Black men could vote on equal terms

Around 1880 a Southern Cheyenne named Howling Wolf sketched this scene recalling the "Great Peace" of 1840. It shows the Cheyennes receiving a gift of horses from the Kiowas. The peace allowed the plains nations, buffeted by epidemic disease and the arrival of Indian nations from east of the Mississippi, to continue to dominate western North America.

with whites in only five New England states. New York imposed a property requirement only on black voters, which disenfranchised the vast majority. In New Jersey, Pennsylvania, and Connecticut, African American men lost the right to vote after having previously enjoyed that privilege.

Black northerners also lacked the basic civil rights that whites enjoyed. Five states prohibited them from testifying against whites, and either law or custom excluded African Americans from juries everywhere except Massachusetts. In addition, several western states passed black exclusion laws prohibiting free African Americans from immigrating into the state. Though seldom enforced, these laws allowed for harassing the African American population in times of social stress.

The free states also practiced segregation, or the physical separation of the races. African Americans sat in separate sections on public transportation. They could not go into most hotels and restaurants, and, if permitted to enter theaters and lecture halls, they squeezed into the corners and balconies. White churches assigned blacks separate pews and arranged for them to take communion after white members. Virtually every community excluded black children from the public schools or forced them to attend overcrowded and poorly funded separate schools. One English visitor commented that "we see, in effect, two nations—one white and another black—growing up together . . . but never mingling on a principle of equality."

BLACK POVERTY Discrimination pushed African American males into the lowest-paying and most unskilled jobs: servants, sailors, waiters, and common laborers. In Philadelphia in 1838, 80 percent of employed black males were unskilled laborers, and three of five black families had less than $60 total wealth. African American women normally continued working after marriage, mostly as servants, cooks, laundresses, and seamstresses, because their wages were critical to the family's economic survival. Blacks were willing strikebreakers, because white workers, fearing economic competition and loss of status, were overtly hostile and excluded them from trade unions. A number of antiblack riots erupted in northern cities during these years. Driven into abject poverty, free blacks in the North suffered from an inadequate diet, were more susceptible to disease, and in 1850 had a life expectancy 8 to 10 years less than that of whites.

THE SPREAD OF WHITE MANHOOD SUFFRAGE

White manhood suffrage became the norm during the Jacksonian era, but in a number of states free black males who had been voting by law or by custom lost the right to vote. After 1821 a $250 property requirement disenfranchised about 90 percent of adult black males in New York. **What prompted the disenfranchisement of free blacks?**

White Male Suffrage (No Property Qualification)

- Before 1800
- 1800 to 1830
- 1830 to 1860
- Concentration of free blacks (approximately 2,000 or more per county)
- Free black male vote in 1789 or when admitted to the Union
- Free black male vote in 1860
- 1810 Date of the abolition of taxpaying qualification. States without a date adopted white male suffrage when admitted to the Union.

AFRICAN COLONIZATION: HOPING FOR THE BEST AND SUSPECTING THE WORST

Henry Clay owned 50 slaves who worked his Kentucky plantation, but he was a lifelong advocate of gradual emancipation and a founder of the American Colonization Society in 1816. He explained his support in 1827. David Walker, a militant leader of the northern free black community, singled out Clay and other colonizationists for sharp criticism.

DOCUMENT 1 In Favor of Colonization: Henry Clay

Numbers of the free African race among us are willing to go to Africa. . . . Why should they not go! Here they are in the lowest state of social gradation; aliens—political, moral, social aliens—strangers though natives. There they would be in the midst of their friends, and their kindred, at home, though born in a foreign land, and elevated above the natives of the country, as much as they are degraded here below the other classes of the community. . . .

What is the true nature of the evil of the existence of a portion of the African race in our population? It is not that there are some, but that there are so many among us of a different caste, of a different physical, if not moral, constitution, who never can amalgate with the great body of our population. Here . . .

the African part of our population bears so large a proportion to the residue, of European origin, as to create the most lively apprehension, especially in some quarters of the Union. Any project, therefore, by which, in a material degree, the dangerous element in the general mass can be diminished or rendered stationary, deserves deliberate consideration.

The Colonization Society has never imagined it to be practicable . . . to transport the whole of the African race within the limits of the United States. Nor is that necessary to accomplish the desirable objects of domestic tranquility, and render us one homogeneous people. Let us suppose . . . that the whole population at present of the United States, is twelve millions of which ten may be estimated of the Anglo-Saxon and two of the

African race. If there could be annually transported from the United States an amount of the African portion equal to the annual increase of the whole of that caste, while the European race should be left to multiply, we should find at the termination of the period . . . that the relative proportion would be as twenty to two. And if the process were continued, during the second term of duplication, the proportion would be forty to two—one which would eradicate every cause of alarm or solicitude from the breasts of the most timid.

Source: Henry Clay, Speech at the Annual Meeting of the American Colonization Society, Washington, January 30, 1827, in The Works of Henry Clay, *ed. Calvin Colton (New York, 1904).*

DOCUMENT 2 Against Colonization: David Walker

Here is demonstrative proof, of a plan got up, by a gang of slaveholders to select the free people of colour from among the slaves, that our more miserable brethren may be the better secured in ignorance and wretchedness, to work their farms and dig their mines, and thus go on enriching the Christians with their blood and groans. What our brethren could have been thinking about, who have left their native land and home and gone away to Africa, I am unable to say. This country is as much ours as it is the whites, whether they will admit it or not they will see and believe it by and by. They tell us about prejudice—what have we to do with it? Their prejudices will be obliged to fall like lightning to the ground, in succeeding generations; not, however, with the will and consent of all the whites, for some will be obliged to hold on to the old adage, viz: the blacks are not men, but were made to be an inheritance to us and our children for ever!!!!!! I hope the residue of the coloured people, will stand still and see the salvation of God and the miracle which he will work for our delivery from wretchedness under the Christians!!!!!! . . .

I shall give an extract from the letter of that truly Reverend Divine, (Bishop [Richard] Allen) of Philadelphia, respecting this trick . . . he says, "Dear Sir, I have been for several years trying to reconcile my mind to the Colonizing of Africans in Liberia, but there have always been and there still remain great and insurmountable objections against the scheme. . . . Can we not discern the project of sending the free people of colour away from their country? Is it not for the interest of the slaveholders to select the free people of colour out of the different states, and send them to Liberia? Will it not make their slaves uneasy to see free men of colour enjoying liberty? It is against the law in some of the Southern States, that a person of colour should receive an education, under a severe penalty. . . . See the thousands of foreigners emigrating to America every year: and if there be ground sufficient for them to cultivate, and bread for them to eat, why would they wish to send the *first tillers* of the land away? Africans have made fortunes for thousands, who are yet unwilling to part with their services; but the free must be sent

away, and those who remain must be *slaves*. I have no doubt that there are many good men who do not see as I do, and who are for sending us to Liberia; but they have not duly considered the subject—they are not men of colour. This land which we have watered with our *tears* and *our blood* is now our *mother country*, and we are well satisfied to stay where wisdom abounds and the gospel is free."

Source: David Walker, Appeal to the Coloured Citizens of the World *(1829).*

Thinking Critically

What were Henry Clay's concerns about free African Americans? Why did he regard colonization as a viable solution to the problems he believed African Americans posed to the United States? What did David Walker and Richard Allen believe to be the true intentions of the colonizationists? Do you believe that they accurately assessed those motives?

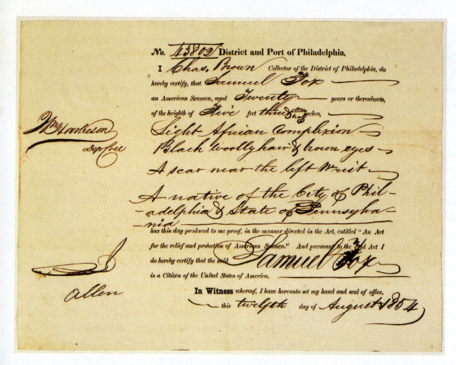

A Protection Certificate for Samuel Fox, a free black sailor

The African American Community

AFRICAN COLONIZATION

Free blacks had long suffered from such oppression and injustice. Between the Revolution and the War of 1812 they had responded by founding schools, churches, and mutual-aid societies to sustain their communities. Some, such as Paul Cuffe, sought to escape white prejudice entirely by establishing settlements of free blacks in West Africa. The Quaker son of a West African father and a Wampanoag Indian mother, Cuffe became a sea captain, and in 1816 his merchant ship brought 38 free black New Englanders to settle in West Africa. Cuffe's venture drew white sympathizers who formed the American Colonization Society (ACS) and

founded Liberia in West Africa in 1821–1822. Several state legislatures in the North and the Upper South as well as all the major Protestant churches endorsed ACS plans to encourage free black emigration, but its members were an unlikely and unstable coalition. Some opposed slavery and hoped that colonization would encourage manumissions and gradual emancipation, while others believed that ridding the nation of free blacks would make it easier for slavery to flourish.

RISE OF BLACK MILITANCY

Even as white support for colonization swelled during the 1820s, black enthusiasm for emigration diminished. Many African American leaders in the North were turning to more confrontational tactics: they advocated resistance to slavery and condemned racism and inequality. Among the most outspoken of this new, more militant generation was David Walker, whose *Appeal to the Colored Citizens of the World* (1829) denounced colonization and urged slaves to use violence to end bondage.

Racism Strikes a Deeper Root

What prompted greater militancy among African Americans after 1820s was also the growth of an increasingly virulent racism among whites. Ironically, the success of efforts to promote education, religious piety, and temperance within the free black community threatened many lower-class whites and intensified their resentment of African Americans. That animosity found vent in race riots, which erupted in Pittsburgh, Boston, Cincinnati, and New Haven.

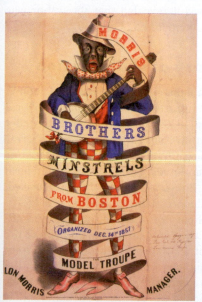

Minstrel sheet music (left) illustrates the racist attitudes that pervaded Jacksonian democracy. Blacks, played by whites, were made to appear ridiculous through grotesque physical features, exaggerated poses, and pretentious airs. In contrast, the confident expression of this African American (right), who had this daguerreotype taken around 1856, evinces the dignity free blacks maintained in the face of unrelenting hostility and discrimination.

APPEAL OF MINSTRELSY The racist attitudes of the day were very much reflected in popular culture, nowhere more than in minstrel shows, the most popular form of entertainment in Jacksonian America. Originating in the 1830s and 1840s, minstrel shows featured white actors performing in blackface. Although popular throughout the country, minstrelsy's primary audience was in northern cities. Its basic message was that African Americans could not cope with freedom and therefore did not belong in the North. Enslaved African Americans were portrayed as happy and contented, whereas free black Americans were caricatured either as strutting dandies or as helpless ignoramuses. Drawing its patrons from workers, Irish immigrants, and the poorer elements in society, minstrelsy assured these white champions of democracy that they remained superior.

DEEPENING RACISM The unsettling economic, social, and political changes of the Jacksonian era heightened white Americans' fear of failure, which stimulated racism. The popular yet unrealistic expectation was that any white man might become rich. Yet in fact, 20 percent or more of white adult males of this era never accumulated any property. Their lack of success encouraged them to relieve personal tensions through increased hostility to their black neighbors. Subjecting black Americans to legal disabilities ensured that even the poorest whites would enjoy an advantage in the race for wealth and status. "The prejudice of race appears to be stronger in the states that have abolished slavery than in those where it still exists," Tocqueville noted. The power of racism in Jacksonian America stemmed, at least in part, from the fact that equality remained part of the nation's creed while it steadily receded as a social reality.

REVIEW

In what ways did Indians and free African Americans attempt to protect their communities in Jacksonian America?

THE NULLIFICATION CRISIS

REMOVAL AND RACISM PROVIDED ONE answer to the question of who would be given equality of opportunity in America's new democracy. Indians and African Americans would not. The issue of nullification raised a different, equally pressing question. As the market revolution propelled the economies of the North, South, and West toward increased specialization, how would various regions or interest groups accommodate their differences?

The Growing Crisis in South Carolina

The depression of 1819 struck hard at South Carolina. And even when prosperity returned to the rest of the nation, many of the state's cotton planters still suffered. With lands exhausted from years of cultivation, they could not compete with the fabulous yields of frontier planters in Alabama and Mississippi.

Increasingly, South Carolinians viewed federal tariffs as the cause of their miseries. When Congress raised the duty rates in 1824, they assailed the tariff as an unfair tax that raised the prices of goods they imported while benefiting other regions of the nation. Other southern states opposed the 1824 tariff as well, though none so vehemently as South Carolina.

DENMARK VESEY ACCUSED The one state in which black inhabitants outnumbered whites, South Carolina had been growing more sensitive about the institution of slavery. In Charleston white anxieties fixed on Denmark Vesey, a literate, well-traveled, free black carpenter. On the flimsiest evidence, much of it extracted by torture, whites accused Vesey and slaves from neighboring plantations of plotting to seize and then burn down the city. Although the accused denied the charges, authorities hanged Vesey and 34 other black men and banished 37 others from the state.

But white South Carolinians worried that other undetected conspirators lurked in their midst. As an additional measure of security, the state's leaders pushed for stronger constitutional protection of slavery. After all, supporters of high tariffs had already claimed that the "implied powers" of the Constitution gave them the right to promote manufacturing. What was to stop this same broad interpretation from being used to end slavery? "In contending against the tariff, I have always felt that we were combatting against the symptom instead of the disease," argued Chancellor William Harper of South Carolina. "Tomorrow may witness [an attempt] to relieve . . . your slaves."

When Congress raised the duty rates still higher in 1828 with the so-called Tariff of Abominations, South Carolina's legislature published the *South Carolina Exposition and Protest*, which outlined for the first time the theory of nullification. Only later was it revealed that its author was Jackson's own vice president, John C. Calhoun.

Calhoun's Theory of Nullification

Educated at Yale and at a distinguished law school, John C. Calhoun was the most impressive intellect of his political generation. During the 1820s the South Carolina leader made a steady journey away from nationalism toward an extreme states' rights position. When he was elected Jackson's vice president, South Carolinians assumed that tariff reform would soon be enacted. But Jackson and Calhoun quarreled, and Calhoun lost all influence in the administration.

MINORITY RIGHTS VS. MAJORITY RULE In his theory of nullification Calhoun addressed the problem of how to protect the rights of a minority in a political system based on the rule of the majority. The Union, he argued, was a compact among sovereign states. Thus the people of each state, acting in special popular conventions, had the right to nullify any federal law that exceeded the powers granted to Congress under the Constitution. The law would then become null and void in that state. In response, Congress could either repeal the law or propose a constitutional amendment expressly giving it the power in question. If the amendment was ratified, the nullifying state could either accept the decision or exercise its ultimate right as a sovereign state and secede from the Union.

NATIONALISTS' THEORY — When Senator Robert Hayne of South Carolina outlined Calhoun's theory in the Senate in 1830, Senator Daniel Webster of Massachusetts replied sharply that the Union was not a compact of sovereign states. The people and not the states, he argued, had created the Constitution. "It is the people's constitution, the people's government, made for the people, made by the people, and answerable to the people." Webster also insisted that the federal government did not merely act as the agent of the states but had sovereign powers in those areas in which it had been delegated responsibility. Finally, Webster endorsed the doctrine of judicial review, which gave the Supreme Court authority to determine the meaning of the Constitution.

The Nullifiers Nullified

When Congress passed another tariff in 1832 that failed to give the state any relief, South Carolina's legislature called for the election of delegates to a popular convention, which overwhelmingly adopted an ordinance in November that declared the tariffs of 1828 and 1832 "null, void, and no law, nor binding upon this state, its officers or citizens" after February 1, 1833.

IDEA OF A PERPETUAL UNION — Jackson, who had spent much of his life defending the nation, was not about to tolerate any defiance of his authority or the federal government's. In his Proclamation on Nullification, issued in December 1832, he insisted that the Union was perpetual. Under the Constitution, there was no right of secession. To reinforce Jackson's announced determination to enforce the tariff laws, Congress passed the Force Bill, reaffirming the president's military powers.

COMPROMISE OF 1833 — Yet Jackson was also a skillful politician. At the same time that he threatened South Carolina, he urged Congress to reduce the tariff rates. With no other state willing to follow South Carolina's lead, Calhoun reluctantly agreed to a compromise tariff, which Jackson signed on March 1, 1833, the same day he signed the Force Bill. South Carolina's convention repealed the nullifying ordinance, and the crisis passed.

Calhoun's doctrine had proved too radical for the rest of the South. Yet the controversy convinced many southerners that they were becoming a permanent minority. "It is useless and impracticable to disguise the fact," concluded nullifier William Harper, "that we are divided into slave-holding and non-slaveholding states, and this is the broad and marked distinction that must separate us at

As Daniel Webster outlines his nationalist theory of the Constitution and the Union, Senator Robert Hayne of South Carolina sits (front, left) with his hands together. Most of the seats in the Senate gallery are occupied by women, evidence of the widespread interest in politics.

last." As that feeling of isolation grew, it was not nullification but the threat of secession that ultimately became the South's primary weapon.

✅ **REVIEW**
What were the issues being contested in the debate over nullification?

THE BANK WAR

JACKSON UNDERSTOOD WELL THE POLITICAL ties that bound the nation. He grasped much less firmly the economic and financial connections that linked different regions of the country through banks and national markets. In particular the president was suspicious of the national bank and the power it possessed. His clash with the Second Bank of the United States brought on the greatest crisis of his presidency.

The National Bank and the Panic of 1819

MONSTER BANK — Chartered by Congress in 1816 for a 20-year period, the Second Bank of the United States at first suffered from woeful mismanagement. During the frenzy of speculation between 1816 and 1818, it recklessly overexpanded its operations. Then it turned about-face and sharply contracted credit by calling in loans when the depression hit in 1819. Senator Thomas Hart Benton of Missouri charged that the national bank foreclosed on so much property that it owned entire towns. To many Americans the Bank had already become a monster.

The psychological effects of the Panic of 1819 were almost as momentous as the economic. To many uneasy farmers and workers the hard times seemed like punishment for losing sight of the old virtues of simplicity, frugality, and hard work. For them banks became a symbol of the commercialization of American society and the passing of a simpler way of life.

Biddle's Bank

FUNCTION AS A CENTRAL BANK In 1823 Nicholas Biddle, a rich 37-year-old Philadelphia businessman, became president of the national bank. Biddle was intelligent and thoroughly familiar with the banking system, but he was also impossibly arrogant. Seeking to restore the Bank's reputation, he set out to provide the nation with a sound currency by regulating the amount of credit available in the economy.

Government revenues were paid largely in banknotes (paper money) issued by state-chartered banks. Because the Treasury Department regularly deposited U.S. funds in the national bank, the notes of state banks from all across the Union came into its possession. If Biddle believed that a state bank was overextended and had issued more notes than was safe, he presented them to that bank and demanded they be redeemed in **specie** (gold or silver). Because banks did not have enough specie reserves to back all the paper money they issued, the only way a state bank could continue to redeem its notes was to call in its loans and reduce the amount of its notes in circulation. This action had the effect of lessening the amount of credit in the economy.

But if Biddle felt that a bank's credit policies were reasonable, he simply returned the state banknotes to circulation without presenting them for redemption. Being the government's official depository gave Biddle's bank enormous power over state banks and over the economy. Under Biddle's direction the Bank became a financial colossus: it had 29 branches and made 20 percent of the country's loans, issued one-fifth of the total banknotes, and held fully a third of all deposits and specie. Yet for the most part, Biddle used the Bank's enormous power responsibly to provide the United States a sound paper currency, which the expanding economy needed.

OPPOSITION TO PAPER Although the Bank had strong support in the business community, workers complained that they were often paid in **depreciated** state banknotes. Such notes could be redeemed for only a portion of their face value, a practice that in effect cheated workers out of part of their wages. Those workers called for a "hard money" currency of only gold and silver. Hard-money advocates viewed bankers and financiers as profiteers who manipulated the paper money system to enrich themselves at the expense of honest, hardworking farmers and laborers.

The Clash between Jackson and Biddle

Jackson's own experiences left him with a deep distrust of banks and paper money. In 1804 his Tennessee land speculations had brought him to the brink of bankruptcy, from which it took years of painful struggle to free himself. Reflecting on his personal situation, he became convinced that banks and paper money threatened to corrupt the Republic.

As president, Jackson called for reform of the banking system from time to time, but Biddle refused even to consider curbing the Bank's powers. Already distracted by the nullification controversy, Jackson warned Biddle not to inject the bank issue into the 1832 campaign. When Biddle went ahead and applied for a renewal of the Bank's charter in 1832, four years early, Jackson was furious. "The Bank is trying to kill me," he stormed to Van Buren, "but I will kill it."

JACKSON'S VETO Despite the president's opposition, Congress passed a recharter bill in the summer of 1832. Immediately Jackson vetoed it as unconstitutional, rejecting Chief Justice Marshall's ruling in *McCulloch v. Maryland* (1819) that Congress had the right to establish the Bank. Condemning the Bank as an agent of special privilege, the president pledged to protect "the humble members of society—the farmer, mechanics, and laborers." The message completely ignored the Bank's vital services in the economy.

The Bank Destroyed

When Congress failed to override Jackson's veto, the recharter of the Bank became a central issue of the 1832 campaign. Jackson's opponent was Henry Clay, a National Republican who eagerly accepted the financial support of Biddle and the national bank. Clay went down to defeat, and once reelected, Jackson was determined to destroy the Bank. A private corporation should not possess the power to influence government policy and the economy, he believed. And he was justly incensed over the Bank's heavy-handed attempt to influence the election.

REMOVAL OF THE DEPOSITS To cripple the Bank, the president simply ordered all the government's federal deposits withdrawn. Because such an act clearly violated federal law, Jackson was forced to transfer one secretary of the treasury and fire another before he finally found in Roger Taney someone willing to take the job and carry out the edict. Taney (pronounced "Taw-ney") began drawing against the government's funds to pay its debts while depositing new revenues in selected state banks.

Biddle fought back by deliberately precipitating a brief financial panic in 1833. "Go to Biddle," Jackson snapped to businesspeople seeking relief. "I never will restore the deposits. I never will recharter the United States Bank, or sign a charter for any other bank." Eventually Biddle had to relent, and Jackson's victory was complete. When the Bank's charter expired in 1836, no national banking system

HISTORIAN'S TOOLBOX

BIDDLE AND JACKSON TAKE THE GLOVES OFF

Photographs of these two allies of Biddle can be found in Chapter 14, when they are much older. Who are they?

Can you identify this future president? What does he mean, "hit him in the breadbasket, it will make him throw up his deposits"?

This frontiersman bears the name of "Joe Tammany." The members of the original Tammany Society of New York rejected the aristocratic philosophy of the Federalist Party.

The caption where this cartoon originally appeared refers to this woman as "Mother Bank."

Port

"Old Monongahela Whiskey"

By their nature cartoons deal in visual symbols; to be accessible to their readers, the symbols cannot be subtle. For present-day viewers, however, some decoding is needed; and historians draw on their knowledge of the period to make sense of the symbols. This 1834 cartoon pits President Andrew Jackson (in black tights) against Nicholas Biddle in a bare-knuckled boxing match. Both the woman holding the bottle of port and the frontiersman (a cat on his hat, no less!) look ridiculous. But the cartoon definitely favors one of the fighters. Can you suggest several details that are tip-offs to the artist's point of view?

Thinking Critically

One key detail revolves around what the supporters are drinking. Why would it matter whether one drank port or whiskey? (For a suggestion, see the Daily Lives feature, Chapter 8.) Why draw Jackson facing the audience and Biddle with his back to us? What are the larger cultural values at the center of the cartoon's message?

replaced it. Instead, Jackson continued depositing federal revenues in selected state banks. Democrats controlled a large majority of these "pet banks."

Jackson's Impact on the Presidency

STRENGTHENING
OF PRESIDENTIAL
POWERS

Jackson approached the end of his administration in triumph. He had seen Indian removal nearly to completion; he had confounded the nullifiers; and he had destroyed "Monster Bank." In the process, Jackson immeasurably enlarged the power of the presidency. "The President is the direct representative of the American people," he lectured the Senate when it opposed him. "He was elected by the people, and is responsible to them." With this declaration, Jackson redefined the character of the presidential office and its relationship to the people.

Jackson also converted the veto into an effective presidential power. During his two terms in office he vetoed 12 bills, compared with only 9 for all previous presidents combined. And whereas his predecessors had vetoed bills only on strict constitutional grounds, Jackson felt free to block laws simply because he thought them bad policy. The threat of such action became an effective way to shape legislation to his liking, which fundamentally strengthened the power of the president over Congress. The development of the modern presidency began with Andrew Jackson.

"Van Ruin's" Depression

With the controls of the national bank removed, state banks rapidly expanded the amount of paper money in circulation. The total value of banknotes jumped from $82 million in January 1835 to $120 million in December 1836. As the currency expanded, so did the number of banks: from 329 in 1829 to 788 in 1837. A spiraling **inflation** set in as prices rose 50 percent after 1830 and interest rates by half as much.

SPECIE
CIRCULAR

As prices rose sharply, so did speculative fever. By 1836 land sales, which had been only $2.6 million four years earlier, approached $25 million. Buyers purchased almost all these lands entirely on credit with banknotes, many of which had little value. Settlers seeking land poured into the Southwest, and as one observer wryly commented, "under this stimulating process prices rose like smoke." In an attempt to slow the economy, Jackson issued the Specie Circular in July 1836, which decreed that the government would

| This Whig cartoon blames the Democratic Party for the depression that began during Van Buren's administration. Barefoot workers go unemployed, and women and children beg and sleep in the streets. Depositors clamor for their money from a bank that has suspended specie payments, while the pawnbroker and liquor store do a thriving business and the sheriff rounds up debtors.

accept only specie for the purchase of public land. Land sales drastically declined, but the speculative pressures in the economy were already too great.

WHIG PARTY — During Jackson's second term, his opponents had come together in a new party, the Whigs. Led by Henry Clay they charged that "King Andrew I" had dangerously concentrated power in the presidency. The Whigs also embraced Clay's "American System," designed to spur national economic development, particularly manufacturing. To do this the Whigs advocated a protective tariff, a national bank, and federal aid for internal improvements. In 1836 the Democrats nominated Martin Van Buren, who triumphed over three Whig sectional candidates.

DEPRESSION — Van Buren had less than two months in office to savor his triumph before the speculative mania collapsed, and with it the economy. After a brief recovery the bottom fell out of the international cotton market in 1839, and the country entered a serious depression. Arising from causes that were worldwide, the depression demonstrated how deeply the market economy had penetrated American society. Thousands of workers were unemployed, and countless businesses failed. Nationally wages fell 30 to 50 percent. "Business of all kinds is completely at a stand," wrote one business leader in 1840, "and the whole body politic sick and infirm, and calling aloud for a remedy."

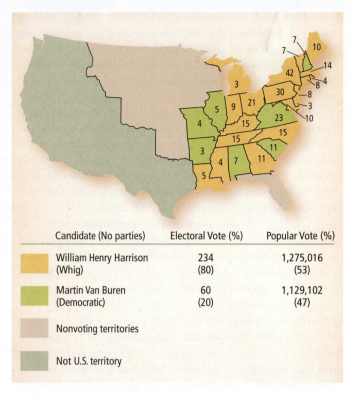

Candidate (No parties)	Electoral Vote (%)	Popular Vote (%)
William Henry Harrison (Whig)	234 (80)	1,275,016 (53)
Martin Van Buren (Democratic)	60 (20)	1,129,102 (47)
Nonvoting territories		
Not U.S. territory		

ELECTION OF 1840

The Whigs' Triumph

FIRST MODERN PRESIDENTIAL CAMPAIGN — With the nation stuck in the worst depression of the century, the Whigs approached the election of 1840 in high spirits. To oppose Van Buren, they turned to William Henry Harrison, the military leader who had won fame defeating the Shawnee Indians at Tippecanoe. Using the democratic electioneering techniques that Jackson's supporters had first perfected, they portrayed Harrison as a man of the people while painting Van Buren as an aristocrat who wore a corset, ate off gold plates with silver spoons, and used cologne. Shades of Franklin Plummer!

Whig rallies featured hard cider and log cabins to reinforce Harrison's image as a man of the people. Born into one of Virginia's most aristocratic families, he lived in a 16-room mansion in Ohio. But the Whig campaign, by portraying the election as a contest between aristocracy and democracy, was perfectly attuned to the prevailing national spirit.

WOMEN AND THE CAMPAIGN — Both parties used parades, barbecues, liberty pole raisings, party songs, and mass meetings to stir up enthusiasm. Deeming themselves the party of morality, Whigs appealed directly to women for support, urging them to become politically informed in order to instruct their husbands. Women attended Whig rallies, conducted meetings, made speeches, and wrote campaign pamphlets, many activities that before had been solely the duties of men. Democrats had no choice but to eventually follow suit.

Just as the Panic of 1819 had roused the voters to action, the depression and the two parties' response to it sparked mass interest. The result was a record turnout, as some 900,000 new voters were mobilized between 1836 and 1840 and nearly four-fifths of the eligible voters went to the polls. Although the popular vote was fairly close (Harrison led by about 150,000 votes out of 2.4 million cast), in the Electoral College Harrison won an easy victory, 234 to 60.

The "log cabin" campaign marked the final transition from the deferential politics of the Federalist era to the egalitarian politics that had emerged in the wake of the Panic of 1819. As the *Democratic Review* conceded after the Whigs' victory in 1840, "We have taught them how to conquer us."

 REVIEW

Why did Jackson oppose the Second Bank of the United States?

THE JACKSONIAN PARTY SYSTEM

THE SOCIAL AND ECONOMIC STRAINS of an expanding nation directly shaped the new political system. Whigs and Democrats held different attitudes toward the changes brought about by the market, banks, and commerce.

Democrats, Whigs, and the Market

DEMOCRATIC IDEOLOGY — The Democrats tended to view society as a continuing conflict between "the people"— farmers, planters, and workers—and a set of greedy aristocrats. The last group was not Europe's landed aristocrats, of course, but a "paper money aristoc- racy" of bankers and investors, who manipulated the banking system for profit. For Democrats, the Bank War became a battle to restore the old Jeffersonian republic with its values of simplicity, frugality, hard work, and independence.

Jackson understood the dangers that private banks posed to a democratic society. Yet Democrats, in effect, wanted the rewards of the market without sacrificing the features of a simple agrarian republic. They wanted the wealth and goods that the market offered without the competitive, changing society, the complex dealings, the dominance of urban cen- ters, and the loss of independence that came with it.

WHIG IDEOLOGY Whigs were more comfortable with the market. They envisioned no conflict between farmers and mechanics on the one hand and businesspeo- ple and bankers on the other. Economic growth would benefit everyone by creating jobs, stimulating demand for agricultural products, and expanding opportunity. The government's responsibility was to provide a well-regulated economy that guaranteed opportunity for citizens of ability. In such an economy, banks and corporations were not only useful but necessary. Whigs and Democrats also disagreed over how active government should be. Despite Andrew Jackson's inclination to be a strong president, Democrats as a rule believed in limited government. Gov- ernment's role in the economy was to promote competi- tion by destroying monopolies and special privileges.

In *Charles River Bridge v. Warren Bridge* (1837) the Supreme Court strengthened the vision of an expanding capitalistic society undergirded by free competition. At is- sue was whether in authorizing construction of a free bridge Massachusetts violated the rights of the owners of a nearby toll bridge. Declaring that the public interest was the overriding concern, Chief Justice Roger Taney, whom Jackson had appointed to succeed John Marshall, struck down the idea of implied monopolies. The Court thus sought to promote equality of opportunity and economic progress.

In keeping with this philosophy of limited government, Democrats also rejected the idea that moral beliefs were the proper sphere of govern- ment action. Religion and politics, they be- lieved, should be kept clearly separate, and they generally opposed humani- tarian legislation as an interference with personal freedom. But they supported debtor relief, which in their view curbed the wealthy aris- tocrats who tyrannized the com- mon worker.

WHIG BELIEF IN ACTIVE GOVERNMENT By contrast, the Whigs viewed government power positively. They believed that it should be used to protect indi- vidual rights and public liberty

and that it had a special role when individual effort was ineffective. By regulating the economy and competition, the government could ensure equal opportunity. Indeed, for Whigs the concept that the government would promote the general welfare went beyond the economy. Northern Whigs in particular also believed that government power should be used to foster the moral welfare of the country. They were much more likely to favor temperance or anti- slavery legislation and aid to education. Whigs portrayed themselves not only as the party of prosperity but also as the party of respectability and proper behavior.

The Social Bases of the Two Parties

In some ways the social makeup of the two parties was sim- ilar. To be competitive Whigs and Democrats both had to have significant support among farmers, the largest group in society, and workers. Neither party could carry an elec- tion by appealing exclusively to the rich or the poor.

ATTITUDES TOWARD THE MARKET ECONOMY But the Whigs enjoyed disproportionate strength among the business and commer- cial classes, especially following the Bank War. Whigs appealed to planters who needed credit to finance their cotton and rice trade in the world market, to farmers who were eager to sell their surpluses, and to workers who wished to improve their so- cial position. Democrats attracted farmers isolated from the market or uncomfortable with it, workers alienated from the emerging industrial system, and rising entrepreneurs who wanted to break monopolies and open the economy to newcomers like them. The Whigs were strongest in the towns, cities, and rural areas that were fully integrated into the market economy, whereas Democrats dominated areas of semisubsistence farming that were more isolated and languishing eco- nomically. Attitude toward the market, rather than economic position, was more important in determining party affiliation.

RELIGIOUS AND ETHNIC FACTORS Religion and ethnic identities also shaped partisanship. As the self-proclaimed "party of re- spectability," Whigs attracted the support of high-status native-born church groups, including the Congregational- ists and the Unitarians in New England and Presbyterians and Episcopalians elsewhere. The party also attracted immigrant groups that most easily merged into the dominant Anglo- Protestant culture, such as the English, Welsh, and Scots. Demo- crats, in contrast, recruited more Germans and Irish, whose more lenient observance of the Sab- bath and (among Catholics) use of parochial schools generated native-born hostility. Democrats

| Whigs drew strongly from the business and commercial classes who were eager to improve themselves. This sculpture from the 1840s suggests the respectable, upright, middle-class outlook characteristic of many Whigs.

appealed to the lower-status Baptists and Methodists, particularly in states where they earlier had been subjected to legal disadvantages. Both parties also attracted freethinkers and the unchurched, but the Democrats had the advantage, because they resisted demands for temperance and sabbatarian laws, such as the prohibition of Sunday travel. In states where they could vote, African Americans were solidly Whig in reaction to the Democratic Party's strong racism and hostility to black rights.

✓ REVIEW

What were the major differences between the Whigs and the Democrats?

CONCLUSION

THE WORLD AT LARGE

In the Americas and in Europe the rise of democratic governance and the spread of market economies developed in similar ways over the same half century. Andrew Jackson's triumph, with the common people trampling the White House furniture, was only the latest in a series of upheavals stretching back to the American and French Revolutions of the eighteenth century. Latin America, too, experienced democratic revolutions. From 1808 to 1821 Spain's American provinces declared their independence one by one, taking inspiration from the writings of Jefferson and Thomas Paine as well as the French *Declaration of the Rights of Man*. Democracy did not always root itself in the aftermath of these revolutions, but democratic ideology remained a powerful social catalyst.

In the United States, the parallel growth of national markets and democratic institutions combined similar ups and downs. If Jackson championed the cause of the "common people," he also led the movement to remove Indians from their lands. The poorest white American might vote for "Old Hickory" and yet reassure himself that African Americans could never rise as high as he did in an increasingly racist society. And the advance of the market created social strains, including the increasing gap between the richest and the poorest.

Still, Americans were evolving a system of democratic politics to deal with the conflicts of the new order. The new national parties, like the new markets, became essential structures uniting the American nation. They advanced an ideology of equality and opportunity, competed vigorously with one another, and involved large numbers of ordinary Americans in the political process. Along with the market, democracy became an integral part of American life. ∞∞∞

CHAPTER SUMMARY

BEGINNING IN THE 1820S THE United States experienced a democratic revolution that was identified with Andrew Jackson.

■ The rise of democracy was stimulated by the Panic of 1819, which caused Americans to look toward both politicians and the government to address their needs.

■ The new political culture of democracy included the use of conventions to make nominations, the adoption of white manhood suffrage, and the acceptance of political parties as essential for the working of the constitutional system.

■ The new politics had distinct limits, however. Women were not given the vote, and racism intensified.

  • The eastern Indian tribes were forced to move to new lands west of the Mississippi River.

  • Free African Americans were subject to increasingly harsh discrimination and exclusion.

■ Andrew Jackson came to personify the new democratic culture. Through his forceful leadership, he expanded the powers of the presidency.

  • Jackson threatened to use force against South Carolina when it tried to nullify the federal tariff.

- In response to John C. Calhoun's theory of nullification, nationalists advanced the idea of the perpetual Union.
- Jackson vetoed a bill to recharter the Second Bank of the United States and destroyed the Bank by removing its federal deposits.

■ Under President Martin Van Buren, the nation entered a severe depression.

■ Capitalizing on hard times and employing the democratic techniques pioneered by the Democrats, the Whigs gained national power in 1840.

■ By 1840 the two parties had developed different ideologies.
- The Whigs were more comfortable with the mechanisms of the market and linked commerce with progress.
- The Democrats were uneasy about the market and favored limited government.

ADDITIONAL READING

THE MOST COMPREHENSIVE REINTERPRETATION OF antebellum political history from Jackson to Lincoln is Sean Wilentz, *The Rise of Democracy* (2005). A contrasting interpretation of the period, more sympathetic to the Whigs, can be found in Daniel Walker Howe, *What Hath God Wrought?* (2007). For a broader perspective on the evolution of American political culture throughout the nineteenth century, see Glenn Altschuler and Stuart Blumin, *Rude Republic* (2000). A good interpretation of Jacksonian politics is Harry Watson, *Liberty and Power* (1990), and important discussions of party ideologies include Marvin Meyers, *The Jacksonian Persuasion* (1957); Daniel Walker Howe, *The Political Culture of American Whigs* (1979); and Lawrence Frederick Kohl, *The Politics of Individualism* (1988). For the history of the Whig Party, the book to read is Michael Holt, *The Rise and Fall of the American Whig Party* (1999).

The best account of the nullification crisis is still William Freehling, *Prelude to the Civil War* (1966), and Robert Remini offers a succinct analysis of the banking controversy in *Andrew Jackson and the Bank War* (1967). Paul Goodman, *Towards a Christian Republic* (1988), is the most valuable study of Anti-Masonry. A useful overview of the free black community in the North is James and Lois Horton, *In Hope of Liberty* (1997). For the hardening of racist attitudes among whites, see Bruce Dain, *A Hideous Monster of the Mind* (2003), and for a full treatment of white and black involvement in the colonization movement, see Richard S. Newman, *The Transformation of American Abolitionism* (2002). On Indian removal in the South, see John Ehle, *The Trail of Tears* (1997), and Robert Remini, *Andrew Jackson and His Indian Wars* (2001).

For a fuller list of readings, see the Bibliography at www.mhhe.com/eh8e.

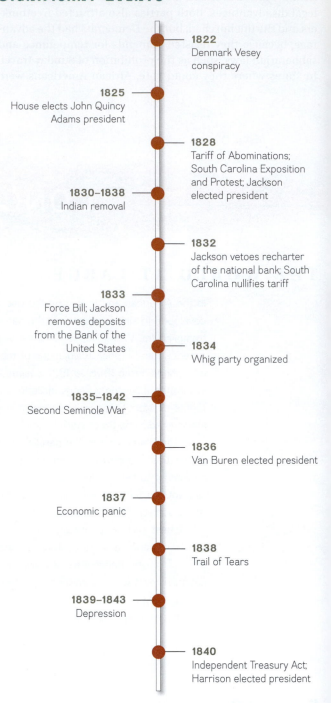

SIGNIFICANT EVENTS

1822
Denmark Vesey conspiracy

1825
House elects John Quincy Adams president

1828
Tariff of Abominations; South Carolina Exposition and Protest; Jackson elected president

1830–1838
Indian removal

1832
Jackson vetoes recharter of the national bank; South Carolina nullifies tariff

1833
Force Bill; Jackson removes deposits from the Bank of the United States

1834
Whig party organized

1835–1842
Second Seminole War

1836
Van Buren elected president

1837
Economic panic

1838
Trail of Tears

1839–1843
Depression

1840
Independent Treasury Act; Harrison elected president

WINNERS	WHY	LOSERS	WHY
Ordinary white men	Expanding franchise; direct election of presidents		
Martin Van Buren	Epitomized the new professional politician; won the presidency	John Quincy Adams	Estranged from the new political culture and refused to become a party leader; lost the presidency to Jackson
Southern speculators and farmers	Removal opened up land once owned by the Indians	Native Americans east of the Mississippi	Jackson's support for removal forced them off their lands.
Southern masters, northern whites	Democrats' support for slavery, hostility to black rights	Free blacks and slaves	Democrats' support for slavery, hostility to black rights, growing racism in white society
Federal officeholders	Democrats' support for the spoils system	Southern supporters of nullification	Jackson's opposition to nullification and his compromise tariff
Workers who advocated a "hard money" currency and opposed the Second Bank of the United States	Before the Second Bank was abolished, workers often received their pay in depreciated state bank notes.	Nicholas Biddle, Henry Clay, and businessmen who supported the Second Bank of the United States	Jackson's determination to destroy the Bank

Bursting with energy and enthusiasm, Methodists head toward a camp meeting in 1819. At a time when the nation had lurched into an economic "panic," the bonds of unity created by this revival and others like it brought a sense of stability and peace amid widespread change. Such revivals also motivated believers to create a better world around them.

Afire with Faith

What's to Come

∞∞∞ **AN AMERICAN STORY** ∞∞∞

THE BEECHERS AND THE KINGDOM OF GOD

In 1826 the Reverend Lyman Beecher was probably the most celebrated minister of the Republic, and the pulpit of Hanover Street Church was his to command. Beecher looked and spoke like a pious farmer, but every Sunday he was transformed when he mounted the pulpit of Boston's most imposing church. From there he would blaze forth denunciations of dancing, drinking, dueling, and "infidelity," all the while punctuating his sermon with pump-handle strokes of the right hand.

Lyman Beecher (center) with his family in 1855. Catharine and Isabella hold his hand; Harriet and Henry are at far right.

Nor were Beecher's ambitions small. His goal was nothing less than to bring the kingdom of Christ to the nation and the world. Like many ministers, Beecher had studied the intriguing final book of the New Testament, the Revelation to John. The Revelation foretold in the latter days of Earth a glorious **millennium**— a thousand years of peace and triumph—when the saints would rule and evil would be banished from the world. Beecher was convinced that the long-awaited millennium might well begin in the United States.

Beecher's boundless energy went into more than devout preaching. He also raised a family of 11 children, every one of whom he prayed would lead in bringing the kingdom of God to America. He loved to wrestle on the floor with his sons, climb the highest trees, or go "berrying" with his daughters. Still, the religious dimension of their lives was constant. The family attended two services on Sunday, a weekly prayer meeting, and a monthly "concert of prayer," where the devout met to pray for the conversion of the world. To usher in that kingdom, Beecher joined other Protestant ministers in supporting a host of religious reforms and missionary efforts. By 1820 voluntary organizations were blanketing the United States with tracts and Bibles, sending missionaries to every corner of the globe, promoting Sunday schools for children, ministering to sailors and the poor, reforming drunkards, and stopping business on the Sabbath. To Beecher, the organizations constituting this loosely united "Benevolent Empire" were signs of the coming kingdom.

As the new pastor at Hanover Street, Beecher also directed his artillery on a host of social evils. With scorn he attacked Unitarians, whose liberal, rational creed rejected the divinity of Jesus. In Boston Unitarians were mainly upper class and cultured. But Beecher also highlighted the "sinful" pastimes of the lower class: playing cards, gambling, and drinking. And he denounced Roman Catholic priests and nuns as superstitious, devious agents of "Antichrist."

These efforts at "moral reform" antagonized many immigrants and other working folk who enjoyed their lotteries or liquor. In disdain they referred to Hanover Street Church, with its imposing stone tower, as Beecher's "stone jug"—where its pastor drank most deeply of his religious spirits. In 1830 a blaze broke out in the basement and spread upward. Along with a mob, firefighters rushed to the scene—but did little more than watch the blaze and make jokes about "Old Beecher" and "hell-fire." If the reverend had little respect for their ways, they had little respect for his. The fiery heat cracked the stone tower top to bottom, and the church burned into ruins. Beecher put a brave face on matters. "Well, my jug's broke; just been to see it," he reported cheerfully the morning after. But the setback was sobering. Beecher was only beginning to learn that spiritual fires, as much as real ones, could spread in unpredictable ways. What did it mean, after all, to make a heaven on earth? Even the devout found it hard to agree. ⚬⚬⚬⚬⚬

The Transformation of American Evangelicalism

Lyman Beecher embodied the spirit of antebellum evangelical Protestantism. At the core of evangelicalism was the conviction that divine grace brought about a new birth, one that enabled belief in Jesus Christ. That conviction also committed the individual convert to reforming his or her own vices as well as the faults of others. But evangelicalism changed over the course of Beecher's long life. As it did, so did its influence on Christian believers. Early-nineteenth-century evangelical leaders such as Beecher sought to convert individuals through revivals and then to turn their energies toward reforming others through the voluntary associations of the Benevolent Empire. Their conservative aim, as he expressed it, was to restore America to "the moral government of God."

But the next generation of evangelical leaders, Beecher's children among them, sought not merely to convert individuals to Christianity but also to reform the most fundamental institutions structuring American society—slavery, the family, and the political and legal subordination of women. By the 1840s they were joined by many other believers in faiths both secular and religious—Unitarians and Transcendentalists, Shakers and socialists, Oneidans and Mormons. All were afire with the faith that they could radically remake the United States.

Before about 1800 most American evangelicals embraced the doctrines of Calvinism (see page 42, Chapter 2). Calvinists believed that God had determined which individuals were destined to be damned or saved and that no human effort could alter those eternal fates. They believed that individuals could do nothing to bring about their own salvation.

But such propositions seemed increasingly unreasonable to the proud American heirs of a revolution that celebrated human equality, free will, and reason. By the beginning of the nineteenth century a growing number of evangelicals moved toward a new outlook. It did not deny the sinfulness of human nature and the necessity of divine grace for salvation. But it did grant more power to free will and human effort. That more democratic belief—that all men and women might choose and win salvation, that each individual should take an active responsibility for redemption—came to characterize the religious views of most evangelicals among the ranks of Congregationalists, Presbyterians, Baptists, and Methodists. Over the course of the Second Great Awakening, their more optimistic view of human potential fostered revivals and sparked ambitious programs for reforming individuals and society.

Charles Grandison Finney and Modern Revivalism

The man who embodied this transformed evangelicalism was Charles Grandison Finney, the founder of modern revivalism. In 1821, as a young man, Finney experienced a soul-shattering conversion that led him to give up his law practice to become an itinerant minister. Eventually he was ordained in the Presbyterian Church, although he lacked any formal theological training. He first attracted national attention when in the mid-1820s and early 1830s he conducted a series of spectacular revivals in the booming port cities along the new Erie Canal.

Finney's New Measures Like George Whitefield before him, Finney had an entrancing voice that carried great distances. His power over an audience was such that when he described the descent of a sinner into hell, those in the back of the hall rose to witness the final plunge. His success also resulted from his use of special techniques—"the new measures."

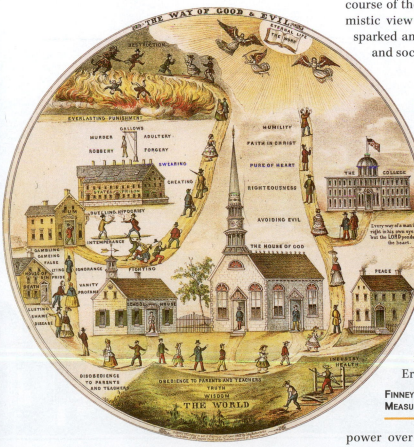

In The Way of Good and Evil *devout Christians are all helped on the path to millennial perfection (right) by the virtues of family, religion, education, and hard work. Sinners on the left, however, take the path of disobedience, intemperance, and lying—straight to hell.*

These methods of encouraging conversion had been developed during the frontier revivals of the Second Great Awakening (pages 227–228). Finney's contribution was to popularize the techniques and use them systematically. He held "protracted meetings" night after night to build up excitement. Speaking boldly and bluntly, he prayed for sinners by name, encouraged women to testify in public gatherings, and placed those struggling with conversion on the "anxious bench" at the front of the church. Whereas the leaders of the first Great Awakening had looked on revivals as god-sent outpourings of grace, Finney viewed them as the consequence of human agency. "A revival is not a miracle," he coolly declared, "it is a purely scientific result of the right use of constituted means."

Like other evangelical revivalists of his day, Finney looked to help individuals undergo an emotionally wrenching conversion experience and be reborn. In doing so, he left little role for the deity in the drama of human deliverance. He endorsed free will and preached that all men and women who wanted to could be

| Charles Grandison Finney, about 1834

saved. To those anxious about their salvation, he thundered, "Do it!"

With salvation within reach of every individual, what might be in store for society at large? "If the church would do her duty," Finney confidently predicted, "the millennium may come in this country in three years."

The Appeal of Evangelicalism

The revivals of the Second Great Awakening drew converts from every segment of American society. Men, women and children, whites, African Americans and Indians, northerners and southerners, slave and free—all joined evangelical churches in unprecedented numbers during the opening decades of the nineteenth century. Evangelicalism proved a potent and protean faith, one that could be

| In the winter of 1830–1831, Charles Finney preached frequently in Rochester, the nation's first inland boomtown.

CENTRAL PART OF BUFFALO STREET, ROCHESTER, N. Y.

The view shows the central part of the city, near the junction of State and Exchange streets, with Buffalo street. The spire House is seen on the right; part of the Methodist church, and other public buildings, on the left.

adapted to answer both the spiritual strivings and needs and the worldly anxieties and sufferings of diverse groups.

MEN AND THE MARKET In the North, middle-class white men under intense pressure from the market economy—lawyers, merchants, and manufacturers—found in evangelicalism's celebration of human ability the assurance that they could contend with the uncertainties in their lives. The emerging urban working class, struggling to stay afloat in the face of industrialization, found in evangelicalism's moral code a discipline that called for self-control and self-improvement. Rural southerners—planters and farmers alike—found their mastery over wives, children, and blacks confirmed by evangelical teachings. And white men of all classes, in North and South, found that church membership and the reputation it conferred for sobriety, honesty, and respectability often helped them to get ahead in a rootless, competitive society.

AFRICAN AMERICAN CHURCHES Blacks, both free and enslaved, joined antebellum churches in impressive numbers, even as they continued to forge a distinctive and liberating faith by infusing evangelicalism with African religious traditions. (For a discussion of religion among slaves, see Chapter 13, as well as "After the Fact," pages 204–207.) Sharpening racial tensions led to the formation of black Methodist and Baptist churches in a number of northern and southern cities. The most important was the African Methodist Episcopal (AME) Church, organized at Philadelphia in 1816. Richard Allen, a former Delaware slave who bought his freedom, became that denomination's first bishop. Growing fears for the security of slavery caused southern white communities, especially in the Deep South, to suppress independent black churches after 1820. But black evangelical churches continued to grow in the North and to serve as organizing centers for the swelling African American opposition to slavery. By 1856 the AME Church boasted some 20,000 members.

Despite the prominence of men as both clerical and lay leaders in the Second Great Awakening, it was women—black and white, northern and southern—whose presence dominated antebellum revivals and churches. In most revivals, female converts outnumbered males by about three to two. Usually the first convert in a family was a woman, and many men who converted were related to women who had come forward earlier.

WOMEN, MARRIAGE, AND CONVERSION Women played an important role in the Awakening partly because of changes in their own social universe. Instead of parents arranging the marriages of their children, couples were beginning to wed more often on the basis of affection. Under such conditions, a woman's prospects for marriage became less certain, and in older areas such as New England and the coastal South, the migration of so many young men to the West compounded this uncertainty. Yet marriage was deemed important for a woman's happiness, and it remained essential for her economic security.

The unpredictability of these social circumstances drew young women toward religion. Women between the ages of 12 and 25 were especially susceptible to conversion. Joining a church heightened a young woman's feeling of initiative and gave her a sense of purpose. By establishing respectability and widening her social circle of friends, church membership also enhanced her chances of marriage. And before and after marriage, it opened opportunities to participate in benevolent and reform associations that took women outside the domestic circle and into a realm of public activism.

The Significance of the Second Great Awakening

As a result of the Second Great Awakening, the dominant form of Christianity in America became evangelical Protestantism. Membership in the major Protestant churches—Congregational, Presbyterian, Baptist, and Methodist—soared during the first half of the nineteenth century. By 1840 an estimated half of the adult population was connected to some church, with the Methodists emerging as the largest Protestant denomination in both the North and the South. Observers such as Alexis de-Tocqueville noted the striking contrast with Europe, where adherence to Christianity declined sharply over the same decades.

INSTITUTIONAL INFLUENCE Not only their sheer numbers but also their institutional presence made evangelicals a formidable force. Their organizations to distribute tracts and Bibles, organize Sunday schools and staff missions, encourage temperance and promote Sabbath observance all operated at a national level. The only other institutions able to make such a claim were the Second Bank of the United States and the Post Office. Evangelical publications dominated the markets for both religious periodicals and books.

St. James AME Zion Church, built in 1833 in Ithaca, New York, became an important transfer point for fugitive slaves heading north. Harriet Tubman visited the church often in her efforts to guide slaves north.

PLEAS FOR AND AGAINST FOREIGN MISSIONS

Gardiner Spring, a New York Presbyterian minister, endorsed missions in 1820 with an urgency that appealed to many Americans. But not everyone was persuaded by evangelical ambitions, and among the doubters was the anonymous author of an essay published the same year in Philadelphia.

DOCUMENT 1   For Foreign Missions: Gardiner Spring

Men are not apt enough to lay out their plans for extended action. In this respect, how much wiser are the men of the world, in their generation, than the children of light? How magnificent the plans, how unwearied the watchfulness, how persevering the efforts after worldly aggrandizement? How ardent the hopes, how inspirited, how confident the expectation of men in the eager pursuit of the meat that perisheth, and the crown that fadeth away? Ah, what a weight of reproach falls upon the head of that Christian who can quietly see the interests of his Master's kingdom languish for the want of determined exertion? "EXPECT GREAT THINGS—ATTEMPT GREAT THINGS" should be the sacred and unalterable motto of men in every department of active labour, who have consecrated themselves to Jesus Christ. . . .

There is mighty work yet to be accomplished for the redemption of fallen men. Though a few sections of the globe have been delivered from their galling manacles, whole kingdoms are to the present hour in the bonds of iniquity. "Darkness covereth the earth, and gross darkness the people." According to the most judicious calculations, the population of the earth may be computed at eight hundred millions. . . . The proportion

of these who bear the Christian name, has been judged to be,

In Asia	2,000,000
Africa	3,000,000
Europe	177,000,000
America	18,000,000
In all	200,000,000,

leaving six hundred millions who are destitute of the gospel. Let any man whom "the day spring from on high hath visited," survey these regions of darkness and earth without emotion, if he can. Eighteen hundred years have passed away since the blood of propitiation was shed for the sins of the world, and three-fourths of the world are at the present hour ignorant of the stupendous sacrifice [of Jesus Christ]. The single empire of China contains more immortal beings, than there are expectants of a happy immortality on the face of the whole earth. . . .

One would think there were enough in the contemplation of pagan pollution and wretchedness, to prove an effectual excitement to missionary exertion. . . .

If the world we inhabit is not under the obscure dominion of chance, but the direction of a wise and holy Governor, a new era is one day to open upon the earth. Moralists have taught, and poets have sung, that this iron age is to pass away, and notwithstanding this dreadful perspective, that the golden age of light and love is yet to stretch its splendours from pole to pole. . . . Nor is it difficult to see that these predictions are in a train of accomplishment. Long as the event has been delayed, long as the prince of darkness has reigned almost without molestation; the kingdom of Christ even now begins to extend its authority, and the glories of that kingdom to look toward their consummation. Within these last eight and twenty years, God has been bringing into view, more distinctly than ever, his own omnipotent hand, in governing the world for the sake of the church. . . .

Is it not high time for every rational man to say, I lay it down as a maxim of my life, and will hereafter regard it as one of the principles of my conduct, that the world is to be converted to Christ?

Source: Gardiner Spring, *Memoirs of the Rev. Samuel Mills . . .* (New York: New York Evangelical Missionary Society, 1820), pp. 242–247. Available online.

DOCUMENT 2   Against Foreign Missions (Anonymous)

What advantage would it be to the heathen, if they were all to take upon them such a religion as now prevails in those called Christian lands? Is it probable they would be any better? Is there any less integrity or uprightness among them, than among ourselves? Let us look at home; and let those who account themselves spiritual physicians, heal their own maladies, and correct the disorders in their own borders, before they undertake to cure others in distant lands, and set them right.

Are not many of those sent to propagate christianity among the heathen, mere men of the world, who differ as greatly from the apostles in their pride, as they do in the expense with which they undertake to propagate it? The apostles were humble men; and instead of being borne about on the shoulders of their fellow beings in splendid *palanquins,* like some of our modern missionaries

to the east, they went about on foot. Thousands of money were not furnished them to preach among the heathen. . . .

People, in general, come into these missionary undertakings much in the same manner as they come into the fashions of the time; and in order to keep up one's popularity, and to be esteemed of some account it is necessary to take an active part in, or to applaud them. I feel no pleasure in making these remarks—I know they must give offence, and endanger the publication in which they may be inserted, but I am sensible that something ought to be said on the subject with all plainness. . . . Indeed, I seriously fear that the spirit and the way in which the missionary and other great undertakings, now going forward in christendom, are carried on, is very little better, or will accomplish very little more in behalf of true Christianity

in the end, than the Croisades [Crusades] or holy wars of former times.

Source: Anonymous, "A Candid Address to Christians in General," *Reformer,* January 1, 1820, p. 6ff. Available through American Periodical Series Online.

Thinking Critically

What arguments and emotional appeals did Spring use to instill in his readers a devotion to the cause of missions? In what ways did he try to persuade them that the conversion of the world to Christianity was an achievable goal? Why did the anonymous author oppose foreign missions? What did he imply by suggesting that those missions could produce the same negative outcome as the Crusades of the Middle Ages?

Few were more aware of the scope of evangelicalism's sway than Lyman Beecher. Earlier in his career, he had lamented the collapse of state-supported Congregationalist religious establishments throughout New England. But looking back in later years, he realized that the churches did not need government support to figure as powerful forces in the United States. To his delight, Beecher concluded that evangelicals had, in fact, gained "deeper influence" since disestablishment "by voluntary efforts, societies, missions, and revivals."

 REVIEW

How did evangelical Protestants change their doctrines to appeal to new social conditions in the early decades of the nineteenth century?

REVIVALISM AND THE SOCIAL ORDER

HOW RIGHT BEECHER WAS. The revivals of the Second Great Awakening had profound and lasting consequences. Its effects went well beyond the churching of hundreds of thousands of American men, women, and children and the spectacular growth of evangelical Protestant denominations. Religious commitment fundamentally reshaped antebellum society because, to keep the fervor afire, Beecher, Finney, and their fellow revivalists channeled the energies of their converts into an array of benevolent and reform societies. But zealous evangelicals did a great deal more than teach Sunday school at home and dispatch missionaries abroad. As early as the 1820s and 1830s their activism had already significantly affected three aspects of American culture: drinking habits, ideals of women and the family, and Protestant attitudes toward a growing population of Roman Catholics.

The Temperance Movement

The temperance campaign, a reform dear to the heart of Lyman Beecher and other evangelical clergy, effected a sweeping change in the personal habits of many Americans.

Until the mid-eighteenth century most colonials (and Europeans) considered spirits an essential supplement to their diet. Liquor flowed freely at ministerial ordinations in New England towns, court days in the South, house-raisings, corn-huskings, and quilting bees on the frontier, not to mention weddings, elections, and militia musters everywhere. Colonial Americans did not condone public drunkenness, but they saw nothing amiss in the regular use of alcohol or even in occasional intoxication.

But alcohol consumption soared after the Revolution, so that by 1825 the average American over the age of 15 consumed seven gallons of absolute alcohol a year, the highest level in American history and nearly triple present-day

levels. Anne Royall, whose travels took her cross-country by stage, reported, "When I was in Virginia, it was too much whiskey—in Ohio, too much whiskey—in Tennessee, it is too, too much whiskey!"

SOCIAL COSTS OF DRINKING The social costs for such habits were high: broken families, abused and neglected wives and children, sickness and disability, poverty, and crime. The temperance movement undertook to eliminate these problems by curbing drinking.

Led largely by clergy, the movement at first focused on drunkenness and did not oppose moderate drinking. But in 1826 the American Temperance Society was founded, taking voluntary abstinence as its goal. During the next decade approximately 5,000 local temperance societies were founded. As the movement gained momentum, annual per capita consumption of alcohol dropped sharply. By 1845 it had fallen below two gallons a year.

The temperance movement lasted longer and attracted many more supporters than other reforms did. It appealed to young and old, to urban and rural residents, to workers and businesspeople. Moreover, it was one of the few reform movements with significant support in the South. Its success came partly for social reasons. Democracy necessitated sober voters; factories required sober workers. In addition, temperance attracted the upwardly mobile—professionals, small businesspeople, and skilled artisans anxious to improve their social standing. Finally, temperance advocates stressed the suffering that men inflicted on women and children, and thus

Annual Consumption of Distilled Spirits, per Capita, 1710–1920

Beginning in 1790, per capita levels of drinking steadily rose, until 1830, when the temperance movement produced a sharp decline over the next two decades.

the movement appealed to women as a means to defend the home and carry out their domestic mission.

Ideals of Women and the Family

Evangelicals also contributed substantially to a new ideal of womanhood, one being elaborated by the clergy and female authors in sermons, advice manuals, magazine articles, and novels during the first half of the nineteenth century. Called the "cult of **domesticity**" or "true womanhood" or "evangelical womanhood," that ideal cast wives and mothers as the "angels" of their households, the sex ideally suited to serve as dispensers of love, comfort, and moral instruction to husbands and children. The premise of that new ideal was that men and women, by their very nature, inhabited separate spheres. The rough-and-tumble world of business and politics was the proper province of husbands and fathers, while women ruled the domestic sphere of home and family. "Love is our life our reality, business yours," Mollie Clark told one suitor.

As business affairs grew increasingly separate from the family in the nineteenth century, the middle-class home became a female domain. A woman's role as a wife and mother was to dispense love and moral guidance to her husband and her children. As this domestic scene makes clear, she was at the very center of the world of the family.

This new ideal also held that women were by nature morally stronger and more religious than men. That view reversed the negative medieval and early modern views of women as the sinful daughters of the temptress Eve, more passionate by nature and thus less morally restrained and spiritually inclined than men. But the new ideal also held antebellum women to a higher standard of sexual purity. A man's sexual infidelity, although hardly condoned, brought no lasting shame. But a woman who engaged in sexual relations before marriage or was unfaithful afterward was threatened with everlasting disgrace. Under this new double standard, women were to be pure, passionless, and passive: they were to submerge their identities in those of their husbands.

SEPARATION OF THE WORKPLACE AND HOME Advocates of the new ideal of womanhood and the notion of separate spheres beamed their message mainly at elite and middle-class women. And that message found an impressionable audience among wives and daughters in the urbanizing Northeast. There the separation of the workplace from the home was most complete. As a result of industrialization, many men worked outside the home, while the rise of factories also led to a decline in part-time work such as spinning, which women had once performed to supplement family income. Home manufacturing was no longer essential, for, except on the frontier, families could easily purchase those articles that women previously had made, such as cloth, soap, and candles. "The transition from mother-and-daughter power to water-and-steam power," one New England minister noted, produced "a complete revolution of domestic life." This growing separation of the household from the workplace in the Northeast made it that much easier for the home to be idealized as a place of "domesticity," a haven away from the competitive, workaday world, with the mother firmly at its center.

 DOMESTICITY IN EUROPE The celebration of domesticity was not unique to the United States. The middle class became increasingly important in Europe, so that after 1850 it was culturally dominant. Employment opportunities expanded for women as industrialization accelerated, yet the social expectation among the middle class was that women would not be employed outside the home. This redefinition of women's roles was more sweeping in Europe because previously, middle-class women had left the task of child-raising largely to hired nurses and governesses. By midcentury these mothers devoted much more time to domestic duties, including rearing the children. Family size also declined, both in France and in England. The middle class was most numerous in England; indeed, the importance of the middle class in Britain during Queen Victoria's reign (1837–1901) gave these ideals the label **Victorianism**.

The Middle-Class Family in Transition

THE RISE OF PRIVACY AND SMALLER FAMILIES As elite and middle-class homes came to be seen as havens of moral virtue, those domestic settings developed a new structure and new set of attitudes closer in spirit to those

| Piecework quilts such as this one became affordable to produce only when cheap manufactured cloth was available. Just as the Industrial Revolution encouraged a cult of domesticity to shelter families from the harsh industrial workplace, so, too, did factory-made cloth encourage the making of piecework quilts.

of the modern family. One basic change was the rise of privacy. The family was increasingly seen as a sheltered retreat from the outside world. In addition, the pressures to achieve success led middle-class young adults to delay marriage, since a husband was expected to have the financial means to support his wife. Smaller family size resulted, since wives, especially those among the urban middle class, began to use birth control to space children farther apart and to minimize the risks of pregnancy. In addition, it has been estimated that before 1860 one abortion was performed for every five or six live births. With smaller families, parents could tend more carefully to their children's success. Increasingly, middle-class families took on the expense of additional education to prepare their sons for a career in business. They also frequently equalized inheritances rather than favoring the eldest son or favoring sons over daughters.

Most women in the United States did not have time to make domesticity the center of their lives. Farmers' wives and enslaved women had to work constantly, whereas lower-class families could not get by without the wages of female members. Still, some elite and middle-class women tried to live up to the new ideals, though many found the effort confining. "The great trial is that I have nothing to do," one complained. "Here I am with abundant leisure and capable, I believe, of accomplishing some good, and yet with no object on which to expend my energies."

In response to those frustrations, Lyman Beecher's eldest daughter, Catharine (who never married), made a career out of assuring women that the proper care of household and children was their sex's crucial responsibility. Like the earlier advocates of "republican motherhood" (see Chapter 8), Catharine Beecher supported women's education and argued that women exercised power as moral guardians of the nation's future. She also wrote several books on efficient home management. "There is no one thing more necessary to a housekeeper in performing her varied duties, than a habit of system and order," she told readers. "For all the time afforded us, we must give account to God."

But many women yearned to exert moral authority outside the confines of their households, and, ironically, the new host of benevolent and reform societies allowed them that unprecedented opportunity. Devout wives and daughters, particularly those from middle-class families, flocked to these voluntary associations, many of which had separate women's chapters. By serving in such organizations, they gained the practical experience of holding office on governing boards, conducting meetings, drafting policy statements, organizing reform programs, and raising money. Evangelicalism thus enabled women to enter public life and to make their voices heard in ways that were socially acceptable. After all, evangelical teachings affirmed that they were the superior sex in piety and morality, a point often repeated by those very women who devoted much of their time to benevolence and reform. They justified such public activism as merely the logical extension of their private responsibility to act as spiritual guides to their families.

Protestants and Catholics

Women's piety and their spiritual influence was surely on the mind of Isaac Bird one Saturday morning in the autumn of 1819. A devout evangelical preparing for the ministry, he had wandered into a Roman Catholic church in Boston and now watched with rapt attention a ritual, conducted entirely in Latin, in which two women "took the veil" and became nuns. Bird often visited Boston on his vacations to proselytize its poorest inhabitants. Many were Catholics, as he noted, some of them recent Irish and German immigrants and others African American, including a man who asked him many intelligent questions about religion and "treated me respectfully but seemed to feel that Protestants were all making a trade of preaching and praying." It troubled Bird, this gathering presence of devout Catholics.

Protestants had a long history of hostility toward Roman Catholics, especially in New England. Every November, colonial Bostonians had celebrated "Pope's Day" with boys decked out as the devil's imps parading through the streets with a cart carrying an effigy of the pope. The uproar over the Quebec Act in 1774 also bore loud witness to anti-Catholic sentiments. But before the beginning of the nineteenth century the number of Catholics had been small: in 1815, there were only 150,000 scattered throughout the United States, and they often had little access to priests or public worship.

That had begun to change by 1820. French-Canadian Catholic immigrants were filtering into New England in growing numbers, an incoming tide that would rise sharply during the 1840s and 1850s, with a new wave of Catholic immigrants from the British Isles and German-speaking countries. By 1830 the Catholic population had jumped to 300,000, and by 1850 Catholics accounted for 8 percent of the U.S. population—the same proportion as Presbyterians. As these newcomers settled in eastern cities and on

PRIVACY BEGINS AT HOME

In 1831 Olive Walkley made a significant decision: she moved the bed in which she and her husband, Stephen, slept out of the parlor and replaced it with a carpet. She also had the unfinished upstairs plastered and partitioned into bedrooms for their children. The Walkleys were farmers in Southington, Connecticut, but like middle-class urban families they were influenced by the new movement to separate public and private space in the home.

When the Walkleys were married in 1811, Americans were accustomed to living in close quarters, because most houses had few rooms. Further, the limited light and heat forced members to congregate. Parents and sometimes the entire family slept in the parlor, where visitors were also entertained and where the family's most valuable possessions, including its best bed, were proudly displayed. Even in the wealthiest households, usually only the parents enjoyed separate sleeping quarters, and in most homes beds could be found in virtually every room.

In the years after 1820, however, the American home was reshaped to create specialized regions of privacy, service, and socializing. Although houses increasingly faced the road, new designs provided greater privacy by creating an entry hall that served as a transition space from the outside world to the various parts of the house and by separating living and cooking quarters from areas for entertainment.

An architect confers with builders about the plans as a new house goes up in the background.

A sitting room was for the family's everyday use, whereas the parlor was reserved for public activity, including receiving company, giving recitals, and performing ceremonies such as weddings and funerals. As Americans developed a new sense of privacy, the parents' bed and the intimate activities associated with it were placed out of sight. In more prosperous homes an upholstered mahogany sofa replaced the bed in the parlor, and the floor was covered with a carpet, as much a symbol of the family's refinement as the mantel clock was of its modern outlook.

Food preparation and domestic work were done in a separate kitchen and adjoining back rooms. Although rural families often continued to eat in the sitting room, houses more frequently contained a separate dining room. Stoves, which enlarged usable space by radiating heat, became common in more affluent homes, while the hearth and its fire—once the main source of food, heat, and light—ceased to be the center of the family's life together.

The new standards of domestic life also emphasized cleanliness and decoration. Lydia Maria Child's popular *The American Frugal Housewife* offered families of modest means numerous tips on cleaning and scouring as well as decorating.

In short, a home's floor plan and furnishings not only determined comfort but also defined a family's status and increasingly middle-class aspirations.

Thinking Critically

What economic, social, and intellectual developments in the early nineteenth century fostered the new concern for privacy?

---

western frontiers, there were an increasing number of priests, nuns, and churches to minister to their spiritual needs.

CATHOLICISM AND PROTESTANTISM COMPARED

The differences between Roman Catholicism and Protestantism—especially evangelicalism—were substantial. Whereas evangelicals stressed the inward transformation of conversion, Catholics emphasized the importance of outward religious observances, such as faithfully attending mass and receiving the sacraments, as essential to salvation. Whereas evangelicals insisted that individuals read the Bible to discover God's will, Catholics urged their faithful to heed church teachings and traditions.

Whereas Catholics believed that human suffering could be a penance paving the way toward redemption, evangelicals regarded it as an evil to be alleviated. Whereas evangelicals looked toward an imminent millennium, Catholics harbored no such expectation and played almost no role in antebellum benevolence and reform movements.

To Protestants, many elements of Catholicism seemed superstitious and even subversive. They rejected the Catholic doctrine of transubstantiation, which held that the bread and wine consecrated by the priest during mass literally turned into the body and blood of Jesus Christ. They condemned as idolatry the Catholic veneration of the Virgin Mary and the saints. They regarded Catholic nuns

HISTORIAN'S TOOLBOX

THE PRINTER'S ANGEL

Printing press, other printers

What is indicated by these mosques and minarets?

A girl in the United States— What is conveyed by her reading a scroll similar to the one in the angel's hands?

Illustration from the American Tract Society, undated (American Antiquarian Society).

The American Tract Society (ATS), one of the many evangelical Protestant voluntary associations founded in the early nineteenth century, celebrated its mission with this illustration. An allegorical rendering of the power of print to convert the world, it shows an angel delivering a scroll, presumably God's word inscribed in the Bible, to a printer's outstretched hands. Although other voluntary associations printed Bibles, the ATS produced millions of tracts, small booklets narrating experiences of religious conversion or inculcating moral lessons. Children in the United States, especially those attending Sunday schools, were among the ATS's target audiences: tracts aimed at boys and girls were often illustrated with woodcuts and covered in brightly colored paper. By 1850 millions of copies of children's tracts had flown off the ATS presses, along with millions more for children and adults translated into several languages. As the mother and son shown in the right-hand corner indicate, the ATS shared the aim of other Protestant voluntary associations to hasten the millennium by persuading Jews and Muslims, pagans and Roman Catholics, to embrace the beliefs of evangelical Protestants.

Thinking Critically

What message is conveyed by positioning a Protestant church and a Muslim mosque on opposite sides of the illustration? Why are a woman and a boy—but no adult men—the recipients of tracts in the lower-right scene? Does this image of an angel recall any biblical scene often depicted by Roman Catholic artists? Why would the Protestant illustrator wish to evoke that association?

and convents as threats to the new ideals of womanhood and domesticity. They found it amiss that Catholic laymen had no role in governing their own parishes and dioceses, entrusting that responsibility entirely to priests and bishops.

But the worst fears of Protestants fastened on what they saw as the political dangers posed by Catholics, especially immigrants. Alarmed as Irish and German settlers poured into the West, Lyman Beecher warned that "the world has never witnessed such a rush of dark-minded population from one country to another, as is now leaving Europe and dashing upon our shores." Beecher foresaw a sinister plot hatched by the pope to snuff out American liberty. For what else would follow in a nation overwhelmed by Catholicism, "a religion which never prospered but in alliance with despotic government, has always been and still is the inflexible enemy of liberty of conscience and free enquiry, and at this moment is the mainstay of the battle against republican institutions?"

The Reverend Lyman Beecher's Hanover Street church—his "stone jug"—was an early example of Gothic Revival architecture, with its medieval stone battlements atop a massive tower and pointed windows. Such a church stood in stark contrast to the plain Congregational meetinghouses of the Puritans (see page 89). On the one hand, Beecher railed against the evils of Catholicism. On the other, he recognized the attraction of such imposing architecture. "If you want to get martins about your house," he commented, comparing his own church flock to the swallows who were so particular about where they nested, "you must put up a martin box."

HANOVER CHURCH.

Evangelical missionaries dispatched abroad also fueled anti-Catholic sentiment at home. Their reports from the mission field, widely circulated in religious magazines, regaled readers with accounts of clashes with Catholic missionaries and ridiculed Catholic beliefs and rituals. Among them was Isaac Bird, who became a missionary in present-day Lebanon: he charged Catholic missionaries there with scheming to get him in trouble with local authorities and to prevent him from distributing Bibles. And he blamed the Catholic laypeople in the Middle East for discouraging the conversion of Jews and Muslims by practicing so "corrupt" a form of Christianity.

It was all the more appalling to evangelicals, then, that some Protestants found Catholic teachings appealing. So attractive that some 57,000 converted to Catholicism in the thirty years after 1830. In response to those defections, many Protestants, believing that converts were drawn by the artistic beauties of Catholic worship, began to include in their own churches recognizably Catholic elements, such as the symbol of the cross, the use of candles and flowers, organ and choir music, stained glass windows, and Gothic architecture. One such church was none other than Lyman Beecher's "Stone Jug," the Hanover Street Congregational Church in Boston.

ATTACKS ON CATHOLICS Other Protestants attacked Catholicism directly. Writing under the name "Maria Monk," a team of evangelical ministers produced a lurid account of life in a convent, replete with sex orgies involving priests and nuns and a cellar planted with dead babies. Published in 1836, it outsold every other book except *Uncle Tom's Cabin* in the years before the Civil War. And with anti-Catholic sentiment running so high, predictably, there was violence. In 1834 a mob in Charlestown, Massachusetts, burned a convent to the ground. The sisters and

their students escaped injury, but during the summer of 1844 in Philadelphia, two separate outbreaks of anti-Catholic violence left 14 people dead, as well as two churches and three dozen homes in smoldering ruins.

Most antebellum Protestants condoned neither violence against Catholics nor the later nativist movement of the 1850s. But even liberal Protestants mistrusted the religion of Rome: in 1821 the Unitarian John Adams asked Thomas Jefferson whether "a free government [can] possibly exist with a Roman Catholic religion." Anti-Catholicism had emerged as a defining feature of American Protestant identity, and the alienation of the two groups ran deep, enduring far into the twentieth century.

 **REVIEW**

Name at least two ways in which evangelical activists influenced American culture during the 1830s and 1840s.

VISIONARIES

INCREASINGLY HOSTILE TO ROMAN CATHOLICS, evangelicals also stood at odds with other groups in antebellum America who envisioned new ways of improving individuals and society. Although often expressing optimism about the prospects for human betterment, these other reformers—Unitarians and Transcendentalists, socialists and communitarians—had little else in common with evangelicals.

The Unitarian Contribution

During the opening decades of the nineteenth century the religious division among Americans that produced the fiercest debates pitted evangelicals against deists, Unitarians, and other rational Christians. A majority only in eastern Massachusetts, Unitarians denied the divinity of Jesus while affirming the ability and responsibility of humankind to follow his moral teachings. Disdainful of the emotionalism of revivals, they were also inclined to interpret the Bible broadly rather than literally. To most Americans, such views were so suspect that the presidents who adhered to Unitarianism—John Adams, Thomas Jefferson, and John Quincy Adams—did not wish to publicize their beliefs.

Despite their many differences, Unitarians shared with evangelicals an esteem for the power of human agency and a commitment to the goal of social betterment. Small though their numbers were, Unitarians made large contributions to the cause of reform. Among their ranks were Dorothea Dix, a Boston schoolteacher who took the lead in creating state-supported asylums to treat the mentally ill; Samuel Gridley Howe, who promoted education for the blind and the deaf; and Horace Mann, who strove to give greater access to public schooling to children of poor and working-class families.

| Dorothea Dix

Unitarians made an equally important contribution to American literature; from their ranks came many of the Transcendentalists—novelists and poets, critics and philosophers—who led the artistic movement that later came to be known as the American Renaissance.

From Unitarianism to Transcendentalism

EMERSON'S DIVINITY SCHOOL ADDRESS   What sparked Transcendentalism was an address delivered by a disenchanted Unitarian minister named Ralph Waldo Emerson to the students of Harvard Divinity School on a warm summer evening in July 1838. Outside, nature's world was alive and vibrant, he told his young audience: "The grass grows, the buds burst, the meadow is spotted with fire and gold in the tint of flowers." But from the pulpits of too many congregations came lifeless preaching. "In how many churches, by how many prophets, tell me," Emerson demanded, "is man made sensible that he is an infinite Soul?" Leaving the shocked audience to ponder his message, Emerson and his wife drove home beneath a night sky illuminated by the northern lights. Emerson's Divinity School Address glowed much like that July aurora and, in its own bold way, reflected the influence of Romanticism on American thinkers.

Romanticism began in Europe as a reaction against the Enlightenment. The Enlightenment had placed reason at the center of human achievement; Romanticism instead emphasized the importance of emotion and intuition as sources of truth. It gloried in the unlimited potential of the individual, who might soar if freed from the restraints of institutions. It extolled humanitarianism and sympathized with the oppressed. It elevated inner feelings and heartfelt convictions. Philosophically, its influence was strongest among intellectuals who took part in the Transcendentalist movement.

Transcendentalism is difficult to define, because it produced individualists who resisted being lumped together. It blossomed in the mid-1830s, when a number of Unitarian clergy such as George Ripley and Ralph Waldo Emerson resigned their pulpits, loudly protesting the church's teachings. The new "Transcendentalist Club" attracted a small following among other discontented Boston intellectuals, including Margaret Fuller, Bronson Alcott, and Orestes Brownson.

Like European Romantics, American Transcendentalists emphasized feeling over reason, seeking a spiritual communion with nature. By transcend they meant to go beyond or to rise above—specifically above reason and beyond the material world. As part of creation, every human being contained a spark of divinity, Emerson avowed. Transcendentalists also shared in Romanticism's glorification of the individual. "Trust thyself. Every heart vibrates to that iron string," Emerson advised. If freed from the constraints of traditional authority, the individual had infinite potential. Like the devout at Finney's revivals, who sought to improve themselves and society, listeners who flocked to Emerson's lectures were infused with the spirit of optimistic reform.

The American Renaissance

As the currents of Romanticism percolated through American society, the country's literature came of age. In 1820 educated Americans still tended to ape the fashions of Europe and to read British books. But as the population grew, education increased, and the country's literary market expanded; American writers looked with greater interest at the customs and character of their own society. Emerson's address "The American Scholar" (1837) constituted a declaration of literary independence. "Our long dependence, our long apprenticeship to the learning of other lands draws to a close," he proclaimed. "Events, actions arise, that must be sung, that will sing themselves."

NATURE AND CIVILIZATION CLASH   Many writers of the American Renaissance betrayed a concern that the advance of civilization, with its smoke-belching factories and crowded urban centers, might destroy both the natural simplicity of the land and the liberty of the individual. A compelling commentator on those themes was Henry David Thoreau, who became part of Emerson's circle. In 1845 he built a cabin on the edge of Walden Pond near Concord, Massachusetts, living there in relative solitude for 16 months to demonstrate the advantages of self-reliance. In *Walden*

In the summer of 1858 members of the cultural Saturday Club of Boston made an excursion to the Adirondacks to observe nature. In *Philosopher's Camp, painted by William J. Stillman,* who organized the expedition, a group on the left dissects a fish under the supervision of the famous scientist Louis Agassiz, while on the right others practice firing rifles. Symbolically, Ralph Waldo Emerson stands alone in the center of the painting in a contemplative mood.

(1854) Thoreau argued that only in nature could one find true independence. By living simply, one could master oneself and the world. He denounced Americans' frantic competition for material goods and wealth: "Money is not required to buy one necessity of the soul," Thoreau maintained. Trapped by property, possessions, and the market, "the mass of men lead lives of quiet desperation."

Thoreau's individualism was so extreme that he rejected any institution that contradicted his personal sense of right. "The only obligation which I have a right to assume, is to do at any time what I think right," he wrote in his essay "On Civil Disobedience." Voicing the anti-institutional impulse of Romanticism, he took individualism to its antisocial extreme.

WHITMAN'S SELF-RELIANT SONGS In contrast to Thoreau's exclusiveness, Walt Whitman was all-inclusive, embracing American society in its infinite variety. A journalist and laborer in the New York City area, Whitman was inspired by the common people, whose "manners, speech, dress, friendships . . . are unrhymed poetry." In taking their measure in *Leaves of Grass* (1855), he pioneered a new, modern form of poetry, unconcerned with meter and rhyme and filled with frank imagery and sexual references.

| Walt Whitman, poet of democracy

Conceiving himself the representative of all Americans, Whitman exuberantly titled his first major poem "Song of Myself."

> I am your voice—It was tied in you—In me it began to talk.
> I celebrate myself to celebrate every man and woman alive.

DARKER SOULS Whitman, like the Transcendentalists, exalted the emotions, nature, and the individual, endowing these ideas with a joyous, democratic spirit. More brooding souls were Nathaniel Hawthorne and Herman Melville, two authors who did not share the Transcendentalists' sunny optimism. Hawthorne wrote of the power of the past to shape future generations. In *The Scarlet Letter* (1850), set in New England's Puritan era, Hawthorne probed the sufferings of a woman who bore an illegitimate child as well as the hypocrisy of the Puritan neighbors who condemned her. Herman Melville's dark masterpiece, *Moby-Dick* (1851), drew on his youthful experiences aboard a whaling ship. The novel's Captain Ahab relentlessly drives his ship in pursuit of the great white whale Moby-Dick. In Melville's telling, Ahab becomes a powerful symbol of American character: the prototype of the ruthless businessman despoiling nature's resources in his pursuit of success.

Ahab is Emerson's self-reliant man, but in him, self-reliance is transformed into a monomania that eventually destroys his ship, its crew, and him.

But with so many opportunities opening before them, most Americans were not attuned to searching criticism. They preferred to celebrate, with Emerson, the glories of democracy and the quest for self-improvement.

Secular Utopian Communities

Both evangelicals and Unitarians focused their early reform efforts on improving individuals. But some antebellum believers, followers of both secular and religious faiths, sought to remake society at large by forming communities intended as examples to the rest of the world.

Herman Melville

BROOK FARM Even some Transcendentalists attempted a utopian venture. During the early 1840s Emerson's friend George Ripley organized Brook Farm, a community near Boston where members could live "a more wholesome and simple life than can be led amidst the pressure of our competitive institutions." Margaret Fuller and, even more surprisingly, Nathaniel Hawthorne, lived and labored there for a time, but, predictably, these Romantic individualists could not sustain the group cooperation essential for success.

SOCIALIST COMMUNITIES Some secular thinkers shared the Transcendentalists' view that competition, inequality, and acquisitiveness were corrupting American society. Among those critics were socialists, and their goal was to defend the interests of American workers from the ravages of industrialization. The most radical voice raised in their behalf belonged to Thomas Skidmore: in 1829 he published *The Rights of Man to Property,* which compared workers laboring for a daily wage to slaves and demanded that the government confiscate private property and redistribute it equally.

More influential was Robert Owen, the unlikely founder of America's first socialist community. A Welsh industrialist who had made a fortune manufacturing textiles, Owen then turned to realizing his vision of a just society—one in which property was held in common and work equally shared. Such a benign social environment, he believed, would foster tolerant, rational human beings capable of self-government. What better place than America to make this dream come true?

NEW HARMONY Initially, Owen received a warm reception. John Quincy Adams not only attended both lectures that Owen delivered at the Capitol but also displayed a model of his proposed community in the White House. A few months later about 900 volunteers flocked to Owen's community at New Harmony, Indiana.

Alas, most lacked the skills and commitment to make it a success, and bitter factions soon split the settlement. Owen made matters worse by announcing that he rejected both the authenticity of the Bible and the institution of marriage. New Harmony dissolved in 1827, but Owen's principles inspired nearly 20 other short-lived experiments.

Owen's followers coined the term "socialism," but it was Charles Fourier, a French theorist, whose ideas interested even more Americans in collectivist communities during the 1840s. His disciples in the United States, most notably, Albert Brisbane, founded nearly 30 planned communities devoted to the principle that work should be satisfying and socially useful. But again, schisms ensured that none survived for more than a dozen years.

The United States proved to be a poor proving-ground for socialist experiments. Wages were too high and land too cheap for such communities to interest most Americans. And individualism was too strong to create a commitment to cooperative action. Communities founded by believers in religious rather than secular faiths proved far more enduring. Their common spiritual convictions muted individualism, and their charismatic leaders held divisions at bay.

Religious Utopian Communities

THE SHAKERS Among the most successful of these religiously based communal groups were the Shakers. Ann Lee, the illiterate daughter of an English blacksmith, believed that God had a dual nature, part male and part female, and that her own life would reveal the feminine side of the divinity, just as Christ had revealed the masculine. In 1774 she led a small band of disciples to America. Her followers sometimes shook in the fervent public demonstration of their faith—hence the name Shakers.

As the Second Great Awakening crested, recruits from revivals swelled Shaker ranks, and their new adherents founded about 20 villages. Members held the community's property in common, worked hard, and lived simply.

Convinced that the end of the world was at hand and that there was no need to perpetuate the human race, Shakers practiced celibacy. Men and women normally worked apart, ate at separate tables in silence, entered separate doorways, and had separate living quarters. Shakers also accorded women unusual authority and equality. Elders typically assigned tasks by gender, with women performing household chores and men laboring in the fields, but leadership of the church was split equally between men and women. By the mid-nineteenth century a majority of members were female. Lacking any natural

Dancing was an integral part of the Shakers' religion, as this picture of a service at Lebanon, New York, indicates. In worshiping, men and women formed separate lines with their hands held out and moved back and forth in rhythm while singing religious songs. One Shaker hymn proclaimed, "With ev'ry gift I will unite, / And join in sweet devotion / To worship God is my delight, / With hands and feet in motion." Note the presence of African Americans in the community.

increase, membership began to decline after 1850, from a peak of about 6,000 members.

John Humphrey Noyes, a revival convert of Charles Finney, also set out to alter the relationship between the sexes, though in a markedly different way. While many evangelicals believed that men and women should strive for moral perfection, Noyes announced that he had actually reached this blessed state. Settling in Putney, Vermont, and, after 1848, in Oneida, New York, Noyes set out to create a community organized on his religious ideals.

COMPLEX MARRIAGE AT ONEIDA

In pursuit of greater freedom, Noyes preached the doctrine of "complex marriage." Commune members could have sexual relations with one another but only with the approval of the community and after a searching examination of the couple's motives. Noyes eventually undertook experiments in planned reproduction by selecting "scientific" combinations of parents to produce morally perfect children.

Under his charismatic leadership the Oneida Community grew to more than 200 members in 1851. But in 1879 an internal dispute drove him from power, and without his guiding hand the community fell apart. In 1881 its members reorganized as a business enterprise.

The Mormon Experience

The most spectacularly successful antebellum religious community—one that mushroomed into a denomination whose followers now number in the millions around the world—is the Church of Jesus Christ of Latter-Day Saints. The Mormons, as they are generally known, took their rise from the visions of a young man named Joseph Smith in Palmyra, in western New York, where the religious fires of revivalism often flared. The son of a poor farmer, Smith was robust, charming, almost hypnotic in his appeal. In 1827, at the age of only 22, he announced that he had discovered and translated a set of golden tablets on which was written the Book of Mormon. The tablets told the story of a band of Hebrews who in biblical times journeyed to America, splitting into two groups, the Nephites and the Lamanites. The Nephites established a Christian civilization, only to be exterminated by the Lamanites, whose descendants were said to be the Indians of the Americas.

| The Mormon temple at Nauvoo, Illinois, was adorned with this sun stone and other celestial carvings drawn from a dream vision by Joseph Smith.

Seeking to reestablish the true church, Smith gathered a group of devoted followers.

Like nineteenth-century evangelicalism, Mormonism proclaimed that salvation was available to all. Mormon culture also upheld the middle-class values of hard work, thrift, and self-control. It partook of the optimistic, materialist attitudes of American society. And by teaching that Christ would return to rule the earth, it shared in the hope of a coming millennial kingdom.

MOVEMENT TO RESTORE THE ANCIENT CHURCH

Yet Mormonism was less an outgrowth of evangelicalism than of the primitive gospel movement, which sought to reestablish the ancient church. In restoring what Smith called "the ancient order of things," he created a **theocracy** uniting church and state, reestablished biblical priesthoods and titles, and adopted temple rituals.

Like Roman Catholics, the Mormons drew bitter opposition—and armed attacks. Smith's unorthodox teachings provoked persecution wherever he and his followers went, first to Ohio and then to Missouri. Mob violence finally hounded him out of Missouri in 1839. Smith then established a new holy city, which he named Nauvoo, located on the Mississippi River in Illinois.

Reinforced by a steady stream of converts from Britain, Nauvoo became the largest city in Illinois, with a population of 10,000 by the mid-1840s. There, Smith introduced the most distinctive features of Mormon theology, including baptism for the dead, eternal marriage, and polygamy, or plural marriage. As a result, Mormonism increasingly diverged from traditional Christianity and became a distinct new religion. To bolster his authority as a prophet, Smith established a theocratic political order under which church leaders controlled political offices and governed the community, with Smith as mayor.

Neighboring residents, alarmed by the Mormons' growing political power and reports that church leaders were practicing polygamy, demanded that Nauvoo's charter be revoked and the church suppressed. In 1844, while in jail for destroying the printing press of dissident Mormons in Nauvoo, Smith was murdered by an anti-Mormon mob. In 1846 the Mormons abandoned Nauvoo, and the following year Brigham Young, Smith's successor, led them westward to Utah.

✓ REVIEW

In what ways did Transcendentalism shape the themes of writers of the American Renaissance? Who were the major communitarian reformers of the era?

RADICAL REFORM

LATE IN THE FALL OF 1834 Lyman Beecher was in the midst of his continuing efforts to "overturn and overturn" on behalf of the kingdom of God. He had left Boston for Cincinnati to assume leadership of Lane Seminary. The school had everything that an institution for training ministers to convert the West needed—everything, that is, except students. In October 1834 all but 8 of Lane's 100 scholars had departed after months of bitter fighting with Beecher and the trustees over the issue of abolition.

Beecher knew the source of his troubles: a scruffy, magnetic convert of Finney's revivals named Theodore Dwight Weld. Weld had fired up his classmates over the need to end slavery immediately. In doing so, he echoed the arguments of William Lloyd Garrison, whose abolitionist writings had sent shock waves across the entire nation. Indeed, Beecher's troubles at Lane Seminary provided only one example of how the flames of reform could spread along paths not anticipated by those who had kindled them.

The Beginnings of the Abolitionist Movement

William Lloyd Garrison symbolized the transition from a moderate antislavery movement to the more militant abolitionism of the 1830s. A sober, religious youngster deeply influenced by his Baptist mother, Garrison in the 1820s edited a newspaper sympathetic to many of the new reforms. In 1829 he was enlisted in the antislavery cause by Benjamin Lundy, a Quaker who edited a Baltimore antislavery newspaper, *The Genius of Universal Emancipation*. Calling for a gradual end to slavery, Lundy supported colonization, hoping to overcome southern fears of emancipation by transporting free black Americans to Africa.

Garrison went to Baltimore to help edit Lundy's paper, and for the first time he encountered the opinions of free African Americans. To his surprise, Garrison discovered that most of them strongly opposed the colonization movement as proslavery and antiblack. Under their influence,

Garrison soon developed views far more radical than Lundy's. Within a year of moving to Baltimore the young firebrand was convicted of libel and imprisoned. On his release Garrison hurried back to Boston, determined to publish a new kind of antislavery journal.

GARRISON'S IMMEDIATISM On January 1, 1831, the first issue of *The Liberator* appeared, and abolitionism was born. In appearance the bespectacled Garrison seemed frail, almost mousy. But in print, he was abrasive, withering, and uncompromising. "On this subject, I do not wish to think, or speak, or write with moderation," he proclaimed. "I am in earnest—I will not equivocate—I will not excuse—I will not retreat a single inch—AND I WILL BE HEARD." Repudiating gradual emancipation and embracing "immediatism," Garrison insisted that slavery end at once. He denounced colonization as a racist, antiblack movement and upheld the principle of racial equality. To those who suggested that slaveowners should be compensated for freeing their slaves, Garrison was firm. Southerners ought to be convinced by "moral suasion" to renounce slavery as a sin. Virtue was its own reward.

| William Lloyd Garrison (shown, left, at age 30) and Theodore Dwight Weld (right) represented different wings of the abolitionist movement. Garrison's growing radicalism led him to repudiate organized religion in the struggle against slavery. Weld, however, preferred to work through the evangelical churches and cooperate with the clergy.

Garrison attracted the most attention, but other abolitionists spoke with equal conviction. Wendell Phillips, from a socially prominent Boston family, held listeners spellbound with his speeches. Lewis Tappan and his brother Arthur, two New York City silk merchants, boldly placed their wealth behind a number of humanitarian causes, including abolitionism. James G. Birney, an Alabama slaveholder, converted to abolitionism after wrestling with his conscience, and Angelina and Sarah Grimké, the daughters of a South Carolina planter, left their native state to speak against the institution. And there was Angelina's future husband, Theodore Weld, the restless student at Lane Seminary who had fallen so dramatically under Garrison's influence.

To abolitionists, slavery was a moral, not an economic, question. The institution seemed a contradiction of the principle of the American Revolution that all human beings had been created with natural rights. Then, too, it went against the Romantic spirit of the age, which celebrated the individual's freedom and self-reliance. Abolitionists condemned slavery because of the breakup of marriages and families by sale, the harsh punishment of the lash, slaves' lack of access to education, and the sexual abuse of black women. Most of all, they denounced slavery as outrageously contrary to Christian teaching. As one Ohio antislavery paper declared: "We believe slavery to be a sin, always, everywhere, and only, sin—sin, in itself." So persistent were abolitionists in their religious objections that they forced the churches to face the question of slavery head-on. In the 1840s the Methodist and Baptist churches each split into northern and southern organizations over the issue.

The Spread of Abolitionism

ABOLITIONISTS' PROFILE After helping organize the New England Anti-Slavery Society in 1832, Garrison joined with Lewis Tappan and Theodore Weld the following year to establish a national organization, the American Anti-Slavery Society. It coordinated a loosely affiliated network of state and local groups. During the years before the Civil War, perhaps 200,000 northerners belonged to an abolitionist society.

Abolitionists were concentrated in the East, especially New England, and in areas that had been settled by New Englanders, such as western New York and northern Ohio. The movement was not strong in cities or among businesspeople and workers. Most abolitionists were young, being generally in their 20s and 30s when the movement began, and had grown up in rural areas and small towns in middle-class families. Intensely religious, many had been profoundly affected by the revivals of the Second Great Awakening. More and more they came to

| In 1850 the Boston Museum's "New Hall of Wax Statuary" featured seven figures portraying the "Horrors of Slavery," indicating a heightened awareness of the institution's evils on the part of the northern public.

Black abolitionist Frederick Douglass (second from left at the podium) was only one of nearly 50 runaway slaves who appeared at an abolitionist convention held in August 1850 in Cazenovia, New York. Other runaways included Emily and Mary Edmonson (both in plaid dresses). When the Edmonsons' attempt at escape failed, Henry Ward Beecher (Lyman Beecher's son) rallied his congregation in Brooklyn to raise the money to purchase the girls' freedom.

feel that slavery was the fundamental cause of the Republic's degraded condition.

Theodore Weld was cut from this mold. After enrolling in Lane Seminary in 1833 he promoted immediate abolitionism among his fellow students. When Lyman Beecher assumed the Lane presidency a year later, he confronted a student body dominated by committed abolitionists, impatient of any position that stopped short of Garrison's immediatism.

LANE SEMINARY REBELLION The radicalism of Lane students was also made clear in their commitment to racial equality. Unlike some abolitionists, who opposed slavery but disdained blacks as inferior, Lane students mingled freely with Cincinnati's free black community. Alarmed by rumors in the summer of 1834 that the town's residents intended to demolish the school, Beecher and Lane's trustees forbade any discussion of slavery on campus, restricted contact with the black community, and ordered students to return to their studies. "Who that has an opinion and a soul will enter L. Sem now?" one rebel asked. "Who can do it without degrading himself?" All except a few left the school and enrolled at Oberlin College. That debt-ridden institution agreed to their demands for guaranteeing freedom of speech, admitting black students, and hiring Charles Finney as professor of theology.

But Finney fared no better than Beecher with the Lane rebels. In the end, he, too, concluded that reform generated discord, distracting Christians from the greater good of promoting revivals. Both men conceived of sin in terms of individual immorality, not unjust social institutions. To the abolitionists, however, America could never become a godly nation until slavery was abolished. "Revivals, moral Reform, etc. will remain stationary until the temple is cleansed," Weld bluntly concluded.

BLACK ABOLITIONISTS Free African Americans, who made up the majority of subscribers to Garrison's *Liberator,* provided important support and leadership for the movement. Frederick Douglass assumed the greatest prominence. Having escaped from slavery in Maryland, he became an eloquent critic of its evils. Initially a follower of Garrison, Douglass eventually broke with him and started his own newspaper in Rochester. Other important black abolitionists included Martin Delany, William Wells Brown, William Still, and Sojourner Truth. Aided by many other African Americans, these men and women battled against racial discrimination in the North as well as slavery in the South.

UNDERGROUND RAILROAD A network of antislavery sympathizers also developed in the North to convey runaway slaves to Canada and freedom. Although not as extensive or as tightly organized as contemporaries claimed, the Underground Railroad hid fugitives and transported them northward from one station to the next. Free African Americans, who were more readily trusted by wary slaves, played a leading role in the Underground Railroad. One of its most famous conductors was Harriet Tubman, an escaped slave who repeatedly returned to the South and eventually escorted to freedom more than 200 slaves.

Opponents and Divisions

The drive for immediate abolition faced massive obstacles within American society. With slavery increasingly important to the South's economy, southerners forced opponents of slavery to flee the region. In the North, where racism was equally entrenched, abolitionism provoked bitter resistance. Even abolitionists such as Garrison treated blacks paternalistically, contending that they should occupy a subordinate place in the antislavery movement.

On occasion, northern resistance turned violent. A hostile Boston mob seized Garrison in 1835 and paraded him with a rope around his body before he was finally rescued. Another anti-abolitionist mob burned down the headquarters of the American Anti-Slavery Society in Philadelphia. And in 1837 in Alton, Illinois, Elijah Lovejoy was murdered when he tried to protect his printing press from an angry crowd. The leaders of these mobs were not from the bottom of society but, as one of their victims noted, were "gentlemen of property and standing." Prominent leaders in the community, they reacted vigorously to the threat that abolitionists posed to their power and prosperity and to the established order.

DIVISIONS AMONG REFORMERS

But abolitionists were also hindered by divisions among reformers. At Oberlin College, Charles Finney preferred revivalism over Theodore Weld's abolitionism. Within another decade Lyman Beecher would see his daughter Harriet Beecher Stowe write the most successful piece of antislavery literature in the nation's history, *Uncle Tom's Cabin*. Even the abolitionists themselves splintered, shaken by the opposition they encountered and unable to agree on the most effective response. More conservative reformers wanted to work within established institutions, using the churches and political action to end slavery. But for Garrison and his followers, the mob violence demonstrated that slavery was only part of a deeper national disease, whose cure required the overthrow of American institutions and values.

By the end of the decade Garrison had worked out a program for the total reform of society. He embraced perfectionism and pacifism, denounced the clergy, urged members to leave the churches, and called for an end to all government. Condemning the Constitution as proslavery—"a covenant with death and an agreement with hell"—he publicly burned a copy one July 4th. No person of conscience, he argued, could vote or otherwise participate in the corrupt political system. This platform was radical enough on all counts, but the final straw for Garrison's opponents was his endorsement of women's rights as an inseparable part of abolitionism.

The Women's Rights Movement

Women faced many disadvantages in American society. They were kept out of most jobs, denied political rights, and given only limited access to education beyond the elementary grades. When a woman married, her husband became the legal representative of the marriage and gained complete control of her property. If a marriage ended in divorce, the husband was awarded custody of the children. Any unmarried woman was made the ward of a male relative.

When abolitionists divided over the issue of female participation, women found it easy to identify with the situation of slaves, since both were victims of male tyranny. Sarah and Angelina Grimké took up the cause of women's

rights after they were criticized for speaking to audiences that included men as well as women. Sarah responded with *Letters on the Condition of Women and the Equality of the Sexes* (1838), arguing that women deserved the same rights as men. Abby Kelly, another abolitionist, remarked that women "have good cause to be grateful to the slave," for in "striving to strike his irons off, we found most surely, that we were manacled ourselves."

SENECA FALLS CONVENTION

Two abolitionists, Elizabeth Cady Stanton and Lucretia Mott, launched the women's rights movement after they were forced to sit behind a curtain at a world antislavery convention in London. In 1848 Stanton and Mott organized a conference in Seneca Falls, New York, that attracted about a hundred supporters. The meeting issued a Declaration of Sentiments, modeled after the Declaration of Independence, that began: "All men and women are created equal."

The Seneca Falls Convention called for educational and professional opportunities for women, laws giving them control of their property, recognition of legal equality, and repeal of laws awarding the father custody of the children in divorce. The most controversial proposal, and the only resolution that did not pass unanimously, was one demanding the right to vote. The Seneca Falls Convention established the arguments and the program for the women's rights movement for the remainder of the century.

Elizabeth Cady Stanton, one of the instigators and guiding spirits at the Seneca Falls Convention, photographed with two of her children about that time.

In response several states gave women greater control over their property, and a few made divorce easier or granted women the right to sue in courts. But disappointments and defeats outweighed these early victories. Still, many of the important leaders in the crusade for women's rights that emerged after the Civil War had already taken their places at the forefront of the movement. They included Stanton, Susan B. Anthony, Lucy Stone, and—as Lyman Beecher by now must have expected, one of his daughters—Isabella Beecher Hooker.

The Schism of 1840

It was Garrison's position on women's rights that finally split antislavery ranks already divided over other aspects of his growing radicalism. The showdown came in 1840 at the national convention of the American Anti-Slavery Society, when delegates debated whether women could hold office in the organization. Some of Garrison's opponents favored women's rights but opposed linking the question to the slavery issue, insisting that it would drive off potential supporters. By packing the convention, Garrison carried the day. His opponents, led by Lewis Tappan, resigned to found the rival American and Foreign Anti-Slavery Society.

The schism of 1840 lessened the influence of abolitionism as a reform movement. Although abolitionism heightened moral concern about slavery, it failed to convert the North to its program, and its supporters remained a tiny minority. Despite the considerable courage of its leaders, the movement lacked a realistic, long-range plan for eliminating such a deeply entrenched institution. Abolitionism demonstrated the limits of voluntary persuasion and individual conversions as a solution to deeply rooted social problems.

✔ REVIEW

What helped spark the growth of an abolitionist movement? What factors caused the movement to splinter?

REFORM SHAKES THE PARTY SYSTEM

"WHAT A FOG-BANK WE ARE in politically. Do you see any head-land or light—or can you get an observation—or soundings?" The words came from a puzzled Whig politician writing a friend after the Massachusetts state elections of 1853. He was in such a confused state because reformers were increasingly entering the political arena to achieve results.

The Turn toward Politics

The crusading idealism of revivalists and reformers inevitably collided with the hard reality that society could not be perfected by converting individuals. Several movements, including those to establish public schools and erect asylums, had operated within the political system from the beginning. But a growing number of other frustrated reformers were abandoning the principle of voluntary persuasion and looking to government coercion to achieve their goals.

Politicians did not particularly welcome the new interest. Because the Whig and Democratic parties both drew on evangelical and nonevangelical voters, heated moral debates over the harmful effects of drink or the evils of slavery threatened to detach regular party members from their old loyalties and disrupt each party's unity. The strong opposition of German and Irish immigrants to temperance stimulated antiforeign sentiment among reformers and further divided both party coalitions, particularly the Democrats. "The temperance question is playing havock in the old party lines," commented one Indiana politician. The issue of abolition seemed even more disruptive.

WOMEN AND THE RIGHT TO VOTE — Because women could not vote, they felt excluded when the temperance and abolitionist movements turned to electoral action to accomplish their goals. By the 1840s female reformers increasingly demanded the right to vote as the means to change society. Nor were men blind to what was at stake: one reason they so strongly resisted female suffrage was that it would give women real power.

The Maine Law

The political parties could resist the women's suffrage movement, because most of its advocates lacked the right to vote. Less easily put off were temperance reformers. Although drinking had significantly declined in American society by 1840, it had hardly been eliminated. After 1845 the arrival of large numbers of German and Irish immigrants, who were accustomed to consuming alcohol, made voluntary prohibition even more remote. In response temperance advocates proposed state laws that would outlaw the manufacture and sale of alcoholic beverages.

Party leaders tried to dodge the question of prohibition, since large numbers of Whigs and Democrats were found on both sides of the issue. Temperance advocates countered by seeking pledges from candidates to support a prohibitory law. To win additional recruits, temperance leaders adopted techniques used in political campaigns, including house-to-house canvasses, parades and processions, bands and singing, banners, picnics, and mass rallies.

The movement's first major triumph came in 1851. The Maine Law, as it was known, authorized search and seizure of private property in that state and provided stiff penalties for selling liquor. In the next few years a number of states enacted similar laws, although most were struck down by the courts or later repealed. Prohibition remained a controversial political issue throughout the century.

TEMPERANCE DISRUPTS THE PARTIES — Although prohibition was temporarily defeated, the issue badly disrupted the Whig and Democratic Parties. It greatly increased party switching and brought to the polls a large number of new voters, including many "wets" who wanted to preserve their right to drink. By dissolving the

THE GREAT REPUBLICAN REFORM PARTY,

| By the 1850s a new antislavery party, the Republicans, was running John Frémont (far right) for president. This cartoon manages to tie just about every reform movement of the era to the Republicans—and in so doing, exhibits the usual stereotypical caricatures. Can you link each of Frémont's petitioners with one of the movements discussed in this chapter? How are the stereotypes being conveyed visually?

ties between so many voters and their parties, the temperance issue played a major role in the eventual collapse of the Jacksonian party system in the 1850s.

Abolitionism and the Party System

Slavery proved even more divisive. In 1835 abolitionists distributed more than a million pamphlets, mostly in the South, through the Post Office. A wave of excitement swept the South when the first batches arrived addressed to white southerners. Former senator Robert Hayne led a Charleston mob that burned sacks of U.S. mail containing abolitionist literature, and postmasters in other southern cities refused to deliver the material. The Jackson administration allowed southern states to censor the mail, leading abolitionists to protest that their civil rights had been violated. In reaction, the number of antislavery societies in the North nearly tripled.

With access to the mails impaired, abolitionists began flooding Congress with petitions against slavery. Asserting that Congress had no power over the institution, angry southern representatives demanded action, and the House

in response adopted the so-called gag rule in 1836. It automatically tabled without consideration any petition dealing with slavery. But southern leaders had made a tactical blunder. The gag rule allowed abolitionists not only to attack slavery but also to speak out as defenders of white civil liberties. The appeal of the antislavery movement was broadened, and in 1844 the House finally repealed the controversial rule.

Many abolitionists outside Garrison's extreme circle began to feel that an antislavery third party offered a more effective means of attacking slavery. In 1840 these political abolitionists founded the Liberty Party and nominated for president James Birney, a former slaveholder who had converted to abolitionism. Birney received only 7,000 votes, but the Liberty Party was the seed from which a stronger antislavery political movement would grow. From 1840 onward, abolitionism's importance would be in the political arena rather than as a voluntary reform organization.

 REVIEW

How did reform movements create instability in the political system?

CONCLUSION

THE WORLD AT LARGE

The ferment of reform during the decades from 1820 to 1850 reflected a multitude of attempts to deal with transformations working through not just the United States but also Europe. Americans crowded the docks of New York City eagerly awaiting the latest installment of Charles Dickens's novels from England, tales often set amid urban slums and dingy factories. European middle classes embraced the home as a domestic refuge, as did their counterparts in America. The "benevolent empire" of American reform organizations drew inspiration from similar British campaigns. Robert Owen launched his utopian reforms in New Lanark, Scotland, before his ideas were tried out at New Harmony, Indiana, and disciples of the French socialist Charles Fourier founded communities in the United States.

Abolition was potentially the most dangerous of these transatlantic reforms because slavery was so deeply and profitably intertwined with the industrial system. Slave labor produced cotton for the textile factories of New England, Great Britain, and Europe; plantation economies supplied the sugar, rice, tea, and coffee that were a part of European and American diets. Revolutionary France had abolished slavery in 1794, but Napoleon reinstated it, along with the slave trade. Great Britain outlawed the trade in 1808 (as did the United States) and then freed nearly 800,000 slaves in its colonies in 1834.

Any move for emancipation in the United States seemed out of the question, and as late as 1840 abolition lacked the power to threaten the political system. Birney's small vote, coupled with the disputes between the two national antislavery societies, encouraged political leaders to believe that the party system had turned back this latest threat of sectionalism. But the growing northern concern about slavery highlighted differences between the two sections. Despite the strength of evangelicalism in the South, the reform impulse spawned by the revivals found little support there, since reform movements were discredited by their association with abolitionism. The party system confronted the difficult challenge of holding together sections that, although sharing much, were also diverging in important ways. To the residents of both sections, the South increasingly appeared to be a unique society with its own distinctive way of life. ∞∞∞

CHAPTER SUMMARY

THE JACKSONIAN ERA PRODUCED THE greatest number of significant reform movements in American history.

■ The Second Great Awakening, which preached the doctrine of salvation available to all and the coming of the millennium, encouraged revivals and reform.

• Revivals drew converts from every segment of American society and spoke to their spiritual needs.

• Women were most prominent among revival converts.

• The Second Great Awakening made evangelicals the dominant religious subculture in the United States.

• Benevolence and reform societies decisively changed drinking habits and the ideals of womanhood and the family.

• Evangelical religious fervor also fueled anti-Catholicism, although many Protestants adopted elements of Catholic art and rituals into their services and church architecture.

■ Unitarianism and Transcendentalism, which emphasized the unlimited potential of each individual, also strengthened reform.

■ Utopian communities sought to establish a model society for the rest of the world to follow.

■ Mormons developed the most significant following among utopian communities but also drew persecution.

■ Temperance, abolitionism, and women's rights movements each turned to political action to accomplish their goals.

• Abolitionism precipitated both strong support and violent opposition, and the movement split in 1840.

• Although it survived, the party system was seriously weakened by these reform movements.

ADDITIONAL READING

GOOD INTRODUCTIONS TO ANTEBELLUM EVANGELICAL religion and reform include Robert Abzug, *Cosmos Crumbling* (1994); Charles Hambrick-Stowe, *Charles G. Finney and the Spirit of American Evangelicalism* (1996); and Bertram Wyatt-Brown, *Lewis Tappan and the Evangelical War Against Slavery* (1971). For suggestive analyses of the relationship between antebellum evangelicalism and the sweeping changes in economic and political life, consult Richard Carwardine, *Evangelicals and Politics in Antebellum America* (1997); Candy Gunther Brown, *The Word in the World* (2004); and Paul Johnson and Sean Wilentz, *The Kingdom of Matthias* (1994). The best studies of the role of women in evangelical churches and reform societies are Anne Boylan, *The Origins of Women's Activism* (1988); Lori Ginzberg, *Women and the Work of Benevolence* (1990); and Nancy Hewitt, *Women's Activism and Social Change* (1984). To understand the link between reformist activism and the early women's rights movement, begin with Lori Ginzberg, *Untidy Origins* (2005), and Nancy Isenberg, *Sex and Citizenship in the United States* (1998).

Despite the dominant influence of evangelical Protestants, both Roman Catholics and Mormons attracted a growing number of adherents during the antebellum period. For a fascinating account of the origins and rise of Mormonism, see John Brooke, *The Refiner's Fire* (1996), and for a compelling account of how American Protestants responded to the growth of Roman Catholicism after the 1830s, see Ryan Smith, *Gothic Arches, Latin Crosses* (2006). To explore the reasons why a small but influential minority of nineteenth-century Americans rejected all forms of Christianity in favor of agnosticism or atheism, rely on James Turner, *Without God, Without Creed* (1985).

For a fuller list of readings, see the Bibliography at www.mhhe.com/eh8e.

SIGNIFICANT EVENTS

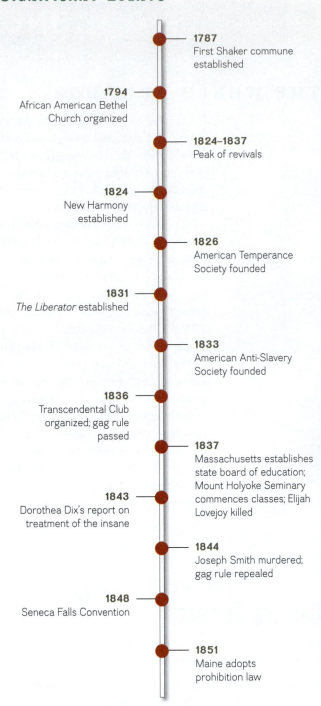

1787
First Shaker commune established

1794
African American Bethel Church organized

1824–1837
Peak of revivals

1824
New Harmony established

1826
American Temperance Society founded

1831
The Liberator established

1833
American Anti-Slavery Society founded

1836
Transcendental Club organized; gag rule passed

1837
Massachusetts establishes state board of education; Mount Holyoke Seminary commences classes; Elijah Lovejoy killed

1843
Dorothea Dix's report on treatment of the insane

1844
Joseph Smith murdered; gag rule repealed

1848
Seneca Falls Convention

1851
Maine adopts prohibition law

REVIEW

Varieties of Antebellum Reform

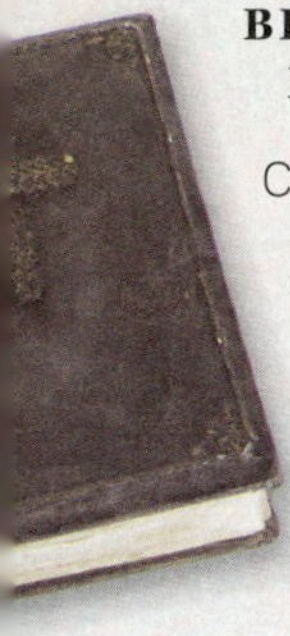

BENEVOLENCE AND MORAL REFORM	HUMANITARIAN REFORM	RADICAL REFORM
Circulation of Bible, tracts	Asylum care for the insane	Socialist rejection of private property
Christian missions to the Indians, foreign nations	Improvement of public education, high schools	Women's rights and suffrage
Campaign to end business on the Sabbath, to found Sunday schools	Education for the blind and deaf	Complex marriage at Oneida; plural marriage among Mormons
Temperance	Prison reform	Prohibition
Missions to sailors, the poor	Antislavery, colonization	Abolitionism

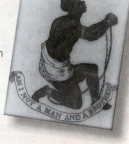

A nurse and child, about 1850. Because it took minutes to expose a daguerreotype print, the nurse is holding the child's hand still. Although the South encompassed a wide variety of subregions, classes of people, crops, and climates, its "peculiar institution," slavery, came to deeply shape its identity in the decades before the Civil War. As this portrait indicates, relations between the free and enslaved were closely, and often ambiguously, intertwined. What ambiguities are suggested by the daguerreotype?

The Old South

1820–1860

What's to Come

⊗⊗⊗⊗ AN AMERICAN STORY ⊗⊗⊗

WHERE IS THE REAL SOUTH?

The impeccably dressed Colonel Daniel Jordan, master of 261 slaves at Laurel Hill, strolls down his oak-lined lawn to the dock along the Waccamaw River, a day's journey north of Charleston, South Carolina, to board the steamship *Nina*. On Fridays, it is Colonel Jordan's custom to visit the exclusive Hot and Hot Fish Club, founded by his fellow low-country planters, to play a game of lawn bowling or billiards and be waited on by black servants in livery as he sips a mint julep in the refined atmosphere that for him is the South.

Several hundred miles west another steamboat, the *Fashion,* makes its way along the Alabama River. One of the passengers is upset by the boat's slow pace. "Time's money, time's money!" he mutters, eager to get back to his plantation in the Red River country of Texas. "Time's worth more'n money to me now; a hundred percent more, 'cause I left my niggers all alone; not a damn white man within four mile on 'em." When asked what they are doing, since the cotton crop has already been picked, he says, "I set 'em to clairin', but they ain't doin' a damn thing. . . . I know that as well as you do. . . . But I'll make it up, I'll make it up when I get thar, now you'd better believe." For this Red River planter, time is money and cotton is his world—indeed, cotton is what the South is all about.

"I am a cotton man, I am, and I don't care who knows it," he proclaims. "I know cotton, I do. I'm dam' if I know anythin' but cotton."

At the other end of the South, the slave Sam Williams works in the intense heat of Buffalo Forge, an iron-making factory in the Shenandoah Valley. As a refiner, Williams heats pig iron in the white-hot coals, then slings the ball of glowing metal on an anvil, where he pounds it with huge, water-powered hammers to remove the impurities. Ambitious and hardworking, he earns extra money (at the same rate paid to whites) for any iron he produces beyond his weekly quota. In some years his extra income is more than $100. His wife, Nancy, in charge of the dairy, earns extra money as well, and the additional income allows them to buy extra food and items for themselves and their daughters. More important, it helps keep their family intact in an unstable environment. Their owner is very unlikely to sell slaves who work so hard. For Sam and Nancy Williams, family ties, worship at the local Baptist church, and socializing with their fellow slaves are what make life meaningful.

In the bayous of the Deep South, where the Mississippi delta meets the Gulf, Octave Johnson hears the dogs coming. For a year Johnson has been a runaway slave. He fled from a Louisiana plantation when the work bell rang before daybreak and the overseer threatened to whip him for staying in bed. To survive, he hides in the swamps 4 miles behind the plantation—stealing turkeys, chickens, and pigs and trading with other slaves. Nearly 30 other slaves have joined him over the past year. The howling dogs warn Johnson and his companions that the hound master Eugene Jardeau is out again. This time when the pack bursts upon them, the slaves do not flee but kill as many dogs as possible. Then they plunge into the bayou, and as the hounds follow, alligators make short work of another six. For Octave Johnson the real South is a matter of weighing one's prospects between the uncertainties of alligators and the overseer's whip—and deciding when to say no.

Selling snacks at the Richmond rail station

Ferdinand Steel and his family are not forced, by the flick of the lash, to rise at five in the morning. They rise because the land demands it. Steel, in his 20s, owns 170 acres of land in Carroll County, Mississippi. Unmarried, he moved there from Tennessee with his widowed mother, sister, and brother, only a few years after the Choctaws had been forced to give up the region and march west. His life is one of continuous hard work, caring for the animals and tending the crops. His mother and sister have plenty to keep them busy: making soap, fashioning dippers out of gourds, or sewing. The Steel family grows cotton, too, but their total crop amounts to only five or six bales—never enough profit to consider buying even one slave. But the five bales at least mean cash, and cash means that when he goes to market, he can buy sugar and coffee, gunpowder and lead, a yard or two of calico, and quinine to treat the malaria that is common in those parts. Though fiercely independent, Steel and his scattered neighbors help one another to raise houses, clear fields, shuck corn, and quilt. They are bound together by blood, religion, obligation, and honor. For small farmers such as Ferdinand Steel, these ties constitute the real South. ∞∞∞

THE SOCIAL STRUCTURE OF THE COTTON KINGDOM

THE PORTRAITS COULD GO ON and on. Different people, different Souths, all real. Such contrasts show how difficult it can be to define a regional identity. Encompassing in 1860 the 15 slave states plus the District of Columbia, the South was a land of great geographic diversity. It extended from the Tidewater coastal plain along the Atlantic Seaboard to the prairies of Texas, from the Kentucky bluegrass region to the Gulf coast, from the mountains of western Virginia to the semitropical swamps of the Mississippi delta. Yet despite its differences, the South was bound together by ties so strong, they eventually outpulled those of the nation itself. At the heart of this unity was an agricultural system made possible by the region's warm climate and long growing season. Within the United States, cotton, rice, and sugar could be grown only in the South. Most important, this rural agricultural economy was based on the institution of slavery, which affected all aspects of southern society. It shaped not only the culture of the slaves but also the lives of their masters and mistresses, and even the ways of farm families and herders in the hills who saw few slaves from day to day.

Of all the South's crops, cotton called the tune. Its spread through the region stimulated the nation's remarkable economic growth after the War of 1812. Demand spurred by the textile industry sent the price of cotton soaring on the international market, and white southerners scrambled into the unplanted lands of the Southwest to reap the profits to be made in the cotton sweepstakes.

THE COTTON ENVIRONMENT

This new cultivation dramatically transformed the South's landscape, denuding countless acres covered with trees, vines, and brush. Cotton also imposed a demanding work discipline on slaves, who cultivated hundreds of acres, and white farming families, who tended many fewer. Typically they planted the newly cleared land in corn for a year, just long enough for tree stumps to decompose. In the next spring season, a heavy plow pulled by oxen or mules cleaved the fields into deep furrows, followed by workers who pitched cottonseed between the ridges. Then began the battle to protect the tender, newly sprouted plants. In the spring it was crucial to thin the excess cotton shoots and to yank out weeds throughout the summer. In years of heavy rains, when such competing vegetation flourished, masters put even their house slaves into the fields. Otherwise, a fungus might rot the cotton boll in wet weather, or beetles like the boll weevil attack the cotton buds, or—worst of all—the dreaded army worm invade, stripping field after field of its cotton.

Paradoxically, the more planters succeeded in opening new lands, the easier it was for the worm (and its parent moth) to spread across an entire region. During a summer in the 1850s, slaves on one plantation dug a deep trench

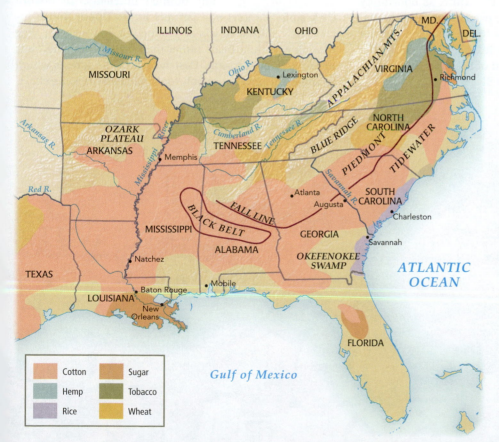

COTTON AND OTHER CROPS OF THE SOUTH

By 1860 the cotton kingdom extended across the Lower South into the Texas prairie and up the Mississippi River valley. Tobacco and hemp were the staple crops of the Upper South, where they competed with corn and wheat. Rice production was concentrated in the swampy coastal region of South Carolina and Georgia as well as the lower tip of Louisiana. The sugar district was in southern Louisiana. **Why was rice growing concentrated in coastal regions? Which staple crop predominates in the South, according to the map? Why is the answer different in the nineteenth century than it is in the eighteenth?**

between the cotton fields on a neighboring operation, in a desperate attempt to halt the army worms' progress. Into it they tumbled—"in untold millions," one observer reported, until the trench's bottom "for nearly a mile in extent, was a foot or two deep in [a] living mass of animal life." Then the slaves hitched a team of oxen to a heavy log and, as they pulled it through the ditch, "it seemed to float on a crushed mass" of army worms.

An army worm on a cotton boll

The Boom Country Economy

COTTON PUSHES WESTWARD But the difficulties of cultivation did little to discourage white southerners' enthusiasm for cotton. Letters, newspapers, and word of mouth all brought tales of the Black Belt region of Alabama, where the dark soil was particularly suited to growing cotton, and of the tremendous yields from the soils along the Mississippi River's broad reaches. "The *Alabama Feaver* rages here with great violence and has *carried off* vast numbers of our Citizens," a North Carolinian wrote in 1817. A generation later, as the removal of the southern Indian tribes opened vast tracts of land to white settlement, immigrants were still "pouring in with a ceaseless tide," one observer reported, "including 'Land Sharks' ready to swallow up the home of the redmen, or the white, as oportunity might offer." By the 1840s planters even began to leave Mississippi and Alabama to head for the new cotton frontier along the Red River and up into Texas. Amazingly, by the eve of the Civil War nearly a third of the total cotton crop came from *west* of the Mississippi River.

SOUTHERN PROSPERITY As Senator James Henry Hammond of South Carolina boasted in 1858, cotton was king in the Old South. By 1860 the United States produced three-fourths of the world's supply of cotton. This boom fueled the southern economy so strongly that following the depression of 1839–1843, the southern economy grew faster than that in the North. Even so, per capita income in the South remained below that of the free states, and wealth was not as evenly distributed in the plantation South as in northern agricultural areas.

Prosperity masked other basic problems in the economy—problems that would become more apparent after the Civil War. Much of the South's new wealth resulted from migration of its population to more productive western lands. Once that prime agricultural land was settled, the South could not sustain its rate of expansion. Nor did the shift in population alter the structure of the southern economy, stimulate technological change, improve the way goods were produced and marketed, or generate internal markets.

ENVIRONMENTAL IMPACT OF SINGLE-CROP AGRICULTURE The single-crop agriculture practiced by southern farmers rapidly wore out the soil. Tobacco was a particularly exhaustive crop, and corn also rapidly drained nutrients. To restore their soils, planters and farmers in the **Upper South** increasingly shifted to wheat production, but because they now plowed their fields rather than using a hoe, this shift intensified soil erosion. Destruction of the forests where commercial agriculture now took hold had the same effect,

In this romanticized Currier and Ives print of a cotton plantation, field hands are waist-deep in cotton while other slaves haul the picked cotton to be ginned and then pressed into bales. Mounted on a horse, an overseer rides through the field supervising the work while the owner and his wife look on. Picking began as early as August and continued in some areas until late January. Because the bolls ripened at different times, a field had to be picked several times.

and many streams quickly silted up and were no longer navigable. Row-crop agriculture made floods and droughts more common. In addition, reliance on a single crop increased toxins and parasites in the soil, making southern agriculture more vulnerable to destruction than varied agriculture was.

Only the South's low population density lessened the impact on the environment. More remote areas remained heavily forested, wetlands were still common, and as late as 1860, 80 percent of the region was uncultivated (cattle and hogs, however, ranged over much of this acreage). Throughout much of the South, farmers fired the woods in the spring to destroy insects, burn off brush, and increase grass for their browsing stock.

Perhaps the most striking environmental consequence of the expansion of southern society was the increase in disease, especially in the **Deep South.** Epidemic diseases such as malaria, yellow fever, and cholera were brought to the area by Europeans. The clearing of land—which increased runoff, precipitated floods, and produced pools of stagnant water—facilitated the spread of these diseases. In notoriously unhealthy areas, such as the coastal swamps of South Carolina's rice district, wealthy whites fled during the sickly summer months.

The Upper South's New Orientation

As cotton transformed the boom country of the Deep South, agriculture in the Upper South also adjusted (see map, page 325). Improved varieties and more scientific agricultural practices reversed the decline in tobacco that had begun in the 1790s. More important, farmers in the Upper South made wheat and corn their major crops. As early as 1840 the value of wheat grown in Virginia was twice that of tobacco.

SLAVE TRADE Because the new crops required less labor, planters in the Upper South regularly sold their surplus slaves to cotton and sugar planters in the Deep South. Indeed, some planters in the Upper South maintained a profit margin only by these sales. The demand in the Deep South for field hands drove their price steadily up so that by the late 1850s a prime field hand, who would have sold for $600 in the early 1840s, commanded $1,500. Even with increased labor costs, southern agriculture flourished.

The Rural South

LACK OF MANUFACTURING The Old South was dynamic, expanding, and booming economically. But the region remained overwhelmingly rural, with 84 percent of its labor force engaged in agriculture in 1860, compared with 40 percent in the North. Conversely, the South lagged in manufacturing, producing only 9 percent of the nation's manufactured goods. During the 1850s some southern propagandists urged greater investment in industry to diversify the South's economy. But as long as high profits from cotton continued, these advocates made little headway. With so little industry, few cities developed in the South. New Orleans, with a population of 169,000 in 1860, was the only truly southern city of significant size. Only 1 in 10 southerners lived in cities and towns in 1860, compared with 1 out of 3 persons in the North.

LACK OF EDUCATION As a rural society the South showed far less interest in education. Southern colleges were inferior to those in the North, and public secondary schools were virtually nonexistent. Wealthy planters, who hired tutors or sent their children to private academies, generally opposed a state-supported school system. Thus free public schools were rare, especially in the rural districts that made up most of the South. Georgia in

1860 had only one county with a free school system, and Mississippi had no public schools outside its few cities. On average, southern white children spent only one-fifth as much time in school as did their northern counterparts.

The net result was high illiteracy rates. Among native-born white citizens, the 1850 census showed that 20 percent were unable to read and write. The comparable figure was 3 percent in the middle states and 0.4 percent in New England. In some areas of the South, more than a third of all white residents were illiterate.

Distribution of Slavery

Even more than agrarian ways, slavery set the South apart. Whereas in 1776 slavery had been a national institution, by 1820 slavery was confined to the states south of Pennsylvania and the Ohio River. The South's "peculiar institution" bound white and black southerners together in a multitude of ways.

Slaves were not evenly distributed throughout the region. More than half lived in the Deep South, where African Americans outnumbered white southerners in both South Carolina and Mississippi by the 1850s. Elsewhere in the Deep South the black population exceeded 40 percent in all states except Texas. In the Upper South, however, whites greatly outnumbered blacks. Only in Virginia and North Carolina did the slave population top 30 percent.

The distribution of slaves showed striking geographic variations within individual states as well. In areas of fertile

THE SPREAD OF SLAVERY, 1820–1860

Between 1820 and 1860 the slave population of the South shifted southward and westward, concentrating especially heavily in coastal South Carolina and Georgia, in the Black Belt region of central Alabama and Mississippi (so named because of its rich soil), and in the Mississippi valley. Small farms with few slaves predominated in cotton-growing areas that lacked good transportation, such as northern Georgia, and in regions with poor soil, such as the piney woods of southern Mississippi. **Comparing this map with the one on page 325, is a heavy concentration of slaves associated with only some of the South's staple crops? What factors contribute to a heavy concentration of slaves?**

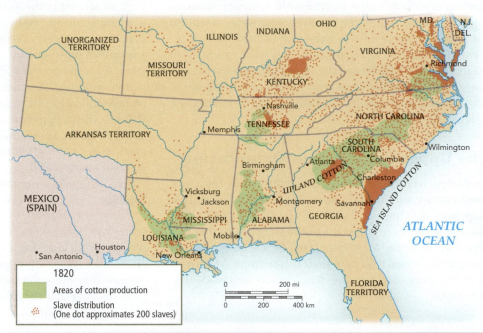

soil, flat or rolling countryside, and good transportation, slavery and the plantation system dominated. In the pine barrens, areas isolated by lack of transportation, and hilly and mountainous regions, small family farms and few slaves were the rule.

SLAVE OCCUPATIONS Almost all enslaved African Americans, male and female, worked in agricultural pursuits, with only about 10 percent living in cities and towns. On large plantations, a few slaves were domestic servants and others were skilled artisans—blacksmiths, carpenters, or bricklayers—but most toiled in the fields.

Slavery as a Labor System

Slavery was, first and foremost, a system to manage and control labor. The plantation system, with its extensive estates and large labor forces, could never have developed without slavery, nor could it have met the world demand for cotton and other staples. Slaves represented an enormous capital investment, worth more than all the land in the Old South.

PROFITABILITY OF SLAVERY Furthermore, slavery remained a highly profitable investment. The average slave-owner spent perhaps $30 to $35 a year to support an adult slave. Allowing for the cost of land, equipment, and other expenses, a planter could expect one of his slaves to produce more than $78 worth of cotton—which meant that about 60 percent of the wealth produced by a slave's labor was clear profit. For those who pinched pennies and drove slaves harder, the gains were even greater.

SLAVERY AND ARISTOCRATIC VALUES By concentrating wealth and power in the hands of the planter class, slavery shaped the tone of southern society. Planters were not aristocrats in the European sense of having special legal privileges or formal titles of rank. Still, the system encouraged southern planters to think of themselves as a landed gentry upholding the aristocratic values of pride, honor, family, and hospitality.

Whereas slavery had existed throughout most of the Americas at the beginning of the century, by the 1850s the United States, Cuba, and Brazil were the only slaveholding nations left in the region. Public opinion in Europe and in the North had grown more and more hostile to the peculiar institution, causing white southerners to feel increasingly like an embattled minority. Yet they clung tenaciously to slavery, for it was the base on which the South's economic growth and way of life rested. As one Georgian observed on the eve of the Civil War, slavery was "so intimately mingled with our social conditions that it would be impossible to eradicate it."

REVIEW

How did the cotton economy shape the South's environment and labor system?

CLASS STRUCTURE OF THE WHITE SOUTH

ONCE A YEAR AROUND CHRISTMASTIME, James Henry Hammond gave a dinner for his neighbors at his South Carolina plantation, Silver Bluff. The richest man for miles around as well as an ambitious politician, the aristocratic Hammond used these dinners to put his neighbors under personal obligation to him as well as receive the honor and respect he believed his due. Indeed, Hammond's social and political ambitions caused him to cultivate his neighbors, despite his low opinion of them, by hiring them to perform various tasks and by providing them a variety of services such as ginning their cotton and allowing them to use his gristmill. These services enhanced his ethic of paternalism, but his less affluent neighbors also displayed a strong personal pride. After he complained about the inconvenience of these services, only three of his neighbors came to his Christmas dinner in 1837, a snub that enraged him. As Hammond's experience demonstrated, class relations among whites in the Old South were a complex blend of privilege, patronage, and equality.

The Slaveowners

In 1860 the region's 15 states had a population of 12 million, of which roughly two-thirds were white, one-third were black slaves, and about 2 percent were free African Americans. Because of the institution of slavery, the social structure of the antebellum South differed in important ways from that of the North. Even so, southern society was remarkably fluid, and as a result, class lines were not rigid.

Of the 8 million white southerners in 1860, only about 2 million (one-quarter) either owned slaves or were members of slaveowning families. And most slaveowners owned only a few slaves. Censuses defined a planter as a person who owned 20 or more slaves; by that measure only about 1 out of every 30 white southerners belonged to families of the planter class.

A planter of consequence needed to own at least 50 slaves, and there were only about 10,000 such families—less than 1 percent of the white population. This privileged group made up the aristocracy at the top of the southern class structure. Owners of large numbers of slaves were rare; only about 2,000 southerners, such as Colonel Daniel Jordan, owned 100 or more slaves. Although limited in size, the planter class nevertheless owned more than half of all slaves and controlled more than 90 percent of the region's total wealth.

PLANTATION ADMINISTRATION The typical plantation had 20 to 50 slaves and 800 to 1,000 acres of land. On an estate larger than that, slaves would have to walk more than an hour to reach the farthest fields, losing valuable work time. Thus larger slaveowners usually owned several plantations, with an overseer to manage the slaves on each while the owner attended to business matters. The slaves were divided into field hands, skilled workers, and house servants, with one or more slaves serving as "drivers" to assist the overseer. Plantations remained labor-intensive operations. Only the production of sugar, among the southern staples, was heavily mechanized.

Tidewater and Frontier

Southern planters shared a commitment to preserve slavery as the source of their wealth and stature. Yet in other ways they were a diverse group. On the one hand, the tobacco and rice planters of the Atlantic Tidewater were part of a settled region and a culture that reached back 150 to 200 years. In contrast, such states as Mississippi and Arkansas were at or just emerging from the frontier stage, since most residents had arrived after 1815.

TIDEWATER SOCIETY It was along the Tidewater, especially the bays of the Chesapeake and the South Carolina coast, that the legendary "Old South" was born. Here, masters erected substantial homes, some of them—especially between Charleston and Columbia—the classic white-pillared mansions in the Greek revival style.

The ideal of the Tidewater South was the English country gentleman. As in England, in the Tidewater South the local gentry often served as justices of the peace, and the Episcopal Church remained the socially accepted road to heaven. Here, too, family names continued to be important in politics.

SOCIETY IN THE COTTON KINGDOM While the newer regions of the South boasted of planters with cultivated manners, as a group the cotton lords were a different breed. Whatever their background, whether planters, farmers, overseers, or businessmen, these entrepreneurs had moved west for the same reason so many other white Americans had: to make their fortunes. By and large, the cotton gentry were self-made men who through hard work, aggressive business tactics, and good luck had risen from ordinary backgrounds. For them, the cotton boom and the exploitation of enslaved men and women offered the opportunity to move up in a new society that lacked an entrenched elite.

SLAVEHOLDERS' VALUES That business orientation was especially apparent in the cotton kingdom, where planters sought to maximize their profits and constantly reinvested their returns in land and slaves. As one visitor said of Mississippi slaveholders: "To sell cotton in order to buy negroes—to make more cotton to buy more negroes, 'ad infinitum,' is the aim and direct tendency of all the operations of the thorough-going cotton planter." And indeed there was money to be made. The combined annual income of the richest thousand families of the cotton kingdom approached $50 million, while the wealth of the remaining 666,000 families amounted to only about $60 million.

Although most planters ranked among the richest citizens in America, their homes were often simple one- or two-story unpainted wooden frame houses, and some were log cabins. A visitor to one Georgia plantation reported that the house did not have a pane of glass in the windows, a door between the rooms, or a ceiling other than the roof. Practical men, few of the new cotton lords had absorbed the culture and learning of the traditional country gentleman.

The Master at Home

Whether supervising a Tidewater plantation or creating a cotton estate on the Texas frontier, the master had to coordinate a complex agricultural operation. He gave daily instructions concerning the work to be done, settled disputes between slaves and the overseer, and generally handed out rewards and penalties. In addition, the owner made the critical decisions concerning the planting, harvesting, and marketing of the crops. Planters also watched investments and expenditures, and they often sought to expand their production by clearing additional fields, buying more land or slaves, or investing in machinery such as cotton gins. As in any business these decisions required a sound understanding of the domestic and international market.

Southern Population, 1860

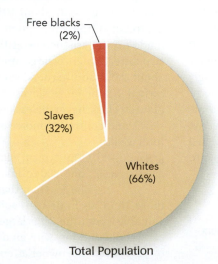

Total Population

White Population

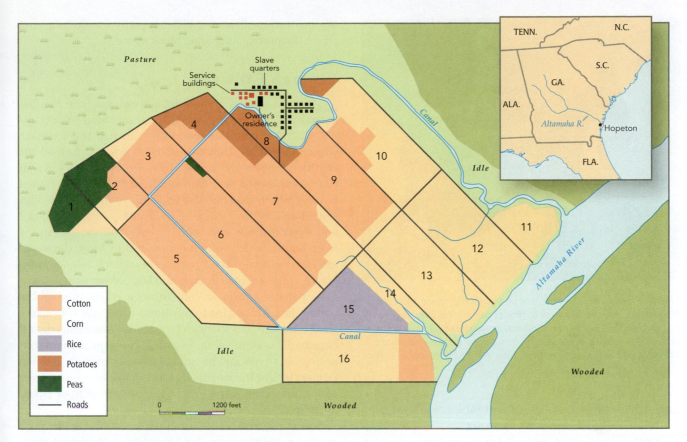

A PLANTATION LAYOUT, HOPETON, GEORGIA

Often covering a thousand acres or more, a plantation was laid out like a small village and contained several fields and usually extensive uncleared woods. Somewhere near the master's "big house" were the quarters—slave cabins clustered along one or more streets. Service buildings might include a smokehouse, stables, a gin house (for cotton) or a rice mill, and an overseer's dwelling. Like most large plantations, Hopeton produced a considerable amount of foodstuffs, but it grew both rice and cotton as staples. Most plantations concentrated on a single cash crop.

PATERNALISM   In performing his duties the plantation owner was supposed to be the "master" of his crops, his family, and his slaves. Defenders of slavery held up this paternalistic ideal—the care and guidance of dependent "children"—maintaining that slavery promoted a genuine affection between caring master and loyal slaves. Yet in real life a concern for money and profits undermined this paternalistic ideal. Some of the most brutal forms of slavery existed on rice plantations in the Tidewater South, where the absenteeism of many owners combined with the sheer numbers of slaves made close personal ties impossible. Owners of large plantations had little contact with their slaves, except for a few domestic servants. Nor could paternalism mask the reality that slavery everywhere rested on violence, racism, and exploitation.

The Plantation Mistress

Upper-class southern white women, like those in the North, grew up with the ideal of domesticity, reinforced by the notion of a paternalistic master who was lord of the plantation. But the plantation mistress soon discovered that, given the demands placed on her, the ideal was hard to fulfill.

MISTRESS'S DUTIES   In her youth a genteel lady enjoyed a certain amount of leisure. But once she married and became a plantation mistress, a southern woman was often shocked by the size of her responsibilities. Nursing the sick, making clothing, tending the garden, caring for the poultry, and overseeing every aspect of food preparation were all her domain. She also had to supervise and plan the work of the domestic servants and distribute clothing. After taking care of breakfast, one harried Carolina mistress recounted that she "had the [sewing] work cut out, gave orders about dinner, had the horse feed fixed in hot water, had the box filled with cork: went to see the carpenters working on the negro houses . . . now I have to cut out the flannel jackets." Sarah Williams, the New York bride of a North Carolina planter, admitted that her mother-in-law "works harder than any Northern farmer's wife I know."

Unlike female reformers in the North, upper-class southern women did not openly challenge their role, but some found their sphere confining, especially the never-ending

Sarah Pierce Vick, the mistress of a plantation near Vicksburg, Mississippi, pauses to speak to one of her slaves, who may be holding feed for her horse. A plantation mistress had many duties and, while enjoying the comforts brought by wealth and status, often found her life more difficult than she had anticipated before marriage.

task of managing slaves. Yet without the labor of slaves, the lifestyle of these women was impossible.

Some women drew a parallel between their situation and that of the slaves. Both were subject to male dominance, and independent-minded women found the subordination of marriage difficult. Susan Dabney Smedes, in her recollection of growing up on an Alabama plantation, recalled that "it was a saying that the mistress of a plantation was the most complete slave on it."

MISCEGENATION Many women were deeply discontented, too, with the widespread double standard for sexual behavior and with the daily reminders of **miscegenation** some had to face. A man who fathered illegitimate children by slave women suffered no social or legal penalties, even in the case of rape (southern law did not recognize such a crime against slave women). In contrast, a white woman guilty of adultery lost all social respectability.

Mary Chesnut, the wife of a South Carolina planter, knew the reality of miscegenation firsthand from her father-in-law's liaisons with slave women. She sneered in her diary at the assumptions of male superiority. "Like the patriarchs of old, our men live all in one house with their wives and concubines; and the mulattoes one sees in every family partly resemble the white children. Any lady is ready to tell you who is the father of all the mulattoes one sees in everybody's household but her own. Those, she seems to think, drop from the clouds. My disgust sometimes is boiling over."

Still, only a small minority of women questioned either their place in southern society or the corrosive influence of slavery. Racism was so pervasive within American society that the few white southern women who privately criticized the institution displayed little empathy for the plight of slaves themselves, including black women.

Yeoman Farmers

FARMERS AND HERDERS In terms of numbers, yeoman farm families were the backbone of southern society, accounting for more than half the southern white population. They owned no slaves and farmed the traditional 80 to 160 acres, like northern farmers. About 80 percent owned their own land, and the rest were tenant farmers who hoped one day to acquire a homestead. They settled almost everywhere in the South, except in the rice and sugar districts and valuable river bottomlands of the Deep South, which were monopolized by large slaveowners. Like Ferdinand Steel, most were semisubsistence farmers who raised primarily corn and hogs, along with perhaps a few bales of cotton or some tobacco, which they sold to obtain the cash needed to buy items like sugar, coffee, and salt. Some were not so much farmers as herdsmen, who set large herds of scrawny cattle or pigs to forage in the woods until it was time for the annual drive to market. Yeoman farmers lacked the wealth of planters, but they had a pride and dignity that earned them the respect of their richer neighbors.

Southern farmers led more isolated lives than their northern counterparts. Yet the social activities of these people were not much different from those of northern farmers. Religion played an important role at camp meetings held in late summer after the crops were laid by and before harvest time. As in the North, neighbors also met to exchange labor and tools, always managing to combine work with fun. A Tennessee plains farmer recalled that his neighbors "seem to take delight in helping each other sutch as lay[ing] railings, cornshucking and house raising[.] [T]hey tried to help each other all they could and dancet all night." Court sessions, militia musters, political rallies—these too were occasions that brought rural folk together.

LIMITS TO ECONOMIC OPPORTUNITY Because yeoman farmers lacked cheap slave labor, good transportation, and access to credit, they could not compete with planters in the production of staples. When it came to selling their corn and wheat, small farmers conducted only limited business with planters, who usually grew as many of their own foodstuffs as possible. In the North, urban centers became a market for small farmers, but in the South the lack of towns limited this internal market.

Thus, while southern yeoman farmers were not poor, they suffered from a chronic lack of money and the absence of conveniences that northern farm families enjoyed, such as cast-iron stoves, sewing machines, specialized tools, and good furniture. A few chafed at the absence of public schools and greater opportunities. Josiah Hinds, who hacked a farm out of the isolated woods of northern Mississippi, worried that his children were growing up "wild." He complained that "education is but little prized by my

MISTRESSES AND HOUSE SERVANTS

Mary Boykin Chesnut was a plantation mistress in South Carolina for many years. Her husband served in the U.S. Senate and later as an aide to Confederate President Jefferson Davis. In this diary excerpt (Document 1), Chesnut compares the conduct of antislavery advocates with that of her mother, grandmother, and mother-in-law. In the second document, an excerpt from a slave narrative, Harriet Ann Jacobs describes the mistress of the plantation where she had been enslaved.

DOCUMENT 1   A Plantation Mistress's View of Living with Slaves

November 27, 1861. "Ye who listen with credulity to the whispers of fancy," pause and look on this picture and that.

On one side Mrs. Stowe, Greeley, Thoreau, Emerson, Sumner* in nice New England homes—clean, clear, sweet-smelling—shut up in libraries, writing books which ease their hearts of their bitterness to us, or editing newspapers—all [of] which pays better than anything else in the world. . . .

What self-denial do they practice? It is the cheapest philanthropy trade in the world—easy. Easy as setting John Brown to come down here [in his 1859 raid on Harpers Ferry] and cut our throats in Christ's name.

Now, what I have seen of my mother's life, my grandmother's, my mother-in-law's:

These people were educated at Northern schools mostly—read the same as their Northern contemners, the same daily newspapers, the same Bible—have the same ideas of right and wrong—are highbred, lovely, good, pious—doing their duty as they con-

ceive it. They live in negro villages. They do not preach and teach hate as a gospel and the sacred duty of murder and insurrection, but they strive to ameliorate the condition of these Africans in every particular. They set them the example of a perfect life—life of utter self-abnegation. Think of these holy New Englanders, forced to have a negro village walk through their houses whenever they saw fit—dirty, slatternly, idle. . . . These women are more troubled by their duty to negroes, have less chance to live their own lives in peace than if they were African missionaries. They have a swarm of blacks about them as children under their care—not as Mrs. Stowe's fancy paints them, but the hard, unpleasant, unromantic, undeveloped savage Africans. And they hate slavery worse than Mrs. Stowe. . . .

I do not do anything whatever but get out of [the way of my slaves]. When I come home, I see the negroes themselves. They look as comfortable as possible and I hear

all they have to say. Then I see the overseer and the Methodist parson. *None* of these complain of each other. And I am satisfied. My husband supported his plantation by his law practice. Now it is running him in debt. We are bad managers. Our people have never earned their own bread. . . .

I say we are no better than our judges in the North—*and no worse.* . . . The slave-owners, when they are good men and women, are the martyrs. And as far as I have seen, the people here are quite as good as anywhere else. I hate slavery. I even hate the harsh authority I see parents think it their duty to exercise *toward their children.*

There now!! What good does it do to write all that?

---

*Harriet Beecher Stowe, author of *Uncle Tom's Cabin;* Horace Greeley, editor of the New York *Tribune;* Henry David Thoreau, Ralph Waldo Emerson, and Senator Charles Sumner of Massachusetts.

Source: Mary Chesnut's Civil War, ed. C. Vann Woodward (New Haven, Conn., 1981), pp. 245–246.

DOCUMENT 2   A Slave's Experience of Living with a Plantation Mistress

Mrs. Flint, like many southern women, was totally deficient in energy. She had not strength to superintend her household affairs; but her nerves were so strong, that she could sit in her easy chair and see a woman whipped, till the blood trickled from every stroke of the lash. She was a member of the church; but partaking of the Lord's supper did not seem to put her in a Christian frame of mind. If dinner was not served at the exact time on that particular Sunday, she would station herself in the kitchen, and wait till it was dished, and then spit in all the kettles and pans that had been used for cooking. She did this to prevent the cook and her children from eking out their meager fare with the remains of the gravy and other scrapings. The slaves could get nothing to eat except what she chose to give them. Provisions were weighed out by the pound and ounce, three times a day. I can assure you she gave them no chance to eat wheat bread from her flour barrel. She knew how many biscuits a quart of flour would make, and exactly what size they ought to be.

Dr. Flint was an epicure. The cook never sent a dinner to his table without fear and trembling; for if there happened to be a dish not to his liking, he would either order her to be whipped, or compel her to eat every mouthful of it in his presence. The poor, hungry creature might not have objected to eating it; but she did object to having her master cram it down her throat till she choked. . . .

From others than the master persecution also comes in [cases of miscegenation]. I once saw a young slave girl dying soon after the birth of a child nearly white. In her agony she cried out, "O Lord, come and take me!" Her mistress stood by, and mocked at her like an incarnate fiend. "You suffer, do you?" she exclaimed. "I am glad of it. You deserve it all, and more too."

The girl's mother said, "The baby is dead, thank God; and I hope my poor child will soon be in heaven, too."

"Heaven!" retorted the mistress. "There is no such place for the like of her and her bastard."

The poor mother turned away, sobbing. Her dying daughter called her, feebly, and as she bent over her, I heard her say, "Don't grieve so, mother; God knows all about it; and HE will have mercy upon me."

Her sufferings, afterwards, became so intense, that her mistress felt unable to stay; but when she left the room, the scornful smile was still on her lips.

Source: Harriet Jacobs, *Incidents in the Life of a Slave Girl. Written by Herself.* L. Maria Child, ed. (Boston, 1861), pp. 22–24.

Thinking Critically

What does Chesnut mean when she says that most plantation mistresses set for their slaves "the example of a perfect life—life of utter self-abnegation"? Why might a mistress have such a cruel reaction to the dying slave girl in Harriet Jacobs's account? How should historians deal with the argument that one or the other account is not representative?

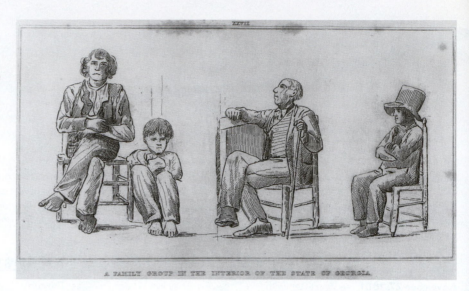

A majority of white southerners were members of nonslaveholding yeoman farm families. Ruggedly independent, these families depended on their own labor and lived under more primitive conditions than large plantation owners or small farmers in the North. Basil Hall, an Englishman traveling through the South in 1827 and 1828, sketched members of this Georgia family with the aid of a camera lucida, an optical device that projected an image from real life onto paper, where it could be traced with accuracy.

A FAMILY GROUP IN THE INTERIOR OF THE STATE OF GEORGIA

neighbours," who were satisfied "if the corn and cotton grows to perfection . . . [and] brings a fare price, and hog meat is at hand to boil with the greens."

ABSENCE OF CLASS CONFLICT

In some ways, then, the worlds of yeoman farmers and upper-class planters were not only different but also in conflict. Still, a hostility between the two classes did not emerge. Yeoman farmers admired planters and hoped that one day they would join the gentry themselves. And even white southerners who owned no slaves accepted slavery as a means of controlling African Americans as members of an inferior social caste based on race. "Now suppose they was free," one poor farmer told Frederick Law Olmsted, a traveler from the North, "You see they'd all think themselves as good as we." Racism and fear of black people were sufficient to keep nonslaveholders loyal to southern institutions.

Poor Whites

LIVES OF POOR WHITES

The poorest white southerners were confined to land that no one else wanted: the wiregrass region of southeastern Georgia, the sand hills of central South Carolina, the pine barrens of the coastal plains from Virginia to southeastern Mississippi. These southerners lived in rough, unchinked, windowless log cabins located in the remotest areas and were often squatters without title to the land they were on. The men spent their time hunting and fishing, while women did the domestic work and what farming they could manage. Largely illiterate, they suffered from malnutrition stemming from a monotonous diet of corn, pork, and whiskey, and they were afflicted with malaria and hookworm, diseases that sapped their energy. Other white southerners scornfully referred to poor whites as crackers, white trash, sand-hillers, and clay-eaters. Numbers are hard to come by, but perhaps 5 percent of the white population comprised these poor folk.

RELATIONS WITH PLANTERS

Because poor whites traded with slaves, exchanging whiskey for stolen goods, contemptuous planters often bought them out simply to rid the neighborhood of them. For their part, poor whites keenly resented planters, but their hostility toward African Americans was even stronger. Poor whites refused to work alongside slaves or perform any work commonly done by them and vehemently opposed ending slavery. Emancipation would remove one of the few symbols of their status—that they were, at least, free.

 REVIEW

What was the relationship between the South's great planters and yeoman farmers?

THE PECULIAR INSTITUTION

SLAVES WERE NOT FREE. THAT overwhelming fact must be understood before anything is said about the kindness or the cruelty that individual slaves experienced; before any consideration of healthy or unhealthy living conditions; before any discussion of how slave families coped with hardship, rejoiced in shared pleasures, or worshiped in prayer. The lives of slaves were affected day in and day out, in big ways and small, by the basic reality that slaves were not their own masters. If a slave's workload was reasonable, it remained so only at the master's discretion, not because the slave determined it to be. If slaves married or visited family or friends on a nearby plantation, they did so only with the master's permission. If they raised a family, they could remain together only as long as the master did not separate them by sale. Whatever slaves wanted to do, they had always to consider the response of their masters.

When power was distributed as unequally as it was between masters and slaves, every action on the part of the enslaved involved a certain calculation, conscious or unconscious. The consequences of every act, of every expression or gesture, had to be considered. In that sense, the line between freedom and slavery penetrated every corner of a slave's life, and it was an absolute and overwhelming distinction.

SLAVERY AND RACE

One other stark fact reinforced the sharp line between freedom and slavery: slaves were distinguished on the basis of color. While the peculiar institution was an economic system of labor, it was also a **caste system** based on race. The color line of slavery made it much easier to brand black people as somehow different. It made it easier to defend the institution and win the support of yeoman farmers and poor white southerners, even though in many ways the system held them back. Hence slavery must be understood on many levels: not only as an economic system but also as a racial and cultural one, not only in terms of its outward conditions of life and labor but also through the inner demands it made on the soul.

Work and Discipline

The conditions slaves encountered varied widely, depending on the size of the farm or plantation, the crop being grown, the personality of the master, and whether he was an absentee owner. On small farms slaves worked in the fields with the owners and had much closer contact with whites. On plantations, in contrast, most slaves dealt primarily with the overseer, who was paid by the size of the harvest he brought in and was therefore often harsh in his approach. The largest plantations, which raised rice and sugar, also required the longest hours and the most grueling labor.

ORGANIZATION OF SLAVE LABOR

House servants and the drivers, who supervised the field hands, were accorded the highest status, and skilled artisans such as carpenters and blacksmiths also received special recognition. Field hands, both men and women, did the hardest work and were sometimes divided into plowhands and hoe gangs. In the summer of 1854 Olmsted watched a group of Mississippi slaves return to work in the fields after a thunderstorm. "First came, led by an old driver carrying a whip, 40 of the largest and strongest women I ever saw together; . . . they carried themselves loftily, each having a hoe over the shoulder, and walking with a free, powerful swing like [soldiers] on the march." Behind them were the plowhands on the mules, "the cavalry, thirty strong, mostly men, but a few of them women." Bringing up the rear was "a lean and vigilant white overseer, on a brisk pony."

Some planters organized their slaves by the gang system, in which a white overseer or a black driver supervised gangs of 20 to 25 adults. Although the approach extracted long hours of hard labor, the slaves had to be constantly supervised and shirkers were difficult to detect. Other planters preferred the task system, under which each slave was given a specific daily assignment to complete, after which he or she was finished for the day. This system allowed slaves to work at their own pace, gave them an incentive to do careful work, and freed overseers from having to closely supervise the work. But, as drivers also discovered, slaves resisted vigorously if masters tried to increase the workload. The task system was most common in the rice fields, whereas the gang system predominated in the cotton districts. Many planters used a combination of the two systems.

| Black slave driver

Toil began just before sunrise and continued until dusk. During cultivation and harvest, slaves were in the field 15 to 16 hours a day, eating a noonday meal there and resting before resuming labor. Work was uncommon on Sundays, and frequently only a half day was required on Saturdays. Even so, the routine was taxing. "We . . . have everybody at work before day dawns," an Arkansas cotton planter reported. "I am never caught in bed after day light nor is any body else on the place, and we continue in the cotton fields when we can have fair weather till it is so dark we can't see to work."

Often masters gave money, additional food, gifts, and time off to slaves who worked diligently, but the threat of punishment was always present. Slaves could be denied passes; their food allowance could be reduced; and if all else failed, they could be sold. The most common instrument of punishment, however, was the whip. The frequency of its use varied from plantation to plantation, but few slaves escaped the lash entirely. "We have to rely more and more on the power of fear," the planter James Henry Hammond acknowledged. "We are determined to continue masters, and to do so we have to draw the rein tighter and tighter day by day to be assured that we hold them in complete check."

Slave Maintenance

CLOTHING AND HOUSING

Planters generally bought rough, cheap cloth for slave clothing and each year gave adults at most only a couple of outfits and a pair of shoes that were worn out by the end of the year. Few had enough clothing or blankets to keep warm when the weather dipped below freezing. Some planters provided well-built housing, but more commonly slaves lived in cramped, poorly built cabins that were leaky in wet weather, drafty in cold, and furnished with only a few crude chairs, benches and a table, perhaps a mattress filled with corn husks or straw, and a few pots and dishes. To keep medical expenses down, slaveowners treated sick slaves themselves and called in a doctor only for serious cases. Conditions varied widely, but on average, a slaveowner spent less than a dollar a year on medical care for each slave.

Even so, the United States was the only slave society in the Americas where the slave population increased naturally—indeed, at about the same rate as the white population. Nevertheless, a deficient diet, inadequate clothing and shelter, long hours of hard toil, and poor medical care resulted in a lower life expectancy among slaves.

Resistance

SLAVE REVOLTS IN LATIN AMERICA

Slaves resisted the bondage imposed on them. The most radical form of resistance was rebellion, which occurred repeatedly in slave societies in the Americas. In Latin America, slave revolts were frequent, involving hundreds and even thousands of slaves and pitched battles in which large numbers were killed. The most successful slave revolt occurred in France's sugar-rich colony Saint-Domingue (the western part of the Caribbean island of Hispaniola). There, free blacks who had fought in the American Revolution because of France's alliance with the United States brought back the ideals of freedom and equality. The brutally overworked population of half a million slaves was ready to revolt and received further encouragement from the example of the French Revolution. Under the leadership of Toussaint L'Ouverture, rebellion led to the establishment of Haiti in 1804, the second independent republic in the Western Hemisphere.

Elsewhere, Jamaica averaged one significant slave revolt every year from 1731 to 1823, while in 1823 thousands revolted in Guiana. Jamaica, too, witnessed an uprising, of some 20,000 slaves in 1831. These revolts, and ones in 1823 and 1824 in British-controlled Demerara, were savagely suppressed. And in Brazil, which had the largest number of slaves outside the United States, the government took 50 years to suppress with military force a colony of about 20,000 slaves who had sought refuge in the mountains.

INFREQUENCY OF REVOLTS IN THE UNITED STATES

In contrast, slave revolts were rare in the United States. Unlike in Latin America, in the Old South whites outnumbered blacks, the government was much more powerful, most slaves were native-born, and family life was much stronger. Slaves recognized the odds against them, and many potential leaders became fugitives instead. In a sense, what is remarkable is that American slaves revolted at all.

Early in the nineteenth century several well-organized uprisings in the United States nearly materialized. In 1800 Gabriel Prosser, a slave blacksmith, recruited perhaps a couple hundred slaves in a plan to march on Richmond and capture the governor. But a heavy thunderstorm postponed the attack and a few slaves then betrayed the plot. Prosser and other leaders were eventually captured and executed. Denmark Vesey's conspiracy in Charleston in 1822 met a similar fate (see page 286).

NAT TURNER'S REBELLION

The most famous slave revolt, led by a literate slave preacher named Nat Turner, was smaller and more spontaneous. Turner, who lived on a farm in southeastern Virginia, was given unusual privileges by his master, whom he described as a kind and trusting man. Spurred on by an almost fanatic mysticism, Turner became convinced that God intended to punish white people. One night in 1831 following an eclipse of the sun, he and six confederates stole out and murdered Turner's master and family. Gaining some 70 recruits as they went, Turner's band killed 57 white men, women, and children. Along the way, the members voiced their grievances against slavery and announced that they intended to confiscate their masters' wealth.

Although the uprising was put down and Turner executed, it left white southerners throughout the region with a haunting uneasiness. Nat Turner had seemed a model slave, yet who could read a slave's true emotions behind the mask of obedience?

Slaves resisted their masters by fleeing to nearby swamps or forests. Masters often used specially trained dogs to track them. Those shown here were imported from Cuba, and Zachary Taylor, who was elected president of the United States in 1848, was among the planters who imported them.

DAILY LIVES

A Slave's Daily Bread

Once a week on most plantations, slaves lined up to receive their rations from the master. Each adult could expect to receive about a peck of cornmeal, 3 or 4 pounds of bacon or salt pork, and molasses for sweetener. Some masters added vegetables, fruits, or sweet potatoes in season, but only on rare occasions did slaves receive wheat flour, beef, lean meat, poultry, or eggs. Milk, when available at all, was reserved for children and was usually sour.

In terms of simple calories, this ration was ample enough to sustain life. A modern study of the slave diet has concluded that on the eve of the Civil War, adult slaves received almost 5,400 calories, which exceeds today's recommended levels of consumption. But the monotonous fare of corn and pork lacked several essential nutrients as well as enough protein, afflicting many slaves with diet-related diseases such as pellagra and beriberi. (Although slaveowners and their families enjoyed more variety in their food and better cuts of meat, they, too, lacked a balanced diet.)

On some plantations masters left all cooking to the slaves, who, before going to work in the morning, would eat breakfast and prepare their noon meal to take with them to eat in the fields. At night, they came home to fix a light supper. Other masters established a plantation kitchen where cooks prepared breakfast and dinner, though supper remained the responsibility of the individual slave or family. On these plantations a noon meal was brought to the fields. In general, the quality of food preparation was better under this system because slaves were often too exhausted after work to put much time or care into cooking. Naturally enough,

slaves preferred to fix meals according to their own taste and eat as a family in some privacy. Fanny Kemble reported that on her husband's Georgia plantation the slaves sat "on the earth or doorsteps, and ate out of their little cedar tubs or an iron pot, some few with broken iron spoons, more with pieces of wood, and all the children with their fingers."

Wherever their masters permitted it, slaves tended their own vegetable gardens after work or raised chickens and other animals. Not only did this practice provide eggs and other items not included in the weekly rations, but it also enabled slaves to sell their surplus to the master or in town and use their earnings to buy occasional luxuries such as coffee, sugar, and tobacco. Slaves also raided the master's smokehouse, secretly slaughtered his stock and killed his poultry, and stole from neighboring plantations. Richard Carruthers, a former slave, recalled, "If they didn't provision you 'nough, you just had to slip round and get a chicken."

Slaves who worked all day still had plenty of incentive to stir out at night to fish or to hunt raccoon or opossum. "The flesh of the coon is palatable," admitted one slave, "but verily there is nothing in all butcherdom so delicious as a roasted 'possum." Along with such meat might come "hoecakes," a popular dish made by slapping cornmeal dough on the blade of a hoe and holding it over the coals.

On holidays the master usually provided a banquet for all hands on the plantation. Slaves filled up on beef, mutton, roast pig, coffee, wheat bread, pies, and other dishes only rarely tasted. Feasting was one of the

Slaves in the Edgefield district of South Carolina fashioned these "face jugs" out of the area's clay. The jugs could be used in the fields to provide water to laborers. But they may also have possessed ritualistic functions, helping their owner protect against magic spells of enemies or provide powers of healing.

slaves' "princi[pal] sources of comfort," one former slave testified. "Only the slave who has lived all the year on his scanty allowance of meal and bacon, can appreciate such suppers."

Thinking Critically

What was the masters' purpose in providing holiday banquets for their slaves?

DAY-TO-DAY RESISTANCE

Beyond outright rebellion, there were other, more subtle, ways of resisting a master's authority. Running away was one. With the odds stacked heavily against them, few runaways escaped safely to freedom except from the border states. More frequently, slaves fled to nearby woods or swamps to avoid punishment or protest their treatment. Some runaways stayed out only a few days; others held out for months.

Many slaves resisted by abusing their masters' property. They mishandled animals, broke tools and machinery, misplaced items, and worked carelessly in the fields. Slaves also sought to trick the master by feigning illness

or injury and by hiding rocks in the cotton they picked. Slaves complained directly to the owner about an overseer's mistreatment, thereby attempting to drive a wedge between the two.

The most common form of resistance, and a persistent annoyance to slaveowners, was theft. Slaves took produce from the garden, raided the master's smokehouse, secretly slaughtered his stock, and killed his poultry. "They always told us it was wrong to lie and steal," recalled Josephine Howard, a former slave in Texas, "but why did the white folks steal my mammy and her mammy? They lived over in Africa. . . . That's the sinfullest stealing there is."

Slaves learned to outwit their masters by wearing an "impenetrable mask" around whites, one bondsman recalled. "How much of joy, of sorrow, of misery and anguish have they hidden from their tormentors." Frederick Douglass, the most famous fugitive slave, explained that "as the master studies to keep the slave ignorant, the slave is cunning enough to make the master think he succeeds."

✓ **REVIEW**

In what ways did slaves resist their oppression?

SLAVE CULTURE

TRAPPED IN BONDAGE, FACED WITH the futility of revolt, slaves could at least forge a culture of their own. By the nineteenth century, American slaves had been separated from much of their traditional African heritage, but that did not mean they had fully accepted the dominant white culture. Instead, slaves combined strands from their African past with customs that evolved from their life in America. This slave culture was most distinct on big plantations, where the slave population was large and slaves had more opportunity to live apart from white scrutiny.

The Slave Family

BREAKUP OF FAMILIES Maintaining a sense of family was one of the most remarkable achievements of African Americans in bondage, given the obstacles that faced them. Southern law did not recognize slave marriages as legally binding, nor did it allow slave parents complete authority over their children. Black women faced the possibility of rape by the master or overseer without legal recourse, and husbands, wives, and children had to live with the fear of being sold and separated. From 1820 to 1860 more than 2 million slaves were sold in the interstate slave trade. Such sales separated perhaps 600,000 husbands and wives.

FAMILY TIES IN SLAVERY Despite their vulnerability, family ties remained strong, as slave culture demonstrated. The marriage ceremony among slaves varied from a formal religious service to jumping over a broomstick in front of the slave community to nothing more than the master giving verbal approval. Whatever the ceremony, slaves viewed the ritual as a public affirmation of the couple's commitment to their new responsibilities. Rather than adopting white norms, slaves developed their own moral code concerning sexual relations and marriage. Although young slaves often engaged in premarital sex, they were expected to choose a partner and become part of a stable family. It has been estimated that at least one in five slave women had one or more children before marriage, but most of these mothers eventually married. "The negroes had their own ideas of morality, and they held them very strictly," the daughter of a Georgia planter recalled. Black churches played a leading role in condemning adultery.

GENDER ROLES The traditional nuclear family of father, mother, and children was the rule, not the exception, among slaves. Within the marriage the father was viewed as the traditional head of the family; wives were to be submissive and obey their husbands. Labor in the quarters was divided according to sex. Women did the indoor work, such as cooking, washing, and sewing, and men

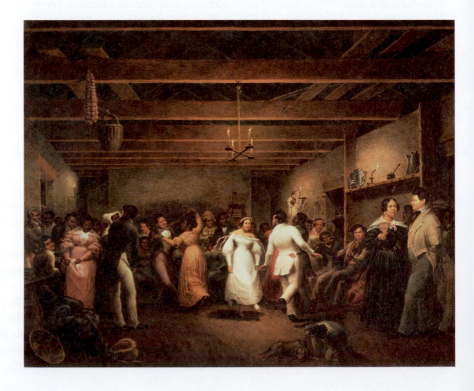

Students of this painting speculate that the participants in this Kitchen Ball at White Sulphur Springs included both free blacks and slaves who had accompanied their masters to this resort in present-day West Virginia (then part of Virginia). Note the individuality of the faces and figures represented here—a striking contrast to the minstrelsy caricatures of blacks in the painting of the frontier quilting party (page 221).

performed outdoor chores, such as gathering firewood, hauling water, and tending the animals and garden plots. The men also hunted and fished to supplement the spare weekly rations.

Beyond the nuclear family, slaves developed strong kinship networks that promoted a sense of community. Aunts and uncles looked after children who lost their parents through death or sale. When children were sold to a new plantation, a family in the slave quarters took them in. Thus all members of the slave society drew together in an extended network of mutual obligation.

Slave Songs and Stories

PROTEST AND CELEBRATION In the songs they sang, slaves expressed some of their deepest feelings about love and work and the joys and pain of life. "The songs of the slave represent the sorrows of his heart," commented Frederick Douglass. Surely there was bitterness as well as sorrow when slaves sang:

> We raise the wheat
> They give us the corn
> We bake the bread
> They give us the crust
> We sift the meal
> They give us the husk
> We peel the meat
> They give us the skin
> And that's the way
> They take us in

Yet songs were also central to the celebrations held in the slave quarters: for marriages, Christmas revels, and after harvest time. And a slave on the way to the fields might sing:

> Saturday night and Sunday too
> Young gals on my mind.
> Monday morning 'way 'fore day,
> Old master's got me gwine.
> Peggy does you love me now?

FOLKTALES Slaves expressed themselves through stories as well as song. Most often these folktales used animals as symbolic models for the predicaments in which slaves found themselves. In the best known of these, the cunning Brer Rabbit was a weak fellow who defeated larger animals like Brer Fox and Brer Bear by using his wits. Other stories were less symbolic and contained more overt hostility to white people; slaves usually told them only among themselves. But the message, whether direct or symbolic, was much the same: to laugh at the master's shortcomings and teach the young how to survive in a hostile world.

Steal Away to Jesus

At the center of slave culture was religion. The Second Great Awakening, which had begun on the southern frontier, converted many slaves, most of whom joined the Methodist and Baptist churches. Slaves constituted more than a quarter of the members of both of these southern churches.

Some slaveowners encouraged religion among slaves as one means of social control. Masters provided slaves with a minister (often white), set the time and place of services, and usually insisted that a white person be present. "Church was what they called it," one former slave protested, "but all that preacher talked about was for us slaves to obey our masters and not to lie and steal." In response, some slaves rejected all religion, while others continued to believe in conjuring, voodoo, and various practices derived from African religion.

SLAVE RELIGION But most slaves sought a Christianity firmly their own, beyond the control of the master. On many plantations they met secretly at night, in the quarters or at "hush harbors" in the safety of the woods, where they broke into rhythmic singing and dancing, modeled on the ring shout of African religion. Even regular services generated intense enthusiasm. "The way in which we worshiped is almost indescribable," one slave preacher

Slave or free? In 1863 artist Eastman Johnson sketched this confident black man, whose high boots, high-buttoned shirt, and jacket suggest he might have driven a carriage or perhaps was a freedman who worked in the army during the Civil War. We don't know the man's identity, and the boundary line between slave and free was sometimes stretched, especially for slaves whose job required them to travel unsupervised.

recalled. "The singing was accompanied by a certain ecstasy of motion, clapping of hands, tossing of heads. . . ." In an environment where slaves, for most of the day, were prevented from expressing their deepest feelings, such meetings served as a satisfying emotional release.

Religion also provided slaves with values and gave them a sense of self-worth. Slaves learned that God would redeem the poor and downtrodden and raise them one day to honor and glory. Rejecting the teaching of some white ministers that slavery was punishment, slave preachers assured their congregations that they were the chosen people of God. "This is one reason why I believe in hell," a former slave declared. "I don't believe a just God is going to take no such man as my former master into His Kingdom."

SLAVE SPIRITUALS Again, song played a central role. Slaves sang religious "spirituals" at work and at play as well as in religious services. Seemingly meek and otherworldly, the songs often contained a hidden element of protest. Frederick Douglass disclosed that when slaves sang longingly of "Canaan, sweet Canaan," they were thinking not only of the Bible's Promised Land but also of the North and freedom. When slaves heard "Steal Away to Jesus" sung in the fields, they knew that a secret devotional meeting was scheduled that evening. Songs became one of the few ways that slaves could openly express, in the approved language of Christianity, their yearning for freedom.

The Slave Community

HIERARCHY Although slaves managed with remarkable success to preserve a sense of self-worth in a religion and a culture of their own, the hard reality of slavery made it impossible to escape fully from white control. Even the social hierarchy within the slave quarters never was entirely free from the white world. Slave preachers, conjurers, and herb doctors held status that no white conferred, but the prestige of a slave driver rested ultimately on the authority of the white master. Similarly, skilled slaves and house servants often felt superior to other slaves, an attitude masters consciously promoted. "We house slaves thought we was better'n the others what worked in the field," one personal servant confessed. Light-skinned slaves sometimes deemed their color a badge of superiority. Fanny Kemble recorded that one woman begged to be relieved of field labor, which she considered degrading, "on 'account of her color.'"

Lucy Skipworth, who was the daughter of a driver and had been educated by her mistress, was a member of the slave elite on both counts. At Hopewell plantation in Alabama, she was in full charge of the main residence during her master's frequent absences. She ran a plantation school (despite white opposition) and, as a devout Baptist, supervised her fellow slaves' religious life. Eager for her master's approval, Skipworth on several occasions reported slave disobedience, which temporarily estranged her from the slave community. Yet in the end she was always welcomed

back. While Skipworth never rebelled or apparently never considered running away, she was far from submissive. She defied white authority, protected her family, and used her influence to get rid of an overseer the slaves disliked. Like many house servants, she lived between two worlds—her master's and the slave quarters—and was never entirely comfortable in either.

But the realities of slavery and white racism inevitably drove black people closer together in a common bond. Walled in from the individualistic white society beyond, slaves out of necessity created a community of their own.

Free Black Southerners

Of the 4 million African Americans living in the South in 1860, only 260,000—about 7 percent—were free. More than 85 percent of them lived in the Upper South, with almost 200,000 in Maryland, Virginia, and North Carolina alone. Free black southerners were also much more urban than the southern white and slave populations. As a rule, free African Americans were more literate than slaves, and they were disproportionately female and much more likely to be of mixed ancestry.

Most free black southerners lived in rural areas, although usually not near plantations. A majority eked out a living farming or in low-paying unskilled jobs, but some did well enough to own slaves themselves. In 1830 about 3,600 did, although commonly their "property" was their wives or children, purchased because they could not be emancipated under state laws. Only a few were full-blown slaveowners.

BETWEEN FREEDOM AND SLAVERY The boundary sometimes blurred between free and enslaved African Americans. Sally Thomas of Nashville was technically a slave, but in the 1830s and 1840s her owner allowed her to ply her trade as a laundress and keep some of her wages. (She saved some $350, which she used to purchase the freedom of one of her sons.) The boundary stretched especially for African Americans working along rivers and the seashore in the fishing trades, as pilots or seamen, or as "watermen" ferrying supplies and stores in small boats. Under such conditions, laborers preserved more freedom and initiative than did most agricultural workers.

Along Albemarle Sound in North Carolina, free blacks and slaves flocked from miles around to "fisherman's courts," a kind of annual hiring fair. Amid an atmosphere of drinking, carousing, cockfighting, and boxing, men who ran commercial fishing operations signed up workers. The crews would then go down to the shore in late February or early March to net vast schools of fish, hauling up onto the beach over 100,000 herring in four to seven hours. Women and children then headed, gutted, cleaned, and salted the fish. A good "cutter" might head tens of thousands of herring a day. In such settings African Americans, both free and slave, could share news with folk they did not regularly see.

Following Nat Turner's Rebellion of 1831, southern legislatures increased the restrictions on free African Americans.

| This painting shows a free African-American market woman in Baltimore. Urban blacks in the South, including slaves, enjoyed greater personal freedom and access to more social activities but had only limited economic opportunity.

They were forbidden to enter a new state, had to carry their free papers, could not assemble when they wished, were subject to a curfew, often had to post a bond and be licensed to work, and could not vote, hold office, or testify in court against white people.

Free African Americans occupied an uncertain position in southern society, well above black slaves but distinctly beneath even poorer white southerners. They were victims of a society that had no place for them.

 **REVIEW**

In what ways did the culture and communities created by blacks help to sustain them in slavery?

SOUTHERN SOCIETY AND THE DEFENSE OF SLAVERY

FROM WEALTHY PLANTERS TO YEOMAN farmers, from free black slaveholders to white mountaineers, from cotton field hands to urban craftworkers, the South was a remarkably diverse region. Yet it was united by its dependence on staple crops and above all by the institution of slavery. As the South's economy became more and more dependent on slave-produced staples, slavery became more central to the life of the South, to its culture and its identity.

The Virginia Debate of 1832

At the time of the Revolution, the leading critics of slavery had been southerners—Jefferson, Washington, Madison, and Patrick Henry among them. But beginning in the 1820s, in the wake of the controversy over admitting Missouri as a

slave state (see pages 235–236), southern leaders became less apologetic about slavery and more aggressive in defending it. The turning point occurred in the early 1830s, when the South found itself increasingly under attack. It was in 1831 that William Lloyd Garrison began publishing his abolitionist newspaper, *The Liberator*. In that year, too, Nat Turner launched the revolt that frightened so many white southerners.

SIGNIFICANCE OF THE VIRGINIA DEBATE

In response to the Turner insurrection, a number of Virginia's western counties, where there were few slaves, petitioned the legislature to adopt a program for gradual emancipation. Between January 16 and 25, 1832, the House of Delegates engaged in a remarkable debate over the merits of slavery. In the end, however, the legislature refused, by a vote of 73 to 58, to consider legislation to end slavery. The debate marked the last significant attempt of white southerners to challenge the peculiar institution.

In its aftermath most felt that the subject was no longer open to debate. Instead, during the 1830s and 1840s, southern leaders defended slavery as a positive good, not just for white people but for black people as well. As John C. Calhoun proclaimed in 1837, "I hold that in the present state of civilization, where two races . . . distinguished by color and other physical differences, as well as intellectual, are brought together, the relation now existing in the slave-holding states between the two is, instead of an evil, a good—a positive good."

The Proslavery Argument

RELIGIOUS, SOCIAL, AND RACIAL ARGUMENTS

Politicians like Calhoun were not alone. White southern leaders justified slavery in a variety of ways. Ministers argued that none of the biblical prophets or Christ himself had ever condemned slavery. They also pointed out that classical Greece and Rome depended on slavery. They even cited John Locke, that giant of the Enlightenment, who had recognized slavery in the constitution he drafted for the colony of Carolina. African Americans belonged to an intellectually and emotionally inferior race, slavery's defenders argued, and therefore lacked the ability to care for themselves and required white guardianship.

Proslavery writers sometimes argued that slaves in the South lived better than factory workers in the North. Masters cared for slaves for life, whereas northern workers had no claim on their employer when they were unemployed, old, or no longer able to work. In advancing this argument, white southerners exaggerated the material comforts of slavery and minimized the average worker's standard of living—to say nothing of the psychological value of freedom. Still, to many white southerners, slavery seemed a more humane system of labor relations.

Defenders of slavery did not really expect to influence public opinion in the North. Their target was more often the slaveowners. As one southern editor explained: "We must satisfy the consciences, we must allay the fears of our own

HISTORIAN'S TOOLBOX

George Washington, Slaveholder

This image is a lithograph of a painting. What's a lithograph? (Well worth it to Google "lithograph.")

Washington himself. Why so formally dressed for the hay field?

A young neighbor, perhaps Washington's overseer or a yeoman or tenant farmer

Washington's two step-grandchildren

Credit: Claude Regnier after Junius Brutus Stearns, *Life of George Washington: the Farmer* (lithograph, 1853) Library of Congress.

Advocates of the proslavery argument made strategic use of anecdotes and images portraying George Washington as the master of Mount Vernon, his plantation—without mentioning that upon his death, his will freed all his slaves. Based on a painting of 1851, this 1853 lithograph and others conveying a similar proslavery message found their way into thousands of southern parlors and libraries before the Civil War. (Historians of technology tell us that lithography came into widespread use in the early nineteenth century, allowing for the cheap mass production of images as well as print.) Such stories and pictures portrayed Washington as a benevolent patriarch—a father to his slaves as well as to his country—and depicted slavery as a benevolent institution. At the center of this scene, a group of hale, neatly outfitted black men refresh themselves with water brought by a slave woman, demurely dressed right up to her head covering. Judging by the riding crop in his hand and the horse (far left), Washington has just dismounted, perhaps to give some instructions to his overseer, a young man who holds not a whip but a rake—to help the slaves with the hay-gathering.

Thinking Critically

What is the significance of placing whites in the foreground of the painting? What point was the artist making by drawing Washington's two step-grandchildren happily at play in the left corner? What was the artist implying by portraying Washington and the young man (who is plainly of lesser status), talking with easy familiarity?

people. We must satisfy them that slavery is of itself right—that it is not a sin against God—that it is not an evil, moral or political. In this way only," he went on, "can we prepare our own people to defend their institutions."

Closing Ranks

Not all white southerners could quell their doubts. Still, a striking change in southern opinion seems to have occurred in the three decades before the Civil War. Outside the border states, few white southerners after 1840 would admit even in private that slavery was wrong. Those who continued to oppose slavery found themselves harassed, assaulted, and driven into exile. Southern mobs destroyed the presses of antislavery papers and threatened the editors into either keeping silent or leaving the state. Southern mails were forcibly closed to abolitionist propaganda, and defenders of the South's institutions carefully scrutinized textbooks and faculty members in southern schools.

Increasingly, too, the debate over slavery spread to the national political arena. Before 1836 Andrew Jackson's enormous popularity in the South blocked the formation of a competitive two-party system there. The rise of the abolitionist movement in the 1830s, however, left many southerners uneasy, and when the Democrats nominated the northerner Martin Van Buren in 1836, southern Whigs seized on the issue of the security of slavery and charged that Van Buren could not be counted on to meet the abolitionist threat. The Whigs made impressive gains in the South in 1836, carrying several states and significantly narrowing the margin between the two parties.

During the Jacksonian era, most southern political battles did not revolve around slavery. Even so, southern politicians in both parties had to be careful to avoid the stigma of antislavery, since they were under mounting pressure from John Calhoun and his followers. Frustrated in his presidential hopes by the nullification crisis in 1832–1833 (pages 286–287), Calhoun sought to unite the South behind his leadership by agitating the slavery issue, introducing inflammatory resolutions in Congress, seizing on the abolitionist mailing campaign to demand censorship of the mails, and insisting on a gag rule to block antislavery petitions. During the 1830s and early 1840s few southern politicians followed his lead, but they did become extremely careful about being in the least critical of southern institutions. They knew quite well that even if their constituents were not as fanatical as Calhoun, southern voters overwhelmingly supported slavery.

> ✓ **REVIEW**
> How did southern whites defend slavery as a positive good?

CONCLUSION

THE WORLD AT LARGE

Two remarkable transformations were sweeping the world in the first half of the nineteenth century. The first was a series of political upheavals leading to increased democratic participation in many nation-states. The second, the Industrial Revolution, applied machine labor and technological innovation to commercial and agricultural economies.

Although it is common to identify the Industrial Revolution with New England's factories and the North's cities, that revolution transformed the rural South too. Cotton could not have become king without the demand created by textile factories or without the ability to "gin" the seeds out of cotton by Eli Whitney's invention. Nor could cotton production flourish without industrial advances in transportation, which allowed raw materials to be shipped worldwide. As for democratic change, the suffrage was extended in Britain by the Reform Bill of 1832, and popular uprisings spread across Europe in 1830 and 1848. In the United States, white southerners and northerners participated in the democratic reforms of the 1820s and 1830s.

The industrial and democratic revolutions thus transformed the South as well as the North, though in different ways. Increasingly, slavery became the focus of disputes between the two sections. The Industrial Revolution's demand for cotton increased the demand for slave labor and the profits to be gained from it. Yet the spread of democratic ideology worldwide increased pressure to abolish slavery. France and Britain had already done so. In eastern Europe the near-slavery of feudal serfdom was being eliminated as well: in 1848 within the Hapsburg empire; in 1861 in Russia; in 1864 in Romania.

In the mid-1840s the contradictory pressures of the industrial and democratic revolutions would begin to sharpen, as the United States embarked on a new program of westward expansion that thrust the slavery issue into the center of politics. Americans were forced to debate how much of the newly won territory should be open to slavery; and in doing so, some citizens began to question whether the Union could permanently endure, half slave and half free. ∞∞∞

Chapter Summary

THE OLD SOUTH WAS A complex, biracial society that increasingly diverged from the rest of the United States in the years before 1860.

- Southerners placed heavy emphasis on agriculture. Given this rural way of life, few cities and towns developed.

  - Southern commercial agriculture produced staple crops for sale in northern and European markets: tobacco, sugar, rice, and, above all, cotton.

  - As southern agriculture expanded into the fresh lands of the Deep South, the slave population moved steadily westward and southward, and the Upper South became more diversified agriculturally.

- Slavery played a major role in shaping the class structure of the Old South.

  - Ownership of slaves brought privilege and status.

  - Planters on the older Eastern Seaboard enjoyed a more refined lifestyle than those on the new cotton frontier.

- Most slaveowners, however, owned only a few slaves, and the majority of southern whites were nonslaveowning yeoman farmers.

- The institution of slavery was both a labor system and a social system, regulating relations between the races.

  - Slaves resisted bondage in many ways. Slave revolts, however, were rare.

  - Slaves developed their own culture in which family, religion, and songs all helped cope with the pressures of bondage.

- As slavery came under mounting attack, white southerners developed a set of arguments defending slavery as a positive good.

Additional Reading

THE REPORTS OF FREDERICK LAW Olmsted, who traveled through the South in the 1850s, make a fascinating jumping-off point for a first look at the region. Much of Olmsted's material is conveniently collected in Lawrence Powell, ed., *The Cotton Kingdom* (1984). A contrasting approach to traveling about is to stay at one plantation, as Erskine Clarke does in his brilliant *Dwelling Place: A Plantation Epic* (2005). Based on meticulous research, this upstairs/downstairs saga profiles the intertwined lives of masters and slaves on a Georgia coastal plantation from 1805 to 1869. James Oakes, *Slavery and Freedom* (1990), and William W. Freehling, *The Road to Disunion* (1990), are good syntheses that analyze the diversity and the contradictions of the antebellum South.

Although old, Frank Owsley's *Plain Folk of the Old South* (1949), about southern yeoman farmers, is still useful and can be supplemented by Samuel C. Hyde Jr., ed., *Plain Folk of the South Revisited* (1997), and Jeff Forret, *Race Relations at the Margins* (2006), a study of poor whites and blacks. The lives of upper-class southern white women and their servants are analyzed in

Elizabeth Fox-Genovese, *Within the Plantation Household* (1988), and Victoria E. Bynum, *Unruly Women* (1992), deals with white and black women of lower status.

The best exploration of slavery as a labor system remains Kenneth M. Stampp, *The Peculiar Institution* (1956), but the most perceptive treatment of slave culture is Eugene D. Genovese, *Roll, Jordan, Roll* (1974). Charles Joyner, *Down by the Riverside* (1984), sensitively re-creates slave culture in the rice districts, and Steven Hahn, *A Nation under Our Feet* (2003), illuminates black political struggles in the rural South throughout the nineteenth century. John Hope Franklin and Loren Schweninger, *Runaway Slaves* (1999), details an important aspect of slave resistance. Walter Johnson, *Soul by Soul: Life Inside the Antebellum Slave Market* (1999), provides a concrete and chilling view of the trade that helped sustain the "peculiar institution." Melvin Patrick Ely, *Israel on the Appomattox* (2004), is an excellent account of southern free blacks. For the proslavery argument, see Lacy K. Ford, *Deliver Us from Evil* (2009), and James Oakes, *The Ruling Race* (1982).

For a fuller list of readings, see the Bibliography at www.mhhe.com/eh8e.

Significant Events

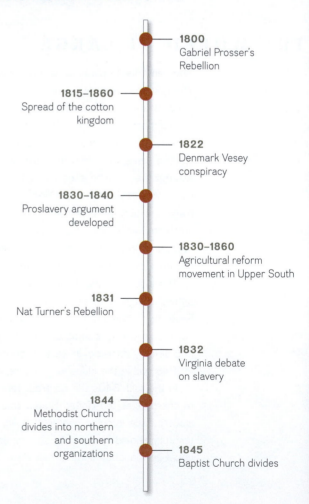

1800 Gabriel Prosser's Rebellion

1815–1860 Spread of the cotton kingdom

1822 Denmark Vesey conspiracy

1830–1840 Proslavery argument developed

1830–1860 Agricultural reform movement in Upper South

1831 Nat Turner's Rebellion

1832 Virginia debate on slavery

1844 Methodist Church divides into northern and southern organizations

1845 Baptist Church divides

THE SPREAD OF COTTON AND SLAVERY		POLITICAL FLASHPOINTS	
1793	Cotton gin sparks spread of crop	1820	Missouri Compromise
1815–1830s	Land rush into Alabama, Mississippi	1831	Garrison publishes *Liberator*; Nat Turner Rebellion
1830–1838	Indian removal accelerates the rush	1832	Virginia Debate over slavery and emancipation
1840s	Spread to Red River, Arkansas, and east Texas	1836	Abolitionist mailing campaign; southerners pass "gag rule" on antislavery petition
1860	U.S. produces 75% of the world's cotton	1840s	Methodist and Baptist churches split into northern and southern organizations

The Hidatsa Indians retreated to these well insulated earth lodges in the forested and more sheltered river bottoms to escape the fierce winter storms of the Plains. The Hidatsa survived on stores of dried beans, corn, squash, and meat. Swiss artist Karl Bodmer painted this scene after a visit in 1833–1834.

CHAPTER 14

Western Expansion and the Rise of the Slavery Issue

1820–1850

What's to Come

∞∞∞ **AN AMERICAN STORY** ∞∞∞

STRANGERS ON THE GREAT PLAINS

At first the Indians of the Great Plains paid little attention to the new people moving out from the forests far to the east. After all, for as long as they could remember, nations such as the Crow had called the plains their own. But the new arrivals came armed with superior weapons and brought a great many women and children. And they seemed to have an unlimited appetite for land. They attacked the villages of the Plains Indians, massacred women and children, and forced defeated enemies to live on reservations. In little more than a century and a half—from the first days when only a handful of their hunters had come into the land—they had become the masters of the northern plains.

The invaders who established this political and military dominance were *not* the strange "white men," who also came from the forest. During the 1830s and early 1840s whites were still few in number. The more dangerous people—the ones who truly worried the Plains tribes—were the Sioux.

| Pouch made from a white skunk skin. The skin, plus the decorative beads, were obtained from a white trapper. The pouch probably held tobacco, also a trade good.

Westward expansion is often told as a one-dimensional tale, centering on the wagon trains pressing toward the Pacific. But frontiers are the transition lines between different cultures or environments, and during the nineteenth century those frontiers were constantly shifting. They moved not only east to west, as with the white and the Sioux migrations, but also south to north, as Spanish culture diffused, and west to east, as Asian immigrants came to California. Furthermore, frontiers marked not only human but also animal boundaries. Horses, cattle, and pigs, all species imported from Europe, moved across the continent, usually in advance of European settlers. Frontiers could be technological, as in the case of trade goods like firearms. Moreover, disease frontiers created disastrous consequences for natives who had not acquired immunity to European microorganisms.

Three frontiers revolutionized the lives of the Sioux: those of the horse, the gun, and disease. Horses spread from the southwest, ahead of the Spanish who had originally brought them. Unlike English and French traders, however, Spanish colonists generally refused to sell firearms to Indians, so the gun frontier moved in the opposite direction, from northeast to southwest. The two waves crossed along the upper Missouri during the first half of the eighteenth century. Horses provided Indians with greater mobility, both for hunting bison and for fighting. Guns, too, conferred obvious advantages, and the arrival of these new elements sparked an extremely unsettled era for Plains Indian cultures.

The Sioux were first lured from the forest onto the Minnesota prairie during the early 1700s to hunt beaver, whose pelts could be exchanged with white traders for guns and other manufactured goods. The Sioux then drove the Omahas, Otos, Cheyennes, and Missouris (who had not yet acquired guns) south and west. But by the 1770s any further advance was blocked by the powerful Mandan, Hidatsa, and Arikara peoples. They were primarily horticultural, raising corn, beans, and squash and living in well-fortified towns. They also owned more horses than the Sioux; thus it was easier for them to resist attacks.

But the third frontier, disease, threw the balance of power toward the Sioux after 1779. That year, a continental smallpox pandemic struck the plains via Louisiana. Those who raised crops were hit especially hard because they lived in densely populated villages, where the epidemic spread more easily. By the time Lewis and Clark came through in 1804, the Sioux controlled much of the upper Missouri, for their nomadic life, centered on the buffalo hunt, enabled them to avoid the worst ravages of disease, especially the smallpox epidemic of 1837, which ravaged Plains Indian populations. And as white Americans moved westward, their own frontier lines produced similar disruptions, not only between white settlers and Indians but also between Anglo-American and Hispanic cultures. The relations between Indian peoples and Mexico were also in flux, as many tribes across the plains began attacking Mexicans during the 1830s. There would even be a frontier moving west to east, as thousands of Chinese were drawn, as were other immigrants from North and South America, Australia, and Hawaii, to gold fields discovered after 1849.

Ironically, perhaps the greatest instability created by the moving frontiers occurred in established American society. As the political system of the United States struggled to incorporate territories, the North and South engaged in a fierce debate over whether the new lands should become slave or free. Just as the Sioux's cultural identity was brought into question by moving frontiers, so too was the identity of the American Republic. ∞∞∞

Manifest (and Not so Manifest) Destiny

MANIFEST DESTINY

"MAKE WAY . . . FOR THE YOUNG American Buffalo—he has not yet got land enough," roared one American politician in 1844. In the space of a few years, the United States acquired Texas, New Mexico, California, the lower half of the Oregon Territory, and the lands between the Rockies and California: nearly 1.5 million square miles in all. John L. O'Sullivan, a prominent Democratic editor in New York, struck a responsive chord when he declared that it had become the United States' "manifest destiny to overspread the continent allotted by Providence for the free development of our yearly multiplying millions." The cry of **Manifest Destiny** soon echoed in other editorial pages and in the halls of Congress.

The Roots of the Doctrine

Many Americans had long believed that their country had a special, even divine, mission, which could be traced back to the Puritans' attempt to build a "city on a hill." Manifest Destiny also contained a political component, inherited from the ideology of the Revolution. In the mid-nineteenth century, Americans spoke of extending democracy, with widespread suffrage among white males, no king or aristocracy, and no established church, "over the whole North American continent."

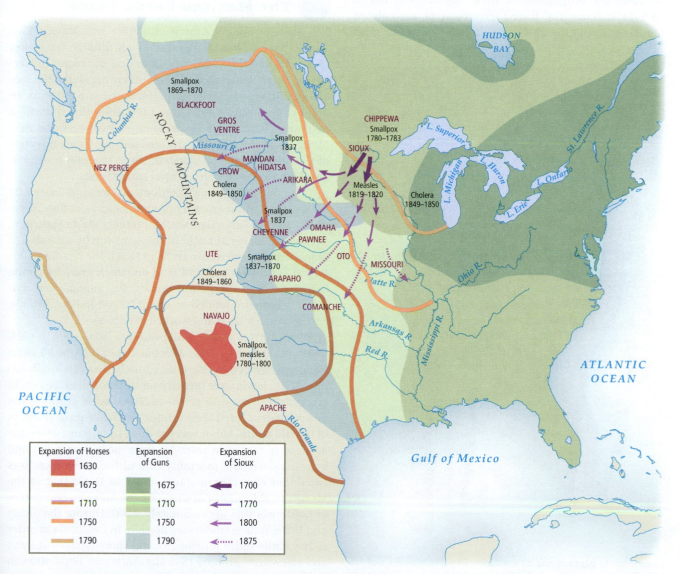

SIOUX EXPANSION AND THE HORSE AND GUN FRONTIERS

In 1710 the horse and gun frontiers had not yet crossed, but by 1750 the two waves began to overlap. The Sioux pushed west during the early eighteenth century thanks to firearms; they were checked from further expansion until the 1770s, when smallpox epidemics again turned the balance in their favor. **Why did the Sioux population survive better than the Mandan, Hidatsa, and Arikara peoples?**

Americans believed that their social and economic system, too, should spread around the globe. They pointed to its broad ownership of land, individualism, and free play of economic opportunity as superior features of American life. More importantly, Manifest Destiny was about power, especially economic power. American business interests recognized the value of the fine harbors along the Pacific coast, which promised a lucrative trade with Asia, and they hoped to make those harbors American.

RACISM Finally, underlying the doctrine of Manifest Destiny was a widespread racism. The same belief in racial superiority that was used to justify Indian removal under Jackson, to uphold slavery in the South, and to excuse segregation in the North also proved handy to defend expansion westward. The United States had a duty to regenerate the backward peoples of America, declared politicians and propagandists. Their reference was not so much to Indians: the forced expulsion of assimilated Cherokees during Indian removal made clear what most

American policy makers thought about Indian "regeneration." By the 1840s it was rather the Mexicans who had caught the attention of Manifest Destiny's prophets of progress. The Mexican race "must amalgamate and be lost, in the superior vigor of the Anglo-Saxon race," proclaimed O'Sullivan's *Democratic Review,* "or they must utterly perish."

Before 1845 most Americans assumed that expansion would be achieved without international war. American settlement would expand westward, and when the time was right, neighboring provinces, like ripe fruit, would fall naturally into American hands. Texas, New Mexico, Oregon, and California—areas that were sparsely populated and weakly defended—dominated the American expansionist imagination. With time, Americans became less willing to wait patiently for the fruit to fall.

The Mexican Borderlands

The heart of Spain's American empire was Mexico City, where spacious boulevards spread out through the center of the city and the University of Mexico, the oldest university in North America, had been accepting students since 1553, a full 85 years earlier than Harvard. From the Mexican point of view, the frontier was 1,000 miles to the north, a four-week journey to Texas, another two weeks to New Mexico, and three months by land and sea to the missions of California. Being so isolated, these Mexican provinces developed largely free from royal supervision.

CALIFORNIO SOCIETY California's settlements were anchored by four coastal *presidios,* or forts, at San Diego, Santa Barbara, Monterey, and San Francisco. Between them lay 21 Catholic missions run by a handful of Franciscans (there were only 36 in 1821). The missions controlled enormous tracts of land on which grazed gigantic herds of cattle, sheep, and horses. The animals and irrigated fields were tended by about 20,000 Indians, who in certain regards lived and worked like slaves.

When Mexico won its independence from Spain in 1821, California at first was little affected. But in 1833 the Mexican Congress stripped the Catholic Church of its vast landholdings. These lands were turned over to Mexican cattle ranchers, usually in massive grants of 50,000 acres or more. The new *rancheros* ruled their estates much like great planters of the Old South. Labor was provided by Indians, who once again were forced to work for little more than room and board. Indeed, the mortality rate of Indian workers was twice that of southern slaves and four times that of the Mexican Californians. At this time the Mexican population of California was approximately 4,000. During the 1820s and 1830s Yankee traders set up shop in California in order to buy cattle hides for the growing shoe industry at Lynn and elsewhere. Still, in 1845 the American population in California amounted to only 700.

NEW MEXICO Spanish settlement of New Mexico was denser than that of California: the province had about 44,000 Spanish-speaking inhabitants in 1827. But as in California, its society was dominated by *ranchero*

| In addition to baptism and an education in certain crafts and skills, Christian missions in California and elsewhere offered native people food, clothing, and sanctuary in a rapidly changing world. Often missions were also places of harsh discipline, physical coercion, and rampant disease. The Ohlone, or Costanoan, people pictured here are native to northern California and were drawn or coerced into missions starting in the 1760s.

Throughout the Spanish and Mexican periods, town life in California, New Mexico, and Texas revolved around central plazas and their churches. One of the first structures built in Santa Fe, the Mission Church of San Miguel (est. ca. 1610), is today the oldest church building in the present-day United States.

families that grazed large herds of sheep along the upper Rio Grande valley between El Paso and Taos. A few individuals controlled most of the wealth, while their workers eked out a meager living. Mining of copper and gold was a side industry, and here too the profits enriched a small upper class. Spain had long outlawed any commerce with Americans, but after Mexico declared its independence in 1821, yearly caravans from the United States began making the long journey along the Santa Fe Trail. Although this trade flourished over the next two decades, developments in the third Mexican borderland, neighboring Texas, worsened relations between Mexico and the United States.

The Texas Revolution

AMERICAN IMMIGRATION TO TEXAS

At first, the new government in Mexico encouraged American immigration to Texas, where only about 3,000 Mexicans, mostly ranchers, lived. In 1821 Moses Austin, an American, received a grant from the Spanish government to establish a colony. After his death, his son Stephen took over the project, laying out the little town of San Felipe de Austin along the Brazos River and offering large grants of land at almost no cost. By 1824 the colony's population exceeded 2,000. Stephen Austin was only the first of a new wave of American land agents, or *empresarios,* that obtained permission from Mexican authorities to settle families in Texas. Ninety percent of the new arrivals came from the South. Many, intending to grow cotton, brought slaves.

ILLEGAL IMMIGRATION IN TEXAS
Tensions between Mexicans and American immigrants grew with the Texas economy. Most settlers from the States were Protestant. Although the Mexican government did not insist that all new citizens become Catholic, it did officially bar Protestant churches. In 1829 Mexico abolished slavery, then looked the other way when Texas slaveholders evaded the law. In the early 1830s the Mexican government began to have second thoughts about American settlement and passed laws prohibiting any new immigration. Austin likened the new anti-immigration laws to "trying to stop the Mississippi with a dam of straw." It was an apt metaphor: between 1830 and 1833, illegal American immigrants and their slaves flooded into Mexican Texas, nearly doubling its colonial population.

GROWING TENSIONS
Admitting that the new regulations had served only to inflame Texans, Mexico repealed them in 1833. But by then colonial ill-will had ballooned along with the population. By mid-decade the American white population of 40,000 was nearly 10 times the number of Mexicans in the territory. Once again Mexico's government talked of abolishing slavery in Texas. Even more disturbing to the American newcomers, in 1834 President Antonio López de Santa Anna and his allies in the Mexican Congress began passing legislation that took power away from the states and concentrated it in Mexico City. Texans had been struggling for more autonomy, not less. When Santa Anna brutally suppressed an uprising against the central government in the state of Zacatecas, Texans grew all the more nervous. Finally, when conflicts over taxes led Santa Anna to march an army north and enforce his new regime, a ragtag Texas army drove back the advance party and then captured Mexican troops in nearby San Antonio. A full-scale rebellion was under way.

The Texas Republic

THE ALAMO
As Santa Anna massed his forces, a provisional government on March 2, 1836, proclaimed Texan independence. The document was signed by a number of prominent **Tejanos,** Mexican residents of Texas. The constitution of the new Texas Republic borrowed heavily from the U.S. Constitution, except that it explicitly prohibited the new Texas Congress from interfering with slavery. Meanwhile, Santa Anna's troops overran a Texan garrison at an old mission in San Antonio, known as the Alamo, and killed all of its 187 defenders—including the famous backwoodsman and U.S. congressman, Davy Crockett. The Mexicans, however, paid dearly for the victory, losing

more than 1,500 men. The massacre of another force at Goliad after it surrendered further inflamed American resistance.

SAM HOUSTON
But anger was one thing; organized resistance was another. The commander of the Texas forces was Sam Houston, a former governor of Tennessee. Physically gifted and something of an eccentric, Houston had a flair for wearing colorful clothing to attract attention. His political career in Tennessee might have continued, except that the failure of his marriage led him to resign abruptly as governor and go to live with the Cherokees. Eventually he made his way to Texas, where his intellectual ability and unexcelled talent as a stump speaker propelled him to the forefront of the independence movement. Steadily retreating eastward, Houston tried to discipline his fighting force and wait for an opportunity to counterattack.

That opportunity came in late April. Reinforced by eager volunteers from the United States, Houston's army surprised Santa Anna's force when spies revealed that they were resting unaware near the San Jacinto River. Admonished to "remember the Alamo," Houston's men burst upon the stunned Mexican force, killing dozens in a brief battle. Driven by revenge, the Texans then pursued the fleeing Mexican soldiers and massacred hundreds. By day's end 630 Mexicans lay dead on the field (compared to only nine Texans), and a humiliated Santa Anna had been taken into custody.

TEXAN INDEPENDENCE
Threatened with execution, the Mexican commander signed treaties recognizing Texan independence and ordering his remaining troops south of the Rio Grande. Texans would later claim that Santa Anna thereby acknowledged the Rio Grande to be Texas's southern boundary. The Mexican Congress repudiated the agreement, especially the claim to the Rio Grande. Over the next decade both sides engaged in low-level border conflict, but neither had the power to mount a successful invasion. In the meantime, Houston assumed office in October 1836 as president of the new republic, determined to bring Texas into the American Union as quickly as possible.

As an old Tennessee protégé of Andrew Jackson, Houston assumed that the United States would quickly annex such a vast and inviting territory. But Jackson worried that any such move would revive sectional tensions and hurt Martin Van Buren's chances in the 1836 presidential election. Only on his last day in office did he extend formal diplomatic recognition to the Texas Republic. Van Buren, distracted by the economic panic that broke out shortly after he entered office, took no action during his term. Rebuffed, Texans decided to go their own way. In the 10 years following independence, the Lone Star Republic attracted more than 100,000 immigrants by offering free land to settlers. Mexico refused to recognize Texan independence,

Sam Houston

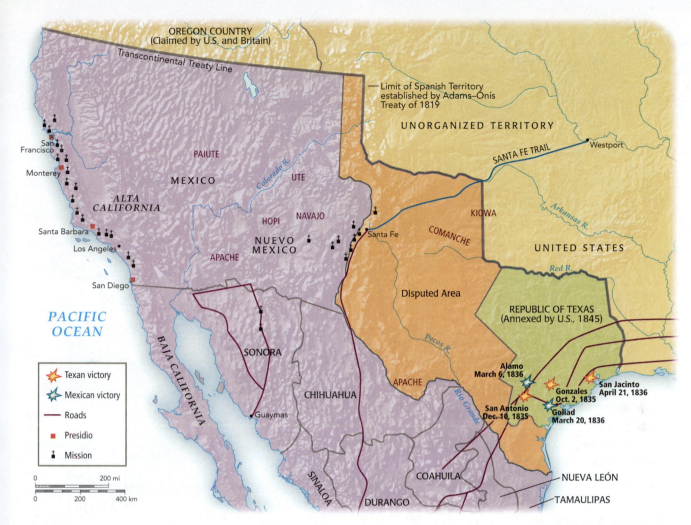

THE MEXICAN BORDERLANDS

and the vast majority of its citizens still wished to join the United States, where most of them, after all, had been born. There matters stood when the Whigs and William Henry Harrison won the presidency in 1840.

> ### REVIEW
> What regions made up the Spanish borderlands; and why did Mexico lose Texas?

THE TREK WEST

AS THOUSANDS OF WHITE AMERICANS were moving into Texas, and increasingly bringing slaves with them, a much smaller trickle headed toward the Oregon Country. Since 1818 the United States and Great Britain had occupied that territory jointly, as far north as latitude 54°40′. Although white settlement remained sparse, by 1836 American settlers outnumbered the British in the Willamette valley.

Pushed by the Panic of 1837 and six years of depression and pulled by tales of Oregon's lush, fertile valleys and the healthy, frost-free climate along California's Sacramento River, many American farmers struck out for the West Coast. Missouri was "cleaned" out of money, worried farmer Daniel Waldo, and his wife was even more adamant about heading west: "If you want to stay here another summer and shake your liver out with the fever and ague, you can do it," she announced to her husband, "but in the spring I am going to take the children and go to Oregon, Indians or no Indians." The wagon trains began rolling west.

The Overland Trail

MIGRATION WEST

Only a few hundred emigrants reached the West in 1841 and 1842, but in 1843 more than 800 followed the Overland Trail across the mountains to Oregon. From then on, they came by the thousands. Every spring brought a new rush of families to Independence or later to St. Joseph, Missouri, or to Council Bluffs, Iowa, where they waited for the spring rains to end and the trails to become passable. The migration was primarily a family enterprise, and many couples had only recently married. Most adults were between 20 and 50 years

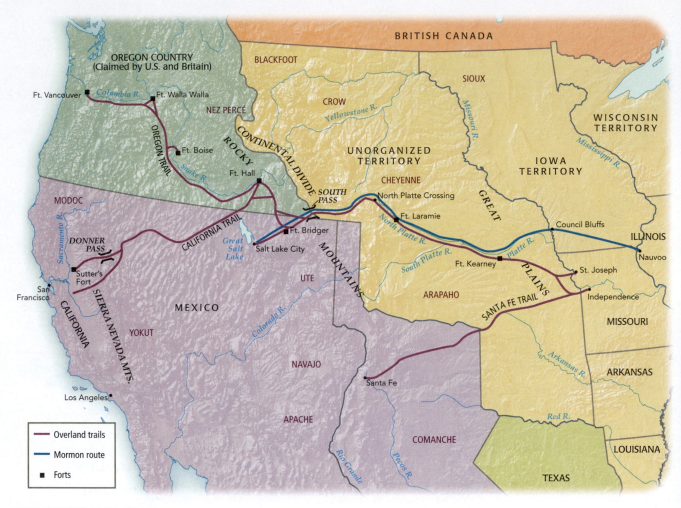

THE OVERLAND TRAIL

Beginning at several different points, the Overland Trail followed the Platte and Sweetwater Rivers across the plains to South Pass, where it crossed the Continental Divide. The trail split again near Fort Hall. Between 1840 and 1860 more than a quarter of a million emigrants made the trek. Following news of the gold strikes in 1848, the flow of westward emigrants increased and shifted toward California.

old; the hard journey discouraged the elderly. Furthermore, a family of four needed about $600 to outfit its journey, an amount that excluded the poor.

Caravans of 20 to 30 wagons were not uncommon the first few years, but after 1845 parties traveled in smaller trains of 8 to 10 wagons. The livestock of large companies ate up the prairie grass quickly, disagreements were more likely, and breakdowns (and hence halts) were more frequent. The trip itself lasted about 6 months, since the wagons normally covered only 15 miles a day, and the weather, repairs, deaths, and other eventualities necessitated occasional halts.

Women on the Overland Trail

The journey west often placed a special strain on women. Few wives were as eager as Daniel Waldo's to undertake the journey. "Poor Ma said only this morning, 'Oh I wish we

never had started,'" one daughter reported, "and she looks so sorrowful and dejected." In one study of Oregon-bound parties, three-fourths of the women did not want to make the move.

BREAKDOWN OF WOMEN'S TRADITIONAL ROLE

At first, parties divided work by gender, as had been done back home. Women cooked, washed, sewed, and took care of the children, while men drove the wagons, cared for the stock, stood guard, and did the heavy labor. Necessity placed new demands on women, however, and eventually altered their roles. Within a few weeks, they found themselves helping to repair wagons and construct bridges. When men became exhausted, sick, or injured, women stood guard and drove the oxen. The change in work assignments proceeded only in one direction, however, for few men undertook "women's work."

As women strove to maintain a semblance of home on the trail, they often experienced a profound sense of loss.

Trains often worked or traveled on the Sabbath, which had been ladies' day back home and an emblem of women's moral authority. Women also felt the lack of close companions to whom they could turn for comfort. One woman, whose husband separated their wagon from the train after a dispute, sadly watched the other wagons pull away: "I felt that indeed I had left all my friends to journey over the dreaded plains without one female acquaintance even for a companion—of course I wept and grieved about it but to no purpose."

Indians and the Trail Experience

PRESSURES ON PLAINS INDIANS The nations whose lands were crossed by white wagon trains reacted in a number of ways to the westward tide. The Sioux, who had long been trading with whites, were among the peoples who regularly visited overlanders to trade for blankets, clothes, cows, rifles, and knives. But the white migrants took a heavy toll on the Plains Indians' way of life: emigrant parties scared off game and reduced buffalo herds, overgrazed the grass, and depleted the supply of wood. Having petitioned unsuccessfully in 1846 for government compensation, some Sioux decided to demand payment from the wagon trains crossing their lands. Whether parties paid or not depended on the relative strength of the two groups, but whites complained bitterly of what seemed to them outright robbery.

Their fears aroused by sensational stories, overland parties were wary of Indians, but this menace was greatly exaggerated, especially on the plains. Few wagon trains were attacked by Indians, and less than 4 percent of deaths on the trail were caused by Indians. In truth, emigrants killed more Indians than Indians killed emigrants. For overlanders the most aggravating problem posed by native peoples was theft of stock. Many companies received valuable assistance from Indians, who acted as guides, directed them to grass and water, and transported stock and wagons across rivers.

As trail congestion and conflict increased, the government constructed a string of protective forts and in 1851 summoned Plains Indians to a conference at Fort Laramie. The U.S. government agreed to make an annual payment as compensation for the damages caused by the wagon trains but also required tribes to confine themselves to areas north or south of a corridor through which the Overland Trail ran. Some tribes were unwilling to surrender their freedom of movement and refused to agree. The Sioux, the most powerful people on the plains, signed and then ignored the terms.

REVIEW

What motivated men and women from the United States to migrate on overland trails?

THE POLITICAL ORIGINS OF EXPANSION

PRESIDENT WILLIAM HENRY HARRISON MADE the gravest mistake of his brief presidential career when he ventured out one raw spring day, bareheaded and without an overcoat, to buy groceries at the Washington markets. He developed pneumonia and died only one month after his inauguration.

TYLER BECOMES PRESIDENT For the first time in the nation's history, a vice president succeeded to the nation's highest office on the death of the president. John Tyler of Virginia had been a Democrat who supported states' rights so strongly that, during the nullification crisis, he was the only senator to vote against the Force Bill (page 287). After that, Jackson and the Democrats would have nothing to do with him, so Tyler joined the Whigs despite his strict constructionist principles. In 1840 the Whigs put him on the ticket

Women were often more reluctant to leave behind the moral support of communities for an unknown land. When they ventured west, they often worked hard to reestablish that community. For many, such as Susannah Bristow, bringing the family china was an important marker of tradition and civility. The blue china plate was part of Bristow's dowry, which she had brought to her marriage in 1812. She had already transported it from Tennessee to Kentucky and then to Illinois in previous moves. And when she joined her husband in Oregon, the china came with her, too, sheltered in this leather-covered trunk.

SEEING THE ELEPHANT ON THE OVERLAND TRAIL

In an era when traveling circuses proved a welcome though rare attraction, Americans used the expression "I have seen the elephant" to indicate they had gotten all—or considerably more than—they had bargained for. To the quarter of a million men and women who migrated overland to the Pacific coast, "seeing the elephant" meant ceasing to be a greenhorn by overcoming hardship and succeeding. The greeting "Have you seen the elephant?" became the unofficial password of the Overland Trail.

Some walked, rode horseback, or accompanied mule pack trains, but the overwhelming majority of emigrants traveled in wagons. Wagons could haul more pounds per animal, did not have to be packed each day, could carry the sick and injured, and could be arranged in a defensive circle at night. Most often, emigrants modified a common farm wagon, about 10 feet long. The wooden wagon bed, made of seasoned hardwood to withstand extreme heat, cold, and moisture, was arched over by cloth or waterproofed canvas that could be closed at each end.

Pulled usually by four to six oxen, one wagon could carry provisions and gear for a family of four. Most farm families were larger, however, and took at least one additional wagon. Packed within was a supply of bacon, breadstuffs (mostly flour), and coffee. For sleeping, families brought blankets and frequently a tent; a well-equipped wagon might have a feather bed laid over the packed possessions in the wagon. Parents normally slept there for privacy while children used the tent.

As the journey settled into a routine, women rose before daybreak to cook breakfast and food for lunch; the men followed around five to care for the animals; the train was off at seven with the call of a bugle. Men and older sons walked alongside the team or herded stock in the rear. Women and children could ride in the wagon as it jolted along, but before long they walked as much as possible to conserve the animals' strength. After a noonday stop for a cold lunch, the journey resumed;

Joseph Goldsborough Bruff, who traveled the Overland Trail to California, drew this picture of a Platte River crossing.

by midafternoon the men seemed almost asleep as they plodded under the baking sun beside their teams. At evening camp the men attended to the animals while the women and children collected buffalo dung for fuel and hauled water. Women cooked the evening meal and afterward washed the dishes, took care of the bedding, cleaned the wagons, aired provisions, and mended clothes. After a guard was posted, the exhausted emigrants turned in for the night.

The final third of the route lay across deserts, along twisting rivers with difficult crossings, on paths barely wide enough for a wagon. Wagons had to be double- and triple-teamed up steep grades and hoisted over canyon walls with ropes, chains, and winches. Because most wagons lacked brakes, drivers locked the wheels when going down steep slopes, dragged a weight behind, or lowered the wagon by a rope attached to a tree.

Improvements in the 1850s shortened the trip and reduced the hardships. Still, it required considerable courage to embark on the journey. "To enjoy such a trip," an anonymous overlander testified, "a man must be able to endure heat like a Salamander, . . . dust like a toad, and labor like a jackass. He must learn to eat with his unwashed fingers, drink out of the same vessel with his mules, sleep on the ground when it rains, and share his blanket with vermin. . . . It is a hardship without glory." When they reached their new homes, those who traveled the Overland Trail could boast that they had, indeed, seen the elephant.

Thinking Critically

Did the overland journey promote individualism or cooperation?

with Harrison in order to balance the ticket sectionally. In the rollicking 1840 campaign, the Whigs sang all too accurately: "And we'll vote for Tyler, therefore, / Without a why or wherefore."

Tyler's Texas Ploy

TYLER BREAKS WITH THE WHIGS

Tyler's courteous manner and personal warmth masked a rigid mind. Repeatedly, when Henry Clay and the Whigs in Congress passed a major bill, Tyler opposed it. After Tyler twice vetoed bills to charter a new national bank, disgusted congressional Whigs formally expelled their president from the party. Most Democrats, too, avoided him as an untrustworthy "renegade." A man without a party, Tyler decided that he could revive his reputation with a great accomplishment—the annexation of Texas.

He found support from Democrats disgruntled with their former leader, Martin Van Buren. Jackson's successor was, in their eyes, an ineffective leader who had stumbled through a depression and in 1840 gone down in ignominious defeat. "They mean to throw Van overboard," reported one delighted Whig, who caught wind of the plans. Meanwhile, Tyler's allies launched rumors designed to frighten southerners into pushing for annexation. Britain was ready to offer economic aid if Texas would abolish slavery, they claimed. (The rumor was false.) In April 1844 Tyler sent to the Senate for ratification a treaty he had secretly negotiated to bring Texas into the Union.

Van Overboard

The front-runners for the Whig and Democratic presidential nominations were Clay and Van Buren. Although rivals, they were both moderates who feared the slavery issue. Apparently by prearrangement, both men issued letters opposing annexation on the grounds that it threatened the Union and would provoke war with Mexico.

POLK'S NOMINATION

As expected, the Whigs unanimously nominated Clay on a platform that ignored the expansion issue entirely. The Democrats, however, had a more difficult time. Those who opposed Van Buren persuaded the Democratic convention to adopt a rule requiring a two-thirds vote to nominate a candidate. That blocked Van Buren's nomination. On the ninth ballot the delegates finally turned to James K. Polk of Tennessee, who was pro-Texas. The 1844 Democratic platform called for the "reannexation" of Texas (under the dubious claim it had been part of the Louisiana Purchase) and the "reoccupation" of Oregon, all the way to its northernmost boundary at 54°40′.

Angered by the convention's outcome, Van Buren's supporters in the Senate joined the Whigs in decisively defeating Tyler's treaty of annexation. Tyler eventually withdrew

James K. Polk

from the race as an independent candidate, but the Texas issue would not go away. Henry Clay found many southerners slipping out of his camp because he opposed annexation; backtracking, he announced that he would be glad to see Texas annexed if it could be done without war or dishonor and without threatening the Union. And in the North, a few antislavery Whigs turned to James G. Birney, running on the Liberty Party ticket.

ELECTION OF 1844

In the end, Polk squeaked through by 38,000 votes out of nearly 3 million cast. If just half of Birney's 15,000 ballots in New York had gone to Clay, he would have carried the state and been narrowly elected president. Indignant Whigs charged that by refusing to support Clay, political abolitionists had made the annexation of Texas, and hence the addition of slave territory to the Union, inevitable. And indeed, Tyler again asked Congress to annex Texas—this time by a joint resolution, which required only a majority in both houses rather than a two-thirds vote for a treaty in the Senate. In the new atmosphere following Polk's victory, the resolution narrowly passed, and on March 3, 1845, his last day in office, Tyler invited Texas to enter the Union.

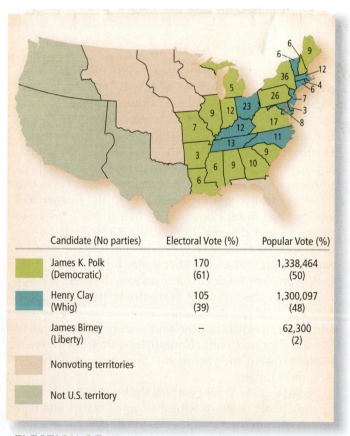

Candidate (No parties)	Electoral Vote (%)	Popular Vote (%)
James K. Polk (Democratic)	170 (61)	1,338,464 (50)
Henry Clay (Whig)	105 (39)	1,300,097 (48)
James Birney (Liberty)	–	62,300 (2)
Nonvoting territories		
Not U.S. territory		

ELECTION OF 1844

To the Pacific

Polk pursued his objectives as president with a dogged determination. Humorless, calculating, and often deceitful, he was not particularly brilliant in his maneuvering. But the life of politics consumed him, he knew his mind, and he could take the political pounding by his opponents. Embracing a continental vision of the United States, Polk not only endorsed Tyler's offer of annexation but also looked beyond, hoping to gain the three best harbors on the Pacific: San Diego, San Francisco, and Puget Sound. That meant wresting Oregon from Britain and California from Mexico.

Claiming that the American title was "clear and unquestionable," the new president brushed aside any notion of continuing joint occupation of Oregon with Britain. To pressure the British, he induced Congress to give the required one-year notice terminating the joint occupation of Oregon. His blustering was reinforced by the knowledge that American settlers in Oregon outnumbered the British 5,000 to 750. On the other hand, Polk hardly wanted war with a nation as powerful as Great Britain. So when the British offered, in June 1846, to divide the Oregon Territory along the 49th parallel, he readily agreed (see map, page 371). Britain retained Vancouver Island, where the Hudson's Bay Company's headquarters was located. But the arrangement gave the United States Puget Sound, which had been the president's objective all along.

Provoking a War

 DISPUTED BOUNDARY OF TEXAS

The Oregon settlement left Polk free to deal with Mexico. In 1845 Congress admitted Texas to the Union as a slave state, but Mexico had never formally recognized Texas's independence. Mexico insisted, moreover, that Texas's southern boundary was the Nueces River, not the Rio Grande, 130 miles to the south, as claimed by Texas. In reality, Texas had never controlled the disputed region; the Nueces had always been Texas's boundary when it was a Mexican province; and if taken literally, the Rio Grande border incorporated most of New Mexico, including Santa Fe, Albuquerque, Taos, and other major towns. Few Texans had ever even been to these places. Indeed, the one time Texas tried to exert authority in the region, New Mexicans had to ride out onto the plains to save the lost and starving expedition, and ultimately sent the men to Mexico City in chains. Nonetheless, Polk was already looking toward the Pacific and thus supported the Rio Grande boundary.

As soon as the Texans entered the Union, Mexico broke off diplomatic relations with the United States, and Polk sent American troops under General Zachary Taylor into the newly acquired state. At the same time, knowing that the unstable Mexican government desperately needed money, he attempted to buy territory to the Pacific. Sending John Slidell of Louisiana to Mexico as his special minister, Polk was prepared to offer $2 million in return for clear title to the Rio Grande boundary, $5 million for the remaining part of New Mexico, and up to $25 million for California. But the Mexican public overwhelmingly opposed ceding any more territory to the land-hungry "Yankees" from the United States, and the government refused to receive Slidell. "Depend upon it," reported Slidell, as he departed from Mexico in March 1846, "we can never get along well with them, until we have given them a good drubbing."

Blocked on the diplomatic front, Polk ordered Taylor, who had already crossed the Nueces with 4,000 troops, to proceed south to the Rio Grande. From the Mexican standpoint, the Americans had invaded their country and occupied their territory. For his part, Polk wanted to be in position to defend the disputed region if the two countries went to war. More importantly, once he realized that Mexico would not cave in to bullying diplomacy, Polk hoped that Taylor's position on the Rio Grande would provoke the Mexican army into starting a war.

By May 9 Polk and his cabinet had lost patience with the plan and decided to submit a war message to Congress without Mexican action. But on that day word arrived that two weeks earlier Mexican forces had crossed the Rio Grande and attacked some of Taylor's troops, killing 11 Americans. The president quickly rewrote his war message, placing the entire blame for the war on Mexico. "Mexico has passed the boundary of the United States, has invaded our territory, and shed American blood upon American soil," he told Congress on May 11. "War exists, and notwithstanding all our efforts to avoid it, exists by the act of Mexico herself." The administration sent a bill to Congress calling for volunteers and requesting money to supply American troops.

Indians and Mexicans

Mexican forces would often outnumber their American enemies in battle, but Mexico nonetheless suffered from critical disadvantages in the war. Chronic instability in its central government left the nation divided against itself in its moment of crisis. An empty national treasury fueled this instability and made it difficult to mobilize an effective response to the U.S. invasion. Mexico was also at a disadvantage in terms of military technology. While Mexican forces had to rely on bulky, fixed cannons, the U.S. Army employed new light artillery that could be repositioned quickly as battles progressed. Light artillery would tip the balance in several crucial engagements.

Finally, much of Mexico had to fight two wars at once. While Mexico enjoyed formal diplomatic title to most of the present-day American West, Indians still controlled the vast majority of that territory, and Mexico had seen

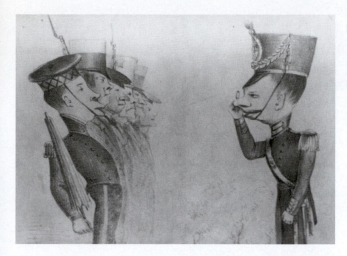

| The U.S.-Mexican War divided Americans, as this cartoon shows by mocking early recruits. One soldier holds a parasol instead of a rifle while his prissy commander squints through a monocle.

its relations with these Indians collapse in the 15 years before the U.S. invasion. During the late eighteenth century, Comanches, Navajos, Utes, and several different tribes of Apaches had made peace with Spanish authorities, ending decades of destructive war. Spaniards provided Indian leaders with gifts, guaranteed fair trade, and even handed out rations to minimize the animal thefts that could spark conflict.

THE END OF A FRAGILE PEACE This expensive and delicate system began to falter once Mexico achieved independence in 1821. Lacking the finances, the political unity, the stability, and the diplomatic resources of their Spanish predecessors, Mexican authorities watched the peace with northern Indians slip away. By the early 1830s, Native men were traveling hundreds of miles to raid Mexican ranches, haciendas, and towns, killing or capturing the people they found there, and stealing or destroying animals and other property. Whenever they were able, Mexicans did the same things to their Indian enemies. American markets helped drive the increasing violence, as Indian or white traders from the United States eagerly purchased horses and mules stolen from Mexico and supplied the raiders' arms and ammunition in return. By the eve of the U.S. invasion of Mexico, the violence encompassed all or parts of nine Mexican states and had claimed thousands of Mexican and Indian lives.

THE U.S.-MEXICAN WAR Thus, when American troops invaded northern Mexico they were literally marching in the footsteps of Comanches and Apaches, traversing territory that had already endured more than a decade of war. As Indian peoples pursued their own political, strategic, and economic goals, they made it far easier for the United States to achieve its goals. Impoverished, exhausted, and divided, and facing ongoing Indian raids, few northern Mexicans were willing or able to resist the U.S. conquest and occupation.

Opposition to the War

The war with Mexico posed a dilemma for Whigs. They were convinced (correctly) that Polk had provoked the conflict in order to acquire more territory from Mexico, and many northern Whigs accused the president of seeking to extend slavery. But they remembered, too, that the Federalist Party had doomed itself to extinction by opposing the War of 1812. Throughout the conflict, they strenuously attacked the conduct of "Mr. Polk's War." But they could not bring themselves to cut off funding for the war.

Pro-war sentiment was strongest in the Old Southwest and most of the Old Northwest. It was much weaker in the East, where antislavery "Conscience Whigs" were prominent. "If I were a Mexican," Senator Thomas Corwin of Ohio affirmed in the Senate, "I would tell you, . . . 'we will greet you with bloody hands and welcome you to hospitable graves.'" With their party deeply divided over the issue of the expansion of slavery, Whigs opposed the acquisition of any territory from Mexico.

The Price of Victory

Even before any word of hostilities arrived in California, a group of impetuous American settlers around Sacramento launched the "Bear Flag Revolt." In June 1846 they proclaimed California an independent republic. American forces in the area soon put down any Mexican resistance, and by the following January California was safely in American hands.

CONQUEST OF MEXICO Meanwhile, Taylor moved south from the Rio Grande and won several battles. At each town conquered or surrendered, he read statements provided in advance by President Polk and the War Department, promising to respect private property and protect the long-suffering residents from Indian attack. Taylor's campaign culminated in a narrow victory over General Antonio López de Santa Anna at Buena Vista in southern Coahuila. Polk had gained the territory he sought to reach the Pacific and wanted an end to the war. But Mexico refused to surrender, so Polk ordered an invasion into the heart of the country.

 TREATY OF GUADALUPE HIDALGO After an American army commanded by General Winfield Scott captured Mexico City on September 14, 1847, Mexico agreed to come to terms. The two nations ratified a peace treaty in 1848. Including Texas, which Mexico had continued to lay claim to, the Treaty of Guadalupe Hidalgo transferred half of Mexico's territory— more than half a million square miles—to the United States. In return the United States recalled its army and ended its aggressive war. It also assumed all the outstanding claims that U.S. citizens had against Mexico and gave the Mexicans 15 million dollars.

The war had cost the United States $97 million and 13,000 American lives, mostly as a result of disease. Yet

DUELING DOCUMENTS

IN WHAT COUNTRY DID THE U.S.-MEXICAN WAR BEGIN?

When President Polk insisted that Mexico had "shed American blood upon American soil," his critics demanded proof. Everyone acknowledged that the initial clash occurred just north of the Rio Grande. But did the boundary of Texas (and hence the boundary of the United States) extend to the Rio Grande, as Polk insisted, or only to the Nueces River, as had been internationally recognized before the Texas rebellion? Nearly all Mexicans believed that the fighting happened in Mexico, and some prominent Americans agreed. Among their number was a freshman member of Congress, Abraham Lincoln, whose "spot resolutions" took Polk to task. The dispute was motivated partly by politics: Lincoln, a Whig, happily criticized the Democratic Polk. Still, Lincoln's resolutions reflected genuine doubts about the war's legitimacy.

DOCUMENT 1   The War Began in the United States: President James K. Polk

The existing state of the relations between the United States and Mexico renders it proper that I should bring the subject to the consideration of Congress. . . . An envoy of the United States repaired to Mexico with full powers to adjust every existing difference. But though present on Mexican soil by agreement between the two Governments, invested with full powers, and bearing evidence of the most friendly dispositions, his mission has been unavailing. The Mexican Government not only refused to receive him or listen to his propositions, but after a long-continued series of menaces have at last invaded our territory and shed the blood of our fellow-citizens on our own soil. . . . In my message at the commencement of the present session I informed you that upon

the earnest appeal both of the Congress and convention of Texas I had ordered an efficient military force to take a position "between the Nueces and Del Norte." This had become necessary to meet a threatened invasion of Texas by the Mexican forces, for which extensive military preparations had been made. The invasion was threatened solely because Texas had determined, in accordance with a solemn resolution of the Congress of the United States, to annex herself to our Union, and under these circumstances it was plainly our duty to extend our protection over her citizens and soil. . . . Meantime Texas, by the final act of our Congress, had become an integral part of our Union. The Congress of Texas, by its act of December 19, 1836, had declared the

Rio del Norte to be the boundary of that Republic. Its jurisdiction had been extended and exercised beyond the Nueces. The country between that river and the Del Norte had been represented in the Congress and in the convention of Texas, had thus taken part in the act of annexation itself, and is now included within one of our Congressional districts. Our own Congress had, moreover, with great unanimity, by the act approved December 31, 1845, recognized the country beyond the Nueces as a part of our territory by including it within our own revenue system, and a revenue officer to reside within that district had been appointed by and with the advice and consent of the Senate. It became, therefore, of urgent necessity to provide for the defense

---

the real cost was even higher. By bringing vast new territories into the Union, the war forced the explosive slavery issue to the center of national politics and threatened to upset the balance of power between North and South. Ralph Waldo Emerson had been prophetic: "The United States will conquer Mexico," he wrote when the U.S.-Mexican War began, "but it will be as the man who swallows the arsenic which brings him down in turn. Mexico will poison us."

The Rise of the Slavery Issue

When the second party system emerged during the 1820s, Martin Van Buren had championed political parties as one way to forge links between North and South that would strengthen the Union. But the Texas movement increased

sectional suspicions, and President Polk did nothing to ease this problem.

NORTHERN DISCONTENT

Polk was a politician to his bones: constantly maneuvering, promising one thing, doing another, making a pledge, taking it back—using any means to accomplish his ends. Discontent over his double-dealing finally erupted in August 1846, when Polk requested $2 million from Congress, as he vaguely explained, to "facilitate negotiations" with Mexico. It was widely understood that the money was to be used to bribe the Mexican government to cede territory to the United States.

WILMOT PROVISO

On August 8 David Wilmot, an obscure Pennsylvania congressman, startled Democratic leaders by introducing an amendment to the bill that barred slavery from any territory acquired of that portion of our country. . . . But no open act of hostility was committed until the 24th of April. On that day General [Mariano] Arista, who had succeeded to the command of the Mexican forces, communicated to General Taylor that "he considered hostilities commenced and should prosecute them." A party of dragoons of 63 men and officers were on the same day dispatched from the American camp up the Rio del Norte, on its left bank, to ascertain whether the Mexican troops had crossed or were preparing to cross the river, "became engaged with a large body of these troops, and after a short affair, in which some 16 were killed and wounded, appear to have been surrounded and compelled to surrender."

Source: Message to Congress, Washington, May 11, 1846. In James D. Richardson, ed., *A Compilation of the Messages and Papers of the Presidents*, Volume 4 (New York: Bureau of National Literature and Art, 1908), pp. 437–443.

DOCUMENT 2   The "Spot" was beyond the U.S. Borders: Representative Abraham Lincoln

---

Whereas the President of the United States, in his message of May 11, 1846, has declared that "the Mexican Government not only refused to receive him, [the envoy of the United States,] or listen to his propositions, but, after a long-continued series of menaces, has at last invaded *our territory* and shed the blood of our fellow-citizens on our *own soil.*"

And again, in his message of December 8, 1846, that "we had ample cause of war against Mexico long before the breaking out of hostilities; but even then we forbore to take redress into our own hands until Mexico herself became the aggressor, by invading *our soil* in hostile array, and shedding the blood of our citizens:"

And yet again, in his message of December 7, 1847, that "the Mexican Government refused even to hear the terms of adjustment which he [our minister of peace] was authorized to propose, and finally, under wholly unjustifiable pretexts, involved the two countries in war, by invading the territory of the State of Texas, striking the first blow, and shedding the blood of our citizens on *our own soil.*"

And whereas this House is desirous to obtain a full knowledge of all the facts which go to establish whether the particular spot on which the blood of our citizens was so shed was or was not at that time *our own soil.* Therefore,

Resolved By the House of Representatives, That the President of the United States be respectfully requested to inform this House—
1st. Whether the spot on which the blood of our citizens was shed, as in his messages declared, was or was not within the territory of Spain, at least after the treaty of 1819, until the Mexican revolution.
2d. Whether that spot is or is not within the territory which was wrested from Spain by the revolutionary Government of Mexico.
3d. Whether that spot is or is not within a settlement of people, which settlement has existed ever since long before the Texas revolution, and until its inhabitants fled before the approach of the United States army.
4th. Whether that settlement is or is not isolated from any and all other settlements by the Gulf and the Rio Grande on the south and west, and by wide uninhabited regions on the north and east.
5th. Whether the people of that settlement, or a majority of them, or any of them, have ever submitted themselves to the government or laws of Texas or the United States, by consent or compulsion, either by accepting office, or voting at elections, or paying tax, or serving on juries, or having process served upon them, or in any other way.
6th. Whether the people of that settlement did or did not flee from the approach of the United States army, leaving unprotected their homes and their growing crops, *before*

the blood was shed, as in the messages stated; and whether the first blood, so shed, was or was not shed within the enclosure of one of the people who had thus fled from it.
7th. Whether our *citizens,* whose blood was shed, as in his message declared, were or were not, at that time, armed officers and soldiers, sent into that settlement by the military order of the President, through the Secretary of War.
8th. Whether the military force of the United States was or was not sent into that settlement after General Taylor had more than once intimated to the War Department that, in his opinion, no such movement was necessary to the defence or protection of Texas.

Resolutions introduced into the House of Representatives Dec. 22, 1847.

Source: http://teachingamericanhistory.org/library/index.asp?document=2463.

Thinking Critically

How does Polk justify Taylor's presence on the Rio Grande? How does Lincoln critique Taylor's presence on the Rio Grande? Do they disagree over facts, or over which facts matter? What more information would you need to decide who makes the more persuasive case?

---

from Mexico. The Wilmot Proviso, as the amendment became known, passed the northern-controlled House of Representatives several times, only to be rejected in the Senate, where the South had more power. As such, it revealed mounting sectional tensions.

Wilmot himself was hardly an abolitionist. Indeed, he hoped to keep not only slaves but all black people out of the territories. Denying any "morbid sympathy for the slave," he declared, "I would preserve for white free labor a fair country . . . where the sons of toil, of my own race and color, can live without the disgrace which association with negro slavery brings upon free labor." The Wilmot Proviso aimed not to destroy slavery in the South but to confine the institution to those states where it already existed. Still, abolitionists had long contended that southern slaveholders—the "Slave Power"—were plotting to extend their sway over the rest of the country. The political maneuverings of slaveholders such as Tyler, and especially Polk, convinced growing numbers of northerners that the Slave Power did indeed exist and that it was aggressively looking to expand its influence.

NEW LANDS, NEW TENSIONS   The status of slavery in the territories became more than an abstract question once the peace with Mexico had been finalized. The United States gained title to an immense territory, including all of what would become the states of California, Nevada, and Utah, nearly all of New Mexico, most of Arizona and Colorado, and parts of Wyoming, Kansas, and Oklahoma. These territories included some of the finest natural harbors in the world, regions of immense agricultural potential, and vast, still-hidden riches in oil, gas, and mineral wealth. With the United States in control of the

SETTAN ANNUAL CALENDAR OF THE KIOWA

The black bars represent trees without leaves, indicating winter.

Winter of 1839–1840: what might this pictograph of a man covered in red spots represent?

"Hide-quiver expedition winter"

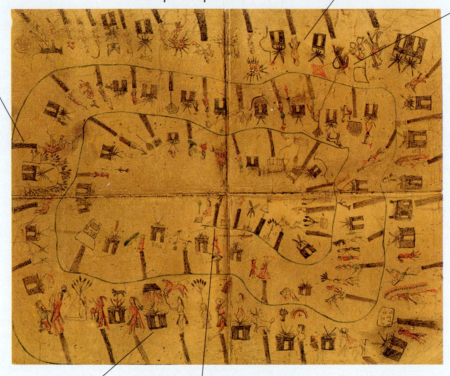

What year is the last winter represented on the calendar?

The recurring pictograph of a medicine bundle atop a lodge represents the Sun Dance, a sacred ceremony Kiowas held in summer.

Kiowas kept pictographic calendars painted on hides. The pictographs memorialized two key events each year, one for summer and one for winter. A Kiowa named Settan (Little Bear) produced the one above, which proceeds in a spiral beginning with the summer of 1832 in the upper-left corner. The calendar marks the winter of 1840–1841 as "Hide-quiver expedition winter." What does that signify? By the 1840s young Kiowa warriors preferred quivers made from sleek leather or panther skin to those made from rougher buffalo hide, which only old men used. "Hide-quiver war expedition winter" refers to a campaign made up of older men

who headed south into Mexico. Traditionally, Kiowas and Comanches would leave older men behind to protect women and children and guard their herds of horses and mules. But in 1840 a peace agreement with their traditional Cheyenne and Arapaho enemies left the Kiowas and Comanches feeling more secure. When winter came, even aged warriors rode off with their hide quivers to steal horses and mules from Mexicans hundreds of miles below the Rio Grande. Indirectly, attacks such as these helped the United States win its own war against Mexico.

Source: www.texasbeyondhistory.net/plateaus/peoples/images/calendar-full.html.

Thinking Critically

Kiowas passed on their history through spoken word. How could a calendar such as this enhance oral tradition? Does the selection of events in the calendar indicate a very different approach to historical memory than the one in this textbook? How would a historian use a document such as this? What other kinds of evidence could historians put this calendar in conversation with?

THE U.S.-MEXICAN WAR

How would the climate of the lands conquered by the United States be likely to affect the issue of slavery?

Pacific Coast from San Diego to Puget Sound, Polk's continental vision had become a reality. But slavery would once again dominate national politics.

NEW SOCIETIES IN THE WEST

As HISPANIC, INDIAN, ASIAN, AND Anglo-American cultures interacted, the patterns of development along the frontier varied widely. Some newcomers re-created the farm economies and small towns of the Anglo-American East; others continued the cattle-ranching life of the Hispanic West. In California the new settlements were overwhelmingly shaped by the rush for gold after 1848. And in the Great Basin around Salt Lake the Mormons established a society

whose sense of religious mission was as strong as that of the Puritans.

Farming in the West

The overlanders expected to replicate the societies they had left behind. When a wagon train arrived at its destination, members had usually exhausted their resources and thus quickly scattered in search of employment or a good farm site. "Friday, October 27.—Arrived at Oregon City at the falls of the Willamette," read one pioneer diary. "Saturday, October 28.—Went to work."

NEW SOCIETIES
IN THE WEST

In a process repeated over and over, settlers in a new area set up the machinery of government. Although violence was common on the frontier, farming communities tended to resolve problems by traditional means. Churches took longer to establish, for ministers were hard to recruit and congregations were often not large enough to support a church. As the population grew, however, a more conventional society evolved. Towns and a middle class developed, the proportion of women increased, schools were established, and the residents became less mobile.

Although opportunity was greater on the frontier and early arrivals had a special advantage, more and more the agricultural frontier of the West resembled the older society of the East. With the development of markets and transportation, wealth became concentrated, some families fell to the lower rungs of society, and those who were less successful left, seeking yet another fresh start.

The Gold Rush

In January 1848, while constructing a sawmill along the American River, James Marshall noticed gold flecks in the millrace. More discoveries followed, and when the news reached the East, it spread like wildfire. The following spring the Overland Trail was jammed with eager "forty-niners." Some 80,000 emigrants journeyed to California that year, about 55,000 of whom took the overland route. In only two years, from 1848 to the end of 1849, California's population jumped from 14,000 to 100,000. By 1860 it stood at 380,000.

With their distinctive clothing and bamboo hats, Chinese miners could be seen throughout the diggings. Chinese immigration reached a peak in 1852, when 20,000 arrived in California. In the heyday of the mining camps, perhaps 20 percent of the miners were Chinese. Confronted with intense hostility from other miners, they worked abandoned claims and unpromising sites with primitive and less expensive equipment.

LIFE IN THE MINING CAMPS

Among those who went to California was William Swain, a 27-year-old farmer in western New York. Deciding that he had had enough of the hard work of farming, he bid good-bye to his wife and daughter in 1849 and set off for the gold fields to make his fortune. On his arrival in November he entered a partnership and staked a claim along the Feather River, but after several months of backbreaking work in icy waters, he and his partners discovered that their claim was "worth nothing." He sold out and joined another company, but early rains soon forced them to stop work. In October 1850, after less than a year in the diggings, Swain decided to return home. With only a few hundred dollars to show for his labor, he counted himself one of the vast majority of miners who had seen "their bright daydreams of golden wealth vanish like the dreams of night." He arrived home the following February and resumed farming.

Predictably, "mining the miners" offered a more reliable road to prosperity. Perhaps half the inhabitants of a mining town were shopkeepers, businesspeople, and professionals who provided services for prospectors. Also conspicuous were gamblers, card sharks, and other outcasts, all bent on separating the miner from his riches.

 NATIVIST AND RACIAL PREJUDICES

More than 80 percent of the prospectors who poured into the gold country were Americans, including free blacks. Mexicans, Australians, Argentinians, Hawaiians, Chinese, French, English, and Irish also came. Observers praised the diggings' democratic spirit. Yet such assertions overlooked strongly held nativist prejudices: when frustrated by a lack of success, American miners directed their hostility toward foreigners. Mob violence drove Mexicans out of nearly every camp, and the Chinese were confined to claims abandoned by Americans as unprofitable. The state eventually enacted a foreign miners' tax that fell largely on the Chinese. Free African Americans felt the sting of discrimination as well, both in the camps and in state law. White American miners proclaimed that "colored men were not privileged to work in a country intended only for American citizens."

WOMEN IN THE CAMPS

Only about 5 percent of gold rush emigrants were women or children; given this relative scarcity, men were willing to pay top dollar for women's domestic skills. Women supported themselves by cooking, sewing, and washing, as well as by running hotels and boardinghouses. "A smart woman can do very well in this country," one woman informed a friend in the East. "It is the only country I ever was in where a woman received anything like a just compensation for work." Women went to the mining frontier to be with their husbands, to make money, or to find adventure. But the class most frequently seen in the diggings was prostitutes, who numbered perhaps 20 percent of female Californians in 1850.

 **MINING'S ENVIRONMENTAL LEGACY**

Before long, the most easily worked claims had been played out and large corporations moved in heavy equipment to get at hidden ore. Shafts were dug deep into the ground, high-pressure water jets tore away ore-bearing gravel, and veins of quartz rock were blasted out and crushed in large stamping mills. This type of mining left a lasting environmental legacy. Abandoned prospect holes and diggings pockmarked the gold fields and created piles of debris that heavy rains would wash down the valley, choking streams and ruining lands below. Excavation of hillsides, construction of dams to divert rivers, and the destruction of the forest cover to meet the heavy demand for lumber and firewood caused serious erosion of the soil and severe flooding in the spring.

Instant City: San Francisco

When the United States assumed control of California, San Francisco had a population of perhaps 200. But thousands of emigrants took the water route west, passing through San Francisco's harbor on their way to the diggings. By 1856 the city's population had jumped to an astonishing 50,000. In a mere 8 years the city had attained the size New York City had taken 190 years to reach.

SAN FRANCISCO'S CHAOTIC GROWTH

The product of economic self-interest, San Francisco developed in helter-skelter fashion. Land prices soared, speculation was rampant, and commercial forces became paramount. Residents lived in tents or poorly constructed, half-finished buildings. To enlarge the commercial district, hills began to be leveled, with the dirt used to fill in the bay (thereby creating more usable land). Since the city government took virtually no role in directing development, almost no land was reserved for public use. Property owners defeated a proposal to widen the streets, prompting the city's leading newspaper to complain, "To sell a few more feet of lots, the streets were compressed like a cheese, into half their width."

The Migration from China

The gold rush that swelled San Francisco's streets was a global phenomenon. Americans predominated in the mining population, but Latin Americans, Europeans, Australians, and Chinese swarmed into California. An amazing assortment of languages could be heard on the city's streets: indeed, in 1860 San Francisco's inhabitants were 50 percent foreign-born.

 CONDITIONS IN CHINA

The most distinctive ethnic group was the Chinese. They had come to Gum San, the land of the golden mountain. Those who arrived in California overwhelmingly hailed from the area of southern China around Canton—and not by accident. Although other provinces of China also suffered from economic distress, population pressures, social unrest, and political upheaval, Canton had a large European presence, since it was the only port open to outsiders. That situation changed after the first Opium War (1839–1842), when Britain forced China to open other ports to trade. For Cantonese, the sudden loss of their trade monopoly produced widespread economic hardship. At the same time, a series of religious and political revolts in the region led to severe fighting that devastated the countryside. A growing number of residents concluded that emigration was the only way to survive, and the presence of Western ships in the harbors of Canton and nearby Hong Kong (a British possession since 1842) made it easier to migrate to California rather than to southeast Asia.

Between 1849 and 1854, some 45,000 Chinese flocked to California. Among those who went was 16-year-old Lee Chew, who left for California after a man from his village returned with great wealth from the "country of the American wizards." Like the other gold seekers, these Chinese immigrants were

San Francisco in 1850: chaos and crowding

overwhelmingly young and male, and they wanted only to accumulate savings and return home to their families. (Indeed, only 16 Chinese women arrived before 1854.) Generally poor, Chinese immigrants arrived already in debt, having borrowed the price of their steamship ticket; they fell further into debt to Chinese merchants in San Francisco, who loaned them money to purchase needed supplies.

OCCUPATIONS When the Chinese were harassed in the mines, many opened laundries in San Francisco and elsewhere, since little capital was required—soap, scrub board, iron, and ironing board. The going rate at the time for washing, ironing, and starching shirts was an exorbitant $8 per dozen. Many early San Franciscans actually found it cheaper to send their dirty laundry to Canton or Honolulu, to be returned several months later. Other Chinese around San Francisco set up restaurants or worked in the fishing industry. In these early years they found Americans less hostile, as long as they stayed away from the gold fields. As immigration and the competition for jobs increased, however, anti-Chinese sentiment intensified.

Gradually, San Francisco took on the trappings of a more orderly community. The city government established a public school system, erected streetlights, created a municipal water system, and halted further filling in of the bay. Industry was confined to the area south of the city; several new working-class neighborhoods grew up near the downtown section. Fashionable neighborhoods sprouted on several hills, as high rents drove many residents from the developing commercial center, and churches and families became more common. By 1856, the city of the gold rush had been replaced by a new city whose stone and brick buildings gave it a new sense of permanence.

California Genocide

Eager to possess native land, resources, and even Indian slaves; determined to avenge Indian thefts or attacks (real or imagined); or anxious about purported Indian conspiracies, many white Californians attempted to exterminate the state's indigenous population.

GOVERNMENT SUPPORT In 1859 California's governor hired notorious Indian killer Walter S. Jarboe to kill or capture any Yuki Indians found outside their newly established reservation. After four months Jarboe boasted that he and his men had killed or captured nearly 500 Yuki. "However cruel it may be," Jarboe candidly explained, "nothing short of extermination will suffice to rid the Country of them." Some white Californians protested Jarboe's "deliberate, cowardly, brutal massacre of defenseless men, women, and children." But others celebrated, and the state legislature reimbursed Jarboe and men like him for their expenses. Washington encouraged extermination by rejecting treaties that might have provided Indians some land and security, ignoring the pleas of dismayed federal Indian agents. The federal government reimbursed California nearly $1.5 million for the costs of its ongoing Indian campaigns.

LAW AND CATASTROPHE Survivors lived to see the seizure of their historic territories, the destruction of the animals they relied upon, profound ecological transformation through overgrazing and hydraulic mining, and the dissolution of families through kidnapping and enslavement. In 1850 the California legislature passed the "Act for the Government and Protection of Indians." The measure legalized the seizure and forced labor of Indian children, as well as the capture of native men and women for loitering, begging, or leading "an immoral or profligate course of life." People seized on these counts were leased out to the highest bidder, for a four-month term of forced labor. By the late 1850s white observers reported Indian villages comprised almost totally of adults, most of the children "doubtless having been stolen and sold."

Though population estimates are imprecise, few historians doubt that California's Indians experienced a

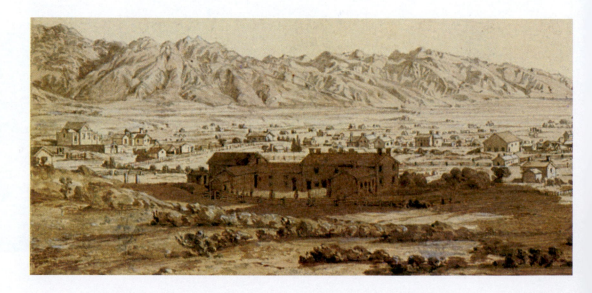

Salt Lake City in 1853: planned, spacious, and orderly

demographic, social, and spiritual catastrophe in the mid-nineteenth century. In the twenty years following the U.S.-Mexican War, homicide, displacement, captivity, forced labor, malnutrition, disease, and social trauma reduced the state's native population from perhaps 150,000 to some 30,000. That said, men like Jarboe and their patrons in state and national government failed to "exterminate" California's Indians. Native men, women, and children employed a host of tactics to protect their families and preserve their cultures and values. Today hundreds of thousands of Californians self-identify as Native American, many of them descended from survivors of the California genocide.

The Mormons in Utah

The makeshift, often chaotic society spawned by the gold rush was a product of largely uncontrolled economic forces. In contrast, the society evolving in the Great Basin of Utah exhibited an entirely different but equally remarkable growth. Salt Lake City became the center of a religious kingdom established by the Church of Jesus Christ of Latter-Day Saints.

STATE OF DESERET

After Joseph Smith's death in 1844 (see page 313), the Mormon Church was led by Brigham Young, who lacked Smith's religious mysticism but was a brilliant organizer. Young decided to move his followers to the Great Basin, an isolated area a thousand miles from the settled parts of the United States. In 1847 the first thousand settlers arrived, the vanguard of thousands more who extended Mormon settlement throughout the valley of the Great Salt Lake and the West. Church officials also held the government positions, and Young had supreme power in legislative, executive, and judicial matters as well as religious affairs. In 1849 the state of Deseret was officially established, with Brigham Young as governor. It applied for admission to the Union.

POLYGAMY

The most controversial church teaching was the doctrine of polygamy, or plural marriage, which Young finally sanctioned publicly in 1852. Visitors reported with surprise that few Mormon wives seemed to rebel against the practice. Some plural wives developed close friendships; indeed, in one sample almost a third of plural marriages included at least two sisters. Moreover, because polygamy distinguished Mormonism from other religions, plural wives saw it as an expression of their religious faith. "I want to be assured of *position in God's estimation*," one such wife explained. "If polygamy is the Lord's order, we must carry it out."

IRRIGATION AND COMMUNITY

The Mormons connected control of water to their sense of mission and respect for hierarchy. The valley of the Great Salt Lake, where the Mormons established their holy community, lacked significant rivers or abundant sources of water. Thus success depended on irrigating the region, something never before attempted. When the first Mormons arrived from the East, they began constructing a coordinated series of dams, aqueducts, and ditches, bringing life-giving water to the valleys of the region. Fanning out from their original settlement, they founded a series of colonies throughout the West, all tied to Salt Lake City and joined by ribbons of water. Mormon farmers grew corn, wheat, hay, and an assortment of fruits and vegetables. By 1850 there were more than 16,000 irrigated acres in what would eventually become the state of Utah. The Mormons were the first Anglos to extensively use irrigation in North America.

Control of water reinforced the Mormons' sense of hierarchy and group discipline. Centralization of authority in the hands of church officials made possible an overall plan of development, allowed for maximum exploitation of resources, and freed communities from the disputes over water rights that plagued many settlements in the arid West. In a radical departure from American ideals,

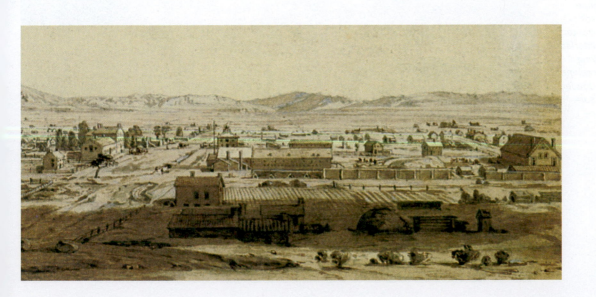

church leaders insisted that water belonged to the community, not individuals, and vested this authority in the hands of the local bishop. Control of water resources, which were vital for survival in the desert, reinforced the power of the church hierarchy over not just the faithful but dissidents as well. Community needs, as interpreted by church leaders, took precedence over individual rights. Thus irrigation did more than make the desert bloom. By checking the Jeffersonian ideal of an independent, self-sufficient farmer, it also made possible a centralized, well-regulated society under the firm control of the church.

Mexican-American Rights and Property

At the conclusion of the U.S.-Mexican War, some 100,000 Mexican citizens suddenly found themselves living inside the newly expanded United States. The Treaty of Guadalupe Hidalgo guaranteed them "the free enjoyment of their liberty and property." Mexican negotiators understood how critical that was: without land, their former citizens would enjoy neither economic security nor political influence in their new country. But the treaty said little about how Mexican Americans would prove their ownership of land. They rarely had the sort of documentation that American courts expected. Differences in legal culture, combined with racism and pervasive fraud, led to the dispossession and impoverishment of most Spanish-speaking property holders in the Southwest.

LEGAL FEES AND LAND LOSS California's Land Act of 1851 required everyone with Spanish or Mexican era claims to document them within two years. Hundreds failed to file claims in the time allotted, and by the terms of the Land Act all their territories passed into the public domain. The board eventually confirmed three-quarters of the claims it did receive. But resolution often took years and proved to be enormously expensive. Property owners had to mortgage their lands to pay legal fees, and in the end the great majority were ruined. Claimants in New Mexico likewise lost vast tracts of lands to Anglo ranchers and, especially, to lawyers. The lengthy and expensive review process left Mexican and Pueblo Indian claimants holding only about 6 percent of the lands they had possessed before the U.S. invasion.

TEJANO RESISTANCE Tejanos faced similar pressures. Stigmatized and despised by whites as racial inferiors, they were the poorest group in free society. One response to this dislocation, an option commonly taken by persecuted minorities, was social banditry. An example was the folk hero Juan Cortina. A member of a displaced landed family in southern Texas, Cortina was driven into resistance in the 1850s by American harassment. He began stealing from wealthy Anglos to aid poor Mexicans, proclaiming, "To me is entrusted the breaking of the chains of your slavery." Cortina continued to raid Texas border settlements until finally he was imprisoned by Mexican authorities. While failing to produce any lasting change, Cortina demonstrated the depth of frustration and resentment among Hispanics over their abuse at the hands of the new Anglo majority.

✅ **REVIEW**

Who were the winners and losers in the California gold rush?

Town plazas, such as this one in San Felipe, Coahuila (in Mexico), were commercial centers in the Mexican borderlands. Traders from outlying ranchos enjoy refreshments while their goods, loaded on oxcarts, await sale.

Escape from Crisis

Issue of
Slavery's
Extension

With the return of peace, Congress confronted the problem of whether to allow slavery in the newly acquired territories. David Wilmot, in his controversial proviso, had already proposed to outlaw slavery throughout the Mexican cession. John C. Calhoun, representing the extreme southern position, countered that slavery was legal in all territories. The federal government had acted as the agent of all the states in acquiring the land, he argued, and southerners had a right to take their property there, including slaves. Only when the residents of a territory drafted a state constitution could they decide the question of slavery.

Between these extremes were two moderate positions. One proposed extending the Missouri Compromise line of 36°30′ to the Pacific, which would have continued the earlier policy of dividing the national domain between the North and the South. The other proposal, championed by Senator Lewis Cass of Michigan and Senator Stephen A. Douglas of Illinois, was to allow the people of the territory rather than Congress to decide the status of slavery. This solution, which became known as **popular sovereignty,** was deliberately ambiguous, since its supporters refused to specify whether the residents could make this decision at any time or only when drafting a state constitution, as Calhoun insisted.

When Congress organized the Oregon Territory in 1848, it prohibited slavery there, since even southerners admitted that the region was too far north to grow the South's staple crops. But this seemingly straightforward decision made it impossible to apply the Missouri Compromise line to the other territories. Without Oregon as a part of the package, the bulk of the remaining land would be open to slavery, something at which the North balked. Almost inadvertently, one of the two moderate solutions had been discarded by the summer of 1848.

A Two-Faced Campaign

In the election of 1848 both major parties tried to avoid the slavery issue. The Democrats nominated Lewis Cass, a supporter of popular sovereignty, while the Whigs bypassed all their prominent leaders and selected General Zachary Taylor, who had taken no position on any public issue and who remained silent throughout the campaign. The Whigs adopted no platform and planned instead to emphasize the general's war record.

Free Soil
Party

But the slavery issue would not be ignored. A new antislavery coalition, the **Free Soil Party** helped force the issue. Alienated by Polk's policies and still angry over the 1844 convention, northern Democrats loyal to Van Buren spearheaded its creation. They were joined by "Conscience Whigs," who disavowed Taylor's nomination because he was a slaveholder. Furthermore, political abolitionists like Salmon P. Chase left the Liberty party in favor of this broader coalition. To widen its appeal, the Free Soil platform focused on the dangers of extending slavery rather than on the evil of slavery itself. Ironically, the party's convention named as its candidate Martin Van Buren—the man who for years had struggled to keep the slavery issue out of politics.

Election of
1848

With the Free Soilers strongly supporting the Wilmot Proviso, the Whigs and Democrats could not ignore the slavery question. The two major parties responded by running different

| The Great Triumvirate—Clay, Webster, and Calhoun—served together in public life for almost four decades. Clay (left) and Webster (center) supported the Compromise of 1850, whereas in his last speech in the Senate, the dying Calhoun (right) opposed it. By midcentury, power was passing to a new generation of politicians more accustomed to sectional conflict and less amenable to compromise.

campaigns in the North and the South. To southern audiences, each party promised that it would protect slavery in the territories; to northern voters, each claimed that it would keep the territories free. In this two-faced, sectional campaign, the Whigs won their second national victory. Taylor held on to the core of Whig voters in both sections (Van Buren and Cass, after all, had long been Democrats). But in the South, where the contest pitted a southern slaveholder against two northerners, Taylor won many more votes than Clay had in 1844. As one southern Democrat complained, "We have lost hundreds of votes, solely on the ground that General Cass was a Northerner and General Taylor a Southern man." Furthermore, Van Buren polled five times as many votes as the Liberty Party had four years earlier. It seemed that the national system of political parties was being gradually pulled apart.

The Compromise of 1850

Once he became president, Taylor could no longer remain silent. The territories gained from Mexico had to be organized; furthermore, by 1849 California had gained enough residents to be admitted as a state. In the Senate the balance of power between North and South stood at 15 states each. California's admission would break the sectional balance.

TAYLOR'S PLAN Called "Old Rough and Ready" by his troops, Taylor was a forthright man of action, but he was politically inexperienced and he oversimplified complex problems. Since even Calhoun conceded that entering states had the right to ban slavery, Taylor proposed that the way to end the sectional crisis was to skip the territorial stage by combining all the Mexican cession into two very large states, New Mexico and California. So the president sent agents to California and New Mexico with instructions to set the machinery in motion for both territories to draft constitutions and apply for statehood directly. Even more shocking to southern Whigs, he proposed to apply the Wilmot Proviso to the entire area, since he was convinced that slavery would never flourish there. By the time Congress convened in December 1849, California had drafted a constitution and applied for admission as a free state. Taylor reported that New Mexico (which included most of Arizona, Utah, and Colorado) would soon do the same and recommended that both be admitted as free states. The president's plan touched off the most serious sectional crisis the Union had yet confronted.

Into this turmoil stepped Henry Clay, now 73 years old and nearing the end of his career. A savvy card player all his life, Clay loved politics: the bargaining, the wheeling and dealing, the late-night trade-offs eased along by a bottle of bourbon. Thirty years earlier he had engineered the Missouri Compromise, and in 1833 he had helped defuse the nullification crisis. Clay decided that a grand compromise was needed to save the Union. Already, Mississippi had summoned other southern states to meet in a convention at Nashville to discuss the crisis, and southern extremists were pushing for secession. The points of disagreement went beyond the question of the western territories. Many northerners considered it disgraceful that slaves were bought and sold in the nation's capital, where slavery was still permitted. Southerners complained bitterly that northern states ignored the 1793 Fugitive Slave Law and prevented them from reclaiming runaway slaves.

CLAY'S COMPROMISE Clay's compromise, submitted in January 1850, addressed all these concerns. California, he proposed, should be admitted as a free state, which represented the clear wishes of most settlers there. The rest of the Mexican cession would be organized as two territories, New Mexico and Utah, under the doctrine of popular sovereignty. Thus slavery would not be prohibited from these regions. Clay also proposed that Congress abolish the slave trade but not slavery itself in the District of Columbia and that a new, more rigorous fugitive slave law be passed to enable southerners to reclaim runaway slaves. To reinforce the idea that both North and South were yielding ground, Clay combined those provisions that dealt with the former Mexican territory and several others adjusting the Texas–New Mexico boundary into a larger package known as the Omnibus Bill.

With the stakes so high, the Senate debated the bill for six months. Daniel Webster of Massachusetts, always deep-voiced, seemed more somber than usual when he delivered a pro-Compromise speech on the seventh of March. "I wish to speak today not as a Massachusetts man, not as a Northern man, but as an American. . . . I speak today for the preservation of the Union. Hear me for my cause." Calhoun, whose aged, crevassed face mirrored the lines that had been drawn so deeply between the two sections, was near death and too ill to deliver his final speech to the Senate, which a colleague read for him as he listened silently. The "cords of Union," he warned—those ties of interest and affection that held the nation together—were snapping one by one. Only equal rights for the South and an end to the agitation against slavery could preserve the Union.

Clay, wracked by a hacking cough, spent long hours trying to line up the needed votes. But for once, the great card enthusiast had misplayed his hand. The Omnibus Bill required that the components of the compromise be approved as a package. Extremists in Congress from both regions, however, combined against the moderates and rejected the bill.

PASSAGE OF THE COMPROMISE OF 1850 With Clay exhausted and his strategy in shambles, Democrat Stephen A. Douglas assumed leadership of the pro-Compromise forces. The sudden death in July of President Taylor, who had threatened to veto Clay's plan, aided the

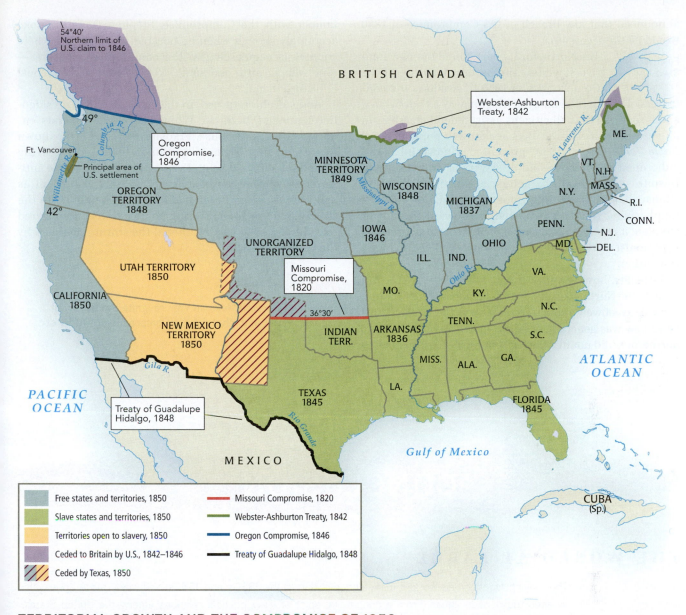

TERRITORIAL GROWTH AND THE COMPROMISE OF 1850

The Webster-Ashburton Treaty established Maine's northern boundary as well as the American-Canadian boundary west of the Great Lakes.

compromise movement. One by one, Douglas submitted the individual measures for a vote. Northern representatives provided the necessary votes to admit California and abolish the slave trade in the District of Columbia, while southern representatives supplied the edge needed to organize the Utah and New Mexico territories and pass the new fugitive slave law. On the face of it, everyone had compromised. But in truth, only 61 members of Congress, or 21 percent of the membership, had not voted against some part of the Compromise.

By September 17 all the separate parts of the Compromise of 1850 had passed and been signed into law by the new president, Millard Fillmore. The Union, it seemed, was safe.

Away from the Brink

REJECTION OF SECESSION
The general public, both North and South, rallied to the Compromise. At the convention of southern states in Nashville, the fire-eaters—the radical proponents of states' rights and secession—found themselves voted down by more moderate voices. Even in the Deep South, coalitions of pro-Compromise Whigs and Democrats soundly defeated secessionists in the state elections that followed. Still, most southerners felt that a firm line had been drawn. With California's admission, they were now outnumbered in the Senate, so it was critical that slaveholders be granted equal legal access to the territories. They

announced that any breach of the Compromise of 1850 would justify secession.

FUGITIVE SLAVE LAW The North, for its part, found the new fugitive slave law the hardest measure of the Compromise of 1850 to swallow. The controversial law denied an accused runaway a trial by jury, and it required that all citizens assist federal marshals in its enforcement. Harriet Beecher Stowe's popular novel *Uncle Tom's Cabin* (1852) presented a powerful moral indictment of the law—and of slavery as an institution. Despite sentimental characters, a contrived plot, and clumsy dialect, the book profoundly moved its readers. Emphasizing the duty of Christians toward the downtrodden, it reached a greater audience than any previous abolitionist work and heightened moral opposition to the institution.

In reality, however, fewer than 1,000 slaves a year ran away to the North, many of whom did not succeed. Despite some cases of well-publicized resistance, the 1850 Fugitive Slave Law was generally enforced in the free states. Many northerners did not like the law, but they were unwilling to tamper with the Compromise. Stephen Douglas spoke accurately enough when he boasted in 1851, "The whole country is acquiescing in the compromise measures—everywhere, North and South. Nobody proposes to repeal or disturb them."

And so calm returned. In the lackluster 1852 presidential campaign, both the Whigs and the Democrats endorsed the Compromise. Franklin Pierce, a little-known New Hampshire Democrat, soundly defeated the Whig candidate, Winfield Scott. Even more significant, the antislavery Free Soil candidate received only about half as many votes as Van Buren had four years before. With the slavery issue seemingly losing political force, it appeared that the Republic had weathered the storm unleashed by the Wilmot Proviso.

✓ **REVIEW**

How did the U.S.-Mexican War re-ignite the sectional controversy, and what did the Compromise of 1850 do to ease it?

CONCLUSION

THE WORLD AT LARGE

The moving frontier had worked many changes during the 1830s and 1840s; and many more upheavals awaited the decade ahead. From a continental point of view, political relations among the United States, Mexico, and the Indian peoples had shifted significantly. Indian attacks on Mexico in the 1820s and 1830s had weakened Mexico's ability to repel an invasion by the United States. And with the Treaty of Guadalupe Hidalgo, the United States gained over half a million square miles. Its frontier had leaped from the Mississippi valley to the Pacific, but in between remained territory still unorganized and still controlled by formidable Indian peoples. And as the North became increasingly industrialized and the South more firmly committed to an economy based on cotton and slavery, the movement of Americans into those territories would revive growing conflict between the two sections over slavery. The disputes would shatter the Jacksonian party system, reignite the slavery issue, and shake the Union to its foundation. ∞∞∞

Chapter Summary

In the 1840s the United States expanded to the Pacific, a development that required an aggressive war and that led to the rise of the slavery issue in national politics.

- In the 1840s Americans proclaimed that it was the United States' Manifest Destiny to expand across the North American continent.

- Americans in Texas increasingly clashed with Mexican authorities, and in 1836 Texans revolted and established an independent republic.

- Americans headed for Oregon and California on the Overland Trail.

  - The journey put special pressures on women as the traditional division of labor by gender broke down.

  - White migration also put pressure on Plains Indians' grazing lands, wood supplies, and freedom of movement.

  - The gold rush spawned a unique society that was overwhelmingly male, highly mobile, and strongly nativist and racist. There was Indian genocide in California.

  - Led by Brigham Young, the Mormons established a tightly organized, centrally controlled society in the Great Basin of Utah.

  - Throughout the Southwest the Hispanic population suffered at the hands of the new Anglo majority, as did the Chinese immigrants who flocked to California.

- President James K. Polk entered office with a vision of the United States as a continental nation.

  - He upheld President John Tyler's annexation of Texas and agreed to divide the Oregon country with Britain.

  - Polk instigated a war with Mexico in order to obtain that country's northern territories.

  - Divided, impoverished, and distracted by ongoing wars with Indians, Mexico was forced to surrender more than half a million square miles of territory in the aftermath of the war.

- The U.S.–Mexican War reinjected the slavery issue into American national politics.

  - The Wilmot Proviso sought to prohibit slavery from any territory acquired from Mexico.

  - The struggle over the Proviso eventually disrupted both major parties.

  - Congress momentarily stilled the sectional crisis with the Compromise of 1850.

Additional Reading

For the Sioux, see the enduring article by Richard White, "The Winning of the West: The Expansion of the Western Sioux in the Eighteenth and Nineteenth Centuries," *Journal of American History* (1978), 319–343. See also Colin G. Calloway, *One Vast Winter Count: The Native American West before Lewis and Clark* (2003). David J. Weber, *The Mexican Frontier, 1821–1846* (1982), is a superb study of the Southwest prior to American control. For a more recent account, with a transnational interpretation of the Texas Rebellion, see Andrés Reséndez, *Changing National Identities at the Frontier* (2005). For the Overland Trail, see John Mack Faragher, *Women and Men on the Overland Trail* (1979). Leonard J. Arrington and Davis Bitton, *The Mormon Experience*, 2nd ed. (1992), is a good survey. For California's missions, see Steven W. Hackel's *Children of Coyote, Missionaries of St. Francis* (2005). Susan Lee Johnson's *Roaring Camp* (2001) explores social interaction during the California gold rush. For the environmental consequences of mining, see Andrew Insenberg's *Mining California* (2005). Robert V. Hine and John Mack Faragher, *Frontiers* (2008), is an excellent synthesis of the region's history.

The fullest treatment of American life in this period is Daniel Walker Howe's magisterial book *What Hath God Wrought* (2007). Thomas R. Hietala offers a stimulating analysis of the social roots of expansionism in *Manifest Design* (1985). For Indians and the geopolitics of the era, see Brian DeLay, *War of a Thousand Deserts: Indian Raids and the U.S.-Mexican War* (2008). The drive to annex Texas is carefully untangled in Joel H. Silbey, *Storm over Texas* (2005). The best discussions of Polk's handling of the Oregon and Texas issues remain Charles G. Sellers, Jr., *James K. Polk, Continentalist, 1843–1846* (1966), and David M. Pletcher, *The Diplomacy of Annexation* (1973). Michael F. Holt presents a powerful analysis of the Whig Party's difficulties in this decade in *The Rise and Fall of the American Whig Party* (1999). For the California Indian genocide, see Benjamin Madley, "California's Yuki Indians: Defining Genocide in Native American History," *Western Historical Quarterly* 39, no. 3 (2008): 303–332. Howard Lamar's classic account *The Far Southwest* (1966) explores political and economic power in the territories after conquest, and Richard Griswold del Castillo's *The Treaty of Guadalupe Hidalgo* (1990) explores the history and legacy of that critical document. For more recent work on the region's postwar history, see Samuel Truett and Elliott Young, *Continental Crossroads* (2004). Holman Hamilton, *Prologue to Conflict* (new ed., 2005), is an excellent study of the Compromise of 1850.

For a fuller list of readings, see the Bibliography at www.mhhe.com/eh8e.

SIGNIFICANT EVENTS

1821
Mexico wins independence; Santa Fe trade opens

1823
First American settlers enter Texas

1831
Violence between northern Mexicans and Indians begins to increase dramatically

1836
Texas Republic established; Battle of the Alamo; Santa Anna defeated at San Jacinto

1843
Large-scale migration to Oregon begins

1844
Polk elected president

1845
United States annexes Texas; phrase *Manifest Destiny* coined

1846
U.S. declares war against Mexico; Bear Flag Revolt in California; Oregon Treaty with Britain ratified; Wilmot Proviso introduced

1847
Mormon migration to Utah; U.S. troops occupy Mexico City

1848
Gold discovered in California; Treaty of Guadalupe Hidalgo approved; Free Soil Party founded; Taylor elected president

1849
Gold rush

1850
Compromise of 1850 enacted

Territorial Transformations in the American West, 1819–1850

DATE	EVENT	SIGNIFICANCE
1819	Transcontinental Treaty (Adams-Onís Treaty)	Establishes the boundary between northern New Spain and the western U.S.; gives U.S. formal access to the Pacific (see map, page 235).
1821	Mexican independence	Independent Mexico assumes rights to all North American territory formerly claimed by Spain.
1820s and 1830s	Indian removal	Responding to threats, incentives, and, finally, military coercion, tens of thousands of eastern Indians relocate to present-day Oklahoma. Change fuels conflict and eventually accommodation with western Indians.
1836	Texan independence	Republic of Texas claims sovereignty over what had been Mexican Texas and insists on the Rio Grande from source to mouth as its western and southern border.
1840	"Great Peace" on the Arkansas	Peace between Comanches and Kiowas on the Southern Plains and Southern Cheyennes and Arapahos on the Central Plains puts an end to struggle in the Arkansas Valley; resulting security and trade opportunities encourage Indian raids into Mexico.
1845	Texas annexed to United States	Federal government under Polk pledges to uphold Texas's claims to the Rio Grande; Mexico severs diplomatic relations.
1846	Oregon Treaty	Settles dispute between Great Britain and U.S. over Oregon territory; fixes boundary at 49th parallel, but Britain retains all of Vancouver Island. Oregon organized as a territory in 1848.
1847	Mormon migration to Great Basin	Beginning of migration that would involve many thousands into the Valley of the Great Salt Lake; state of Deseret proclaimed in 1849.
1848	Treaty of Guadalupe Hidalgo	At the close of the U.S.-Mexican War, Republic of Mexico surrenders more than 750,000 square miles of land to the United States (including Texas), amounting to more than half of Mexico's national territory.
1850	Compromise of 1850	Texas relinquishes claim to Rio Grande as western boundary but is given El Paso; California admitted as state; New Mexico and Utah organized as territories.

As Kansas became a battleground over whether slavery would expand into the new territories, pro- and anti-slavery factions armed themselves for open conflict. This drawing depicts the so-called "Border Ruffians" from Missouri destroying the Free State Hotel. What evidence from the opening narrative suggests that the artist took liberties with this illustration? Does the drawing betray northern or southern sympathies? Why?

The Union Broken

1850–1861

∞∞∞ AN AMERICAN STORY ∞∞∞

THE SACKING OF A TOWN IN KANSAS

Into town they rode, several hundred strong, their faces flushed with excitement. They were unshaven, rough-talking men, "armed . . . to the teeth with rifles and revolvers, cutlasses and bowie-knives." At the head of the procession an American flag flapped softly in the warm May breeze. Alongside it was another with a crouching tiger emblazoned on black and white stripes, followed by banners proclaiming "Southern Rights" and "The Superiority of the White Race." At the rear rolled five artillery pieces, which were quickly dragged into range of the town's main street. Watching intently from a window in his office, Josiah Miller, the editor of the Lawrence *Kansas Free State,* predicted, "Well, boys, we're in for it."

For the residents of Lawrence, Kansas, the worst seemed at hand. The town had been founded by the New England Emigrant Aid Company, a Yankee association that recruited settlers in an effort to keep Kansas Territory from becoming a slave state. Accepting Stephen Douglas's idea that the people should decide the status of slavery, the town's residents intended to see to it that under this doctrine of popular sovereignty Kansas entered the Union as a free state. Emigrants from the neighboring slave state of Missouri were equally determined that no "abolition tyrants" or "negro thieves" would control the territory. There had been conflict in Kansas almost immediately: land disputes, horse thievery, shootings on both sides.

In the ensuing turmoil, the federal government seemed to back the proslavery forces. In the spring of 1856 a U.S. district court indicted several of Lawrence's leading citizens for treason, and federal marshal Israel Donaldson led a posse, swelled by volunteers from across the Missouri border, to Lawrence on May 20 to make the arrests.

Meanwhile, Lawrence's "committee of safety" had agreed on a policy of nonresistance. Most of those indicted had fled, but Donaldson arrested two men without incident. Then he dismissed his posse.

The posse, however, was not ready to go home. Already thoroughly liquored up, it marched into town cheering. Ignoring the pleas of some leaders, its members smashed the presses of two newspapers, the *Herald of Freedom* and the *Kansas Free State*. Then the horde unleashed its wrath on the now-deserted Free State Hotel, which more closely resembled a fort. The invaders unsuccessfully attempted to batter it down with cannon fire and blow it up with gunpowder; finally they put a torch to the building. When the mob finally rode off, it left the residents of Lawrence unharmed but thoroughly terrified.

A proslavery newspaper. Missouri was never invaded.

Startling News!
OUR BORDER IN DANGER!!
Missouri to be Invaded!

We have authority which will not admit of doubt, for stating that Lane, with 3000 lawless abolitionists, and 10 pieces of artillery, is about to march into Missouri, and sack the border towns of Lexington, Independence, Westport, and New Santa Fe. This is no idle rumor; and there can be no doubt of it. These desperadoes swear they wil carry everything before them, and spare nothing.

Retaliation by free-state partisans was not long in coming. Hurrying north along a different road to Lawrence, an older man with a grim face and steely eyes heard the news the next morning that the town had been attacked. "Old Man Brown," as everyone called him, was on his way with several of his sons to provide reinforcements. A severe, God-fearing Calvinist, John Brown was also a staunch abolitionist who had once remarked to a friend that he believed "God had raised him up on purpose to break the jaws of the wicked." Brooding over the failure of the free-staters to resist the "slave hounds" from Missouri, Brown headed toward Pottawatomie Creek on the night of May 24, 1856, with half a dozen others, including his sons. Announcing that they were "the Northern Army" come to serve justice, they burst into the cabin of James Doyle, a proslavery man from Tennessee, with cutlasses drawn. As Brown marched off Doyle and his three sons, Doyle's terrified wife, Mahala, begged him to spare her youngest, and the old man relented. The others were led no more than 100 yards down the road before Owen and Salmon Brown hacked them to death with broadswords. Old Man Brown then walked up to James Doyle's body and put a bullet through his forehead. Before the night was done, two more cabins had been visited and two more proslavery settlers brutally executed. Not one of the five murdered men owned a single slave or had any connection with the raid on Lawrence.

Brown's action precipitated a new wave of fighting in Kansas, and controversy throughout the nation. "Everybody here feels as if we are upon a volcano," remarked one congressman in Washington.

The country was indeed atop a smoldering volcano that would finally erupt in the spring of 1861, showering civil war, death, and destruction across the land. Popular sovereignty, the last remaining moderate solution to the controversy over the expansion of slavery, had failed dismally in Kansas. The violence and disorder in the territory provided a stark reply to Stephen Douglas's proposition: What could be more peaceable, more fair than the notion of popular sovereignty? ◦◦◦◦◦

SECTIONAL CHANGES IN AMERICAN SOCIETY

THE ROAD TO WAR WAS not a straight or short one. Six years elapsed between the Compromise of 1850 and the crisis in "Bleeding Kansas." Another five years would pass before the first shot was fired. And the process of separation involved more than ineffective politicians and an unwillingness to compromise. As we have seen, Americans were bound by a growing transportation network, by national markets, and by a national political system. These social and political ties—the "cords of Union," the powerful South Carolina senator John C. Calhoun called them—could not be severed all at once. Increasingly, however, the changes occurring in American society heightened sectional tensions. As the North continued to industrialize, its society came into conflict with that of the South. The Old Northwest, which had long been a political ally of the South, became more closely linked to the East. The coming of civil war, in other words, involved social and economic changes as well as political ones.

The Growth of a Railroad Economy

By the time the Compromise of 1850 produced a lull in the tensions between North and South, the American economy had left behind the depression of the early 1840s and was roaring again. Its basic structure, however, was changing. Cotton remained the nation's major export, but it was no longer the driving force for American economic growth. After 1839 this role was taken over by the construction of a vast railroad network covering the eastern half of the continent. By 1850 the United States possessed more than 9,000 miles of track; 10 years later it had over 30,000 miles, more than the rest of the world combined. Much of the new construction during the 1850s occurred west of the Appalachian Mountains.

Because western railroads ran through less settled areas, they were especially dependent on public aid. State and local governments made loans to rail companies and sometimes exempted them temporarily from taxes. About a quarter of the cost of railroad construction came from state and local governments, but federal land grants were crucial, too. By mortgaging or selling the land to farmers, the rail companies raised construction capital and also stimulated settlement, which increased its business and profits.

On a national map, the rail network in place by 1860 looked impressive, but these lines were not fully integrated. A few trunk-line roads such as the New York Central had combined a number of smaller lines to facilitate the shipment of freight. But roadbeds had not yet been standardized, so that no fewer than 12 different gauges, or track widths, were in use. Moreover,

cities at the end of rail lines jealously strove to maintain their commercial advantages, not wanting to connect with competing port cities for fear that freight would pass through to the next city down the line.

RAILROADS' IMPACT ON THE ECONOMY

The effect of the new lines rippled outward through the economy. Farmers along the tracks began to specialize in cash crops and market them in distant locations. With their profits they purchased manufactured goods that earlier they might have made at home. Before the railroad reached Athens, Tennessee, the surrounding counties produced about 25,000 bushels of wheat, which sold for less than 50 cents a bushel. Once the railroad came, farmers in these same counties grew 400,000 bushels and sold their crop at a dollar a bushel. Railroads also stimulated other areas of the economy, notably the mining and iron industries.

REORIENTATION OF WESTERN TRADE

The new rail networks shifted the direction of western trade. In 1840 most northwestern grain was shipped down the Mississippi River to the bustling port of New Orleans. But low water made steamboat travel risky in summer, and ice shut down traffic in winter. Products such as lard, tallow, and cheese quickly spoiled if stored in New Orleans's sweltering warehouses. Increasingly, traffic from the Midwest flowed west to east, over the new rail lines. Chicago became the region's hub, linking the farms of the upper Midwest to New York and other eastern cities by more than 2,000 miles of track in 1855. Thus, while the value of goods shipped by river to New Orleans continued to increase, the South's overall share of western trade dropped dramatically.

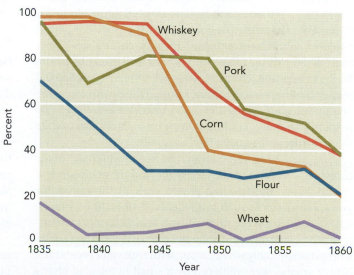

Proportion of Western Exports Shipped via New Orleans, 1835–1860

In 1835 nearly 100 percent of western exports of corn, pork, and whiskey were being shipped via New Orleans. By 1860 only about 40 percent of pork and whiskey and 20 percent of flour and corn were. The change in shipping patterns weakened the political ties between the South and the Old Northwest.

These new patterns of commerce and agriculture weakened the traditional political alliance between the South and the West, which had been based on shared economic interests. "The power of cotton over the financial affairs of the Union has in the last few years rapidly diminished," the *Democratic Review* remarked in 1849, "and breadstuffs will now become the governing power."

Railroads and the Prairie Environment

As railroad lines fanned out from Chicago, farmers began to acquire open prairie land in Illinois and then Iowa, putting its deep black soil into production. Commercial agriculture transformed this remarkable treeless environment.

To settlers accustomed to woodlands, the thousands of square miles of tall grass were an awesome sight. Indian grass, Canadian wild rye, and native big bluestem all grew higher than a person. In 1838 Edmund Flagg gazed upon "the tall grasstops waving in . . . billowy beauty in the breeze; the narrow pathway winding off like a serpent over the rolling surface, disappearing and reappearing till lost in the luxuriant herbage." Long-grass prairies had their perils too: summer or winter storms sent travelers searching for the shelter of trees along river valleys. Dewitt Smith recalled the fierce green-headed flies awaiting the unsuspecting. "A journey across the big praries was, in the summer time, undertaken only at night," he recalled, "because on a hot summer day horses would be literally stung and worried to death."

IMPACT OF TECHNOLOGY Because eastern plows could not penetrate the densely tangled roots of prairie grass, the earliest settlers erected farms along the boundary separating the forest from the prairie. In 1837, however, John Deere patented a sharp-cutting steel plow that sliced through the sod without soil sticking to the blade. In addition, Cyrus McCormick refined a mechanical reaper that harvested 14 times more wheat with the same amount of labor. By the 1850s McCormick was selling 1,000 reapers a year and could not keep up with demand, while Deere turned out 10,000 plows annually.

CHANGES IN THE LANDSCAPE The new commercial farming fundamentally altered the landscape and the environment. Indians had grown corn in the region for years, but never in such large fields as did white farmers, whose surpluses were shipped east. Prairie farmers also introduced new crops that were not part of the earlier ecological system, notably wheat, along with fruits and vegetables. Native grasses were replaced by a small number of plants cultivated as commodities.

Western farmers also altered the landscape by reducing the annual fires, often set by Indians, that had kept the prairie free from trees. In the fires' absence, trees reappeared on land not in cultivation and, if undisturbed, eventually formed woodlots. The earlier unbroken landscape gave way to independent farms, each fenced in the precise checkerboard pattern established by the Northwest Ordinance. It was an artificial ecosystem of animals, woodlots, and crops whose large, uniform layout made western farms more efficient than the irregular farms in the East.

Railroads and the Urban Environment

INFLUENCE ON LOCATION OF TOWNS Railroads transformed the urban environment as well. Communities soon recognized that their economic survival depended on creating adequate rail links to the countryside and to major urban markets. Large cities feared they would be left behind in the struggle to be the dominant city in the region. Smaller communities saw their very survival at stake in the battle for rail connections. When the new railroad line bypassed the prairie village of Auburn, Illinois, its fate was sealed, and residents quickly abandoned it for more promising locations.

Even communities that obtained rail links found the presence of this new technology difficult to adjust to. When a railroad began serving nearby Jacksonville, Illinois, merchants complained about the noise, dirt, and billowing smoke when locomotives hissed through the business district. "Many of the people were as much scared as the horses at the steaming monster," recalled one resident. After a few years, the tracks were relocated on the outskirts of town. Jacksonville's experience became the norm: increasingly, communities kept railroads away from fashionable neighborhoods and shopping areas. As the tracks became a physical manifestation of social and economic divisions, the notion of living "on the wrong side of the tracks" became crucial to defining the urban landscape.

Rising Industrialization

On the eve of the Civil War, 60 percent of American laborers worked on farms. In 1860, for the first time, that figure dropped below 50 percent in the North. The expansion of commercial agriculture spurred the growth of industry. Of the 10 leading American industries, 8 processed raw materials produced by agriculture, including flour milling and the manufacture of textiles, shoes, and woolens. (The only exceptions were iron and machinery.) Industrial growth also spurted during the 1850s as water power was increasingly replaced by steam, since there were only a fixed number of water-power sites.

Most important, the factory system of organizing labor and the technology of interchangeable parts spread to other areas of the economy. Many industries during the 1850s adopted interchangeable parts. Isaac Singer began using them in 1851 to mass-produce sewing machines, which made possible the ready-made clothing industry, while workers who assembled farm implements performed a single step in the process over and over again. By 1860 the United States had nearly a billion dollars invested in manufacturing, almost twice as much as in 1849.

RAILROADS, 1850 AND 1860, WITH TRACK GAUGES

During the 1850s a significant amount of railroad track was laid, but total track mileage is misleading, because the United States lacked a fully integrated rail network in 1860. A few trunk-line roads had combined a number of smaller lines into a single system to facilitate shipment. The Pennsylvania Railroad, for example, connected Philadelphia and Pittsburgh. But the existence of five major track gauges as well as minor ones meant that passengers and freight often had to be transferred from one line to the next. And north-south traffic was further disrupted by the lack of bridges over the Ohio River. *How many changes in railroad cars does the map indicate would have to be made for freight to ship from Chicago to New York City? from St. Louis to New Orleans?*

BRANDIED CHERRIES AND BUTTONS

Brandied cherries from France

Buttons matched patterns on calico print dresses.

Arabia Steamboat Museum, 400 Grand Boulevard, Kansas City, MO 64106. Photos by Greg Hawley.

The brandy, the tight seal, and the steamboat's location in cold, wet silt preserved most cargo well. A bottle of pickles remained edible.

How many button patterns are shown?

Although railroads reshaped the U.S. economy, steamboats continued to play a major role—as demonstrated by the remarkable case of the *Arabia*. In 1856 the steamboat sank in shallows along the Missouri River, its hull punctured by a sunken tree. Over 130 years later, a group of ambitious amateur historians located the wreck, buried 35 feet deep in a Kansas cornfield (the river's course having changed). Excavators painstakingly restored and preserved a cargo that illustrates the quantity and variety of goods being shipped up the Missouri: not only the expected guns, axes, and saddles but also brandied cherries and sardines from France, preserved pie fruits from Baltimore, 35,000 buttons to be sewn on dresses, perfumes (their scents preserved), shoes and boots (5,000), rubbers, bleeding knives (used for medicinal purposes), and some 5 million glass beads for trade to Indians. The Arabia Steamboat Museum in Kansas City now showcases this treasure trove of material culture, a snapshot of antebellum America's dynamic economy.

Thinking Critically

How could historians use such evidence as an old bottle of brandied cherries or a pair of shoes to understand life in the western territories during this period? How might it help to know the relative numbers of various goods being shipped? Their origins?

Immigration

The surge of industry required a large factory labor force. Natural increase helped swell the population to more than 30 million by 1860, but only in part, since the birthrate had begun to decline. On the eve of the Civil War the average white mother bore five children, compared to seven at the turn of the century. It was the beginning of mass immigration to America during the mid-1840s that kept population growth soaring.

 INFLUX FROM ABROAD In the 20 years from 1820 to 1840, about 700,000 newcomers had entered the United States. That figure jumped to 1.7 million in the 1840s, then to 2.6 million in the 1850s. Though even greater numbers arrived after the Civil War, as a percentage of the nation's total population, the wave from 1845 to 1854 was the largest influx of immigrants in American history. Most newcomers were young people in the prime of life: out of 224,000 arrivals in 1856, only 31,000 were under 10 and only 20,000 were over 40.

Certainly the booming economy and the lure of freedom drew immigrants, but they were also pushed by deteriorating conditions in Europe. In Ireland, a potato blight created *an Gorta Mór*—the "Great Famine," leaving potatoes rotting in the fields. The blight may well have spread from the United States and Canada, and it also infected Europe generally. But Ireland suffered more, because nearly a third of its population depended almost entirely on the potato for food. "They are all gone—clean gone," wrote a priest in the Irish town of Galway. "If travelling by night, you would know when a potato field was near by the smell." In 1846 and for several years following, as many as a million Irish perished, while a million and a half more emigrated, two-thirds to the United States.

NEW SOURCES OF IMMIGRATION The Irish tended to be poorer than other immigrant groups in the mid nineteenth century. Although the Protestant Scots-Irish continued as before to emigrate, the decided majority of the Irish who came after 1845 were Catholic. The newcomers were generally mostly unmarried younger sons and daughters of hard-pressed rural families. Because they were poor and unskilled, the Irish congregated in the cities, where the women performed domestic service and took factory jobs and the men did manual labor.

Germans and Scandinavians also had economic reasons for leaving Europe. They included small farmers whose lands had become marginal or who had been displaced by landlords, and skilled workers thrown out of work by industrialization. Others fled religious persecution. Some, particularly among the Germans, left after the liberal revolutions of 1848 failed, in order to live under the free institutions of the United States. Since coming to America, wrote a Swede who settled in Iowa in 1850, "I have not been compelled to pay a penny for the privilege of living. Neither is my cap worn out from lifting it in the presence of gentlemen."

THE REVOLUTIONS OF 1848 Unprecedented unrest and upheaval prevailed in Europe in 1848, the so-called year of revolutions. The famine that had driven so many Irish out of their country was part of a larger food shortage caused by a series of poor harvests. Mounting unemployment and overburdened relief programs increased suffering. In this situation middle-class reformers, who wanted civil liberty and a more representative government, joined forces with lower-class workers to overthrow several regimes, sometimes by also appealing to nationalist feelings. France, Austria, Hungary, Italy, and Prussia all witnessed major popular uprisings. Although these revolts succeeded at first, they were all crushed by the forces of the old order. Liberal hopes for a more open, democratic society suffered a severe setback.

In the aftermath of this failure, a number of hard-pressed German workers and farmers, as well as disillusioned radicals and reformers, emigrated to the United States, the

German immigrants enjoyed gathering for music and conversation in beer gardens. One of the most elegant and spacious of its day was New York City's German Winter-Garden in the Bowery neighborhood, shown in this watercolor by Fritz Meyer. "These are immense buildings," wrote one American, "fitted up in imitation of a garden. . . . Germans carry their families there to spend a day, or an evening."

symbol of democratic liberalism in the world. They were joined by the first significant migration from Asia, as thousands of Chinese headed to the gold rush in California and other strikes (see pages 365–366). This migration was simply part of a century-long phenomenon, as approximately 50 million Europeans, largely from rural areas, would migrate to the Western Hemisphere.

IMMIGRANTS AND INDUSTRIALIZATION Factories came more and more to depend on immigrant labor, including children, since newcomers would work for lower wages and were less prone to protest harsh working conditions. The shift to an immigrant workforce could be seen most clearly in the textile industry, where by 1860 more than half the workers in New England mills were foreign-born. Tensions between native- and foreign-born workers, as well as among immigrants of various nationalities, made it difficult for workers to unite.

URBAN RESOURCES STRAINED The sizable foreign-born population in many American cities severely strained urban resources. Immigrants who could barely make ends meet were forced to live in overcrowded, unheated tenement houses, damp cellars, and even shacks— "the hall was dark and reeking with the worst filth," reported one New York journalist; the house was "filled with little narrow rooms, each one having five or six occupants; all very filthy." Urban slums became notorious for crime and drinking, which took a heavy toll on families and the poor. In the eyes of many native-born Americans, immigrants were to blame for driving down factory wages and pushing American workers out of jobs. Overshadowing these complaints was a fear that America might not be able to **assimilate** the new groups, with their unfamiliar social customs, strange languages, and national pride. These fears sparked an outburst of political **nativism** in the mid-1850s.

Southern Complaints

With British and northern factories buying cotton in unprecedented quantities, southern planters prospered in the 1850s. Their operations, like those of northern commercial farmers, became more highly capitalized to keep up with the demand. But instead of machinery, white southerners invested in slaves. During the 1850s the price of prime field hands reached record levels.

Nonetheless, a number of southern nationalists, who advocated that the South should become a separate nation, pressed for greater industrialization to make the region more independent. "At present, the North fattens and grows rich upon the South," one Alabama newspaper complained in 1851, noting that "we purchase all our luxuries and necessities from the North," including clothing, shoes, implements and machinery, saddles and carriages, and even books. But most southerners ignored such pleas. As long as investments in cotton and slaves absorbed most of the South's capital, efforts to promote southern industry made little headway.

SOUTHERN ECONOMIC DEPENDENCE Despite southern prosperity, the section's leaders complained that the North used its power over banking and commerce to convert the South into a colony. In the absence of any significant southern shipping, northern intermediaries controlled the South's commodities through a complex series of transfers from planter to manufacturer. Storage and shipping charges, insurance, port fees, and commissions together added an estimated 20 percent to the cost of cotton and other commodities. These revenues went into the pockets of northern merchants, shippers, and bankers. The idea that the South was a colony of the North was inaccurate, but southern whites found it a convincing explanation of the North's growing wealth.

Prices of Cotton and Slaves

From 1815 to 1850, cotton and slave prices generally moved together, as southerners plowed their profits from growing cotton into buying more land and slaves. During the 1850s, however, the booming southern economy and bumper cotton crops drove the price of slaves steeply upward compared to cotton prices, squeezing slaveowners' profit margins and heightening southern anxieties about the future.

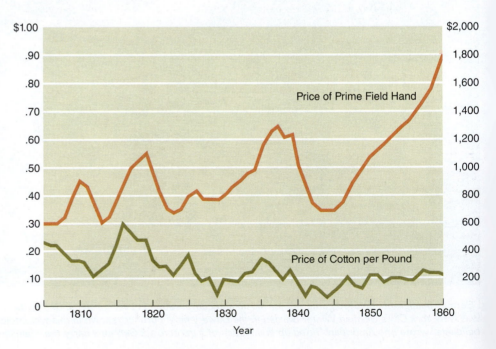

More important, it reinforced their resistance to federal aid for economic development, which they were convinced would inevitably enrich the North at southern expense. This attitude further weakened the South's political alliance with the West, which needed federal aid for transportation.

White southerners also feared that the new tide of immigration would shift the sectional balance of power. Some immigrants did settle in the South's few cities, but most shunned the region, because they did not want to compete with cheap slave labor. The lack of industry and the limited demand for skilled labor also shunted immigrants northward. As a result, the North surged even further ahead of the South in population, thereby strengthening its control of the House of Representatives and heightening southern concern that the North would rapidly settle the western territories.

 REVIEW

How did the new railroads affect urban and prairie environments? How did they increase sectional tensions?

THE POLITICAL REALIGNMENT OF THE 1850S

WHEN FRANKLIN PIERCE (he pronounced it "Purse") assumed the presidency in 1853, he was only 48 years old, the youngest man yet to be elected president. He was also a supporter of the "Young America" movement of the Democratic Party, which eagerly looked to spread democracy across the globe by annexing additional territory to the United States.

GADSDEN
PURCHASE

The believers in Young America felt it idle to argue about slavery when the nation could be developing new resources. But they failed to appreciate how each new plan for expansion would stir up the slavery issue. In 1853 Pierce did manage to conclude the Gadsden Purchase, thereby gaining control of about 45,000 square miles of Mexican desert that contained the most practical southern route for a transcontinental railroad (see map, page 386).

OSTEND
MANIFESTO

Pierce had no success, however, with his major goal, the acquisition of Cuba. Spain rebuffed all efforts to purchase the rich sugar-producing region in which slavery had once been strong and still existed. Then, in 1854, the American ministers meeting at Ostend in Belgium confidentially recommended that if Spain would not sell Cuba, the island should be seized. The contents of the "Ostend Manifesto" soon leaked, and Pierce was forced to renounce any notion of acquiring Cuba by force. In any case the president soon had his hands full with the proposals of another Democrat of the Young America stamp, Senator Stephen A. Douglas of Illinois.

The Kansas-Nebraska Act

Known as the Little Giant, Douglas was ambitious, bursting with energy, and impatient to get things done. As chairman of the Senate's Committee on Territories, he was eager to organize federal lands west of Missouri as part of his program for economic development. And as a citizen of Illinois, he wanted Chicago selected as the eastern terminus of the transcontinental railroad to California. Chicago would never be chosen over St. Louis and New Orleans, however, unless the rest of the Louisiana Purchase was organized, for any northern rail route would have to run through that region.

REPEAL OF THE
MISSOURI
COMPROMISE

Under the terms of the Missouri Compromise of 1820, slavery was prohibited in this portion of the Louisiana Purchase. Douglas had already tried in 1853 to organize the area while keeping a ban on slavery—only to have his bill voted down by southern opposition in the Senate. Bowing to southern pressure, the Illinois leader removed the prohibition on slavery that had been in effect for 34 years. The Kansas-Nebraska Act was passed in May 1854.

POPULAR
SOVEREIGNTY

The new act created two territories: Kansas, directly west of Missouri, and a much larger Nebraska Territory, located west of Iowa and the Minnesota Territory. The Missouri Compromise was explicitly repealed. Instead, popular sovereignty was to determine the status of slavery in both territories, though it was left unclear whether residents of Kansas and Nebraska could prohibit slavery at any time or only at the time of statehood, as southerners insisted. Still, most members of Congress assumed that Douglas had split the region into two territories so that each section could claim another state: Kansas would be slave and Nebraska free.

The Kansas-Nebraska Act outraged northern Democrats, Whigs, and Free Soilers alike. Critics rejected Douglas's contention that popular sovereignty would keep the territories free. As always, most northerners spoke little of the moral evils of slavery; it was the chance that the Slave Power might gain new territory that concerned them. So great was the northern outcry that Douglas joked he could "travel from Boston to Chicago by the light of my own [burning] effigy."

The Collapse of the Second American Party System

POLITICAL
REALIGNMENT

The furor over the Kansas-Nebraska Act laid bare the underlying social and economic tensions that had developed between the North and the South. These tensions put mounting pressure on the political parties, and in the 1850s the Jacksonian party system collapsed. Voters who had been loyal to one party for years, even decades, began switching allegiances, while new voters were mobilized. By the time the process of realignment was completed, a new party system

THE KANSAS-NEBRASKA ACT

When the Kansas-Nebraska Act of 1854 opened the remaining portion of the Louisiana Purchase to slavery under the doctrine of popular sovereignty, conflict between the two sections focused on control of Kansas, directly west of the slave state of Missouri. **Which part of the map indicates the unorganized portion of the Louisiana Purchase? How did the doctrine of popular sovereignty effectively repeal the Missouri Compromise?**

had emerged, divided this time along clearly sectional lines.

DISILLUSIONMENT WITH THE PARTIES — In part, the old party system decayed because new problems had replaced the traditional economic issues of both Whigs and Democrats. The Whigs alienated many of their traditional Protestant supporters by openly seeking the support of Catholics and recent immigrants. Then, too, the growing agitation by Protestant reformers for the prohibition of alcohol divided both parties, especially the Whigs. But the Kansas-Nebraska Act provided the final blow, dividing the two major parties along sectional lines. Northern congressional Whigs, who unanimously opposed the bill, found themselves deserted by virtually all their southern colleagues. And fully half the northern Democratic representatives in the House voted against Douglas's bill.

The Know-Nothings

In such an unstable atmosphere, independent parties flourished. The most dramatic challenge to the Whigs and Democrats came first from a movement worried about the recent flood of immigrants.

New York City was the primary gateway for immigrants, and it was here that the American Party, a secret nativist society, first organized. Its members were sworn to secrecy and instructed to answer inquiries by replying "I know nothing." In 1853 the Know-Nothings, as they were quickly dubbed, began organizing in several other states; after only a year they had become the fastest-growing party in the nation. Significantly, 1854 also marked the peak of the new wave of immigration.

NATIVIST IMPULSE — Taking as its slogan "Americans should rule America," the American Party advocated that immigrants be forced to wait not 5 but 21 years before becoming naturalized citizens. It also called on voters to oust from office politicians who openly bid for foreign and Catholic votes. Know-Nothings denounced illegal voting by immigrants, the rising crime and disorder in urban areas, and immigrants' heavy drinking. They were also strongly anti-Catholic, convinced that the "undemocratic" hierarchy of priests, bishops, and archbishops controlled by the pope in Rome was conspiring to undermine American democracy.

To young native-born American workers, the Know-Nothing message was particularly appealing. It was they who bore the brunt of the economic dislocations caused by

DAILY LIVES

UNCLE TOM BY FOOTLIGHTS

In 1850 theaters remained a controversial if popular form of entertainment. The Puritans had roundly condemned plays of any sort, and many religious critics still frowned on theatergoing. Nevertheless, with the rise of cities the stage became a medium for mass entertainment and increasingly attracted the urban middle class.

In 1852 George C. Howard, the head of the Museum Theater in Troy, New York, was looking for new material. He was attracted to the issue of slavery by a controversial new novel, *Uncle Tom's Cabin*. Written by Harriet Beecher Stowe, one of the Reverend Lyman Beecher's energetic sons and daughters (see page 372), the book was a runaway bestseller, with more than 300,000 copies printed in the first year.

The book's plot followed a host of characters to a multitude of locales. George and Eliza Harris, a mulatto slave couple, learn that their young son is to be sold. Eliza flees with her child across the ice-choked Ohio River to freedom, while George escapes separately. At the same time, Tom, an older slave and a devout Christian, is sold and taken to Louisiana. He is bought by the father of Evangeline St. Clare, an innocent, golden-haired child who treats Tom kindly, but after both Evangeline and her father die, Tom is sold to Simon Legree, a hard-drinking, blasphemous Yankee. When Tom refuses to whip other slaves on the plantation, Legree beats him to death; Tom is a martyr to his faith in God and his love for his fellow man.

Compressing this complex story was not easy. Then, too, no American play on the subject of slavery had been produced before, and many theater managers believed that the public would not accept a black hero. But Howard wanted to cast his four-year-old daughter, Cordelia (already an experienced trouper), as young Eva, and so he produced an adaptation that focused on Tom's experiences in the St. Clare household.

The play's success prompted a sequel based on the Legree section of the novel; finally Howard combined the two plays into a 6-act, 30-scene epic that took an entire evening to perform. From Troy the production moved to New York City, where it ran for an unprecedented 325 performances and then achieved similar triumphs in other northern cities. No play had ever attracted such large audiences.

The production had a good eye for the dramatic: a slave auction, Eva's death after a long illness, and Tom's defiance of Legree when threatened with a whipping. ("My soul a'nt yours, mas'r; you haven't bought it—ye can't buy it.") Eliza's flight across the icy Ohio River—described in two paragraphs in the book—became one of the major scenes, with a pack of bloodhounds added for good measure. As in minstrel shows, blacks were played by whites wearing lampblack.

Howard worked hard to attract a new middle-class audience. He banned the prostitutes who frequented theaters and in the lobby displayed the endorsements of prominent religious leaders and reformers on posters. A further innovation, matinee performances, attracted women and children. Blacks, who normally were barred from New York theaters, were seated in a segregated section.

The play moved audiences of all backgrounds. After wrestling with his religious scruples, John Kirk, a salesman, finally went to see a Chicago production. "The appeals of the dying little Eva to her father, for Uncle Tom's freedom, were overwhelmingly affecting," he testified. "I never saw so many white pocket handkerchiefs in use at the same time. . . . I was not the only one in that large audience to shed tears I assure you." Equally striking, the play affected the workers and apprentices who made up the theater's normal clientele. Traditionally hostile to abolitionism, these groups cheered wildly over Eliza's escape. By providing vivid images of the cruelty of slavery, theatrical presentations of *Uncle Tom's Cabin,* even more than the book, heightened the sectional tensions that divided the nation in the 1850s.

Thinking Critically

Since northern states were already free states, and Uncle Tom's Cabin *didn't play in southern states, how did it help the cause of antislavery?*

In this playbill advertising a dramatic production of Uncle Tom's Cabin, *vicious bloodhounds pursue the light-skinned Eliza, who clutches her child as she frantically leaps to safety across the ice-choked Ohio River.*

Edward Beecher, one of Lyman Beecher's sons, in 1854 published the inflammatory Papal Conspiracy Exposed. *Protestant Bibles had been widely distributed and in northern New York, not far from heavily Catholic Quebec, a renegade friar gathered up a handful of copies and burned them. The story, magnified in the retelling, fanned anti-Catholic and nativist sentiment.*

CATHOLIC PRIESTS BURNING BIBLES AT CHAMPLAIN, N. Y., 1842.

industrialization and who had to compete with immigrants for jobs. In the 1854 elections the Know-Nothings won a series of remarkable victories, as former Whigs flocked to the new party in droves. Fueled by its success the American Party turned its attention south, and in a few months it had organized in every state of the Union. With perhaps a million voters enrolled in its lodges in 1855, Know-Nothing leaders confidently predicted that they would elect the next president.

KNOW-NOTHINGS' DECLINE

Yet only a year later the party had collapsed as quickly as it had risen. Many Know-Nothing officeholders proved woefully incompetent. Voters deserted them when the party failed to enact its program. But the death knell of the party was rising sectional tensions. In 1856 most northern delegates walked out of the American Party's national convention when it adopted a proslavery platform. Significantly, they deserted to the other new party, the Republicans. This party, unlike the Know-Nothings, had no base in the South. It intended to elect a president by sweeping the free states, which controlled a majority of the electoral votes.

The Republicans and Bleeding Kansas

Initially, the Republican Party made little headway in the North. Many moderate Whigs and Democrats viewed it as too radical. A Democratic newspaper expressed the prevailing view when it declared, "Nobody believes that this Republican movement can prove the basis of a permanent party."

Such predictions, however, did not reckon with the emotions stirred up by developments in Kansas. Most early settlers migrated to Kansas for the same reasons other white

Americans headed west—the chance to prosper in a new land. But Douglas's idea of popular sovereignty transformed the process of settlement into a referendum on slavery in the territories. A race soon developed between northerners and southerners to settle Kansas first. To the proslavery residents of neighboring Missouri, free-state communities such as Lawrence seemed ominous threats. "We are playing for a mighty stake," former senator David Rice Atchison insisted. "If we win, we carry slavery to the Pacific Ocean; if we fail we lose Missouri, Arkansas and Texas and all the territories; the game must be played boldly."

TURMOIL IN KANSAS

When the first Kansas elections were held in 1854 and 1855, Missourians poured over the border, seized the polls, and stuffed the ballot boxes. This massive fraud tarnished popular sovereignty at the outset and greatly aroused public opinion in the North. It also provided proslavery forces with a commanding majority in the Kansas legislature, where they promptly expelled the legally elected free-state members and enacted a strict legal code limiting such time-honored rights as freedom of speech, impartial juries, and fair elections. Mobilized into action, the free-staters in the fall of 1855 organized a separate government, drafted a state constitution prohibiting slavery, and asked Congress to admit Kansas as a free state. In such a polarized situation, violence quickly broke out between the two factions, leading to the proslavery attack on Lawrence and to John Brown's reprisals (see page 378).

The Caning of Charles Sumner

In May 1856, only a few days before the proslavery attack on Lawrence, Republican Senator Charles Sumner of Massachusetts delivered a scathing speech, "The Crime against

The caning of Senator Charles Sumner of Massachusetts by Representative Preston S. Brooks of South Carolina inflamed public opinion. In this northern drawing, the fallen Sumner, a martyr to free speech, raises his pen against Brooks's club. In the background, several prominent Democrats look on in amusement. Printmakers, rushing to capitalize on the furor, did not know what the obscure Brooks looked like and thus had to devise ingenious ways of portraying the incident. In this print, Brooks's face is hidden by his raised arm.

SOUTHERN CHIVALRY — ARGUMENT versus CLUB'S.

Kansas." Sumner not only condemned slavery, but he also deliberately insulted the state of South Carolina and one of its senators, Andrew Butler. Preston S. Brooks, a South Carolina congressman who was related to Butler, was outraged that Sumner had insulted his relative and mocked his state.

Several days later, Brooks strode into the Senate after it had adjourned, went up to Sumner, who was seated at his desk, and proceeded to beat the Massachusetts leader over the head with his cane. The cane shattered from the violence of the attack, but Brooks, swept up in the emotion of the moment, continued hitting Sumner until the senator collapsed to the floor, drenched in blood.

SIGNIFICANCE OF THE CANING Northerners were shocked to learn that a senator of the United States had been beaten unconscious in the Senate chamber. But what caused them even greater consternation was southern reaction to Sumner's caning—for in his own region, Preston Brooks was lionized as a hero. Instantly, the Sumner caning breathed life into the fledgling Republican Party. Its claims about "Bleeding Kansas" and the Slave Power now seemed credible. Sumner, reelected in 1857 by the Massachusetts legislature, was unable to return to the Senate until 1860, his chair left vacant as a symbol of southern brutality.

The Election of 1856

Given the storm that had arisen over Kansas, Democrats concluded that no candidate associated with the repeal of the Missouri Compromise

JOHN

AND

JESSIE.

A campaign badge supporting John C. Frémont

had a chance to win. So the Democrats turned to James Buchanan of Pennsylvania as their presidential nominee. Buchanan's supreme qualification was having the good fortune to have been out of the country when the Kansas-Nebraska Act was passed. The American Party, split badly by the Kansas issue, nominated former president Millard Fillmore. The Republicans chose John C. Frémont, a western explorer who had helped liberate California during the Mexican War. The party's platform denounced slavery as a "relic of barbarism" and demanded that Kansas be admitted as a free state. Throughout the summer the party hammered away on Bleeding Sumner and Bleeding Kansas.

IDEOLOGY OF THE REPUBLICAN PARTY A number of principles guided the Republican Party, including the ideal of free labor. Slavery degraded labor, Republicans argued, and would inevitably drive free labor out of the territories. Condemning the South as stagnant, hierarchical, and economically backward, Republicans praised the North as a society of opportunity where enterprising individuals could rise through hard work and self-discipline. Stopping the expansion of slavery, they argued, would preserve this heritage of economic independence for white Americans. Republicans by and large remained blind to ways in which industrialization was closing off avenues of social mobility for poor workers.

Also important was the moral opposition to slavery, which such works as Harriet Beecher Stowe's *Uncle Tom's Cabin* had strengthened. Republican speakers and editors stressed that slavery was a moral wrong, that it was incompatible with the ideals of the Republic and Christianity. "Never forget," Republican leader Abraham Lincoln declared on one occasion, "that we have before us this whole matter of the right and wrong of slavery in this Union, though the immediate question is as to its spreading out into new Territories and States."

CONCEPT OF THE
SLAVE POWER

More negatively, Republicans gained support by shifting their attacks from slavery itself to the Slave Power, or the political influence of the planter class. Pointing to the Sumner assault and the incidents in Kansas, Republicans contended that the Slave Power had set out to destroy the liberties of northern whites. "The question has passed on from that of slavery for negro servants, to that of tyranny over free white men," one Republican insisted in the 1856 campaign.

HERITAGE OF
REPUBLICANISM

All these fears played on a strong northern attachment to the heritage of the American Revolution. Just as the nation's founders had battled against slavery, tyranny, aristocracy, and minority rule, so the North faced the unrepublican Slave Power. "The liberties of our country are in tenfold the danger that they were at the commencement of the American Revolution," warned one Republican paper. "We then had a distant foe to contend with. Now the enemy is within our borders."

In the election, Buchanan all but swept the South (losing only Maryland to Fillmore) and won enough free states to push him over the top, with 174 electoral votes to Frémont's 114 and Fillmore's 8. Still, the violence in Kansas and Sumner's caning nearly carried Frémont into the presidency. He ran ahead of both Buchanan and Fillmore in the North and won 11 free states out of 16. Had he carried Pennsylvania plus one more state, he would have been elected. For the first time in American history, an antislavery party based entirely in the North threatened to elect a president and snap the bonds of union.

> ✓ **REVIEW**
>
> What events led the political realignment of the 1850s to at first favor the Know-Nothings? What events led the Republicans to emerge as a powerful party?

THE WORSENING CRISIS

BUCHANAN'S
CHARACTER

JAMES BUCHANAN HAD SPENT MUCH of his life in public service: more than 20 years in the House and the Senate, secretary of state under Polk, and minister to Russia and to Great Britain. A tall, heavyset man with flowing white hair, he struck White House visitors as exceptionally courteous: an eye defect caused him to tilt his head slightly forward and to one side, which reinforced the impression of deference and attentiveness. A dutiful party member, he had over the years carefully cultivated wide personal support, yet he was a cautious and uninspiring leader who

had a strong stubborn streak and deeply resented opposition to his policies.

Moderates in both sections hoped that the new president would thwart Republican radicals and secessionists of the Deep South, popularly known as "fire-eaters." Throughout his career, however, Buchanan had taken the southern position on sectional matters. Moreover, on March 6, 1857, only two days after Buchanan's inauguration, the Supreme Court gave the new administration an unintended jolt with one of the most controversial decisions in its history.

The *Dred Scott* Decision

The owner of a Missouri slave named Dred Scott had taken him to live for several years in Illinois, a free state, and in the Wisconsin Territory, in what is now Minnesota, where slavery had been banned by the Missouri Compromise. Scott had returned to Missouri with his owner, only to sue eventually for his freedom on the grounds that his residence in a free state and a free territory had made him free. His case ultimately went to the Supreme Court. Two northern justices joined all five southern members of the Court in ruling 7 to 2 that Scott remained a slave. The majority opinion was written by Chief Justice Roger Taney of Maryland, who argued that under Missouri law, which took precedence, Scott was still a slave.

PROTECTION OF
SLAVERY

Had the Court stopped there, the public outcry would have been minimal. But the Court majority believed that they had a responsibility to deal with the larger controversy between the two sections. In particular, Chief Justice Taney wanted to strengthen the judicial protection of slavery. Taney, a former Maryland slaveowner who had freed his slaves, ruled that African Americans could not be and never had been citizens of the United States. Instead, he insisted that at the time the Constitution was adopted, they were "regarded as beings of an inferior order, so far inferior that they had no rights which the white man was bound to respect." In

Dred Scott

Chief Justice Roger Taney

addition, the Court ruled that the Missouri Compromise was unconstitutional. Congress, it declared, had no power to ban slavery from *any* territory of the United States.

REACTION TO THE DECISION

While southerners rejoiced at this outcome, Republicans denounced the Court. Their platform declared, after all, that Congress ought to prohibit slavery in all territories. "We know the court . . . has often over-ruled its own decisions," Abraham Lincoln observed, "and we shall do what we can to have it over-rule this." But the decision was sobering. If all territories were now open to slavery, how long would it be before a move was made to reintroduce slavery in the free states? For Republicans, the Court's decision foreshadowed the spread of slavery throughout the West and even throughout the nation.

But the decision also threatened Douglas's more moderate solution of popular sovereignty. If Congress had no power to prohibit slavery in a territory, how could it authorize a territorial legislature to do so? Although the Court did not rule on this point, the clear implication of the *Dred Scott* decision was that popular sovereignty was also unconstitutional. The Court, in effect, had endorsed John C. Calhoun's radical view that slavery was legal in all the territories. It had intended to settle the question of slavery in the territories once and for all. Instead, the Court succeeded only in strengthening the forces of extremism in American politics.

The Panic of 1857

ECONOMIC ISSUES INCREASE SECTIONAL TENSIONS

As the nation grappled with the *Dred Scott* decision, an economic depression aggravated sectional conflict. Once again, boom gave way to bust as falling wheat prices and contracted credit hurt commercial farmers and overextended railroad investors. The Panic of 1857 was nowhere near as severe as the depression of 1837–1843. But the psychological results were far-reaching, for the South remained relatively untouched. With the price of cotton and other southern commodities still high, southern secessionists hailed the panic as proof that an independent southern nation was economically workable. Insisting that cotton sustained the international economy, James Henry Hammond, a senator from South Carolina, boasted: "What would happen if no cotton was furnished for three years? England would topple headlong and carry the whole civilized world with her save the South. No, you dare not make war on cotton. No power on earth dares to make war on it. Cotton is king."

For their part, northerners urged federal action to spur the economy. Southerners defeated an attempt to increase the tariff duties, at their lowest level since 1815, and Buchanan, under southern pressure, vetoed bills to improve navigation on the Great Lakes and to give free farms to western settlers. Many businesspeople and conservative ex-Whigs condemned these southern actions and now endorsed the Republican Party.

The Lecompton Constitution

ATTEMPT TO MAKE KANSAS A SLAVE STATE

Although the *Dred Scott* decision and economic depression weakened the bonds of the Union, Kansas remained at the center of the political stage. In June 1857, when the territory elected delegates to draft a state constitution, free-state voters boycotted the election, thereby giving proslavery forces control of the convention that met in Lecompton. The delegates drafted a constitution that made slavery legal. Even more boldly, they scheduled a referendum in which voters could choose only whether to admit additional slaves into the territory. They could not vote against the constitution, and they could not vote to get rid of slavery entirely. Once again, free-staters boycotted the election, and the Lecompton constitution was approved.

DEFEAT OF THE LECOMPTON CONSTITUTION

As a supporter of popular sovereignty, President Buchanan had pledged a free and fair vote on the Lecompton constitution. But the outcome offered him the unexpected opportunity to satisfy his southern supporters by pushing the Lecompton constitution through Congress. This action was too much for Douglas, who broke party ranks and denounced the Lecompton constitution as a fraud. Nevertheless, the administration prevailed in the Senate. Buchanan now pulled out all the stops to gain the necessary votes in the House to admit Kansas as a slave state. But the House, where northern representation was much stronger, rejected the constitution. In a compromise, Congress, using indirect language, returned the constitution to Kansas for another vote. This time it was decisively defeated, 11,300 to 1,788. No doubt remained that as soon as Kansas had sufficient population, it would come into the Union as a free state.

The attempt to force slavery on the people of Kansas drove many conservative northerners into the Republican Party. And Douglas, once the Democrats' strongest potential candidate in 1860, now found himself assailed by the southern wing of his party. On top of that, in the summer of 1858, Douglas faced a desperate fight in his race for reelection to the Senate against Republican Abraham Lincoln.

The Lincoln-Douglas Debates

LINCOLN'S VIEW OF THE CRISIS

"He is the strong man of his party . . . and the best stump speaker, with his droll ways and dry jokes, in the West," Douglas commented when he learned of Lincoln's nomination to oppose him. "He is as honest as he is shrewd, and if I beat him my victory will be hardly won." Tall (6 feet 4 inches) and gangly, Lincoln had a gaunt face, high cheekbones, deep-socketed gray eyes, and a shock of unruly hair. He appeared awkward as he spoke, never knowing quite what to do with his large, muscular hands. Yet his finely honed logic, his simple, eloquent language, and his sincerity carried the audience with him. His sentences, as spare as the man himself, had none of the oratorical flourishes common in that day. "If we could first know *where* we are, and *whither* we are tending, we could then better judge *what* to do, and *how* to do it," Lincoln began, in accepting his party's nomination for senator from Illinois in 1858. He quoted a proverb from the Bible:

> A house divided against itself cannot stand.
>
> I believe this government cannot endure, permanently half *slave* and half *free.*
>
> I do not expect the Union to be *dissolved*—I do not expect the house to *fall*—but I *do* expect it will cease to be divided.
>
> It will become *all* one thing, or *all* the other.
>
> Either the *opponents* of slavery, will arrest the further spread of it, and place it where the public mind shall rest in the belief that it is in course of ultimate extinction; or its *advocates* will push it forward, till it shall become alike lawful in all the States, *old* as well as new—*North* as well as *South.*

The message echoed through the hall and across the pages of the national press.

LINCOLN'S
CHARACTER

Born in the slave state of Kentucky, Lincoln had grown up mostly in southern Indiana and central Illinois. He could split rails with the best frontier farmer, loved telling stories, and was at home mixing with ordinary folk. Yet his intense ambition had lifted him above the backwoods from which he came. He compensated for a lack of formal schooling through disciplined self-education, and he became a shrewd courtroom lawyer of respectable social standing. Known for his sense of humor, he was nonetheless subject to chronic depression, and his eyes often mirrored a deep melancholy.

DOUGLAS AND
LINCOLN ON
THE SLAVERY
ISSUE

At the age of 25 Lincoln entered the state legislature and soon became an important Whig strategist. After the party's decline he joined the Republicans and became one of their key leaders in Illinois. In a series of seven joint debates Lincoln challenged Douglas to discuss the issues of slavery and the sectional controversy. Douglas joined the debate by portraying Lincoln as a radical whose "House Divided" speech preached sectional warfare. The nation *could* endure half slave and half free, Douglas declared, as long as states and territories were left alone to regulate their own affairs. Accusing Lincoln of believing that blacks were his equal, Douglas countered that the American government had been "made by the white man, for the white man, to be administered by the white man."

Lincoln responded by denying any intention to interfere with slavery in the South, but he insisted that the spread of slavery to the territories was a blight on the Republic. Douglas could not be counted on to oppose slavery's

Superb debaters, Douglas and Lincoln nevertheless had very different speaking styles. The deep-voiced Douglas was constantly on the attack, drawing on his remarkable memory and showering points like buckshot in all directions. Employing sarcasm and ridicule rather than humor, he never tried to crack a joke. Lincoln, who had a high-pitched voice and a rather awkward platform manner, developed his arguments more carefully and methodically, and he relied on his sense of humor and unmatched ability as a storyteller to drive his points home to the audience.

expansion, Lincoln warned, for he had already admitted that he didn't care whether slavery was voted "down or up." For his part, Lincoln denied any "perfect equality between the negroes and white people" and opposed allowing blacks to vote, hold office, or intermarry with whites. But, he concluded,

> notwithstanding all this, there is no reason in the world why the negro is not entitled to all the natural rights enumerated in the Declaration of Independence, the right to life, liberty and the pursuit of happiness. . . . I agree with Judge Douglas [that the negro] is not my equal in many respects—certainly not in color, perhaps not in moral or intellectual endowment. But in the right to eat the bread, without leave of anybody else, which his own hand earns, *he is my equal and the equal of Judge Douglas, and the equal of every living man.*

FREEPORT DOCTRINE

At the debate held at Freeport, Illinois, Lincoln asked Douglas how under the *Dred Scott* decision the people of a territory could lawfully exclude slavery before statehood. Douglas answered, with what became known as the Freeport Doctrine, that slavery could exist only with the protection of law and that slaveowners would never bring their slaves into an area that did not have a slave code. Therefore, Douglas explained, if the people of a territory refused to pass a slave code, slavery would never be established there.

In a close race, the legislature elected Douglas to another term in the Senate.* But Democrats from the South angrily repudiated him and condemned the Freeport Doctrine. Although Lincoln lost, Republicans thought his performance marked him as a presidential contender for 1860.

The Beleaguered South

While northerners increasingly feared that the Slave Power was conspiring to extend slavery into the free states, southerners worried that the "Black Republicans" would hem them in and undermine their political power. The very factors that brought prosperity during the 1850s stimulated the South's sense of crisis. As the price of slaves rose sharply, the proportion of southerners who owned slaves had dropped almost a third since 1830. Land also was being consolidated into larger holdings, evidence of declining opportunity for ordinary white southerners. Furthermore, California and Kansas had been closed to southern slaveholders—unfairly, in

*State legislatures elected senators until 1913, when the Seventeenth Amendment was adopted. While Lincoln and Douglas both campaigned for the office, Illinois voters actually voted for candidates for the legislature who were pledged to one of the senatorial candidates.

their eyes. Finally, Douglas's clever claim that a territory could effectively outlaw slavery using the Freeport Doctrine seemed to negate the *Dred Scott* decision that slavery was legal in all the territories.

FAILED SOLUTIONS

The South's growing sense of moral and political isolation made this crisis more acute. By the 1850s slavery had been abolished throughout most of the Americas, and in the United States the South's political power was steadily shrinking. Only the expansion of slavery held out any promise of new slave states needed to preserve the South's political power and protect its way of life. "The truth is," fumed one Alabama politician, ". . . the South is excluded from the common territories of the Union. The right of expansion claimed to be a necessity of her continued existence, is practically and effectively denied the South."

✓ **REVIEW**

How did the Lecompton constitution and the Lincoln-Douglas debates affect the debate over slavery in the territories?

THE ROAD TO WAR

JOHN BROWN'S RAID

IN 1857 JOHN BROWN—THE abolitionist firebrand—had returned to the East from Kansas, consumed with the idea of attacking slavery in the South itself. With financing from a number of prominent northern reformers, Brown gathered 21 followers, including 5 free blacks, in hope of fomenting a slave insurrection. On the night of October 16, 1859, the group seized the unguarded federal armory at Harpers Ferry in Virginia. But no slaves rallied to Brown's standard: few even lived in the area to begin with. Before long the raiders found themselves holed up in the armory's engine house with hostile townspeople taking potshots at them. Charging with bayonets fixed, federal troops commanded by Colonel Robert E. Lee soon captured Brown and his band.

Brown's raid at Harpers Ferry was yet another blow weakening the forces of compromise and moderation at the nation's political center. The invasion itself was a dismal failure, as were most of the enterprises Brown undertook in his troubled life. But the old man knew how to bear himself with a martyr's dignity. "Had I so interfered in behalf of the rich, the powerful, the intelligent, the so-called great," he declared at his trial, ". . . it would have been all right. . . . [T]o have interfered as I have done in behalf of [God's] despised poor, is no wrong, but a right." On December 2, 1859, the state of Virginia hanged Brown for treason.

| John Brown

REACTION TO
THE RAID

Republicans made haste to denounce Brown's raid, lest they be tarred as radicals, but other northerners were less cautious. Ralph Waldo Emerson described Brown as a "saint, whose martyrdom will make the gallows as glorious as the cross," and on the day of his execution, church bells tolled in many northern cities. Only a minority of northerners endorsed Brown, but southerners were shocked by such public displays of sympathy. And they were firmly convinced that the Republican Party was secretly connected to the raid.

A Sectional Election

When Congress convened in December, there were ominous signs everywhere of the growing sectional rift. Intent on destroying Douglas's Freeport Doctrine, southern radicals demanded a congressional slave code to protect slavery in the territories. To northern Democrats, such a platform spelled political death. As one Indiana Democrat put it, "We cannot carry a single congressional district on that doctrine in the state."

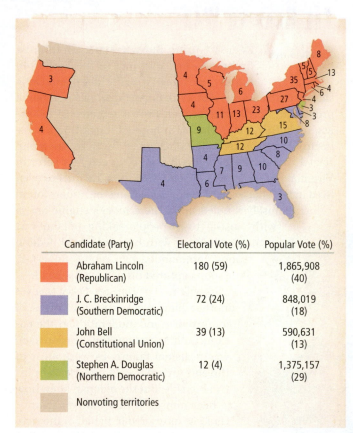

Candidate (Party)	Electoral Vote (%)	Popular Vote (%)
Abraham Lincoln (Republican)	180 (59)	1,865,908 (40)
J. C. Breckinridge (Southern Democratic)	72 (24)	848,019 (18)
John Bell (Constitutional Union)	39 (13)	590,631 (13)
Stephen A. Douglas (Northern Democratic)	12 (4)	1,375,157 (29)
Nonvoting territories		

ELECTION OF 1860

Although Lincoln did not win a majority of the popular vote, he still would have been elected even if the votes for all three of his opponents had been combined, because he won a clear majority in every state he carried except California, Oregon, and New Jersey (whose electoral votes he split with Douglas).

DISRUPTION OF
THE DEMOCRATIC
PARTY

At the Democratic Convention in April in Charleston, South Carolina, southern radicals boldly pressed their demand for a federal slave code. After a heated debate, however, the convention adopted the Douglas platform upholding popular sovereignty, whereupon the delegations from eight southern states walked out. Unable to agree on a candidate, the convention finally reassembled two months later in Baltimore and nominated Douglas. At this point most of the remaining southern Democrats left in disgust. Joining with the Charleston seceders, they nominated their own candidate, Vice President John C. Breckinridge of Kentucky, on a platform supporting a federal slave code. The last major national party had shattered.

In May the Republicans met in Chicago, where they turned to Abraham Lincoln, a moderate on the slavery issue who was strong in Illinois and the other northern states the party had lost in 1856. The election that followed was really two contests in one. In the North, which had a majority of the electoral votes, only Lincoln and Douglas had any chance of carrying a state. In the South the race pitted Breckinridge against John Bell of Tennessee, the candidate of the new conservative Constitutional Union Party. Although Lincoln received less than 40 percent of the popular vote and had virtually no support in the South, he won 180 electoral votes, 27 more than needed for election. For the first time, the nation had elected a president who headed a completely sectional party and who was committed to stopping the expansion of slavery.

Secession

SOUTHERN
FEARS

Although the Republicans had not won control of either house of Congress, Lincoln's election struck many southerners as a blow of terrible finality. Lincoln had been lifted into office on the strength of the free states alone. With Republicans opposed to slavery's expansion, the South's power base could only shrink. It was not unrealistic, many fire-eaters argued, to believe that Lincoln would use federal aid to induce the border states to voluntarily free their slaves. Once slavery disappeared there, and new states were added, the necessary three-fourths majority would exist to approve a constitutional amendment abolishing slavery. Or perhaps Lincoln might send other John Browns into the South to stir up more slave insurrections. The Montgomery (Alabama) *Mail* accused Republicans of intending "to free the negroes and force amalgamation between them and the children of the poor men of the South."

CONFEDERATE
STATES OF
AMERICA

Secession seemed the only alternative left to protect southern equality and liberty. South Carolina, which had challenged federal authority in the nullification crisis, was determined to force the other southern states to act. On December 20, 1860, a popular convention unanimously passed a resolution seceding from the Union. The rest of the Deep South followed, and on February 7, 1861, the

In Iowa, a somber young member of the Republicans' "Wide-Awake" marching club, shows his support for Lincoln in the 1860 election.

have just carried an election on principles fairly stated to the people," Lincoln wrote in opposing compromise. "Now we are told in advance, the government shall be broken up, unless we surrender to those we have beaten, before we take the offices. If we surrender, it is the end of us, and of the government." Only the unamendable amendment passed, but war ended any possibility that it would be ratified.

The Outbreak of War

As he prepared to take office, Lincoln pondered what to do about secession. In his inaugural address on March 4, he sought to reassure southerners that he had no intention, "directly or indirectly, to interfere with the institution of slavery in the States where it exists." But he maintained that "the Union of these states is perpetual," echoing Andrew Jackson's Proclamation on Nullification, and that no state could leave the Union by its own action. He also announced that he intended to "hold, occupy and possess" federal property and collect customs duties under the tariff. He closed by calling for a restoration of the "bonds of affection" that united all Americans.

FORT SUMTER The new president hoped for time to work out a solution, but on his first day in office he was handed a dispatch from Major Robert Anderson, commander of the federal garrison at Fort Sumter in Charleston harbor. Sumter was one of the few remaining federal outposts in the South. Anderson informed the government that he was almost out of food and that, unless resupplied, he would have to surrender in six weeks. For a month Lincoln looked for a peaceful resolution, but he finally felt compelled to send a relief expedition. As a conciliatory gesture, he notified the governor of South Carolina that supplies were being sent and that if the fleet were allowed to pass, only food, and not men, arms, or ammunition, would be landed.

UPPER SOUTH SECEDES The burden of decision now shifted to Jefferson Davis. From his point of view, secession was a constitutional right and the Confederacy was a legitimate government. To allow the United States to hold property and maintain military forces within the Confederacy would destroy its claim of independence. Davis therefore instructed the Confederate commander at Charleston to demand the immediate surrender of Fort Sumter and, if refused, to open fire. When Anderson declined the ultimatum, Confederate batteries began shelling the fort on April 12 at 4:30 a.m. Some 33 hours later Anderson surrendered. When in response Lincoln called for 75,000 volunteers to put down the rebellion, four states in the Upper South, led by Virginia, also seceded. Matters had passed beyond compromise.

states stretching from South Carolina to Texas organized the Confederate States of America and elected Jefferson Davis president.

But the Upper South and the border states declined to secede, hoping that once again Congress could patch together a settlement. Senator John Crittenden of Kentucky proposed a constitutional amendment extending to California the old Missouri Compromise line of 36°30′. Slavery would be prohibited north of this line and given federal protection south of it in all territories, including any acquired in the future. Furthermore, Crittenden proposed an "unamendable amendment" to the Constitution, forever preserving slavery in states where it already existed.

CRITTENDEN COMPROMISE FAILS But the Crittenden Compromise was doomed for the simple reason that the two groups who were required to make concessions— Republicans and secessionists—had no interest in doing so. "The argument is exhausted," representatives from the Deep South announced, even before Crittenden had introduced his legislative package. "We

DUELING DOCUMENTS

SLAVERY AND SECESSION

The two highest officials of the Confederacy provide contrasting opinions on slavery's relation to the Civil War. The first, Alexander Stephens, delivered his remarks (which came to be known as the "Cornerstone Speech") in Savannah, Georgia, shortly after being elected vice president of the new government. Jefferson Davis, president of the Confederacy, published his reflections after the war.

DOCUMENT 1   Slavery Is the Cornerstone: Alexander Stephens

The new Constitution [of the Confederate States of America] has put at rest *forever* all the agitating questions relating to our peculiar institutions—African slavery as it exists among us—the proper *status* of the negro in our form of civilization. *This was the immediate cause of the late rupture and present revolution.* JEFFERSON, in his forecast, had anticipated this, as the "rock upon which the old Union would split." He was right. What was conjecture with him, is now a realized fact. But whether he fully comprehended the great truth upon which that rock *stood* and *stands,* may be doubted. *The prevailing ideas entertained by him and most of the leading statesmen at the time of the formation of the Old Constitution were, that the enslavement of the African was in violation of the laws of*

nature; that it was wrong in principle, socially, morally and politically. It was an evil they knew not well how to deal with; but the general opinion of the men of that day was, that, somehow or other, in the order of Providence, the institution would be evanescent and pass away. This idea, though not incorporated in the Constitution, was the prevailing idea at the time. . . . *Those ideas, however, were fundamentally wrong. They rested upon the assumption of the equality of races. This was an error.* It was a sandy foundation, and the idea of a Government built upon it—when the "storm came and the wind blew, it fell."

Our new Government is founded upon exactly the opposite ideas; its foundations are laid, its cornerstone rests, upon the

great truth that the negro is not equal to the white man; that slavery, subordination to the superior race, is his natural and moral condition. This, our new Government, is the first, in the history of the world, based upon this great physical philosophical and moral truth. . . .

It is the first Government ever instituted upon principles in strict conformity to nature, and the ordination of Providence, in furnishing the materials of human society. Many Governments have been founded upon the principles of certain classes; but the classes thus enslaved, were of the same race, and in violation of the laws of nature. Our system commits no such violation of nature's laws. The negro by nature, or by the curse against Canaan, is fitted for that

THE PATTERN OF SECESSION

Led by South Carolina, the Deep South seceded between Lincoln's election in November and his inauguration in March. The Upper South did not secede until after the firing on Fort Sumter. The four border slave states never seceded and remained in the Union throughout the war. As the map indicates, secession sentiment was strongest in states where the highest percentage of white families owned slaves.

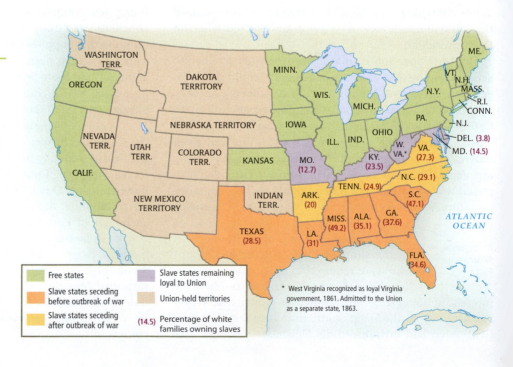

Legend:
- Free states
- Slave states seceding before outbreak of war
- Slave states seceding after outbreak of war
- Slave states remaining loyal to Union
- Union-held territories
- (14.5) Percentage of white families owning slaves

* West Virginia recognized as loyal Virginia government, 1861. Admitted to the Union as a separate state, 1863.

condition which he occupies in our system. . . . The substratum of our society is made of the material fitted by nature for it, and by experience we know that it is the best, not only for the superior but for the inferior race, that it should be so.

Source: Alexander Stephens, speech delivered March 21, 1861, Savannah, Georgia. Frank Moore, ed., *The Rebellion Record* (New York, 1861–1868), vol. 1, pp. 45–46.

DOCUMENT 2   Slavery Did Not Cause the Civil War: Jefferson Davis

The reader of many of the treatises on these events, which have been put forth as historical . . . might naturally enough be led to the conclusion that the controversies which arose between the States, and the war in which they culminated, were caused by efforts on the one side to extend and perpetuate human slavery, and on the other to resist it and establish human liberty. The Southern States and Southern people have been sedulously represented as "propagandists" of slavery, and the Northern as the defenders and champions of universal freedom. . . .

I have not attempted, and shall not permit myself to be drawn into any discussion of the merits or demerits of slavery as an ethical or even as a political question. It would be foreign to my purpose, irrelevant to my subject, and would only serve—as it has invariably served in the hands of its agitators—to "darken counsel" and divert attention from the genuine issues involved. . . .

As a mere historical fact, we have seen that African servitude among us—confessedly the mildest and most humane of all institutions to which the name "slavery" has ever been applied—existed in all the original States, and that it was recognized and protected in the fourth article of the Constitution. Subsequently, for climatic, industrial, and economical—not moral or sentimental—reasons, it was abolished in the Northern, while it continued to exist in the Southern States. . . . Eleven years after the agitation on the Missouri [Compromise of 1820], when the subject first took a sectional shape, the abolition of slavery was proposed and earnestly debated in the Virginia Legislature, and its advocates were so near the accomplishment of their purpose, that a declaration in its favor was defeated only by a small majority. . . . At a still later period, abolitionist lecturers and teachers were mobbed, assaulted, and threatened with tar and feather in New York, Pennsylvania, Massachusetts, New Hampshire, Connecticut, and other States. . . .

These facts prove incontestably that the sectional hostility which exhibited itself in 1820, on the application of Missouri for admission into the Union, which again broke out on the proposition for the annexation of Texas in 1844, and which reappeared after the Mexican war . . . was not the consequence of any difference on the abstract question of slavery. It was the offspring of sectional rivalry and political ambition. It would have manifested itself just as certainly if slavery had existed in all the States, or if there had not been a negro in America. . . .

It was not slavery that threatened a rupture in 1832 [during the Nullification crisis], but the unjust and unequal operation of a protective tariff. . . .

The truth remains intact and incontrovertible, that the existence of African servitude was in no wise the cause of the conflict, but only an incident. In the later controversies that arose, however, its effect in operating as a lever upon the passions, prejudices, or sympathies of mankind, was so potent that it has been spread, like a thick cloud, over the whole horizon of historical truth.

Source: Jefferson Davis, *The Rise and Fall of the Confederate Government* (New York, 1881), vol. 1, pp. 77–80.

Thinking Critically

What does Stephens mean by "the curse against Canaan"? How do Davis and Stephens differ in discussing the underlying causes of the Civil War? Does the date when each man delivered his opinion suggest a reason for the attitudes toward slavery and the reasons for secession? What evidence would you seek to decide the question of whether the dispute over slavery was the primary motivation for seceding?

The Roots of a Divided Society

And so the Union was broken. After 70 years, the forces of sectionalism and separatism had finally outpulled the ties binding "these United States." Why did affairs come to such a pass?

In some ways, as we have seen, the revolution in markets that transformed the nation during these years served to link together northerners and southerners. The cotton planter in Chapter 10 who rode the steamship *Fashion* along the Alabama River ("Time's money! Time's money!") was wearing ready-made clothes manufactured in New York from southern cotton. Chauncey Jerome's clocks from Connecticut were keeping time not only for commercial planters but also for Lowell mill workers like Mary Paul, who learned to measure her lunch break in minutes. Farmers in both Tennessee and Iowa were interested in the price of wheat in New York, for it affected the profits that could be made shipping their grain by the new railroad lines. American society had become far more specialized, and therefore far more interdependent, since the days of Hector St. John de Crèvecoeur's idealized self-sufficient farmer of the 1780s.

| When news of secession spread, many southern white women wore decorative cockades made of woven palmetto leaves and silk.

DIVERGING ECONOMIES

But a specialized economy had not brought unity. For the North, specialization meant more factories, a higher percentage of urban workers, and a greater number of cities and towns. Industry affected midwestern farmers as well, for their steel plows and McCormick reapers allowed them to farm larger holdings and required greater capital investment in the new machinery. For its part, the South was transformed by the Industrial Revolution, too, as textile factories made cotton the booming mainstay of its economy. But for all its growth, the region remained largely a rural society. Its prosperity stemmed from expansion westward into new areas of cotton production, not new forms of production or technology. The dominant planter class reinforced its traditional concepts of honor, hierarchy, and deference.

Above all, the intensive labor required to produce cotton, rice, and sugar made slavery an inseparable part of the southern way of life—"so intimately mingled with our social conditions," as one Georgian admitted, "that it would be impossible to eradicate it." An increasing number of northerners viewed slavery as evil, not so much out of high-minded sympathy toward slaves but as a labor system that threatened the republican ideals of white American society.

WEAKNESSES OF THE POLITICAL SYSTEM

It fell to the political system to try to resolve sectional conflict through a system of national parties that represented various interest groups and promoted democratic debate. But the political system had critical weaknesses. The American process of electing a president gave the winning candidate a state's entire electoral vote, regardless of the margin of victory. That procedure made a northern sectional party possible, since the Republicans could never have carried an election on the basis of a popular vote alone. In addition, the four-year fixed presidential term

AN EMINENT SOUTHERN CLERGYMAN, During an eloquent discourse, is wonderfully assisted in finding scriptural authority for Secession and Treason, and the divine ordination of Slavery.

Northerners reacted differently to secession. Envelopes like the one shown here portrayed a secessionist southern preacher inspired by the devil to give "an eloquent discourse" on "Treason" and God's approval of slavery.

allowed Presidents Pierce and Buchanan to remain in office, pursuing disruptive policies on Kansas even after the voters had rejected those policies in the midterm congressional elections in 1854 and 1858. Finally, since 1844 the Democratic party had required a two-thirds vote to nominate its presidential candidate. Unintentionally, this requirement made it difficult to pick any truly forceful leader and gave the South a veto over the party's candidate. Yet the South, by itself, could not elect a president.

BELIEF IN CONSPIRACIES AGAINST LIBERTY

The nation's republican heritage also contributed to the political system's vulnerability. Ever since the Revolution, when Americans accused the king and Parliament of deliberately plotting to deprive them of their liberties, Americans were on the watch for political conspiracies. Such an outlook often stimulated exaggerated fears, unreasonable conclusions, and excessive reactions. For their part, Republicans emphasized the existence of the Slave Power bent on eradicating northern rights. Southerners, on the other hand, accused the Black Republicans of conspiring to destroy southern equality. Each side viewed itself as defending the country's republican tradition from an internal threat.

✓ **REVIEW**

Why did Lincoln's election cause the southern states to secede from the Union?

CONCLUSION

THE WORLD AT LARGE

But in the end, the threat to the Union came not from within but from beyond its borders. As the nation expanded in the 1840s, it incorporated vast new territories, becoming a truly continental republic. And that forced the Union, in absorbing new lands, to define itself anew. If the American frontier had not swept so quickly toward the Pacific, the nation might have been able to postpone the day of reckoning on slavery until some form of gradual emancipation could be adopted. But the luxury of time was not available. The new territories became the battlegrounds for two contrasting ways of life, with slavery at the center of the debate. Elsewhere in the world the push toward abolition grew louder, whether of serfdom in eastern Europe or of slavery across the globe. Americans who saw the issue in moral terms joined that chorus. They saw no reason why the abolition of slavery should be postponed.

In 1850, supporters and opponents of slavery were still willing to compromise on how "the peculiar institution" could expand into the new territories. But a decade later, many Americans both North and South had come to accept the idea of an irrepressible conflict between two societies, one based on freedom, the other on slavery, in which only one side could ultimately prevail. At stake, it seemed, was control of the nation's future. Four years later, as a weary Abraham Lincoln looked back to the beginning of the conflict, he noted, "Both parties deprecated war, but one of them would *make* war rather than let the nation survive, and the other would *accept* war rather than let it perish, and the war came." ∞∞∞∞

CHAPTER SUMMARY

IN THE 1850S THE SLAVERY issue reemerged in national politics and increasingly disrupted the party system, leading to the outbreak of war in 1861.

- Fundamental economic changes heightened sectional tensions in the 1850s.

  - The construction of a vast railroad network reoriented western trade from the South to the East.

  - A tide of new immigrants swelled the North's population (and hence its political power) at the expense of the South, thereby stimulating southern fears.

- The old Jacksonian party system was shattered by the nativist movement and by a renewed controversy of the expansion of slavery.

  - In the Kansas-Nebraska Act, Senator Stephen A. Douglas tried to defuse the slavery debate by incorporating popular sovereignty (the idea that the people of a territory should decide the status of slavery there). This act effectively repealed the Missouri Compromise.

  - Popular sovereignty failed in the Kansas Territory, where fighting broke out between proslavery and antislavery partisans.

- Sectional violence reached a climax in May 1856 with the attack on Lawrence, Kansas, and the caning of Senator Charles Sumner of Massachusetts by Representative Preston S. Brooks of South Carolina.

- Sectional tensions sparked the formation of a new antislavery Republican party, and the party system realigned along sectional lines.

  - The Supreme Court's *Dred Scott* decision, the Panic of 1857, the congressional struggle over the proslavery Lecompton constitution, and John Brown's attack on Harpers Ferry in 1859 strengthened the two sectional extremes.

- In 1860 Abraham Lincoln became the first Republican to be elected president.

  - Following Lincoln's triumph, the seven states of the Deep South seceded.

  - When Lincoln sent supplies to the Union garrison in Fort Sumter in Charleston harbor, Confederate batteries bombarded the fort into submission.

  - The North rallied to Lincoln's decision to use force to restore the Union, and in response the four states of the Upper South seceded.

ADDITIONAL READING

THE PROBLEM OF THE COMING of the Civil War has attracted considerable historical attention over the years. John Ashworth, *The Republic in Crisis* (2012), is a lucid, recent interpretation. The political aspects of the conflict also take center stage in Michael F. Holt's brief and incisive work, *The Fate of Their Country: Politicians, Slavery Extension, and the Coming of the Civil War* (2004). Holt stresses the self-interest of the political leaders and plays down the larger structural economic and social factors. A contrasting and similarly brief study can be found in Don E. Fehrenbacher, *Sectional Crises and Southern Constitutionalism* (1995).

The heavy immigration during these years is explored in Raymond L. Cohn, *Mass Migration under Sail* (2009). For slavery's mounting implications for American politics, see Eric Foner, *The Fiery Trial* (2011).

Paul Quigley's *Shifting Grounds* (2012) puts the idea of southern nationalism in a broad spatial context. The most thorough examination of the blend of factors that produced the Republican Party is William E. Gienapp, *The Origins of the Republican Party, 1852–1856* (1987). Eric Foner's classic *Free Soil, Free Labor, Free Men* (1970), focuses on the ideas of Republican Party leaders. For the turbulent history of Kansas in this period, see Nicole Etcheson, *Bleeding Kansas* (2006). The critical events of 1857 are the focal point of Kenneth M. Stampp's *America in 1857* (1990). William W. Freehling's two-volume work *The Road to Disunion* (1991, 2007) offers a broad perspective on the secessionist project, and Charles B. Dew provides a regional view by examining the role of the secession commissioners appointed by the Confederacy to persuade wavering southerners in *Apostles of Secession* (2001). Adam Goodheart's *1861: The Civil War Awakening* (2011) presents a rich portrait of the war's beginnings. For a discussion of the broader issue of why the South chose secession and fought the Civil War, see Gary W. Gallagher and Alan T. Nolan, eds., *The Myth of the Lost Cause and Civil War History* (2000).

For a fuller list of readings, see the Bibliography at www.mhhe.com/eh8e.

SIGNIFICANT EVENTS

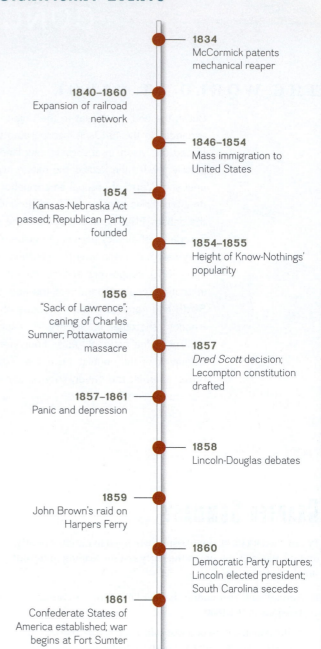

1834
McCormick patents mechanical reaper

1840–1860
Expansion of railroad network

1846–1854
Mass immigration to United States

1854
Kansas-Nebraska Act passed; Republican Party founded

1854–1855
Height of Know-Nothings' popularity

1856
"Sack of Lawrence"; caning of Charles Sumner; Pottawatomie massacre

1857
Dred Scott decision; Lecompton constitution drafted

1857–1861
Panic and depression

1858
Lincoln-Douglas debates

1859
John Brown's raid on Harpers Ferry

1860
Democratic Party ruptures; Lincoln elected president; South Carolina secedes

1861
Confederate States of America established; war begins at Fort Sumter

1854

Kansas-Nebraska Act opens debate over status of new territories; Missouri Compromise repealed

1855

Proslavery forces stuff ballot boxes in Kansas elections, expel free-state members of legislature; free-staters organize separate government

1856

Lawrence, Kansas, sacked by proslavery forces; John Brown's Pottawatomie Massacre; Charles Sumner beaten unconscious on Senate floor

1857

Dred Scott decision; Court rules that Congress cannot ban slavery in any territory; Missouri Compromise unconstitutional

1858

Lincoln and Douglas debate slavery; Douglas suggests "Freeport Doctrine" as a way to block slavery, angering southern Democrats

1859

John Brown launches raid on Harpers Ferry; Brown caught, tried, and executed

1860

Republican Abraham Lincoln wins presidency without support of any southern states; South Carolina secedes

1861

Confederate States of America organized; Fort Sumter attacked; war commences

Longer-term factors

Slavery gradually extinguished in the North (1770s–1840s); abolitionist movement expands (1830s–1850s)
Railroads link Northwest more closely to Northeast (1840s–1850s)
Second party system (Whigs vs. Democrats) disintegrates over slavery disputes (1840s–1850s)
Electoral College system makes a northern sectional party possible (1850s)

absence of meat from the market, the desperation on people's faces. Some of the residents of Richmond "look like vagabonds," Jones noted in his diary.

Nowhere were the profound effects of war more complete than within the Confederacy. These changes were especially ironic because the southern states had seceded in order to preserve their traditional ways. Not only did the war send hundreds of thousands of "Johnny Rebs" off to the front; it also put extreme burdens on the women and families at home. It fundamentally transformed the southern economy and forced the Confederate government to become more centralized. And, of course, it ended by destroying the institution of slavery, which the South had gone to war to preserve.

The New Economy

With the Union blockade tightening, the production of foodstuffs became crucial to the South's economy. Many men who normally worked in the fields had gone into the army, and with the lessening of discipline, slaves became increasingly assertive and independent. More and more plantations switched from growing cotton to raising grain and livestock. As a result, cotton production dropped from 4.5 million bales in 1861 to 300,000 in 1864. Even so, food production declined. By the last two years of the war, the shortage was serious.

ATTEMPTS TO INDUSTRIALIZE The Union blockade also made it impossible to rely on European manufactured goods. So the Confederate War Department built and ran factories, took over the region's mines, and regulated private manufacturers so as to increase the production of war goods. Although the Confederacy never became industrially self-sufficient, it sustained itself far better in industrial goods than it did in agricultural produce. It was symbolic that when Lee surrendered, his troops had sufficient guns and ammunition to continue, but they had not eaten in two days.

New Opportunities for Southern Women

Southern white women took an active role in the war. Some gained notoriety as spies; others smuggled military supplies into the South. Women also spent a good deal of time knitting and sewing clothes for soldiers. "We never went out to pay a visit without taking our knitting along,"

| "Nannie" McKenzie Semple was one of many southern white women who worked for the Confederate government. Semple's salary, from working as a "Treasury Girl," netted her more than what the average soldier received.

recalled a South Carolina woman. Perhaps most important, with so many men fighting, women took charge of agricultural production. On a plantation the mistress often supervised the slaves as well as the wrenching shift from cotton to foodstuffs.

One such woman was 33-year-old Emily Lyles Harris, the wife of a small slaveowner and farmer in upcountry South Carolina. When her husband joined the army in 1862, she was left to care for their seven children as well as supervise the slaves and manage the farm. Despite the disruptions of wartime, she succeeded remarkably, one year producing the largest crop of oats in the neighborhood and always making enough money for her family to live decently. She took little pride, however, in her achievements. "I shall never get used to being left as the head of affairs at home," she wrote on one occasion. "The burden is very heavy, and there is no one to smile on me as I trudge wearily along in the dark with it. . . . I am not an independent woman nor ever shall be." Self-doubt, lack of privacy, and the burdens of responsibility left her depressed, and while she persevered, by 1865 she openly hoped for defeat.

The war also opened up new jobs for women off the farm. Given the manpower shortage, "government girls" became essential to fill the growing Confederate bureaucracy. At first women were paid half the wages of male coworkers, but by the end of the war they had won equal pay. White women also staffed the new factories springing up in southern cities and towns, undertaking even dangerous work that normally would have been considered off-limits. A majority of the workers in the South's munitions factories were women, some of whom lost their lives in accidental explosions.

Confederate Finance and Government

The most serious domestic problem the Confederate government faced was finance, for which officials at Richmond never developed a satisfactory program. The South had few banks and only $27 million in specie when the war began. European governments refused to float major loans, which left taxation as the unappealing alternative. Only in 1863 did the government begin levying a **graduated income tax** (from 1 to 15 percent) and a series of excise taxes. Most controversial, the government resorted to a tax-in-kind on farmers that, after exempting a certain portion, took one-tenth of their agricultural crops. Even more unpopular was the policy of impressment, which allowed the army to seize private property for its own use, often with little or no compensation.

FACE VALUE?

"Act of Feby 25, 1862"

Why is Alexander Hamilton on the bill?

"Confederate States of America will pay to the bearer on demand"

Why is this man on the bill? (Hint: Chapter 14 includes his photograph.)

Hand-signed and hand-numbered

A government at war can survive only if it maintains its credit—not only with its bankers but with its citizens as well. Both the Union and the Confederacy issued paper money to finance the war, and by examining the bills' designs, historians can appreciate the issuers' efforts to appear creditworthy. The Union note uses Alexander Hamilton to vouch for its reliability—the Republic's first treasury secretary, who during the 1790s stabilized the nation's shaky finances. It announces the act of Congress that allows the government to issue the notes: the Legal Tender Act, passed February 25, 1862. And the intricate engraving and red treasury seal made the bill harder to counterfeit. The Confederacy had more difficulty issuing bills because few skilled engravers lived in the South. To help prevent counterfeiting, the Confederacy followed the older tradition of signing each bill individually, employing as many as 200 secretaries to do the tedious work. (The Union's signatures were printed.) But by war's end, so many Confederate notes had been issued that they were carted about in wheelbarrows to pay the hugely inflated prices for goods. In the end, mere symbols of credit could not obliterate the realities on the ground.

Thinking Critically

The fine print located above the Confederate promise to "pay on demand" reads "Six months after a ratification of a Treaty of Peace between The Confederate States & The United States of America." What effect does this condition have? Who are the people portrayed at the center of the Confederate bill? Why choose to include them?

SOARING INFLATION

Above all, the Confederacy financed the war effort simply by printing paper money not backed by specie, some $1.5 billion, which amounted to three times more than the federal government issued. The result was runaway inflation, so that by 1865 a Confederate dollar was worth only 1.7 cents in gold and prices had soared to 92 times their prewar base. Prices were highest in Richmond, where flour sold for $275 a barrel by early 1864 and coats for $350. By the end of the war, flour had reached an astronomical $1,000 a barrel. Inflation that ate away at their standard of living was one of the great wartime hardships borne by southerners.

CENTRALIZATION OF POWER

In politics even more than in finance the Confederacy exercised far greater powers than those of the federal government before 1861. Indeed, Jefferson Davis strove to meet the demands of total war by transforming the South into a centralized, national state. He sought to limit state authority over military units, and in April 1862 the Confederacy passed the first national **conscription** law in American history, drafting all white males between 18 and 35 unless exempted. As conditions worsened, those age limits widened to 17 and 50, mobilizing virtually the entire military-age white population. Civilians, too, felt the effects of government control, for in 1862 the Congress authorized Davis to invoke martial law and suspend the writ of habeas corpus.

OPPOSITION TO DAVIS Critics protested that Davis was destroying states' rights, the cardinal principle of the Confederacy. Concerned foremost about their states' safety, governors wanted to be able to recall troops if their own territory was threatened. When President Davis suspended the writ of habeas corpus, his vice president, Alexander H. Stephens, accused him of aiming at a dictatorship. Davis used those powers for a limited time, yet in practice it made little difference whether the writ was suspended or not. With disloyalty a greater problem than in the Union, Confederate authorities more stringently regulated civil liberties, and the army arrested thousands of civilians.

HOSTILITY TO CONSCRIPTION But the Confederate draft, more than any other measure, produced an outcry. The law allowed the rich to provide substitutes. On the open market, the price for recruiting such a substitute eventually rose to $6,000. The Confederacy eventually abolished this privilege, but as one Georgia leader complained, "It's a notorious fact if a man has influential friends—or a little money to spare he will never be enrolled." Most controversially, the draft exempted from service one white man on every plantation with 20 or more slaves (later reduced to 15). This law was designed to preserve control of the slave population, but more and more non-slaveholders complained that it was a rich man's war and a poor man's fight. "All they want is to git you pumped up and go to fight for their infernal negroes and after you do their fighting you may kiss their hind parts for all they care," one Alabama farmer complained. In some counties where the draft was unenforceable, conscription officers ventured only at risk to their own safety.

Hardship and Suffering

By the last year of the conflict, food shortages had become so severe that ingenious southerners concocted various substitutes: parched corn in place of coffee, strained blackberries in place of vinegar. One scarce item for which there was no substitute was salt, which was essential for curing meat. The high prices and food shortages led to riots in several cities, most seriously in Richmond early in April 1863. There, about 300 women and children chanting "Bread!" looted a number of stores.

REVIEW
In what ways did the Confederacy, which championed states' rights, become a more centralized, national government?

THE UNION HOME FRONT

BECAUSE THE WAR WAS FOUGHT mostly on southern soil, northern civilians rarely felt its effects directly. Yet to be effective, the North's economic resources had to be organized and mobilized.

Government Finances and the Economy

MEASURES TO RAISE MONEY To begin with, the North required a comprehensive system to finance its massive campaign. Taxing the populace was an obvious means, and taxes paid for 21 percent of Union war expenses, compared with only 1 percent of the Confederacy's. In August 1861 Congress passed the first federal income tax, 3 percent on all incomes over $800 a year. When that, along with increased tariff duties, proved insufficient, Congress enacted a comprehensive tax law in 1862 that for the first time brought the tax collector into every northern household. Excise fees taxed virtually every occupation, commodity, or service; income and inheritances were taxed, as were corporations and consumers. A new bureaucracy, the Internal Revenue Bureau, oversaw the collection process.

The government also borrowed heavily, through the sale of some $2.2 billion in **bonds,** and financed the rest of the war's cost by issuing paper money. In all, the Union printed $431 million in greenbacks (so named because of their color on one side). Although legal for the payment of debts, they could not be redeemed in specie, and therefore their value fluctuated. Also, by taxing state banknotes out of circulation, Congress for the first time created a uniform national currency, as well as a national banking system.

WESTERN DEVELOPMENT During the war the Republican-controlled Congress encouraged economic development. Tariffs to protect industry from foreign competition rose to an average rate of 47 percent, compared to 19 percent in 1860. To encourage development of the West, the Homestead Act of 1862 granted 160 acres of public land—the size of the traditional American family farm—to anyone (including women) who settled and improved the land for five years. Over a million acres were distributed during the war years alone. In addition, the Land Grant College Act of 1862 donated the proceeds from certain land sales to finance public colleges and universities, creating 69 in all, many in the West.

A Rich Man's War

Over the course of the war the government purchased more than $1 billion worth of goods and services. In response to this heavy demand, the economy boomed and

| The superiority of northern industry was an important factor in the war's eventual outcome. Here molten ore is cast into cannons at a foundry in West Point, New York. This factory produced 3,000 cannons during the war.

and guns that would not fire. At least 20 percent of government expenditures involved fraud.

Stocks and dividends rose with the economy as investors scrambled after profitable new opportunities. An illegal cotton trade flourished in the Mississippi valley, where northern agents bribed military authorities for passes to go through the lines in order to purchase cotton bales from southern planters. The Confederate government quietly traded cotton for contraband such as food, medicine, and enough arms and equipment to maintain an army of 50,000 men.

Women and the Workforce

Even more than in the South, the war opened new opportunities for northern women. Countless wives ran farms while their husbands were away at war. One traveler in Iowa reported, "I met more women driving teams on the road and saw more at work in the fields than men." The war also stimulated the shift to mechanization, which made the northern labor shortage less severe. By 1865 three times as many reapers and harvesters were in use as in 1861.

Beyond the farm women increasingly found work in industry, filling approximately 100,000 new jobs during the war. Like women in the South, they worked as clerks in the expanding government bureaucracy. The work was tedious and the workload heavy, but the new jobs offered good wages, a sense of economic independence, and a pride in having aided the war effort.

business and agriculture prospered. Wages increased 42 percent between 1860 and 1864, but because prices rose faster than wages, workers' real income dropped almost 30 percent, from $363 in 1860 to $261 in 1865. That meant the working class paid a disproportionate share of the war's costs.

CORRUPTION AND FRAUD

The Republican belief that government should play a major role in the economy also fostered a cozy relationship between business and politics. In the rush to profit from government contracts, some suppliers sold inferior goods at inflated prices. Uniforms made of "shoddy"—bits of unused thread and recycled cloth—were fobbed off in such numbers that the word became an adjective describing inferior quality. Unscrupulous dealers sold clothing that dissolved in the rain, shoes that fell apart, spoiled meat, broken-down horses,

WOMEN AND MEDICINE

The war also allowed women to enter and eventually dominate the profession of nursing. "Our women appear to have become almost wild on the subject of hospital nursing," protested one army physician, who like many others opposed the presence of women in military hospitals. Led by Drs. Emily and Elizabeth Blackwell, Dorothea Dix, and Mary Ann Bickerdyke, women fought the bureaucratic inefficiency of the army medical corps. Their service in the wards of the maimed and dying reduced the hostility to women in medicine.

Clara Barton, like so many other nurses, often found herself in battlefield hospitals, amid massive death and suffering. During the Battle of Fredericksburg she wiped the

| Field hospitals were often makeshift, like this house where the surgeon operates in front on a table. The only anesthetic is to the right of the patient's head: a bottle of whiskey. Often, wounded soldiers lay untended or waited so long for help that their open wounds teemed with maggots "as though a swarm of bees had settled" on them. Confederate Walter Lenoir had his wounded leg sawn off below the knee and then endured a 20-mile ride in a rude farm wagon, every jolt causing "a pang which felt as if my stump was thrust into liquid fire."

brows of the wounded and dying, bandaged wounds, and applied tourniquets to stop the flow of blood. She later recalled that as she rose from the side of one soldier, "I wrung the blood from the bottom of my clothing, before I could step, for the weight about my feet." She steeled herself at the sight of amputated arms and legs casually tossed in piles outside the front door as the surgeons cut away, yet she found the extent of suffering overwhelming. She was jolted by the occasional familiar face among the tangled mass of bodies: the sexton of the church in her hometown, his face caked in blood, or a wayward boy she had befriended years ago. Sleeping in a tent nearby, she drove herself to the brink of exhaustion until the last patients were transferred to permanent hospitals. She then returned to her home in Washington, D.C., where she broke down and wept.

WOMEN AND TEACHING Before 1861 teaching, too, had been dominated by males, but the shortage of men forced school boards in both sections to turn to women, who were paid half to two-thirds of what men received. After the war teaching increasingly became a female profession, as many women came to see it as a career and not just a temporary occupation. Women also contributed to the war effort through volunteer work. The United States Sanitary Commission was established in 1861 to provide medical supplies and care. Much of its work was performed by women volunteers, who raised funds, collected supplies, and toiled in hospitals alongside paid nurses.

Civil Liberties and Dissent

SUSPENSION OF THE WRIT OF HABEAS CORPUS In order to mobilize northern society, Lincoln did not hesitate to curb dissenters. Shortly after the firing on Fort Sumter, he suspended the writ of habeas corpus in specified areas, which allowed the indefinite detention of anyone suspected of disloyalty or activity against the war. Although the Constitution permitted such suspension in time of rebellion or invasion, Lincoln did so without consulting Congress (unlike President Davis), and he used his power far more broadly, expanding it in 1862 to cover the entire North for cases involving antiwar activities. Lincoln also decreed that those arrested under its provisions could be tried under the stricter rules of martial law by a military court. Eventually more than 20,000 individuals were arrested, most of whom were never charged with a specific crime or brought to trial.

Democrats attacked Lincoln as a tyrant bent on destroying the Constitution. Among those arrested was Clement Vallandigham, a Democratic member of Congress from Ohio who called for an armistice in May 1963. He was convicted by a military commission and banished to the Confederacy (in 1864 he returned to the North). The Supreme Court refused to review the case, but once the war was over, it ruled in *Ex parte Milligan* (1866) that as long as the regular courts were open, civilians could not be tried by military tribunals.

THE COPPERHEADS Republicans labeled those who opposed the war **Copperheads,** conjuring up the image of a venomous snake waiting to strike the Union. Copperheads constituted the extreme peace wing of the Democratic Party. Often they had been hurt by the economic changes of the war, but more crucial was their bitter opposition to emancipation and also the draft, which they condemned as a violation of individual freedom and an instrument of special privilege. According to the provisions enacted in 1863, a person would be exempt from the present (but not any future) draft by paying a commutation fee of $300, about a year's wages for a worker or a typical farmer. Or those drafted could hire a substitute, the cost of which was beyond the reach of all but the wealthy. Despite this criticism, in reality poor men also bought their way out of the draft, often by pooling their resources; in addition, the government of some communities paid the commutation fee for any resident who was drafted. In all, approximately 118,000 men provided substitutes, and another 87,000 paid the commutation fee. Perhaps another 160,000 northerners illegally evaded the draft. Only 46,000 men were actually drafted into the Union army, out of more than 2 million who served.

NEW YORK CITY DRAFT RIOT In July 1863, when the first draftees' names were drawn in New York City, workers in the Irish quarter rose in anger. Rampaging through the streets, the mob attacked draft officials and prominent Republicans, ransacked African American

HOW FREE BALLOT IS PROTECTED!

This anti-Republican cartoon from Philadelphia expresses the fears of many Copperhead Democrats that the war for Union had been subverted by becoming a war on slavery. A caricatured black soldier tries to prevent a legless Union veteran from voting for General George McClellan, Lincoln's opponent in the election of 1864. The election clerk beside the stuffed ballot box is told to "pretend you see nothing" of the ballot stuffing.

neighborhoods, and lynched black residents who fell into its hands. By the time order was restored four days later, at least 105 people had been killed, the worst loss of life from any riot in all of American history. (See pages 434–437.)

 **REVIEW**

How did the war affect women in the workforce? How were civil liberties compromised?

GONE TO BE A SOLDIER

MARCUS SPIEGEL CAME TO THE United States after the revolution of 1848 failed in Germany. The son of a rabbi, Spiegel married an American woman, became a naturalized citizen, and was trying to make it in the warehouse business in Ohio when the war began. As an immigrant, he considered it his duty to preserve the Union for his children,

and the regular pay of an officer was also enticing, so he enlisted in November 1861. Eventually he became one of the few Jewish colonels in the army. A loyal Democrat, Spiegel did not go to war to end slavery and flatly proclaimed that black people were not "worth fighting for." By early 1864, however, his views had changed. He had "learned and seen more of what the horrors of Slavery was than I ever knew before," and though he still doubted African Americans' capabilities, he now was "in favor of doing away with the institution of Slavery." He assured his wife that "this is no hasty conclusion but a deep conviction." A few weeks later, Marcus Spiegel died of wounds he received while fighting in Louisiana.

Soldiering and Suffering

Fervently committed or not, by war's end about 2 million men had served the Union cause and another million, the Confederate. They were mostly young; almost 40 percent of

DAILY LIVES

Hardtack, Salt Horse, and Coffee

"If a person wants to know how to appreciate the value of good vi[c]tuals he had better enlist," a Vermont soldier declared. "I have seen the time when I would have been glad to [have] picked the crusts of bread that mother gives to the hogs." Whether in the field or in quarters, food was generally Johnny Reb's and Billy Yank's first concern.

At the beginning of the war, the prescribed daily allowance for each soldier included 12 ounces of pork or 20 ounces of beef, a pound or more of bread or flour, and ample quantities of rice, beans, sugar, and coffee. In general northern soldiers had more food and greater variety than their opponents. As the war ground on, the Confederacy was forced to reduce sharply the daily ration because of shortages.

Meat, bread, and coffee: these were the soldier's mainstays. The meat was either pork or beef and was usually salted to preserve it. Soldiers, who called salt pork "sowbelly" and pickled beef "salt horse," preferred the former, since the beef was so briny that it was inedible unless thoroughly soaked in water. Many soldiers left salted beef in a creek overnight before they tried to eat it.

Union soldiers normally were given wheat bread or flour, but for Confederates cornbread was the standby. This monotonous fare prompted a Louisiana soldier near the end of the war to grumble, "If any person offers me cornbread after this war comes to a close I shall *probably* tell him to—go to hell." Both armies often replaced bread with hardtack, crackers half an inch thick that were so hard, soldiers dubbed them "teeth-dullers." The crackers became moldy and worm-infested with age, and hence veterans preferred to eat them in the dark.

Coffee was the other main staple, eagerly consumed. Because of the Union blockade, the Confederacy could not get enough, and Rebel troops resorted to various unappealing substitutes. Despite official opposition, troops often fraternized during lulls in the fighting, swapping tobacco, which was in short supply on the Union side, for coffee and sugar, which Confederates desired most. When the two armies spent the winter of 1862 camped on opposite sides of the Rappahannock River, enlisted men ferried cargoes of sugar and coffee to one bank and tobacco to the other, using makeshift toy boats.

Members of both armies supplemented their diet by foraging (the army's polite term for stealing), although Union soldiers, being most often in enemy territory, relied more heavily on this tactic. Hungry troops regularly raided pigpens, poultry houses, orchards, gardens, cornfields, and smokehouses.

During training and in winter quarters, cooks normally prepared food for an entire company. Neither army, however, established a cooks' or bakers' school, and troops contended that officers regularly selected

Hardtack—often dubbed "teeth dullers"

the poorest soldiers to be cooks. "A company cook is a most peculiar being," one soldier recalled after the war. "He generally knows less about cooking than any other man in the company. Not being able to learn the drill, and too dirty to appear on inspection, he is sent to the cook house to get him out of the ranks." Once the army went on the march, men usually cooked for themselves or formed a mess of four to eight soldiers, taking turns cooking. Either way, food was rarely prepared with any skill.

By war's end, soldiers on both sides had developed a new appreciation for food. A poetic Yankee summed up the situation succinctly:

The soldiers' fare is very rough,
is hard, the beef is tough;
If they can stand it, it will be,
Through love of God, a mystery.

Thinking Critically

What are victuals, and how do you pronounce the word? What specific factors generally gave the North the advantage in supplying themselves with victuals?

Soldiers leaving for war often had their pictures taken with their loved ones. Such photographs are reminders of how much the war and its mounting death toll touched civilians as well as soldiers on both sides.

entering soldiers were age 21 or younger. They were not drawn disproportionately from the poor, and in both the North and the South, farmers and farm laborers accounted for the largest group of soldiers. Unskilled workers, who were poorer than other groups, were actually underrepresented in the ranks. It is also a myth that the North hired an army of foreign-born mercenaries. The overwhelming majority of those who wore the blue and the gray were native-born, and the proportion of immigrants in both armies was roughly the same as in the eligible military population.

Most soldiers, like Marcus Spiegel, took patriotism seriously, although officers tended to be more ideological. Enlisted men usually expressed their motivation for fighting in general terms, either to defend the Union or to protect the South. But as Union soldiers personally witnessed the effects of slavery, the majority of them, like Spiegel, came to endorse ending slavery as a war aim.

DISEASE AND MEDICAL CARE On average, soldiers spent 50 days in camp for every day in battle. Camp life was often unhealthy as well as unpleasant. Poor sanitation, miserable food, exposure to the elements, and primitive medical care contributed to widespread sickness. Officers and men alike regarded army doctors as quacks and tried to avoid them. It was a common belief that if a fellow went to the hospital, "you might as well say good bye." Conditions were even worse in the Confederate hospitals, for the Union blockade produced a shortage of medical supplies. Twice as many soldiers died from dysentery, typhoid, and other diseases as from wounds.

Treatment at field hospitals was a chilling experience. Ignorance was responsible for the existing conditions and practices, because nothing was known about germs or how wounds became infected. Years later an appalled federal surgeon recounted:

> We operated in old blood-stained and often pus-stained coats. . . . We used undisinfected instruments . . . and still worse, used marine sponges which had been used in prior pus cases and had been only washed in tap water. . . . Our silk to tie blood vessels was undisinfected. . . . We dressed the wounds with clean but undisinfected sheets, shirts, tablecloths, or other old soft linen rescued from the family ragbag. . . . We knew nothing about antiseptics and therefore used none.

DECLINE OF MORALITY The boredom of camp life, the horrors of battle, and the influence of an all-male society all corrupted morals. Swearing and heavy drinking were common, and one Mississippian reported that after payday games of chance were "running night and day, with eager and excited crowds standing around with their hands full of money." Prostitutes flooded the camps of both armies, and an Illinois private stationed in Pulaski, Tennessee, wrote home that the price schedule in each of the brothels in town was quite reasonable. "You may think I am a hard case," he conceded, "but I am as pious as you can find in the army."

With death so near, some soldiers sought solace in religion. Religious fervor was greater in the Confederate camps, and a wave of revivals swept the ranks during the last two winters of the war, producing between 100,000 and 200,000 conversions. Significantly, the first major revivals occurred after the South's twin defeats at Vicksburg and Gettysburg. Then, too, as battle after battle thinned Confederate ranks, death became much more likely.

Death on the Field and at Home

The Civil War compelled the divided nation to confront death as never before. North and South, battle front and home front, slave and free, men and women, rich and poor: nearly all Americans living through the Civil War found themselves surrounded by the immediate reality of death or its profound and multiplying consequences at every turn.

CARNAGE AT THE FRONT Most obviously, Americans at the front produced death and bore witness to it on a staggering scale. Upwards of three-quarters of a million men died in the war. The conflict lasted 1,458 days, claiming more than 500 lives each day on average. But of course the war's carnage did not unfold gradually. The scale of the violence increased as the conflict ground on, and much of the dying came in staggering, appalling surges at places thereafter synonymous with death—places like Bull Run, Shiloh, Antietam, Gettysburg.

Technological advances in the tools of destruction helped account for staggering losses. Smoothbore muskets, which at first served as the basic infantry weapon, gave way to the rifle, so named because of the grooves etched into the barrel to give a bullet spin. A new bullet, the minié ball, allowed the rifle to be easily loaded, and the invention of the percussion cap rendered it serviceable in wet weather. More important, the new weapon had an effective range of 400 yards—four times greater than that of the old musket. As a result, soldiers fought each other from greater distances and hit their targets far more frequently. Battles took much longer to fight and produced vastly more casualties. Under such conditions, the defense became a good deal stronger than the offense. The larger artillery pieces also adopted rifled barrels, but they lacked good fuses and accurate sighting devices and could not effectively support attacking troops. Artillery remained a deadly defensive weapon, however, one that devastated advancing infantry at close range. More than 100 regiments on both sides suffered in excess of 50 percent casualties in a single battle.

As the haze of gunfire covered the land and the constant spray of bullets mimicked rain pattering through the treetops, soldiers discovered that their romantic notions about war had no place on the battlefield. Men witnessed horrors they had never envisioned as civilians and choked from the stench of decaying flesh and mortal slaughter. They realized that their efforts to convey to those back home the gruesome truth of combat were inadequate. "No tongue can tell, no mind can conceive, no pen portray the horrible sights I witnessed this morning," a Union soldier wrote after Antietam. And still they tried.

Trenches like this Confederate fortification at the Battle of Petersburg disrupted both the land and the forests that supplied the wood.

An Indiana soldier at Perryville (7,600 casualties): "It was an awful sight to see there men torn all to pieces with cannon balls and bom shells[.] [T]he dead and wounded lay thick in all directions." An Ohio soldier at Antietam (23,000 casualties), two days after the fighting: "The smell was offul . . . there was about 5 or 6,000 dead bodes decaying over the field. . . . I could have walked on the boddees all most from one end too the other." A Georgian, the day after Chancellorsville (30,000 casualties): "It looked more like a slaughter pen than anything else. . . . The shrieks and groans of the wounded . . . was heart rending beyond all description." A Maine soldier who fought at Gettysburg (50,000 casualties): "I have Seen . . . men rolling in their own blood, Some Shot in one place, Some another . . . our dead lay in the road and the Rebels in their hast to leave dragged both their baggage wagons and artillery over them and they lay mangled and torn to pieces so that Even friends could not tell them. You can form no idea of a battlefield."

Surrounded by the wreckage of war, amid the sounds and smells and sight of thousands of dead or dying men, soldiers who fell on the battlefield struggled to die as they thought they should. If they made it to a camp hospital, they might look to exhausted nurses, doctors, or aides to stay with them in their final moments. They might give comrades or outright strangers messages for kin—parents, wives, siblings, and children they knew they would never see again. Many tens of thousands simply died where they fell; some immediately, others more slowly, and some others granted final moments with treasured photographs or with letters from people they loved. Survivors became hardened through horror. "The daily sight of blood and mangled bodies," observed a Rhode Island soldier, "so blunted their finer sensibilities as almost to blot out all love, all sympathy from the heart."

THE BUSINESS OF GRIEF

This multitude of war dead forced immense tasks upon the living. Millions of people across the country would spend years and lifetimes grieving as a consequence of the war. They wanted to know how their loved ones died, wanted to know where their bodies were, and, increasingly, wanted to retrieve those bodies and bury them closer to home. The railroad network and the new practice of embalming made this heartfelt desire possible for the first time in the history of warfare. Volunteers like Clara Barton organized to help grieving families locate the bodies of their fallen soldiers. A feverish alliance of shipping agents and undertakers emerged to meet demand. Embalmers propped up the preserved corpses of unknown dead in shop windows to advertise their services. Responding to popular pressure, the U.S. government pledged to help in the task of identification and recovery—eventually spending $4 million to identify the resting places of half the Union's fallen soldiers and to reburying most of them. Not until 1906 would the national government assume the same responsibilities for Confederate dead. Instead, such tasks fell to state governments and, after the war, to civic organizations like the Daughters of the Confederacy.

 **REVIEW**

How did the massive and constant presence of death change Civil War Americans?

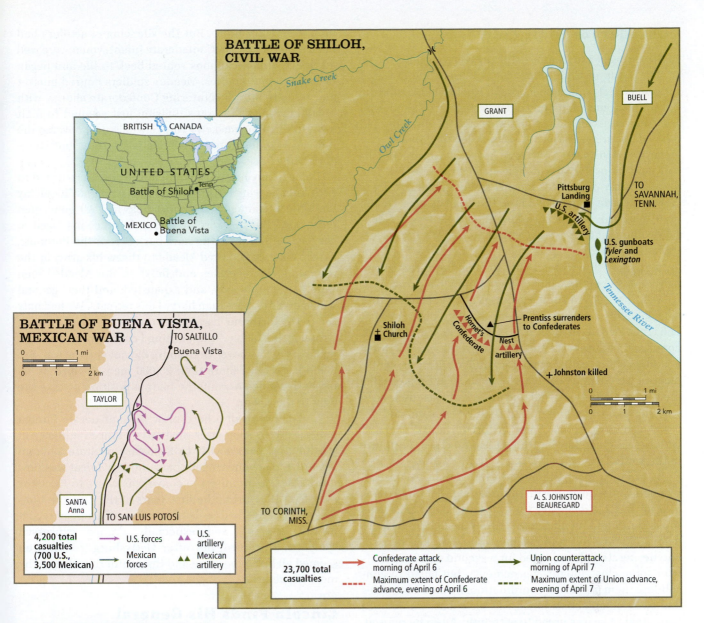

BATTLE OF SHILOH, CIVIL WAR

BRITISH CANADA

UNITED STATES

Battle of Shiloh — Tenn.

MEXICO

Battle of Buena Vista

Snake Creek

Owl Creek

GRANT

BUELL

Pittsburg Landing

U.S. artillery

TO SAVANNAH, TENN.

U.S. gunboats *Tyler* and *Lexington*

Tennessee River

Shiloh Church

Hornet's

Confederate

Prentiss surrenders to Confederates

Nest artillery

Johnston killed

TO CORINTH, MISS.

A. S. JOHNSTON BEAUREGARD

BATTLE OF BUENA VISTA, MEXICAN WAR

0   1 mi
0   1   2 km

TO SALTILLO

Buena Vista

TAYLOR

SANTA Anna

TO SAN LUIS POTOSÍ

| 4,200 total casualties (700 U.S., 3,500 Mexican) | U.S. forces | U.S. artillery |
| | Mexican forces | Mexican artillery |

0   1 mi
0   1   2 km

| 23,700 total casualties | Confederate attack, morning of April 6 | Union counterattack, morning of April 7 |
| | Maximum extent of Confederate advance, evening of April 6 | Maximum extent of Union advance, evening of April 7 |

A NEW MAGNITUDE OF BATTLE

During the U.S.-Mexican War at Buena Vista, the American army of 4,800 men was overextended trying to defend a 2-mile line against 15,000 Mexicans. At Shiloh, in contrast, battle lines stretched almost 6 miles. (The maps are drawn to the same scale.) Against 40,000 Confederates, Grant galloped back and forth, rallying some 35,000 troops organized under five subordinates and coordinating the overnight reinforcement of 25,000 troops. The size of the armies, the complexity of their organization, the length of battle lines, and the number of casualties all demonstrate the extent to which the magnitude of battle had changed.

THE UNION'S TRIUMPH

WHILE TALKING TO A NEIGHBOR in Covington, Georgia, Dolly Lunt suddenly saw the bluecoats coming down the road. Thinking to herself, "Oh God, the time of trial has come!" she ran home as fast as she could. William Tecumseh Sherman's dreaded army had arrived at her gate. As the Union troops swarmed over the yard, they cleaned out the smokehouse and dairy, stripped the kitchen and cellar of their contents, and killed her fowl and hogs. They broke open locks, smashed down doors, seized items of no military value such as kitchen utensils and even a doll, and marched off some of the male slaves. Not content with plundering the main house, the troops entered the slave cabins and rifled them of every valuable, even the money some of the slaves had made by doing extra work. Lunt spent a supperless night huddled in the house with her remaining slaves, who were clutching their meager possessions. As darkness descended, she reported, "the heavens from every point were lit up with flames from burning buildings." The war had come to Dolly Lunt's doorstep.

Confederate High Tide

In the spring of 1863 matters still looked promising for Lee. At the Battle of Chancellorsville, he brilliantly defeated Lincoln's latest commander, Joseph Hooker. But during the fighting the ingenious and relentless General Stonewall Jackson was accidentally shot by his own men, and he died a few days later—a grievous setback for the Confederacy. Determined to take the offensive, Lee made a characteristically audacious decision and invaded Pennsylvania in June with an army of 75,000. Lincoln's newest general, George Gordon Meade, warily shadowed the Confederates. On the first of July, advance parties from the two armies accidentally collided at the town of Gettysburg, and the war's greatest battle ensued.

THE BATTLE OF GETTYSBURG The iconic battle unfolded over the course of three bloody days. Confederate forces enjoyed some successes at first, before either side had all its troops in position, and these successes left Lee emboldened. He instructed General Richard Ewell, in command of Stonewall Jackson's corps, to seize a critical Union position called Cemetery Ridge, "if practicable." Jackson would have taken this for an order and charged his men up the hill. But Ewell, far more cautious, took Lee's wording as a suggestion rather than a command and decided against an attack. Some historians have speculated whether this inaction was the critical missed opportunity in the battle.

By day two most Union and Confederate troops had reached Gettysburg. Northern forces arrayed themselves in a formidable defensive line—so formidable that Lee's top subordinate urged him to withdraw and find a more defensible position somewhere to the east. Lee refused, and desperate fighting raged for a second day. The rebels won some close-fought engagements, but failed to consolidate them for lack of coordination. By dusk both sides had endured great casualties, but the robust Union lines held. Again Lee was urged to withdraw. Again he refused. Convinced that he had left Union men bloodied and demoralized, he decided to mass his forces for a coordinated attack on Meade's center the following day. It would prove to be the costliest mistake of his military career.

Day three opened with some surprising Union victories, including one led by a dashing 23-year-old General named George Armstrong Custer. Not until early afternoon did Lee's plan become clear. Around 1 p.m. he gave the order and the sky exploded as massed Confederate artillery blasted away at the Union center. Meade responded in kind, and for an hour Gettysburg was a deafening furnace of explosions and shattering bodies. Then, one by one, the Union guns fell silent. Convinced that he had disabled Meade's artillery and believing victory was at hand, Lee ordered three Confederate divisions to take the Union positions. Remembered as "Pickett's Charge," after General George Pickett, the effort started off confidently with some 12,500 Confederate soldiers marching up to Cemetery Ridge. But the silencing of artillery had been a ruse; once the Confederate infantrymen were well advanced, union cannons roared back to life and began blasting them to pieces. Meade's soldiers poured musket and rifle fire into the cratering Confederate charge, with horrible results. "Pickett's division just seemed to melt away in the blue musketry smoke which now covered the hill," one Confederate officer wrote. "Nothing but stragglers came back."

Indeed, only half of the men in the charge returned to Lee's lines, leaving the great general distraught. "It's all my fault," he exclaimed. "You must help me. All good men must rally." But there would be no rally. Lee managed to get most of his surviving men back across the Potomac, barely. Lincoln implored Meade to throw his army at the retreating Confederates and finish it. But Meade's men were battered, bloody, and exhausted; and their general would do little more than harry Lee's retreat. "We had only to stretch forth our hands and they were ours," Lincoln wrote, inconsolably. "And nothing I could say or do could make the Army move." Gettysburg did not end the war. But it did rob Lee of more than 25,000 men—a third of his force. Never again would he be in a position to take the fight to the North.

Gettysburg dealt a hard blow to Confederate foreign policy as well. Soon after the battle, France's minister in Washington paid a visit to Secretary of State William Seward and acknowledged that southern defeat was now inevitable. He promised to convey his views to Emperor Napoléon III. During the first years of the war, the Confederacy had worked tirelessly to secure European recognition. England and especially France expressed sympathy in return, but after Gettysburg, recognition seemed all but impossible and the southern cause all the more desperate.

Lincoln Finds His General

CAPTURE OF VICKSBURG To the west, Grant had been trying for months to capture Vicksburg, a Rebel stronghold on the Mississippi. In a daring maneuver, he left behind his supply lines and marched inland, calculating that he could feed his army from the produce of Confederate farms, weakening southern resistance in the process. These actions were the tactics of total war, and seldom had they been tried before Grant used them. His troops drove the defenders of Vicksburg back into the city and starved them into submission. On July 4, the city surrendered. With the fall of Port Hudson, Louisiana, four days later, the Mississippi was completely in Union hands. Grant had divided the Confederacy and isolated Arkansas, Texas, and part of Louisiana from the rest of the South.

He followed up this victory by rescuing Union forces holed up in Chattanooga. His performance confirmed Lincoln's earlier judgment that "Grant is my man, and I am his the rest of the war." Congress now revived the rank of

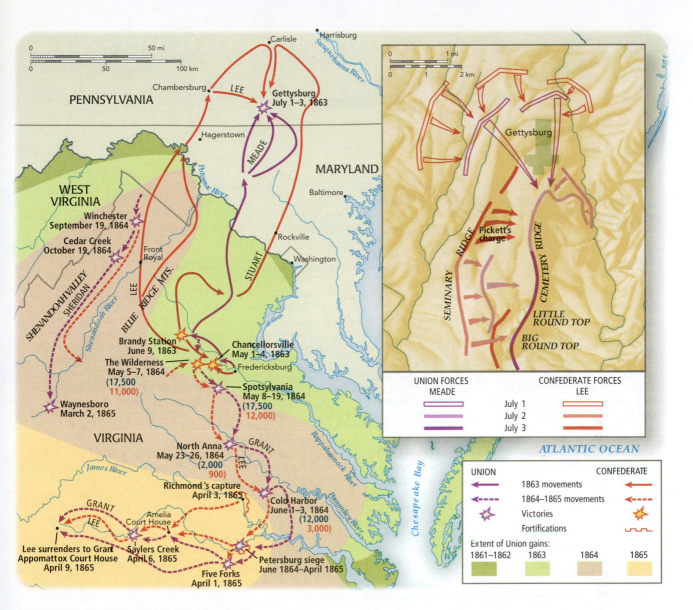

THE WAR IN THE EAST, 1863–1865

Lee won his most brilliant victory at Chancellorsville, then launched a second invasion of the North, hoping to score a decisive victory. When the two armies accidentally collided at Gettysburg on July 1, 1863, the Union's Army of the Potomac took up a strong defensive position, shaped like a fishhook and anchored by a hill at each end (see map inset). On July 2 the Confederate attack drove back the Union's left flank but failed to dislodge the right. Lee's assault on the center of the Union line on July 3 ended in a shattering defeat, and the Army of Northern Virginia retreated to Virginia. In 1864 Grant delivered a series of heavy blows against Lee's outnumbered forces in Virginia. Despite staggering losses, Grant relentlessly pressed on. Note the casualties listed for the spring and summer of 1864; from mid-May to mid-June, Grant lost nearly 60,000 men, equal to Lee's strength (listed in parentheses). Sheridan's raids against the civilian farms of the Shenandoah Valley helped deprive Lee of desperately needed supplies. In April 1865, too weak to defend Richmond any longer, Lee surrendered at the Appomattox Court House.

lieutenant general, held before only by George Washington, which Lincoln bestowed on Grant. In March 1864 Lincoln brought him east and put him in command of all the Union armies.

GRANT IN COMMAND Grant recognized that the Union possessed the resources to wear down the Confederacy but that its larger armies had "acted independently and without concert, like a balky team, no two ever pulling together." He intended to change that.

While he launched a major offensive against Lee in Virginia, William Tecumseh Sherman, who replaced Grant as commander of the western army, would drive a diagonal wedge through the Confederacy from Tennessee across Georgia. Grant's orders to Sherman were as blunt as his response had been that rainy night when the two had conferred at Shiloh: "Get into the interior of the enemy's country so far as you can, inflicting all the damage you can against their war resources."

DUELING DOCUMENTS

INVADERS AND DEFENDERS

William Christie from Minnesota was one of the Union soldiers under Grant's army as it besieged and then occupied Vicksburg. His letter shows the mixture of hardship, boredom, horror, and hilarity that were the lot of ordinary soldiers. Nancy Emerson lived in Augusta County, Virginia, in the Shenandoah Valley. She was a fervent Confederate who found Union raiders at her doorstep.

DOCUMENT 1   A Union View of Occupying Vicksburg: William Christie

July 19th Dear Brother I once more resume my pen, to scrible a few lines to you. We are much Pleased here with the Prospects in Tenn: and Penn, and are well satisfied with our own achievements. . . . The Mississippi River is oppen and the Southern Confedracy is cut in twain, it will be out of the question to think that the Pesky critter can live without the tail, and if Meade only gives the Head a scrunch with his heel we will soon make away with the Body.

This city is very nicely sittuated, and has been very handsome Before the war. I have been over the whole Place and I have changed my mind in regard to its appearance. Tis very filthy and although large gangs of Negroes have been employed in cleaning the streets, there has been But little, apparently, (comparitivly speaking) done the Rebels have been very filthy [during the siege], and it has just been here as every

where else. We have been driven to a great Deal of work for healths sake. There are waggon loads of old rags of clothing, full of vermin and disgusting to Behold, there are one or two Rebel hospitals in town, and you can tell long before you come near them By the odorous stench, where they are, and let me assure you that they as a general thing have a Peculiar odor, belong[ing] to their camps and hospitals, and you can tell when Passing through a country, where troops of Both sides have been camped. the difference, between each camp By the smell even before you see a scrap of clothing or anything else to tell the difference by. . . .

You complain of having nothing to write about, what do you suppose we Poor Devils have to write about, nothing only drumming here: and drumming there, drumming everywhere, and fiffing for the same. . . . Next we might tell of transport hot weather, then of

the daily arrivals of Contraband, from the cane brakes, where they have been hid away by there masters, untill so near dead with exposure and want, poisoned by vines of various kinds, and in such horrid Plight, that numbers drop Dead in the streets, or lie down in some unoccupied house, and die. Is this war too much for the Nation, that has had such a system in it that bears such fruits. No, and untill this accursed thing is Put from among us there will be no end to the war. . . .

My letters are wearisome, I know. But there is only one excuse for me writing and that is it lets you know I am well, I am also light in weight, (not to say or imply anything else) Being, only 140 lbs. By the scales so you see I am But a bunch of Bones: But lively and well. . . . Be Patient in all things, is my advice to you and if I had only written so at the head of this letter you would have been profittably warned and spared you

---

UNION'S SUMMER OFFENSIVE

In May and June 1864 Grant tried to maneuver Lee out of the trenches and into an open battle. But Lee was too weak to win head-on, so he opted for a strategy of attrition, hoping to inflict such heavy losses that the northern will to continue fighting would break. It was a strategy that nearly worked, for Union casualties were staggering. In a month of fierce fighting, the Army of the Potomac lost 60,000 men— the size of Lee's entire army at the beginning of the campaign. Yet at the end of the campaign Grant's reinforced army was larger than when it started, whereas Lee's was significantly weaker.

After especially bloody losses at the Battle of Cold Harbor, Grant changed tactics. He marched his army around Richmond and settled into a siege of Petersburg, which guarded Richmond's last remaining rail link to the south. A siege would be agonizingly slow, but he counted on his numerical superiority to eventually stretch Lee's line

to the breaking point. In the west, meanwhile, the gaunt and grizzled Sherman fought his way by July to the outskirts of Atlanta, which was heavily defended. "Our all depends on that army at Atlanta," wrote Mary Chesnut in August, based on her conversations with Confederate leaders. "If that fails us, the game is up."

War in the Balance

The game was nearly up for Lincoln as the 1864 election approached. In 1863 the victories at Gettysburg and Vicksburg sparked Republican victories, indicating that public opinion seemed to be swinging toward emancipation. But as the Union war machine swept more and more northerners south to their deaths and as Grant and Sherman bogged down on the Virginia and Georgia fronts, even leaders in Lincoln's own party began to mutter out loud that Lincoln was not equal to the task.

self the trouble of reading such a jumble of nonsense, Read and forgive, and Remember me to all,

Believe me your affecttionate Brother

Wm G. Christie

Source: Letter of William G. Christie, July 16 [and 19], 1862. Minnesota Historical Society, facsimile text at www.mnhs.org/library/Christie/letters/0716631.html.

DOCUMENT 2   A Confederate View of Union Raiders: Nancy Emerson

Our friends at the North have probably been thinking some about us of late, hearing that the Yankees have taken Staunton, though *what* they have thought is beyond my power to divine, ignorant as we are of each others feelings. Sister C. & I very often talk of them, wonder how they fare & what they think of us, whether they set us down for incorrigible rebels against "the best government in the world," always winding up however by arguing that we do not & cannot believe they favor this unjust & abominable war, though such strange things happen these days that nothing ought to astonish us. . . .

The first day, they came in from the West, across the mountain. A party of 40 or 50 perhaps, came riding up, dismounted & rushed in. "Have you got any whiskey" said they, "got any flour? got any bacon?" with plenty of oaths "Come on boys," says one, "we'll find it all" With that, they pushed rudely by Sister C. who was terribly alarmed, & had been from the first news of their coming, & spread them selves nearly all over the house. Finding their way to a fine barrel of flour which a neighbor had given us, they proceeded to fill their sacks & pillow cases, scattering a large percent on the floor, till it was nearly exhausted. . . . Some went upstairs, opened every trunk & drawer & tossed things upside down or on the floor, even my nice bonnets, pretending to be looking for arms. . . . We did not say anything to provoke them, but did not disguise our sentiments. They went peeping under the beds,

looking for rebels as they said. Baxter told them there were no rebels here (meaning rebel soldiers) Cate spoke & said *We are all rebels.* Ellen spoke & said "Yes Baxter, I am a rebel." The Yankee looked up from her drawer, which he was searching just then, & said "That's right." Cate then said, "I am a rebel too & I *glory* in it." . . .

At one of our neighbors, they took every thing they had to eat, all the pillow cases & sheets but what were on the beds, & the towels & some of the ladies stockings. . . . At another neighbors, they took all of their meat (some 30 pieces of bacon) & nearly everything else they had to eat, all their horses (4) & persuaded off their two negro men. One of these was afterwards seen by one of our men crying to come back, but was watched so closely that he could not escape. No wonder he cried. He has been twice on the brink of the grave with pneumonia, & was nursed by his mistress as tenderly as if he had been a brother, & she was always kind to him, his master also. He will not find such treatment anywhere else. . . .

Some hid their things & had them discovered but we were more fortunate. (Some were betrayed by their servants) Some hid nothing, thinking they would not be disturbed but found themselves woefully mistaken. Others thought they might be worse dealt with if they hid anything. A lady near Staunton a little time since had two Yankee officers come to take tea with her. She was

strong "secesh," but she got them a good supper. It was served up in very plain dishes. They perceived that she was wealthy, & inquired if she had not hid her plate &c. She told them she had. They asked *where.* She told them in the ash heap. They said "That is not a good place. It is the first place searched." They then very kindly & politely showed her a good place (in their opinion). She followed their advice & saved her things. In another instance, some Yankee officers politely showed a lady where to hide her silver &c. The soldiers came & searched in vain. Just as they were going away, a little black chap who had followed them around says to them in a tone of triumph, "Ah you did not find Missis things hid inside the "

Source: The Diary of Nancy Emerson, Albert and Shirley Small Special Collections Library, University of Virginia, Charlottesville, Virginia. Available online at http://valley.lib.virginia.edu/papers/EmeDiar#n5.

Thinking Critically

What is the "Pesky critter" in William Christie's first paragraph? What does he mean by "this accursed thing" in the second to last paragraph? Nancy Emerson indicates that she is strongly "secesh." But in what ways is she ambivalent about Northerners? What range of experiences do these documents reveal in the behavior of slaves?

1864 ELECTION   Perhaps the most remarkable thing about the 1864 election is that it was held at all. Indeed, before World War II, the United States was the only democratic government in history to carry out a general election in wartime. But Lincoln firmly believed that to postpone it would be to lose the priceless heritage of republicanism itself: "We cannot have free government without elections, and if the rebellion could force us to forego or postpone a national election, it might fairly claim to have already conquered and ruined us." Exploiting his control of the party machinery, Lincoln easily won the Republican nomination, and he made certain that the Republican platform called for the adoption of a constitutional amendment abolishing slavery. To balance the ticket, the convention selected Andrew Johnson, the military governor of Tennessee and a pro-war Democrat, as his running mate. The two men ran under the label of the "Union" Party.

The Democrats nominated George McClellan, the former Union commander. Their platform pronounced the war a failure and called for an armistice and a peace conference. Warned that a cessation of fighting would lead to disunion, McClellan partially repudiated this position, insisting that "the Union is the one condition of peace—we ask no more." In private he made it clear that if elected he intended to restore slavery. Late in August, Lincoln was still gloomy about his prospects as well as those of the Union itself. But Admiral David Farragut won a dramatic victory at Mobile Bay, and a few weeks later, in early September, Sherman finally captured Atlanta. As Secretary of State Seward gleefully noted, "Sherman and Farragut have knocked the bottom out of the Chicago [Democratic] nominations."

SIGNIFICANCE OF LINCOLN'S REELECTION   Polling an impressive 55 percent of the popular vote, Lincoln won 212 electoral votes to McClellan's 21. Eighteen states allowed soldiers to vote in the field, and Lincoln

Union soldiers vote in the election of 1864, in a camp near Petersburg, Virginia. The troops gave strong support to Lincoln—nearly 80 percent, compared to 55 percent of the popular vote.

received nearly 80 percent of their ballots. One lifelong Democrat described the sentiment in the army: "We all want peace, but none any but an honorable one. I had rather stay out here a lifetime (much as I dislike it) than consent to a division of our country." Jefferson Davis remained defiant, but the last hope of a Confederate victory was gone.

THIRTEENTH AMENDMENT Equally important, the election of 1864 ended any doubt that slavery would be abolished in the reconstructed Union. The Emancipation Proclamation had not put an end to the question, for its legal status remained unclear. Lincoln and the Republicans insisted that a constitutional amendment was necessary to secure emancipation. After the election, the president threw all his influence behind the drive to round up the necessary votes, and the measure passed the House on January 31, 1865. By December enough states had ratified the Thirteenth Amendment to make it part of the Constitution.

 ABOLITION AS A GLOBAL MOVEMENT The abolition of slavery in the United States was part of a worldwide trend. The antislavery movement was spearheaded in Britain, where Parliament abolished slavery in the empire in 1833. The other colonial powers were much slower to act. Portugal did not end slavery in its New World colonies until 1836, Sweden in 1847, Denmark and France in 1848, Holland in 1863, and Spain not until 1886. Most of the Latin American republics had ended slavery when they threw off Spanish or Portuguese control, but the institution remained important in Cuba and Brazil; Spain abolished slavery in Cuba in 1886, and Brazil ended the institution in 1888. European reformers also crusaded against slavery in Africa and Asia, and indeed the antislavery movement increased European presence in Africa. At the same time, European nations ended the medieval institution of serfdom. In Russia, where serfdom had most closely approximated slavery, Czar Alexander II emancipated the serfs in 1861,

an act that led him to strongly favor the Union in the American Civil War.

The Twilight of the Confederacy

CONFEDERACY'S ABANDONMENT OF SLAVERY For the Confederacy the outcome of the 1864 election had a terrible finality. At the beginning of the war, Vice President Stephens had proclaimed slavery the cornerstone of the Confederacy, but in March 1865 the Confederate Congress authorized recruiting 300,000 slaves for military service. When signing the bill, Davis announced that freedom would be given to those who volunteered and to their families. That same month he offered through a special envoy to abolish slavery in exchange for British diplomatic recognition. A Mississippi paper denounced this proposal as "a total abandonment of the chief object of this war." The British rejected the offer, and the war ended before any slaves were mustered into the Confederate army, but the abandonment of slavery surely completed the Confederacy's internal revolution. The demands of total war had forced Confederate leaders to forsake the Old South's fundamental values and institutions.

In the wake of Lincoln's reelection the Confederate will to resist rapidly disintegrated. White southerners had never fully united behind the war effort, but the large majority had endured great suffering to uphold it. As Sherman pushed deeper into the Confederacy and General Philip Sheridan mounted his devastating raid on the Shenandoah Valley, the war came home to southern civilians as never before. "We haven't got nothing in the house to eat but a little bit o meal," wrote the wife of one Alabama soldier in December 1864. "Try to get off and come home and fix us all up some and then you can go back. . . . If you put off a-coming, 'twont be no use to come, for we'll all . . . [be] in the grave yard." He deserted. In the last months of the fighting, more than half the Confederacy's soldiers were absent without leave.

MARCH TO THE SEA After the fall of Atlanta, Sherman gave a frightening demonstration of total war. Imitating Grant's strategy he abandoned his supply lines for an audacious 300-mile march to the sea. Sherman intended to deprive Lee's army of the supplies it desperately needed to continue and to break the southern will to resist. Or as he bluntly put it, "to whip the Rebels, to humble their pride, to follow them to their recesses, and make them fear and dread us."

Moving in four columns, Sherman's army covered about 10 miles a day, cutting a path of destruction 50 miles wide. "We had a gay old campaign," one of his soldiers wrote. "Destroyed all we could not eat, stole their niggers, burned their cotton and gins, spilled their sorghum, burned and twisted their railroads and raised Hell generally." Sherman estimated that his men did $100 million in damage, of which $20 million was necessary to supply his army and the rest was wanton destruction.

After he captured Savannah in late December, he turned north and wreaked even greater havoc in South Carolina, which Union troops considered the seedbed of the rebellion.

By December the interior of the Confederacy was essentially conquered. Only Lee's army remained, entrenched around Petersburg, Virginia, as Grant relentlessly extended his lines, stretching the Confederates thinner and thinner. On April 2 Confederate forces evacuated Richmond.

LEE'S SURRENDER Grant doggedly pursued the Army of Northern Virginia westward for another hundred miles. After Union forces captured supplies waiting for Lee at Appomattox Court House, the weary gentleman from Virginia asked to see Grant. Lee surrendered on April 9, 1865. As the vanquished foe mounted his horse, Grant saluted by raising his hat; Lee raised his respectfully and rode off at a slow trot. "On our part," one federal officer wrote, there was "not a sound of trumpet . . . nor roll of drum; not a cheer . . . but an awed stillness rather." The guns were quiet.

With Lee's army gone, resistance throughout the Confederacy collapsed within a matter of weeks. Visiting the captured city of Richmond on April 4, Lincoln was enthusiastically greeted by the black population. He looked "pale, haggard, utterly worn out," noted one observer. The lines in his face showed how much the war had aged him in only four years. Often his friends had counseled rest, but Lincoln had observed that "the tired part of me is *inside* and out of reach." Day after day, the grim telegrams had arrived at the War Department, or mothers had come to see him, begging him to spare their youngest son because the other two had died in battle. The burden, he confessed, was almost too much to bear.

LINCOLN'S ASSASSINATION Back in Washington the president received news of Lee's surrender with relief. The evening of April 14, Lincoln, seeking a welcome escape, went to see a comedy at Ford's Theater. In the midst of the performance John Wilkes Booth, a mentally unstable actor and Confederate sympathizer, slipped into the presidential box and shot him. Lincoln died the next morning. As he had called upon his fellow Americans to do in his Gettysburg Address, the sixteenth president had given his "last full measure of devotion" to the Republic.

✅ **REVIEW**

What decisions by Grant and Lincoln led the Union to victory?

General William Sherman demonstrated the tactics of total war in the autumn of 1864. "Destroyed all we could not eat . . . burned their cotton and gins . . . burned and twisted their railroads . . . ," wrote one of Sherman's soldiers. This drawing, done by a Union private, depicts a similar destructive raid on a plantation along Virginia's James River in 1862, and by the spring of 1865 Confederate armies were increasingly unable to resist Union might.

TROOPS BURNING "THE COLE HOUSE" and PLANTATION. OPPOSITE HARRISON'S

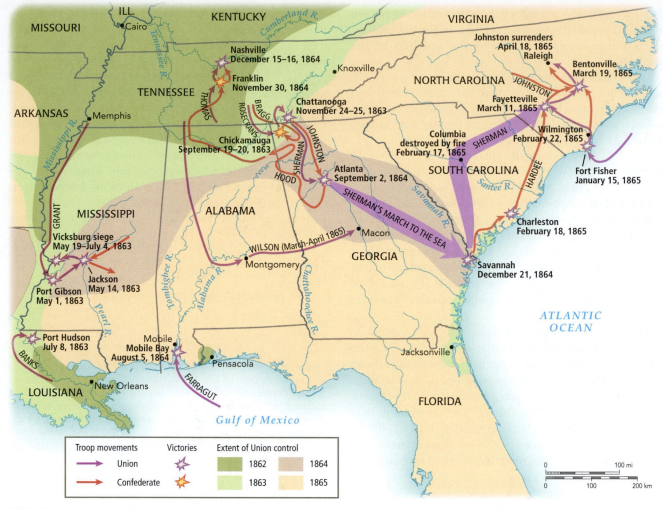

THE WAR IN THE WEST, 1863–1865

The Union continued its war of mobility in the western theater, bringing more Confederate territory under its control. After Grant captured Vicksburg, the entire Mississippi lay in Union hands. His victories at Lookout Mountain and Missionary Ridge, near Chattanooga, ended the Confederate threat to Tennessee. In 1864 Sherman divided the Confederacy by seizing Atlanta and marching across Georgia; then he turned north. When Joseph Johnston surrendered several weeks after Lee's capitulation at Appomattox, the war was effectively over.

The war's greatest generals, Ulysses S. Grant (left) and Robert E. Lee (right), confronted each other in the eastern theater during the last year of the war. A member of a distinguished Virginia family, the tall, impeccably dressed Lee was every inch the aristocratic gentleman. Grant, a short, slouched figure with a stubby beard, dressed indifferently, often wearing a private's uniform with only the stars on his shoulders to indicate his rank. But his determination is readily apparent in this picture, taken at his field headquarters in 1864.

CONCLUSION

THE WORLD AT LARGE

The assassination, which capped four years of bloody war, left a tiredness in the nation's bones—a tiredness "inside" and not easily within reach. In every way the conflict had produced fundamental, often devastating changes. There was, of course, the carnage. Hundreds of thousands of men on both sides lost their lives, almost as many as in all the other wars the nation has fought from the Revolution through Vietnam combined. In material terms, the conflict cost an estimated $20 billion, or about 10 times the value of all slaves in the country in 1860 and more than 11 times the total amount spent by the federal government from 1789 to 1861. Even without adding the market value of freed slaves, southern wealth declined 43 percent, transforming what had been the richest section in the nation (on a white per-capita basis) into the poorest.

The Civil War reordered not only the national economy but also economic relations worldwide. Manufacturers were forced to supply the army on an unprecedented scale over great distances. One consequence was the creation of truly national industries in flour milling, meat packing, clothing and shoe manufacture, and machinery making.

People across the globe felt the effects of the war, particularly due to changes in the cotton trade. By 1860 the South was supplying more than three-quarters of all cotton imported by Britain, France, Germany, and Russia. When the war cut off that supply, manufacturers scrambled to find new sources. India, Egypt, and Brazil all improved their railroad facilities and ports in order to encourage planters to open new cotton fields. The effect of the trade on Egypt was so great, historians of that nation rank the American Civil War along with the construction of the Suez Canal as the most crucial events in its nineteenth-century history.

Politically, the war dramatically changed the balance of power. The South lost its substantial influence, as did the Democratic Party, while the Republicans emerged in a dominant position. The Union's military victory also signaled the triumph of nationalism. The war destroyed the idea that the Union was a voluntary confederacy of sovereign states. The Union was perpetual, as Andrew Jackson had first suggested—truly an indivisible nation.

In the short run the price was disillusionment and bitterness. The war's corrosive effect on morals corrupted American politics, destroyed idealism, and crippled humanitarian reform. Millennialism and perfectionism were victims of the war's appalling slaughter, forsaken for a new emphasis on practicality, order, materialism, and science.

George Ticknor, a prominent critic of the day, reflected on the changes that had shaken the nation. The war, it seemed to him, had left "a great gulf between what happened before it in our century and what has happened since. . . . It does not seem to me as if I were living in the country in which I was born." ∞∞∞

CHAPTER SUMMARY

FOR THE FIRST TOTAL WAR in history, the Civil War's outcome depended not just on armies but also on the mobilization of each society's human, economic, and intellectual resources.

- Confederate president Jefferson Davis's policy of concentrating power in the government at Richmond, along with the resort to a draft and impressment of private property, provoked strong protests from many southerners.

- Abraham Lincoln's suspension of habeas corpus and interference with civil liberties were equally controversial.

- But Lincoln skillfully kept the border states in the Union.

- Lincoln at first resisted pressure to make emancipation a Union war aim, but he eventually issued the Emancipation Proclamation, which transformed the meaning of the war.

- African Americans helped undermine slavery and contributed vitally to the Union's military victory.

- On the home front, women confronted new responsibilities and enjoyed new occupational opportunities.

- Confederate financial and tax policies and the tightening Union blockade increased hardships within the Confederacy.

- Technology, particularly the use of rifles and rifled artillery, revolutionized the tactics of warfare.

- The Union victory at Gettysburg and Lincoln's choice of Grant to lead Union forces marked the turning point of the war. Union success relied in part on the strategy of attacking the civilian population of the South.

ADDITIONAL READING

A GOOD SINGLE-VOLUME HISTORY OF the Civil War remains James M. McPherson's *Battle Cry of Freedom* (1988). Some historians have questioned whether the conflict should be considered a "total war." McPherson argues that it should in *Drawn with the Sword* (1996); Mark Neely makes the opposite case in *The Civil War and the Limits of Destruction* (2007). For the evolution of the Union's strategy toward southern civilians, see Mark Grimsley, *The Hard Hand of War* (1995).

The best biography of Lincoln is David Donald, *Lincoln* (1995). William E. Gienapp, *Abraham Lincoln and Civil War America* (2002), is concise and focuses on the presidential years. The president's complex thinking on slavery is the subject of Eric Foner's masterful book *The Fiery Trial* (2011). For the contradictions of the southern project, see Stephanie McCurry, *Confederate Reckoning* (2010). Drew Gilpin Faust, *Mothers of Invention* (1996), is an imaginative study of slaveholding women; Edward Ayers, *In the Presence of Mine Enemies* (2003), examines the consequences of war in Virginia and Pennsylvania. For the northern home front, see J. Matthew Gallman, *The North Fights the Civil War* (1994). Chandra Manning, in *What This Cruel War Was Over* (2007), argues that Union rank-and-file widely believed in emancipation as early as the end of 1861. Drew Gilpin Faust, *This Republic of Suffering* (2008), brilliantly explores how death, grieving, and belief were changed by this most deadly of wars. For Britain's critical role in the diplomacy of the Civil War, see Amanda Foreman's *A World on Fire* (2011).

For a fuller list of readings, see the Bibliography at www.mhhe.com/eh8e.

SIGNIFICANT EVENTS

1861
Border states remain in the Union; Battle of Bull Run

1862
Forts Henry and Donelson captured; Battle of Shiloh; New Orleans captured; McClellan's peninsula campaign fails; Battle of Antietam; Lincoln suspends writ of habeas corpus throughout the Union; Battle of Fredericksburg

1863
Emancipation Proclamation issued; Union institutes conscription; Confederacy enacts general tax laws, initiates impressment; bread riots in the Confederacy; Battle of Gettysburg; Vicksburg captured; New York City draft riots

1864
Grant becomes Union general in chief; Grant's Virginia offensive; siege of Petersburg; fall of Atlanta; Lincoln reelected; Sherman's march to the sea

1865
Sherman's march through the Carolinas; Lee surrenders; Lincoln assassinated; Thirteenth Amendment ratified

	MILITARY	POLITICAL	SOCIAL/ECONOMIC
1861	Naval blockade set up	Lincoln secures border states for Union; First Confiscation Act frees slaves used for Confederate military purposes	Wartime demand sparks economic boom in industry and agriculture
1862	Grant succeeds in his western campaigns	Legal Tender Act; first federal income tax	Northern factories turn out military supplies; railroad construction
1863	Stonewall Jackson dies; Battles of Gettysburg and Vicksburg	Emancipation Proclamation issued	African Americans increasingly defect from southern plantations, join Union forces
1864	Grant given command of Union armies; Sherman marches through Georgia, captures Atlanta	Lincoln wins election in middle of war	Broader public support as military victories buoy North
1865	Sherman drives through Carolinas; Appomattox Court House		

the sale was so unusual that the parties involved agreed to keep it secret, since the Montgomerys were black, and Mississippi law prohibited African Americans from owning land.

Though a slave, Montgomery had been the business manager of the two Davis plantations before the war. He had also operated a store on Hurricane Plantation for white as well as black customers with his own line of credit in New Orleans. In 1863 Montgomery fled to the North, but when the war was over, he returned to Davis Bend, where the federal government was leasing plots of the land on confiscated plantations, including Hurricane and Brierfield, to black farmers. Montgomery quickly emerged as the leader of the African American community at the Bend.

Then, in 1866, President Andrew Johnson pardoned Joseph Davis and restored his lands. By then Davis was over 80 years old and lacked the will and stamina to rebuild. Yet unlike many ex-slaveholders, he still felt bound by obligations to his former slaves. He was convinced that with proper encouragement African Americans could succeed economically in freedom. Only when the law prohibiting African Americans from owning land was overturned in 1867 did Davis publicly confirm the sale to his former slave.

For his part, Montgomery undertook to create a model society at Davis Bend based on mutual cooperation. He rented land to black farmers, hired others to work his own fields, sold supplies on credit, and ginned and marketed the crops. To the growing African American community, he preached the gospel of hard work, self-reliance, and education.

Various difficulties dogged these black farmers, including the destruction caused by the war, several disastrous floods, insects, droughts, and declining cotton prices. Yet before long, cotton production exceeded that of the prewar years, and in 1870 the black families at Davis Bend produced 2,500 bales. The Montgomerys eventually acquired another plantation and owned 5,500 acres, which made them reputedly the third-largest planters in the state. They won national and international awards for the quality of their cotton. Their success demonstrated what African Americans, given a fair chance, might accomplish.

| Benjamin Montgomery

The experiences of Benjamin Montgomery during the years after 1865 were not those of most black southerners, who did not own land or have a powerful white benefactor. Yet Montgomery's dream of economic independence was shared by all African Americans. As one black veteran noted, "Every colored man will be a slave, and feel himself a slave until he can raise him own bale of cotton and put him own mark upon it and say dis is mine!" Blacks could not gain effective freedom simply through a proclamation of emancipation. They needed economic power, including their own land that no one could unfairly take away.

For nearly two centuries the laws had prevented slaves from possessing such economic power. If those conditions were to be overturned, black Americans needed political power too. Thus the Republic would have to be reconstructed to give African Americans political power that they had been previously denied.

War, in its blunt way, had roughed out the contours of a solution, but only in broad terms. Clearly, African Americans would no longer be enslaved. The North, with its industrial might, would be the driving force in the nation's economy and retain the dominant political voice. But, beyond that, the outlines of a reconstructed Republic remained vague. Would African Americans receive effective power? How would the North and the South readjust their economic and political relations? These questions lay at the heart of the problem of Reconstruction. ∞∞∞

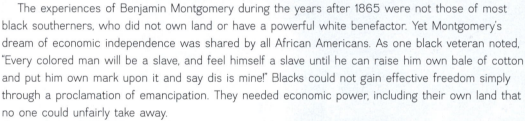

PRESIDENTIAL RECONSTRUCTION

THROUGHOUT THE WAR ABRAHAM LINCOLN had considered Reconstruction his responsibility. Elected with less than 40 percent of the popular vote in 1860, he was acutely aware that once the states of the Confederacy were restored to the Union, the Republicans would be weakened unless they ceased to be a sectional party. By a generous peace, Lincoln

hoped to attract former Whigs in the South, who supported many of the Republicans' economic policies, and build up a southern wing of the party.

Lincoln's 10 Percent Plan

Lincoln outlined his program in a Proclamation of **Amnesty** and Reconstruction issued in December 1863. When a

| A Visit from the Old Mistress, *by Winslow Homer, captures the conflicting, often awkward, emotions felt by both races after the war.*

minimum of 10 percent of the qualified voters from 1860 took a **loyalty oath** to the Union, they could organize a state government. The new state constitution had to be republican in form, abolish slavery, and provide for black education, but Lincoln did not insist that high-ranking Confederate leaders be barred from public life.

Lincoln indicated that he would be generous in granting pardons and did not rule out compensation for slave property. Moreover, while he privately suggested permitting some black men to vote in the disloyal states, "as for instance, the very intelligent and especially those who have fought gallantly in our ranks," he did not demand social or political equality for black Americans, and he recognized pro-Union governments in Louisiana, Arkansas, and Tennessee that allowed only white men to vote.

RADICAL REPUBLICANS The Radical Republicans found Lincoln's approach much too lenient. Strongly antislavery, Radical members of Congress had led the struggle to make emancipation a war aim. Now they were in the forefront in advocating rights for the freed people. Lincoln argued that the executive branch should bear the responsibility for restoring proper relations with the former Confederate states. The Radicals, on the other hand, believed that it was the duty of Congress to set the terms under which states would regain their rights in the Union. Though the Radicals often disagreed on other matters, they were united in a determination to readmit southern states only after slavery had been ended, black rights protected, and the power of the planter class destroyed.

WADE-DAVIS BILL Under the direction of Senator Benjamin Wade of Ohio and Representative Henry Winter Davis of Maryland, Congress formulated a much stricter plan of Reconstruction. It proposed that Confederate states be ruled temporarily by a military governor, required half the white adult males to take an oath of allegiance before drafting a new state constitution, and restricted political power to the hard-core Unionists in each state. When the Wade-Davis bill passed on the final day of the 1864 congressional session, Lincoln exercised his right of a **pocket veto.** Still, his own program could not succeed without the assistance of Congress, which refused to seat Unionist representatives who had been elected from Louisiana or Arkansas. As the war drew to a close, Lincoln appeared ready to make concessions to the Radicals. At his final cabinet meeting, he approved placing the defeated South temporarily under military rule. But only a few days later Booth's bullet found its mark, and Lincoln's final approach to Reconstruction would never be known.

The Mood of the South

In the wake of defeat, the immediate reaction among white southerners was one of shock, despair, and hopelessness. Some former Confederates, of course, were openly antagonistic. A North Carolina innkeeper remarked bitterly that Yankees had stolen his slaves, burned his house, and killed all his sons, leaving him only one privilege: "To hate 'em. I git up at half-past four in the morning, and sit up till twelve at night, to hate 'em." Most Confederate

The mood of white southerners at the end of the war was mixed. Many, like the veteran caricatured here by northern cartoonist Thomas Nast, remained hostile. Others, like Texas captain Samuel Foster, came to believe that the institution of slavery "had been abused" and that men "who actually owned and held slaves up to this time,—have now changed in their opinions regarding slavery . . . to see that for a man to have property in man was wrong, and that the 'Declaration of Independence' meant more than they had ever been able to see before."

soldiers were less defiant, having had their fill of war. Even among hostile civilians the feeling was widespread that the South must accept northern terms.

This psychological moment was critical. To prevent a resurgence of resistance, the president needed to lay out clearly what white southerners had to do to regain their old status in the Union. Any wavering on the peace terms could only increase the likelihood of resistance. Perhaps even a clear and firm policy would not have been enough. But with Lincoln's death, the executive power came to rest in far less capable hands.

Johnson's Program of Reconstruction

JOHNSON'S CHARACTER AND VALUES

Andrew Johnson, the new president, had been born in North Carolina and eventually moved to Tennessee, where he worked as a tailor. Barely able to read and write when he married, he rose to political power by portraying himself as the champion of the people against the wealthy planter class. "Some day I will show the stuck-up aristocrats who is running the country," he vowed as he began his political career. He had not opposed slavery before the war—in fact, he hoped to disperse slave ownership more widely in southern society. Although he accepted emancipation as one consequence of the war, Johnson remained a confirmed racist. "Damn the negroes," he said during the war, "I am fighting these traitorous aristocrats, their masters."

Because Johnson disliked the planter class, Republican Radicals in Congress expected him to uphold their views on Reconstruction. In fact, the new president did speak of trying Confederate leaders and breaking up planters' estates. Unlike most Republicans, however, Johnson strongly supported states' rights. Furthermore, his prickly personality made conflict between the president and Congress

| Andrew Johnson

inevitable. Scarred by his humble origins, Johnson remained an outsider throughout his life. When challenged or criticized he became tactless and inflexible, alienating even those who sought to work with him.

JOHNSON'S PROGRAM

Johnson moved quickly to return the southern states to their place in the Union. He prescribed a loyalty oath that white southerners would have to take to regain their civil and political rights and to have their property, except for slaves, restored. Excluded were high Confederate officials and those with property worth over $20,000, who had to apply for individual pardons. Johnson announced that once a state had drafted a new constitution and elected state officers and members of Congress, he would revoke martial law and recognize the new state government. Suffrage was limited to white citizens who had taken the loyalty oath. This plan was similar to Lincoln's, though more lenient. Only informally did Johnson ask that the southern states renounce their ordinances of secession, repudiate the Confederate debt, and ratify the proposed Thirteenth Amendment abolishing slavery.

The Failure of Johnson's Program

SOUTHERN DEFIANCE

The southern delegates who met to construct new governments were in no frame of mind to follow Johnson's recommendations. Several states merely repealed instead of repudiating their ordinances of secession, rejected the Thirteenth Amendment, or refused to repudiate the Confederate debt.

BLACK CODES

Nor did the new governments allow African Americans any political rights or make any effective provisions for black education. In addition, each state passed a series of laws, often modeled on its old slave code, that applied only to African Americans. These **black codes** did grant African Americans some rights that had not been enjoyed by slaves. They legalized marriages performed under slavery and allowed black southerners to hold and sell property and to sue and be sued in state courts. Yet their primary purpose was to keep African Americans as propertyless agricultural laborers with inferior legal rights. The new freedmen, or freedpeople, could not serve on juries, testify against whites, or work as they pleased. South Carolina forbade blacks to engage in anything other than agricultural labor without a special license; Mississippi prohibited them from buying or renting farmland. Most states ominously provided that black people who were vagrants could be arrested and hired out to land-owners. Many northerners were incensed by the restrictive black codes.

ELECTIONS IN THE SOUTH

Southern voters under Johnson's plan also defiantly elected prominent Confederate military and political leaders to office, headed by Alexander Stephens, the vice president of the Confederacy, who was elected senator from Georgia. At this point, Johnson could have called for new elections or admitted that a different program of Reconstruction was needed. Instead, he caved in. For all his harsh rhetoric, he shrank from the prospect of social upheaval, and he found it enormously gratifying when upper-class planters praised his conduct and requested pardons. As the lines of ex-Confederates waiting to see him lengthened, he began issuing special pardons almost as fast as they could be printed. In the next two years he pardoned some 13,500 former rebels.

| Thaddeus Stevens, Radical leader in the House

In private, Johnson warned southerners against a reckless course. Publicly he put on a bold face, announcing that Reconstruction had been successfully completed. But many members of Congress were deeply alarmed.

Johnson's Break with Congress

The new Congress was by no means of one mind. A small number of Democrats and a few conservative Republicans backed the president's program. At the other end of the spectrum, a larger group of Radical Republicans, led by Thaddeus Stevens, Charles Sumner, Benjamin Wade, and others, was bent on remaking southern society in the image of the North. Reconstruction must "revolutionize Southern institutions, habits, and manners," insisted Representative Stevens, ". . . or all our blood and treasure have been spent in vain." Unlike Johnson, Radicals championed civil and political rights for African Americans and believed that the only way to maintain loyal governments and develop a Republican Party in the South was to give black men the ballot.

As a minority, the Radicals could accomplish nothing without the aid of the moderate Republicans, the largest bloc in Congress. Led by William Pitt Fessenden and Lyman Trumbull, the moderates hoped to avoid a clash with the president, and they had no desire to foster social revolution or promote racial equality in the South. But they wanted to keep Confederate leaders from reassuming power, and they were convinced that the former slaves needed federal protection. Otherwise, Trumbull declared, the freedpeople would "be tyrannized over, abused, and virtually reenslaved."

Moderates agreed that the new southern governments were too harsh toward African Americans, but they feared that too great an emphasis on black civil rights would alienate northern voters.

In December 1865, when southern representatives to Congress appeared in Washington, a majority in Congress voted to exclude them. Congress also appointed a joint committee, chaired by Senator Fessenden, to look into how to implement Reconstruction. The split with the president became clearer when Congress passed a bill extending the life of the Freedmen's Bureau. Created in March 1865, the bureau provided emergency food, clothing, and medical care to war refugees (including white southerners) and took charge of settling freedpeople on abandoned lands. The new bill gave the bureau the added responsibilities of supervising special courts to resolve disputes involving freedpeople and establishing schools for black southerners. Although this bill passed with near unanimous Republican support, Johnson vetoed it. Congress failed to override his veto.

JOHNSON'S VETOES

Johnson also vetoed a civil rights bill designed to overturn the most severe provisions of the black codes. The law made African Americans citizens of the United States and granted them the right to own property, make contracts, and have access to courts as parties and witnesses. For most Republicans Johnson's action was the last straw, and in April 1866 Congress overrode his veto, the first major legislation in American history to be enacted over a presidential veto. Congress then approved a slightly revised Freedmen's Bureau bill in July and promptly overrode the president's veto. Johnson's refusal to compromise drove the moderates into the arms of the Radicals.

The Fourteenth Amendment

To prevent unrepentant Confederates from taking over the reconstructed state governments and denying African Americans basic freedoms, the Joint Committee on Reconstruction proposed an amendment to the Constitution, which passed both houses of Congress with the necessary two-thirds vote in June 1866. The amendment, coupled with the Freedmen's Bureau and civil rights bills, represented the moderates' terms for Reconstruction.

PROVISIONS OF THE AMENDMENT

The Fourteenth Amendment put a number of matters beyond the control of the president. The amendment guaranteed repayment of the national war debt and prohibited repayment of the Confederate debt. To counteract the president's wholesale pardons, it disqualified prominent Confederates from holding office and provided that only Congress by a two-thirds vote could remove this penalty. Because moderates, fearful of the reaction of white northerners, balked at giving the vote to African Americans, the amendment merely gave Congress the right to reduce the representation of any state

DUELING DOCUMENTS

EQUALITY AND THE VOTE IN RECONSTRUCTION

Debate swirled around not only the conditions southern states needed to fulfill to return to the Union but also the rights of citizenship granted to former slaves. At war's end, African Americans held a number of conventions to set forth their views (Document 1). Andrew Johnson privately conveyed to white southern leaders his idea of how they should act (Document 2). And Representative Thaddeus Stevens of Pennsylvania spoke for Radical Republicans (Document 3).

DOCUMENT 1   African Americans Seek the Vote

We, the delegates of the colored people of the State of Virginia . . . solemnly [declare] that we desire to live upon the most friendly and agreeable terms with all men; we feel no ill-will or prejudice towards our former oppressors . . . and that we believe that in this State we have still many warm and solid friends among the white people. . . .

We must, on the other hand, be allowed to aver and assert that we believe that we have among the white people of this State, many who are our most inveterate enemies . . .

who despise us simply because we are black, and more especially, because we have been made free by the power of the United States Government; and that they—the class last mentioned—will not, in our estimation, be willing to accord to us, as freemen, that protection which all freemen must contend for, if they would be worthy of freedom. . . .

We claim, then, as citizens of this State, the laws of the Commonwealth shall give to all men equal protection; that each and every man may appeal to the law for his equal

rights without regard to the color of his skin; and we believe this can only be done by extending to us the elective franchise, which we believe to be our inalienable right as freemen, and which the Declaration of Independence guarantees to all free citizens of this Government and which is the privilege of the nation.

Source: Proceedings of the Convention of the Colored People of Virginia . . . in Philip S. Foner and George E. Walker, eds., Proceedings of the Black State Conventions, 1840–1865 (Philadelphia, 1980), vol. 2, pp. 262–264.

DOCUMENT 2   President Johnson Advises Southern Leaders

I hope that without delay your convention will amend your State constitution . . . [to] adopt the amendment to the Constitution of the United States abolishing slavery. If you could extend the elective franchise to all persons of color who can read the Constitution of the United States in English and write their names, and to all persons of color who own real estate valued at not less

than two hundred and fifty dollars and pay taxes thereon, you would completely disarm the adversary and set an example the other States will follow. This you can do with perfect safety, and you would thus place Southern States in reference to the free persons of color upon the same basis with the free States. . . . And as a consequence the radicals, who are wild upon negro

franchise, will be completely foiled in their attempts to keep the Southern States from renewing their relations to the Union by not accepting their Senators and Representatives.

Source: Walter L. Fleming, ed., Documentary History of Reconstruction (Cleveland, 1906–1907), vol. 1, p. 177.

DOCUMENT 3   Representative Stevens on Equal Privileges

But this is not all that we ought to do before these inveterate rebels are invited to participate in our legislation. We have turned, or are about to turn, loose four million slaves without a hut to shelter them or a cent in their pockets. The infernal laws of slavery have prevented them from acquiring an education, understanding the commonest laws of contract, or of managing the ordinary business of life. This Congress is bound to provide for them until they can take care of themselves. If we do not furnish them with homesteads, and hedge them around with protective laws; if we leave them to the legislation of their late masters, we had better have left them in bondage . . . equal rights to all the privileges of the Government is innate to every immortal being, no matter what the

shape or color of the tabernacle which it inhabits. . . .

If equal privileges were granted to all, I should not expect to any but white men to be elected to office for long ages to come. . . . But it would still be beneficial to the weaker races. In a country where political divisions will always exist, their power, joined with just white men, would greatly modify, if it did not entirely prevent, the injustice of majorities. Without the right of suffrage in the late slave States, (I do not speak of the free States,) I believe the slaves had far better been left in bondage. . . .

[Men of influence] proclaim, "This is a white man's Government," and the whole coil of copperheads echo the same sentiment, and upstart, jealous Republicans join the cry. Is it any wonder ignorant foreigners and

illiterate natives should learn this doctrine, and be led to despise and maltreat a whole race of their fellow men?

Source: Congressional Globe, 39th Congress, 1st Session, 1865, pp. 72–73.

Thinking Critically

Each of the writers recommends that African Americans receive the vote in some way. Which document is the most radical? Which the least so? Who does President Johnson refer to as "the adversary"? How does he intend to "foil" the Radicals? And what does Thaddeus Steven not speak about? Why?

that did not have impartial male suffrage. The practical effect of this provision, which Radicals labeled a "swindle," was to allow northern states to restrict suffrage to whites if they wished, since unlike southern states they had few African Americans and thus would not be penalized.

The amendment's most important provision, Section 1, defined an American citizen as anyone born in the United States or naturalized, thereby automatically making African Americans citizens. Section 1 also prohibited states from abridging "the privileges or immunities" of citizens, depriving "any person of life, liberty, or property, without due process of law," or denying "any person . . . equal protection of the laws." The framers of the amendment probably intended to prohibit laws that applied to one race only, such as the black codes, or that made certain acts felonies when committed by black but not white people, or that decreed different penalties for the same crime when committed by white and black lawbreakers. The framers probably did not intend to prevent African Americans from being excluded from juries or to forbid segregation (the legal separation of the races) in schools and public places.

Nevertheless, Johnson denounced the proposed amendment and urged southern states not to ratify it. Ironically, of the seceded states only the president's own state ratified the amendment, and Congress readmitted Tennessee with no further restrictions. The telegram sent to Congress by a longtime foe of Johnson announcing Tennessee's approval ended, "Give my respects to the dead dog in the White House." The amendment was ratified in 1868.

The Elections of 1866

ANTIBLACK RIOTS

When Congress blocked his policies, Johnson undertook a speaking tour of the East and Midwest in the fall of 1866 to drum up popular support. But the president found it difficult to convince northern audiences that white southerners were fully repentant. News that summer of major race riots in Memphis and New Orleans heightened northern concern. Forty-six African Americans died when white mobs invaded the black section of Memphis, burning homes, churches, and schoolhouses. About the same number were killed in New Orleans when whites attacked both black and white delegates to a convention supporting black suffrage. "The negroes now know, to their sorrow, that it is best not to arouse the fury of the white man," boasted one Memphis newspaper. When the president encountered hostile audiences during his northern campaign, he made matters only worse by trading insults and ranting that the Radicals were traitors. Even supporters found his performance humiliating.

Not to be outdone, the Radicals vilified Johnson as a traitor aiming to turn the country over to rebels and Copperheads. Resorting to the tactic of "waving the **bloody shirt**," they appealed to voters by reviving bitter memories of the war. In a classic example of such rhetoric, Governor Oliver

This politician is literally "waving the bloody shirt"—using the bitter memories of the Civil War to rouse voters to side with Republicans.

Morton of Indiana proclaimed that "every bounty jumper, every deserter, every sneak who ran away from the draft calls himself a Democrat...Every 'Son of Liberty' who conspired to murder, burn, rob arsenals and release rebel prisoners calls himself a Democrat...In short, the Democratic Party may be described as a common sewer."

REPUDIATION OF JOHNSON

Voters soundly repudiated Johnson, as the Republicans won more than a two-thirds majority in both houses of Congress, every northern gubernatorial contest, and control of every northern legislature. The Radicals had reached the height of their power.

✓ **REVIEW**

What were Lincoln's and Andrew Johnson's approaches to Reconstruction, and why did Congress reject Johnson's approach?

CONGRESSIONAL RECONSTRUCTION

WITH A CLEAR MANDATE IN hand, congressional Republicans passed their own program of Reconstruction, beginning with the first Reconstruction Act in March 1867. Like all later pieces of Reconstruction legislation, it was repassed over Johnson's veto.

Placing the 10 unreconstructed states under military commanders, the act directed officials to include black adult males as voters but not former Confederates barred from holding office under the Fourteenth Amendment. State conventions would frame constitutions that provided for black suffrage and that disqualified prominent ex-Confederates from office. The first state legislatures to meet under the new constitution were required to ratify the

Fourteenth Amendment. Once these steps were completed and Congress approved the new state constitution, a state could send representatives to Congress.

RESISTANCE OF SOUTHERN WHITES

White southerners found these requirements so insulting that officials took no steps to register voters. Congress then enacted a second Reconstruction Act, also in March, ordering the local military commanders to put the machinery of Reconstruction into motion. Johnson's efforts to limit the power of military commanders produced a third act, passed in July, that upheld their superiority in all matters. When elections were held to ratify the new state constitutions, white southerners boycotted them in large numbers. Undaunted, Congress passed the fourth Reconstruction Act (March 1868), which required ratification of the constitution by only a majority of those voting rather than those who were registered.

By June 1868 Congress had readmitted the representatives of seven states. Georgia's state legislature expelled its black members once it had been readmitted, granting seats to those barred by Congress from holding office. Congress ordered the military commander to reverse these actions, and Georgia was then admitted a second time in July 1870. Texas, Virginia, and Mississippi did not complete the process until 1869.

Post-Emancipation Societies in the Americas

With the exception of Haiti's revolution (1791–1804), the United States was the only society in the Americas in which the destruction of slavery was accomplished by violence. But the United States, uniquely among these societies, enfranchised former slaves almost immediately after the emancipation. Thus in the United States former masters and slaves battled for control of the state in ways that did not occur in other post-emancipation societies. In most of the Caribbean, property requirements for voting left the planters in political control. Jamaica, for example, with a population of 500,000 in the 1860s, had only 3,000 voters.

Moreover, in reaction to political efforts to mobilize disenfranchised black peasants, Jamaican planters dissolved the assembly and reverted to being a Crown colony governed from London. Of the sugar islands, all but Barbados adopted the same policy, thereby blocking the potential for any future black peasant democracy. Nor did any of these societies have the counterparts of the Radical Republicans, a group of outsiders with political power that promoted the fundamental transformation of the post-emancipation South. These comparisons highlight the radicalism of Reconstruction in the United States, which alone saw an effort to forge an interracial democracy.

The Land Issue

BLACKS' DESIRE FOR LAND

While the political process of Reconstruction proceeded, Congress confronted the question of whether land should be given to former slaves to foster economic independence. At a meeting with Secretary of War Edwin Stanton near the end of the war, African American leaders declared, "The way we can best take care of ourselves is to have land, and till it by our own labor." During the war, the Second Confiscation Act of 1862 had authorized the government to seize and sell the property, including land, of supporters of the rebellion. In June 1866, however, President Johnson ruled that confiscation laws applied only to wartime.

Congress debated land confiscation off and on from December 1865 until early 1867. Thaddeus Stevens, a leading Radical in the House, advocated confiscating 394 million acres of land from about 70,000 of what he termed the "chief rebels" in the South, who made up less than 5 percent of the South's white families. He proposed to give 40 acres to every adult male freedperson and then sell the remaining land, which would amount to nine-tenths of the total, to pay off the public debt, compensate loyal southerners for losses they suffered during the war, and fund Union veterans'

THE SOUTHERN STATES DURING RECONSTRUCTION

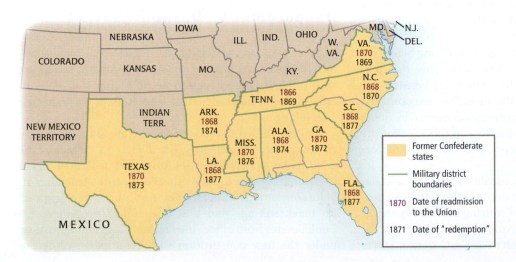

Former Confederate states

Military district boundaries

1870 Date of readmission to the Union

1871 Date of "redemption"

pensions. Land, he insisted, would be far more valuable to African Americans than the right to vote.

FAILURE OF LAND REDISTRIBUTION

But in the end Congress rejected all proposals. Given Americans' strong belief in self-reliance, little sympathy existed for the idea that government should support any group. In addition, land redistribution represented an attack on property rights, another cherished American value. By 1867 land reform was dead.

Few freedpeople acquired land after the war, a development that severely limited African Americans' economic independence and left them vulnerable to white coercion. It is doubtful, however, that this decision was the basic cause of the failure of Reconstruction. In the face of white hostility and institutionalized racism, African Americans probably would have been no more successful in protecting their property than they were in maintaining the right to vote.

Impeachment

TENURE OF OFFICE ACT

Throughout 1867 Congress routinely overrode Johnson's vetoes. Still, the president had other ways of undercutting congressional Reconstruction. He interpreted the new laws as narrowly as possible and removed military commanders who vigorously enforced them. Congress responded by restricting Johnson's power to issue orders to military commanders in the South. It also passed the Tenure of Office Act, which forbade Johnson to remove any member of the cabinet without the Senate's consent. The intention of this law was to prevent him from firing Secretary of War Edwin Stanton, the only Radical in the cabinet.

JOHNSON ACQUITTED

When Johnson tried to dismiss Stanton in February 1868, the determined secretary of war barricaded himself in his office (where he remained night and day for about two months). Angrily, the House of Representatives approved articles of impeachment. The articles focused on the violation of the Tenure of Office Act, but the charge with the most substance was that Johnson had conspired to systematically obstruct Reconstruction legislation. In the trial before the Senate, his lawyers argued that a president could be impeached only for an indictable crime, which Johnson clearly had not committed. The Radicals countered that impeachment applied to political offenses, not merely criminal acts. In May 1868 the Senate voted 36 to 19 to convict, one vote short of the two-thirds majority needed. The seven Republicans who joined the Democrats in voting for acquittal were uneasy about using impeachment as a political weapon.

✓ REVIEW

What was Congress's approach to Reconstruction, and why did it not include a provision for giving land to former slaves?

RECONSTRUCTION IN THE SOUTH

THE REFUSAL OF CONGRESS TO convict Johnson sent a clear signal: the power of the Radicals in Congress was waning. Increasingly the success or failure of Reconstruction hinged on developments not in Congress but in the southern states themselves. Power there rested with the new Republican parties, representing a coalition of black and white southerners and transplanted northerners.

Black Officeholding

Almost from the beginning of Reconstruction, African Americans had lobbied for the right to vote. After they received the **franchise,** black men constituted as much as 80 percent of the Republican voters in the South. They steadfastly opposed the Democratic Party with its appeal to white supremacy.

Throughout Reconstruction, African Americans never held office in proportion to their voting strength. No African American was ever elected governor, and only in South Carolina, where more than 60 percent of the population was black, did they control even one house of the legislature. During Reconstruction between 15 and 20 percent of the state officers and 6 percent of members of Congress (2 senators and 15 representatives) were black. Only in South Carolina did black officeholders approach their proportion of the population.

BACKGROUND OF BLACK POLITICAL LEADERS

Blacks who held office generally came from the top levels of African American society. Among state and federal officeholders, perhaps four-fifths were literate, and more than a quarter had been free before the war, both marks of distinction in the black community. Their occupations also set them apart: two-fifths were professionals (mostly clergy), and of the third who were farmers, nearly all owned land. Among black members of Congress, all but three had a secondary school education, and four had gone to

| Hiram Revels, a minister and educator, became the first African American to serve in the U.S. Senate, representing Mississippi. Later he served as president of Alcorn University.

college. In their political and social values, African American leaders were more conservative than the rural black population was, and they showed little interest in land reform.

White Republicans in the South

Black citizens were a majority of the voters only in South Carolina, Mississippi, and Louisiana. Thus in most of the South the Republican Party had to secure white votes to stay in power. Opponents scornfully labeled white southerners who allied with the Republican Party **scalawags,** yet an estimated quarter of white southerners at one time voted Republican. Although the party appealed to some wealthy planters, they were outnumbered by Unionists from the upland counties and hill areas who were largely yeoman farmers. Such voters were attracted by Republican promises to rebuild the South, restore prosperity, create public schools, and open isolated areas to the market with railroads.

The other group of white Republicans in the South was known as **carpetbaggers.** Originally from the North, they allegedly had arrived with all their worldly possessions stuffed in a carpetbag, ready to plunder the defeated South. Some did, but northerners moved south for a variety of reasons. Those in political office were especially well educated. Though carpetbaggers made up only a small percentage of

Harper's Illustrated Weekly *celebrated African Americans who voted for the first time in 1867. First in line is a skilled craftworker, his tools in his pocket; then an urban resident of some sophistication, followed by a veteran. Why would the artist choose these men as examples?*

Republican voters, they controlled almost a third of the offices in the South. More than half of all southern Republican governors and nearly half of Republican members of Congress were originally northerners.

DIVISIONS AMONG SOUTHERN REPUBLICANS

The Republican Party in the South had difficulty maintaining unity. Scalawags were especially susceptible to the race issue and social pressure. "Even my own kinspeople have turned the cold shoulder to me because I hold office under a Republican administration," testified a Mississippi white Republican. As black southerners pressed for greater recognition and a greater share of the offices, white southerners increasingly defected to the Democrats. Carpetbaggers were less sensitive to race, although most felt that their black allies should be content with minor offices. The friction between scalawags and carpetbaggers, which grew out of their rivalry for party honors, was particularly intense.

The New State Governments

NEW STATE CONSTITUTIONS

The new southern state constitutions enacted several reforms. They put in place fairer systems of legislative representation, allowed voters to elect many officials who before had been appointed, and abolished property requirements for office-holding. In South Carolina, for the first time, voters were allowed to vote for the president, governor, and other state officers. (Previously, presidential electors as well as the governor had been chosen by the South Carolina legislature.) The Radical state governments also assumed some responsibility for social welfare and established the first statewide systems of public schools in the South.

RACE AND SOCIAL EQUALITY

All the new constitutions proclaimed the principle of equality and granted black adult males the right to vote. On social relations they were much more cautious. No state outlawed segregation, and South Carolina and Louisiana were the only states that required integration in public schools (a mandate that was almost universally ignored).

Economic Issues and Corruption

The war left the southern economy in ruins, and problems of economic reconstruction were as difficult as those of politics. The new Republican governments encouraged industrial development by providing subsidies, loans, and even temporary exemptions from taxes. These governments also largely rebuilt the southern railroad system, often offering lavish aid to railroad corporations. The investments in the South helped double its manufacturing establishments in the two decades after 1860. Yet the harsh reality was that the South steadily slipped further behind the booming industrial economy of the North. Between 1854 and 1879, 7,000 miles of railroad track were laid in the South, but in the same period 45,000 miles were constructed in the rest of the nation.

CORRUPTION   The expansion of government services offered temptations for corruption. In many southern states, officials regularly received bribes and kickbacks for their award of railroad charters, franchises, and other contracts. By 1872 the debts of the 11 states of the Confederacy had increased by $132 million, largely because of railroad grants and new social services such as schools. The tax rate grew as expenditures went up; by the 1870s it was four times the rate of 1860.

Corruption, however, was not only a problem in the South: the decline in morality affected the entire nation. During these years in New York City alone, the Democratic Tweed Ring stole more money than all the Radical Republican governments in the South combined. Moreover, corruption in the South was hardly limited to Republicans. Many Democrats and white business leaders participated in the looting. "Everybody is demoralizing down here. Corruption is the fashion," reported Louisiana governor Henry Warmoth.

Corruption in Radical governments existed, but southern whites exaggerated its extent for partisan purposes. Conservatives just as bitterly opposed honest Radical regimes as they did corrupt ones. In the eyes of most white southerners the real crime of the Radical governments was that they allowed black citizens to hold some offices and tried to protect the civil rights of African Americans. Race was the conservatives' greatest weapon. And it would prove the most effective means to undermine Republican power in the South.

✓ REVIEW

What roles did African Americans, southern whites, and northern whites play in the Reconstruction governments of the South?

BLACK ASPIRATIONS

EMANCIPATION CAME TO SLAVES IN different ways and at different times. For some it arrived during the war when Union soldiers entered an area; for others it came some time after the Confederacy's collapse, when Union troops or officials announced that they were free. Whatever the timing, freedom meant a host of precious blessings to people who had been in bondage all their lives.

Experiencing Freedom

The first impulse was to think of freedom as a contrast to slavery. Emancipation immediately released slaves from the most oppressive aspects of bondage—the whippings, the breakup of families, the sexual exploitation. Freedom also meant movement, the right to travel without a pass or white permission. Above all, freedom meant that African Americans' labor would be for their own benefit. One Arkansas freedman, who earned his first dollar working on a railroad, recalled that when he was paid, "I felt like the richest man in the world."

CHANGING EMPLOYMENT   Freedom included finding a new place to work. Changing jobs was one concrete way to break the psychological ties of slavery. Even planters with reputations for kindness sometimes saw their former hands depart. The cook who left a South Carolina family even though they offered her higher wages than her new job explained, "I must go. If I stays here I'll never know I'm free."

IMPORTANCE OF NAMES   Symbolically, freedom meant having a full name, and African Americans now adopted last names. More than a few took the last name of some prominent individual; more common was to take the name of the first master in the family's oral history as far back as it could be recalled. Most, however, retained their first name, especially if the name had been given to them by their parents (as most often had been the case among slaves). It had been their form of identity in bondage, and for those separated from their family it was the only link with their parents. Whatever name they took, it was important to black Americans that they make the decision themselves without white interference.

The Black Family

UPHOLDING THE FAMILY   African Americans also sought to strengthen the family in freedom. Because slave marriages had not been recognized as legal, thousands of former slaves insisted on being married again by proper authorities, even though a ceremony was not required by law. Blacks who had been forcibly separated in slavery and later remarried confronted the dilemma of which spouse to take. Laura Spicer, whose husband had been sold away in slavery, received a series of wrenching letters from him after the war. He had thought her dead, had remarried, and had a new family. "You know it never was our wishes to be separated from each other, and it never was our fault. I had rather anything to had happened to me most than ever have been parted from you and the children," he wrote. "As I am, I do not know which I love best, you or Anna." Declining to return, he closed, "Laura, truly, I have got another wife, and I am very sorry...."

SAML. DOVE wishes to know of the whereabouts of his mother, Areno, his sisters Maria, Neziah, and Peggy, and his brother Edmond, who were owned by Geo. Dove, of Rockingham county, Shenandoah Valley, Va. Sold in Richmond, after which Saml. and Edmond were taken to Nashville, Tenn., by Joe Mick; Areno was left at the Eagle Tavern, Richmond

Respectfully yours,
SAML. DOVE.

Utica, New York, Aug. 5, 1865–3m

A Tennessee newspaper advertisement seeking a family, 1865

Like white husbands, black husbands deemed themselves the head of the family and acted legally for their wives. They often insisted that their wives would not work in the fields as they had in slavery, a decision that had major economic repercussions for agricultural labor. In negotiating contracts, a father also demanded the right to control his children and their labor. All these changes were designed to insulate the black family from white control.

The Schoolhouse and the Church

BLACK EDUCATION
In freedom, the schoolhouse and the black church became essential institutions in the black community. Next to ownership of land, African Americans saw education as the best hope for advancement. At first, northern churches and missionaries, working with the Freedmen's Bureau, set up black schools in the South. Tuition represented 10 percent or more of a laborer's monthly wages. Yet these schools were full. Many parents sent their children by day and attended classes themselves at night. Eventually, the Bureau schools were replaced by the new public school systems, which by 1876 enrolled 40 percent of African American children.

Black adults had good reasons for seeking literacy. They wanted to be able to read the Bible, to defend their newly gained civil and political rights, and to protect themselves from being cheated. One elderly Louisiana freedman explained that giving children an education was better than giving them a fortune, "because if you left them even $500, some man having more education than they had would come along and cheat them out of it all."

TEACHERS IN BLACK SCHOOLS
Teachers in the Freedmen's Bureau schools were primarily northern middle-class white women sent south by northern missionary societies. "I feel that it is a precious privilege," Esther Douglass wrote, "to be allowed to do something for these poor people." Many saw themselves as peacetime soldiers, struggling to make emancipation a reality. Indeed, on more than one occasion, hostile white southerners destroyed black schools and threatened and even murdered white teachers. Then there were the everyday challenges: low pay, dilapidated buildings, lack of sufficient books, classes of 100 or more children, and irregular attendance. Meanwhile, the Freedmen's Bureau undertook to train black teachers, and by 1869 most of the 3,000 teachers in freedmen's schools were black.

INDEPENDENT BLACK CHURCHES
Before the war, most slaves had attended white churches or services supervised by whites. Once free, African Americans quickly established their own congregations led by black preachers. In the first year of freedom, the Methodist Church South lost fully half of its black members. By 1870 the Negro Baptist Church had increased its membership threefold when compared to the membership in 1850, and the African Methodist Episcopal Church expanded at an even greater rate.

Black churches were so important because they were the only major organizations in the African American community controlled by blacks. Black ministers were respected leaders, and many of the black men elected to political office during Reconstruction were preachers. As it had in slavery, religion offered African Americans a place of refuge in a hostile white world and provided them with hope, comfort, and a means of self-identification.

| After living for years in a society where teaching slaves to read and write was usually illegal, freedpeople viewed literacy as a key to securing their newfound freedom. African Americans were not merely "anxious to learn," a school official in Virginia reported, they were "crazy to learn."

New Working Conditions

As a largely propertyless class, blacks in the postwar South had no choice but to work for white landowners. Except for paying wages, whites wanted to retain the old system of labor, including close supervision, gang labor, and physical punishment. Determined to remove all emblems of servitude, African Americans refused to work under these conditions, and they demanded time off to devote to their own interests. Convinced that working at one's own pace was part of freedom, they simply would not work as long or as hard as they had in slavery. Because of shorter hours and the withdrawal of children and women from the fields, work output declined by an estimated 35 percent in freedom. Blacks also refused to live in the old slave quarters located near the master's house. Instead, they erected cabins on distant parts of the plantation. Wages at first were $5 or $6 a month plus provisions and a cabin; by 1867, they had risen to an average of $10 a month.

SHARECROPPING These changes eventually led to the rise of sharecropping. Under this arrangement, African American families farmed discrete plots of land and then at the end of the year split the crop with the white landowner. Sharecropping had higher status and offered greater personal freedom than being a wage laborer. "I am not working for wages," one black farmer declared in defending his right to leave the plantation at will, "but am part owner of the crop and as [such,] I have all the rights that you or any other man has." Although black per-capita agricultural income increased 40 percent in freedom, sharecropping was a harshly exploitative system in which black families often sank into perpetual debt.

The Freedmen's Bureau

The task of supervising the transition from slavery to freedom on southern plantations fell to the Freedmen's Bureau, a unique experiment in social policy supported by the federal government. Assigned the task of protecting freedpeople's economic rights, approximately 550 local agents supervised and regulated working conditions in southern agriculture after the war. The racial attitudes of Bureau agents varied widely, as did their commitment and competence. Then, too, they had to depend on the army to enforce their decisions.

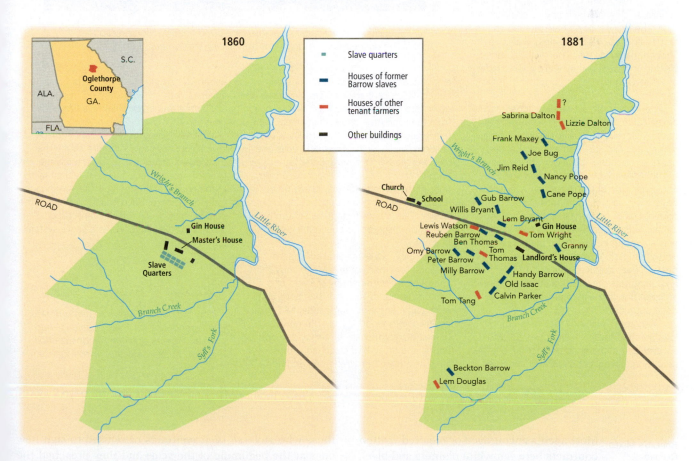

A GEORGIA PLANTATION AFTER THE WAR

After emancipation, sharecropping became the dominant form of agricultural labor in the South. Black families no longer lived in the old slave quarters but dispersed to separate plots of land that they farmed themselves. At the end of the year, each sharecropper turned over part of the crop to the white landowner. **How does the discussion of sharecroppers' cabins in Daily Lives (page 452) explain the difference of household locations on these two maps?**

DAILY LIVES

THE BLACK SHARECROPPER'S CABIN

On the plantations of the Old South slaves had lived in cabins along a central path in the shadow of the white master's "big house." These quarters were the center of their community, where marriages and other festivals were celebrated and family life went on. But with the coming of emancipation, freedpeople looked to leave the old quarters, which stood as a symbol of bondage and of close white supervision. African Americans either built new housing or dismantled their old cabins and hauled them to the plots of land they rented as tenants or sharecroppers. Moving enabled them to live on the land they farmed, just as white farmers and tenants did.

Like slave cabins, most sharecroppers' dwellings were one story high, about 16 feet square, and usually built of logs chinked with mud. The few windows had shutters to protect against the weather; glass was rare. Though the inside walls normally lacked plaster or sheeting, they were given a coat of whitewash annually to brighten the dark interior.

The main room served as kitchen and dining room, parlor, bathing area, and the parents' bedroom. To one side might be a homemade drop-leaf table (essential because of cramped space), which served as a kitchen work counter and a dining table. The other side of the room had a few plain beds, their slats or rope bottoms supporting corn shuck or straw mattresses. The social center of the room was the fireplace, the only source of heat and the main source of light after dark. Pots and pans were hung on the wall near the fireplace, and the mother and daughters did the cooking stooped over an open fire. In the summer, cooking was done outdoors.

The cabin's chimney was made of small logs notched together and covered with several layers of clay to protect it from the heat. Sometimes its height was extended by

Chimneys on sharecroppers' cabins were often titled deliberately so that they could be pushed away from the house quickly if they caught fire.

empty flour barrels. A taller chimney drew better, which kept smoke from blowing back down into the house and kept sparks away from the roof. After the evening meal the family gathered around the fireplace, the children to play with homemade dolls and toys, the mother to sew, and the father perhaps to play the fiddle. At bedtime a trapdoor in the ceiling offered access up a ladder to the loft beneath the gabled roof, where older children slept, usually on pallets on the floor, as had been the case in slavery.

Gradually, as black sharecroppers scraped together some savings, they improved their homes. By the end of the century, frame dwellings were more common, and many older log cabins had been covered with wood siding. The newer homes were generally larger, with wood floors, and often had attached rooms such as a porch or kitchen. In addition,

windows had glass panes, roofs were covered with shingles instead of planking, and stone and brick chimneys were less unusual.

Without question, the cabins of black sharecroppers provided more space than the slave quarters had, and certainly more freedom and privacy. Still, they lacked many of the comforts that most white Americans took for granted. Such housing reflected the continuing status of black sharecroppers as poverty-stricken laborers in a caste system based on race.

Thinking Critically

How did housing serve to demonstrate independence for freedpeople? What other aspects of life in Reconstruction served to demonstrate independence?

BUREAU'S MIXED RECORD Most agents encouraged or required written contracts between white planters and black laborers, specifying not only wages but also the conditions of employment. Although agents sometimes intervened to protect freedpeople from unfair treatment, they also provided important help to planters. They insisted that black laborers not desert at harvest time; they arrested those who violated their contracts or refused to sign new ones at the beginning of the year; and they preached the gospel of work and the need to be orderly and respectful. Given such attitudes, freedpeople increasingly complained that Bureau agents were mere tools of the planter class. "They are, in fact, the planters' guards, and nothing else," claimed the *New Orleans Tribune,* a black newspaper.

END OF THE BUREAU

The primary means of enforcing working conditions were the Freedmen's Courts, which Congress created in 1866 to avoid the discrimination African Americans received in state courts. These new courts functioned as military tribunals, and often the agent was the entire court. The sympathy black laborers received varied from state to state.

But in 1869, with the Bureau's work scarcely under way, Congress decided to shut it down, and by 1872 it had gone out of business. Despite its mixed record, it was the most effective agency in protecting blacks' civil and political rights. Its disbanding signaled the beginning of the northern retreat from Reconstruction.

Planters and a New Way of Life

PLANTERS' NEW VALUES

Planters and other white southerners faced emancipation with dread. "All the traditions and habits of both races had been suddenly overthrown," a Tennessee planter recalled, "and neither knew just what to do, or how to accommodate themselves to the new situation."

The old ideal of a paternalistic planter, which required a facade of black subservience and affection, gave way to an emphasis on strictly economic relationships. Mary Jones, a Georgia slaveholder before the war who did more for her workers than the law required, lost all patience when two workers accused her of trickery and hauled her before a Freedmen's Bureau agent, with whom she won her case. Upon returning home, she announced to the assembled freedpeople that "I have considered them friends and treated them as such but now they were only laborers under contract, and only the law would rule between us." Only with time did planters develop new norms and standards to judge black behavior. What in 1865 had seemed insolence was viewed by the 1870s as the normal attitude of freedom.

Slavery had been a complex institution that welded black and white southerners together in intimate relationships. After the war, however, planters increasingly embraced the ideology of segregation. Because emancipation significantly reduced the social distance between the races, white southerners sought psychological separation and kept dealings with African Americans to a minimum. By the time Reconstruction ended, white planters had developed a new way of life based on the institutions of sharecropping and segregation and undergirded by a militant white supremacy.

Although most planters kept their land, they did not regain the economic prosperity of the prewar years. Rice plantations, unsuitable to tenant farming, largely disappeared after the war. In addition, southern cotton growers faced increased competition from new areas such as India, Egypt, and Brazil. Cotton prices began a long decline, and by 1880 the value of southern farms had slid 33 percent below the level of 1860.

> ✔ **REVIEW**
>
> Why were the church and the school central to African American hopes after the Civil War? To what degree did working conditions for African Americans change?

THE ABANDONMENT OF RECONSTRUCTION

ON CHRISTMAS DAY 1875, A white acquaintance approached Charles Caldwell on the streets of Clinton, Mississippi, and invited him into Chilton's store to have a drink to celebrate the holiday. A former slave, Caldwell was a state senator and the leader of the Republican Party in Hinds County, Mississippi. But the black leader's fearlessness made him a marked man. Only two months earlier, he had been forced to flee the county to escape a white mob angry about a Republican barbecue he and his fellow Republicans had organized. For four days the mob hunted down and killed nearly 40 Republican leaders for presuming to hold a political meeting. Despite that hostility, Caldwell had returned to vote in the November state election. Even more boldly, he had led a black militia company through the streets to help quell the disturbances. Now, as Caldwell and his "friend" raised their glasses in a holiday toast, a gunshot exploded through the window. Caldwell collapsed, mortally wounded from a bullet to the back of his head. He was taken outside, where his assassins riddled his body with bullets.

Charles Caldwell shared the fate of more than a few southern black Republicans. Southern whites used violence, terror, and political assassination to challenge the federal government's commitment to Reconstruction. If northerners had boldly countered such terrorism, Reconstruction might have ended differently. But in the years following President Johnson's impeachment trial in 1868, the influence of Radical Republicans steadily waned. The Republican Party was being drained of the crusading idealism that had stamped its early years.

| Lucy Stone, a major figure in the women's rights movement

The Election of Grant

Immensely popular after the war, Ulysses S. Grant was the natural choice of Republicans to run for president in 1868. Although Grant was elected, Republicans were shocked that despite his great military stature, his popular margin was only 300,000 votes. An estimated 450,000 black Republican votes had been cast in the South, which meant

The Fifteenth Amendment

1 Reading Emancipation Proclamation
2 Life Liberty and Independence
3 We Unite the Bonds of Fellowship
4 Our Charter of Rights the Holy Scriptures

5 Education will prove the Equality of the Races
6 Liberty Protects the Marriage Alter
7 Celebration of Fifteenth Amendment May 19th 1870
8 The Ballot Box is open to us.

9 Our representative Sits in the National Legislature
10 The Holy Ordinances of Religion are free
11 Freedom unites the Family Circle.
12 We will protect our Country as it defends our Rights.

13 We till our own Fields.
14 The Right of Citizens of the U.S. to vote shall not be denied or abridged by the U.S. or any State on account of Race Color or Condition of Servitude 15th Amendment

PUBLISHED & PRINTED BY   THOMAS KELLY 17 BARCLAY ST. N.Y.

| From the beginning of Reconstruction, African Americans demanded the right to vote as free citizens. The Fifteenth Amendment, ratified in 1870, secured that right for black males. In New York, black citizens paraded in support of Ulysses S. Grant for president. Parades played a central role in campaigning: this parade exhibits the usual banners, flags, costumes, and a band. Blacks in both the North and the South voted solidly for the Republican Party as the party of Lincoln and emancipation, although white violence in the South increasingly reduced black turnout.

that a majority of whites casting ballots had voted Democratic. The 1868 election helped convince Republican leaders that an amendment securing black suffrage throughout the nation was necessary.

FIFTEENTH AMENDMENT

In February 1869 Congress sent the Fifteenth Amendment to the states for ratification. It forbade any state to deny the right to vote on grounds of race, color, or previous condition of servitude. Some Radicals had hoped to forbid literacy or property requirements to protect blacks further. Others wanted a simple declaration that all adult male citizens had the right to vote. But the moderates in the party were aware that many northerners were increasingly worried about the number of immigrants who were again entering the country and wanted to be able to restrict their voting. As a result, the final amendment left loopholes that eventually allowed

southern states to **disenfranchise** African Americans. The amendment was ratified in March 1870, aided by the votes of the four southern states that had not completed the process of Reconstruction and thus were also required to endorse this amendment before being readmitted to Congress.

WOMEN'S SUFFRAGE REJECTED

Proponents of women's suffrage were gravely disappointed when Congress refused to prohibit voting discrimination on the basis of sex as well as race. The Women's Loyal League, led by Elizabeth Cady Stanton and Susan B. Anthony, had pressed for first the Fourteenth and then the Fifteenth Amendment to recognize women's public role. But even most Radicals, contending that black rights had to be ensured first, were unwilling to back women's suffrage. The Fifteenth Amendment ruptured the feminist movement. Although disappointed that women were not included in its provisions, Lucy Stone and the American Woman Suffrage Association urged ratification. Stanton and Anthony, however, broke with their former allies among the Radicals, denounced the amendment, and organized the National Woman Suffrage Association to work for passage of a new amendment giving women the ballot. The division hampered the women's rights movement for decades to come.

The Grant Administration

Ulysses Grant was ill at ease with the political process. His simple, quiet manner, while superb for commanding armies, did not serve him as well in public life, and his well-known resolution withered when he was uncertain of his goal. Also, he lacked the moral commitment to make Reconstruction succeed.

CORRUPTION UNDER GRANT A series of scandals wracked Grant's presidency. Although Grant did not profit personally, he remained loyal to his friends and displayed little zeal to root out wrongdoing. His relatives were implicated in a scheme to corner the gold market, and his private secretary escaped conviction for stealing federal whiskey revenues only because Grant interceded on his behalf. His secretary of war resigned to avoid impeachment.

Nor was Congress immune from the lowered tone of public life. In such a climate ruthless state machines, led by men who favored the status quo, came to dominate the party. Office and power became ends in themselves, and party leaders worked in close cooperation with northern industrial interests. The few Radicals still active in public life increasingly repudiated Grant and the Republican governments in the South. Congress in 1872 passed an amnesty act, removing the restrictions of the Fourteenth Amendment on officeholding except for about 200 to 300 ex-Confederate leaders.

As corruption in both the North and the South worsened, reformers became more interested in cleaning up government than in protecting blacks' rights. These liberal Republicans opposed the continued presence of the army in the South, denounced the corruption of southern governments as well as the national government, and advocated free trade and civil service reform. In 1872 they broke with the Republican Party and nominated for president Horace Greeley, the editor of the *New York Tribune*. A onetime Radical, Greeley had become disillusioned with Reconstruction and urged a restoration of home rule in the South as well as adoption of civil service reform. Democrats decided to back the Liberal Republican ticket. The Republicans renominated Grant, who, despite the defection of a number of prominent Radicals, won an easy victory with 56 percent of the popular vote.

Growing Northern Disillusionment

CIVIL RIGHTS ACT OF 1875 During Grant's second term, Congress passed the Civil Rights Act of 1875, the last major piece of Reconstruction legislation. This law prohibited racial discrimination in all public

Grant swings from a trapeze while supporting a number of associates accused of corruption. Among those holding on are Secretary of the Navy George M. Robeson (top center), who was accused of accepting bribes for awarding navy contracts; Secretary of War William W. Belknap (top right), who was forced to resign for selling Indian post traderships; and the president's private secretary, Orville Babcock (bottom right), who was implicated in the Whiskey Ring scandal. Although not personally involved in the scandals during his administration, Grant was reluctant to dismiss supporters accused of wrongdoing from office.

accommodations, transportation, places of amusement, and juries. At the same time, Congress rejected a ban on segregation in public schools, which was almost universally practiced in the North as well as the South. Although some railroads, streetcars, and public accommodations in both sections were desegregated after the bill passed, the federal government made little attempt to enforce the law, and it was ignored throughout most of the South. In 1883 the Supreme Court struck down its provisions except the one relating to juries.

Despite passage of the Civil Rights Act, many northerners were growing disillusioned with Reconstruction. They were repelled by the corruption of the southern governments, they were tired of the violence and disorder in the

South, and they had little faith in black Americans. "We have tried this long enough," remarked one influential northern Republican of Reconstruction. "Now let the South alone."

DEPRESSION AND DEMOCRATIC RESURGENCE

As the agony of the war became more distant, the Panic of 1873 diverted public attention from Reconstruction to economic issues. In the severe depression that followed over the next four years, some 3 million people found themselves out of work. Congress became caught up in the question of whether printing greenbacks would help the economy prosper. Battered by the panic and the corruption issue, the Republicans lost a shocking 77 seats in Congress in the 1874 elections and, along with them, control of the House of Representatives for the first time since 1861. "The truth is our people are tired out with the worn out cry of 'Southern outrages'!!" one Republican concluded. "Hard times and heavy taxes make them wish the 'ever lasting nigger' were in hell or Africa." Republicans spoke more and more about cutting loose the unpopular southern governments.

The Triumph of White Supremacy

As northern commitment to Reconstruction waned, southern Democrats set out to overthrow the remaining Radical governments. White Republicans already in the South felt heavy pressure to desert their party. In Mississippi one party member justified his decision to leave on the grounds that otherwise he would have "to live a life of social oblivion" and his children would have no future.

RACISM

To poor white southerners who lacked social standing, the Democratic appeal to racial solidarity offered great comfort. As one explained, "I may be poor and my manners may be crude, but . . . because I am a white man, I have a right to be treated with respect by Negroes. . . . That I am poor is not as important as that I am a white man; and no Negro is ever going to forget that he is not a white man." The large landowners and other wealthy groups that led southern Democrats objected less to black southerners voting. These well-to-do leaders did not face social and economic competition from African Americans, and in any case, they were confident that if outside influences were removed, they could control the black vote.

Democrats also resorted to economic pressure to undermine Republican power. In heavily black counties, white observers at the polls took down the names of black

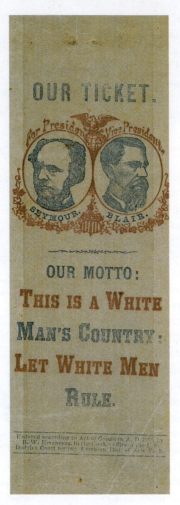

OUR TICKET.

For President · Vice President

SEYMOUR · BLAIR

OUR MOTTO:

THIS IS A WHITE MAN'S COUNTRY: LET WHITE MEN RULE.

Entered according to Act of Congress A. D. 1868 by B. W. Hitchcock, in the Clerk's Office of the U.S. District Court for the Southern Dist. of New York.

| This campaign badge from 1868 made the sentiments of white Democrats clear.

residents who cast Republican ballots and published them in local newspapers. Planters were urged to discharge black tenants who persisted in voting Republican. But terror and violence provided the most effective means to overthrow the Radical regimes. A number of paramilitary organizations broke up Republican meetings, terrorized white and black Republicans, assassinated Republican leaders, and prevented black citizens from voting. The most famous was the Ku Klux Klan, founded in 1866 in Tennessee. It and similar groups functioned as unofficial arms of the Democratic Party.

CONTESTING THE NIGHT

In the war for supremacy, contesting control of the night was of paramount concern to both southern whites and blacks. Before emancipation, masters attempted to control the nighttime hours, with a system of passes and patrols that chased slaves who went hunting or tried to sneak a visit to a family member at a neighboring plantation. For slaves the night provided precious hours not devoted to work: time to read, to meet for worship, school, or dancing. During Reconstruction, African Americans actively took back the night for a host of activities, including a custom that white Americans had enjoyed since the beginning of the republic: torchlight political parades. In Holly Springs, Mississippi, hundreds, even thousands of black citizens filled the streets during campaigns, holding aloft torches and "transparencies"—pictures painted on thin cloth, 10 to 12 feet long—the entire scene lit in an eerie, flickering glow.

Part of the Klan's mission was to recoup this contested ground and to limit the ability of African Americans to use the night as they pleased. Sometimes the Klan's threat of violence was indirect: one or two riders galloping through black neighborhoods rattling fences with lances. Other times several "dens" of the KKK might gather to ride from plantation to plantation over the course of a night, stopping in every black home they could reach and demanding all firearms. Other times the violence was direct: beatings and executions—again, heightened by the dark of night.

Congress finally moved to break the power of the Klan with the Force Act of 1870 and the Ku Klux Klan Act of 1871. These laws made it a felony to interfere with the right to vote; they also authorized use of the army and suspension of the writ of habeas corpus. The Grant administration eventually suspended the writ of habeas corpus in nine South Carolina counties and arrested hundreds of suspected Klan members throughout the South. Although these actions weakened the Klan, terrorist organizations continued to operate underground.

DRESSED TO KILL

Klan members drawn for Harper's Weekly magazine, 1868

Advertisement for a minstrel show, 1864

Why wear a hooded mask? Does the advertisement suggest more than one reason?

The costumes of Ku Klux Klan night riders—pointed hoods and white sheets—have become a staple of history books. But why use such outlandish disguises? To hide the identity of members, according to some accounts, or to terrorize freedpeople into thinking they were being menaced by Confederate ghosts. Historian Elaine F. Parsons has suggested that KKK performances took their cues from American popular culture: the costumes of Mardi Gras and similar carnivals, as well as minstrel shows. In behaving like carnival revelers, KKK members may have hoped to lull northern authorities into viewing the night rides as humorous pranks, not a threat to Radical rule. For southern white Democrats the theatrical night rides helped overturn the social order of Reconstruction, just as carousers at carnivals disrupted the night. The ritual garb provided seemingly innocent cover for what was truly a campaign of terror and intimidation that often turned deadly.

Thinking Critically

In what ways does the advertisement speak of experiences both frightening and humorous? In terms of popular culture, do modern horror films sometimes combine both terror and humor? Assess how this dynamic of horror and jest might have worked in terms of the different groups perceiving the Klan's activities: white northerners, white southerners, and African Americans. If this theory of why the Klan dressed as they did is true, does it make them more effective or less so as a terrorist organization?

MISSISSIPPI PLAN

Then in 1875 Democrats inaugurated what became known as the Mississippi Plan, the decision to use as much violence as necessary to carry the state election. Several local papers trumpeted, "Carry the election peaceably if we can, forcibly if we must." When Republican governor Adelbert Ames requested federal troops to stop the violence, Grant's advisers warned that sending troops to Mississippi would cost the party the Ohio election. In the end the administration told Ames to depend on his own forces. Bolstered by terrorism, the Democrats swept the election in Mississippi. Violence and intimidation prevented as many as 60,000 black and white Republicans from voting, converting the normal Republican majority into a Democratic majority of 30,000. Mississippi had been "redeemed."

The Disputed Election of 1876

With Republicans on the defensive across the nation, the 1876 presidential election was crucial to the final overthrow of Reconstruction. The Republicans nominated Ohio governor Rutherford B. Hayes to oppose Samuel Tilden, Governor of New York. Once again, violence prevented many Republican votes, this time an estimated quarter of a million, from being cast in the South. Tilden had a clear majority of 250,000 in the popular vote, but the outcome in the Electoral College was in doubt because both parties claimed South Carolina, Florida, and Louisiana, the only reconstructed states still in Republican hands. Hayes needed all three states to be elected, for even without them, Tilden had amassed 184 electoral votes, one short of a majority. Republican canvassing boards in power disqualified enough Democratic votes to give each state to Hayes.

To arbitrate the disputed returns, Congress established a 15-member electoral commission: 5 members each from the Senate, the House, and the Supreme Court. By a straight party vote of 8 to 7, the commission awarded the disputed electoral votes—and the presidency—to Hayes.

COMPROMISE OF 1877 — When angry Democrats threatened a filibuster to prevent the electoral votes from being counted, key Republicans met with southern Democrats on February 26 at the Wormley Hotel in Washington. There they reached an informal understanding, later known as the Compromise of 1877. Hayes's supporters agreed to withdraw federal troops from the South and not oppose the new Democratic state governments. For their part, southern Democrats dropped their opposition to Hayes's election and pledged to respect the rights of African Americans.

REDEEMERS TAKE CONTROL — Without federal support, the Republican governments in South Carolina and Louisiana promptly collapsed, and Democrats took control of the remaining states of the Confederacy. By 1877, the entire South was in the hands of the **Redeemers,** as they called themselves. Reconstruction and Republican rule had come to an end.

The Failure of Reconstruction

Reconstruction failed for a multitude of reasons. The reforming impulse that had created the Republican Party in the 1850s had been battered and worn down by the war. The new materialism of industrial America inspired in many Americans a jaded cynicism about the corruption of the age and a desire to forget uncomfortable issues. In the South, African American voters and leaders inevitably lacked a certain amount of education and experience; elsewhere, Republicans were divided over policies and options.

Yet beyond these obstacles, the sad fact remains that the ideals of Reconstruction were most clearly defeated by the deep-seated racism that permeated American life. Racism was why the white South so unrelentingly resisted Reconstruction. Racism was why most white northerners had little interest in black rights except as a means to preserve the Union or to safeguard the Republic. Racism was why northerners were willing to write off Reconstruction and with it the welfare of African Americans. While Congress might pass a constitutional amendment abolishing slavery, it could not overturn at a stroke the social habits of two centuries.

Certainly the political equations of power, in the long term, had been changed. The North had fought fiercely during the war to preserve the Union. In doing so, it had secured the power to dominate the economic and political destiny of the nation. With the overthrow of Reconstruction, the white South had won back some of the power it had lost in 1865. But even with white supremacy triumphant, African Americans did not return to the social position they had occupied before the war. They were no longer slaves, and black southerners who walked dusty roads in search of family members, sent their children to school, or worshiped in churches they controlled knew what a momentous change emancipation was. Even under the exploitative sharecropping system, black income rose significantly in freedom. Then, too, the Fourteenth

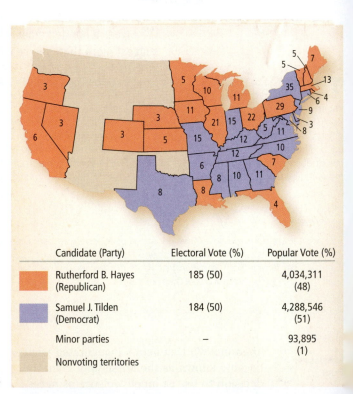

Candidate (Party)	Electoral Vote (%)	Popular Vote (%)
Rutherford B. Hayes (Republican)	185 (50)	4,034,311 (48)
Samuel J. Tilden (Democrat)	184 (50)	4,288,546 (51)
Minor parties	–	93,895 (1)
Nonvoting territories		

ELECTION OF 1876

Amendment principles of "equal protection" and "due process of law" had been written into the Constitution. These guarantees would be available for later generations to use in championing once again the Radicals' goal of racial equality.

END OF THE DAVIS BEND EXPERIMENT — But this was a struggle left to future reformers. For the time being, the clear trend was away from change or hope—especially for former slaves like Benjamin Montgomery and his sons, the owners of the old Davis plantations in Mississippi. In the 1870s bad crops, lower cotton prices, and falling land values undermined the Montgomerys' financial position, and in 1875 Jefferson Davis sued to have the sale of

Brierfield invalidated. A lower court ruled against him, since he had never received legal title to the plantation. Davis appealed to the state supreme court, which, following the overthrow of Mississippi's Radical government, had a white conservative majority. In a politically motivated decision, the court awarded Brierfield to Davis in 1878, and the Montgomerys lost Hurricane as well. Reconstruction was over and done, along with the hopes that came with it.

> ✓ **REVIEW**
> What factors in the North and the South led the federal government to abandon Reconstruction in the South?

CONCLUSION

THE WORLD AT LARGE

The waning days of Reconstruction were filled with such ironies: of governments "redeemed" by violence and Supreme Court decisions using Fourteenth Amendment rights to protect giant corporations rather than individual African Americans. Increasingly, the industrial North focused on the economic task of integrating the South and the West into the Union. Northern factories sought southern and western raw materials (cotton, timber, cattle, and minerals) to produce goods to sell in national and international markets.

This trend was global in scope. During the coming decades European nations also scrambled to acquire natural resources and markets. In the onrushing age of imperialism, Western nations would seek to dominate newly acquired colonies in Africa and Asia. There would be gold rushes in South Africa as well as in the United States, vast cattle ranches in Argentina and Canada as well as across the American Great Plains. Farmers would open up lands in New Zealand and Australia as well as in Oklahoma and Wyoming. And just as racism replaced slavery as the central justification for white supremacy in the South, it promoted the campaigns against Indians and Hispanics in the West and in a belief in "inferior races" to be swept aside by imperialists all across the world. The ideal of a truly diverse and democratic society remained largely unsought and unfulfilled. ∞∞∞

CHAPTER SUMMARY

PRESIDENTS ABRAHAM LINCOLN AND ANDREW Johnson and the Republican-dominated Congress each developed a program of Reconstruction to restore the Confederate states to the Union.

■ Lincoln's 10 percent plan required that 10 percent of qualified voters from 1860 swear an oath of loyalty to begin organizing state government.

■ Following Lincoln's assassination, Andrew Johnson changed Lincoln's terms and lessened Reconstruction's requirements.

■ The more-radical Congress repudiated Johnson's state governments and enacted its own program of Reconstruction, which included the principle of black suffrage.

• Congress passed the Fourteenth and Fifteenth Amendments and also extended the life of the Freedmen's Bureau, a unique experiment in social welfare.

• Congress rejected land reform, however, which would have provided the freedpeople with a greater economic stake.

• The effort to remove Johnson from office through impeachment failed.

■ The Radical governments in the South, led by black and white southerners and transplanted northerners, compiled a mixed record on matters such as racial equality, education, economic issues, and corruption.

■ Reconstruction was a time of both joy and frustration for former slaves.

• Former slaves took steps to reunite their families and establish black-controlled churches.

• They evidenced a widespread desire for land and education.

- Black resistance to the old system of labor led to the adoption of sharecropping.
- The Freedmen's Bureau fostered these new working arrangements and also the beginnings of black education in the South.

■ Northern public opinion became disillusioned with Reconstruction during the presidency of Ulysses S. Grant.

■ Southern whites used violence, economic coercion, and racism to overthrow the Republican state governments.

■ In 1877 Republican leaders agreed to end Reconstruction in exchange for Rutherford B. Hayes's election as president.

■ Racism played a key role in the eventual failure of Reconstruction.

ADDITIONAL READING

HISTORIANS' VIEWS OF RECONSTRUCTION HAVE dramatically changed over the past half century. Modern studies offer a more sympathetic assessment of Reconstruction and the experience of African Americans. Indicative of this trend is Eric Foner, *Reconstruction* (1988), and his briefer treatment (with photographic essays by Joshua Brown) *Forever Free: The Story of Emancipation and Reconstruction* (2005). Michael Les Benedict treats the clash between Andrew Johnson and Congress in *The Impeachment and Trial of Andrew Johnson* (1973). Political affairs in the South during Reconstruction are examined in Dan T. Carter, *When the War Was Over* (1985), and Thomas Holt, *Black over White* (1977), an imaginative study of black political leadership in South Carolina. Hans Trefousse, *Thaddeus Stevens: Nineteenth-Century Egalitarian* (1997), provides a sympathetic reassessment of the influential Radical Republican. Mark W. Summers, *A Dangerous Stir* (2009), deftly examines the ways in which fear and paranoia shaped Reconstruction.

Leon Litwack's Pulitzer Prize–winning *Been in the Storm So Long* (1979) sensitively analyzes the transition of enslaved African Americans to freedom. Heather Andrea Williams, *Self-Taught: African American Education in Slavery and Freedom* (2005), illustrates the black drive for literacy and education. The dialectic of black-white relations is charted from the antebellum years through Reconstruction and beyond in Steven Hahn, *A Nation under Our Feet: Black Political Struggles in the Rural South from Slavery to the Great Migration* (2003). Excellent studies of changing labor relations in southern agriculture include Amy Dru Stanley's *From Bondage to Contract* (1998), Julie Saville's *The Work of Reconstruction* (1995), and John C. Rodrigue's *Reconstruction in the Cane Fields* (2001). For contrasting views of the Freedman's Bureau, see George R. Bentley, *A History of the Freedman's Bureau* (1955)—favorable—and Donald Nieman, *To Set the Law in Motion* (1979)—critical. Heather Cox Richardson explores the postwar context in the North in *The Death of Reconstruction* (2004) and considers Reconstruction in the West in *West from Appomattox* (2008).

For a fuller list of readings, see the Bibliography at www.mhhe.com/eh8e.

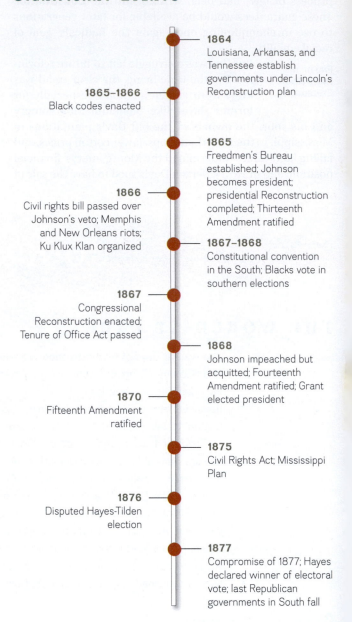

SIGNIFICANT EVENTS

1864
Louisiana, Arkansas, and Tennessee establish governments under Lincoln's Reconstruction plan

1865–1866
Black codes enacted

1865
Freedmen's Bureau established; Johnson becomes president; presidential Reconstruction completed; Thirteenth Amendment ratified

1866
Civil rights bill passed over Johnson's veto; Memphis and New Orleans riots; Ku Klux Klan organized

1867–1868
Constitutional convention in the South; Blacks vote in southern elections

1867
Congressional Reconstruction enacted; Tenure of Office Act passed

1868
Johnson impeached but acquitted; Fourteenth Amendment ratified; Grant elected president

1870
Fifteenth Amendment ratified

1875
Civil Rights Act; Mississippi Plan

1876
Disputed Hayes-Tilden election

1877
Compromise of 1877; Hayes declared winner of electoral vote; last Republican governments in South fall

Major Players in Reconstruction

Radical Republicans	Advocated rights for freedpeople; believed Congress should set terms of Reconstruction
Moderate Republicans	Looked to bar Confederates from regaining power and to give slaves federal protection, but did not favor racial equality
African American officials	15–20 percent of state officeholders, 6 percent of members of Congress; generally more conservative than rural southern blacks
Scalawags	White southern Republicans; mostly yeoman farmers from upland counties; looked to restore prosperity, build railroads and schools
Carpetbaggers	White northerners in the South; made up a small percentage of Republican voters but held disproportionate number of political offices
Teachers, Freedmen's Bureau Schools	At first, northern middle-class white women sent by missionary societies; by 1869 black teachers made up a majority
Ministers, African American churches	Community leaders; black churches spread widely in the South after the war
White planters	Most did not regain prewar prosperity; developed a new way of life based on sharecropping and segregation
Redeemers	White Democrats who ousted Reconstruction governments; KKK and other paramilitary organizations used force to achieve their goals

Appendix

The Declaration of Independence

In Congress, July 4, 1776,

THE UNANIMOUS DECLARATION OF THE THIRTEEN UNITED STATES OF AMERICA

When, in the course of human events, it becomes necessary for one people to dissolve the political bands which have connected them with another, and to assume, among the powers of the earth, the separate and equal station to which the laws of nature and of nature's God entitle them, a decent respect to the opinions of mankind requires that they should declare the causes which impel them to the separation.

We hold these truths to be self-evident, that all men are created equal; that they are endowed by their Creator with certain unalienable rights; that among these, are life, liberty, and the pursuit of happiness. That, to secure these rights, governments are instituted among men, deriving their just powers from the consent of the governed; that, whenever any form of government becomes destructive of these ends, it is the right of the people to alter or to abolish it, and to institute a new government, laying its foundation on such principles, and organizing its powers in such form, as to them shall seem most likely to effect their safety and happiness. Prudence, indeed, will dictate that governments long established, should not be changed for light and transient causes; and, accordingly, all experience hath shown, that mankind are more disposed to suffer, while evils are sufferable, than to right themselves by abolishing the forms to which they are accustomed. But, when a long train of abuses and usurpations, pursuing invariably the same object, evinces a design to reduce them under absolute despotism, it is their right, it is their duty, to throw off such government and to provide new guards for their future security. Such has been the patient sufferance of these colonies, and such is now the necessity which constrains them to alter their former systems of government. The history of the present King of Great Britain is a history of repeated injuries and usurpations, all having, in direct object, the establishment of an absolute tyranny over these States. To prove this, let facts be submitted to a candid world:

He has refused his assent to laws the most wholesome and necessary for the public good.

He has forbidden his governors to pass laws of immediate and pressing importance, unless suspended in their operation till his assent should be obtained; and, when so suspended, he has utterly neglected to attend to them.

He has refused to pass other laws for the accommodation of large districts of people, unless those people would relinquish the right of representation in the legislature; a right inestimable to them, and formidable to tyrants only.

He has called together legislative bodies at places unusual, uncomfortable, and distant from the depository of their public records, for the sole purpose of fatiguing them into compliance with his measures.

He has dissolved representative houses repeatedly for opposing, with manly firmness, his invasions on the rights of the people.

He has refused, for a long time after such dissolutions, to cause others to be elected; whereby the legislative powers, incapable of annihilation, have returned to the people at large for their exercise; the state remaining, in the meantime, exposed to all the danger of invasion from without, and convulsions within.

He has endeavored to prevent the population of these States; for that purpose, obstructing the laws for naturalization of foreigners, refusing to pass others to encourage their migration hither, and raising the conditions of new appropriations of lands.

He has obstructed the administration of justice, by refusing his assent to laws for establishing judiciary powers.

He has made judges dependent on his will alone, for the tenure of their offices, and the amount and payment of their salaries.

He has erected a multitude of new offices, and sent hither swarms of officers to harass our people, and eat out their substance.

He has kept among us, in time of peace, standing armies, without the consent of our legislatures.

He has affected to render the military independent of, and superior to, the civil power.

He has combined, with others, to subject us to a jurisdiction foreign to our Constitution, and unacknowledged by our laws; giving his assent to their acts of pretended legislation:

For quartering large bodies of armed troops among us:

For protecting them by a mock trial, from punishment, for any murders which they should commit on the inhabitants of these States:

For cutting off our trade with all parts of the world:

For imposing taxes on us without our consent:

For depriving us, in many cases, of the benefit of trial by jury:

For transporting us beyond seas to be tried for pretended offences:

For abolishing the free system of English laws in a neighboring province, establishing therein an arbitrary government, and enlarging its boundaries, so as to render it at once an example and fit instrument for introducing the same absolute rule into these colonies:

For taking away our charters, abolishing our most valuable laws, and altering, fundamentally, the powers of our governments:

For suspending our own legislatures, and declaring themselves invested with power to legislate for us in all cases whatsoever.

He has abdicated government here, by declaring us out of his protection, and waging war against us.

He has plundered our seas, ravaged our coasts, burnt our towns, and destroyed the lives of our people.

He is, at this time, transporting large armies of foreign mercenaries to complete the works of death, desolation, and tyranny, already begun, with circumstances of cruelty and perfidy scarcely paralleled in the most barbarous ages, and totally unworthy the head of a civilized nation.

He has constrained our fellow citizens, taken captive on the high seas, to bear arms against their country, to become the executioners of their friends, and brethren, or to fall themselves by their hands.

He has excited domestic insurrections amongst us, and has endeavored to bring on the inhabitants of our frontiers, the merciless Indian savages, whose known rule of warfare is an undistinguished destruction of all ages, sexes, and conditions.

In every stage of these oppressions, we have petitioned for redress, in the most humble terms; our repeated petitions have been answered only by repeated injury. A prince, whose character is thus marked by every act which may define a tyrant, is unfit to be the ruler of a free people.

Nor have we been wanting in attention to our British brethren. We have warned them, from time to time, of attempts made by their legislature to extend an unwarrantable jurisdiction over us. We have reminded them of the circumstances of our emigration and settlement here. We have appealed to their native justice and magnanimity, and we have conjured them, by the ties of our common kindred, to disavow these usurpations, which would inevitably interrupt our connections and correspondence. They, too, have been deaf to the voice of justice and consanguinity. We must, therefore, acquiesce in the necessity which denounces our separation, and hold them as we hold the rest of mankind, enemies in war, in peace, friends.

We, therefore, the representatives of the United States of America, in general Congress assembled, appealing to the Supreme Judge of the world for the rectitude of our intentions, do, in the name, and by the authority of the good people of these colonies, solemnly publish and declare, that these united colonies are, and of right ought to be, free and independent states: that they are absolved from all allegiance to the British Crown, and that all political connection between them and the state of Great Britain is, and ought to be, totally dissolved; and that, as free and independent states, they have full power to levy war, conclude peace, contract alliances, establish commerce, and to do all other acts and things which independent states may of right do. And, for the support of this declaration, with a firm reliance on the protection of Divine Providence, we mutually pledge to each other our lives, our fortunes, and our sacred honor.

The foregoing Declaration was, by order of Congress, engrossed, and signed by the following members:

JOHN HANCOCK

NEW HAMPSHIRE	NEW YORK	DELAWARE	NORTH CAROLINA
Josiah Bartlett	William Floyd	Caesar Rodney	William Hooper
William Whipple	Philip Livingston	George Read	Joseph Hewes
Matthew Thornton	Francis Lewis	Thomas M'Kean	John Penn
	Lewis Morris		
MASSACHUSETTS BAY		MARYLAND	SOUTH CAROLINA
Samuel Adams	NEW JERSEY	Samuel Chase	Edward Rutledge
John Adams	Richard Stockton	William Paca	Thomas Heyward, Jr.
Robert Treat Paine	John Witherspoon	Thomas Stone	Thomas Lynch, Jr.
Elbridge Gerry	Francis Hopkinson	Charles Carroll, of Carrollton	Arthur Middleton
	John Hart		
RHODE ISLAND	Abraham Clark	VIRGINIA	GEORGIA
Stephen Hopkins		George Wythe	Button Gwinnett
William Ellery	PENNSYLVANIA	Richard Henry Lee	Lyman Hall
	Robert Morris	Thomas Jefferson	George Walton
CONNECTICUT	Benjamin Rush	Benjamin Harrison	
Roger Sherman	Benjamin Franklin	Thomas Nelson, Jr.	
Samuel Huntington	John Morton	Francis Lightfoot Lee	
William Williams	George Clymer	Carter Braxton	
Oliver Wolcott	James Smith		
	George Taylor		
	James Wilson		
	George Ross		

Resolved, That copies of the Declaration be sent to the several assemblies, conventions, and committees, or councils of safety, and to the several commanding officers of the continental troops; that it be proclaimed in each of the United States, at the head of the army.

The Constitution of the United States of America[1]

We the People of the United States, in Order to form a more perfect Union, establish Justice, insure domestic Tranquility, provide for the common defence, promote the general Welfare, and secure the Blessings of Liberty to ourselves and our Posterity, do ordain and establish this CONSTITUTION for the United States of America.

ARTICLE I

Section 1. All legislative Powers herein granted shall be vested in a Congress of the United States, which shall consist of a Senate and House of Representatives.

Section 2. The House of Representatives shall be composed of Members chosen every second Year by the People of the several States, and the Electors in each State shall have the Qualifications requisite for Electors of the most numerous Branch of the State Legislature.

No Person shall be a Representative who shall not have attained to the Age of twenty-five Years, and been seven Years a Citizen of the United States, and who shall not, when elected, be an Inhabitant of that State in which he shall be chosen.

[Representatives and direct Taxes[2] shall be apportioned among the several States which may be included within this Union, according to their respective Numbers, which shall be determined by adding to the whole Number of free Persons, including those bound to Service for a Term of Years, and excluding Indians not taxed, three fifths of all other Persons.][3] The actual Enumeration shall be made within three Years after the first Meeting of the Congress of the United States, and within every subsequent Term of ten Years, in such Manner as they shall by Law direct. The Number of Representatives shall not exceed one for every thirty Thousand, but each State shall have at Least one Representative; and until such enumeration shall be made, the State of New Hampshire shall be entitled to chuse three, Massachusetts eight, Rhode-Island and Providence Plantations one, Connecticut five, New York six, New Jersey four, Pennsylvania eight, Delaware one, Maryland six, Virginia ten, North Carolina five, South Carolina five, and Georgia three.

When vacancies happen in the Representation from any State, the Executive Authority thereof shall issue Writs of Election to fill such Vacancies.

The House of Representatives shall chuse their Speaker and other Officers; and shall have the sole Power of Impeachment.

Section 3. The Senate of the United States shall be composed of two Senators from each State, chosen by the Legislature thereof, for six Years; and each Senator shall have one Vote.

Immediately after they shall be assembled in Consequence of the first Election, they shall be divided as equally as may be into three Classes. The Seats of the Senators of the first Class shall be vacated at the Expiration of the second Year, of the second Class at the Expiration of the fourth Year, and of the third Class at the Expiration of the sixth Year, so that one-third may be chosen every second Year; and if Vacancies happen by Resignation, or otherwise, during the Recess of the Legislature of any State, the Executive thereof may make temporary Appointments until the next Meeting of the Legislature, which shall then fill such Vacancies.

No Person shall be a Senator who shall not have attained to the Age of thirty Years, and been nine Years a Citizen of the United States, and who shall not, when elected, be an Inhabitant of that State for which he shall be chosen.

The Vice President of the United States shall be President of the Senate, but shall have no vote, unless they be equally divided.

The Senate shall chuse their other Officers, and also a President pro tempore, in the absence of the Vice President, or when he shall exercise the Office of President of the United States.

The Senate shall have the sole Power to try all Impeachments. When sitting for that purpose they shall be on Oath or Affirmation. When the President of the United States is tried, the Chief Justice shall preside: And no person shall be convicted without the Concurrence of two thirds of the Members present.

Judgment in Cases of Impeachment shall not extend further than to removal from Office, and disqualification to hold and enjoy any Office of honor, Trust, or Profit under the United States: but the Party convicted shall nevertheless be liable and subject to Indictment, Trial, Judgment, and Punishment, according to Law.

Section 4. The Times, Places and Manner of holding Elections for Senators and Representatives, shall be prescribed in each State by the Legislature thereof; but the Congress may at any time by Law make or alter such Regulations, except as to the Places of Chusing Senators.

The Congress shall assemble at least once in every Year, and such Meeting shall be on the first Monday in December, unless they shall by Law appoint a different Day.

Section 5. Each House shall be the Judge of the Elections, Returns and Qualifications of its own Members, and a Majority of each shall constitute a Quorum to do Business; but a smaller number may adjourn from day to day, and may be authorized to compel the Attendance of absent Members, in such Manner, and under such Penalties, as each House may provide.

Each House may determine the Rules of its Proceedings, punish its Members for disorderly Behaviour, and, with the Concurrence of two thirds, expel a Member.

---

[1] This version follows the original Constitution in capitalization and spelling. It is adapted from the text published by the United States Department of the Interior, Office of Education.

[2] Altered by the Sixteenth Amendment.

[3] Negated by the Fourteenth Amendment.

Each House shall keep a Journal of its Proceedings, and from time to time publish the same, excepting such Parts as may in their Judgment require Secrecy; and the Yeas and Nays of the Members of either House on any question shall, at the Desire of one fifth of those Present, be entered on the Journal.

Neither House, during the Session of Congress, shall, without the Consent of the other, adjourn for more than three days, nor to any other Place than that in which the two Houses shall be sitting.

Section 6. The Senators and Representatives shall receive a Compensation for their Services, to be ascertained by Law, and paid out of the Treasury of the United States. They shall in all Cases, except Treason, Felony, and Breach of the Peace, be privileged from Arrest during their Attendance at the Session of their respective Houses, and in going to and returning from the same; and for any Speech or Debate in either House, they shall not be questioned in any other Place.

No Senator or Representative shall, during the Time for which he was elected, be appointed to any civil Office under the Authority of the United States, which shall have been created, or the Emoluments whereof shall have been increased, during such time; and no Person holding any Office under the United States shall be a Member of either House during his continuance in Office.

Section 7. All Bills for raising Revenue shall originate in the House of Representatives; but the Senate may propose or concur with Amendments as on other bills.

Every Bill which shall have passed the House of Representatives and the Senate, shall, before it become a Law, be presented to the President of the United States; If he approve he shall sign it, but if not he shall return it, with his Objections, to that House in which it shall have originated, who shall enter the Objections at large on their Journal, and proceed to reconsider it. If after such Reconsideration two thirds of that House shall agree to pass the bill, it shall be sent, together with the objections, to the other House, by which it shall likewise be reconsidered, and if approved by two thirds of that House, it shall become a Law. But in all such Cases the Votes of both Houses shall be determined by Yeas and Nays, and the Names of the Persons voting for and against the Bill shall be entered on the Journal of each House respectively. If any Bill shall not be returned by the President within ten Days (Sundays excepted) after it shall have been presented to him, the Same shall be a Law, in like Manner as if he had signed it, unless the Congress by their Adjournment prevent its Return, in which Case it shall not be a Law.

Every Order, Resolution, or Vote to which the Concurrence of the Senate and House of Representatives may be necessary (except on a question of Adjournment) shall be presented to the President of the United States; and before the Same shall take Effect, shall be approved by him, or being disapproved by him, shall be repassed by two thirds of the Senate and House of Representatives, according to the Rules and Limitations prescribed in the Case of a Bill.

Section 8. The Congress shall have Power To lay and collect Taxes, Duties, Imposts and Excises, to pay the Debts and provide for the common Defence and general Welfare of the United States; but all Duties, Imposts and Excises shall be uniform throughout the United States;

To borrow money on the credit of the United States;

To regulate Commerce with foreign Nations, and among the several States, and with the Indian Tribes;

To establish an uniform rule of Naturalization, and uniform Laws on the subject of Bankruptcies throughout the United States;

To coin Money, regulate the Value thereof, and of foreign Coin, and fix the Standard of Weights and Measures;

To provide for the Punishment of counterfeiting the Securities and current Coin of the United States;

To establish Post Offices and post Roads;

To promote the Progress of Science and useful Arts, by securing for limited Times to Authors and Inventors the exclusive Right to their respective Writings and Discoveries;

To constitute Tribunals inferior to the Supreme Court;

To define and punish Piracies and Felonies committed on the high Seas, and Offenses against the Law of Nations;

To declare War, grant Letters of Marque and Reprisal, and make Rules concerning Captures on Land and Water;

To raise and support Armies, but no Appropriation of Money to that Use shall be for a longer Term than two Years;

To provide and maintain a Navy;

To make Rules for the Government and Regulation of the land and naval forces;

To provide for calling forth the Militia to execute the Laws of the Union, suppress Insurrections and repel Invasions;

To provide for organizing, arming, and disciplining the Militia, and for government such Part of them as may be employed in the Service of the United States, reserving to the States respectively, the Appointment of the Officers, and the Authority of training the Militia according to the discipline prescribed by Congress;

To exercise exclusive Legislation in all Cases whatsoever, over such District (not exceeding ten Miles square) as may, by Cession of particular States, and the acceptance of Congress, become the Seat of the Government of the United States, and to exercise like Authority over all Places purchased by the Consent of the Legislature of the State in which the Same shall be, for the Erection of Forts, Magazines, Arsenals, Dock-yards, and other needful Buildings;—And

To make all Laws which shall be necessary and proper for carrying into Execution the foregoing Powers, and all other Powers vested by this Constitution in the Government of the United States, or in any Department or Officer thereof.

Section 9. The Migration or Importation of such Persons as any of the States now existing shall think proper to admit, shall not be prohibited by the Congress prior to the Year one thousand eight hundred and eight, but a tax or duty may be imposed on such Importation, not exceeding ten dollars for each Person.

The privilege of the Writ of Habeas Corpus shall not be suspended, unless when in Cases of Rebellion or Invasion the public Safety may require it.

No bill of Attainder or ex post facto Law shall be passed.

No capitation, or other direct, Tax shall be laid unless in Proportion to the Census or Enumeration herein before directed to be taken.

No Tax or Duty shall be laid on Articles exported from any State.

No Preference shall be given by any Regulation of Commerce or Revenue to the Ports of one State over those of another: nor shall Vessels bound to, or from, one State, be obliged to enter, clear, or pay Duties in another.

No Money shall be drawn from the Treasury, but in Consequence of Appropriations made by Law; and a regular Statement and Account of the Receipts and Expenditures of all public Money shall be published from time to time.

No Title of Nobility shall be granted by the United States: And no Person holding any Office of Profit or Trust under them, shall, without the Consent of the Congress, accept of any present, Emolument, Office, or Title, of any kind whatever, from any King, Prince, or foreign State.

Section 10. No State shall enter into any Treaty, Alliance, or Confederation; grant Letters of Marque and Reprisal; coin Money; emit Bills of Credit; make any Thing but gold and silver Coin a Tender in Payment of Debts; pass any Bill of Attainder, ex post facto Law, or Law impairing the Obligation of Contracts, or grant any Title of Nobility.

No State shall, without the Consent of the Congress, lay any Imposts or Duties on Imports or Exports, except what may be absolutely necessary for executing its inspection Laws; and the net Produce of all Duties and Imposts, laid by any State on Imports or Exports, shall be for the use of the Treasury of the United States; and all such Laws shall be subject to the Revision and Control of the Congress.

No state shall, without the Consent of Congress, lay any duty of Tonnage, keep Troops, or Ships of War in time of Peace, enter into any Agreement or Compact with another State, or with a foreign Power, or engage in War, unless actually invaded, or in such imminent Danger as will not admit of delay.

ARTICLE II

Section 1. The executive Power shall be vested in a President of the United States of America. He shall hold his Office during the Term of four years, and, together with the Vice President, chosen for the same Term, be elected, as follows:

Each State shall appoint, in such Manner as the Legislature thereof may direct, a Number of Electors, equal to the whole Number of Senators and Representatives to which the State may be entitled in the Congress: but no Senator or Representative, or Person holding an Office of Trust or Profit under the United States, shall be appointed an Elector.

[The Electors shall meet in their respective States, and vote by Ballot for two persons, of whom one at least shall not be an Inhabitant of the same State with themselves. And they shall make a List of all the Persons voted for, and of the Number of Votes for each; which List they shall sign and certify, and transmit sealed to the Seat of the Government of the United States, directed to the President of the Senate. The President of the Senate shall, in the Presence of the Senate and House of Representatives, open all the Certificates, and the Votes shall then be counted. The Person having the greatest Number of Votes shall be the President, if such Number be a Majority of the whole Number of Electors appointed; and if there be more than one who have such Majority, and have an equal Number of Votes, then the House of Representatives shall immediately chuse by Ballot one of them for President; and if no Person have a Majority, then from the five highest on the List the said House shall in like Manner chuse the President. But in chusing the President, the Votes shall be taken by States, the Representation from each State having one Vote; a quorum for this Purpose shall consist of a Member or Members from two-thirds of the States, and a Majority of all the States shall be necessary to a Choice. In every Case, after the Choice of the President, the Person having the greatest Number of Votes of the Electors shall be the Vice President. But if there should remain two or more who have equal votes, the Senate shall chuse from them by Ballot the Vice President.][4]

The Congress may determine the Time of chusing the Electors, and the Day on which they shall give their Votes; which Day shall be the same throughout the United States.

No person except a natural-born Citizen, or a Citizen of the United States, at the time of the Adoption of this Constitution, shall be eligible to the Office of President; neither shall any Person be eligible to that Office who shall not have attained to the Age of thirty-five years, and been fourteen Years a Resident within the United States.

In Case of the Removal of the President from Office, or of his Death, Resignation, or Inability to discharge the Powers and Duties of the said Office, the same shall devolve on the Vice President, and the Congress may by Law provide for the Case of Removal, Death, Resignation, or Inability, both of the President and Vice President, declaring what Officer shall then act as President, and such Officer shall act accordingly, until the disability be removed, or a President shall be elected.

The President shall, at stated Times, receive for his Services a Compensation, which shall neither be increased nor diminished during the Period for which he shall have been elected, and he shall not receive within that Period any other Emolument from the United States, or any of them.

Before he enter on the execution of his Office, he shall take the following Oath or Affirmation:—"I do solemnly swear (or affirm) that I will faithfully execute the Office of President of the United States, and will, to the best of my Ability, preserve, protect, and defend the Constitution of the United States."

Section 2. The President shall be Commander in Chief of the Army and Navy of the United States, and of the Militia of the several States, when called into the actual Service of the United States; he may require the Opinion, in writing, of the principal Officer in each of the executive Departments, upon any subject relating to the Duties of their respective Offices, and he shall have Power to Grant Reprieves and Pardons for Offenses against the United States, except in Cases of Impeachment.

He shall have Power, by and with the Advice and Consent of the Senate, to make Treaties, provided two-thirds of the Senators present concur; and he shall nominate, and by and with the Advice and Consent of the Senate, shall appoint Ambassadors, other public Ministers and Consuls, Judges of the supreme Court, and all other Officers of the United States, whose Appointments are not herein otherwise provided for, and which shall be established by Law: but the Congress may by Law vest the Appointment of such inferior Officers, as they think proper, in the President alone, in the Courts of Law, or in the Heads of Departments.

The President shall have Power to fill up all Vacancies that may happen during the Recess of the Senate, by granting Commissions which shall expire at the End of their next Session.

Section 3. He shall from time to time give to the Congress Information of the State of the Union, and recommend to their Consideration such Measures as he shall judge necessary and expedient; he may, on extraordinary occasions, convene both Houses, or either of them, and in Case of Disagreement between them, with respect to the Time of Adjournment, he may adjourn them to such Time as he shall think proper; he shall receive Ambassadors and other public Ministers; he shall take care that

[4]Revised by the Twelfth Amendment.

the Laws be faithfully executed, and shall Commission all the Officers of the United States.

Section 4. The President, Vice President and all civil Officers of the United States, shall be removed from Office on Impeachment for, and Conviction of, Treason, Bribery, or other high Crimes and Misdemeanors.

ARTICLE III

Section 1. The judicial Power of the United States, shall be vested in one supreme Court, and in such inferior Courts as the Congress may from time to time ordain and establish. The Judges, both of the supreme and inferior Courts, shall hold their Offices during good Behaviour, and shall, at stated Times, receive for their Services, a Compensation, which shall not be diminished during their Continuance in Office.

Section 2. The judicial Power shall extend to all Cases, in Law and Equity, arising under this Constitution, the Laws of the United States, and Treaties made, or which shall be made, under their Authority;—to all Cases affecting ambassadors, other public ministers and consuls;—to all cases of admiralty and maritime Jurisdiction;—to Controversies to which the United States shall be a Party;—to Controversies between two or more States;—between a State and Citizens of another State;[5]—between Citizens of different States—between Citizens of the same State claiming Lands under Grants of different States, and between a State, or the Citizens thereof, and foreign States, Citizens, or Subjects.

In all Cases affecting Ambassadors, other public Ministers and Consuls, and those in which a State shall be Party, the supreme Court shall have original Jurisdiction. In all the other Cases before mentioned, the supreme Court shall have appellate Jurisdiction, both as to Law and Fact, with such Exceptions, and under such Regulations as the Congress shall make.

The trial of all Crimes, except in Cases of Impeachment, shall be by Jury; and such Trial shall be held in the State where the said Crimes shall have been committed; but when not committed within any State, the Trial shall be at such Place or Places as the Congress may by Law have directed.

Section 3. Treason against the United States, shall consist only in levying War against them, or in adhering to their Enemies, giving them Aid and Comfort. No Person shall be convicted of Treason unless on the Testimony of two Witnesses to the same overt Act, or on Confession in open Court.

The Congress shall have power to declare the Punishment of Treason, but no Attainder of Treason shall work Corruption of Blood, or Forfeiture except during the Life of the Person attainted.

ARTICLE IV

Section 1. Full Faith and Credit shall be given in each State to the public Acts, Records, and judicial Proceedings of every other State. And the Congress may by general Laws prescribe the Manner in which such Acts, Records and Proceedings shall be proved, and the Effect thereof.

Section 2. The Citizens of each State shall be entitled to all Privileges and Immunities of Citizens in the several States.

A Person charged in any State with Treason, Felony, or other Crime, who shall flee from Justice, and be found in another State, shall on demand of the executive Authority of the State from which he fled, be delivered up, to be removed to the State having Jurisdiction of the crime.

No Person held to Service or Labour in one State, under the Laws thereof, escaping into another, shall, in Consequence of any Law or Regulation therein, be discharged from such Service or Labour, but shall be delivered up on Claim of the Party to whom such Service or Labour may be due.

Section 3. New States may be admitted by the Congress into this Union; but no new State shall be formed or erected within the Jurisdiction of any other State; nor any State be formed by the Junction of two or more States, or parts of States, without the Consent of the Legislatures of the States concerned as well as of the Congress.

The Congress shall have Power to dispose of and make all needful Rules and Regulations respecting the Territory or other Property belonging to the United States; and nothing in this Constitution shall be so construed as to Prejudice any Claims of the United States, or of any particular State.

Section 4. The United States shall guarantee to every State in this Union a Republican Form of Government, and shall protect each of them against Invasion; and on Application of the Legislature, or of the Executive (when the Legislature cannot be convened) against domestic Violence.

ARTICLE V

The Congress, whenever two-thirds of both Houses shall deem it necessary, shall propose Amendments to this Constitution, or, on the Application of the Legislatures of two-thirds of the several States, shall call a Convention for proposing Amendments, which, in either Case, shall be valid to all Intents and Purposes, as part of this Constitution, when ratified by the Legislatures of three-fourths of the several States, or by Conventions in three-fourths thereof, as the one or the other Mode of Ratification may be proposed by the Congress; Provided that no Amendment which may be made prior to the Year One thousand eight hundred and eight shall in any Manner affect the first and fourth Clauses in the Ninth Section of the first Article; and that no State, without its Consent, shall be deprived of its equal Suffrage in the Senate.

ARTICLE VI

All Debts contracted and Engagements entered into, before the Adoption of this Constitution, shall be as valid against the United States under this Constitution, as under the Confederation.

This Constitution, and the Laws of the United States which shall be made in Pursuance thereof; and all Treaties made, or which shall be made, under the Authority of the United States, shall be the supreme Law of the Land; and the Judges in every State shall be bound thereby, any Thing in the Constitution or Laws of any State to the Contrary notwithstanding.

The Senators and Representatives before mentioned, and the Members of the several State Legislatures, and all executive and judicial Officers, both of the United States and of the several States, shall be bound by Oath or Affirmation to support this Constitution; but no religious Tests shall ever be required as a qualification to any Office or public Trust under the United States.

---

[5]Qualified by the Eleventh Amendment.

ARTICLE VII

The Ratification of the Conventions of nine States shall be sufficient for the Establishment of this Constitution between the States so ratifying the same.

Done in Convention by the Unanimous Consent of the States present the Seventeenth Day of September in the Year of our Lord one thousand seven hundred and Eighty seven, and of the Independence of the United States of America the Twelfth. In Witness whereof We have hereunto subscribed our Names.[6]

GEORGE WASHINGTON
PRESIDENT AND DEPUTY FROM VIRGINIA

NEW HAMPSHIRE
John Langdon
Nicholas Gilman

MASSACHUSETTS
Nathaniel Gorham
Rufus King

CONNECTICUT
William Samuel Johnson
Roger Sherman

NEW YORK
Alexander Hamilton

NEW JERSEY
William Livingston
David Brearley
William Paterson
Jonathan Dayton

PENNSYLVANIA
Benjamin Franklin
Thomas Mifflin
Robert Morris
George Clymer
Thomas FitzSimons
Jared Ingersoll
James Wilson
Gouverneur Morris

DELAWARE
George Read
Gunning Bedford, Jr.
John Dickinson
Richard Bassett
Jacob Broom

MARYLAND
James McHenry
Daniel of St. Thomas Jenifer
Daniel Carroll

VIRGINIA
John Blair
James Madison, Jr.

NORTH CAROLINA
William Blount
Richard Dobbs Spaight
Hugh Williamson

SOUTH CAROLINA
John Rutledge
Charles Cotesworth Pinckney
Charles Pinckney
Pierce Butler

GEORGIA
William Few
Abraham Baldwin

Articles in Addition to, and Amendment of, the Constitution of the United States of America, Proposed by Congress, and Ratified by the Legislatures of the Several States, Pursuant to the Fifth Article of the Original Constitution[7]

[AMENDMENT I]

Congress shall make no law respecting an establishment of religion, or prohibiting the free exercise thereof; or abridging the freedom of speech, or of the press; or the right of the people peaceably to assemble, and to petition the Government for a redress of grievances.

[AMENDMENT II]

A well regulated Militia, being necessary to the security of a free State, the right of the people to keep and bear Arms shall not be infringed.

[AMENDMENT III]

No Soldier shall, in time of peace, be quartered in any house, without the consent of the Owner, nor in time of war, but in a manner to be prescribed by law.

[AMENDMENT IV]

The right of the people to be secure in their persons, houses, papers, and effects, against unreasonable searches and seizures, shall not be violated, and no Warrants shall issue, but upon probable cause, supported by Oath or affirmation, and particularly describing the place to be searched, and the persons or things to be seized.

[AMENDMENT V]

No person shall be held to answer for a capital or otherwise infamous crime, unless on a presentment or indictment of a Grand Jury, except in cases arising in the land or naval forces, or in the Militia, when in actual service in time of War or public danger; nor shall any person be subject for the same offence to be twice put in jeopardy of life or limb; nor shall be compelled in any criminal case to be a witness against himself, nor be deprived of life, liberty, or property, without due process of law; nor shall private property be taken for public use, without just compensation.

[AMENDMENT VI]

In all criminal prosecutions, the accused shall enjoy the right to a speedy and public trial, by an impartial jury of the State and district wherein the crime shall have been committed, which district shall have been previously ascertained by law, and to be informed of the nature and cause of the accusation; to be confronted with the witnesses against him; to have compulsory process for obtaining witnesses in his favour, and to have the Assistance of Counsel for his defence.

[AMENDMENT VII]

In suits at common law, where the value in controversy shall exceed twenty dollars, the right of trial by jury shall be preserved, and no fact tried by a jury, shall be otherwise reexamined in any Court of the United States, than according to the rules of the common law.

---

[6]These are the full names of the signers, which in some cases are not the signatures on the document.

[7]This heading appears only in the joint resolution submitting the first ten amendments, known as the Bill of Rights.

[AMENDMENT VIII]

Excessive bail shall not be required, nor excessive fines imposed, nor cruel and unusual punishments inflicted.

[AMENDMENT IX]

The enumeration of the Constitution, of certain rights, shall not be construed to deny or disparage others retained by the people.

[AMENDMENT X]

The powers not delegated to the United States by the Constitution, nor prohibited by it to the States, are reserved to the States respectively, or to the people.
[Amendments I–X, in force 1791.]

[AMENDMENT XI][8]

The Judicial power of the United States shall not be construed to extend to any suit in law or equity, commenced or prosecuted against one of the United States by Citizens of another State, or by Citizens or Subjects of any Foreign State.

[AMENDMENT XII][9]

The Electors shall meet in their respective States and vote by ballot for President and Vice-President, one of whom, at least, shall not be an inhabitant of the same State with themselves; they shall name in their ballots the person voted for as President, and in distinct ballots the person voted for as Vice-President, and they shall make distinct lists of all persons voted for as President, and of all persons voted for as Vice-President, and of the number of votes for each, which lists they shall sign and certify, and transmit sealed to the seat of the government of the United States, directed to the President of the Senate;—The President of the Senate shall, in the presence of the Senate and House of Representatives, open all the certificates and the votes shall then be counted;—The person having the greatest number of votes for President, shall be the President, if such number be a majority of the whole number of Electors appointed; and if no person have such majority, then from the persons having the highest numbers not exceeding three on the list of those voted for as President, the House of Representatives shall choose immediately, by ballot, the President. But in choosing the President, the votes shall be taken by states, the representation from each state having one vote; a quorum for this purpose shall consist of a member or members from two-thirds of the states, and a majority of all the states shall be necessary to a choice. And if the House of Representatives shall not choose a President whenever the right of choice shall devolve upon them, before the fourth day of March next following, then the Vice-President shall act as President, as in the case of the death or other constitutional disability of the President.—The person having the greatest number of votes as Vice-President, shall be the Vice-President, if such number be a majority of the whole number of Electors appointed, and if no person have a majority, then from the two highest numbers on the list, the Senate shall choose the Vice-President; a quorum for the purpose shall consist of two-thirds of the whole number of Senators, and a majority of the whole number shall be necessary to a choice. But no person constitutionally ineligible to the office of President shall be eligible to that of Vice-President of the United States.

[AMENDMENT XIII][10]

Section 1. Neither slavery nor involuntary servitude, except as a punishment for crime whereof the party shall have been duly convicted, shall exist within the United States, or any place subject to their jurisdiction.

Section 2. Congress shall have power to enforce this article by appropriate legislation.

[AMENDMENT XIV][11]

Section 1. All persons born or naturalized in the United States, and subject to the jurisdiction thereof, are citizens of the United States and of the State wherein they reside. No State shall abridge the privileges or immunities of citizens of the United States; nor shall any State deprive any person of life, liberty, or property, without due process of law; nor deny to any person within its jurisdiction the equal protection of the laws.

Section 2. Representatives shall be apportioned among the several States according to their respective numbers, counting the whole number of persons in each State, excluding Indians not taxed. But when the right to vote at any election for the choice of electors for President and Vice-President of the United States, Representatives in Congress, the Executive and Judicial officers of a State, or the members of the Legislature thereof, is denied to any of the male inhabitants of such State, being twenty-one years of age, and citizens of the United States, or in any way abridged, except for participation in rebellion, or other crime, the basis of representation therein shall be reduced in the proportion which the number of such male citizens shall bear to the whole number of male citizens twenty-one years of age in such State.

Section 3. No person shall be a Senator or Representative in Congress, or elector of President and Vice-President, or hold any office, civil or military, under the United States, or under any State, who, having previously taken an oath, as a member of Congress, or as an officer of the United States, or as a member of any State legislature, or as an executive or judicial officer of any State, to support the Constitution of the United States, shall have engaged in insurrection or rebellion against the same, or given aid or comfort to the enemies thereof. But Congress may by a vote of two-thirds of each House, remove such disability.

Section 4. The validity of the public debt of the United States, authorized by law, including debts incurred for payment of pensions and bounties for services in suppressing insurrection or rebellion, shall not be questioned. But neither the United States nor any State shall assume or pay any debts or obligation incurred in aid of insurrection or rebellion against the United States, or any claim for the loss or emancipation of any slave; but all such debts, obligations, and claims shall be held illegal and void.

Section 5. The Congress shall have the power to enforce, by appropriate legislation, the provisions of this article.

---

[8]Adopted in 1798.
[9]Adopted in 1804.

[10]Adopted in 1865.
[11]Adopted in 1868.

[AMENDMENT XV][12]

Section 1. The right of citizens of the United States to vote shall not be denied or abridged by the United States or by any State on account of race, color, or previous condition of servitude—

Section 2. The Congress shall have power to enforce this article by appropriate legislation.

[AMENDMENT XVI][13]

The Congress shall have power to lay and collect taxes on incomes, from whatever source derived, without apportionment among the several States, and without regard to any census or enumeration.

[AMENDMENT XVII][14]

The Senate of the United States shall be composed of two Senators from each State, elected by the people thereof, for six years; and each Senator shall have one vote. The electors in each State shall have the qualifications requisite for electors of the most numerous branch of the State legislatures.

When vacancies happen in the representation of any State in the Senate, the executive authority of such State shall issue writs of election to fill such vacancies: Provided, That the legislature of any State may empower the executive thereof to make temporary appointments until the people fill the vacancies by election as the legislature may direct.

This amendment shall not be so construed as to affect the election or term of any Senator chosen before it becomes valid as part of the Constitution.

[AMENDMENT XVIII][15]

Section 1. After one year from the ratification of this article the manufacture, sale, or transportation of intoxicating liquors within, the importation thereof into, or the exportation thereof from the United States and all territory subject to the jurisdiction thereof for beverage purposes is hereby prohibited.

Section 2. The Congress and the several States shall have concurrent power to enforce this article by appropriate legislation.

Section 3. This article shall be inoperative unless it shall have been ratified as an amendment to the Constitution by the legislatures of the several States, as provided in the Constitution, within seven years from the date of the submission hereof to the States by the Congress.

[AMENDMENT XIX][16]

The right of citizens of the United States to vote shall not be denied or abridged by the United States or by any State on account of sex.

Congress shall have power to enforce this article by appropriate legislation.

[AMENDMENT XX][17]

Section 1. The terms of the President and Vice-President shall end at noon on the 20th day of January, and the terms of Senators and Representatives at noon on the 3d day of January, of the years in which such terms would have ended if this article had not been ratified; and the terms of their successors shall then begin.

Section 2. The Congress shall assemble at least once in every year, and such meeting shall begin at noon on the 3d day of January, unless they shall by law appoint a different day.

Section 3. If, at the time fixed for the beginning of the term of the President, the President elect shall have died, the Vice-President elect shall become President. If a President shall not have been chosen before the time fixed for the beginning of his term or if the President elect shall have failed to qualify, then the Vice-President elect shall act as President until a President shall have qualified; and the Congress may by law provide for the case wherein neither a President elect nor a Vice-President elect shall have qualified, declaring who shall then act as President, or the manner in which one who is to act shall be selected, and such person shall act accordingly until a President or Vice-President shall have qualified.

Section 4. The Congress may by law provide for the case of the death of any of the persons from whom the House of Representatives may choose a President whenever the right of choice shall have devolved upon them, and for the case of the death of any of the persons from whom the Senate may choose a Vice-President whenever the right of choice shall have devolved upon them.

Section 5. Sections 1 and 2 shall take effect on the 15th day of October following the ratification of this article.

Section 6. This article shall be inoperative unless it shall have been ratified as an amendment to the Constitution by the legislatures of three-fourths of the several States within seven years from the date of its submission.

[AMENDMENT XXI][18]

Section 1. The eighteenth article of amendment to the Constitution of the United States is hereby repealed.

Section 2. The transportation or importation into any State, Territory, or possession of the United States for delivery or use therein of intoxicating liquors, in violation of the laws thereof, is hereby prohibited.

Section 3. This article shall be inoperative unless it shall have been ratified as an amendment to the Constitution by conventions in the several States, as provided in the Constitution, within seven years from the date of the submission hereof to the States by the Congress.

[AMENDMENT XXII][19]

No person shall be elected to the office of the President more than twice, and no person who has held the office of President, or acted as President, for more than two years of a term to which some other person was elected President shall be elected to the office of the President more than once.

---

[12]Adopted in 1870.
[13]Adopted in 1913.
[14]Adopted in 1913.
[15]Adopted in 1918.
[16]Adopted in 1920.

[17]Adopted in 1933.
[18]Adopted in 1933.
[19]Adopted in 1951.

But this Article shall not apply to any person holding the office of President when this Article was proposed by the Congress, and shall not prevent any person who may be holding the office of President, or acting as President, during the term within which this Article becomes operative from holding the office of President or acting as President during the remainder of such term.

This article shall be inoperative unless it shall have been ratified as an amendment to the Constitution by the legislatures of three-fourths of the several states within seven years from the date of its submission to the states by the Congress.

[AMENDMENT XXIII][20]

Section 1. The District constituting the seat of Government of the United States shall appoint in such manner as the Congress may direct:

A number of electors of President and Vice-President equal to the whole number of Senators and Representatives in Congress to which the District would be entitled if it were a State, but in no event more than the least populous State; they shall be in addition to those appointed by the States, but they shall be considered, for the purpose of the election of President and Vice-President, to be electors appointed by a State; and they shall meet in the District and perform such duties as provided by the twelfth article of amendment.

Section 2. The Congress shall have power to enforce this article by appropriate legislation.

[AMENDMENT XXIV][21]

Section 1. The right of citizens of the United States to vote in any primary or other election for President or Vice-President, for electors for President or Vice-President, or for Senator or Representative in Congress, shall not be denied or abridged by the United States or any state by reason of failure to pay any poll tax or other tax.

Section 2. The Congress shall have the power to enforce this article by appropriate legislation.

[AMENDMENT XXV][22]

Section 1. In case of the removal of the President from office or of his death or resignation, the Vice-President shall become President.

Section 2. Whenever there is a vacancy in the office of the Vice President, the President shall nominate a Vice President who shall take office upon confirmation by a majority vote of both Houses of Congress.

Section 3. Whenever the President transmits to the President Pro Tempore of the Senate and the Speaker of the House of Representatives his written declaration that he is unable to discharge the powers and duties of his office, and until he transmits to them a written declaration to the contrary, such powers and duties shall be discharged by the Vice-President as Acting President.

Section 4. Whenever the Vice-President and a majority of either the principal officers of the executive departments or of such other body as Congress may by law provide, transmit to the President Pro Tempore of the Senate and the Speaker of the House of Representatives their written declaration that the President is unable to discharge the powers and duties of his office, the Vice President shall immediately assume the powers and duties of the office as Acting President.

Thereafter, when the President transmits to the President Pro Tempore of the Senate and the Speaker of the House of Representatives his written declaration that no inability exists, he shall resume the powers and duties of his office unless the Vice President and a majority of either the principal officers of the executive departments or of such other body as Congress may by law provide, transmit within four days to the President Pro Tempore of the Senate and the Speaker of the House of Representatives their written declaration that the President is unable to discharge the powers and duties of his office. Thereupon Congress shall decide the issue, assembling within forty-eight hours for that purpose if not in session. If the Congress, within twenty-one days after receipt of the latter written declaration, or, if Congress is not in session, within twenty-one days after Congress is required to assemble, determines by two-thirds vote of both Houses that the President is unable to discharge the powers and duties of his office, the Vice President shall continue to discharge the same as Acting President; otherwise, the President shall resume the powers and duties of his office.

[AMENDMENT XXVI][23]

Section 1. The right of citizens of the United States, who are eighteen years of age or older, to vote shall not be denied or abridged by the United States or by any State on account of age.

Section 2. The Congress shall have power to enforce this article by appropriate legislation.

[AMENDMENT XXVII][24]

No law, varying the compensation for the services of the Senators and Representatives, shall take effect, until an election of Representatives shall have intervened.

[20]Adopted in 1961.

[21]Adopted in 1964.

[22]Adopted in 1967.

[23]Adopted in 1971.

[24]Adopted in 1992.

Presidential Elections

YEAR	CANDIDATES	PARTIES	POPULAR VOTE	% OF POPULAR VOTE	ELECTORAL VOTE	% VOTER PARTICIPATION
1789	**George Washington**				69	
	John Adams				34	
	Other candidates				35	
1792	**George Washington**				132	
	John Adams				77	
	George Clinton				50	
	Other candidates				5	
1796	**John Adams**	Federalist			71	
	Thomas Jefferson	Dem.-Rep.			68	
	Thomas Pinckney	Federalist			59	
	Aaron Burr	Dem.-Rep.			30	
	Other candidates				48	
1800	**Thomas Jefferson**	Dem.-Rep.			73	
	Aaron Burr	Dem.-Rep.			73	
	John Adams	Federalist			65	
	Charles C. Pinckney	Federalist			64	
	John Jay	Federalist			1	
1804	**Thomas Jefferson**	Dem.-Rep.			162	
	Charles C. Pinckney	Federalist			14	
1808	**James Madison**	Dem.-Rep.			122	
	Charles C. Pinckney	Federalist			47	
	George Clinton	Dem.-Rep.			6	
1812	**James Madison**	Dem.-Rep.			128	
	DeWitt Clinton	Federalist			89	
1816	**James Monroe**	Dem.-Rep.			183	
	Rufus King	Federalist			34	
1820	**James Monroe**	Dem.-Rep.			231	
	John Quincy Adams	Indep.-Rep.			1	
1824	**John Quincy Adams**	Dem.-Rep.	113,122	31.0	84	26.9
	Andrew Jackson	Dem.-Rep.	151,271	43.0	99	
	Henry Clay	Dem.-Rep.	47,136	13.0	37	
	William H. Crawford	Dem.-Rep.	46,618	13.0	41	
1828	**Andrew Jackson**	Democratic	642,553	56.0	178	57.6
	John Quincy Adams	National Republican	500,897	44.0	83	
1832	**Andrew Jackson**	Democratic	701,780	54.5	219	55.4
	Henry Clay	National Republican	484,205	37.5	49	
	William Wirt	Anti-Masonic ⎫	101,051	8.0	7	
	John Floyd	Democratic ⎭			11	
1836	**Martin Van Buren**	Democratic	764,176	50.9	170	57.8
	William H. Harrison	Whig	550,816	49.1	73	
	Hugh L. White	Whig			26	
	Daniel Webster	Whig			14	
	W. P. Mangum	Whig			11	
1840	**William H. Harrison**	Whig	1,275,390	53.0	234	80.2
	Martin Van Buren	Democratic	1,128,854	47.0	60	

YEAR	CANDIDATES	PARTIES	POPULAR VOTE	% OF POPULAR VOTE	ELECTORAL VOTE	% VOTER PARTICIPATION
1844	**James K. Polk**	Democratic	1,339,494	49.6	170	78.9
	Henry Clay	Whig	1,300,004	48.1	105	
	James G. Birney	Liberty	62,300	2.3		
1848	**Zachary Taylor**	Whig	1,361,393	47.4	163	72.7
	Lewis Cass	Democratic	1,223,460	42.5	127	
	Martin Van Buren	Free Soil	291,263	10.1		
1852	**Franklin Pierce**	Democratic	1,607,510	50.9	254	69.6
	Winfield Scott	Whig	1,386,942	44.1	42	
	John P. Hale	Free Soil	155,825	5.0		
1856	**James Buchanan**	Democratic	1,836,072	45.3	174	78.9
	John C. Fremont	Republican	1,342,345	33.1	114	
	Millard Fillmore	American	871,731	21.6	8	
1860	**Abraham Lincoln**	Republican	1,865,908	39.8	180	81.2
	Stephen A. Douglas	Democratic	1,375,157	29.5	12	
	John C. Breckinridge	Democratic	848,019	18.1	72	
	John Bell	Constitutional Union	590,631	12.6	39	
1864	**Abraham Lincoln**	Republican	2,218,388	55.0	212	73.8
	George B. McClellan	Democratic	1,812,807	45.0	21	
1868	**Ulysses S. Grant**	Republican	3,013,650	52.7	214	78.1
	Horatio Seymour	Democratic	2,708,744	47.3	80	
1872	**Ulysses S. Grant**	Republican	3,598,235	55.6	286	71.3
	Horace Greeley	Democratic	2,834,761	43.9	66	
1876	**Rutherford B. Hayes**	Republican	4,034,311	48.0	185	81.8
	Samuel J. Tilden	Democratic	4,288,546	51.0	184	
1880	**James A. Garfield**	Republican	4,446,158	48.5	214	79.4
	Winfield S. Hancock	Democratic	4,444,260	48.1	155	
	James B. Weaver	Greenback-Labor	308,578	3.4		
1884	**Grover Cleveland**	Democratic	4,874,621	48.5	219	77.5
	James G. Blaine	Republican	4,848,936	48.2	182	
	Benjamin F. Butler	Greenback-Labor	175,370	1.8		
	John P. St. John	Prohibition	150,369	1.5		
1888	**Benjamin Harrison**	Republican	5,443,892	47.9	233	79.3
	Grover Cleveland	Democratic	5,534,488	48.6	168	
	Clinton B. Fisk	Prohibition	249,506	2.2		
	Anson J. Streeter	Union Labor	146,935	1.3		
1892	**Grover Cleveland**	Democratic	5,551,883	46.1	277	74.7
	Benjamin Harrison	Republican	5,179,244	43.0	145	
	James B. Weaver	People's	1,029,846	8.5	22	
	John Bidwell	Prohibition	264,133	2.2		
1896	**William McKinley**	Republican	7,108,480	52.0	271	79.3
	William J. Bryan	Democratic	6,511,495	48.0	176	
1900	**William McKinley**	Republican	7,218,039	51.7	292	73.2
	William J. Bryan	Democratic; Populist	6,358,345	45.5	155	
	John C. Wooley	Prohibition	208,914	1.5		
1904	**Theodore Roosevelt**	Republican	7,626,593	57.4	336	65.2
	Alton B. Parker	Democratic	5,082,898	37.6	140	
	Eugene V. Debs	Socialist	402,283	3.0		
	Silas C. Swallow	Prohibition	258,536	1.9		

YEAR	CANDIDATES	PARTIES	POPULAR VOTE	% OF POPULAR VOTE	ELECTORAL VOTE	% VOTER PARTICIPATION
1908	**William H. Taft**	Republican	7,676,258	51.6	321	65.4
	William J. Bryan	Democratic	6,406,801	43.1	162	
	Eugene V. Debs	Socialist	420,793	2.8		
	Eugene W. Chafin	Prohibition	253,840	1.7		
1912	**Woodrow Wilson**	Democratic	6,293,152	42.0	435	58.8
	Theodore Roosevelt	Progressive	4,119,207	28.0	88	
	William H. Taft	Republican	3,484,980	24.0	8	
	Eugene V. Debs	Socialist	900,672	6.0		
	Eugene W. Chafin	Prohibition	206,275	1.4		
1916	**Woodrow Wilson**	Democratic	9,126,300	49.4	277	61.6
	Charles E.. Hughes	Republican	8,546,789	46.2	254	
	A. L. Benson	Socialist	585,113	3.2		
	J. Frank Hanly	Prohibition	220,506	1.2		
1920	**Warren G. Harding**	Republican	16,153,115	60.4	404	49.2
	James M. Cox	Democratic	9,133,092	34.2	127	
	Eugene V. Debs	Socialist	919,799	3.4		
	P. P. Christensen	Farmer-Labor	265,411	1.0		
1924	**Calvin Coolidge**	Republican	15,719,921	54.0	382	48.9
	John W. Davis	Democratic	8,386,704	28.8	136	
	Robert M. La Follette	Progressive	4,831,289	16.6	13	
1928	**Herbert C. Hoover**	Republican	21,437,277	58.2	444	56.9
	Alfred E. Smith	Democratic	15,007,698	40.9	87	
1932	**Franklin D. Roosevelt**	Democratic	22,829,501	57.4	472	56.9
	Herbert C. Hoover	Republican	15,760,684	39.7	59	
	Norman Thomas	Socialist	881,951	2.2		
1936	**Franklin D. Roosevelt**	Democratic	27,757,333	60.8	523	61.0
	Alfred M. Landon	Republican	16,684,231	36.5	8	
	William Lemke	Union	882,479	1.9		
1940	**Franklin D. Roosevelt**	Democratic	27,313,041	54.8	449	62.5
	Wendell L. Wilkie	Republican	22,348,480	44.8	82	
1944	**Franklin D. Roosevelt**	Democratic	25,612,610	53.5	432	55.9
	Thomas E. Dewey	Republican	22,117,617	46.0	99	
1948	**Harry S Truman**	Democratic	24,179,345	50.0	303	53.0
	Thomas E. Dewey	Republican	21,991,291	46.0	189	
	J. Strom Thurmond	States' Rights	1,169,021	2.0	39	
	Henry A. Wallace	Progressive	1,157,172	2.0		
1952	**Dwight D. Eisenhower**	Republican	33,936,234	55.1	442	63.3
	Adlai E. Stevenson	Democratic	27,314,992	44.4	89	
1956	**Dwight D. Eisenhower**	Republican	35,590,472	57.6	457	60.6
	Adlai E. Stevenson	Democratic	26,022,752	42.1	73	
1960	**John F. Kennedy**	Democratic	34,226,731	49.7	303	62.8
	Richard M. Nixon	Republican	34,108,157	49.6	219	
	Harry F. Byrd	Independent	501,643		15	
1964	**Lyndon B. Johnson**	Democratic	43,129,566	61.1	486	61.7
	Barry M. Goldwater	Republican	27,178,188	38.5	52	
1968	**Richard M. Nixon**	Republican	31,785,480	44.0	301	60.6
	Hubert H. Humphrey	Democratic	31,275,166	42.7	191	
	George C. Wallace	American Independent	9,906,473	13.5	46	

YEAR	CANDIDATES	PARTIES	POPULAR VOTE	% OF POPULAR VOTE	ELECTORAL VOTE	% VOTER PARTICIPATION
1972	**Richard M. Nixon**	Republican	47,169,911	60.7	520	55.2
	George S. McGovern	Democratic	29,170,383	37.5	17	
	John G. Schmitz	American	1,099,482	1.4		
1976	**Jimmy Carter**	Democratic	40,830,763	50.1	297	53.5
	Gerald R. Ford	Republican	39,147,793	48.0	240	
1980	**Ronald Reagan**	Republican	43,904,153	51.0	489	52.6
	Jimmy Carter	Democratic	35,483,883	41.0	49	
	John B. Anderson	Independent	5,719,437	7.0	0	
	Ed Clark	Libertarian	920,859	1.0	0	
1984	**Ronald Reagan**	Republican	54,455,075	58.8	525	53.3
	Walter Mondale	Democratic	37,577,185	40.5	13	
1988	**George H. W. Bush**	Republican	48,886,097	53.9	426	48.6
	Michael Dukakis	Democratic	41,809,074	46.1	111	
1992	**William J. Clinton**	Democratic	44,908,254	43.0	370	55.9
	George H. W. Bush	Republican	39,102,343	37.4	168	
	H. Ross Perot	Independent	19,741,065	18.9	0	
1996	**William J. Clinton**	Democratic	45,590,703	49.3	379	49
	Robert Dole	Republican	37,816,307	40.7	159	
	H. Ross Perot	Reform	8,085,294	8.4	0	
2000	**George W. Bush**	Republican	50,456,062	47.9	271	51.2
	Al Gore	Democratic	50,996,582	48.4	266	
	Ralph Nader	Green	2,858,843	2.7	0	
2004	**George W. Bush**	Republican	62,048,610	50.7	286	60.7
	John F. Kerry	Democrat	59,028,444	48.3	251	
	Ralph Nader	Independent	465,650	0.4	0	
2008	**Barack Obama**	Democratic	65,070,487	53	365	63.0
	John McCain	Republican	57,154,810	46	173	
2012	**Barack Obama**	Democrat	65,899,660	51.0	332	58.9
	Mitt Romney	Republican	60,929,152	47.2	206	

Justices of the Supreme Court

	TERM OF SERVICE	YEARS OF SERVICE	LIFE SPAN
John Jay	1789–1795	5	1745–1829
John Rutledge	1789–1791	1	1739–1800
William Cushing	1789–1810	20	1732–1810
James Wilson	1789–1798	8	1742–1798
John Blair	1789–1796	6	1732–1800
Robert H. Harrison	1789–1790	—	1745–1790
James Iredell	1790–1799	9	1751–1799
Thomas Johnson	1791–1793	1	1732–1819
William Paterson	1793–1806	13	1745–1806
*John Rutledge**	1795	—	1739–1800
Samuel Chase	1796–1811	15	1741–1811
Oliver Ellsworth	1796–1800	4	1745–1807
Bushrod Washington	1798–1829	31	1762–1829
Alfred Moore	1799–1804	4	1755–1810
John Marshall	1801–1835	34	1755–1835
William Johnson	1804–1834	30	1771–1834
H. Brockholst Livingston	1806–1823	16	1757–1823
Thomas Todd	1807–1826	18	1765–1826
Joseph Story	1811–1845	33	1779–1845
Gabriel Duval	1811–1835	24	1752–1844
Smith Thompson	1823–1843	20	1768–1843
Robert Trimble	1826–1828	2	1777–1828
John McLean	1829–1861	32	1785–1861
Henry Baldwin	1830–1844	14	1780–1844
James M. Wayne	1835–1867	32	1790–1867
Roger B. Taney	1836–1864	28	1777–1864

	TERM OF SERVICE	YEARS OF SERVICE	LIFE SPAN
Philip P. Barbour	1836–1841	4	1783–1841
John Catron	1837–1865	28	1786–1865
John McKinley	1837–1852	15	1780–1852
Peter V. Daniel	1841–1860	19	1784–1860
Samuel Nelson	1845–1872	27	1792–1873
Levi Woodbury	1845–1851	5	1789–1851
Robert C. Grier	1846–1870	23	1794–1870
Benjamin R. Curtis	1851–1857	6	1809–1874
John A. Campbell	1853–1861	8	1811–1889
Nathan Clifford	1858–1881	23	1803–1881
Noah H. Swayne	1862–1881	18	1804–1884
Samuel F. Miller	1862–1890	28	1816–1890
David Davis	1862–1877	14	1815–1886
Stephen J. Field	1863–1897	34	1816–1899
Salmon P. Chase	1864–1873	8	1808–1873
William Strong	1870–1880	10	1808–1895
Joseph P. Bradley	1870–1892	22	1813–1892
Ward Hunt	1873–1882	9	1810–1886
Morrison R. Waite	1874–1888	14	1816–1888
John M. Harlan	1877–1911	34	1833–1911
William B. Woods	1880–1887	7	1824–1887
Stanley Matthews	1881–1889	7	1824–1889
Horace Gray	1882–1902	20	1828–1902
Samuel Blatchford	1882–1893	11	1820–1893
Lucius Q. C. Lamar	1888–1893	5	1825–1893
Melville W. Fuller	1888–1910	21	1833–1910
David J. Brewer	1890–1910	20	1837–1910
Henry B. Brown	1890–1906	16	1836–1913

*Appointed and served one term, but not confirmed by the Senate.
Note: Chief justices are in italics.

	TERM OF SERVICE	YEARS OF SERVICE	LIFE SPAN
George Shiras Jr.	1892–1903	10	1832–1924
Howell E. Jackson	1893–1895	2	1832–1895
Edward D. White	1894–1910	16	1845–1921
Rufus W. Peckham	1895–1909	14	1838–1909
Joseph McKenna	1898–1925	26	1843–1926
Oliver W. Holmes	1902–1932	30	1841–1935
William R. Day	1903–1922	19	1849–1923
William H. Moody	1906–1910	3	1853–1917
Horace H. Lurton	1909–1914	4	1844–1914
Charles E. Hughes	1910–1916	5	1862–1948
Edward D. White	1910–1921	11	1845–1921
Willis Van Devanter	1911–1937	26	1859–1941
Joseph R. Lamar	1911–1916	5	1857–1916
Mahlon Pitney	1912–1922	10	1858–1924
James C. McReynolds	1914–1941	26	1862–1946
Louis D. Brandeis	1916–1939	22	1856–1941
John H. Clarke	1916–1922	6	1857–1945
William H. Taft	1921–1930	8	1857–1930
George Sutherland	1922–1938	15	1862–1942
Pierce Butler	1922–1939	16	1866–1939
Edward T. Sanford	1923–1930	7	1865–1930
Harlan F. Stone	1925–1941	16	1872–1946
Charles E. Hughes	1930–1941	11	1862–1948
Owen J. Roberts	1930–1945	15	1875–1955
Benjamin N. Cardozo	1932–1938	6	1870–1938
Hugo L. Black	1937–1971	34	1886–1971
Stanley F. Reed	1938–1957	19	1884–1980
Felix Frankfurter	1939–1962	23	1882–1965
William O. Douglas	1939–1975	36	1898–1980
Frank Murphy	1940–1949	9	1890–1949
Harlan F. Stone	1941–1946	5	1872–1946
James F. Byrnes	1941–1942	1	1882–1972

	TERM OF SERVICE	YEARS OF SERVICE	LIFE SPAN
Robert H. Jackson	1941–1954	13	1892–1954
Wiley B. Rutledge	1943–1949	6	1894–1949
Harold H. Burton	1945–1958	13	1888–1964
Fred M. Vinson	1946–1953	7	1890–1953
Tom C. Clark	1949–1967	18	1899–1977
Sherman Minton	1949–1956	7	1890–1965
Earl Warren	1953–1969	16	1891–1974
John Marshall Harlan	1955–1971	16	1899–1971
William J. Brennan Jr.	1956–1990	33	1906–1997
Charles E. Whittaker	1957–1962	5	1901–1973
Potter Stewart	1958–1981	23	1915–1985
Bryon R. White	1962–1993	31	1917–2002
Arthur J. Goldberg	1962–1965	3	1908–1990
Abe Fortas	1965–1969	4	1910–1982
Thurgood Marshall	1967–1991	24	1908–1993
Warren C. Burger	1969–1986	17	1907–1995
Harry A. Blackmun	1970–1994	24	1908–1999
Lewis F. Powell Jr.	1972–1987	15	1907–1998
William H. Rehnquist	1972–1986	14	1924–2005
John P. Stevens III	1975–2010	35	1920–
Sandra Day O'Connor	1981–2006	24	1930–
William H. Rehnquist	1986–2005	18	1924–2005
Antonin Scalia	1986–	—	1936–
Anthony M. Kennedy	1988–	—	1936–
David H. Souter	1990–2009	20	1939–
Clarence Thomas	1991–	—	1948–
Ruth Bader Ginsburg	1993–	—	1933–
Stephen Breyer	1994–	—	1938–
John G. Roberts Jr.	2005–	—	1955–
Samuel A. Alito Jr.	2006–	—	1950–
Sonia Sotomayor	2009–	—	1954–
Elena Kagan	2010–	—	1960–

A Social Profile of the American Republic

YEAR	POPULATION	PERCENT INCREASE	POPULATION PER SQUARE MILE	POPULATION PERCENT URBAN/ RURAL	PERCENT MALE/ FEMALE	PERCENT WHITE/ NONWHITE	PERSONS PER HOUSEHOLD	MEDIAN AGE
1790	3,929,214		4.5	5.1/94.9	NA/NA	80.7/19.3	5.79	NA
1800	5,308,483	35.1	6.1	6.1/93.9	NA/NA	81.1/18.9	NA	NA
1810	7,239,881	36.4	4.3	7.3/92.7	NA/NA	81.0/19.0	NA	NA
1820	9,638,453	33.1	5.5	7.2/92.8	50.8/49.2	81.6/18.4	NA	16.7
1830	12,866,020	33.5	7.4	8.8/91.2	50.8/49.2	81.9/18.1	NA	17.2
1840	17,069,453	32.7	9.8	10.8/89.2	50.9/49.1	83.2/16.8	NA	17.8
1850	23,191,876	35.9	7.9	15.3/84.7	51.0/49.0	84.3/15.7	5.55	18.9
1860	31,443,321	35.6	10.6	19.8/80.2	51.2/48.8	85.6/14.4	5.28	19.4
1870	39,818,449	26.6	13.4	25.7/74.3	50.6/49.4	86.2/13.8	5.09	20.2
1880	50,155,783	26.0	16.9	28.2/71.8	50.9/49.1	86.5/13.5	5.04	20.9
1890	62,947,714	25.5	21.2	35.1/64.9	51.2/48.8	87.5/12.5	4.93	22.0
1900	75,994,575	20.7	25.6	39.6/60.4	51.1/48.9	87.9/12.1	4.76	22.9
1910	91,972,266	21.0	31.0	45.6/54.4	51.5/48.5	88.9/11.1	4.54	24.1
1920	105,710,620	14.9	35.6	51.2/48.8	51.0/49.0	89.7/10.3	4.34	25.3
1930	122,775,046	16.1	41.2	56.1/43.9	50.6/49.4	89.8/10.2	4.11	26.4
1940	131,669,275	7.2	44.2	56.5/43.5	50.2/49.8	89.8/10.2	3.67	29.0
1950	150,697,361	14.5	50.7	64.0/36.0	49.7/50.3	89.5/10.5	3.37	30.2
1960	179,323,175	18.5	50.6	69.9/30.1	49.3/50.7	88.6/11.4	3.33	29.5
1970	203,302,031	13.4	57.4	73.5/26.5	48.7/51.3	87.6/12.4	3.14	28.0
1980	226,545,805	11.4	64.0	73.7/26.3	48.6/51.4	86.0/14.0	2.76	30.0
1990	248,709,873	9.8	70.3	75.2/24.8	48.7/51.3	80.3/19.7	2.63	32.9
2000	281,422,426	13.1	79.6	79.0/21.0	49.0/51.0	81.0/19.0	2.59	35.4
2010	308,745,538	9.7	87.4	80.7/19.3	49.2/50.8	77.1/22.9	2.58	37.2

NA = Not available.

YEAR	BIRTHS	YEAR	VITAL STATISTICS (RATES PER THOUSAND) BIRTHS	DEATHS*	MARRIAGES*	DIVORCES*
1800	55.0	1900	32.3	17.2	NA	NA
1810	54.3	1910	30.1	14.7	NA	NA
1820	55.2	1920	27.7	13.0	12.0	1.6
1830	51.4	1930	21.3	11.3	9.2	1.6
1840	51.8	1940	19.4	10.8	12.1	2.0
1850	43.3	1950	24.1	9.6	11.1	2.6
1860	44.3	1960	23.7	9.5	8.5	2.2
1870	38.3	1970	18.4	9.5	10.6	3.5
1880	39.8	1980	15.9	8.8	10.6	5.2
1890	31.5	1990	16.7	8.6	9.8	4.6
		2000	14.7	8.7	8.5	4.2
		2010	13.8	8.0	6.8	3.6

NA = Not available.
*Data not available before 1900.

YEAR	TOTAL POPULATION	LIFE EXPECTANCY (IN YEARS)			
		WHITE FEMALES	NONWHITE FEMALES	WHITE MALES	NONWHITE MALES
1900	47.3	48.7	33.5	46.6	32.5
1910	50.1	52.0	37.5	48.6	33.8
1920	54.1	55.6	45.2	54.4	45.5
1930	59.7	63.5	49.2	59.7	47.3
1940	62.9	66.6	54.9	62.1	51.5
1950	68.2	72.2	62.9	66.5	59.1
1960	69.7	74.1	66.3	67.4	61.1
1970	70.9	75.6	69.4	68.0	61.3
1980	73.7	78.1	73.6	70.7	65.3
1990	75.4	79.3	75.2	72.6	67.0
2000	76.9	80.0	75.0	74.8	68.3
2010	78.3	80.8	80.3	75.7	74.5

THE CHANGING AGE STRUCTURE

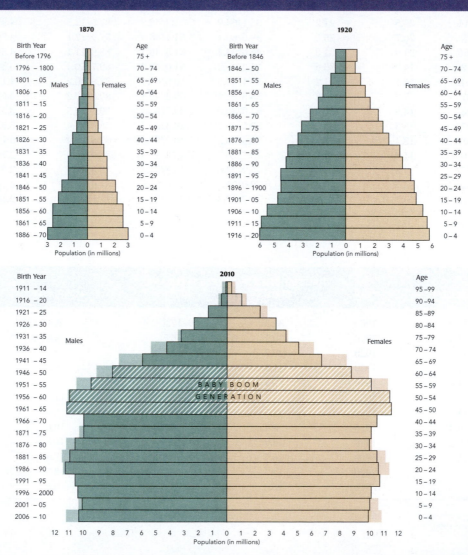

Before the twentieth century, the age distribution of Americans could be charted roughly as a pyramid, as seen in the figures for 1870 and 1920. High birthrates create a broad base at the bottom, while mortality rates winnow the population to a small tip of elderly. But by 2010, the pyramid had been transformed more nearly into a cylinder. Over the past two centuries fertility rates have undergone a steady decline, pulling in the base of the pyramid, while higher living standards have allowed Americans to live longer, broadening the top. Only the temporary bulge of the baby boom distorts the shape.

| YEARS | TOTAL NUMBER OF IMMIGRANTS | REGIONAL ORIGIN OF IMMIGRANTS (PERCENT) EUROPE | | | | WESTERN HEMISPHERE | ASIA |
		TOTAL EUROPE	NORTH AND WEST	EAST AND CENTRAL	SOUTH AND OTHER		
1821–1830	143,389	69.2	67.1	—	2.1	8.4	—
1831–1840	599,125	82.8	81.8	—	1.0	5.5	—
1841–1850	1,713,251	93.8	92.9	0.1	0.3	3.6	—
1851–1860	2,598,214	94.4	93.6	0.1	0.8	2.9	1.6
1861–1870	2,314,824	89.2	87.8	0.5	0.9	7.2	2.8
1871–1880	2,812,191	80.8	73.6	4.5	2.7	14.4	4.4
1881–1890	5,246,13	90.3	72.0	11.9	6.3	8.1	1.3
1891–1900	3,687,546	96.5	44.5	32.8	19.1	1.1	1.9
1901–1910	8,795,386	92.5	21.7	44.5	6.3	4.1	2.8
1911–1920	5,735,811	76.3	17.4	33.4	25.5	19.9	3.4
1921–1930	4,107,209	60.3	31.7	14.4	14.3	36.9	2.4
1931–1940	528,431	65.9	38.8	11.0	16.1	30.3	2.8
1941–1950	1,035,039	60.1	47.5	4.6	7.9	34.3	3.1
1951–1960	2,515,479	52.8	17.7	24.3	10.8	39.6	6.0
1961–1970	3,321,677	33.8	11.7	9.4	12.9	51.7	12.9
1971–1980	4,493,300	17.8	4.3	5.6	8.4	44.3	35.2
1981–1990	7,338,000	10.4	5.9	4.8	1.1	49.3	37.3
1991–2000	9,095,417	14.9	4.8	8.6	1.6	49.3	30.7

Dash indicates less than 0.1 percent.

| RECENT TRENDS IN IMMIGRATION (IN THOUSANDS) | | | | | PERCENT | | |
	1961–1970	1971–1980	1981–1990	1991–2000	1971–1980	1981–1990	1991–2000
All countries	3,321.7	4,493.3	7,338.1	9095.4	100.0	100.0	100.0
Europe	1,123.5	800.4	761.5	1359.7	17.8	10.4	14.9
Austria	20.6	9.5	18.3	15.5	0.2	0.3	0.2
Belgium	9.2	5.3	7.0	7.0	0.1	0.1	0.1
Czechoslovakia	3.3	6.0	7.2	9.8	0.1	0.1	0.1
Denmark	9.2	4.4	5.3	6.0	0.1	0.1	0.1
France	45.2	25.1	22.4	35.8	0.6	1.3	0.4
Germany	190.8	74.4	91.6	92.6	1.7	2.2	1.0
Greece	86.0	92.4	38.3	26.7	2.1	0.4	0.3
Hungary	5.4	6.6	6.5	9.3	0.1	0.1	0.1
Ireland	33.0	11.5	31.9	56.9	0.3	0.9	0.6
Italy	214.1	129.4	67.2	62.7	2.9	0.2	0.7
Netherlands	30.6	10.5	12.2	13.3	0.2	0.1	0.1
Norway	15.5	3.9	4.2	5.1	0.1	1.1	0.5
Poland	53.5	37.2	83.3	163.7	0.8	0.5	1.8
Portugal	76.1	101.7	40.4	22.9	2.3	0.3	0.3
Spain	44.7	39.1	20.4	17.1	0.9	0.2	0.2
Sweden	17.1	6.5	11.0	12.7	0.1	0.1	0.1
Switzerland	18.5	8.2	8.8	11.8	0.2	0.1	0.1
United Kingdom	213.8	137.4	159.2	151.8	3.1	2.2	1.7
USSR	2.5	39.0	57.7	462.8	0.9	0.3	5.1
Yugoslavia	20.4	30.5	18.8	66.5	0.7	0.5	0.7
Other Europe	9.1	18.9	8.2	57.7	0.2	0.0	0.6

RECENT TRENDS IN IMMIGRATION (IN THOUSANDS)

	1961–1970	1971–1980	1981–1990	1991–2000	PERCENT 1971–1980	PERCENT 1981–1990	PERCENT 1991–2000
Asia	427.6	1588.2	2738.1	2795.6	35.2	37.3	30.7
China	34.8	124.3	298.9	419.1	2.8	4.1	4.6
Hong Kong	75.0	113.5	98.2	109.8	2.5	1.3	1.2
India	27.2	164.1	250.7	363.1	3.7	3.4	4.0
Iran	10.3	45.1	116.0	69.0	1.0	1.6	0.8
Israel	29.6	37.7	44.2	39.4	0.8	0.6	0.4
Japan	40.0	49.8	47.0	67.9	1.1	0.6	0.7
Korea	34.5	267.6	333.8	164.2	6.0	4.5	1.8
Philippines	98.4	355.0	548.7	503.9	7.9	7.5	5.5
Turkey	10.1	13.4	23.4	38.2	0.3	0.3	0.4
Vietnam	4.3	172.8	281.0	286.1	3.8	3.8	3.1
Other Asia	36.5	176.1	631.4	735.4	3.8	8.6	8.0
America	1716.4	1982.5	3615.6	4486.8	44.3	49.3	49.3
Argentina	49.7	29.9	27.3	26.6	0.7	0.4	0.3
Canada	413.3	169.9	158.0	192.0	3.8	2.2	2.1
Colombia	72.0	77.3	122.9	128.5	1.7	1.7	1.4
Cuba	208.5	264.9	144.6	169.3	5.9	2.0	1.9
Dominican Rep.	93.3	148.1	252.0	335.3	3.3	3.4	3.7
Ecuador	36.8	50.1	56.2	76.5	1.1	0.8	0.8
El Salvador	15.0	34.4	213.5	215.7	0.8	2.9	2.4
Haiti	34.5	56.3	138.4	179.6	1.3	1.9	2.0
Jamaica	74.9	137.6	208.1	169.2	3.1	2.8	1.9
Mexico	453.9	640.3	1655.7	2249.4	14.3	22.6	24.7
Other America	264.4	373.8	639.3	744.3	8.3	8.7	8.2
Africa	29.0	80.8	176.8	355.0	1.8	2.4	3.9
Oceania	25.1	41.2	45.2	55.8	0.9	0.6	0.6

Figures may not add to total due to rounding.

AMERICAN WORKERS AND FARMERS

YEAR	TOTAL NUMBER OF WORKERS (THOUSANDS)	PERCENT OF WORKERS MALE/ FEMALE	PERCENT OF FEMALE WORKERS MARRIED	PERCENT OF WORKERS IN FEMALE POPULATION	PERCENT OF WORKERS IN LABOR UNIONS	FARM POPULATION (THOUSANDS)	FARM POPULATION AS PERCENT OF TOTAL POPULATION
1870	12,506	85/15	NA	NA	NA	NA	NA
1880	17,392	85/15	NA	NA	NA	21,973	43.8
1890	23,318	83/17	13.9	18.9	NA	24,771	42.3
1900	29,073	82/18	15.4	20.6	3	29,875	41.9
1910	38,167	79/21	24.7	25.4	6	32,077	34.9
1920	41,614	79/21	23.0	23.7	12	31,974	30.1
1930	48,830	78/22	28.9	24.8	7	30,529	24.9
1940	53,011	76/24	36.4	27.4	27	30,547	23.2
1950	59,643	72/28	52.1	31.4	25	23,048	15.3
1960	69,877	68/32	59.9	37.7	26	15,635	8.7
1970	82,049	63/37	63.4	43.4	25	9712	4.8
1980	108,544	58/42	59.7	51.5	23	6051	2.7
1990	117,914	55/45	58.4	44.3	16	3871	1.6
2000	135,208	54/46	61.3	45.7	15	3305	1.1

| | GROSS NATIONAL | FOREIGN TRADE (IN MILLIONS) | | | FEDERAL | FEDERAL | FEDERAL |
YEAR	PRODUCT (GNP) (IN BILLIONS)*	EXPORTS	IMPORTS	BALANCE OF TRADE	BUDGET (IN BILLIONS)	SURPLUS/DEFICIT (IN BILLIONS)	DEBT (IN BILLIONS)
						THE ECONOMY AND FEDERAL SPENDING	
1790	NA	$20	$23	$−3	$0.004	$+0.00015	$0.076
1800	NA	71	91	−20	0.011	+0.0006	0.083
1810	NA	67	85	−18	0.008	+0.0012	0.053
1820	NA	70	74	−4	0.018	−0.0004	0.091
1830	NA	74	71	+3	0.015	+0.100	0.049
1840	NA	132	107	+25	0.024	−0.005	0.004
1850	NA	152	178	−26	0.040	+0.004	0.064
1860	NA	400	362	−38	0.063	−0.01	0.065
1870	$7.4	451	462	−11	0.310	+0.10	2.4
1880	11.2	853	761	+92	0.268	+0.07	2.1
1890	13.1	910	823	+87	0.318	+0.09	1.2
1900	18.7	1499	930	+569	0.521	+0.05	1.2
1910	35.3	1919	1646	+273	0.694	−0.02	1.1
1920	91.5	8664	5784	+2880	6.357	+0.3	24.3
1930	90.7	4013	3500	+513	3.320	+0.7	16.3
1940	100.0	4030	7433	−3403	9.6	−2.7	43.0
1950	286.5	10,816	9125	+1691	43.1	−2.2	257.4
1960	506.5	19,600	15,046	+4556	92.2	+0.3	286.3
1970	992.7	42,700	40,189	+2511	195.6	−2.8	371.0
1980	2631.7	220,783	244,871	+24,088	590.9	−73.8	907.7
1990	5803.2	394,030	495,042	−101,012	1253.1	−220.5	3206.6
2000	9872.9	1,102,900	1,466,900	−364,000	1788.8	+236.4	5629.0

*For 1990 and after, gross domestic product (GDP) is given.

Glossary

A

actual representation   view that the people can be represented only by a person whom they have actually elected to office; this understanding of representation was the consensus among colonials during the imperial crisis and the basis of their objection to the British claim that Americans were virtually represented in Parliament.

affirmative action   practice of actively seeking to increase the number of racial and ethnic minorities, women, persons in a protected age category, persons with disabilities, and disabled veterans in a workplace or school. Such measures sometimes include the setting of quotas or percentages in hiring.

amnesty   general pardon granted by a government, usually for political crimes. Proposals of amnesty were made, with varying degrees of exception for high Confederate officials, by Presidents Lincoln and Johnson as well as by Congress in 1872. President Ford offered conditional amnesty in 1974 to draft evaders at the conclusion of the Vietnam War.

anti-Semitism   hatred, prejudice, oppression, or discrimination against Jews or Judaism. *Semite* originally referred to the descendants of Shem, which included both Jews and Muslims in the Middle East. More recently the term has come to refer primarily to Jews.

appeasement   policy of making concessions to an aggressor nation, as long as its demands appear reasonable, in order to avoid war. Hitler's full conquest of Czechoslovakia, violating his promises given at the Munich Conference in 1938, gave the term its negative connotation.

armistice   mutually agreed-on truce or temporary halt in the fighting of a war so that the combatants may discuss peace.

artisan   skilled craftworker, such as a blacksmith, a cooper, a miller, or a tailor. Master artisans constituted a large segment of the middle classes in American cities and towns from the beginnings of colonial settlement through the 1820s; they owned their own shops and employed a number of younger journeyman artisans, who owned only their tools, and trained even younger and less skilled apprentices in a craft.

assimilate   to absorb a culturally distinct group into the dominant culture. The debate over the process of assimilation, of immigrants "becoming American," has been a persistent fault line in American politics. The debate revolves around what qualities are American and the degree to which a dominant culture should define them. The debate is extremely difficult in a society in which immigration plays a crucial role—in a "nation of nations," as Walt Whitman described the United States.

autonomy   condition of being independent or, in the case of a political structure, the right to self-government.

B

balanced constitution   view that England's constitution gave every part of English society some voice in the workings of its government. While the Crown represented the monarchy and the House of Lords the aristocracy, the House of Commons represented the ordinary people of England.

barter economy   networks of trade based on the mutual exchange of goods and services with little or no use of coin or currency.

behaviorism   school of psychology that measures human behavior, believes it can be shaped, and discounts emotion as subjective. Behaviorism was founded by psychologist John Watson and was first presented in his *Psychology as the Behaviorist Views It* (1913).

benign neglect   policy also known as "salutary neglect," pursued by the British empire in governing its American colonies until the end of the Seven Years' War.

biocentric   life-centered; also a theory of moral responsibility stating that all forms of life have an inherent right to exist and that humanity is not the center of existence.

biogenetic engineering   process of changing the DNA of a plant or an animal to produce desirable characteristics. Examples of desirable characteristics include fast growth and unusually large size. The health and environmental safety of genetically modified food products is a subject of debate in the scientific and lay communities.

black codes   series of laws passed by southern states in 1865 and 1866, modeled on the slave codes in effect before the Civil War. The codes did grant African Americans some rights not enjoyed by slaves, but their primary purpose was to keep African Americans as propertyless agricultural laborers.

bloody shirt   political campaign tactic of "waving the bloody shirt," used by Republicans against Democrats; it invoked the tremendous loss of life and casualties from the Civil War as a reason to vote for Republicans as the party of the Union and not to trust Democrats, who had often opposed the war. The tactic continued to work, with diminishing success, throughout Reconstruction.

bonds   certificates of debt issued by a government or corporation promising to repay the buyers of the bonds their original investment, plus interest, by a specified date of maturity. Bonds have been traditionally used by governments as a way to raise money during wartime or for large-scale projects.

boom-bust economy   periods of expansion and recession or depression that an economy goes through. Also referred to as *business cycle*. Major downturns in the cycle have occurred in the United States beginning in 1819, 1837, 1857, 1873, 1893, 1907, and 1929, the start of the Great Depression.

bootlegging   illegal transport or sale of goods, in this case alcoholic beverages during the 1920s. The term derived from the practice of hiding a container of alcohol in the upper part of a boot.

boycott   tactic used by protesters, workers, and consumers to pressure business organizations through a mass refusal to purchase their products or otherwise do business with them.

brinkmanship policy of pushing a critical situation to the edge of catastrophe by using the implicit threat of nuclear war in order to persuade an opponent to back down. The strategy was developed by Secretary of State John Foster Dulles under President Dwight Eisenhower.

bureaucratic state government run by administrative bureaus or divisions and staffed by nonelected officials.

business cycle *see* **boom-bust economy.**

C

carpetbagger white Republicans, originally from the North, who came to live in the South after the Civil War. They received their nickname from hostile southerners who claimed that the newcomers arrived carrying all that they owned stuffed into a carpetbag and eager to get rich by plundering the South.

cartel organization of private businesses that join to control production, distribution, and prices.

caste system system of social stratification separating individuals by various distinctions, among them hereditary, rank, profession, wealth, and race. Slavery as a caste system not only separated whites from blacks but also assigned value to people according to shadings of color.

cede to give up possession of, usually by treaty.

celibate abstaining from sexual intercourse; also, unmarried. Celibacy is the abstention from intercourse, a state often motivated by religious teachings.

charter document issued by a sovereign ruler, legislature, or other authority creating a public or private corporation. England's rulers issued charters setting forth the authority of corporations or joint stock companies to colonize sections of the Americas; state legislatures have issued charters to corporations; and the British (including American colonials) traced basic rights of representation to the Magna Carta (Great Charter) granted by King John in 1215 CE.

checks and balances mechanism by which each branch of government— executive, legislative, and judicial—keeps the others within the bounds of their constitutional authority; James Madison emphasized this feature of the federal constitution to assure the Anti-Federalists.

Columbian exchange transition of people, plants, insects, and microbes between the two hemispheres, initiated when Columbus reached the Americas in 1492.

commercial economy economy in which individuals are involved in a network of markets and commercial transactions. Such economies are often urban, where goods and services are exchanged for money and credit; agricultural areas are also commercial when crops and livestock are sold in markets rather than consumed by those who grew or raised them. Commercial economies are less egalitarian, because wealth can be concentrated in the hands of fewer individuals. *See also* **semisubsistence economy.**

committees of correspondence strategy devised by Samuel Adams in 1772 to rally popular support among American colonials against British imperial policies. The committees of correspondence drew up statements of American rights and grievances, distributed those documents within and among the colonies, and solicited responses from towns and counties. This committee structure formed a new communications network, one that fostered intercolonial agreement on resistance to British measures and spread the resistance from seaports into rural areas.

community action programs programs designed to identify and organize local leaders to take steps to alleviate poverty and crime in their neighborhoods. Sociologist Saul Alinsky from Chicago organized the Industrial Areas Foundation to support community action programs in the 1960s.

conformity degree to which people adjust their behavior, values, and ideas to fit into a group or society.

conglomerate corporation whose various branches or subsidiaries are either directly or indirectly spread among a variety of industries, usually unrelated to one another. The purpose of a conglomerate is generally to increase shareholder value and ensure against market cycles by spreading its risk, rather than to improve market share or production efficiency by concentrating on excelling within a single industry.

Congregationalists members of a Protestant denomination that originated in sixteenth-century Britain as part of the Puritan movement. While some early Congregationalists, known as Separatists,

concluded that the Church of England was beyond reformation, most strove to reform English religion and society while remaining within the Church of England. Early modern Congregationalists embraced Calvinist theological beliefs and held that each individual congregation should conduct its own religious affairs, answering to no higher authority. The Separatists founded Plymouth, the first northern colony, and the Non-Separating Congregationalists predominated elsewhere in seventeenth-century New England.

conscription act of compulsory enrollment for military service, as opposed to a voluntary enlistment.

consensus point of view generally shared by a group, institution, or even a culture. Scholars have analyzed and debated the institutions that contribute to the construction of a consensus viewpoint, ranging from schools and churches to the media in their various forms.

constitution framework of government establishing the contract between rulers and ruled. American revolutionaries insisted on written constitutions to protect individual rights and liberties; by contrast, Britons understood the term *constitution* to mean the existing arrangement of government—not an actual document but a collection of parliamentary laws, customs, and precedents.

consumer goods products such as food and clothing that fill the needs and wants of individuals. *Producer* or *capital goods,* in contrast, are the factory equipment and other machines used to manufacture or transport other goods or services.

Continental Army main rebel military force, created by the Second Continental Congress in July 1775 and commanded by George Washington. After the 1776 campaign, most enlistments came from the poorest and most desperate in American society, and it was they who shouldered the burden of the fighting. During the harsh winter at Valley Forge in 1778/1779, the army acquired greater discipline and expertise and thereafter scored important military victories in the mid-Atlantic and the South.

contraband goods seized by a government during wartime, when the goods were being used by an enemy nation or being shipped to an enemy nation by a neutral nation. The term was also applied during the Civil War to escaped slaves who fled behind Union lines.

Copperhead derogatory term used by Republicans to label northern Democrats who opposed the war policies of the Lincoln administration and advocated a negotiated peace.

CORE Congress of Racial Equality, an organization founded in Chicago in 1942. The group's inspiration was Krishnalal Shridharani's book *War without Violence,* which outlined Mohandas K. Gandhi's nonviolent philosophy for action. CORE believed that African Americans could use nonviolent civil disobedience to challenge racial segregation.

corporation business entity that has been granted a charter granting it legal rights, privileges, and liabilities distinct from the individual members that are a part of it. A corporation therefore may survive the death of the individuals who created and run it.

Counter-Reformation reform movement within the Roman Catholic Church in response to the Protestant Reformation, seeking to reform and reinvigorate the Church. Religious orders played a large role in the Counter-Reformation, particularly the Jesuit order, known formally as the Society of Jesus, and founded in 1534 by Ignatius of Loyola.

covert operations military or political actions carried out in secret to allow the responsible government or party to deny its role. Governments have often relied on such operations when overt military force is impractical or dangerous or when public negotiations are likely to fail.

D

de facto segregation spatial and social separation of populations brought about by social behavior rather than by laws or legal mechanisms. Segregation (especially in schools) has often existed without being sanctioned by law. When the practice is accomplished through explicit legal means, it is known as *de jure segregation.*

debt peonage paying off a debt through labor when the debtor lacks sufficient cash or other assets.

Deep South South Carolina, Georgia, Florida, Alabama, Mississippi, Louisiana, and Texas.

demographic factors relating to the characteristics of populations. Demography is the study of populations, looking at such aspects as size, growth, density, and age distribution.

depreciated decreased in value owing to market conditions. Depreciation in the value of banknotes can occur when too much paper money is put into circulation or when users doubt the ability of the government to back up the paper currency with reserves of gold or silver.

détente relaxation of strained relations between nations, especially among the United States, the Soviet Union, and China in the 1970s and late 1980s. In seeking détente, once-hostile parties begin to emphasize their common interests and reduce their points of conflict.

deterrence prevention of an action by fear of the consequences; during the cold war, the theory that war could be avoided because each side knew that the other possessed large numbers of nuclear weapons. Thus any nuclear exchange threatened the survival of both sides.

disenfranchise to deny a citizen's right to vote.

disenfranchisement denial of a citizen's right to vote.

doctrine of preemption war undertaken in anticipation of imminent attack or invasion by another nation or in hopes of gaining a strategic advantage when war seems unavoidable. In that sense the Japanese government viewed its attack on Pearl Harbor as preemptive.

domesticity devotion to home life, and a woman's place at the center of that life. The ideal of domesticity became popular during the nineteenth century as industrialization was increasingly separating work and home as individual spheres.

dove *see* **hawks and doves.**

dry farming farming system to conserve water in semiarid regions receiving less than 15 to 20 inches of rain a year. Methods include leaving some fields fallow or unplanted to reduce water use, keeping soil broken to absorb water, and growing drought-resistant crops.

due process constitutional concept, embodied in the Fifth and Fourteenth Amendments, that no person shall be deprived of life, liberty, or property without legal safeguards such as being present at a hearing, having an opportunity to be heard in court, having the opportunity to confront hostile witnesses, and being able to present evidence.

E

ecosystem a community and/or region studied as a system of functioning relationships between organisms and their environments.

ecumenism movement encouraging unity among religions, especially among Christian denominations and between Christians and Jews. Ecumenical movements promote cooperation and better understanding among different religious denominations.

egalitarian exhibiting or asserting a belief in the equality of humans in a social, political, or economic context.

elect in theology, those of the faithful chosen, or "elected," by God for eternal salvation.

elites class of people given special social, economic, or intellectual status within society. The singular noun *elite* can also be used as a plural, as in *the colonial elite.*

embargo government act prohibiting trade with a foreign country or countries, usually to exert economic pressure.

enfranchise *see* **suffrage** and **disenfranchisement.**

Enlightenment intellectual movement that flourished in Europe from the mid-1600s through the eighteenth century and stressed the power of human reason to promote social progress by discovering the laws that governed both nature and society. In the American colonies, the Enlightenment's influence encouraged scientists such as Benjamin Franklin to experiment and discover useful scientific knowledge, and it also persuaded a growing minority to accept more liberal religious views, known as "rational Christianity."

escalation process of steady intensification, rather than a sudden or marked increase, applied to the increasing American military presence in Vietnam. The term derives from an escalator, which gradually lifts its cargo to a higher level. Nuclear theorist Herman Kahn used the term geopolitically in his *On Escalation: Metaphors and Scenarios* (1968).

evangelical term that derives from a Greek word meaning the bringing of good news—in this case, the Gospel. Protestant evangelicals stressed the need for individual conversion and rebirth stemming from an awareness of sinful guilt and Christ's act of atoning, through his death, for their sins.

excise tax internal tax placed on the production or sale of a commodity, usually a luxury item or nonessential.

executive order declaration issued by the president or by a governor possessing the force of law. Executive orders are usually based on existing statutory authority and require no action by Congress or the state legislature to take effect.

expatriate one who leaves the country of one's birth or citizenship to live in another, usually out of a sense of alienation. The term is often applied to the group of writers and artists living in self-imposed exile in Paris during the 1920s and sometimes referred to as the "Lost Generation." That term was coined by the writer Gertrude Lawrence, describing the rootless generation of American expatriates who found life in the United States culturally sterile and promises of postwar freedom and democracy empty.

F

federalism governing principle established by the Constitution in which the national government and the states divide power. A stronger commitment to federalism as the basis of a national republic replaced the system established by the Articles of Confederation, which granted virtually sovereign power to individual states.

fission splitting of a nucleus of an atom into at least two other nuclei, accompanied by the release of a relatively large amount of energy. The splitting of the nucleus of the uranium isotope U-235 or its artificial cousin, plutonium, powered the atomic bomb.

Free Soil Party antislavery party formed in 1848 by northern Democrats disillusioned with southern Democratic support for slavery. The party tried to widen its appeal by focusing less on outright abolition than on opposing the spread of slavery into the territories (the need to protect "free soil" and "free labor"). The party never gained strength, however; the Republican Party in the 1850s attracted the greater number of antislavery voters.

freedmen former slaves; the term came into use during the Civil War, as greater numbers of slaves fled or were freed under the terms of the Emancipation Proclamation, and continued to be widely used during Reconstruction. More recently historians have also used the gender-neutral term, *freedpeople*.

G

graduated income tax tax based on a percentage of an individual's income, the percentage increasing as total income increases. Under such a system, wealthy individuals are taxed at a higher rate than are poorer individuals.

Great Awakening term used by some historians to describe periods of intense religious piety and commitment among Americans that fueled the expansion of Protestant churches. The First Great Awakening extended from the 1730s to the American Revolution; the Second Great Awakening includes the period from about 1790 to the 1840s; the Third Great Awakening took place during the late nineteenth and early twentieth centuries; the Fourth Great Awakening spans the latter half of the twentieth century.

H

habeas corpus Latin phrase meaning, "you have the body." For centuries, the term referred in English law to the right of individuals to be brought before a court and informed of the crime alleged against them. The right of habeus corpus is meant to ensure that the government cannot arbitrarily arrest and imprison a citizen without giving grounds for doing so.

hawks and doves nicknames for the two opposing positions in American policy during the war in Vietnam. Hawks supported the escalation of the war and a "peace with honor." Doves, the peace faction, argued that the United States had intervened in a civil war and should withdraw its troops.

hedge fund an investment fund requiring high minimum contributions and thus used by a limited range of more affluent investors. Hedge funds are very lightly regulated by the government, often secretive, and undertake a range of high-risk investment and trading strategies.

Hessians German soldiers who fought with the British Army during the American Revolution. Some Hessians taken as prisoners of war later served in the Continental Army and settled in the United States after the Revolution.

horizontal combination strategy of business growth (sometimes referred to as "horizontal integration") that attempts to stifle competition by combining more than one firm involved in the same level of production, transportation, or distribution into a single firm.

http:// abbreviation for HyperText Transfer Protocol, the set of Internet rules governing the transfer of data between a server and a computer as well as for exchanging files (text, graphic images, sound, video, and other multimedia files) on the World Wide Web.

I

impeachment under the U.S. Constitution, the process by which members of the House of Representatives bring charges against a high government official for "Treason, Bribery, or other high Crimes and Misdemeanors." Once an individual is impeached, he or she must stand trial before the Senate, where a two-thirds majority vote is required for conviction. Conviction results in removal from office.

imperialism acquisition of control over the government and the economy of another nation, usually by conquest. The United States became an imperialistic world power in the late nineteenth century by gaining control over the Hawaiian Islands and, after the Spanish American War (1898), Guam, the Philippines, Cuba, and Puerto Rico.

indemnity compensation for loss or damage.

indentures contract signed between two parties, binding one to serve the other for a specified period of time. The term originated because two copies of the agreement were made, both indented in the same way at its edges, so that each party was provided an identical record of the agreement.

inflation increase in the overall price of goods and services over an extended period of time; or a similar decrease over time of the purchasing power of money. The latter situation can be caused by an increase of the amount of currency and credit available in an economy. In such cases, when the perceived value of paper money declines (as often happens in wars, when the government tries to raise revenues by printing money), sellers raise the prices of their goods to compensate.

injunction court order requiring individuals or groups to participate in or refrain from a certain action.

interstate commerce trade in goods that crosses state lines. Regulation of interstate commerce is reserved in the Constitution for the federal government and has become the constitutional basis for much of federal regulation of business.

Iroquois League Indian confederacy, also known as the Five Nations, that exerted enormous influence throughout the region. In 1712, a sixth tribe, the Tuscaroras, joined the confederation.

isolationism belief that the United States should avoid foreign entanglements, alliances, and involvement in foreign wars. The tradition had its roots in President George Washington's farewell address, which warned in 1796, "It is our true policy to steer clear of permanent alliances with any portion of the foreign world. . . ."

Issei   *see* **Nisei.**

itinerant   traveling preacher attached to no settled congregation. Itinerants played an important role in the first Great Awakening, taking their inspiration from George Whitefield, who preached up and down the Atlantic seaboard. In the early nineteenth century, many Protestant denominations—especially the Methodists and the Baptists—made strategic use of itinerants to evangelize settlers on the frontier.

J

jihad   Arabic term meaning "striving or struggling in the way of God." Although broadly the term can indicate a spiritual effort on the part of a Muslim believer to come closer to Allah, the expression is also used to denote a Muslim holy war against unbelievers.

joint stock company   business in which capital is held in transferable shares of stock by joint owners. The joint stock company was an innovation that allowed investors to share and spread the risks of overseas investment. Instead of only a few individuals owning a ship and its cargo—which might sink and bring ruin to its investors—joint stock allowed for smaller sums to be invested in a variety of different ventures.

journeyman   person who has served an apprenticeship in a trade or craft and who is a qualified worker employed by another person.

judicial review   doctrine set out by Chief Justice John Marshall in *Marbury v. Madison.* The decision established that the judicial branch of the federal government possesses the power to determine whether the laws of Congress or the actions of the executive branch violate the Constitution.

L

laissez faire   a French term ("allow [people] to do [as they choose]") referring to an economic doctrine that advocates holding government interference in the economy to an absolute minimum and ideally having none at all.

landed states and landless states   some of the 13 colonies that became the United States had originally been granted land

whose western boundaries were vague or overlapped the land granted to other colonies. During the Confederation period, the so-called landless states had boundaries that were firmly drawn on all sides, such as Maryland, New Jersey, and Massachusetts. The so-called landed states possessed grants whose western boundaries were not fixed. (See the map on page 186).

libertarian   advocate of a minimalist approach to governing, in which the freedom of private individuals to do as they please ranks paramount. A libertarian philosophy contrasts with the outlook of modern liberals, in which government plays a more active role in meeting the needs of citizens or in managing social and economic life for the common good.

lien   legal claim against property used to obtain a loan, which must be paid when the property is sold. Developing first in the South after the Civil War, the crop-lien system allowed merchants to claim a portion (or all) of current or future crops as payment for loans to farmers for seed, tools, and fertilizer. Merchants often insisted that indebted farmers raise a single cash crop, frequently cotton. That requirement helped to ensnare farmers in a cycle of debt as the price of such crops fell.

loyalists   supporters of the king and Parliament and known to the rebels as "tories." At the outset of the American Revolution, loyalists made up about one-fifth of the white population, but their ranks diminished steadily after about 1777, as the British army alienated many civilians in every region that they occupied.

loyalty oath   oath of fidelity to the state or to an organization. Plans for Reconstruction insisted that southerners returning to the Union take a loyalty oath of some sort, whether that they would be loyal henceforth to the United States or a more strict "ironclad oath" that they never had aided the Confederacy. At other times of stress—as during the Revolutionary era or during the cold war of the 1950s, loyalty oaths and loyalty investigations have been used by groups or governments to enforce obedience to the state or to a revolutionary movement.

M

managed economy   economy directed by the government with power over prices, allocation of resources, and marketing of goods.

Manifest Destiny   belief, as Democratic editor John L. O'Sullivan put it, that it had

become the United States' "manifest destiny to overspread the continent allotted by Providence for the free development of our yearly multiplying millions." The roots of the doctrine were both religious and political. Protestant religious thinkers had long seen American settlement as setting a pious and virtuous example to the rest of the world. The political ideology of the Revolution encouraged the notion that the benefits of democracy would spread along with the political expansion of the nation. Yet Manifest Destiny was also racist in its assumption of the inferiority of other peoples and cultures; and it encompassed a purely economic desire to expand the nation's commerce and power.

"Maroon" communities   collective attempts at escape typically undertaken by groups of newly arrived African slaves in the American South. Such slaves fled inland, often to the frontiers of colonial settlement, where they attempted to reconstruct the African villages from which they had been taken captive. Because of their size, such communities proved to be short-lived; they were quickly discovered by white slave patrols or by Indian tribes such as the Cherokees, who profited from returning runaways. "Maroon communities" in the Caribbean proved far more enduring and provided the bases for successful slave rebellions during the eighteenth and early nineteenth centuries.

mass media   forms of communication designed to reach a vast audience, generally a nation state or larger, without personal contact between the senders and receivers. Examples would include newspapers, movies, magazines, radio, television, and—today—some sites on the Internet.

mercantilism   European economic doctrine calling for strict regulation of the economy in order to ensure a balance of exports over imports and increase the amount of gold and silver in a nation's treasury.

merchants of death   term popularized in the 1930s to describe American bankers and arms makers whose support for the Allied cause, some historians charged, drew the United States into World War I.

Mesoamerica   the area stretching from present-day central Mexico southward through Honduras and Nicaragua, in which pre-Columbian civilizations developed.

Methodist   denomination that originated as a reform movement within the Church of England during the mid-eighteenth century, much as the Puritans originated as a reform movement within the English church during the mid-sixteenth century. The distinctive features of early Methodism on both sides of the Atlantic included a strict devotional regimen, an ascetic moral discipline, and an emphasis on evangelical conversion. By the Civil War, Methodists had become the largest Protestant denomination in the United States among both whites and African Americans.

military-industrial complex combination of the U.S. armed forces, arms manufacturers, and associated political and commercial interests, which grew rapidly during the cold war era. It is another term for the mutually supportive relationship of military contractors, the Pentagon, and sympathetic members of Congress, an alliance also known as the "Iron Triangle."

militia local defense band of civilians comprising men between the ages of 16 and 65 whose military training consisted only of occasional gatherings known as musters. Militias were organized in towns and counties throughout the American colonies from the beginnings of settlement, but they played a crucial role in the war for independence by supporting the Continental Army whenever the fighting moved into their neighborhoods.

millennialism belief in the thousand-year reign of Christ predicted in the Bible's final book, the Revelation to John. The belief that dedicated Christians could help bring about this reign of holiness by converting the world to Christianity proved to be a powerful impulse to reform.

miscegenation marriage, cohabitation, or sexual relations between persons of different races. Since race is a socially constructed identifier rather than one with any scientific or genetic basis, *miscegenation* as a term is used only in its historical context.

monoculture growth of a single crop to the virtual exclusion of all others, either on a farm or more generally within a region.

mutiny refusal of rank-and-file soldiers to follow the commands of their superior officers. Mutinies plagued the Continental Army between 1779 and 1781 as resentments mounted among soldiers over spoiled food, inadequate clothing, and back pay.

mutually assured destruction (MAD) national defense strategy in which a nuclear attack by one side would inevitably trigger an equal response leading to the destruction of both the attacker and the defender. Deterrence theory suggested that when both sides possessed the capability to inflict nuclear annihilation, even after being hit by a first strike, neither side would dare use such weapons.

national debt cumulative total of all previous annual *federal deficits* or budget shortfalls incurred each year and owed by the federal government.

nativism outlook championing the supremacy of "native" cultural traits and political rights over those of immigrants from different backgrounds. Nativism flourished during the high immigration of the late 1840s and 1850s, evidenced by the rise of the American ("Know-Nothing") party. In the late nineteenth and early twentieth centuries, nativists pressed for the restriction of immigration and won their biggest victories when Congress enacted the National Origins Acts of 1921 and 1924. As immigrant numbers rose again in the late twentieth and early twenty-first centuries, the nativist debate again emerged.

naturalization act of granting full citizenship to someone born outside the country.

navalism theories of warfare and trade that rely on a nation's navy as a principal instrument of policy.

neo-isolationist term applied to those who after World War II believed the United States should avoid foreign entanglements. Neo-isolationists especially condemned the United Nations and its supporters, whom they contemptuously referred to as "one-worlders."

"new" immigrants called "new" because they differed substantially from earlier arrivals who had come mostly from northern and western Europe; these newcomers came to the United States between 1880 and 1920 from eastern and southern Europe. Unlike most earlier immigrants (with the exception of the Irish), these immigrants were non-Protestants: Catholics, Jews, and Russian Orthodox Christians.

Nisei American-born citizens of Japanese ancestry, contrasted with *Issei*, native-born Japanese who had moved to the United States. At the outbreak of World War II, Nisei referred specifically to Japanese Americans who lived on the West Coast (but not in Hawaii or the East Coast), who were interned during the war because of prejudice and the widespread fear that they sympathized with Japan.

nomad a member of a group of people who have no fixed home and who move about, usually seasonally, in pursuit of food, water, and other resources.

normal schools schools that trained teachers, usually for two years and mostly for teaching in the elementary grades.

Northwest Territory present-day states of Ohio, Indiana, Illinois, Michigan, and Wisconsin. The incorporation of this territory into the United States through the Northwest Ordinance of 1785 marked the major achievement of the national government under the Articles of Confederation.

Opposition diverse group of political thinkers and writers in Great Britain, also known as the Country Party and the Commonwealthmen, who elaborated the tradition of classical republicanism from the late seventeenth century through the eighteenth century. They warned that the executive branch of government (the king and his ministers) was conspiring to corrupt and coopt the legislative branch of government (the House of Commons), thereby endangering popular liberties, and they called for political reforms to make Britain's government more representative of and more accountable to the people. Dismissed in England as a disaffected radical minority, the Opposition exerted a decisive influence on the political thinking of an increasing number of American colonials in the decades leading up to the Revolution.

outsourcing the contracting of goods or services from outside a company or organization in order to maintain flexibility in the size of the organization's workforce. Increasingly, outsourcing has used suppliers outside the United States in low-wage countries such as Mexico, India, and China.

pandemic outbreak of disease that spreads across national boundaries or across the world.

partisan warfare armed clashes among political rivals, typically involving guerrilla fighting and the violent intimidation of civilians by militias. Partisan warfare between loyalists and rebels tore apart communities everywhere in the United States during the war for independence, but the fighting was especially fierce and protracted in the South. The success of rebel insurgencies there ultimately convinced many southern whites to support the cause of independence.

patent legal document issued by the government giving the holder exclusive rights to use, make, and sell a process, product, or device for a specified period of time. The first patents in America were issued by colonial governments as early as 1641. Congress enacted the first patent law in 1790.

paternalism attitude or policy of treating individuals or groups in a fatherly manner, by providing for their needs without granting them rights or responsibilities. The relation involves both a dominant and a subordinate party. Sometimes the dominance comes from gender, as in a male patriarchy, whereby females are given subordinate roles. But paternalism can also be expressed in relations between colonial and subject peoples, masters and slaves, or culturally different groups.

pays d'en haut in the seventeenth century, the lands referred to by the French as the "upper country," the land upriver from Montreal as French fur traders passed into the Great Lakes beyond the southern shores of Lake Ontario. The trading lands stretched all the way to the Mississippi River.

peculiar institution euphemism for slavery, perhaps revealing in its use. The institution was "peculiar" to the South in that it had been abolished in the North (and other parts of the world, increasingly). *Peculiar* also suggests the contradiction with the ideals of the Declaration of Independence, that "all men are created equal."

per capita income average yearly income per person in a particular population; it provides one statistical measure of the relative wealth of a region.

pluralism idea that identity cannot be reduced to a single shared essence. Under such a philosophy, distinct ethnic, cultural, and religious groups are tolerated and affirmed within a society. The philosophy contrasts with the belief, in American politics, that citizens should assimilate into a more uniform cultural identity of shared values. Contrasting metaphors portray an assimilationist United States as a melting pot versus a pluralist mixing bowl.

plurality in elections, a candidate who receives a plurality wins more votes than any other candidate but less than half of all votes cast. Receiving more than half of the votes cast is called a *majority*.

pocket veto means of vetoing a bill without formally doing so. Normally, if a president does not veto or sign a bill within 10 days of receiving it, the bill automatically becomes law. If it is received, however, within 10 days of Congress's adjournment, the president can simply "pocket" the bill unsigned, until Congress adjourns, and it does not go into effect.

political culture patterns, habits, institutions, and traits associated with a political system. The political culture of the Jacksonian era, for example, was marked by a number of innovations: political nominating conventions, torchlight parades, campaign songs, badges, and other souvenirs.

political machine hierarchical political organization developed in the nineteenth century that controlled the activities of a political party and was usually headed by a political boss.

popular sovereignty doctrine that a territory could decide by vote whether or not to permit slavery within its boundaries. The doctrine was devised by Senator Stephen Douglas of Illinois as a way to placate southerners who wanted slavery permitted within Kansas Territory, forbidden under the Missouri Compromise. Meant as a compromise measure, the doctrine only inflamed the situation, as both sides worked to win a vote over slavery.

Populism political outlook that supports the rights and powers of the common people in opposition to the interests of the privileged elite. The Populist Party evolved out of the economic distress of the 1890s among farmers and focused its anger against the era's large industrial corporations, railroad monopolies, and banks. But populism as an outlook and philosophy persisted long after the party had dissolved.

pragmatism philosophical movement, led by philosophers Charles S. Peirce and William James, that stressed the visible, real-world results of ideas. Pragmatism was embraced by many progressives who wanted to promote the possibilities of change by abandoning the old notion that events were predetermined and inevitable.

predestination basis of Calvinist theology and a belief that holds that God has ordained the outcome of all human

history before the beginning of time, including the eternal fate of every human being. Believers in this doctrine found comfort and meaning from its assurance that God was directing the fate of nations, individuals, and all of creation toward his divine purposes.

Presbyterians members of a Protestant denomination that originated in sixteenth-century Britain as part of the Puritan movement. Like their fellow Puritan reformers, the Congregationalists, the Presbyterians embraced Calvinist theology beliefs; but unlike the Congregationalists, Presbyterians favored a more hierarchical form of church governance, a system in which individual congregations were guided by presbyteries and synods comprising both laymen and ministers.

presidio military garrison; as Spanish colonizers moved north from central Mexico in the sixteenth and seventeenth centuries, they constructed presidios to consolidate claims over new territory. Presidios often encouraged the growth of nearby towns and ranches and were probably more important as sites of diplomacy with Indians than as centers of military power. Poor funding and political instability led to the decline of the presidios after Mexican independence in 1821.

privatize transferral of an economic enterprise or public utility from the control of the government into private ownership. The Bush plan for Social Security reform sought to place retirement contributions into investment accounts managed privately, rather than into a fund managed by the Social Security Administration.

producer goods goods, such as heavy machinery, used to manufacture other goods, often consumer goods.

psychedelic characterized by or generating shifts in perception and altered states of awareness, often hallucinatory, and usually brought on by drugs such as LSD, mescaline, or psilocybin. Advocates of the psychedelic state spoke of euphoria, mystic visions, and philosophic insights produced. Critical observers pointed to the potential of inducing not only hallucinations but also sometimes psychoses.

public works government-financed construction projects, such as highways and bridges, for use by the public.

Puritans members of a reform movement within the Church of England that originated in the sixteenth century and that ultimately formed the Congregationalist and Presbyterian churches. Calvinist in their theology, the Puritans strove to reform English religion, society, and politics by restricting church membership to the pious and godly, by according the laity greater power in church governance, and by enlisting the state to enforce a strict moral code that prohibited drunkenness, gambling, swearing, and attending the theater.

 Q

Quakers   Protestant sect, also known as the Society of Friends, founded in mid-seventeenth century England. The Quakers believed that the Holy Spirit dwelt within each human being and that religious conviction was the source of their egalitarian social practices, which included allowing women to speak in churches and to preach in public gatherings. Quakers settled the mid-Atlantic colonies in large numbers and founded the colony of Pennsylvania.

R

racialism   *see* **racism.**

racism   form of discrimination based on the belief that one race is superior to another. Racism may be expressed individually and consciously, through explicit thoughts, feelings, or acts; it can be codified into a theory that claims scientific backing for its tenets. It can also be expressed socially and unconsciously, through institutions that promote inequality between races. In the early twentieth century, when racism became much more pronounced, the term *racialism* was also coined.

reconquista   military reconquest of the Iberian Peninsula from Islamic Moors of Africa by European Christian rulers. The campaign lasted on and off from 718 to 1492 CE.

Redeemers   southerners who came to power in southern state governments from 1875 to 1877, claiming to have "redeemed" the South from Reconstruction. The Redeemers looked to undo many of the changes wrought by the Civil War. Their goals included minimizing the role of African Americans in government and reducing their economic independence and strengthening the "New South" through industrial development.

red-light district   area in cities reserved for prostitutes. The term, first employed in the United States, resulted from the use of red lights to show that prostitutes were open for business.

repatriation   act of returning people to their nation of origin. The term often refers to the act of returning soldiers or refugees to their birth country.

republican motherhood   redefinition of the role of women promoted by many American reformers in the 1780s and 1790s, who believed that the success of republican government depended on educated and independent-minded mothers who would raise children to become informed and self-reliant citizens. The ideal of republican motherhood fostered improvements in educational opportunities for women and accorded them an important role in civic life, but it also reinforced the notion that women should confine the sphere of their activities to home and family.

republicanism   belief that representative government safeguards popular liberties more reliably than does either monarchy or oligarchy and that all citizens must practice vigilance and self-denying virtue to prevent their rulers from succumbing to the temptations of power and becoming tyrants. This "classical republicanism" profoundly influenced the political views of many Americans from the middle of the eighteenth century to the middle of the nineteenth century.

Romanticism   intellectual and artistic movement that arose in the early nineteenth century out of a rejection of the Enlightenment values of reason and balance. Romanticism emphasized the individual's expression of emotion and intuition.

 S

sagebrush rebels   group of western cattlemen, loggers, miners, developers, and others who argued that federal ownership of huge tracts of land and natural resources violated the principle of states' rights. This group demanded that government transfer control to individual states, in respect of their right to make decisions about the management of both the land and the natural resources.

scalawag   white southerners who supported the Republican Party. The derisive nickname was given by their opponents. Perhaps a quarter of all white southerners voted Republican at some time during Reconstruction.

scientific management   system of factory production that stresses efficiency.

The system was pioneered by American engineer Frederick Winslow Taylor. In *The Principles of Scientific Management* (1911), his most famous work, he emphasized time-and-motion studies to enhance productivity. The book became the bible of efficiency experts and Taylor the "Father of Scientific Management."

sedition   words or actions that incite revolt against the law or duly constituted government.

segregation   system, imposed through law and custom, of separating people by race; first enacted into law in Tennessee (1875) with a statute separating blacks from whites on trains, one of the most prevalent public spaces for racial mingling.

self-determination   principle in international law that people have a right to determine their own form of government free from outside control. The principle contrasts with colonialism and imperialism, under which people are subject to foreign rulers.

semisubsistence economy   economy in which individuals and families produce most of what they need to live on. Such economies are overwhelmingly rural and also egalitarian, in that wealth is distributed fairly broadly. During the colonial period and early republic, much of the American economy was semisubsistence. *See also* **commercial economy.**

separate but equal   rationale for a policy of segregation granting equal facilities and services to African American and whites in schools, hospitals, transportation and lodging facilities, and other public places. The Supreme Court upheld such laws in *Plessy v. Ferguson* (1896). In practice such facilities were separate but seldom equal.

separation of church and state   principle that religious institutions and their representatives should exercise no civil or judicial powers and that civil governments should give no official sanction, privileges, or financial support to any religious denomination or organization.

separation of powers   principle that each branch of government—the legislature (Congress), the executive (the President), and the judiciary (the Supreme Court)—should wield distinct powers independent from interference or infringement by other branches of government. During the debates of the Constitutional Convention in 1797, James Madison successfully argued that this separation of powers was essential to a balanced republican government.

settlement house   social reform effort that used neighborhood centers in which settlement house workers lived and worked among the poor, often in slum neighborhoods. The first settlement house, Toynbee Hall in London, was founded in 1884. The first settlement house in the United States (The Neighborhood Guild, later University Settlement House) came in 1886 in New York City and was founded by Stanton Coit.

Shi'ite and Sunni   two major branches of Islam, a division not unlike the Protestant-Catholic split in Christianity. After the death of the Prophet Muhammad, followers disagreed over who should be his successor. Most believers accepted the tradition of having their leader chosen by community consensus (the Sunni branch), but a minority supported the claim of Ali, the Prophet's cousin. Over the years theological differences have separated Shi'ite and Sunni Muslims as well. Today the Shi'ites are dominant largely in Iran and southeastern Iraq.

silent majority   phrase coined by President Richard Nixon in a 1969 speech, referring to the large number of Americans who supported his policies but did not express their views publicly.

sit-in   form of direct action in which protesters nonviolently occupy and refuse to leave an area. Mahatma Gandhi employed the tactic during the Indian independence movement, and autoworkers used it in Flint, Michigan, in the late 1930s. Student movements around the world widely adopted the tactic in the 1960s.

social mobility   movement of individuals from one social class to another. In general, the stronger the barriers of class, race, gender or caste, the less social mobility exhibited by a society.

socialism   philosophy of social and economic organization in which the means of producing and distributing goods is owned collectively or by government.

sociological jurisprudence   legal theory that emphasizes the importance not merely of precedent but of contemporary social context in interpreting the law.

specie   coined money of gold or silver. Also referred to as hard money or hard currency. In contrast, banknotes or notes are paper money or paper currency.

sphere of influence   geographic region beyond its border over which a nation exerts political or economic control.

spoils system   practice of rewarding loyal party members with jobs in government. Known more formally as "patronage," the practice drew its name from the old saying "To the victor belong the spoils," in this instance, meaning the rewards of election victories.

steerage   least expensive accommodation on a passenger ship, located below decks and often used by immigrants for passage to the United States in the late nineteenth and early twentieth centuries.

stock exchange   market at which shares of ownership in corporations are bought and sold. The creation of what were markets for investment capital made it easier to raise the large sums of money needed for large industrial projects.

stratified   layered; in this case, according to class or social station. A highly stratified society has a greater variety of social levels, from the richest or most socially esteemed to the poorest or least socially approved. A society can be stratified according to wealth, race, religion, or a number of other social markers.

subsistence farming   see **semisubsistence economy.**

subversive   one who seeks the destruction or overthrow of a legally constituted government; also used as an adjective (for example, *subversive conduct*) to refer more generally to behavior undermining the established social order.

suffrage   right to vote; also referred to as the franchise. To *disenfranchise* is to take away the right to vote.

Sun Belt   areas of the southern and western parts of the United States that experienced significant economic and population growth since World War II. That growth has been a contrast to the relative decline of the *Rust Belt*, the older industrial area from New England to the mid-Atlantic region across the upper Middle West.

Sunni   see **Shi'ite and Sunni.**

supply-side economics   theory that emphasizes tax cuts and business incentives to encourage economic growth rather than deficit spending to promote demand. Businesses and individuals, the theory assumes, will use their tax savings to create new businesses and expand old businesses, which in turn will increase productivity, employment, and general well-being.

T

tariff   duty on trade, the purpose of which is primarily to regulate the flow of commerce rather than to raise a revenue. The Molasses Act of 1733, for example, imposed a hefty customs duty on molasses imported from non-British Caribbean islands to encourage American distillers to purchase molasses exclusively from the British West Indies.

task system   way of organizing slave labor in the South Carolina low country during the eighteenth century. Masters and overseers of rice and indigo plantations assigned individual slaves a daily task, and after its completion, slaves could spend the rest of the day engaged in pursuits of their own choosing. Gang labor, the system practiced in the Chesapeake, afforded slaves less opportunity for freedom within slavery.

taxes   duty on trade (known as external taxation) or a duty on items circulating within a nation or a colony (known as internal taxation) intended primarily to raise a revenue rather than to regulate the flow of commerce. The Sugar Act of 1764 was an external tax, whereas the Stamp Act of 1765 was an internal tax.

Tejano   Texan of Hispanic descent. In the early stages of the rebellion against Santa Anna, more than a few Tejanos supported the Texan drive for independence. But as Americans continued to arrive in Texas in large numbers, many viewed Tejanos with suspicion, and they were marginalized in Texan society.

temperance movement   reform movement, begun in the 1820s, to temper or restrain the sale and use of alcohol. It achieved its greatest success when the Eighteenth Amendment took effect in 1920, outlawing the manufacture, sale, transportation, and importation of alcohol. The amendment was repealed in 1933.

tenement   building, often in disrepair and usually five or six stories in height, in which cheap apartments were rented to tenants. Such dilapidated housing sprang up in cities across the United States in the late nineteenth and early twentieth centuries to lodge the growing numbers of immigrants, African Americans, and other poor populations moving to urban centers.

theocracy   system of government dominated by the clergy.

totalitarian government   system in which the state controls all aspects of economic, political, and even social life, usually through some form of dictatorship. Nazi Germany under Adolf Hitler and the Soviet Union under Joseph Stalin are examples of totalitarian regimes.

trade association   organization of individuals and firms in a given industry that provides statistical, lobbying, and other services to members.

trust   business arrangement in which owners of shares in a business turn over their shares "in trust" to a board with power to control those businesses for the benefit of the trust. Following the example set by John D. Rockefeller and Standard Oil, trusts blossomed in the late nineteenth century as a means of consolidating power over production, marketing, and pricing, often crowding out other competitors.

U

union   organization of workers designed to improve their economic status and working conditions. Such organizations come in two varieties: the horizontal union, in which all members share a common skill or craft, and the vertical union, composed of workers from all across the same industry.

Upper South   the border states (Delaware, Maryland, Kentucky, and Missouri) and Virginia, North Carolina, Tennessee, and Arkansas.

V

vertical integration   strategy of business growth that attempts to reduce costs by gaining control of the successive stages of a business operation,

incorporating into a single firm several firms involved in all aspects of the manufacture of a product—from exploiting raw materials to manufacturing and distribution.

Victorianism   constellation of middle-class values attributed to the proper virtues of Britain's Queen Victoria. Victorianism responded to the instabilities of an industrial age in which factory work dominated the lives of struggling workers and middle-class clerks as well as down-at-the-heels landed gentry. The culture's emphasis on "refinement" and "manners" established a social hierarchy offering some sense of stability.

virgin soil epidemic   epidemic in which the populations at risk have had no previous contact with the diseases that strike them and are therefore immunologically almost defenseless.

virtual representation   view that representation is not linked to election but rather to common interests; for example, during the imperial crisis the British argued that Americans were virtually represented in Parliament, even though colonials elected none of its members, because each member of Parliament stood for the interests of the whole empire. *See also* **actual representation.**

W

"watered" stock   stock issued in excess of the assets of a company. The term derived from the practice of some ranchers who made their cattle drink large amounts of water before weighing them for sale.

welfare capitalism   business practice of providing welfare—in the form of pension and profit-sharing programs, subsidized housing, personnel management, paid vacations, and other services and benefits—for workers. The practice was pioneered by Henry Ford under the philosophy that businesses in a capitalist economy should act for the common good of their workers. The philosophy, if not the businesswide practice, became popular in the 1920s as a way of reducing high rates of turnover among employees and integrating technological change into the workplace.

Wisconsin idea   series of progressive reforms at the state level promoted by Robert La Follette during his governorship of Wisconsin (1901–1906). They included primary elections, corporate property taxes, regulation of railroads and public utilities, and supervision of public resources in the public interest. A nonpartisan civil service group, recruited mostly from faculty at the University of Wisconsin, provided a cadre of expert bureaucrats to run the new programs.

Y

yellow journalism   brand of newspaper reporting that stresses excitement and shock over evenhandedness and dull fact. The term "yellow journalism" derived from the color of the ink used to print the first comic strip, which appeared in William Randolph Hearst's *New York Journal* in 1895. Hearst's newspaper specialized in yellow journalism and is often credited with igniting public passions for war with Spain in 1898.

Credits

Text Credits

CHAPTER 1
Page 17, Dueling Document 1
Quotation from Sherburne F. Cook and Woodrow Borah, *Essays in Population History: Mexico and the Caribbean,* 3 vols. Copyright 1971 by University of California Press—Books. Reproduced with permission of University of California Press—Books via Copyright Clearance Center.

Page 17, Dueling Document 2
Quotation from Massimo Livi-Bacci, "Return to Hispaniola: Reassessing a Demographic Catastrophe," in *Hispanic American Historical Review,* Volume 83, no. 1, pp. 3–51. Copyright, 2003, Duke University Press. All rights reserved. Republished by permission of the copyright holder, Duke University Press. www.dukeupress.edu.

CHAPTER 4
Page 93, Dueling Documents 1 & 2
Quotation from The Salem Witchcraft Papers, Verbatim Transcriptions of the Court Records in three volumes. Edited by Paul Boyer and Stephen Nissenbaum, Da Capo Press, 1977. Salem Witch Trials Documentary Archive, http://etext.virginia.edu/salem/witchcraft.

Photo Credits
Image Researcher: Deborah Bull; Assistant Researcher: Jullie Chung

FRONT MATTER
p. iii (top): The McGraw-Hill Companies; (bottom): Library of Congress (LC-DIG-pga02419); p. iv: Library of Congress; p.xxiv: The Granger Collection, New York; xxvi; National Archives; p. xxvii: Private Collection/The Bridgeman Art Library International; Backgrounds (Laid paper): National Gallery of Art, Washington.

CHAPTER 1
Opener: © Richard A. Cooke/Corbis; p. 4: © Heritage Images/Corbis; p. 5: Adalberto Rios Szalay/Sexto Sol/Getty Images/Getty Images; p. 6: Princeton University Art Museum. Museum purchase, Fowler McCormick, Class of 1921, Fund, in honor of Gillett G. Griffin on his seventieth birthday. Photo: Bruce M. White, © Trustees of Princeton University/Art Resource, NY; p. 7 (top) © Werner Formans/HIP/Image Works; (bottom) © George H. H. Huey/Corbis; p. 8: Courtesy of Cahokia Mounds State Historic Site, Collinsville, Illinois. Painting by William R. Iseminger; p. 9: Ancestor Figure, Kwakwaka'wakw, A50009d. Courtesy UBC Museum of Anthropology, Vancouver, Canada. Photo: Bill McLennan; p. 11: © David Cavagnaro/Visuals Unlimited/Corbis; p. 12 (top): Service Historique de la Marine, Vincennes, France, Giraudon/Bridgeman Art Library; (bottom): © Emmanueal Lattes/Alamy; p. 14: Chaco Culture National Parks Service; p.16: © Danny Lehman/Corbis; p. 21 (left): Ancestor Figure, Kwakwaka'wakw, A50009d. Courtesy UBC Museum of Anthropology, Vancouver, Canada. Photo: Bill McLennan; (right): Service Historique de la Marine, Vincennes, France, Giraudon/The Bridgeman Art Library International; p 23: © Carolina Biological/Visuals Unlimited/Corbis; p. 25: North Star Archaeological Research Program, Department of Anthropology, Texas A&M University. Image © Mike Waters.

CHAPTER 2
Opener: *A Ship Sailing Past Rocks in a Rough Sea,* c. 1620, by Cornelisz Verbeecq. National Maritime Museum, London (BHC0725); p. 28: (detail) The Pierpont Morgan Library/Art Resource, NY; p. 29: Pendant: skull, 1600s. Metal, enamel, 1.3 × 1.2 × 3 cm. The Thomson Collection. Courtesy, Art Gallery of Ontario; p. 30 (left): © Geffrye Museum, London, UK/The Bridgeman Art Library International; (right): Photograph © A. G. Massey. Used by permission; p. 31: SSPL/Science Museum/Art Resource, NY; p. 32: Erich Lessing/Art Resource, NY; p. 33: Library of Congress (3b49587u); p. 35 (left): Document sur l'Aperreamiento, ca. 1540, ms. mex. 374. Bibliothèque Nationale, Paris; (right): Library of Congress; p. 36: The Granger Collection, New York; p. 39: The Pierpont Morgan Library/Art Resource, NY; p. 40: © Dorling Kindersley/Getty Images, RF; p. 42: AGE Fotostock; p. 43: Bildarchiv Preussischer Kulturbesitz/Art Resource, NY; p. 44, 45: Private Collection/The Bridgeman Art Library.

CHAPTER 3
Opener: Art Resource, NY; p. 52: Ashmolean Museum of Art & Archaeology, University of Oxford; p. 53: National Portrait Gallery, Washington, D.C./Art Resource, NY p. 54 (top): © Kevin Moloney; (bottom): © Kevin Fleming/Corbis; p. 56: Service Historique de la Marine, Vincennes, France, Lauros/Giraudon/The Bridgeman Art Library; p. 60: Getty Images; p. 62: Virginia Historical Society, The Center for Virginia History/Courtesy Xanterra Corporation; p. 64 (top): Foto Marburg/Art Resource, NY; (bottom): The Granger Collection, New York; p. 65 (top): Musée d'Histoire de Nantes–Chateau des ducs de Bretagne; (bottom left): John Gabriel Stedman, Narrative of a Five Years Expedition, Plate 53. New York Public Library/Art Resource, NY; (bottom right): Blacks working on the James River by Benjamin Henry Latrobe, 1798-99. The Library of Virginia; p. 66: Image copyright © The Metropolitan Museum of Art/Art Resource, NY; p. 67: The Colonial Williamsburg Foundation (#1975-242); p. 69: The Library Company of Philadelphia (I1 Pome, 95.Q); p. 70: Private Collection/Photo © Christie's Images/The Bridgeman Art Library; p. 73: "View of Mulberry, House and Street, 1805" by Thomas Coram (American, 1756-1811), Oil on paper. Image © Gibbes Museum of Art/Carolina Art Association, 1968.18.01; p. 74: Philip Georg Friedrich von Reck, "Indian Festival," 1736. Watercolor on paper. Royal Library, Copenhagen; p. 77 (left): © Kevin Moloney; (right): Musée du Chateau des ducs de Bretagne Cliché: P. Jean Ville de Nantes.

CHAPTER 4
Opener: © Collection of the New-York Historical Society, USA/The Bridgeman Art Library; p. 80: www.canadianheritage.ca/ID#20640, National Archives of Canada C-37056; p. 81: Musée Marguerite-Bourgeoys; p. 82 (top): The Granger Collection, New York; (bottom):The National Library of Medicine; p. 83: Library of Congress (ct000656 g3300); p. 85: Universal History Archive/UIG/The Bridgeman Art Library; p. 88: © The British Museum; p. 89: © Steve Dunwell; p. 90: Private Collection/The Stapleton Collection/The Bridgeman Art Library; p. 91: © Bettmann/Corbis; p. 94: Library of Congress (cph3b42346); p. 95: The New York Public Library, Astor, Lenox and Tilden Foundation. Print Division, Phillip Stokes Collection of American Historical Prints; p. 97: Prints Collection, Miriam and Ira D. Wallach Division of Arts, Prints and Photographs, New York Public Library, Astor, Lenox and Tilden Foundations; p.98: City of Bristol Museum and Art Gallery, UK/The Bridgeman Art Library; p. 101 (left): © Collection of the New-York Historical Society, USA/The Bridgeman Art Library; (right): Corbis.

CHAPTER 5
Opener: Segesser II. Courtesy Palace of Governors (MNM/DCA) 158345; p. 104: Segesser II. Courtesy Palace of Governors (MNM/DCA) 158345; p. 106: © Gilcrease Museum, Tulsa

Oklahoma (4016.336.12); p. 107: Courtesy of the Private Collection of Mrs. Janis Lyon and the Phoenix Art Museum; p. 110: National Library of Australia (nla.pic-an10333402); p. 112: Library of Congress (3a52292); p. 113: The Maryland Historical Society, XIV.17; p. 116: Courtesy, North Carolina Division of Archives and History; p. 118: The Granger Collection, New York; p. 119: From the Collection of the Henry Ford (THF6826_36.17.1); p. 121: (detail) Abby Aldrich Rockefeller Folk Art Museum, Williamsburg, VA. (T1995-1); p. 123: Private Collection/The Stapleton Collection/The Bridgeman Art Library; p. 125: British Museum, London, UK/The Bridgeman Art Library; p. 126 (top): Clements Library, University of Michigan; (bottom): Mrs. Thomas Cushing's Tea Caddy, Courtesy of The Bostonian Society/Old State House, Boston, MA (1958.0003).

CHAPTER 6
Opener: Fort Necessity Battlefield, National Park Service; (inset): The Granger Collection, New York; p. 132: The Granger Collection, New York; p. 135 (left): © National Gallery of Scotland (PG2190); p. 135 (right): Library of Congress (03847v); p. 136: With permission of the Royal Ontario Museum © ROM; p. 140: Detail, "A View of the Year of 1765", by Paul Revere, 1765. MHS Neg.#1448. Courtesy of the Massachusetts Historical Society; p. 142: (detail) The Colonial Williamsburg Foundation (DS89-328); p. 143: © V&A Images/Victoria and Albert Museum, London; p. 144: Library of Congress (3a22737u); p. 146: The New-York Historical Society (49494); p. 147: © Bettmann/Corbis; p. 149: Library of Congress; p. 150: © Collection of the New-York Historical Society, USA/The Bridgeman Art Library; p. 151: © Philadelphia History Museum at the Atwater Kent,/Courtesy of Historical Society of Pennsylvania Collection/The Bridgeman Art Library; p. 152 (top): Thomas Paine, by Auguste Milliere. By courtesy of the National Portrait Gallery, London (897); (bottom): New York Public Library, USA/The Bridgeman Art Library p. 155: Library of Congress.

CHAPTER 7
Opener: *Attack on Bunker's Hill, with the Burning of Charles Town*, 1783 or after. Oil on canvas, 53.3 × 70.8 cm (21 × 27 7/8 in.) Gift of Edgar William and Bernice Chrysler Garbisch, © 2007 Board of Trustees, National Gallery of Art, Washington. 1953.5.86; p. 158: We Research Pictures, LLC; p. 159: © Corbis; p. 160: © Atwater Kent Museum of Philadelphia/Courtesy of Historical Society of Pennsylvania Collection,/The Bridgeman Art Library ; p. 164: Photograph courtesy of the Pocumtuck Valley Memorial Association, Memorial Hall Museum, Deerfield, Massachusetts.1914.07.28; p. 165: The Dietrich American Foundation (6.7.197-2); p. 167: Image © The Metropolitan Museum of Art,/Art Resource, NY; p. 168: © American Antiquarian Society; p. 169:

Library of Congress; p. 172: Charles Willson Peale (1741-1827). *General Nathanael Greene*, 1783. Oil on Canvas, 22 × 19 inches. Museum purchase: Acquisition Fund, 1961.12. Photo by: Peter Jacobs, 1999. Montclair Art Museum; p. 173: Photo by MPI/Getty Images; p. 174: Virginia General Assembly, Legislative petitions of the General Assembly, "A List of Negroes that Went off to Dunmore, April 14, 1776". State government records collection, The Library of Virginia, Richmond, Va. 23219; p. 176: The Historical Society of Pennsylvania, Bb612 R2997; p. 179: (left): British Grenadier, artist unknown. The Historical Society of Pennsylvania. (HSP). 1931.5 Courtesy of The Historical Society of Pennsylvania Collection, Atwater Kent Museum of Philadelphia.; (right): Library of Congress.

CHAPTER 8
Opener: Courtesy, Winterthur Museum, Painting, *Captain John Purves and his Wife, Eliza Anne Pritchard*, by Henry Benbridge, 1775-1777, Charleston, SC, Bequest of Henry Francis du Pont, 1960.582; p. 182: © Collection of the New-York Historical Society, USA/The Bridgeman Art Library; p. 183: Miriam & Ira D. Wallach Division of Arts, Prints and Photographs. New York Public Library. Astor, Lenox and Tilden Foundations.; p. 184: National Archives (596742); p. 185: unidentified artist, circa 1805. *The Plan of Civilization*. Oil on canvas, 35 7/8 × 49 7/8 inches. Greenville County Museum of Art, Greenville, SC, Gift of The Museum Association, Inc.with funds donated by Corporate Partners: Ernst and Young; Fluor Daniel; Director's Circle Members; Mr. and Mrs. Alester G. Furman, III; Mr. and Mrs. Dexter Hagy; Thomas P. Harntess; Mr. and Mrs. E. Erwin Maddrey, II; Mary M. Pearce; Mr. and Mrs. John D. Pellett, Jr.; Mr. W. Thomas Smith; Mr. and Mrs. Edward H. Stall; Eleanor and Irvine Welling; Museum Antiques Show, 1989, 1990, 1991, Elliott, Davis & Company, CPA's sponsor: Collectors Group 1990, 1991; p. 187: © Bettmann/Corbis; p. 189: © Wilberforce House, Hull City Museums and Art Galleries, UK/The Bridgeman Art Library; p. 190: The Library Company of Philadelphia (W26); p. 191: *The Skater (Portrait of William Grant)*, 1782, by Gilbert Stuart, American, 1755 - 1828. Oil on canvas, 245.5 × 147.4 cm (96 1/4 × 58 in.) Andrew W. Mellon Collection, © 2007 Board of Trustees, National Gallery of Art, Washington. 1950.18.1; p. 192: Courtesy, Winterthur Museum, Painting, *Rebecca Prichard Mills (Mrs. William Mills) and her daughter Eliza Shrewsbury*, by James Earl, 1794-1796, Charleston, SC, Bequest of Henry Francis du Pont, 1960.554; p. 193: Courtesy Winterthur Museum (1954.0093.001); p. 194 (left): Tate Gallery, London/Art Resource, NY; (right): The Library Company of Philadelphia; p. 195: © Reproduced by permission of The Society of the Cincinnati, Washington, D.C. (M1938.482); p. 196: © Francis G. Mayer/Corbis; p. 197: Private Collection/Peter Newark

American Pictures/The Bridgeman Art Library; p. 203 (top): Brand X Pictures/PunchStock; p. 204: Herrnhut, Archiv der Brüder-Unität; p. 205: Virginia Baptist Historical Society at the University of Richmond; p. 206: The Print and Picture Collection, The Free Library of Philadelphia. Will Brown, Photographer; p. 207: The Historic New Orleans Collection, accession no. 1960.46.

CHAPTER 9
Opener: © Collection of the New-York Historical Society, USA/The Bridgeman Art Library; p. 210: The Granger Collection, New York; p. 214: copyright © The Metropolitan Museum of Art/Art Resource, NY; p. 216 (left): Independence National Historical Park; (right): *Alexander Hamilton,* c. 1972, (detail) by John Trumbull. Oil on canvas, 30 1/4 × 24 1/8 in. Gift of Avalon Foundation, © 2000 Board of Trustees, National Gallery of Art, Washington, DC.; p. 217: Private Collection/Archives Charmet/The Bridgeman Art Library; p. 218: Gilbert Stuart (American painter, 1755-1828), *John Adams,* c. 1800/1815, oil on canvas, overall: 73.7 × 61 cm (29 × 24 in.) framed: 97.5 × 84.5 × 10.8 cm (38 3/8 × 33 1/4 × 4 1/4 in.) Gift of Mrs. Robert Homans, National Gallery of Art, Washington, DC; p. 220: Hulton Archive/Getty Images; p. 221: Courtesy, Winterthur Museum, Painting, *The Quilting Frolic,* by John Lewis Krimmel, 1813, Philadelphia, PA, Museum Purchase, 1953.178.2; p. 222: Miniature Panorama Scene (detail): "Scenes from a Seminary for Young Ladies," c. 1810–20. Saint Louis Art Museum, Museum Purchase and funds given by the Decorative Arts Society (89:1976); p. 227, 228: The Granger Collection, New York; p. 233: Library of Congress (ppmsca10755); p. 234 (left): Special Collections and College Archives, Skillman Library, Lafayette College; (right): Collection of the New-York Historical Society (1937.714); p. 239 (left): Library of Congress (LC-USZ62-70508); (right): From the Collection of the Henry Ford; p. 241: Monticello, The Thomas Jefferson Memorial Foundation, Inc.; p. 242: Jefferson, Thomas. Farm Book, 1774–1824; p. 145. Original manuscript from the Coolidge Collection of Thomas Jefferson manuscripts, Courtesy of the Massachusetts Historical Society; p. 243 (top): Howard University/Moorland-Spingarn Research Center; (bottom): Abby Aldrich Rockefeller Folk Art Museum, Colonial Williamsburg Foundation, Williamsburg, VA (#T94-121).

CHAPTER 10
Opener: © Collection of the New-York Historical Society, USA/The Bridgeman Art Library; p. 246: Library of Congress; p. 247: © Bettmann/Corbis; p. 250 (top): Library of Congress (LC-USZ62-103288); (bottom): The Lilly Library, Indiana University, Bloomington, Indiana; p. 252: *Princess*, by Adrien Persac. Louisiana State University Museum of Art, Baton Rouge. Gift of Mrs. Mamie Persac Lusk;

p. 255: Charles Felix, Blauvelt, *A German Immigrant Inquiring His Way*, 1855, Oil on canvas, 36 1/8 × 29 in. (91.8 × 73.7 cm), North Carolina Museum of Art, Purchased with funds from the State of North Caroline, 52.9.2; p. 256: American Textile History Museum, Lowell MA; p. 258: Photo by Jonathan Parker/Lowell National Historic Park/National Park Service; p. 259: Gift of the American Art Council and Mr. and Mrs. J. Douglas Pardee/Digital Image © Museum Associates/LACMA; p. 260: New York Public Library/Art Resource, NY; p. 262: Library of Congress p. 263 (left): Private Collection: (right): Biggs Museum of American Art; p. 265: *Interior of Fort Laramie*, Alfred Jacob Miller. ©Walters Art Museum, Baltimore USA/The Bridgeman Art Library; p. 266: Library of Congress (LC-USZ62-89594).

CHAPTER 11
Opener: SuperStock; p. 272: Courtesy of the Cornell University Library, "Making of America" Digital; Collection; p. 274: © Museum of the City of New York, USA/The Bridgeman Art Library; p. 277 *Politics in an Oyster House*, Richard Caton Woodville. The Walters Art Museum (37.1994); p. 278 (top): *County Election* by George Caleb Bingham, 1851–52. Saint Louis Art Museum, Gift of Bank of America (bottom): The New-York Historical Society, 1858.11; p. 279: The Granger Collection, New York; p. 280: National Museum of the American Indian, Smithsonian Institution (P00452); p. 282: Joslyn Art Museum, Omaha, Nebraska (1991.19.2); p. 285: (top): Library of Congress Manuscript Division (MMC-2503); (bottom left): Library of Congress (LC-USZC4-4438); (bottom right): Courtesy of the J. Paul Getty Museum, Los Angeles, 84.XT.441.3; p. 287: "Webster's Reply to Hayne" Courtesy of The Boston Art Commission, 2004; p. 289: The Library Company of Philadelphia; p. 290: Museum of the City of New York, The J. Clarence Davies Collection/Art Resource, NY; p. 292: Gift of Stephen C. Clark. Fenimore Art Museum, Cooperstown, NY. Photograph by Richard Walker. (N0402.1955) p. 295: Library of Congress (3b35969).

CHAPTER 12
Opener: Library of Congress; p. 298: Harriet Beecher Stowe Center, Hartford, CT; p. 299: Library of Congress (LC-USZC4-2671); p. 300 (top): Allen Memorial Art Museum, Oberlin College, Ohio; Gift of Lewis Tappan to Oberlin College, 1858; (bottom): The Granger Collection, New York; p. 301: Photograph by Richard Pieper. Courtesy of New York Parks, Recreation and Historic Preservation; p. 303: The McGraw-Hill Companies; p. 304: Stock Montage, Inc.; p. 305: From the Collections of Old Sturbridge Village, Sturbridge, MA (26.23.95); p. 306: Image copyright © The Metropolitan Museum of Art/Art Resource, NY; p.307: A6 folio American Tract Society, Boston, MA n.d.s.n. Engraving, 53 × 46.5cm © American Antiquarian Society; p. 308: Connecticut

Historical Society, Hartford, Connecticut (920 B4135be vol. 2); p. 309: Library of Congress (LC-USZC2-9797); p. 310 (top): Courtesy Concord Free Public Library; (bottom): Library of Congress; p. 311: Apic/Getty Images; p. 312: Miriam and Ira D. Wallach Division of Art, Prints and Photographs, The New York Public Library. Astor, Lenox and Tilden Foundations; p. 313: © Lowell Georgia/Corbis; p. 314 (top left): Courtesy of the Trustees of the Boston Public Library/Rare Books. (Ms. B. 10.37); (top right): Library of Congress; (bottom): Photograph courtesy of the Pocumtuck Valley Memorial Association, Memorial Hall Museum, Deerfield, Massachusetts. L05.077 p. 315: Madison County Historical Society, Oneida, NY; p. 316: Coline Jenkins/Elizabeth Cady Stanton Trust; p. 318: Library of Congress (3a12793); p. 321(left): AGE Fotostock; (right): Library of Congress (cph 3a44497).

CHAPTER 13
Opener: 322: The J. Paul Getty Museum, Los Angeles; p. 324: National Archives of Canada, Documentary Art and Photography Division (C128473); p. 326 (top): University of Arkansas Department of Entomology. (IMG9368)/Scott Akin; (bottom): Museum of the City of New York, Harry T. Peters Collection/Art Resource, NY; p. 332: The Historic New Orleans Collection, accession no. 1975.93.5; p. 334: Basil Hall, Etching 25, Forty etchings from sketches made with the camera lucida in North America, in 1827 and 1828. Edinburg, London. William L. Clements Library, University of Michigan; p. 336: © Walker Art Gallery/National Museums, Liverpool The Bridgeman Art Library; p. 337: Face Jug, 1860-1880, Edgefield, South Carolina. Alkaline glazed stoneware and kaolin inserts. Collection of the Chipstone Foundation (photo by Gavin Ashworth); p. 338: De Agostini Picture Library/The Bridgeman Art Library; p. 339: (detail) *Seated Man*, Eastman Johnston. National Gallery of Art, Washington, D.C.; p. 341: "Market Woman," by Thomas Waterman Wood. 1858. Oil on canvas. 23 3/8 × 14 1/2". The Fine Arts Museums of San Francisco, Mildred Anna Williams Collection, 1944.8; p. 342: Library of Congress (LC-DIG-pga02419); p. 345: Photodisc/Getty Images.

CHAPTER 14
Opener: © Historical Picture Archive/Corbis; p. 348: Archive Photos/Getty Images; p. 350: Courtesy of The Bancroft Library, University of California, Berkeley; p. 351: © Andre Jenny/Alamy; p. 352: Library of Congress (cph 3c10029); p. 355: Courtesy of the Lane County Historical Museum (GN10128) (GN4986); p. 356: The Huntington Library, Art Collections, and Botanical Gardens, San Marino, CA/SuperStock; p. 357, 359: Library of Congress; p. 362: National Anthropological Archives, Smithsonian Institution; p. 364: "The 'Heathen Chinee' with Pick and Rocker", from Mining Scenes in California Series, ca. 1868. Photograph by Eadweard J. Muybrige Courtesy

California Historical Society, San Francisco. FN-138990; p. 365: Courtesy of The Bancroft Library, University of California, Berkeley (1905. 16242.106); p. 366: Print Collection, Miriam and Ira D. Wallach Division of Arts, Prints and Photographs. New York Public Library, Astor, Lenox and Tilden Foundations/Art Resource, NY; p. 368: Courtesy of the Witte Museum, San Antonio, Texas; p. 369, 375: Library of Congress.

CHAPTER 15
Opener: Kansas State Historical Society (FK2.83*15); p. 378: Kansas State Historical Society; p. 382: David Hawley/Arabia Steamboat Museum, Kansas City, MO; p. 383: Image © Metropolitan Museum of Art/Art Resource, NY; p. 387: Library of Congress (LC-USZC4-1298); p. 388: American Antiquarian Society, Worcester, Massachusetts, USA/The Bridgeman Art Library; p. 389 (top): Print Collection, Miriam and Ira D. Wallach Division of Arts, Prints and Photographs. New York Public Library, Astor, Lenox and Tilden Foundations.; (bottom): © David J. & Janice L. Frent Collection/Corbis; p. 390 (left): (detail) Missouri Historical Society (1897.9.1); (right): Library of Congress; p. 392, 393: Library of Congress; p. 395: Thompson Library, OSU Rare Books and Manuscripts, Ohio State University Library (ambrotype382); p. 397: The Museum of the Confederacy, Richmond, Virginia. Photography by Katherine Wetzel; p. 398: The New-York Historical Society, PR-022-3-45-13 p. 401: Library of Congress.

CHAPTER 16
Opener: The Granger Collection, New York; p. 404, 406: Library of Congress; p. 407 (top): © Corbis; (bottom): Library of Congress; p. 408, 410, 412: Library of Congress; p. 413: © Corbis; p. 414: The Museum of the Confederacy, Richmond, Virginia; p. 415 (left): American Numismatic Association, Edward C. Rochette Money Museum (Fr-61 [face]); (right): Library of Congress (cph 3c25842); p. 417: John Ferguson Weir, "The Gun Foundry". Putnam County Historical Society, Cold Spring, NY 10516; p. 418, 419: Library of Congress ; p. 420 (top): The Museum of the Confederacy, Richmond, VA; (bottom): Library of Congress; p. 422: National Archives (NWDNS-111-B-372); p. 428: Library of Congress (LC-DIG-ppmsca-21711); p. 429: © 2014 Virginia Historical Society; p. 430 (left): Library of Congress; (right): © Corbis; p. 433 (left): Library of Congress (cwpb 01058); p. 433 (top): Library of Congress; p. 433 (bottom): © Corbis; p. 434: Library of Congress (LC-USZ62-47037) 437: Harper's Weekly.

CHAPTER 17
Opener: Library of Congress (LC-DIG-cwpb-00468); p. 440: Library of Congress; p. 441: Smithsonian American Art Museum, Washington, DC/Art Resource, NY; p. 442 (top): Harper's Weekly; (bottom): Library of

Congress (LC-B8184-10690); p. 443: Library of Congress; p. 445: Puck, 1890; p. 447: "Portrait of Hiram Rhoades Revels," by Theodor Kaufmann, 1870. Oil on millboard, 12" × 10". Courtesy of the Herbert F. Johnson Museum of Art, Cornell University, Ithaca. NY. Transferred from the Olin 69.170.; p. 448: The Granger Collection, New York; p. 450: © Corbis; p. 452: The New-York Historical Society (50475); p. 453: Schlesinger Library, Radcliffe Institute, Harvard University/The Bridgeman Art Library; p. 454: Library of Congress; p. 455: The Granger Collection, New York; p. 456: © David

J. & Janice L. Frent Collection/Corbis; p. 457 (center): The New York Public Library/Art Resource, NY; (left and right): Library of Congress (cph 3c19565); p. 461: Library of Congress (cph 3a36683).

ADDITIONAL CREDITS
Globe icon: Cartesia/Getty Images
Sun icon: Photodisc/Getty Images
Daily Lives (field): Design Pics/Michael Interisano/Getty Images
Dueling Documents (swords): Civil War Archive/Getty Images

Conclusion (map): Royalty-Free/Corbis
Historian's Toolbox (weathered wood): Darrin Kilmek/Getty Images

After the Fact images:
Magnifying glass: Richard Hutchings
Blank parchment paper: Christine Balderas/Getty Images
Roll of parchment, background: Oleksiy Maksymenko/Alamy
Antique books: Ingram Publishing/SuperStock
Row of books: Tetra Images/Getty Images

Index

Note: Page numbers in *italics* indicate illustrations and their captions; numbers followed by *m* indicate maps; page numbers followed by *n* indicate material in footnotes; page numbers followed by *t* indicate material in tables.

election of 1796 and, 218, *218*
federal court system and, *220*, 220–221
ratification of Constitution and, 199
split within, 220, 220*m*
suppression of disloyalty, 219–220
"The Female Advocate," 223
Ferdinand, King of Spain, 30, 33
Ferdinando, Simon, 45, 46
Fessenden, William Pitt, 443
Fifteenth Amendment, 454, *454*, A-9
Fillmore, Millard, 371, 389, 390
Finney, Charles Grandison, 299–300, *300*, 303, 312, 313, 315, 316
First Amendment, 219, A-7
First Bank of United States, 214–215, 225, 247, 251
First Continental Congress, 150–151, 154
First Great Awakening, 123, *123*, 204
Fitch, Caroline, 253–254
Flagg, Edmund, 380
Fletcher v. Peck (1810), 253
Florida, 23, 135, 236, 279
as Spanish colony, 55, *56*, 57*m*, 75, 77
Spanish expeditions, 39–40
Force Act of 1870, 456
Force Bill, 287, 355
Fort Bent, 282
Fort Caroline, 42–43, 55
Fort Detroit, 111
Fort Donelson, 408, 409*m*
Fort Duquesne, 132
Forten, James, 221
Fort Frontenac, capture of, 134*m*, 135
Fort Henry, 408, 409*m*
Fort Laramie, 355
Fort McHenry, 234
Fort Mims, 233
Fort Necessity, 132, 133
Fort Pitt, 138, 210
Fort Sumter, 395
Foster, Capt. Samuel, *442*
Foster, Eugene A., 242
Fourier, Charles, 311, 319
Fourteenth Amendment, 443, 445–446, 455, 458–459, A-8
Fowler, John, 274
Fox, Samuel, *285*
Foxe, John, 85, *85*
France, 28, 30, 407, 428
alliance with American rebels, *167*, 167–168, 219
colonization in North America, 80–84, 99
attempts in Southwest, 103–105
maps of, 83, 83*m*, 105*m*, 129*m*
engaged in piracy, 42–43
explorations in North America, 41, 83, 83*m*, 104
French Revolution, 217, *217*, 236, 237
Louisiana Purchase, 225–227, 226*m*, 230
rivalry with Britain, 113–114, 132
war with Great Britain, 217, 230
Franchise, 447

Franciscan missionaries, 55, 56–57, 71, 81, 106
in California, 107, 110, 129*m*
in New Mexico, 55, 56, 57*m*, 75
Francis I, King of France, 30
Franklin, Abraham, 435
Franklin, Benjamin, 122, 123, 124, 133, 196, 275
at Constitutional Convention, 198
Declaration of Independence and, 159, *160*
negotiates Treaty of Paris, 175
negotiations with France, *167*, 167–168, 234
Franquelin, Jean Baptiste Louis, 83*m*
Fredericksburg, Battle of, 410, 411*m*
Freedmen, *285*, 412–413, 459–460
black codes and, 442–443
employment of, 340, 449, 451, *451*, 452
minstrel shows, *285*, 286
in North, 282–283, 283*m*
in Old South, 329, 340–341, *341*
Freedmen's Bureau, 443, 451–453, 461
Freedmen's Courts, 443, 453
Freedom of press, 219
Freedom of speech, 219
Freeman's Farm, battle of, 167
Freemanship, 88
Freemasons, 275
Freeport Doctrine, 393, 394
Free Soil Party, 369, 370, 372, 385
Free State Hotel, *376–377*, 378
Frémont, John C., *318*, 389, *389*, 390
French Revolution, 217, *217*, 236, 237
Frontier, 74, 138, 192
life in backcountry, 115–116, *116*
Northwest Territory, 188*m*, 188–189
settlement of, 114–116, 117*m*, 185, *187*, 225, 227, 254
Fugitive Slave Law of 1793, 370
Fugitive Slave Law of 1850, 370, 372
Fuller, Margaret, 309, 311
Fulton, Robert, 250
Fundamental Constitutions, 70–71
Fur trade, 81, 105*m*, 265–266, *266*

G

Gadsden Purchase, 385
Gage, Gen. Thomas, 151, 157–158
Galloway, Joseph, 150
Gang system of labor, 335, 451
Garcia, Pedro, 58
Gardoqui, Don Diego de, 195
Gaspee (ship), 147
Gaspee Commission, 147, 150
Gates, Gen. Horatio, 167, 172, 177
Gender segregation, 354–355
The Genius of Universal Emancipation, 313
Genocide, of Indians, 366–367
Genographic Project of National Geographic Society, 25

Gentry, *67*, 67–68, 124
Geographic mobility, *253*, 253–254
George II, King of England, 73–74
George III, King of England, 142, 145, 146, 150, 175, *183*, 253
appointment of Pitt, 143
criticism of, 149, 152, 159–160
Georgia, 39–40, 162, 279, 446
founding of, 73–74, 77
public schools in, 327–328
Sherman's march through, 425*m*, 429
Germain, Lord George, 159, 165, 175
German immigrants, 96–97, 116, 117*m*, *383*, 383–384
Germantown, battle of, 166, 166*m*
Gerry, Elbridge, 197
Gettysburg, Battle of, 421, 422, 424, 425*m*
Ghent, Treaty of, 235
Gibbons v. Ogden (1824), 251, 253
Gilbert, Humphrey, 28, 34*m*, 43, 44, 46
Global issues
abolitionist movement, 319, 428
American sectionalism, 397–398
Civil War, 431
Jacksonian era, 293
market economy, 267
The Old South, 343
Reconstruction, 459
western expansion, 372
Glorious Revolution, 98–99
Goddard, Robert, 148
Godey's Lady's Book, 274
Gold, 33, *39*, 40*m*
Gold Coast of Africa, 64*m*
Gold mining, *39*, 351, 364–365
Gold rush, 348, 363, *364*, 364–365, 384
Goliad, battle of, 352, 353*m*
Gordon-Reed, Annette, 241–242, 243
Government(s), 141, 183, *215*, 292, 455
colonial, 37, 70–71, 89, 97–98, 151
representative, 95, 99, 125–126
royal government, 73, 98–99
English constitution, 124–125
federal government, 287, 366
state governments, 96, *183*, 183–184, 448
Governors, 183
Graduated income tax, 414
Grand Canyon, 40
Grant, Ulysses S., 453–455, *454*
as general, 407–409, 409*m*, 424–426, *430*, 432
as president, *455*, 455–456, 460
Grasse, comte de, 175
Great Awakening
First, 123, *123*, 204
Second, 227, 299–300, 301, 303, 314–315, 339
Great Basin, 9
early civilizations of, 5, 18, 18*m*, 21*t*
Mormon settlement in, 363, *366–367*, 367–368, 375

Plummer, Franklin E., 272, *272*, 273, 276, 291
Plymouth Colony, 3, 86*m*, 86–87, 94, 98
Pneumonia, 13
Pocket veto, 441
Political autonomy, 126
Political conventions, 275
Political culture, 221, 273–276, 293
Political parties, 275, 276, 398
   disillusionment with, 385–386
   emergence of, 216–224
   Jacksonian party system, 291–293, 318
   radical reform and, 317–318, *318,* 319
   See also specific parties
Polk, James K., 357, 357*m,* 358–361, 363, 369, 373
Polygamy, 313, 367
Ponce de León, Juan, 39
Pondicherry, battle of, 134*m*
Pontiac (Ottawa chief), 138, 139*m*
Pontiac's Rebellion, 138–140, 139*m,* 153
Poor whites, 334, 456
Popé, 57, 58, 104
Pope, Gen. John, 410
Pope's Day parades, 146, *146, 176,* 305
Popular sovereignty, 369, 378, 385, 386*m,* 391, 399
Population. *See* Demographics
Portolá, Gaspar de, 107
Portugal, 28, 31–33, 41, 46, 48, 127*m,* 428
Postal system, 250–251, 318, 343
Potatoes, 11, 383
Potawatomi Indians, 138, 230
Potosí, 37
Pottawatomie Creek massacre, 378, 401
Poverty, 255
Poverty Point (La.), 8, 10*m*
Power printing press, 250
Powhatan, *50–51,* 51–53, 60
Powhatan confederacy, *50–53,* 51–53, 60
Prairie, destruction of, 380, 381*m*
Pratt, Micajah, 258–259
Predestination, 42, 85, 299
Presbyterian Church, 84, 85, 123, 204–207, 299–300, *300*
Prescott, Col. William, 158
Presidential elections
   of 1796, 218, *218*
   of 1800, 220, 220*m,* 221, 224
   of 1804, 230
   of 1808, 231
   of 1824, 274–275, 275*m*
   of 1828, 277
   of 1844, 357, 357*m*
   of 1852, 372
   of 1856, *389,* 389–390
   of 1860, 394, 394*m,* 395
   of 1864, 426–427
   of 1868, 453–455, *454*
   of 1872, 455
   of 1876, 458, 458*m,* 460
   changes in process, 275

indirect election of president, 198
   summary of, A-11–A-14
Presidios, 106, 107, 110, 350
Press gangs, 119
Preston, Capt. Thomas, 148
Princeton, Battle of, 165, *165, 166m*
Privacy norms, 305, 306, *306*
Proclamation of 1763, 137*m,* 138, 139*m,* 139–140
Proclamation of Amnesty and Reconstruction, 440–441
Proclamation on Nullification, 287, 395
Proctor, John, 92, 93
The Prophet, *227,* 229*m,* 229–230, 237
Prosperity, *265,* 266, 326
Prosser, Gabriel, 336
Prostitution, 255, 364, 421
Protection certificates, *285*
Protestant(s), 305–308
Protestant Reformation, 41–43, 99
Provincial Congress, 151
Pueblo Bonito, *7*
Pueblo Indians, 103, 368
   revolt of, 56–57, 58, 104
   Spanish colonizers and, *54,* 54–55
Puerto Rico, 35, 68
Puritans, 43, 99
   disagreements among, 89, 91
   Puritan movement, 84–86, *85*
   similarities with Indians, 92–93
Purves, Anne Pritchard, *180–181*
Purves, John, *180–181*
Put-In Bay, Battle of, 232*m,* 233
Putnam, Ann, 92–93
Putting-out system, 260

Q

Quadroons, 240
Quakers, 90, 95, 189
   founding of Pennsylvania, 95–96
   political strife among, 96–97
   women speakers at meetings, 91, *91*
Quartering Act of 1765, 140, 144, 149, 153, 155
Quebec, 80, 84, 134*m,* 135, *136*
Quebec Act of 1774, 149, 305
Queen Anne's War, 114, 128
Quincy, Josiah, Jr., 148
Quitrents, 60
Quivira (rumored kingdom), 40–41

R

Race, 108–109, 279–286, 335
Race riots, 283, 285, 445
Racism, 67, 332, 413, 447, 458
   in Jacksonian era, 282, *285,* 285–286
   Manifest Destiny and, 350
   minstrel shows and, *285,* 286
Radical Republicans, 441–443, 445, *445,* 449, 455, 459, 460

Raguieneau, Paul, 82
Railroads, 249–250, 254
   expansion of, 250, *250*
   growth of railroad economy, *379,* 379–385, 381*m*
   incompatible track gauges, 381*m*
Raleigh, Sir Walter, 28, 34*m, 44,* 44–46
Rancheros, 350–351
Randal, Henry, 241
Randolph, Ellen Coolidge, 241
Randolph, Martha Jefferson, 240
Randolph, Thomas Jefferson, 241
Ranney, William, *173*
Rape, 166, 171, 332, 338
Rational Christianity, 122
Reapers, 380, 417
Reconstruction, 439–460, *460,* 461
   abandonment of, 453–459
   African Americans. *See* African Americans
   congressional plan, 445–447, 446*m*
   effects on South, 447–449
   global perspective of, 459
   presidential plans, 440–446
Redeemers, 458, 459, 461
"Red Stick" Creeks, 233
Reform Act of 1832 (Gr. Britain), 275, 343
Reformers, 259, 455
Reform movements, 41–43, 319, 321
   abolitionist. *See* Abolitionist movement
   American Renaissance and, 309–311, *310*
   efforts at moral reform, 297–298, *298*
   party system and, 317–318, *318,* 319
   radical reform, 313–317, 321
   Transcendentalism, 309
   Unitarian contributions, 309, *309*
Regnies, Nicolas, *32*
Religion, 6, 81, 367
   camp meetings. *See* Camp meetings
   churches. *See* Churches
   evangelicalism. *See* Evangelicalism
   Great Awakening. *See* Great Awakening
   missionaries. *See* Missionaries
   in New England colonies, 89, *89*
   political views and, 292–293
   Protestant Reformation, 41–43
   Puritan movement, 84–86, *85*
   revivalism, 123, 299–300, *300*
   society under control of, 367–368
   in South, 204–207, 330, 339–340
   utopian communities, 311–312
   witchcraft, 29, 30, *30,* 90, *90,* 91–93
Religious art, 107, *107*
Religious freedom, 60
Representation, 142–143, 197, 198
Representative governments, 141
Republicanism, 141, 184, 202, 398
   election of 1864 and, 427
   Southern attachment to, 390
   views on property, 189–190

Ships and shipbuilding, 31, 248m, 252, 252–254
Shoe industry, 350
Siberia, 23–24, 25
Silver, 37, 39, 40m, 42, 106
Silver Bluff plantation, 329
Singer, Isaac, 380
Sioux Indians, 282, 347–348, 348, 349m, 355
Sixteenth Amendment, A-9
The Skater (Stuart), *191*
Skelton, Martha Wayles (Jefferson), 240, 243, *243*
Skidmore, Thomas, 311
Skipworth, Lucy, 340
Slater, Samuel, 256
Slave(s), 159, 324, 328, 335, 340
    African vs. native born, 120–121
    maintenance of, 335–336, 337, *337*
    rebellions by, 68, 113, 122, 128, 222, 336
        running away, 336, *336*, 337
        White fears of, 174–175
    runaways, 177, 182, 324
        Dunmore's recruitment of, 173–175, *174*
        Maroon communities, *64, 65*, 121
        as rebellion, 336, *336*, 337
Slave drivers, 330, 335, *335*, 340
Slaveholders, 224, *336*, 340
    class structure of South, 329–330, *330*
    encouragement of religion, 339
Slave Power, 361, 389, 390
Slave quarters, *331*
Slavery, 7, 9, *9*, 37, 62–68, *67*, 70, *189*
    abolition of, 74, 189, 352, 428
    of *conquistadores* in Texas, 39
    defense of, 341–343
    Denmark Vesey case, 286
    distribution of power in, 334–335
    in eighteenth-century seaports, 117
    in French Louisiana, 113–114
    Indians as slave owners, 280, *280*
    Missouri Compromise and, 235m, 235–236
    in Old South, 329, 334–341, 344
    as "peculiar institution," 190, 328, 334–335
    plantation monocultures and, 53
    secession and, 396–397
    sectionalism and, 189–190, 360–361, 363
    slave laws and codes, 67, 73, 282–283
    slave wars in Carolinas, 71
    systems of labor in, 120, 335, 451
    Western expansion and, 352, 359, 369–372, 375
Slave societies, 117, 119–122, *121*, 190, *190*
Slave trade, 31–33, 63, 327
    abolition of, 222, 235
    Atlantic slave trade, 63–68
    cost of slaves, *384*, 393
Slidell, John, 358
Smallpox epidemics, 13, 71, 115, 348, 349m
    during American Revolution, 170, 170m
    Indians and, 82, *82*, 281–282

in Spanish colonies, 37, 56, 106
    trade routes and, 226
Smedes, Susan Dabney, 332
Smith, Adam, 57
Smith, Capt. John, 52, *53*, 87
Smith, Dewitt, 380
Smith, Jedediah, 265
Smith, Joseph, 312–313, *313*, 367
Smith, Rev. James, 4
Smith, Venture, 222
Smuggling, 126
Social class, 272, 274, *274*
    class conflict, 259
    in colonial seaports, 118–119
    in England and America, 124
    middle class. *See* Middle class
    political parties and, 292–293
    of Whites in Old South, 329–334, 398
Social control, 367–368
Socialists, 311
Social mobility, 263, 264
Society, 116
    Chesapeake Bay colonies, 57, 59–61, 61m, 77, 120
    of early republic, 182, *191*, 191–195, 227, 228, *228*
    evangelicalism and, *303–307*, 303–308
    French Louisiana, *113*, 113–114
    market society, 245–267, *268*
    of Old South, 325m, 325–329, 328m
    pre-Civil War changes, 379–385, 381m
    social structure of Old South, 323–324, *324*
    Western expansion and, 363–368
Society of Cincinnati, 195, *195*
Society of Friends. *See* Quakers
Society of Jesus (Jesuits), 43, 55, 81
Sofaer, Anna, 14
Soil erosion, 326
Soldiers
    African American, 234–235
        American Revolution, *173*, 177
        Civil War, 413, *413*
    Civil War, 402–403, 419–422
        black soldiers, 413, *413*
        casualties, 404, 421–422, *422*, 423m
        diet of, 420, *420*
        hardships, 419, *420*, 421, 426–427
"Song of Myself" (Whitman), 310, *310*
Sons of Liberty, 142, 144
Soto, Hernán de, 39–40, *40*
The South, 214, 398
    biracial worship in, 204–207, *204–207*
    colonial era, 51–75, 119–122
    market economy and, 247, 249, 251
    pre-Civil War, *384*, 384–385, 393
    during Reconstruction, 441–443, *442*
    temperance movement in, *303*, 303–304
    Tidewater region, 212m, 212–213, 330, 331
    upper South, 326–327, 340, 395, 396m
    See also Confederate States of America; The Old South

South Carolina, 39–40, 68, 70–71, 72m, 442
    black majority of voters, 447, 448
    distribution of slavery in, 328, 328m
    nullification crisis, 286–287
    Sherman's march through, 425m, 429
South Carolina Exposition and Protest (Calhoun), 286
Southern Baptist Church, 204–207
The Southwest, 6, 7, *7*, 40–41, 107
    French attempt to colonize, 103–105
    Spanish colonization of. *See* New Spain
Sovereign powers, 287
Spain, 30, 33–35, 127m, 428
    allegiance of Indians to, *185*, 186
    control of Mississippi River, 186–187
    exploration of New World, 33–41, 34m, 48, 104
        conquistadores, 28, 41, 46
        search for Indian empires, 37, 39–41, 40m
    Huguenots as threat to, 42–43
    North American colonies of, 53–57, 57m, 58, 75, 104
    in Seven Years' War. *See* Seven Years' War
Specie, 288
Specie Circular, 290–291
Spiegel, Marcus, 419, 421
Spinning bees, 164, *164*
Spirituals, 340
Spoils system, 277–278
Sports and fitness, 6, *6*
Spot resolutions, 360, 361
Spring, Gardiner, 302
Squanto (Wampanoag Indian), 87
St. Augustine (Florida), 43, 55, 57m, 71
St. Clair, Gen. Arthur, 225
St. Kitts, 68, 72m
St. Lawrence River, 111, 129m, 135
Stamp Act of 1765, *140*, 140–144, 153, 155
Stamp Act riot, *140*
Stanton, Edwin, 446, 447
Stanton, Elizabeth Cady, 316, *316*, 317, 454, 455
State(s)
    constitutions, 182–184, *183*, 352, 448
    disputes among, 186–187
    governments, 96, *183*, 183–184, 448
    importance in postwar period, 182
    laws of, 317–318
"Steal Away to Jesus," 340
Steam power, 380
Steam-powered ships, 248m, 252, 252–254
Steel, Ferdinand, 324, 332
Stephens, Alexander, 396–397, 416, 428, 443, *443*
Steuben, Baron von, 169, 172, 177
Stevens, Thaddeus, 443, 444, 446
Stiles, Ezra, 187
Still, William, 315
Stillman, William J., *310*
Stone, Lucy, *453*, 455